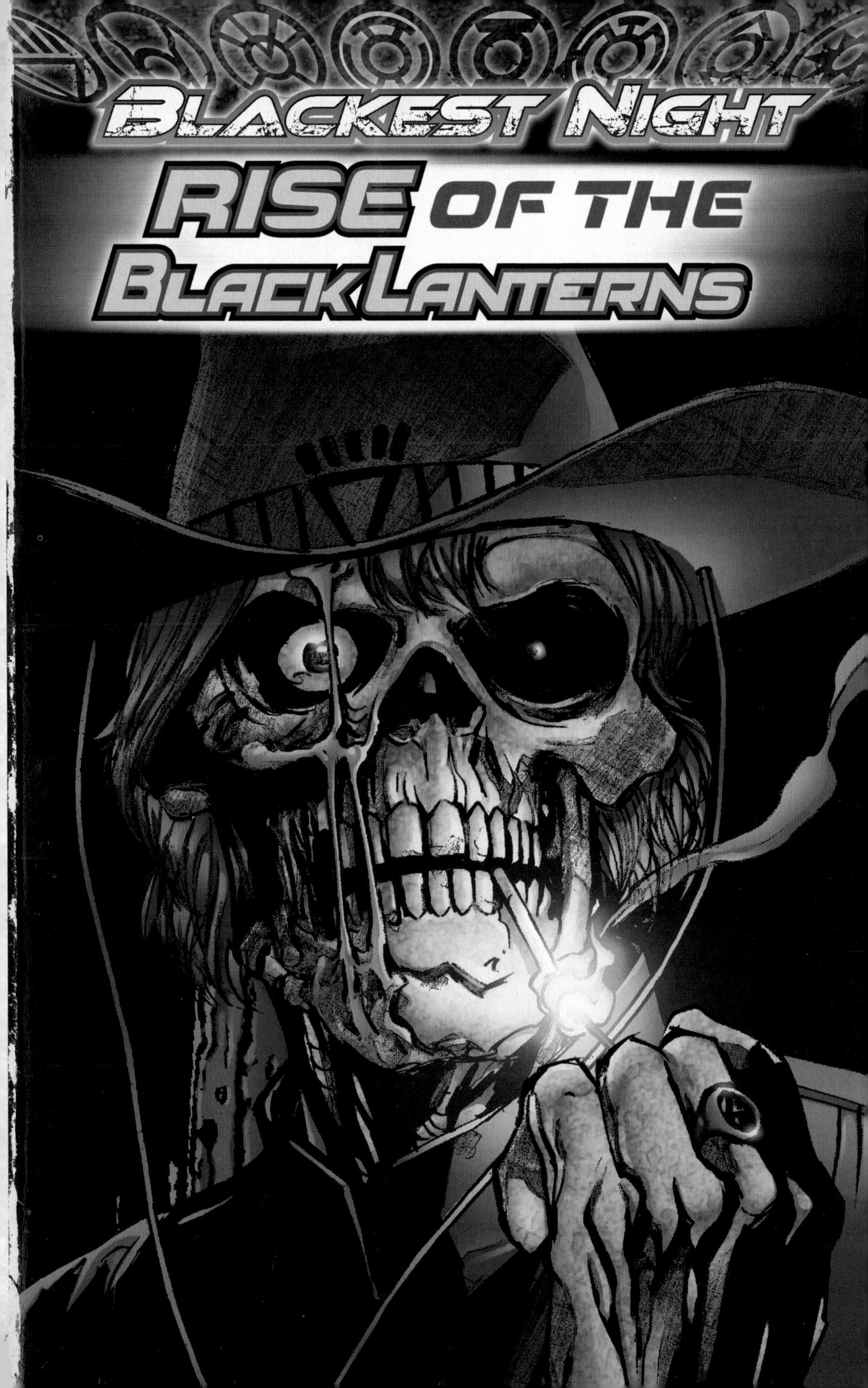
BLACKEST NIGHT
RISE OF THE
BLACK LANTERNS

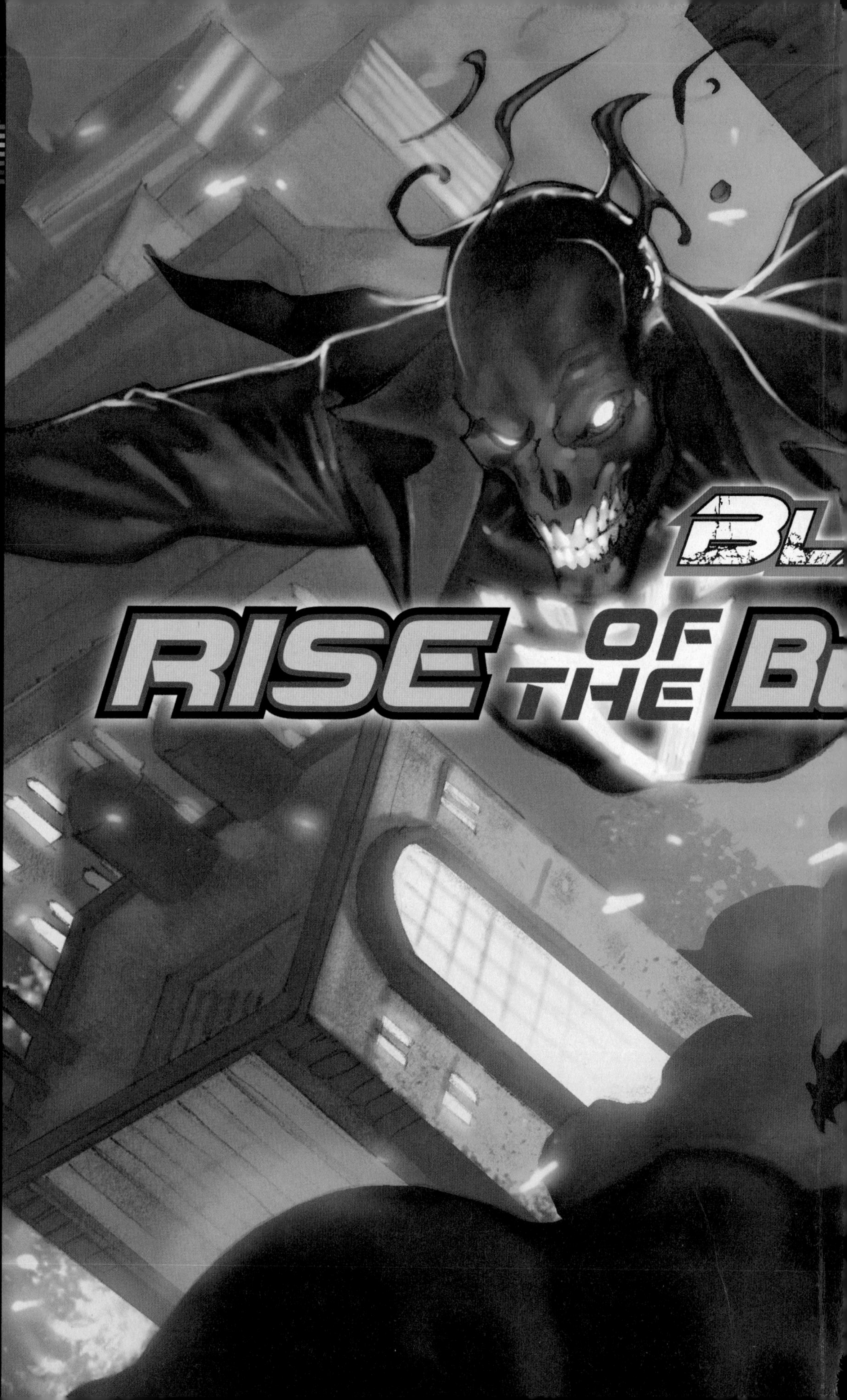
RISE OF THE

GEOFF JOHNS
TONY BEDARD
DAN DIDIO
J.T. KRUL
DENNIS O'NEIL &
GREG RUCKA
JAMES ROBINSON
PETER J. TOMASI
ERIC WALLACE
WRITERS

ACKEST NIGHT
ackLanterns

RENATO ARLEM   MICHAEL BABINSKI
VICENTE CIFUENTES   DENYS COWAN
FERNANDO DAGNINO   LUCIANA DEL NEGRO
FABRIZIO FIORENTINO   DON KRAMER
MARCOS MARZ   FERNANDO PASARIN
IBRAIM ROBERSON   BILL SIENKIEWICZ
RYAN SOOK   JOHN STANISCI
ARDIAN SYAF   DIOGENES NEVES
RUY JOSÉ   TRAVIS MOORE   DAN GREEN
KEITH CHAMPAGNE   BOB WIACEK
ARTISTS

ULISES ARREOLA   DAVID BARON
HI-FI DESIGNS   MATT HOLLINGSWORTH
FRANK MARTIN   CHUCK PIRES
ROD REIS   JD SMITH
CHUCK PIRES   BRIAN BUCCELLATO
COLORISTS

JARED K. FLETCHER   JOHN J. HILL
ROB LEIGH   KEN LOPEZ
NICK J. NAPOLITANO   STEVE WANDS
SAL CIPRIANO
LETTERERS

JACK KNIGHT CREATED BY
JAMES ROBINSON & TONY HARRIS
THE ATOM/RAY PALMER AND HAWKMAN CREATED BY
GARDNER FOX

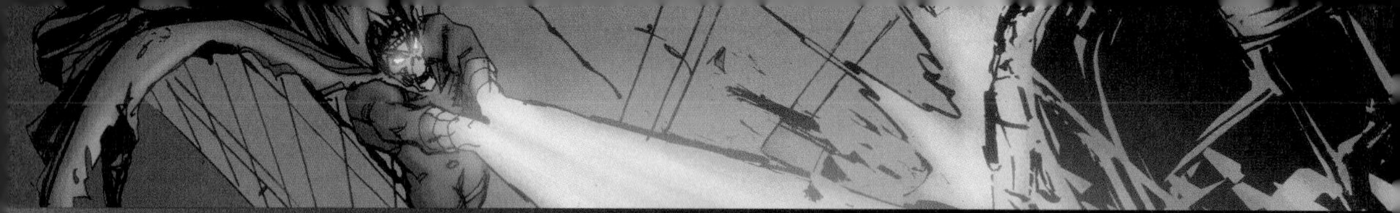

Eddie Berganza Mike Carlin Brian Cunningham Matt Idelson Adam Schlagman
Michael Siglain *Editors-original series* / Rachel Gluckstern *Associate Editor-original series*
Wil Moss Rex Ogle Harvey Richards *Assistant Editors-original series*
Bob Harras *Group Editor-Collected Editions* / Anton Kawasaki *Editor* / Robbin Brosterman *Design Director-Books*

DC COMICS / Diane Nelson *President* / Dan DiDio and Jim Lee *Co-Publishers*
Geoff Johns *Chief Creative Officer* / Patrick Caldon *EVP–Finance and Administration*
John Rood *EVP–Sales, Marketing and Business Development* / Amy Genkins *SVP–Business and Legal Affairs*
Steve Rotterdam *SVP–Sales and Marketing* / John Cunningham *VP–Marketing*
Terri Cunningham *VP–Managing Editor* / Alison Gill *VP–Manufacturing* / David Hyde *VP–Publicity*
Sue Pohja *VP–Book Trade Sales* / Alysse Soll *VP–Advertising and Custom Publishing*
Bob Wayne *VP–Sales* / Mark Chiarello *Art Director*

Cover by Rodolfo Migliari after Ivan Reis

BLACKEST NIGHT: RISE OF THE BLACK LANTERNS Published by DC Comics.

DC COMICS 1700 Broadway, New York, NY 10019 A Warner Bros. Entertainment Company

Printed by RR Donnelley, Salem, VA, USA. 6/23/10. First printing.

HC ISBN: 978-1-4012-2789-0
SC ISBN: 978-1-4012-2806-4

SUSTAINABLE FORESTRY INITIATIVE
Certified Chain of Custody
Promoting Sustainable Forest Management
www.sfiprogram.org

Fiber used in this product line meets the sourcing requirements of the SFI program.
www.sfiprogram.org NFS-SPICOC-C0001801

THE STORY SO FAR...

Billions of years ago, the self-appointed Guardians of the Universe recruited thousands of sentient beings from across the cosmos to join their intergalactic police force: the Green Lantern Corps.

Chosen because they are able to overcome great fear, the Green Lanterns patrol their respective space sectors armed with power rings capable of wielding the emerald energy of willpower into whatever constructs they can imagine.

Hal Jordan is the greatest of them all.

When the dying Green Lantern Abin Sur crashed on Earth, he chose Hal Jordan to be his successor, for his indomitable will and ability to overcome great fear. As the protector of Sector 2814, Hal has saved Earth from destruction, even died in its service and been reborn.

Thaal Sinestro of Korugar was once considered the greatest Green Lantern of them all.

As Abin Sur's friend, Sinestro became Jordan's mentor in the Corps. But after being sentenced to the Anti-Matter Universe for abusing his power, Sinestro learned of the yellow light of fear being mined on Qward. Wielding a new golden power ring fueled by terror, Sinestro drafted thousands of the most horrific, psychotic and sadistic beings in the universe, and with their doctrine of fear, burned all who opposed them.

When the Green Lantern Corps battled their former ally during the Sinestro Corps War, the skies burned with green and gold as Earth erupted into an epic battle between good and evil. Though the Green Lanterns won, their brotherhood was broken and the peace they achieved was short-lived. In its aftermath, the Guardians rewrote the Book of Oa, the very laws by which their corps abides, and dissent grew within their members.

Now Hal Jordan will face his greatest challenge yet, as the prophecy foretold by

The emotional spectrum has splintered into seven factions. Seven corps were born.

The Green Lanterns. The Sinestro Corps. Atrocitus and the enraged Red Lanterns. Larfleeze, the avaricious keeper of the Orange Light. Former Guardians Ganthet and Sayd's small but hopeful Blue Lantern Corps. The Zamarons and their army of fierce and loving Star Sapphires. And the mysterious Indigo Tribe.

As the War of Light ignited between these Lantern bearers, the skies on every world darkened. In Sector 666, on the planet Ryut, a black lantern grew around the Anti-Monitor's corpse, using his vast energies to empower it.

The first of the Black Lanterns, the Black Hand, has risen from the dead, heralding a greater power that will extinguish all of the light—and life—in the universe.

Now across thousands of worlds, the dead have risen, and Hal Jordan and all of Earth's greatest heroes must bear witness to Blackest Night, which will descend upon them all, without prejudice, mercy or reason.

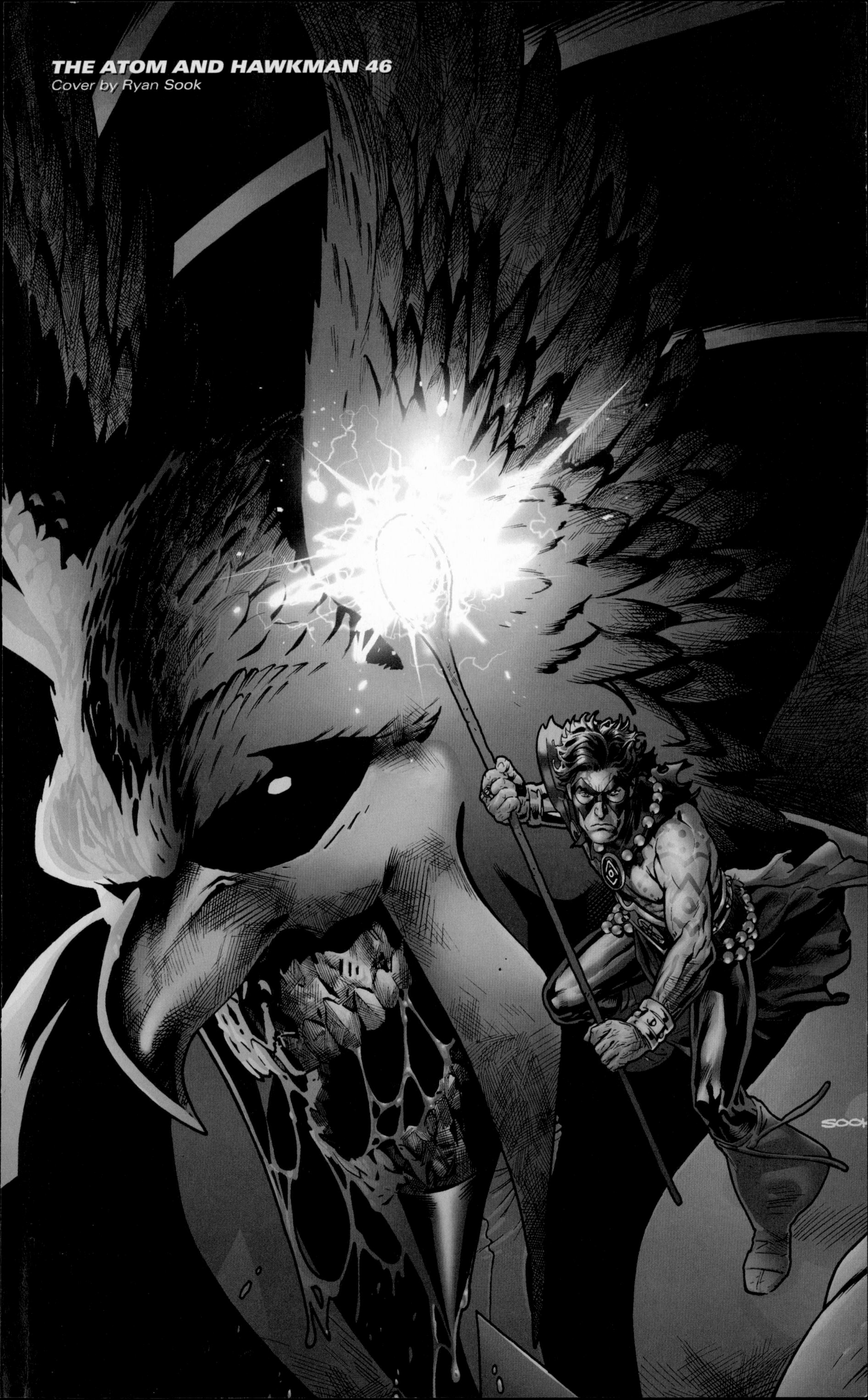

THE ATOM AND HAWKMAN 46
Cover by Ryan Sook

BYE BYE BIRDIE!

GEOFF JOHNS
WRITER

RYAN SOOK
FERNANDO PASARIN
ARTISTS

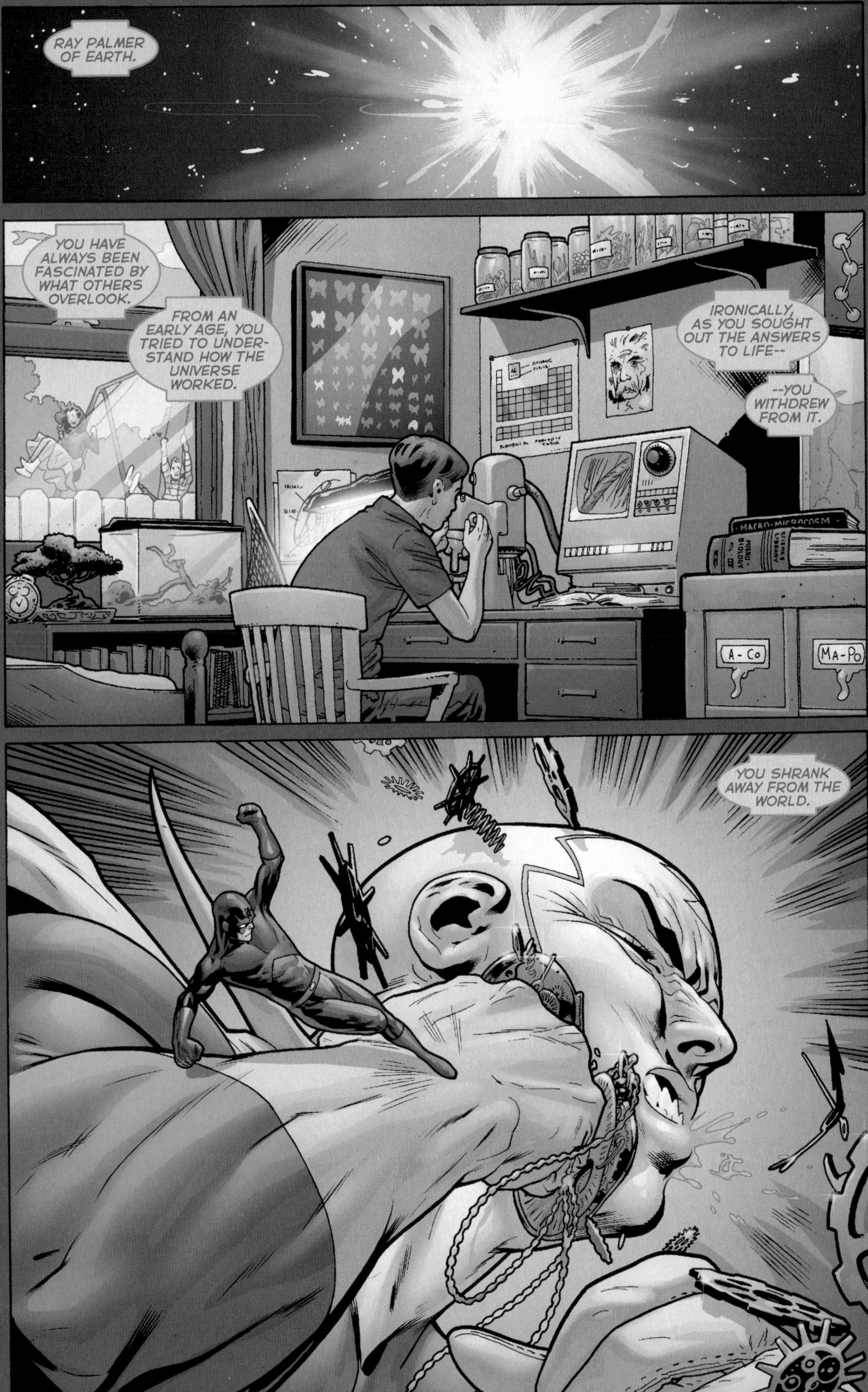
RAY PALMER OF EARTH.
YOU HAVE ALWAYS BEEN FASCINATED BY WHAT OTHERS OVERLOOK.
FROM AN EARLY AGE, YOU TRIED TO UNDERSTAND HOW THE UNIVERSE WORKED.
IRONICALLY, AS YOU SOUGHT OUT THE ANSWERS TO LIFE--
--YOU WITHDREW FROM IT.
MACRO-MICROCOSM
A-Co
MA-Po
YOU SHRANK AWAY FROM THE WORLD.

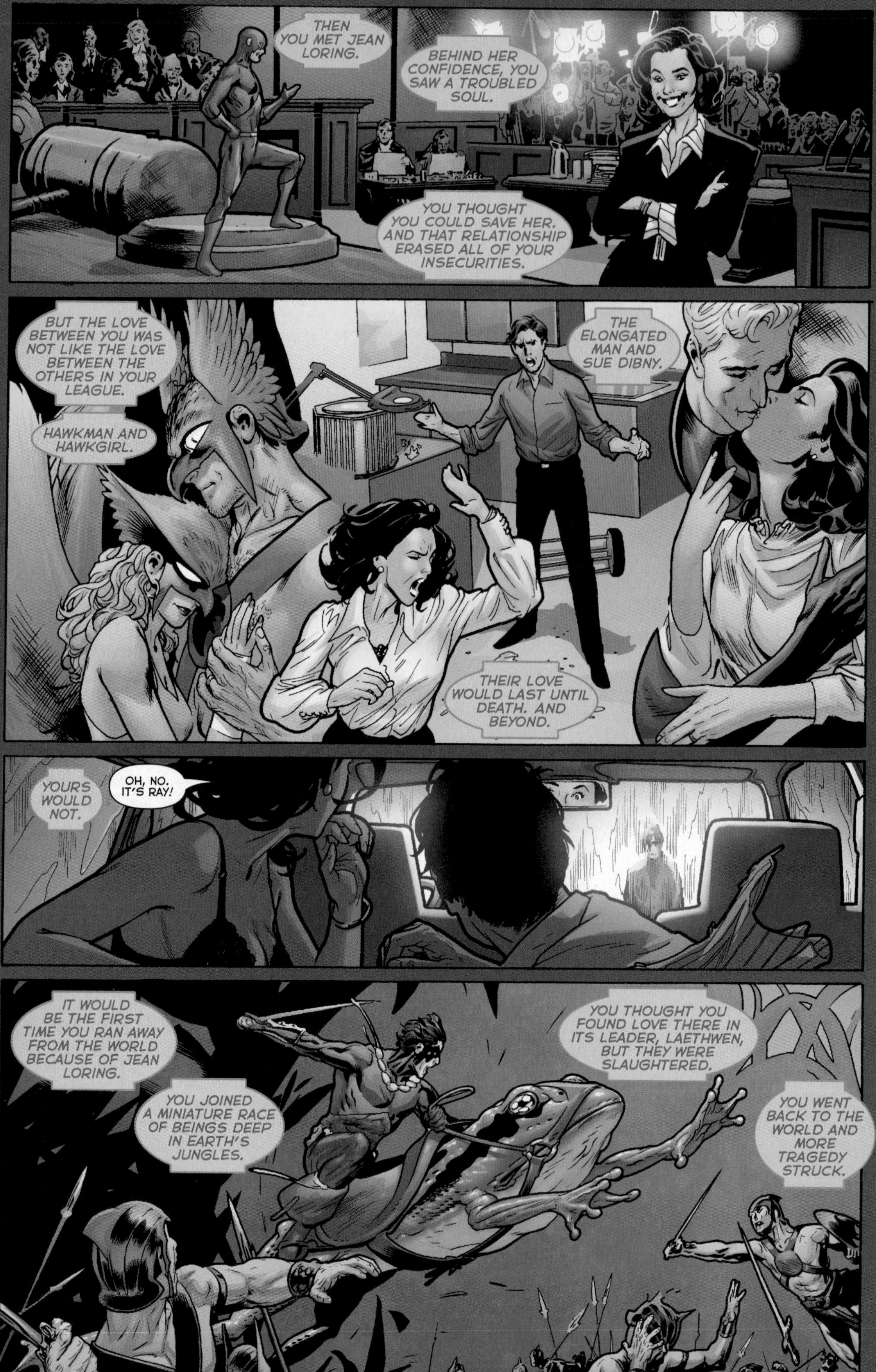
THEN YOU MET JEAN LORING.
BEHIND HER CONFIDENCE, YOU SAW A TROUBLED SOUL.
YOU THOUGHT YOU COULD SAVE HER. AND THAT RELATIONSHIP ERASED ALL OF YOUR INSECURITIES.
BUT THE LOVE BETWEEN YOU WAS NOT LIKE THE LOVE BETWEEN THE OTHERS IN YOUR LEAGUE.
HAWKMAN AND HAWKGIRL.
THE ELONGATED MAN AND SUE DIBNY.
THEIR LOVE WOULD LAST UNTIL DEATH. AND BEYOND.
YOURS WOULD NOT.
OH, NO. IT'S RAY!
IT WOULD BE THE FIRST TIME YOU RAN AWAY FROM THE WORLD BECAUSE OF JEAN LORING.
YOU JOINED A MINIATURE RACE OF BEINGS DEEP IN EARTH'S JUNGLES.
YOU THOUGHT YOU FOUND LOVE THERE IN ITS LEADER, LAETHWEN, BUT THEY WERE SLAUGHTERED.
YOU WENT BACK TO THE WORLD AND MORE TRAGEDY STRUCK.

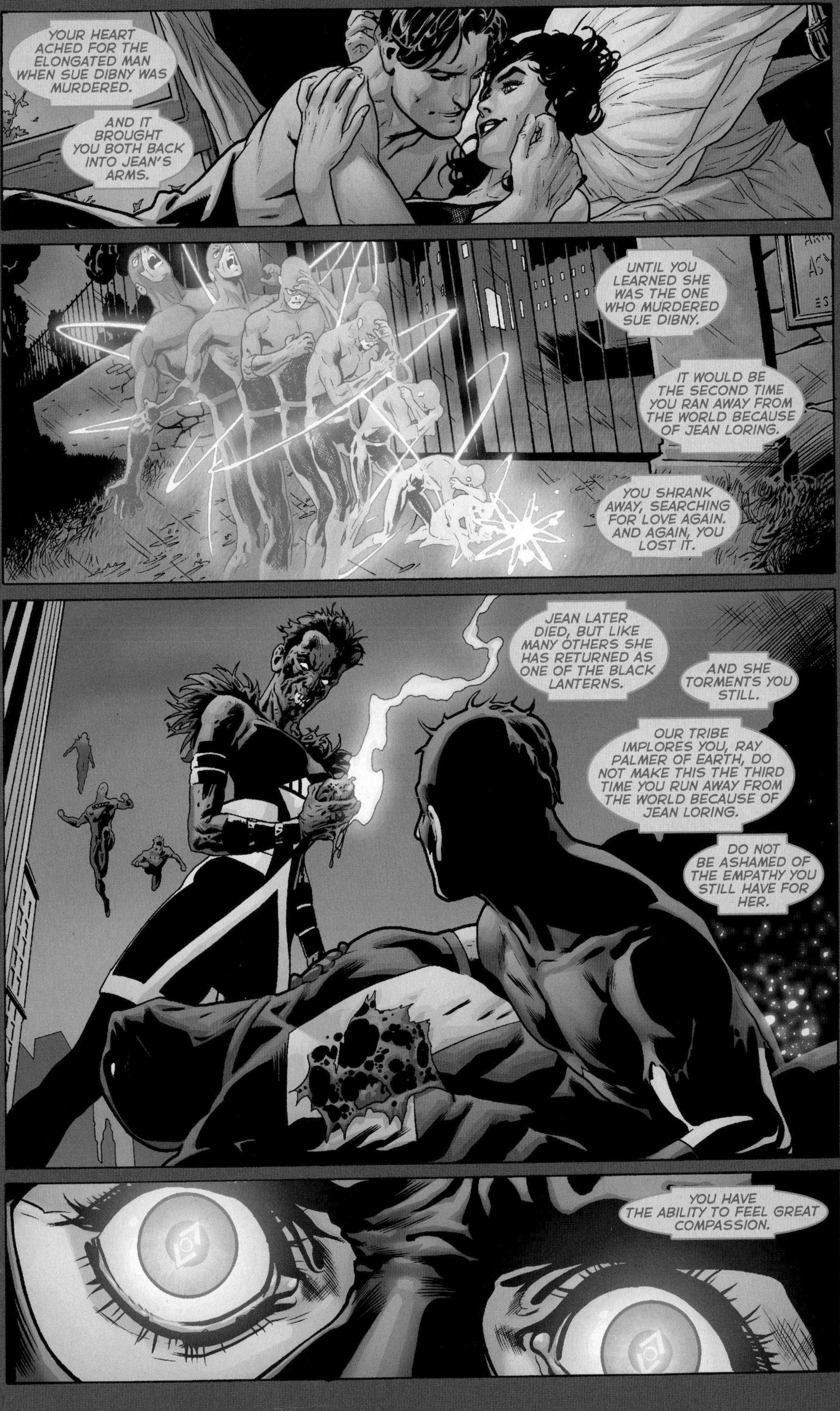
YOUR HEART ACHED FOR THE ELONGATED MAN WHEN SUE DIBNY WAS MURDERED.
AND IT BROUGHT YOU BOTH BACK INTO JEAN'S ARMS.
UNTIL YOU LEARNED SHE WAS THE ONE WHO MURDERED SUE DIBNY.
IT WOULD BE THE SECOND TIME YOU RAN AWAY FROM THE WORLD BECAUSE OF JEAN LORING.
YOU SHRANK AWAY, SEARCHING FOR LOVE AGAIN. AND AGAIN, YOU LOST IT.
JEAN LATER DIED, BUT LIKE MANY OTHERS SHE HAS RETURNED AS ONE OF THE BLACK LANTERNS.
AND SHE TORMENTS YOU STILL.
OUR TRIBE IMPLORES YOU, RAY PALMER OF EARTH, DO NOT MAKE THIS THE THIRD TIME YOU RUN AWAY FROM THE WORLD BECAUSE OF JEAN LORING.
DO NOT BE ASHAMED OF THE EMPATHY YOU STILL HAVE FOR HER.
YOU HAVE THE ABILITY TO FEEL GREAT COMPASSION.

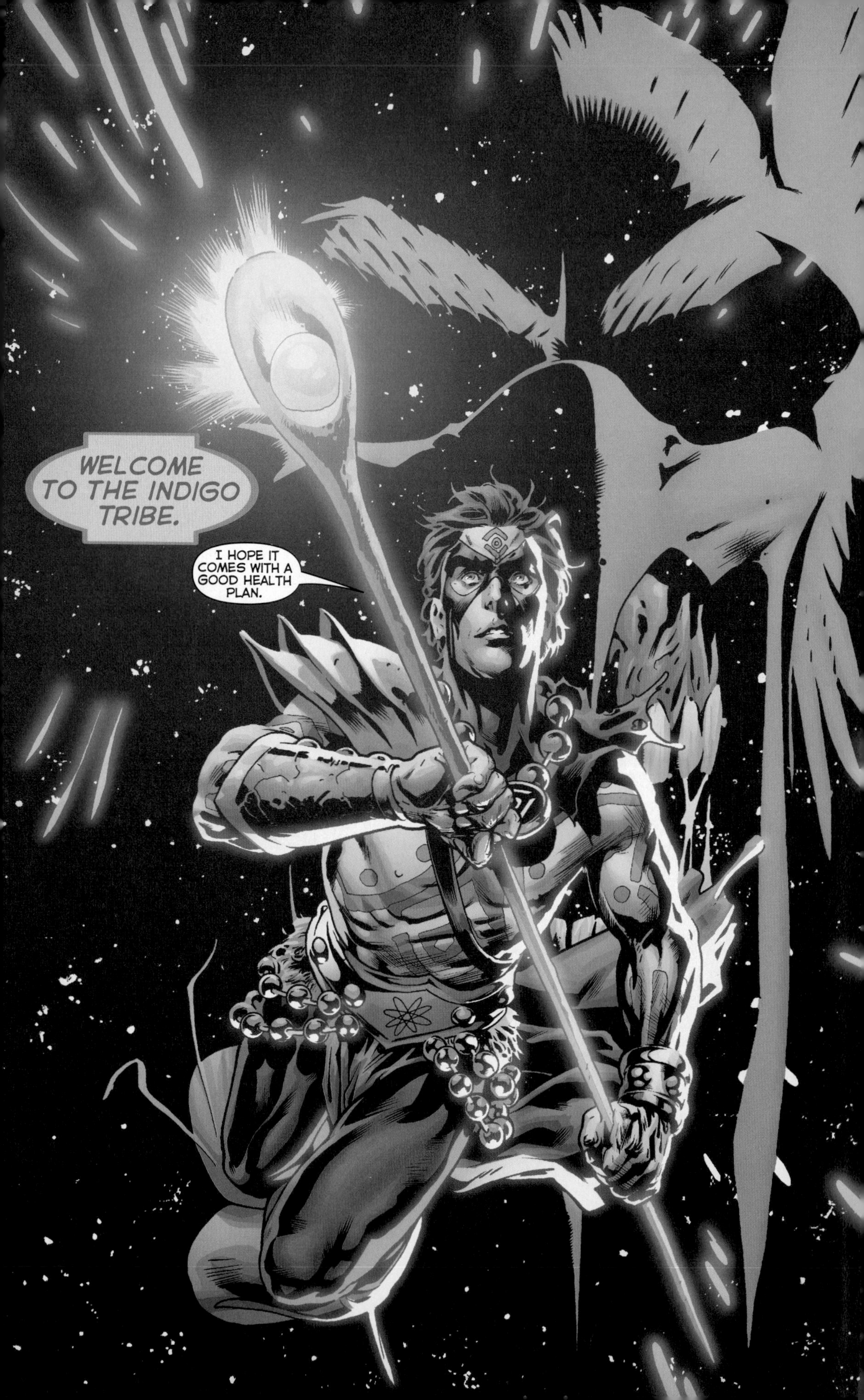
WELCOME TO THE INDIGO TRIBE.
I HOPE IT COMES WITH A GOOD HEALTH PLAN.

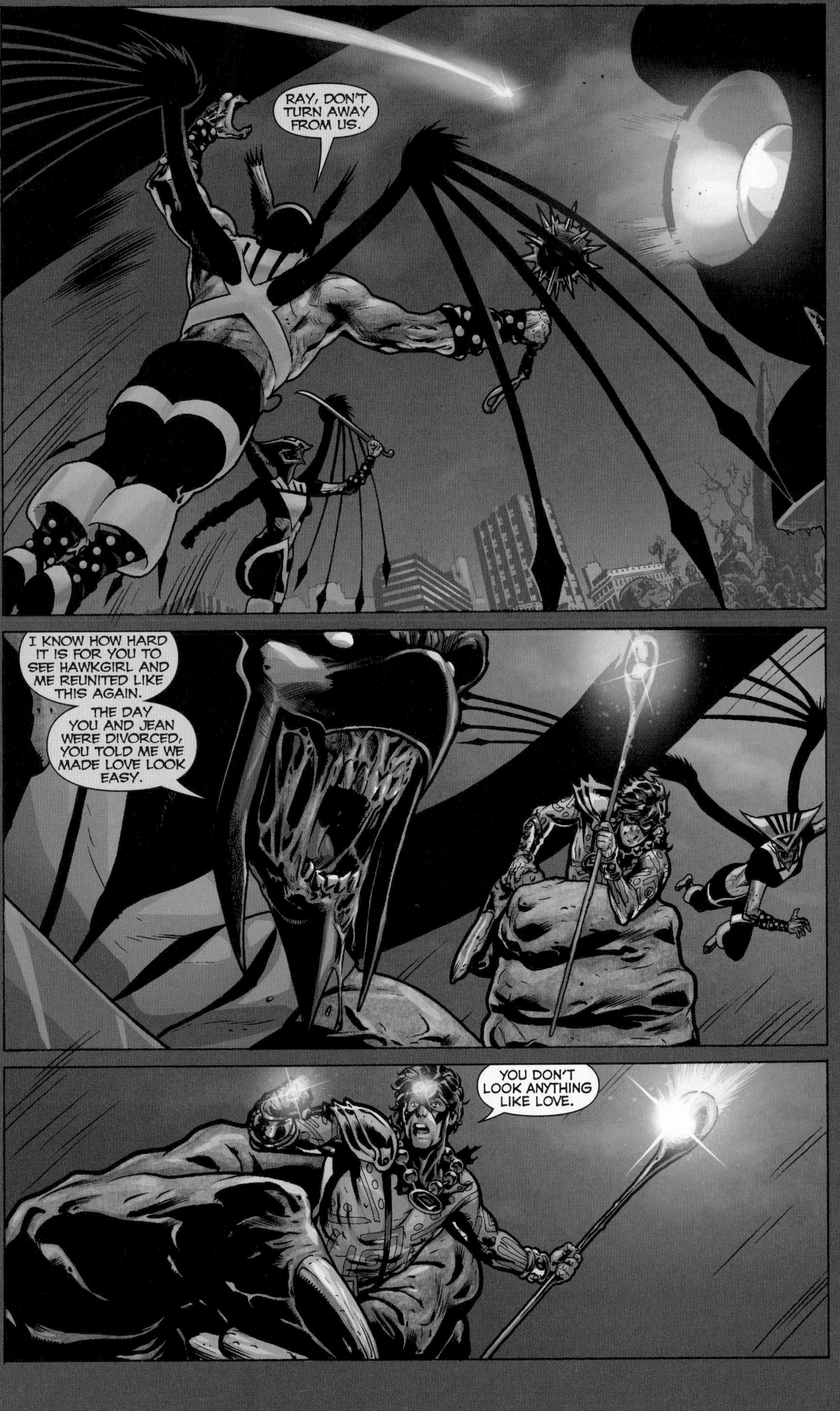

RAY, DON'T TURN AWAY FROM US.
I KNOW HOW HARD IT IS FOR YOU TO SEE HAWKGIRL AND ME REUNITED LIKE THIS AGAIN.
THE DAY YOU AND JEAN WERE DIVORCED, YOU TOLD ME WE MADE LOVE LOOK EASY.
YOU DON'T LOOK ANYTHING LIKE LOVE.

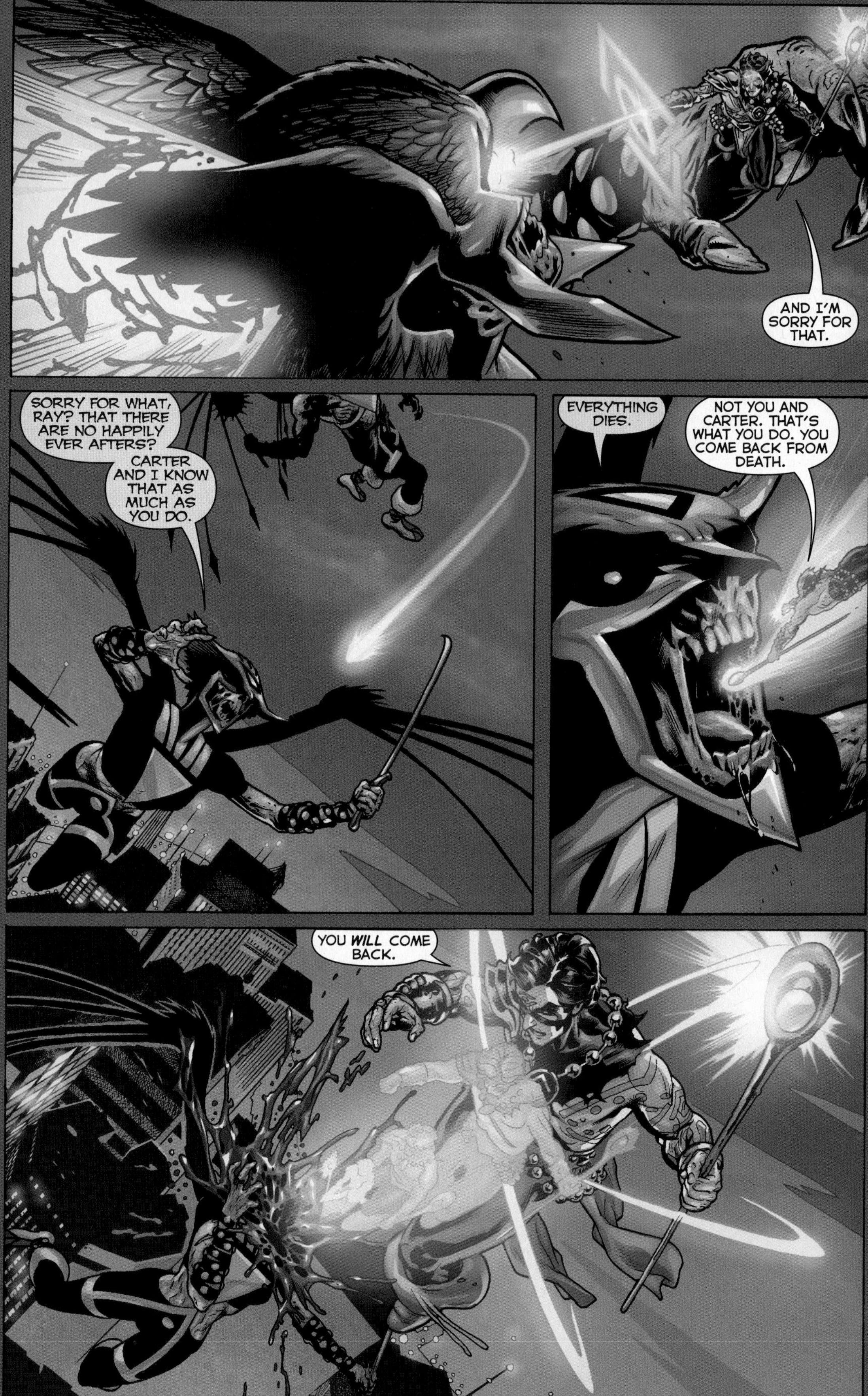

AND I'M SORRY FOR THAT.
SORRY FOR WHAT, RAY? THAT THERE ARE NO HAPPILY EVER AFTERS?
CARTER AND I KNOW THAT AS MUCH AS YOU DO.
EVERYTHING DIES.
NOT YOU AND CARTER. THAT'S WHAT YOU DO. YOU COME BACK FROM DEATH.
YOU *WILL* COME BACK.

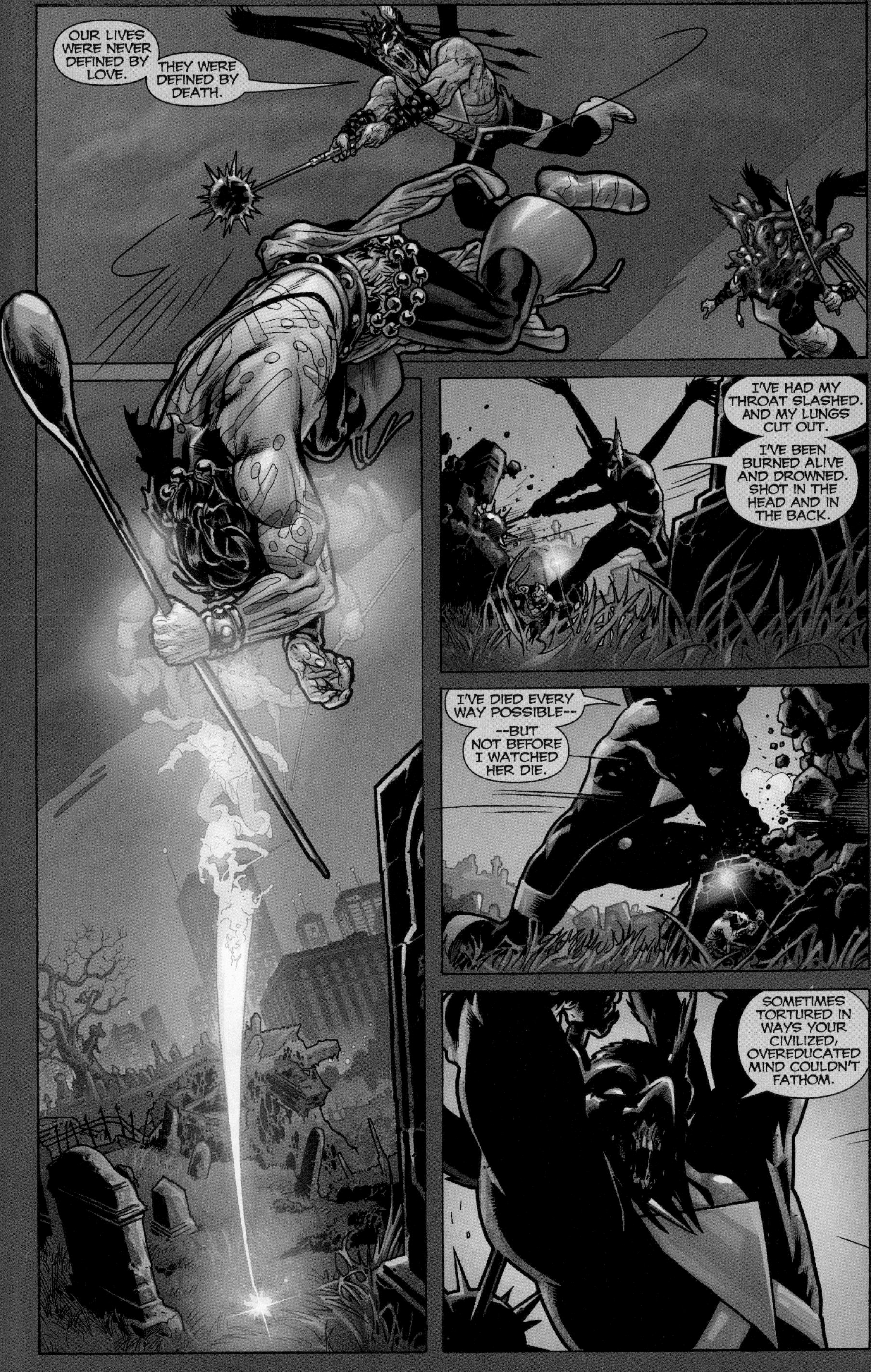

OUR LIVES WERE NEVER DEFINED BY LOVE.
THEY WERE DEFINED BY DEATH.
I'VE HAD MY THROAT SLASHED. AND MY LUNGS CUT OUT.
I'VE BEEN BURNED ALIVE AND DROWNED. SHOT IN THE HEAD AND IN THE BACK.
I'VE DIED EVERY WAY POSSIBLE--
--BUT NOT BEFORE I WATCHED HER DIE.
SOMETIMES TORTURED IN WAYS YOUR CIVILIZED, OVEREDUCATED MIND COULDN'T FATHOM.

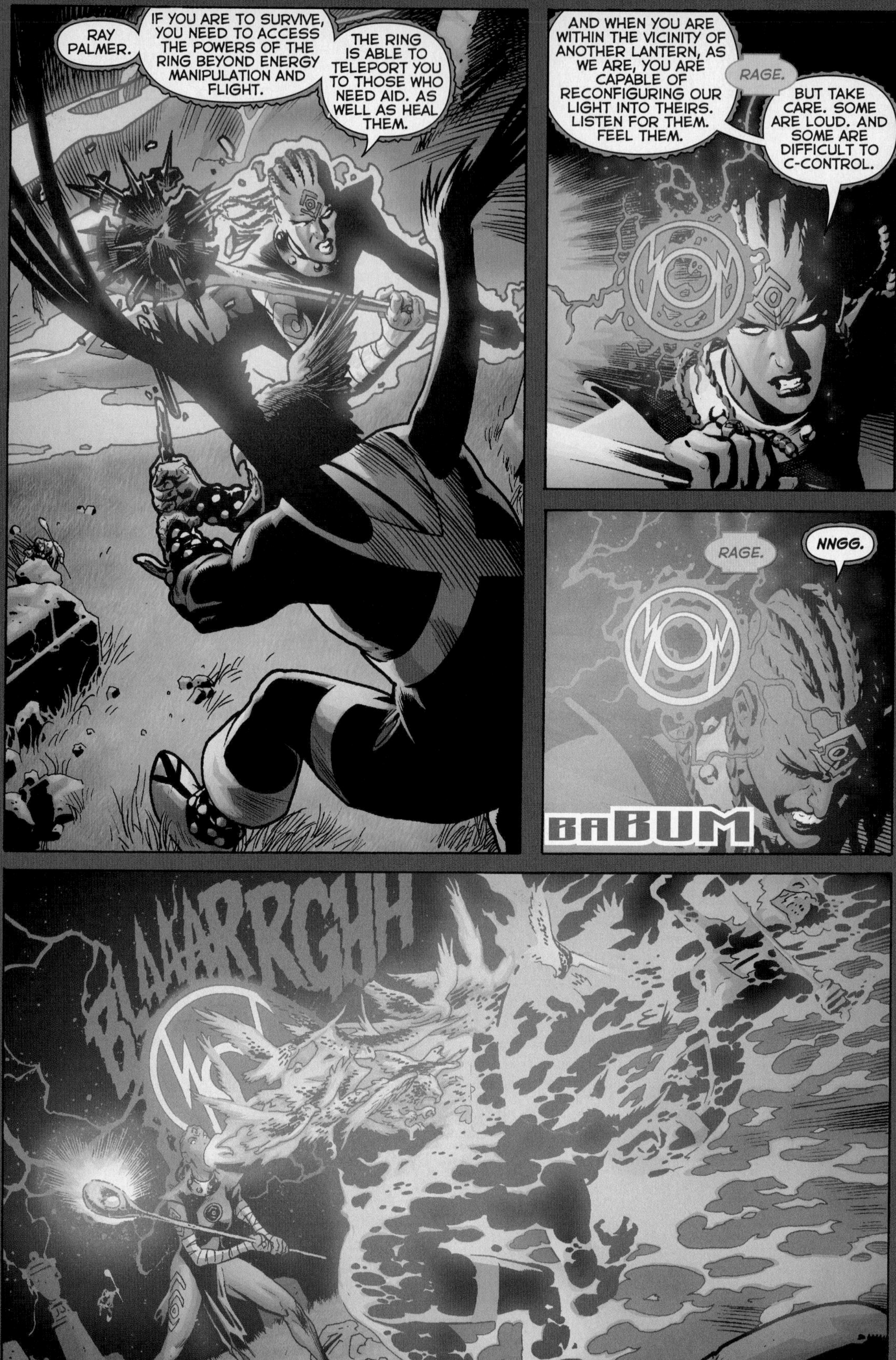
RAY PALMER.
IF YOU ARE TO SURVIVE, YOU NEED TO ACCESS THE POWERS OF THE RING BEYOND ENERGY MANIPULATION AND FLIGHT.
THE RING IS ABLE TO TELEPORT YOU TO THOSE WHO NEED AID. AS WELL AS HEAL THEM.
AND WHEN YOU ARE WITHIN THE VICINITY OF ANOTHER LANTERN, AS WE ARE, YOU ARE CAPABLE OF RECONFIGURING OUR LIGHT INTO THEIRS. LISTEN FOR THEM. FEEL THEM.
RAGE.
BUT TAKE CARE. SOME ARE LOUD. AND SOME ARE DIFFICULT TO C-CONTROL.
RAGE.
NNGG.
BABUM
BLAARRGHH

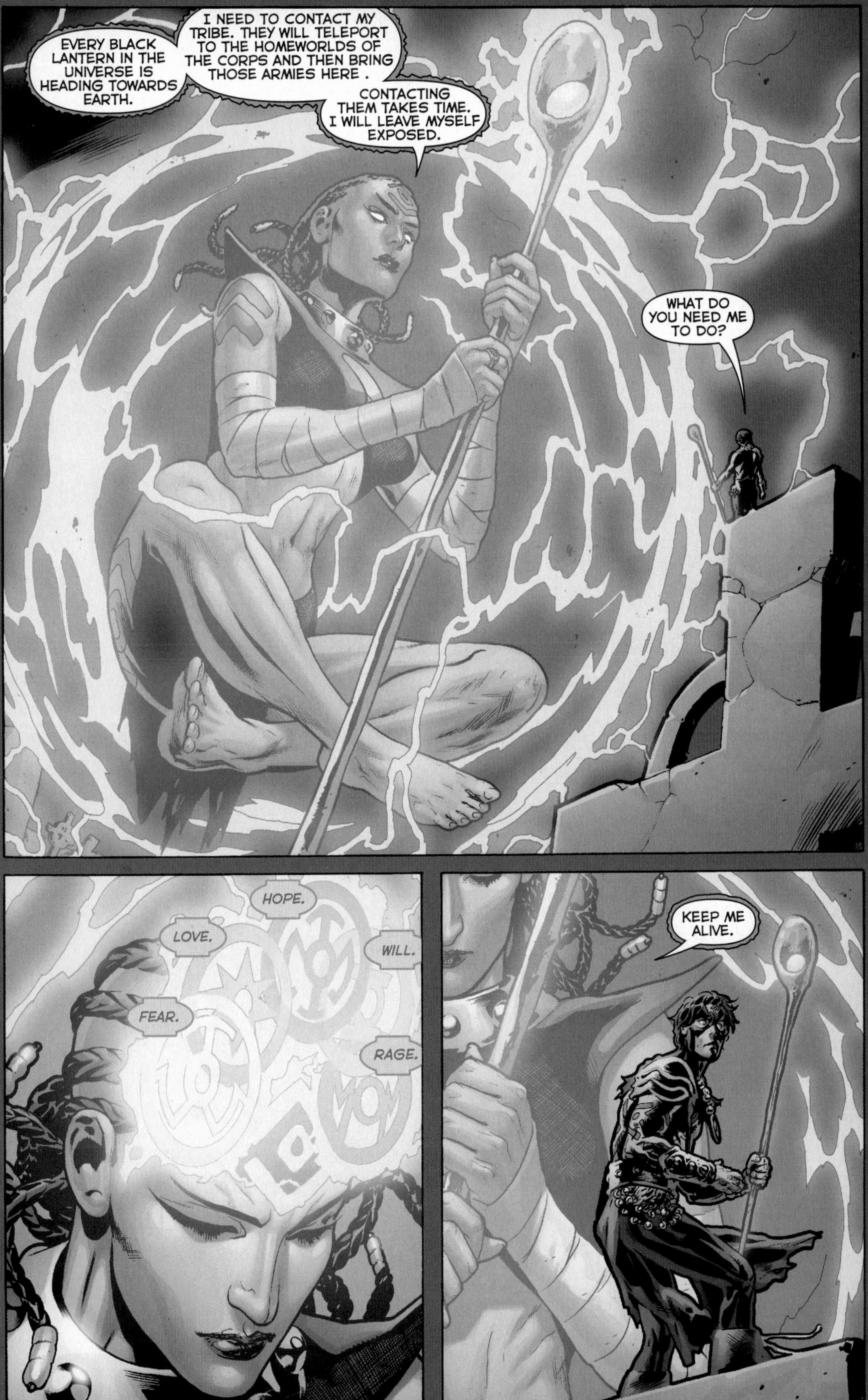
EVERY BLACK LANTERN IN THE UNIVERSE IS HEADING TOWARDS EARTH.
I NEED TO CONTACT MY TRIBE. THEY WILL TELEPORT TO THE HOMEWORLDS OF THE CORPS AND THEN BRING THOSE ARMIES HERE .
CONTACTING THEM TAKES TIME. I WILL LEAVE MYSELF EXPOSED.
WHAT DO YOU NEED ME TO DO?
HOPE.
LOVE.
WILL.
FEAR.
RAGE.
KEEP ME ALIVE.

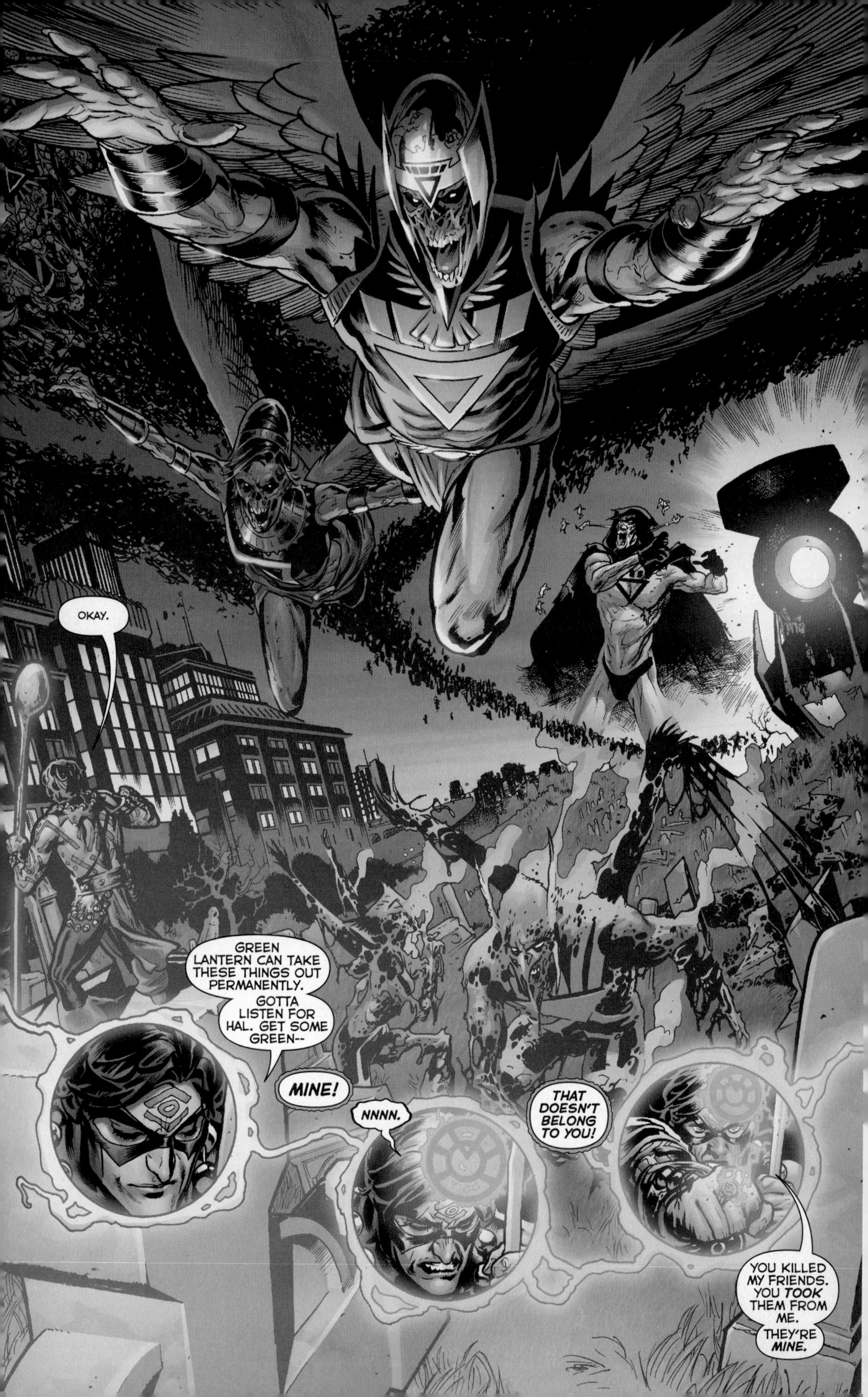
OKAY.
GREEN LANTERN CAN TAKE THESE THINGS OUT PERMANENTLY.
GOTTA LISTEN FOR HAL. GET SOME GREEN--
MINE!
NNNN.
THAT DOESN'T BELONG TO YOU!
YOU KILLED MY FRIENDS. YOU TOOK THEM FROM ME.
THEY'RE MINE.

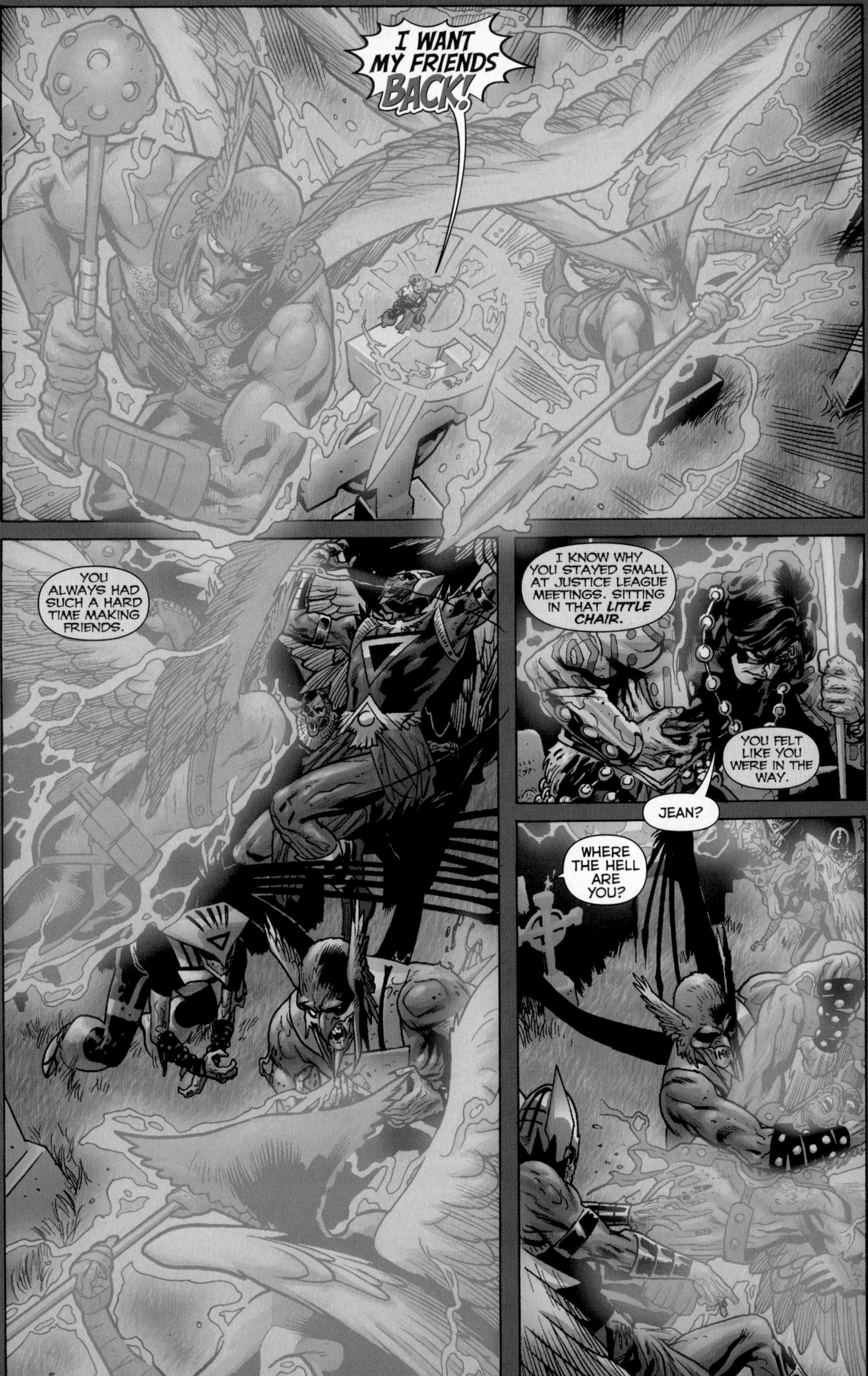
I WANT MY FRIENDS BACK!
YOU ALWAYS HAD SUCH A HARD TIME MAKING FRIENDS.
I KNOW WHY YOU STAYED SMALL AT JUSTICE LEAGUE MEETINGS. SITTING IN THAT LITTLE CHAIR.
YOU FELT LIKE YOU WERE IN THE WAY.
JEAN?
WHERE THE HELL ARE YOU?

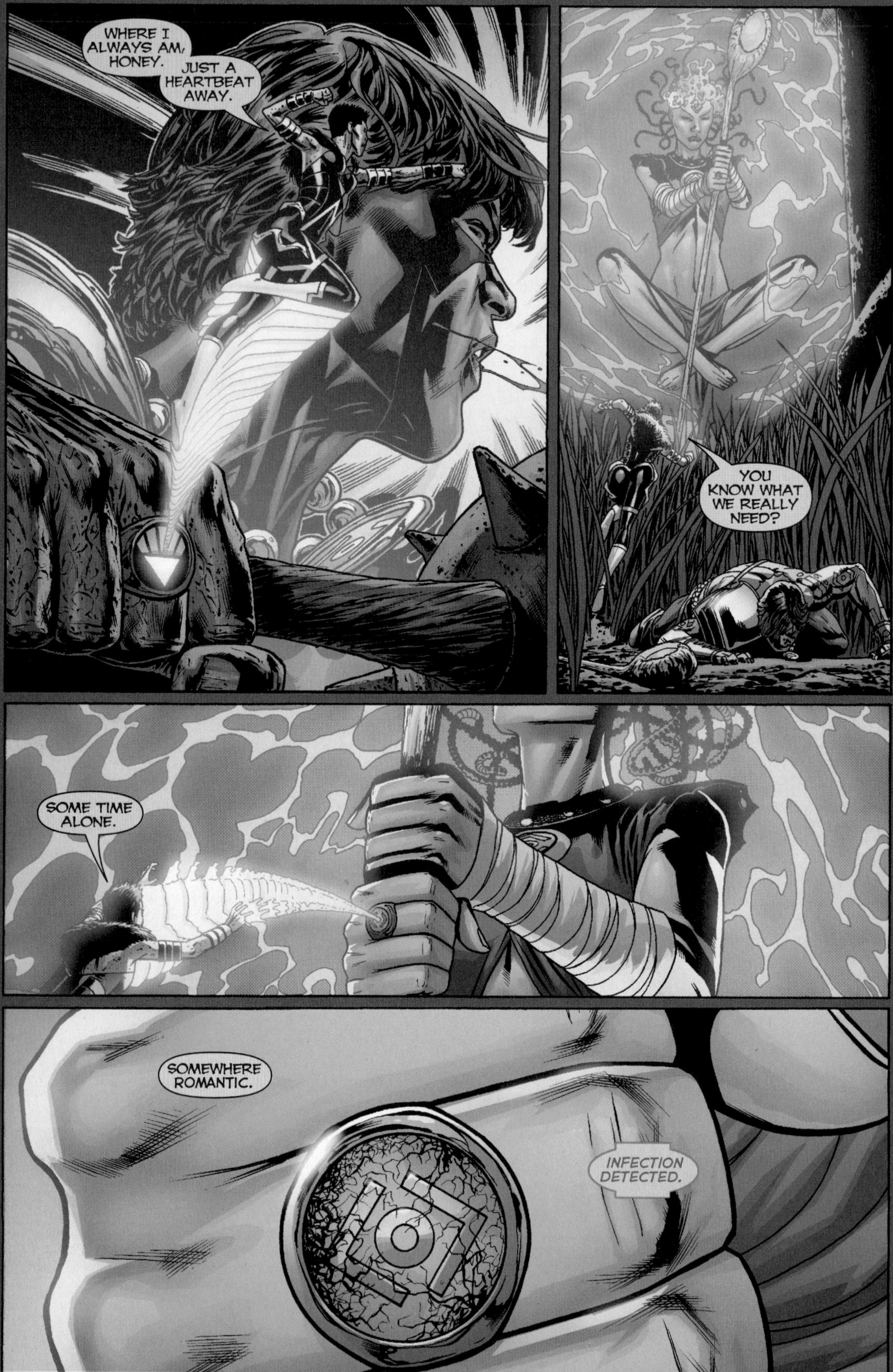
WHERE I ALWAYS AM, HONEY.
JUST A HEARTBEAT AWAY.
YOU KNOW WHAT WE REALLY NEED?
SOME TIME ALONE.
SOMEWHERE ROMANTIC.
INFECTION DETECTED.

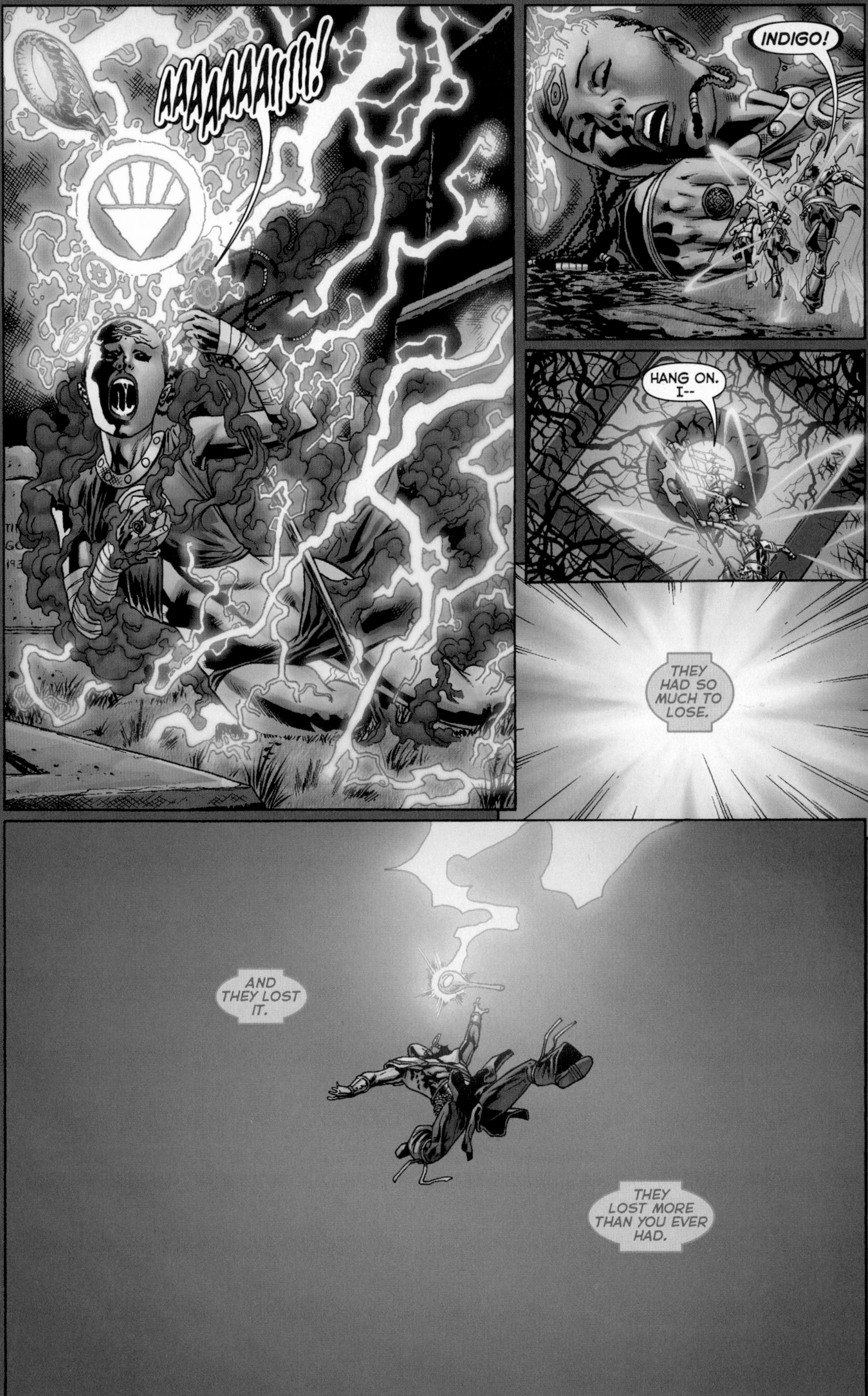
AAAAAAIIII!
INDIGO!
HANG ON. I--
THEY HAD SO MUCH TO LOSE.
AND THEY LOST IT.
THEY LOST MORE THAN YOU EVER HAD.

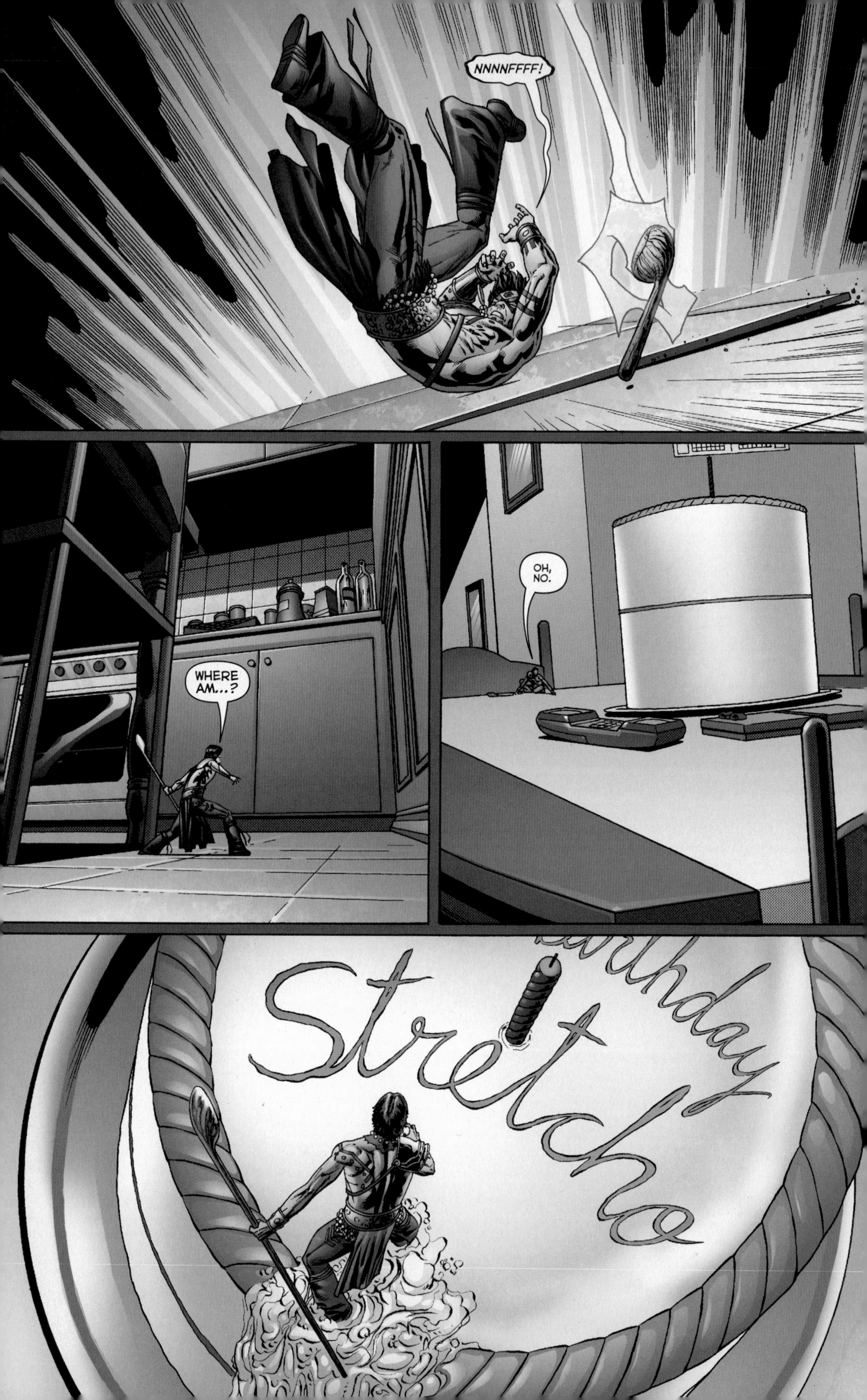
NNNNFFFF!
WHERE AM...?
OH, NO.
Stretcho

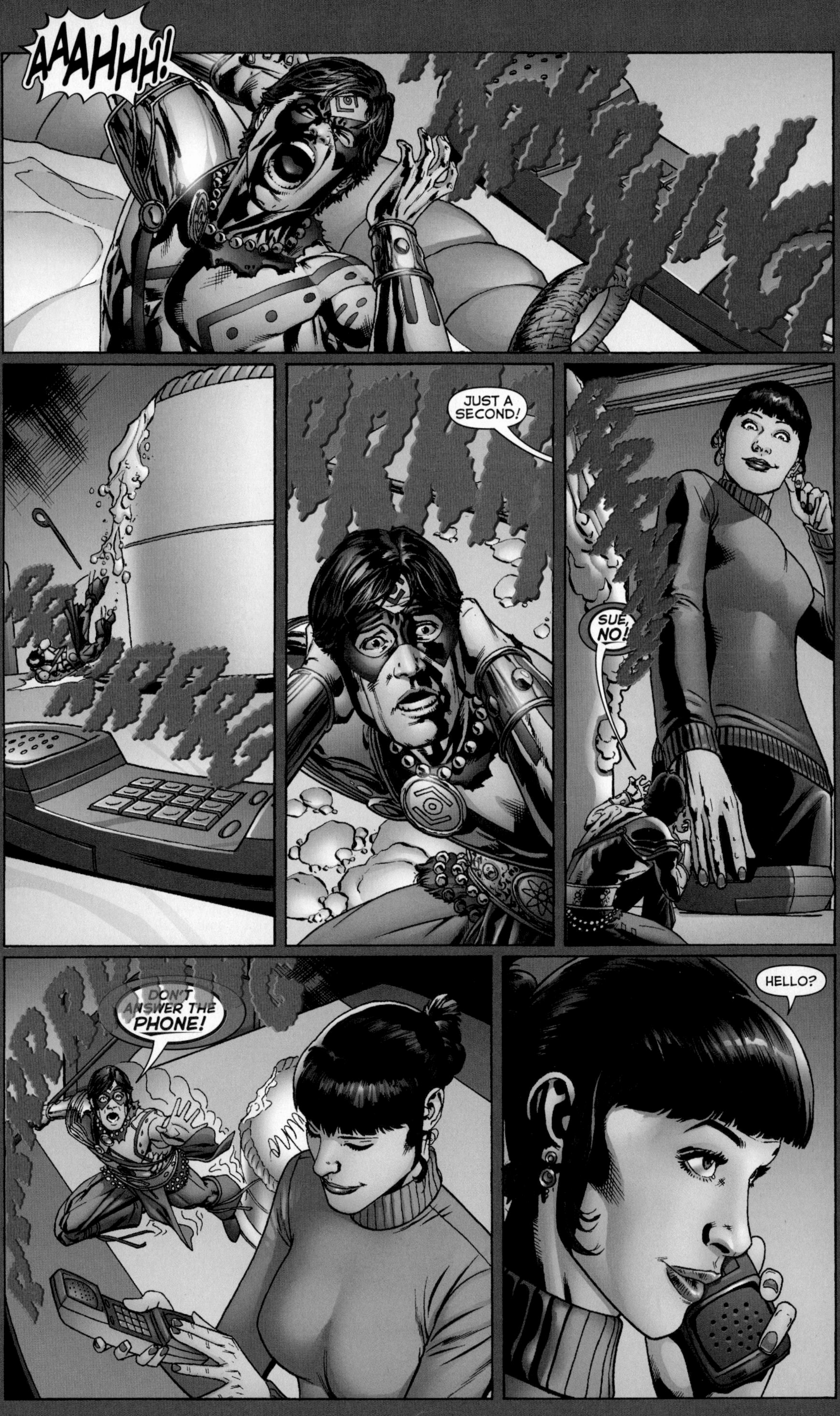
AAAHHH!
JUST A SECOND!
SUE, NO!
DON'T ANSWER THE PHONE!
HELLO?

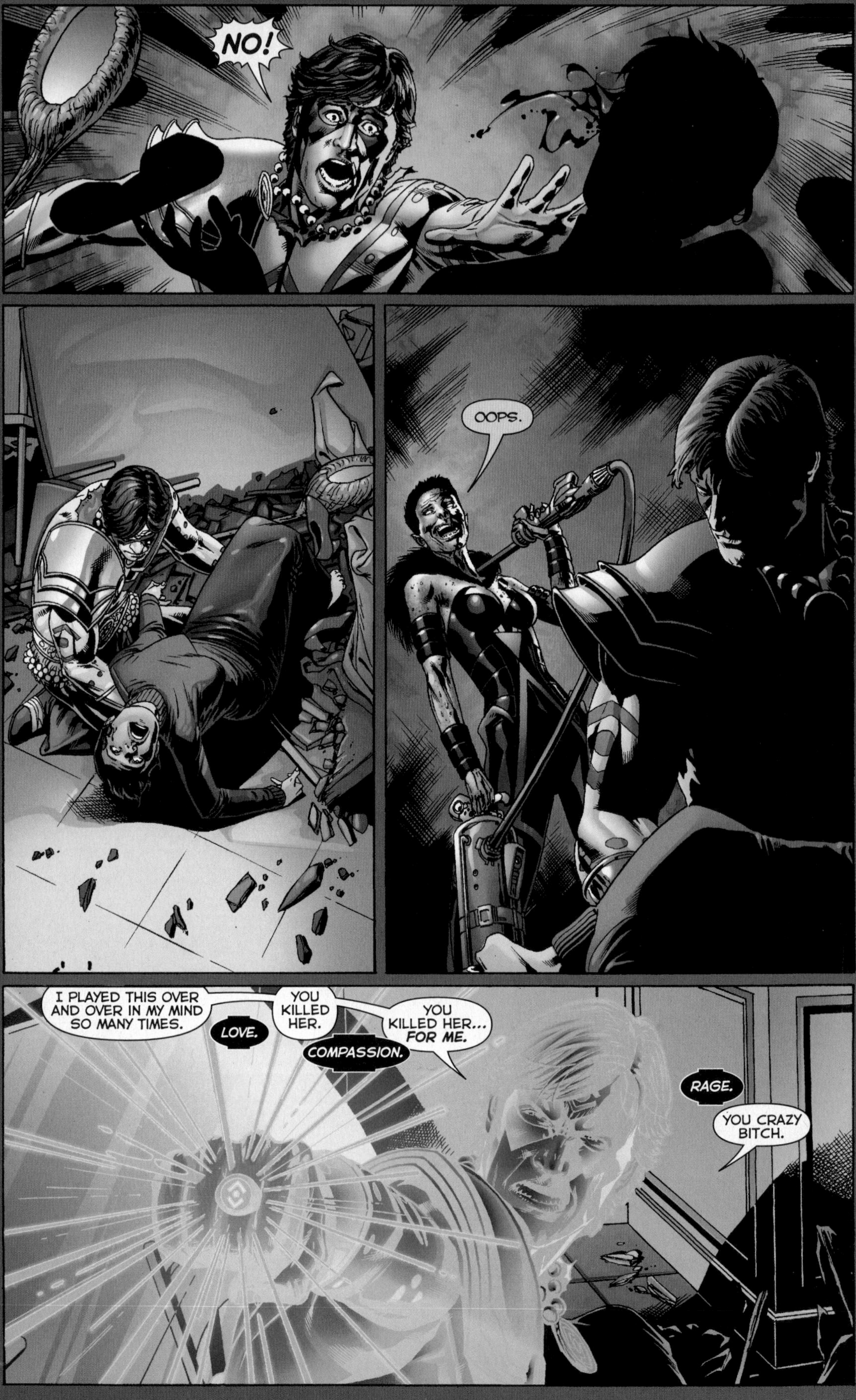
NO!
OOPS.
I PLAYED THIS OVER AND OVER IN MY MIND SO MANY TIMES.
LOVE.
YOU KILLED HER.
COMPASSION.
YOU KILLED HER... FOR ME.
RAGE.
YOU CRAZY BITCH.

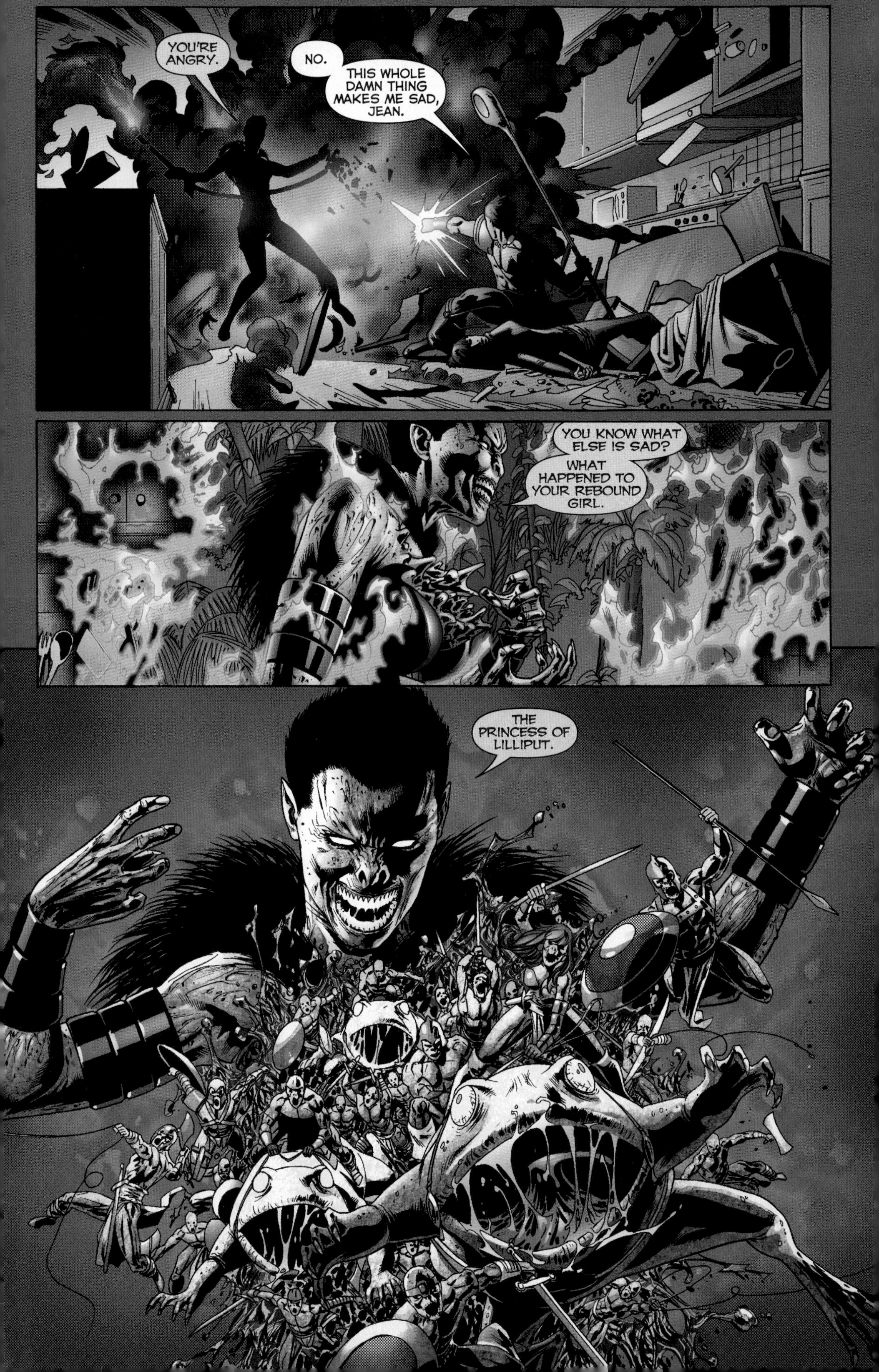
YOU'RE ANGRY.
NO.
THIS WHOLE DAMN THING MAKES ME SAD, JEAN.
YOU KNOW WHAT ELSE IS SAD?
WHAT HAPPENED TO YOUR REBOUND GIRL.
THE PRINCESS OF LILLIPUT.

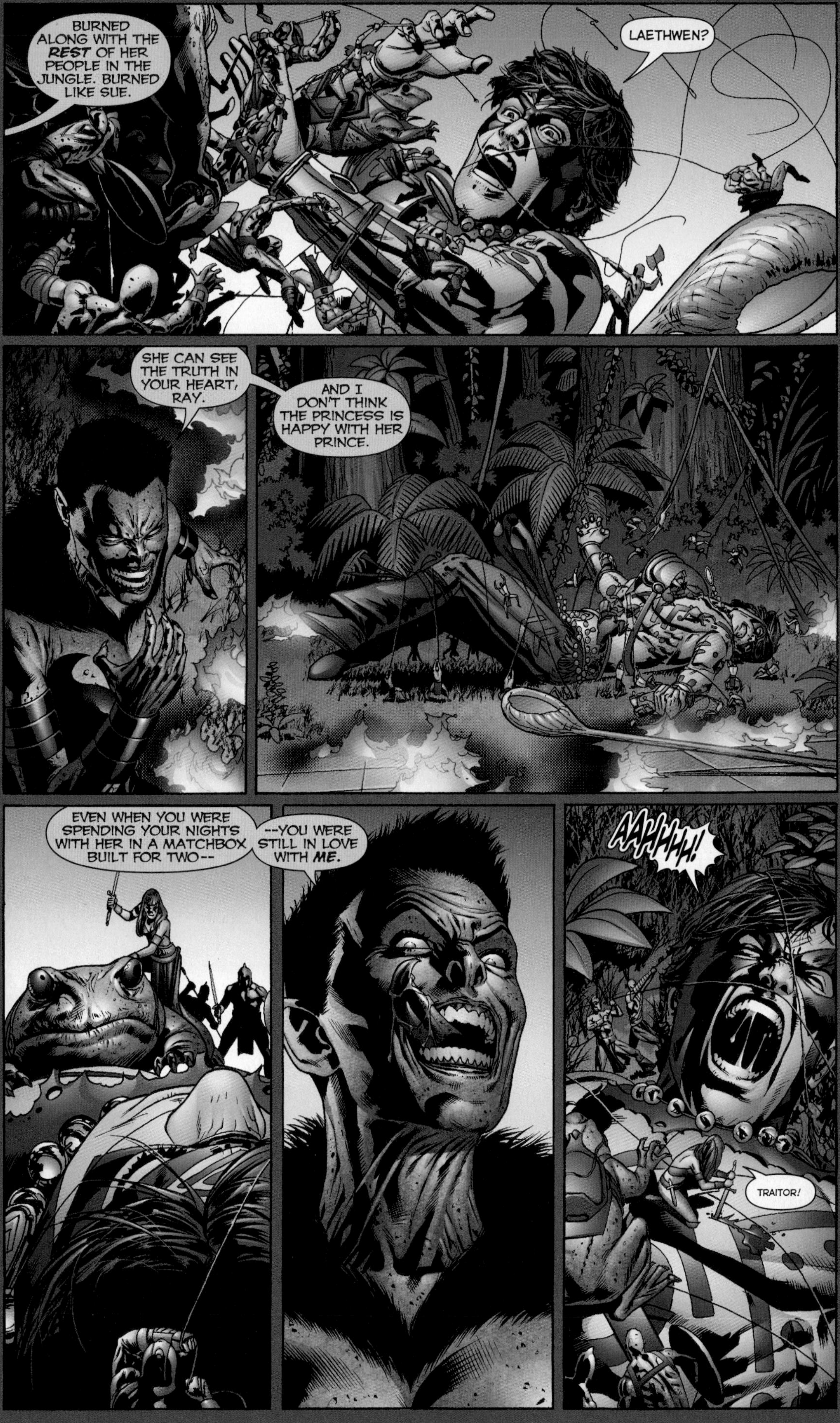

BURNED ALONG WITH THE *REST* OF HER PEOPLE IN THE JUNGLE. BURNED LIKE SUE.
LAETHWEN?
SHE CAN SEE THE TRUTH IN YOUR HEART, RAY.
AND I DON'T THINK THE PRINCESS IS HAPPY WITH HER PRINCE.
EVEN WHEN YOU WERE SPENDING YOUR NIGHTS WITH HER IN A MATCHBOX BUILT FOR TWO--
--YOU WERE STILL IN LOVE WITH *ME*.
AAHHHH!
TRAITOR!

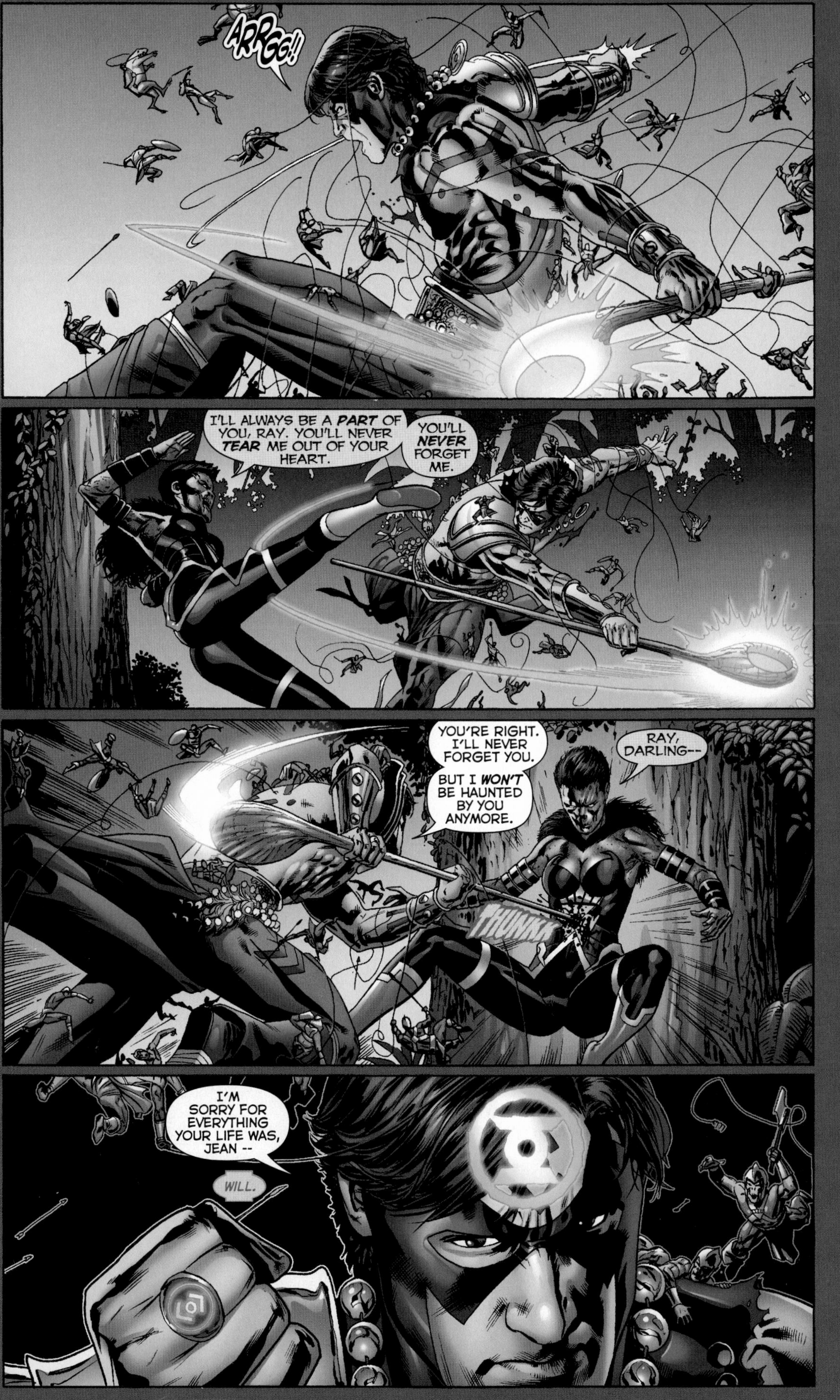
ARRGG!!
I'LL ALWAYS BE A PART OF YOU, RAY. YOU'LL NEVER TEAR ME OUT OF YOUR HEART.
YOU'LL NEVER FORGET ME.
YOU'RE RIGHT. I'LL NEVER FORGET YOU.
BUT I WON'T BE HAUNTED BY YOU ANYMORE.
RAY, DARLING--
THUNKK
I'M SORRY FOR EVERYTHING YOUR LIFE WAS, JEAN --
WILL.

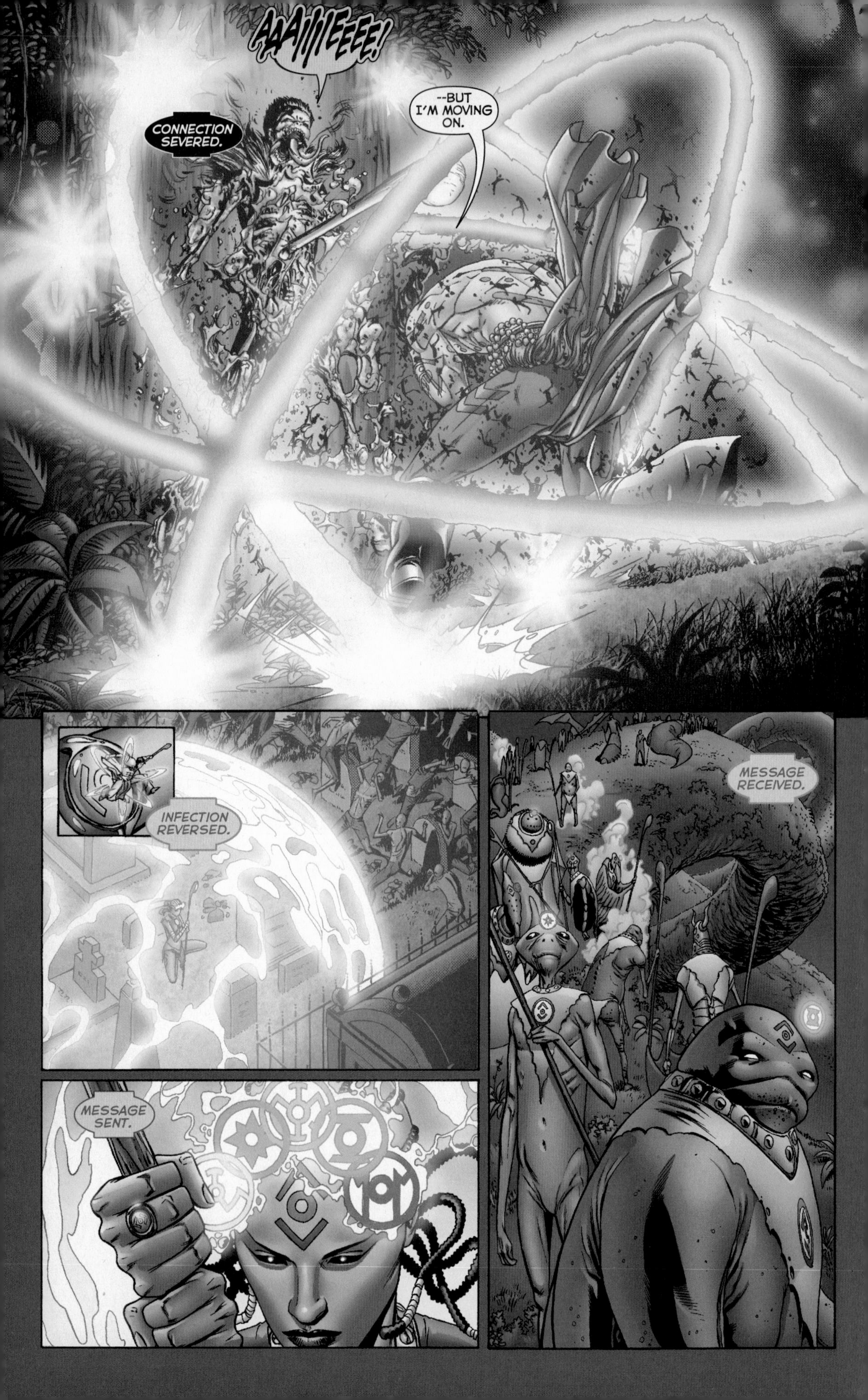
AAAIIIIEEEE!
CONNECTION SEVERED.
--BUT I'M MOVING ON.
INFECTION REVERSED.
MESSAGE SENT.
MESSAGE RECEIVED.

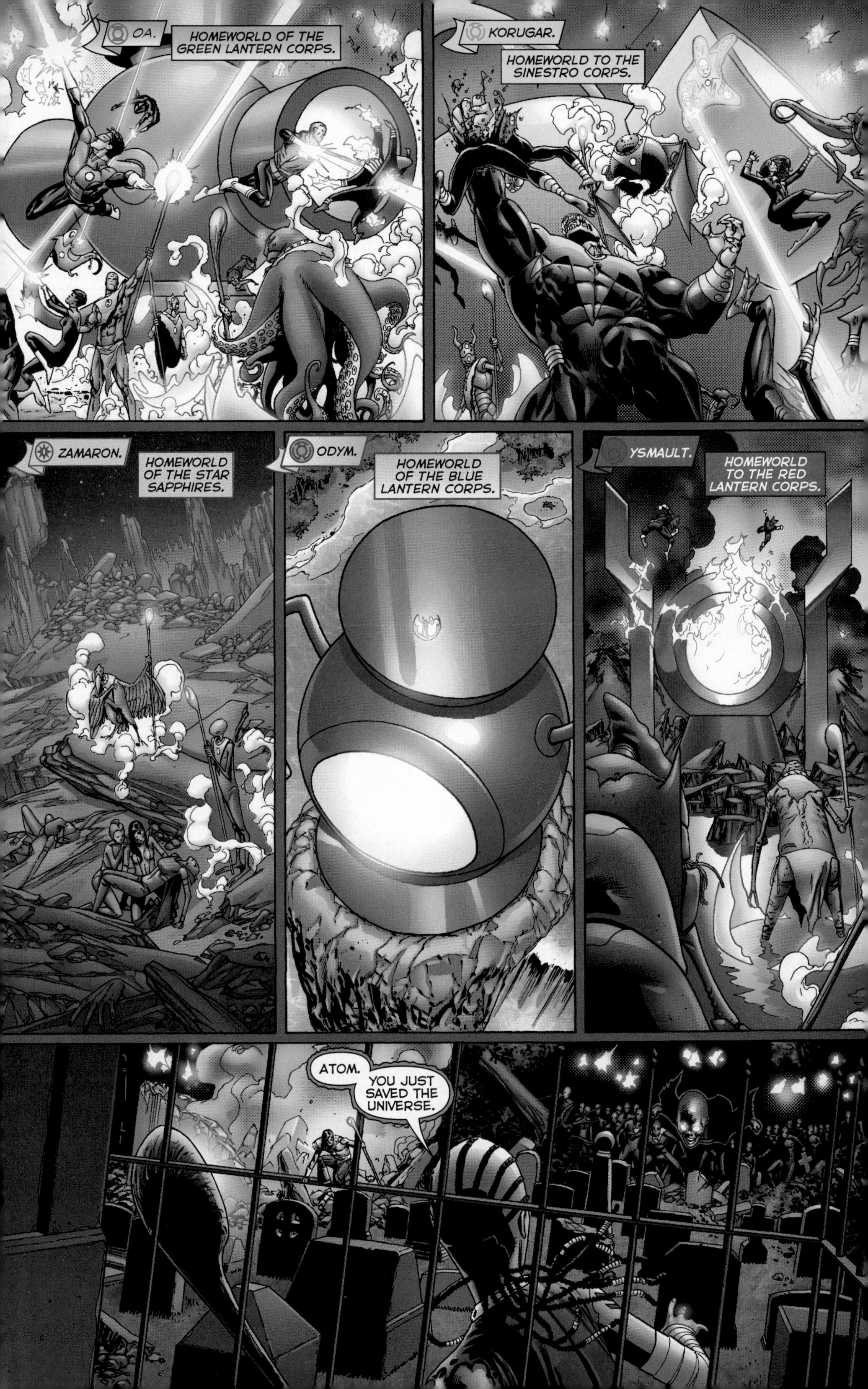
OA.
HOMEWORLD OF THE GREEN LANTERN CORPS.
KORUGAR.
HOMEWORLD TO THE SINESTRO CORPS.
ZAMARON.
HOMEWORLD OF THE STAR SAPPHIRES.
ODYM.
HOMEWORLD OF THE BLUE LANTERN CORPS.
YSMAULT.
HOMEWORLD TO THE RED LANTERN CORPS.
ATOM.
YOU JUST SAVED THE UNIVERSE.

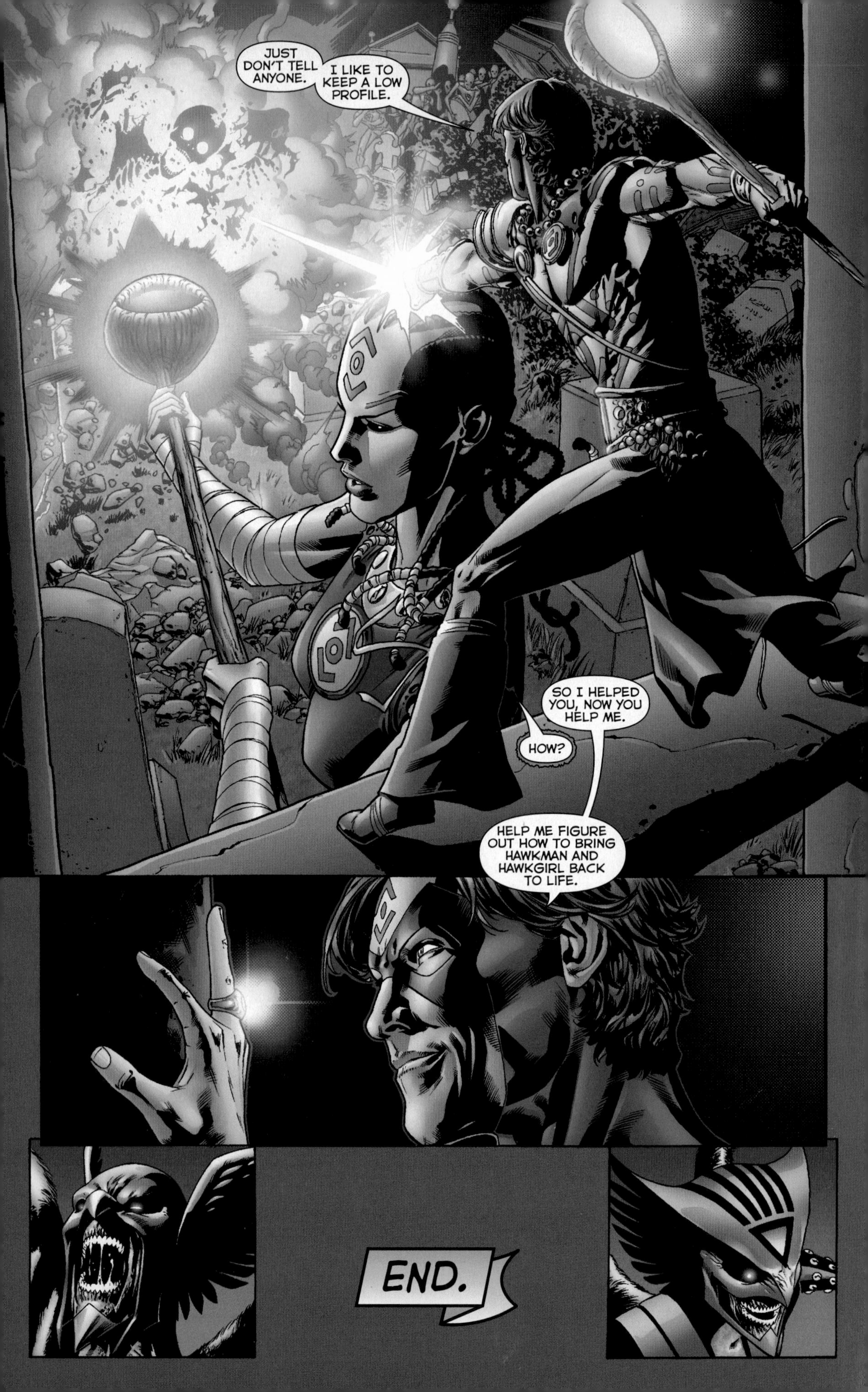
JUST DON'T TELL ANYONE.
I LIKE TO KEEP A LOW PROFILE.
SO I HELPED YOU, NOW YOU HELP ME.
HOW?
HELP ME FIGURE OUT HOW TO BRING HAWKMAN AND HAWKGIRL BACK TO LIFE.
END.

THE PHANTOM STRANGER 42
Cover by Ardian Syaf & Vicente Cifuentes
with Ulises Arreola

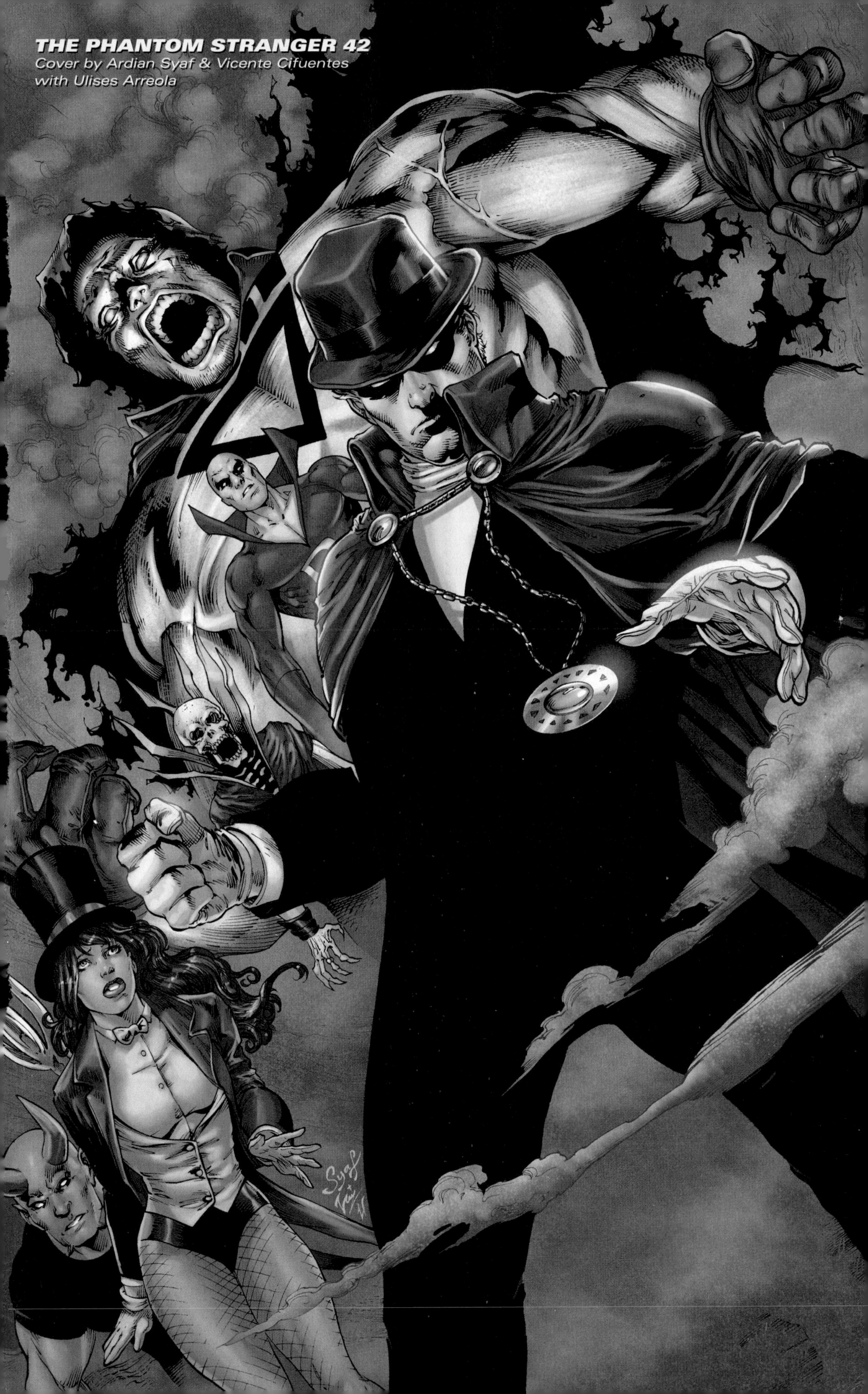

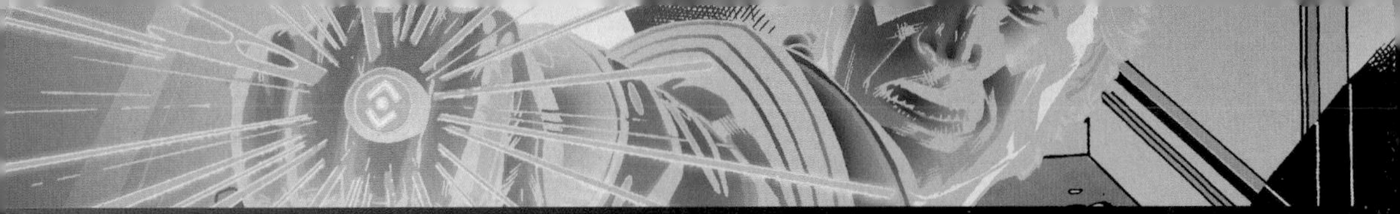

DEADMAN WALKING

PETER J. TOMASI
WRITER

ARDIAN SYAF
PENCILS

VICENTE CIFUENTES
INKS

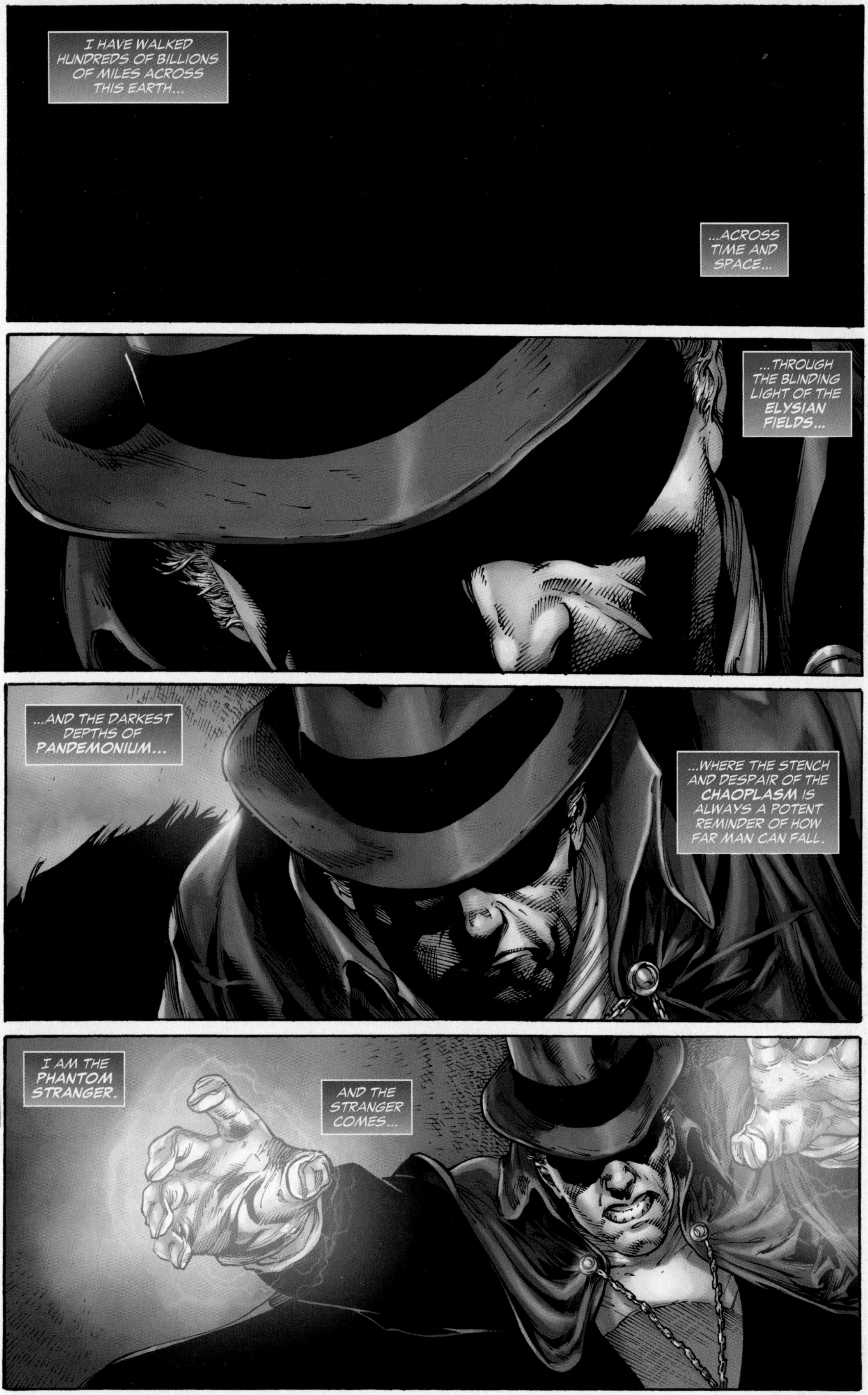
I HAVE WALKED HUNDREDS OF BILLIONS OF MILES ACROSS THIS EARTH...
...ACROSS TIME AND SPACE...
...THROUGH THE BLINDING LIGHT OF THE ELYSIAN FIELDS...
...AND THE DARKEST DEPTHS OF PANDEMONIUM...
...WHERE THE STENCH AND DESPAIR OF THE CHAOPLASM IS ALWAYS A POTENT REMINDER OF HOW FAR MAN CAN FALL.
I AM THE PHANTOM STRANGER.
AND THE STRANGER COMES...

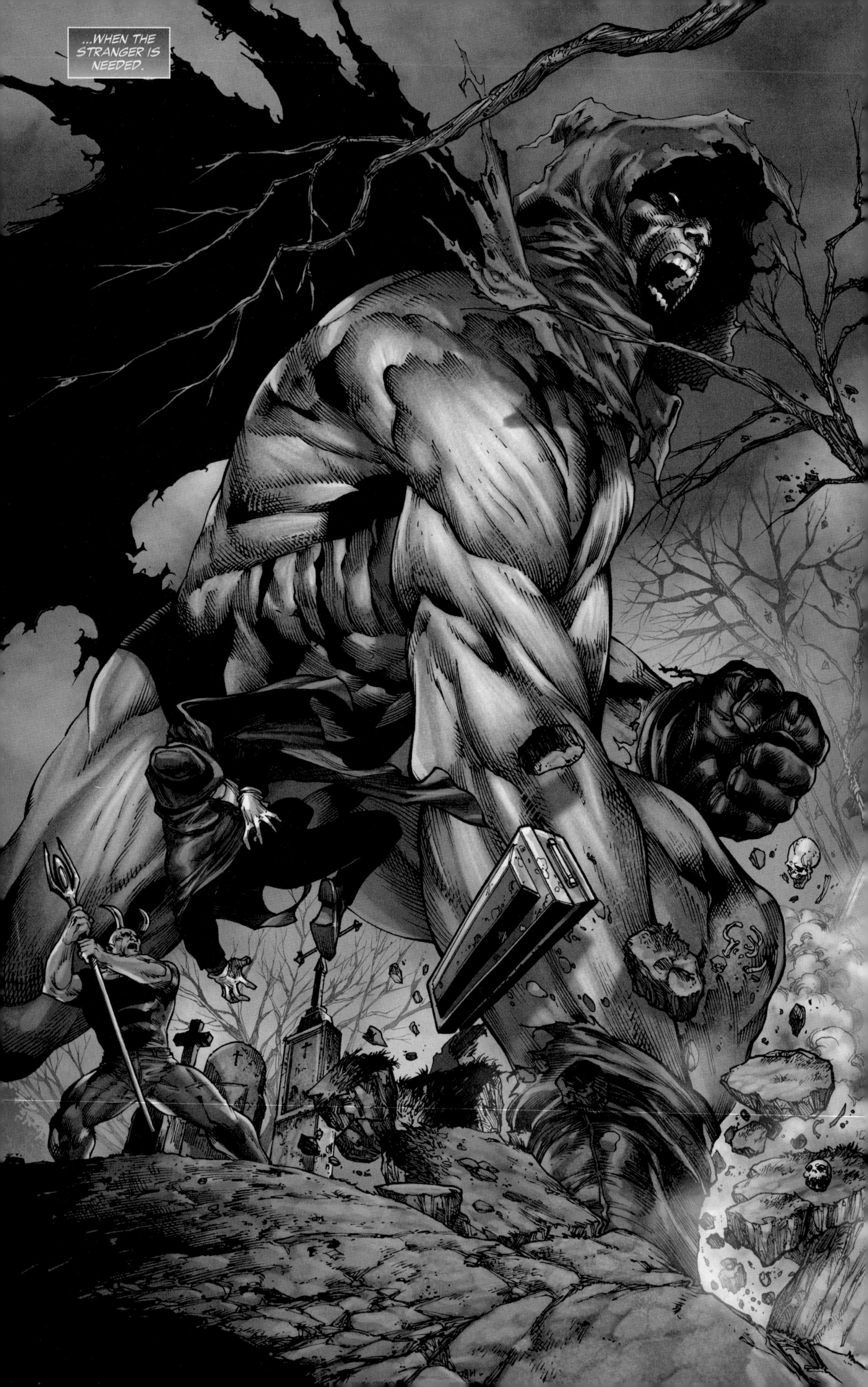
...WHEN THE STRANGER IS NEEDED.

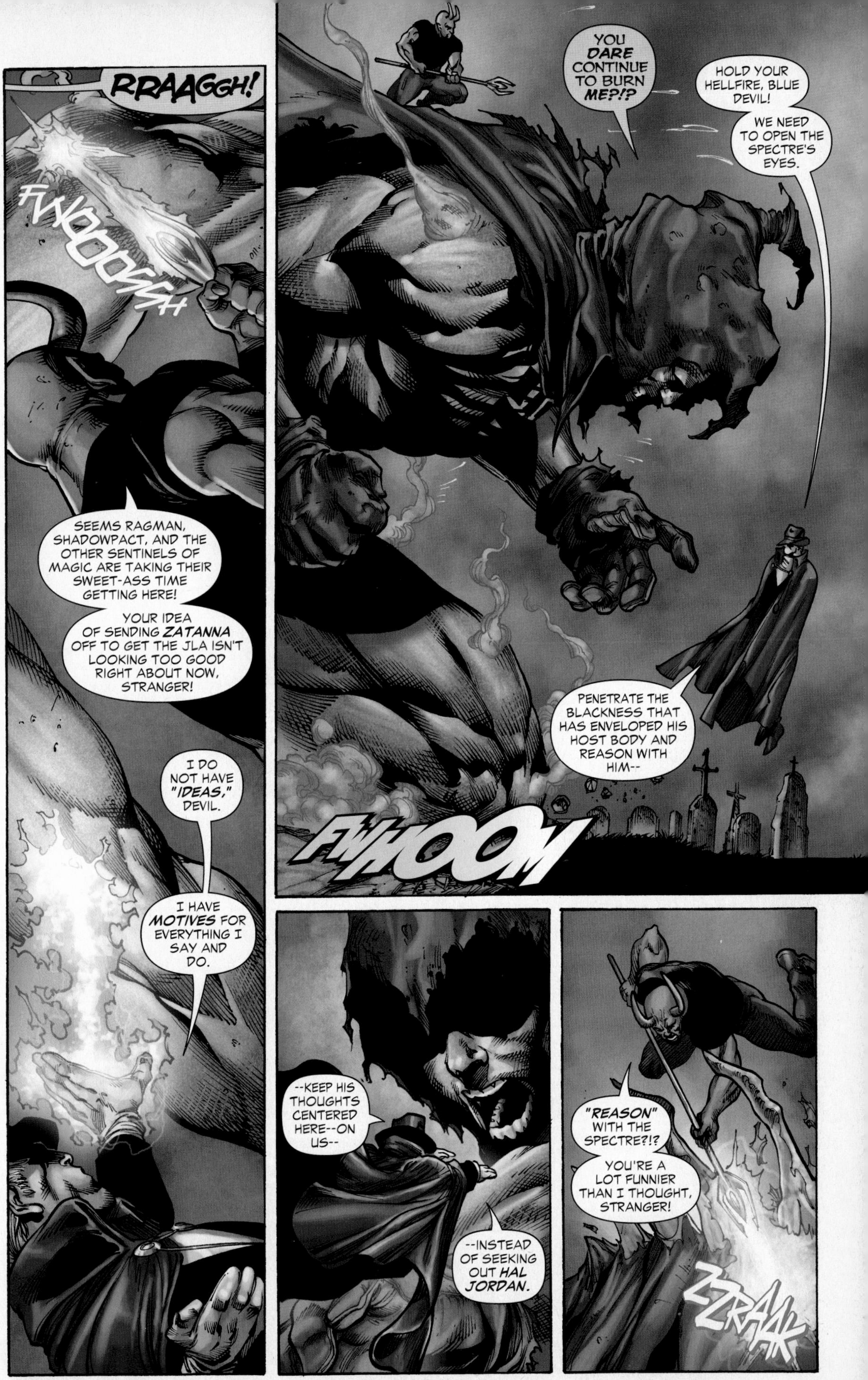
RRAAGGH!
FWOOOSH
SEEMS RAGMAN, SHADOWPACT, AND THE OTHER SENTINELS OF MAGIC ARE TAKING THEIR SWEET-ASS TIME GETTING HERE!
YOUR IDEA OF SENDING ZATANNA OFF TO GET THE JLA ISN'T LOOKING TOO GOOD RIGHT ABOUT NOW, STRANGER!
I DO NOT HAVE "IDEAS," DEVIL.
I HAVE MOTIVES FOR EVERYTHING I SAY AND DO.
YOU DARE CONTINUE TO BURN ME?!?
HOLD YOUR HELLFIRE, BLUE DEVIL!
WE NEED TO OPEN THE SPECTRE'S EYES.
PENETRATE THE BLACKNESS THAT HAS ENVELOPED HIS HOST BODY AND REASON WITH HIM--
FWHOOM
--KEEP HIS THOUGHTS CENTERED HERE--ON US--
--INSTEAD OF SEEKING OUT HAL JORDAN.
"REASON" WITH THE SPECTRE?!?
YOU'RE A LOT FUNNIER THAN I THOUGHT, STRANGER!
ZZRAAK

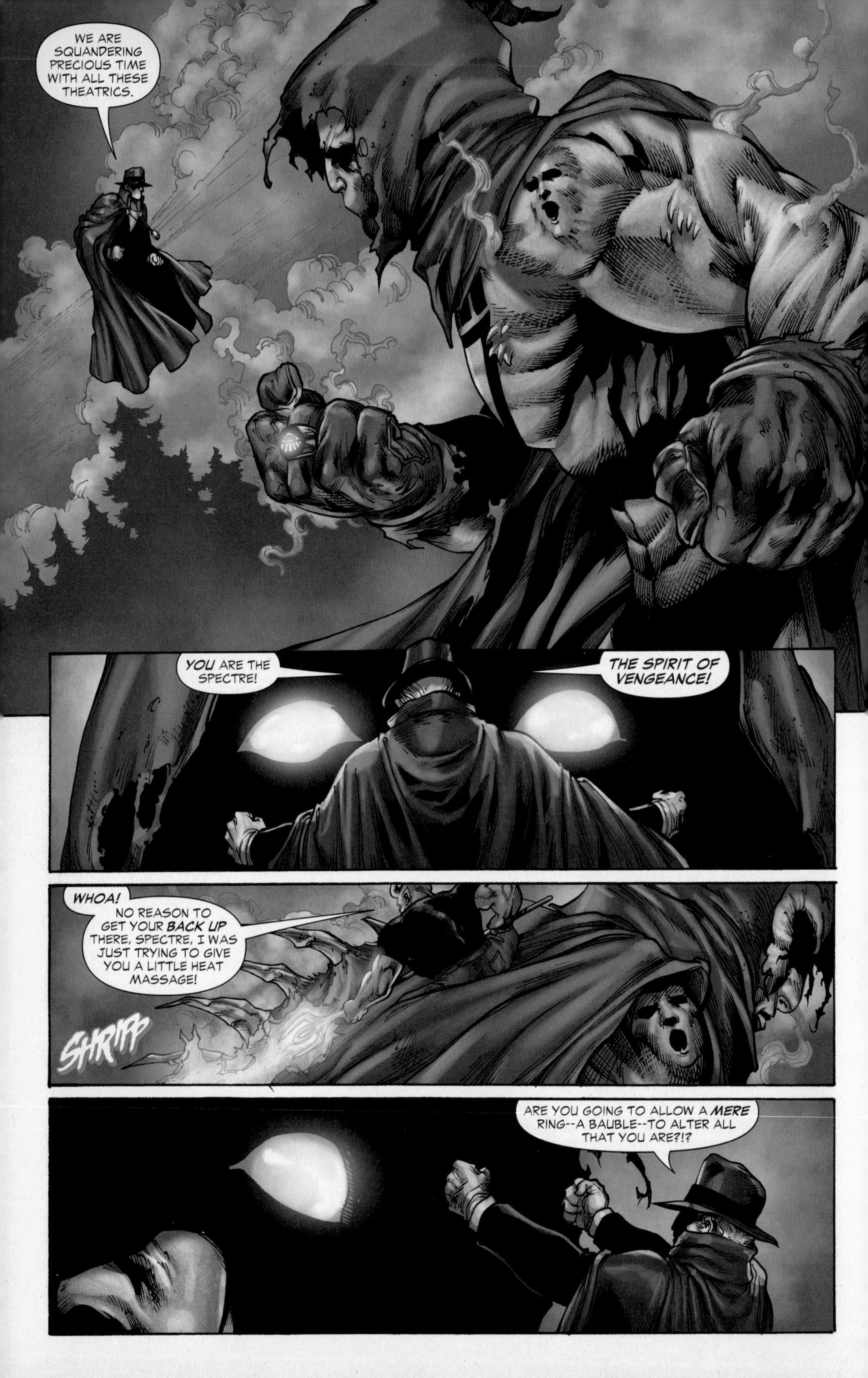
WE ARE SQUANDERING PRECIOUS TIME WITH ALL THESE THEATRICS.
YOU ARE THE SPECTRE!
THE SPIRIT OF VENGEANCE!
WHOA! NO REASON TO GET YOUR ***BACK UP*** THERE, SPECTRE, I WAS JUST TRYING TO GIVE YOU A LITTLE HEAT MASSAGE!
SHRIPP
ARE YOU GOING TO ALLOW A ***MERE*** RING--A BAUBLE--TO ALTER ALL THAT YOU ARE?!?

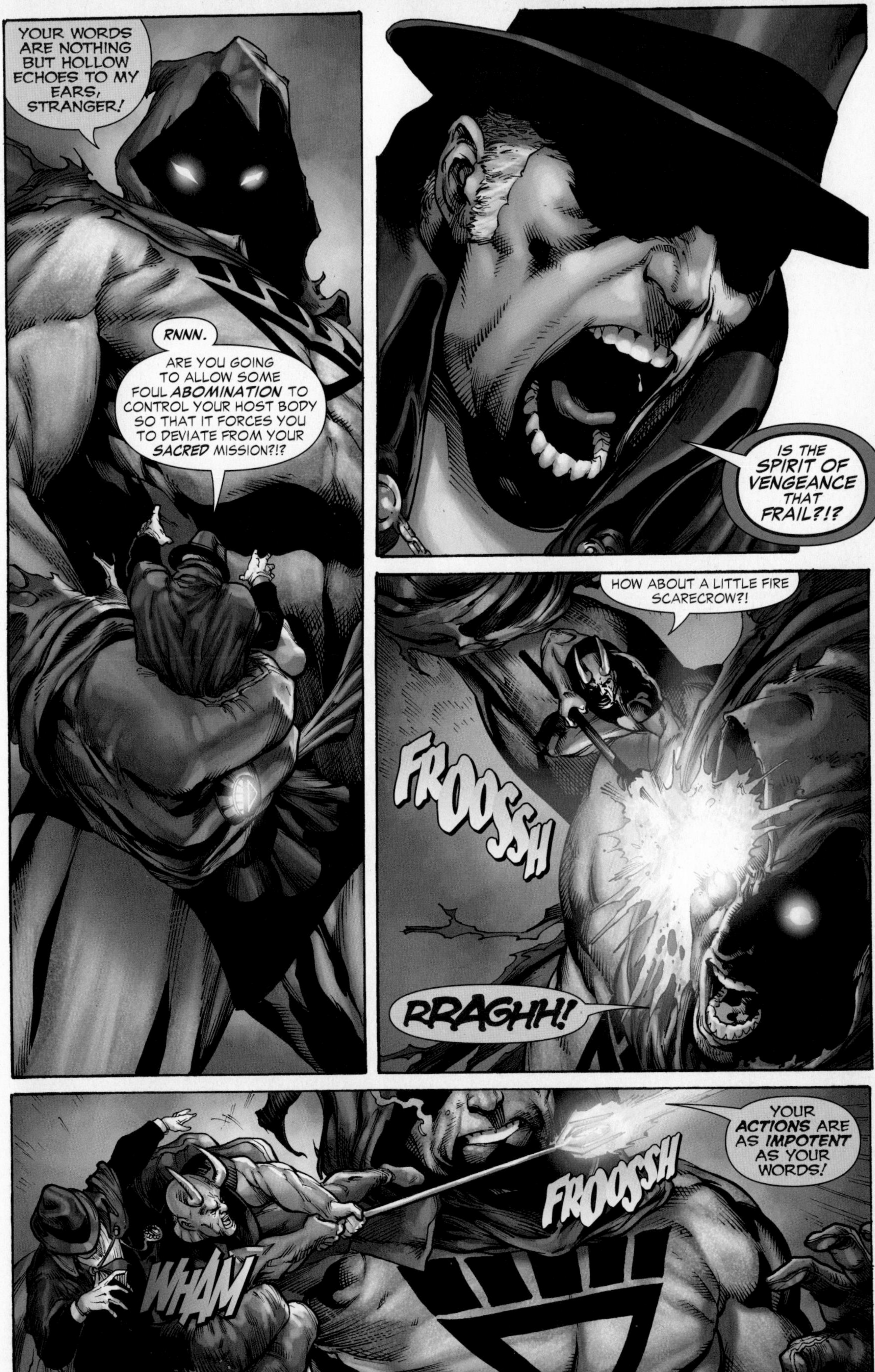
YOUR WORDS ARE NOTHING BUT HOLLOW ECHOES TO MY EARS, STRANGER!
RNNN.
ARE YOU GOING TO ALLOW SOME FOUL ABOMINATION TO CONTROL YOUR HOST BODY SO THAT IT FORCES YOU TO DEVIATE FROM YOUR SACRED MISSION?!?
IS THE SPIRIT OF VENGEANCE THAT FRAIL?!?
HOW ABOUT A LITTLE FIRE SCARECROW?!
FROOSSH
RRAGHH!
YOUR ACTIONS ARE AS IMPOTENT AS YOUR WORDS!
FROOSSH
WHAM

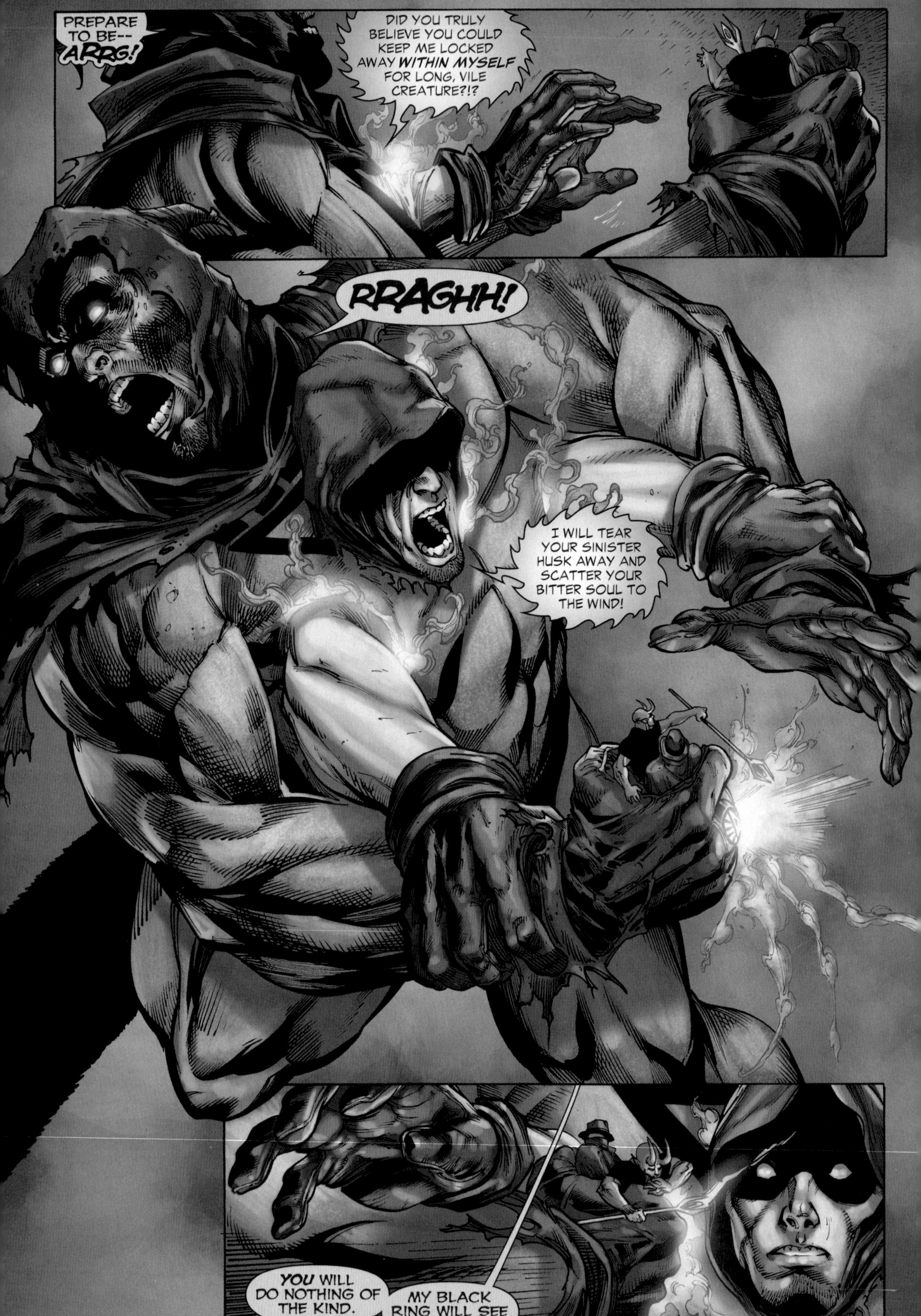
PREPARE TO BE-- ARRG!
DID YOU TRULY BELIEVE YOU COULD KEEP ME LOCKED AWAY WITHIN MYSELF FOR LONG, VILE CREATURE?!?
RRAGHH!
I WILL TEAR YOUR SINISTER HUSK AWAY AND SCATTER YOUR BITTER SOUL TO THE WIND!
YOU WILL DO NOTHING OF THE KIND.
MY BLACK RING WILL SEE TO THAT!

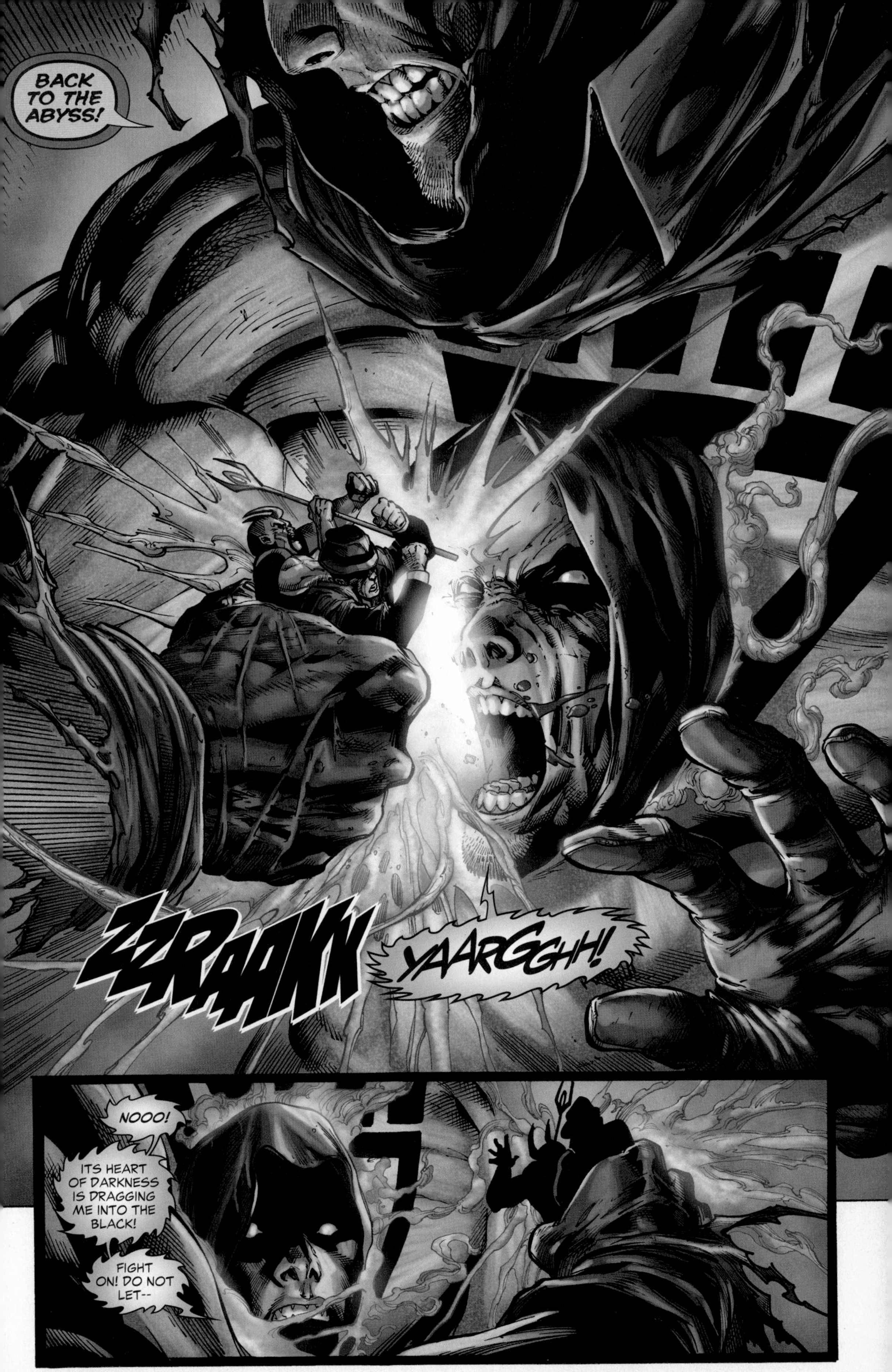
BACK TO THE ABYSS!
ZZRAAKK
YAARGGHH!
NOOO!
ITS HEART OF DARKNESS IS DRAGGING ME INTO THE BLACK!
FIGHT ON! DO NOT LET--

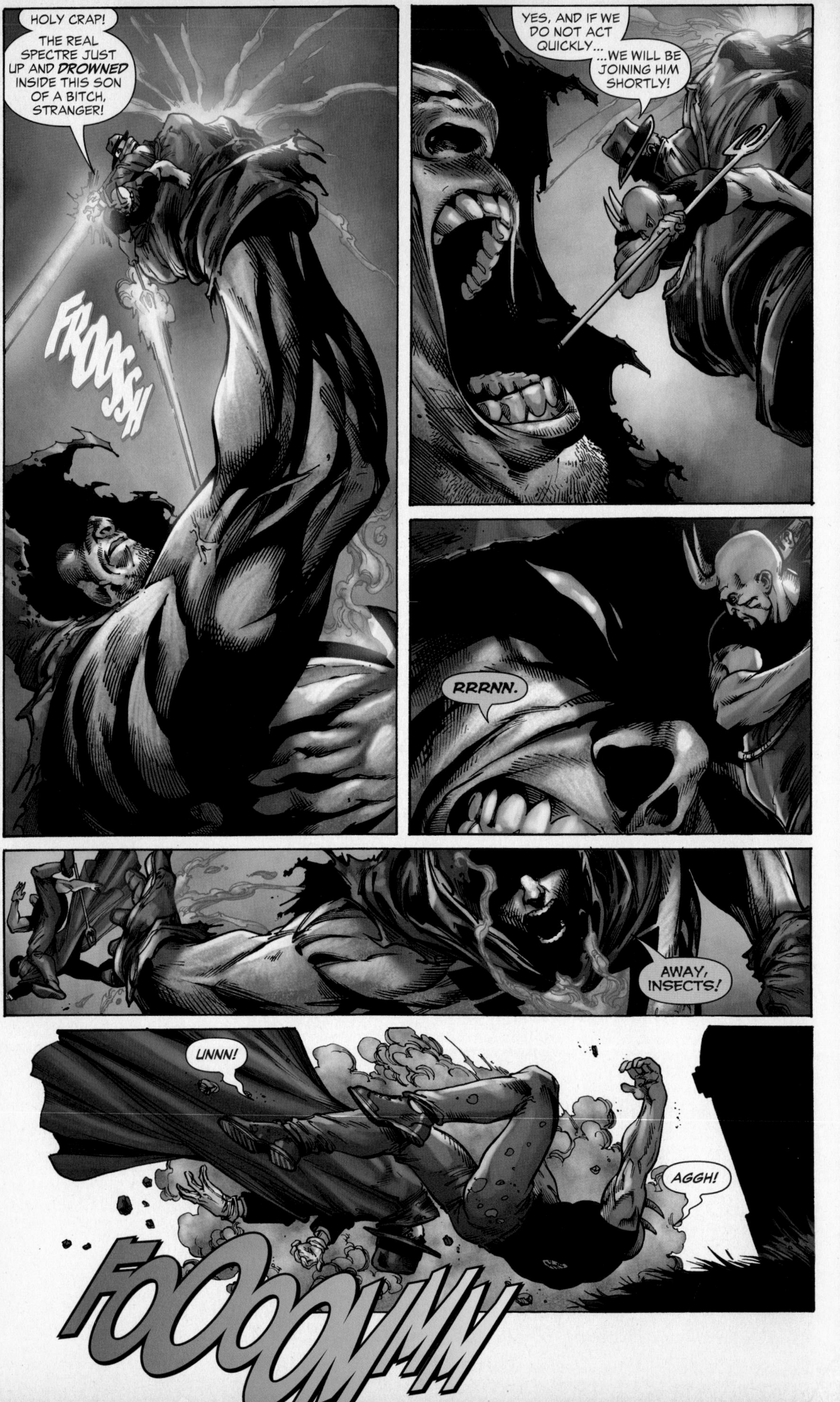

HOLY CRAP!
THE REAL SPECTRE JUST UP AND DROWNED INSIDE THIS SON OF A BITCH, STRANGER!
FROOSSH
YES, AND IF WE DO NOT ACT QUICKLY...
...WE WILL BE JOINING HIM SHORTLY!
RRRNN.
AWAY, INSECTS!
UNNN!
AGGH!
FOOOOMMM

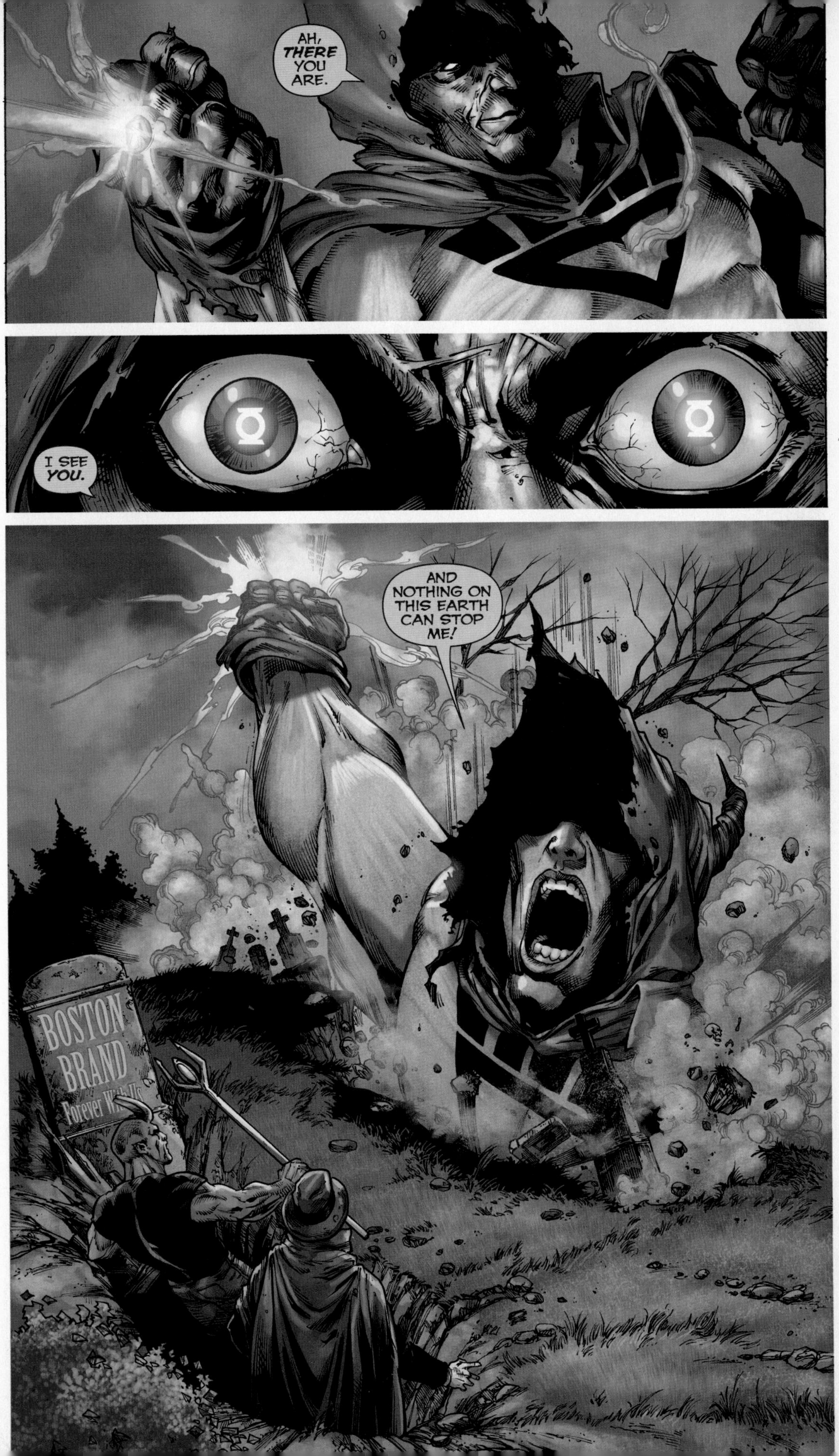
AH, THERE YOU ARE.
I SEE YOU.
AND NOTHING ON THIS EARTH CAN STOP ME!
BOSTON BRAND

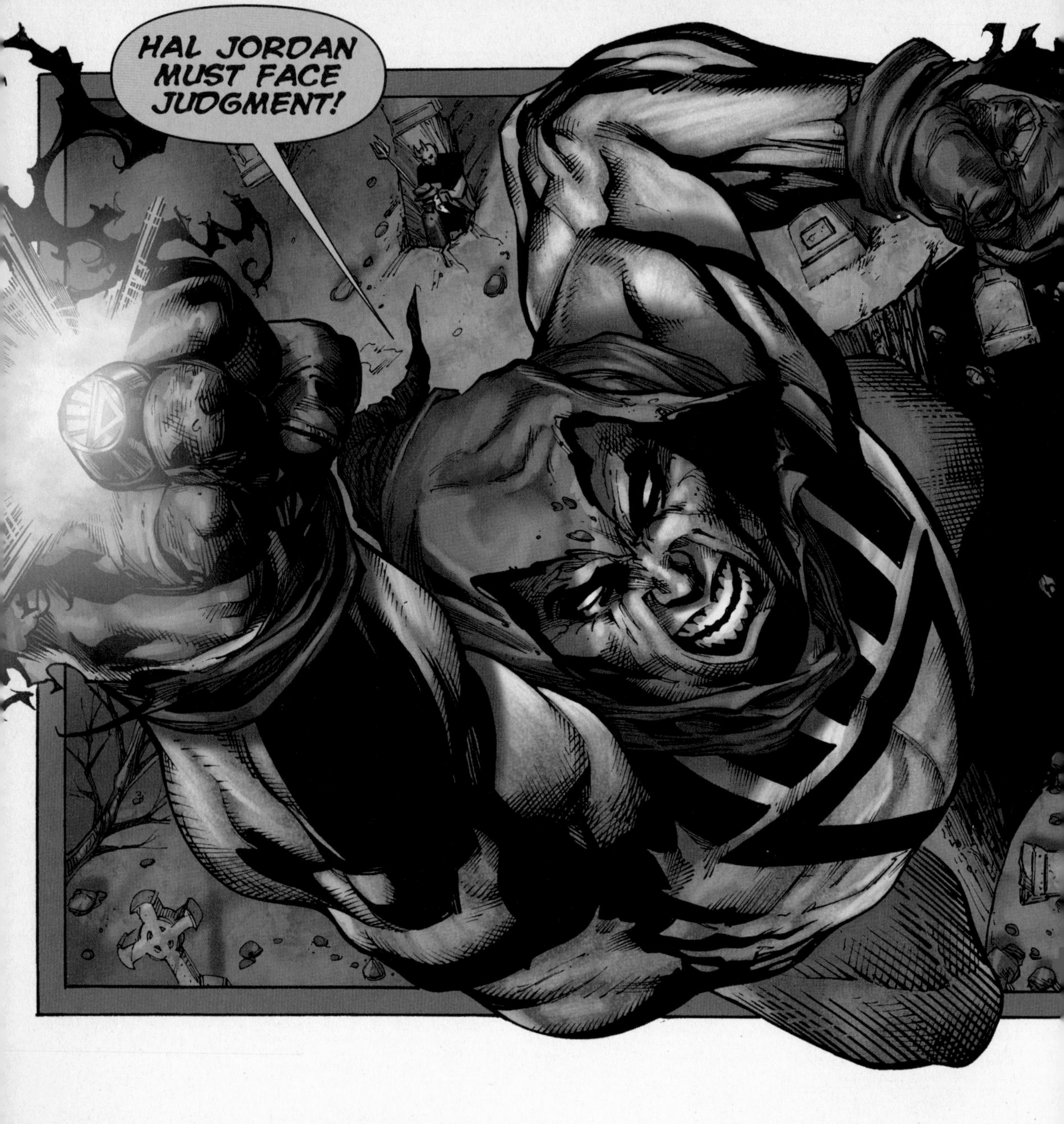
HAL JORDAN MUST FACE JUDGMENT!

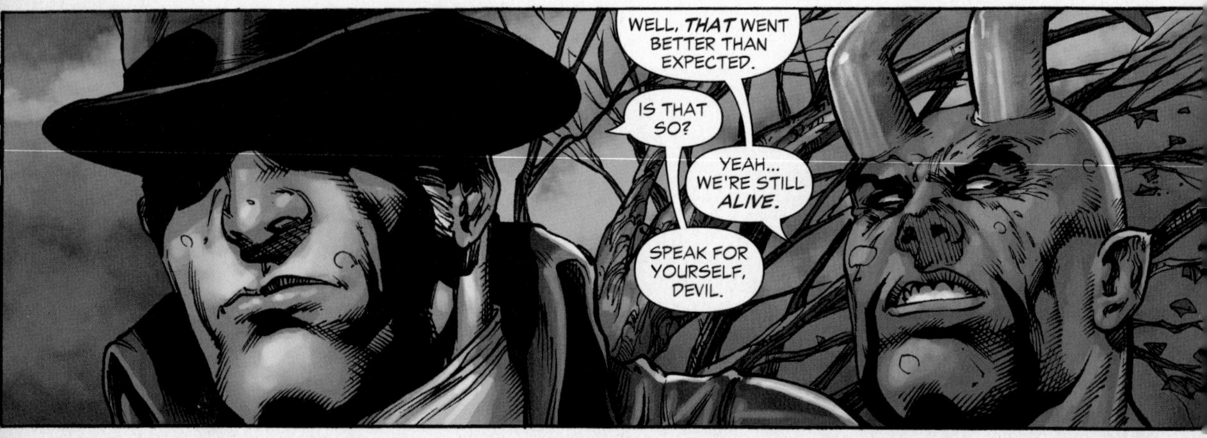
WELL, THAT WENT BETTER THAN EXPECTED.
IS THAT SO?
YEAH... WE'RE STILL ALIVE.
SPEAK FOR YOURSELF, DEVIL.

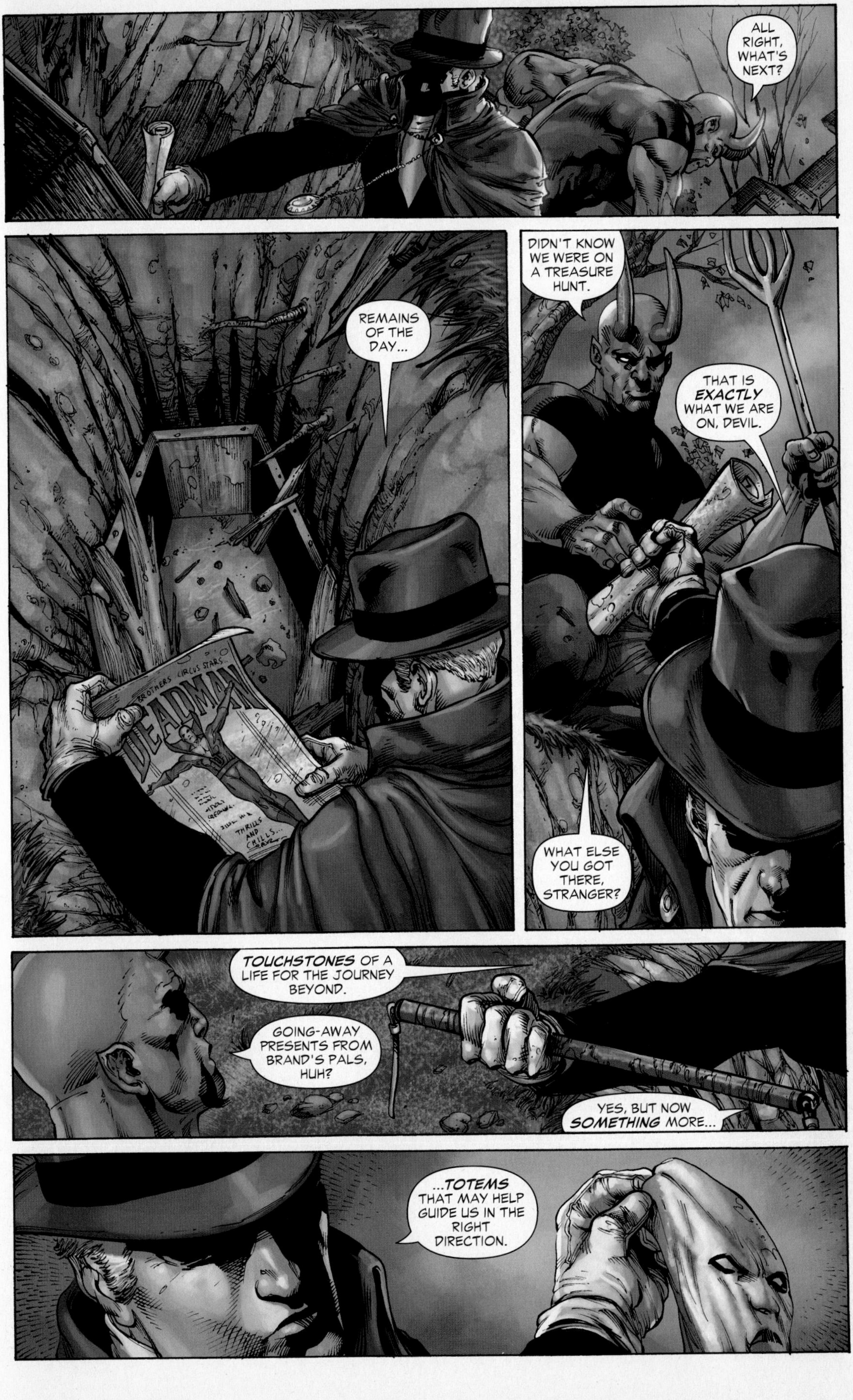
ALL RIGHT, WHAT'S NEXT?
REMAINS OF THE DAY...
DEADMAN
THRILLS AND CHILLS...
DIDN'T KNOW WE WERE ON A TREASURE HUNT.
THAT IS *EXACTLY* WHAT WE ARE ON, DEVIL.
WHAT ELSE YOU GOT THERE, STRANGER?
TOUCHSTONES OF A LIFE FOR THE JOURNEY BEYOND.
GOING-AWAY PRESENTS FROM BRAND'S PALS, HUH?
YES, BUT NOW *SOMETHING* MORE...
...*TOTEMS* THAT MAY HELP GUIDE US IN THE RIGHT DIRECTION.

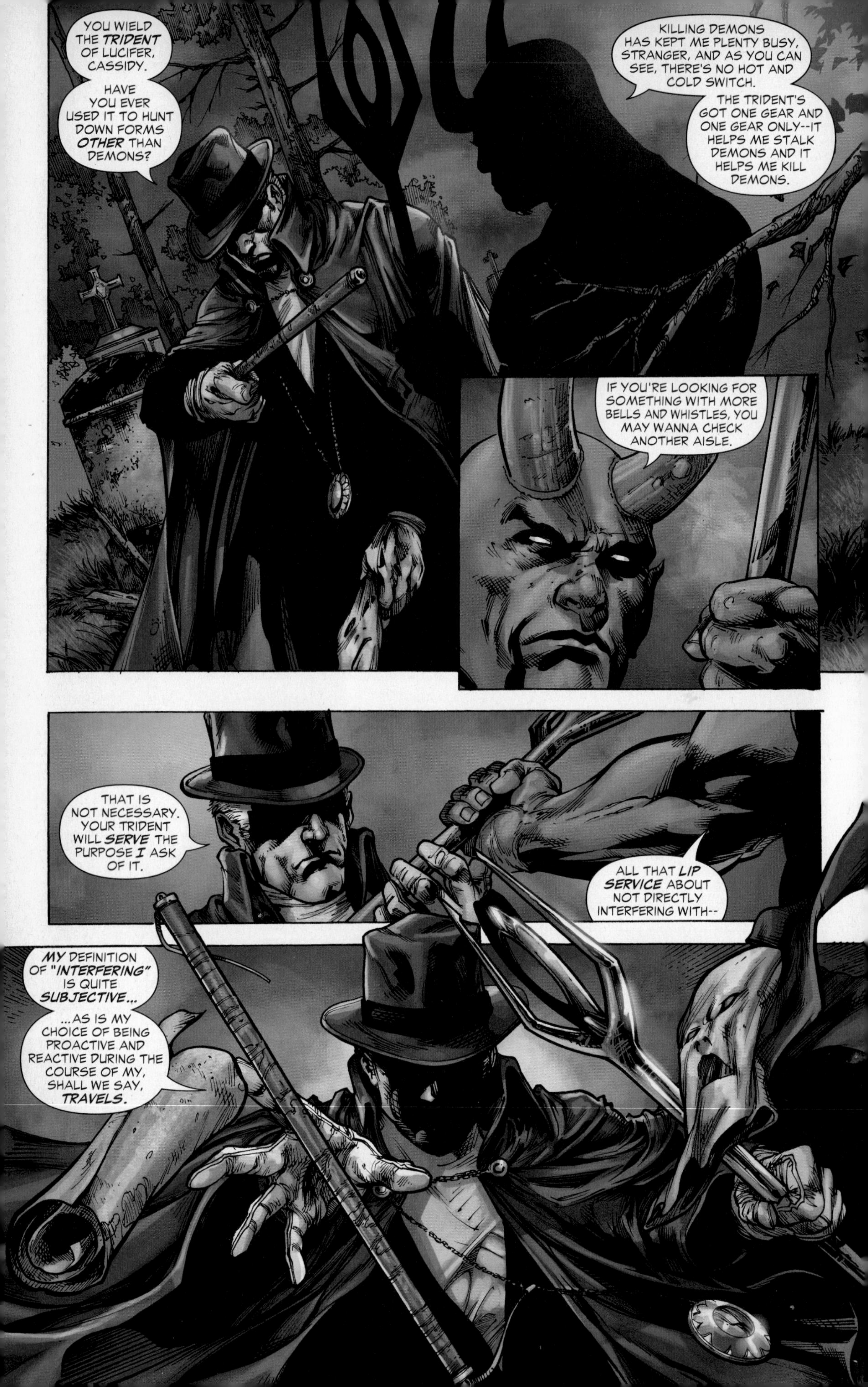
YOU WIELD THE TRIDENT OF LUCIFER, CASSIDY.
HAVE YOU EVER USED IT TO HUNT DOWN FORMS OTHER THAN DEMONS?
KILLING DEMONS HAS KEPT ME PLENTY BUSY, STRANGER, AND AS YOU CAN SEE, THERE'S NO HOT AND COLD SWITCH.
THE TRIDENT'S GOT ONE GEAR AND ONE GEAR ONLY--IT HELPS ME STALK DEMONS AND IT HELPS ME KILL DEMONS.
IF YOU'RE LOOKING FOR SOMETHING WITH MORE BELLS AND WHISTLES, YOU MAY WANNA CHECK ANOTHER AISLE.
THAT IS NOT NECESSARY. YOUR TRIDENT WILL SERVE THE PURPOSE I ASK OF IT.
ALL THAT LIP SERVICE ABOUT NOT DIRECTLY INTERFERING WITH--
MY DEFINITION OF "INTERFERING" IS QUITE SUBJECTIVE...
...AS IS MY CHOICE OF BEING PROACTIVE AND REACTIVE DURING THE COURSE OF MY, SHALL WE SAY, TRAVELS.

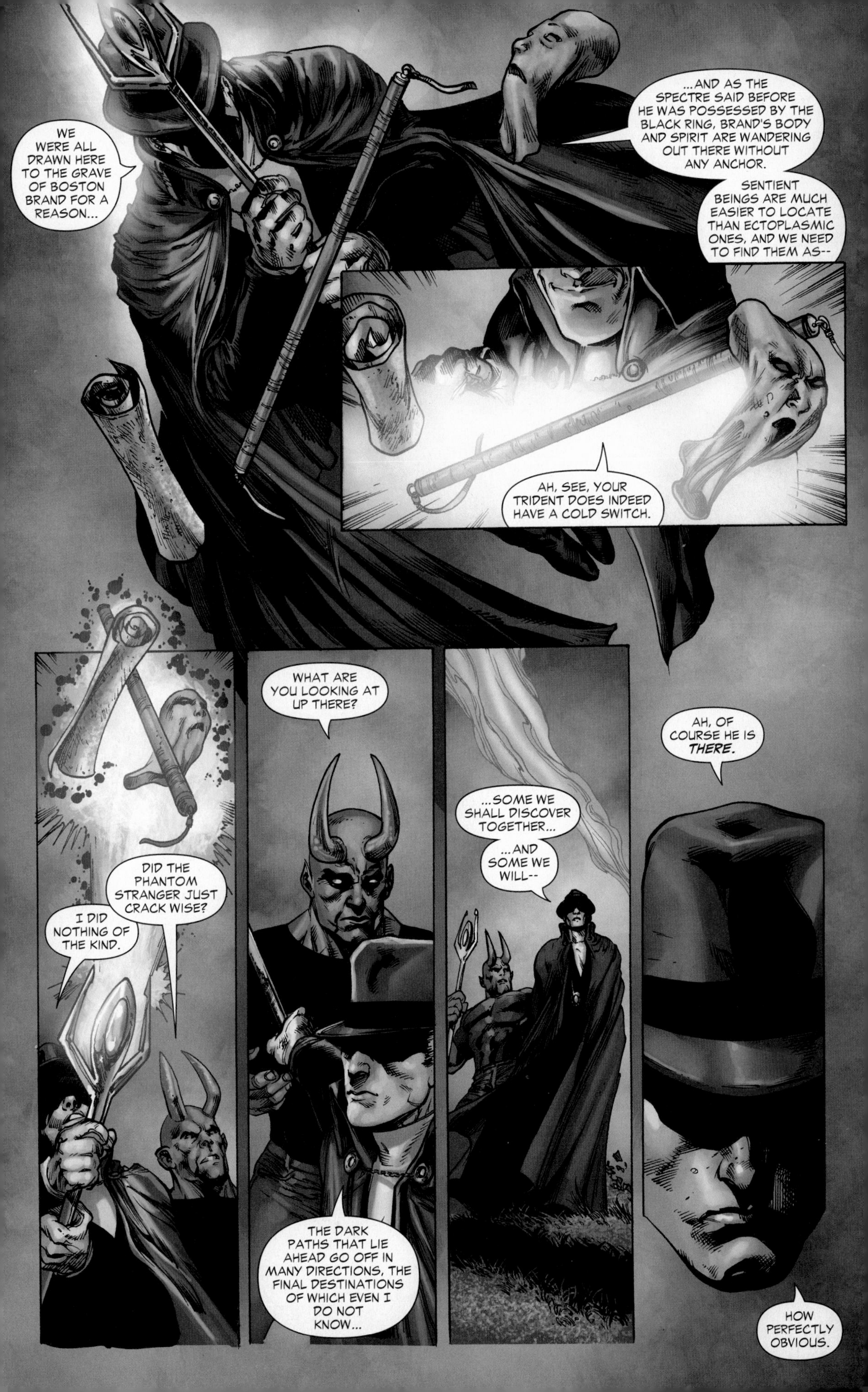

WE WERE ALL DRAWN HERE TO THE GRAVE OF BOSTON BRAND FOR A REASON...
...AND AS THE SPECTRE SAID BEFORE HE WAS POSSESSED BY THE BLACK RING, BRAND'S BODY AND SPIRIT ARE WANDERING OUT THERE WITHOUT ANY ANCHOR.
SENTIENT BEINGS ARE MUCH EASIER TO LOCATE THAN ECTOPLASMIC ONES, AND WE NEED TO FIND THEM AS--
AH, SEE, YOUR TRIDENT DOES INDEED HAVE A COLD SWITCH.
DID THE PHANTOM STRANGER JUST CRACK WISE?
I DID NOTHING OF THE KIND.
WHAT ARE YOU LOOKING AT UP THERE?
THE DARK PATHS THAT LIE AHEAD GO OFF IN MANY DIRECTIONS, THE FINAL DESTINATIONS OF WHICH EVEN I DO NOT KNOW...
...SOME WE SHALL DISCOVER TOGETHER...
...AND SOME WE WILL--
AH, OF COURSE HE IS *THERE.*
HOW PERFECTLY OBVIOUS.

TALK TO ME!

RRARR!

I'LL KEEP TEARING YOU APART AS FAST AS YOU CAN PUT YOURSELVES BACK TOGETHER!

ONE BLACK INFESTED HEART AT A TIME!

BECAUSE TIME IS ALL I GOT--

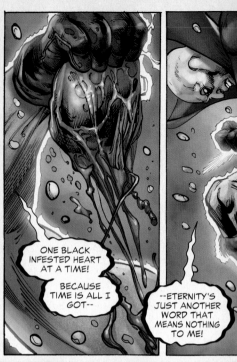

--ETERNITY'S JUST ANOTHER WORD THAT MEANS NOTHING TO ME!

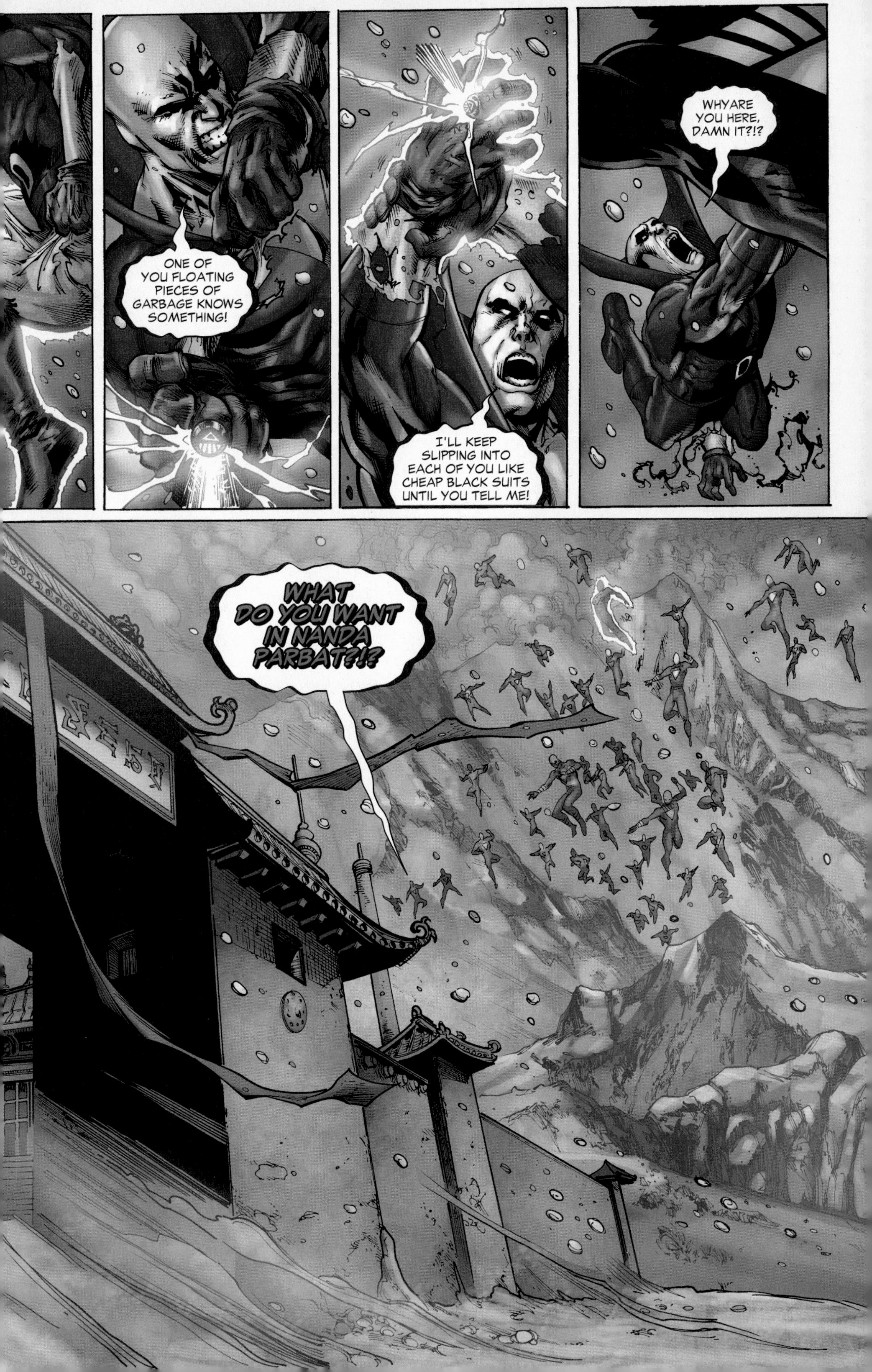
ONE OF YOU FLOATING PIECES OF GARBAGE KNOWS SOMETHING!
I'LL KEEP SLIPPING INTO EACH OF YOU LIKE CHEAP BLACK SUITS UNTIL YOU TELL ME!
WHYARE YOU HERE, DAMN IT?!?
WHAT DO YOU WANT IN NANDA PARBAT?!?

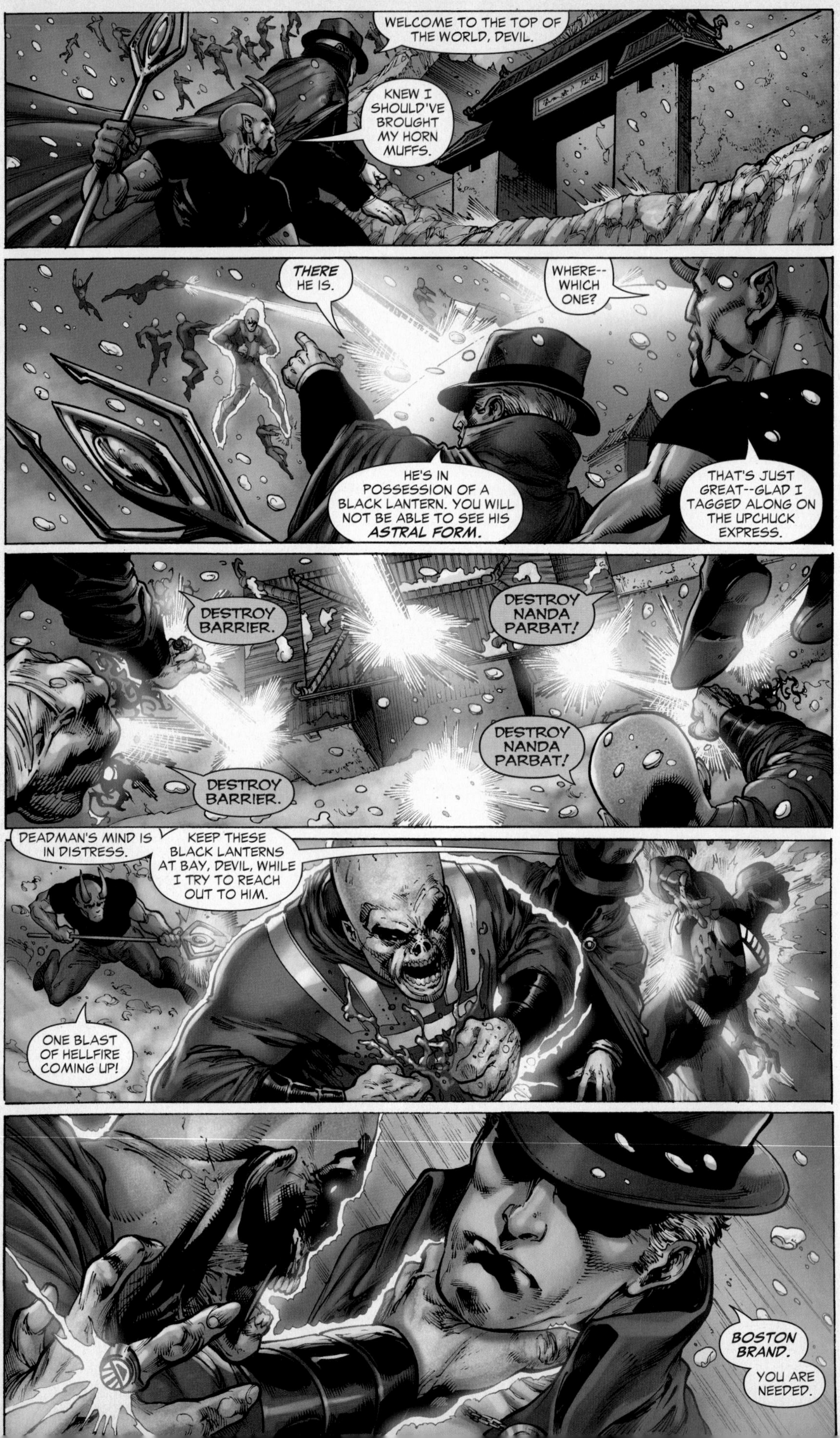
WELCOME TO THE TOP OF THE WORLD, DEVIL.
KNEW I SHOULD'VE BROUGHT MY HORN MUFFS.
THERE HE IS.
WHERE-- WHICH ONE?
HE'S IN POSSESSION OF A BLACK LANTERN. YOU WILL NOT BE ABLE TO SEE HIS ASTRAL FORM.
THAT'S JUST GREAT--GLAD I TAGGED ALONG ON THE UPCHUCK EXPRESS.
DESTROY BARRIER.
DESTROY NANDA PARBAT!
DESTROY NANDA PARBAT!
DESTROY BARRIER.
DEADMAN'S MIND IS IN DISTRESS.
KEEP THESE BLACK LANTERNS AT BAY, DEVIL, WHILE I TRY TO REACH OUT TO HIM.
ONE BLAST OF HELLFIRE COMING UP!
BOSTON BRAND.
YOU ARE NEEDED.

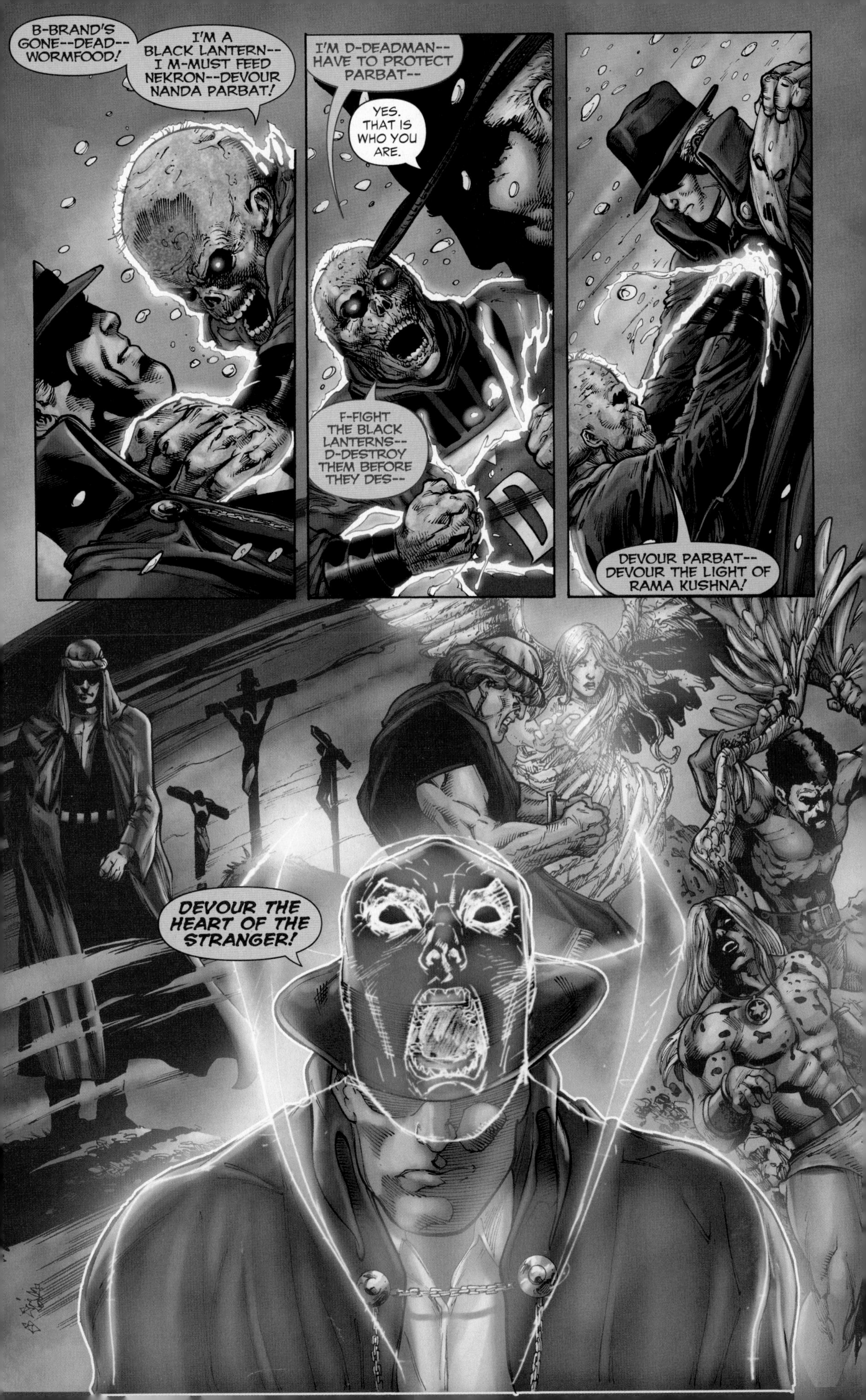

B-BRAND'S GONE--DEAD--WORMFOOD!
I'M A BLACK LANTERN--I M-MUST FEED NEKRON--DEVOUR NANDA PARBAT!
I'M D-DEADMAN--HAVE TO PROTECT PARBAT--
YES. THAT IS WHO YOU ARE.
F-FIGHT THE BLACK LANTERNS--D-DESTROY THEM BEFORE THEY DES--
DEVOUR PARBAT--DEVOUR THE LIGHT OF RAMA KUSHNA!
DEVOUR THE HEART OF THE STRANGER!

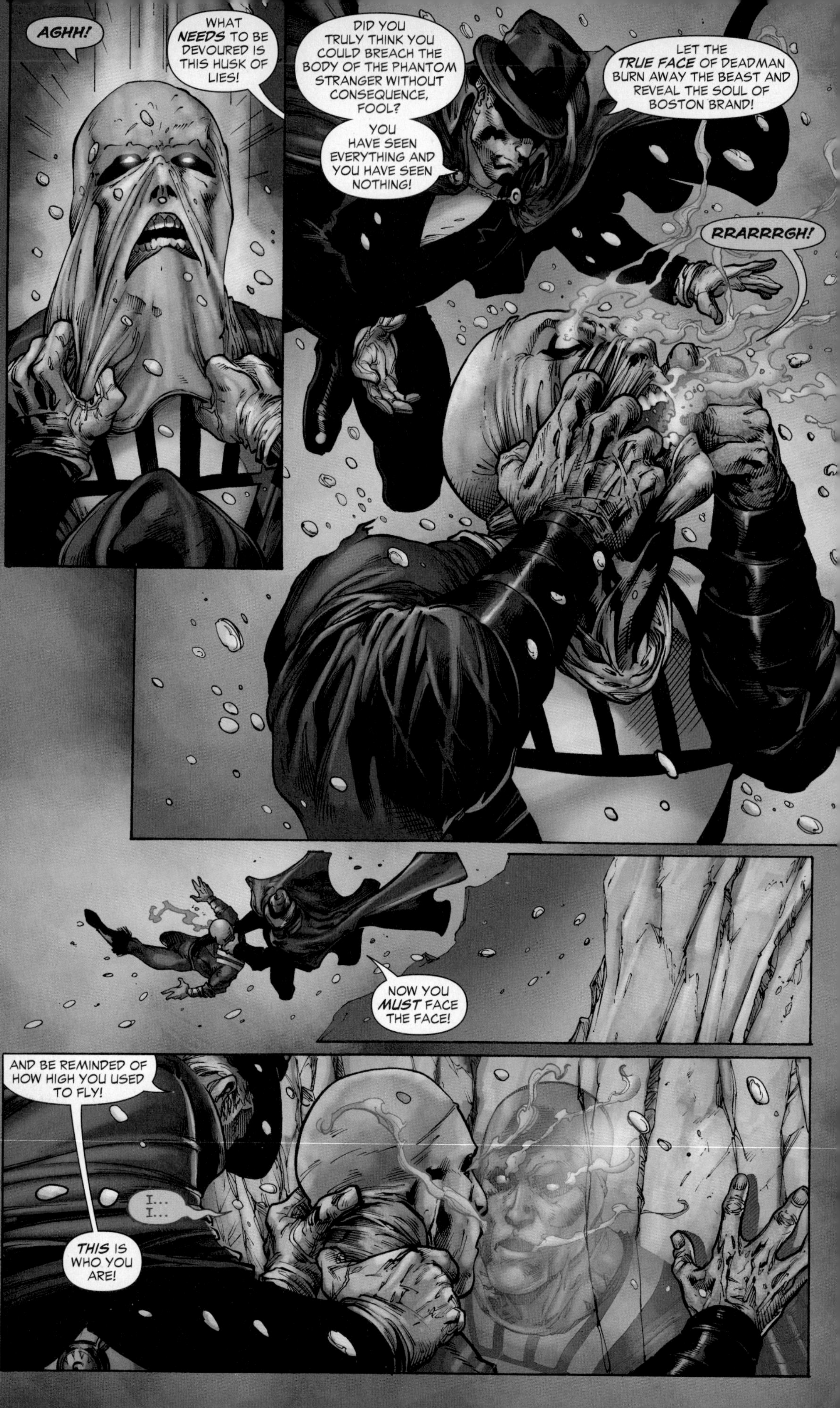
AGHH!
WHAT NEEDS TO BE DEVOURED IS THIS HUSK OF LIES!
DID YOU TRULY THINK YOU COULD BREACH THE BODY OF THE PHANTOM STRANGER WITHOUT CONSEQUENCE, FOOL?
YOU HAVE SEEN EVERYTHING AND YOU HAVE SEEN NOTHING!
LET THE TRUE FACE OF DEADMAN BURN AWAY THE BEAST AND REVEAL THE SOUL OF BOSTON BRAND!
RRARRRGH!
NOW YOU MUST FACE THE FACE!
AND BE REMINDED OF HOW HIGH YOU USED TO FLY!
I... I...
THIS IS WHO YOU ARE!

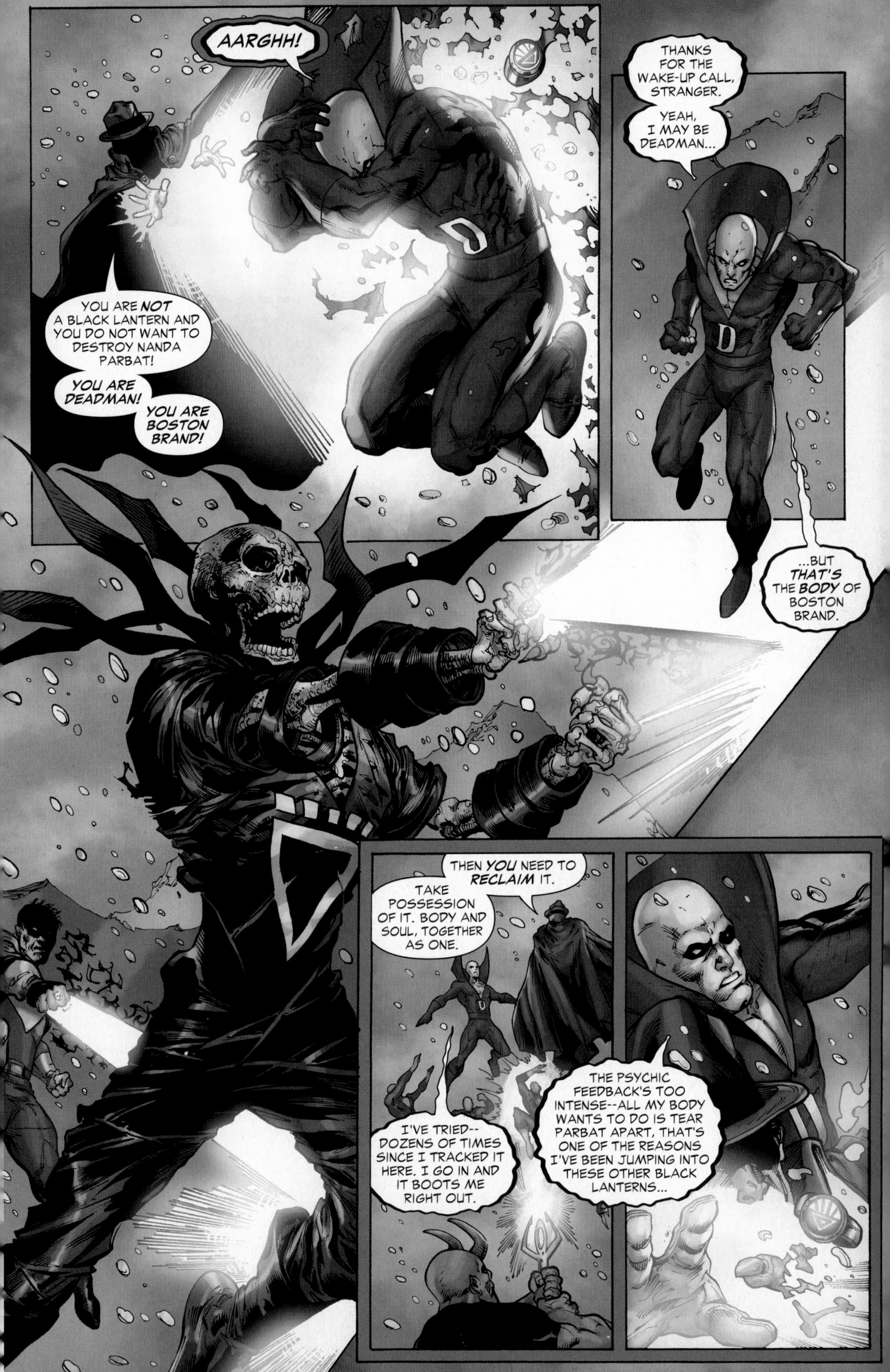
AARGHH!
THANKS FOR THE WAKE-UP CALL, STRANGER.
YEAH, I MAY BE DEADMAN...
YOU ARE NOT A BLACK LANTERN AND YOU DO NOT WANT TO DESTROY NANDA PARBAT!
YOU ARE DEADMAN!
YOU ARE BOSTON BRAND!
...BUT THAT'S THE BODY OF BOSTON BRAND.
THEN YOU NEED TO RECLAIM IT.
TAKE POSSESSION OF IT. BODY AND SOUL, TOGETHER AS ONE.
I'VE TRIED-- DOZENS OF TIMES SINCE I TRACKED IT HERE. I GO IN AND IT BOOTS ME RIGHT OUT.
THE PSYCHIC FEEDBACK'S TOO INTENSE--ALL MY BODY WANTS TO DO IS TEAR PARBAT APART, THAT'S ONE OF THE REASONS I'VE BEEN JUMPING INTO THESE OTHER BLACK LANTERNS...

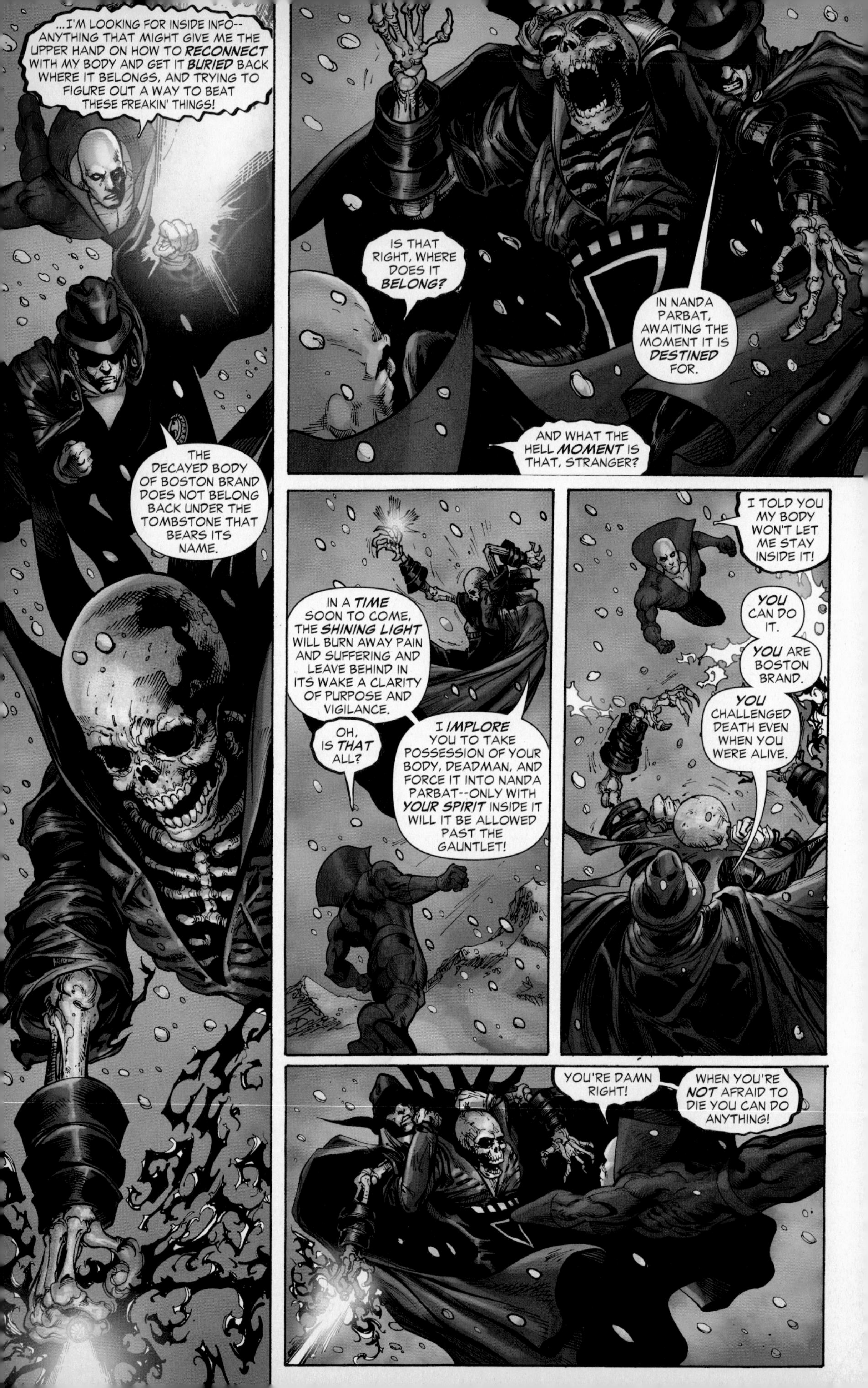
...I'M LOOKING FOR INSIDE INFO--ANYTHING THAT MIGHT GIVE ME THE UPPER HAND ON HOW TO RECONNECT WITH MY BODY AND GET IT BURIED BACK WHERE IT BELONGS, AND TRYING TO FIGURE OUT A WAY TO BEAT THESE FREAKIN' THINGS!
THE DECAYED BODY OF BOSTON BRAND DOES NOT BELONG BACK UNDER THE TOMBSTONE THAT BEARS ITS NAME.
IS THAT RIGHT, WHERE DOES IT BELONG?
IN NANDA PARBAT, AWAITING THE MOMENT IT IS DESTINED FOR.
AND WHAT THE HELL MOMENT IS THAT, STRANGER?
IN A TIME SOON TO COME, THE SHINING LIGHT WILL BURN AWAY PAIN AND SUFFERING AND LEAVE BEHIND IN ITS WAKE A CLARITY OF PURPOSE AND VIGILANCE.
OH, IS THAT ALL?
I IMPLORE YOU TO TAKE POSSESSION OF YOUR BODY, DEADMAN, AND FORCE IT INTO NANDA PARBAT--ONLY WITH YOUR SPIRIT INSIDE IT WILL IT BE ALLOWED PAST THE GAUNTLET!
I TOLD YOU MY BODY WON'T LET ME STAY INSIDE IT!
YOU CAN DO IT.
YOU ARE BOSTON BRAND.
YOU CHALLENGED DEATH EVEN WHEN YOU WERE ALIVE.
YOU'RE DAMN RIGHT!
WHEN YOU'RE NOT AFRAID TO DIE YOU CAN DO ANYTHING!

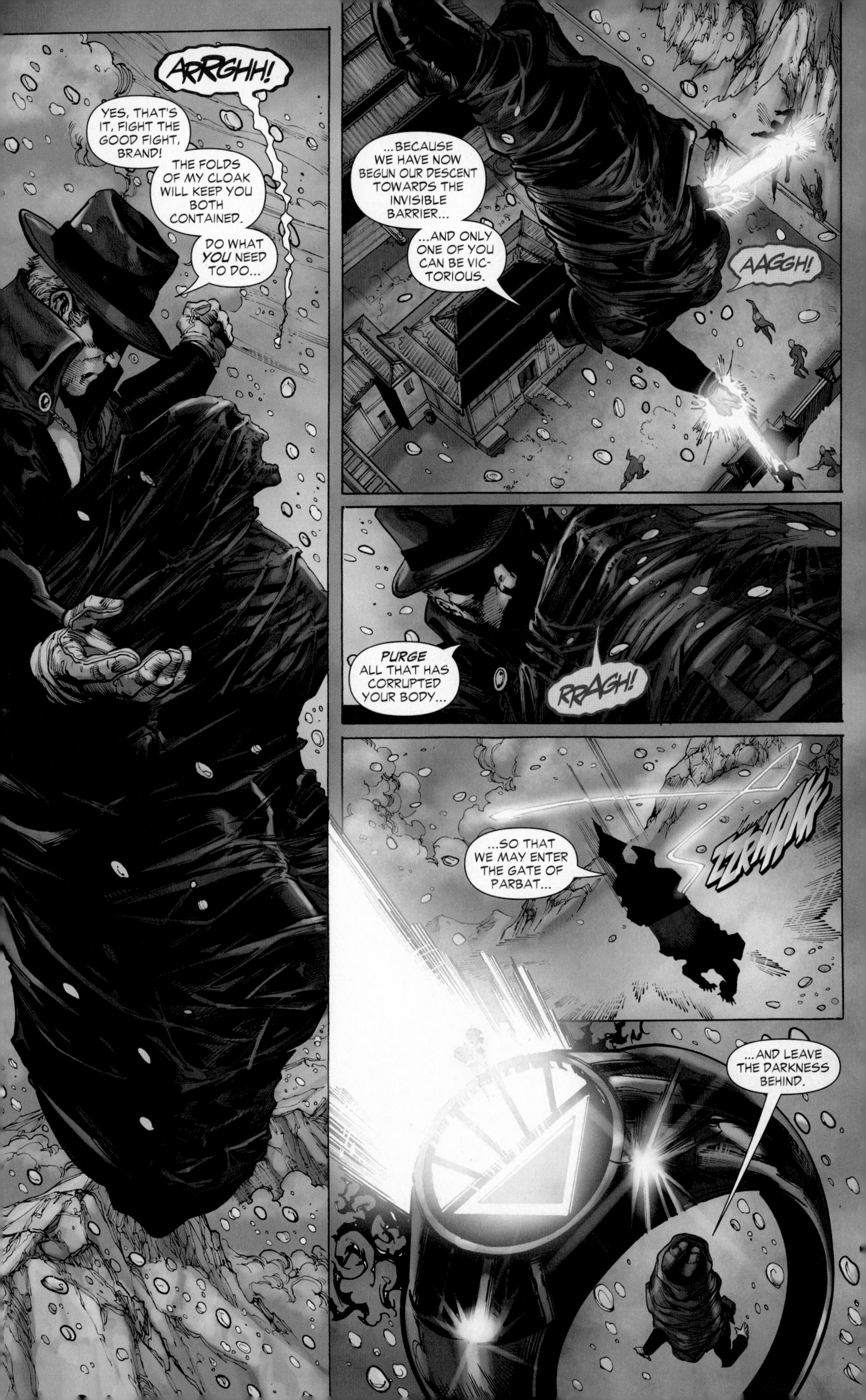
ARRGHH!
YES, THAT'S IT, FIGHT THE GOOD FIGHT, BRAND!
THE FOLDS OF MY CLOAK WILL KEEP YOU BOTH CONTAINED.
DO WHAT *YOU* NEED TO DO...
...BECAUSE WE HAVE NOW BEGUN OUR DESCENT TOWARDS THE INVISIBLE BARRIER...
...AND ONLY ONE OF YOU CAN BE VICTORIOUS.
AAAGGH!
PURGE ALL THAT HAS CORRUPTED YOUR BODY...
RRAGH!
...SO THAT WE MAY ENTER THE GATE OF PARBAT...
SZZRAAAK!
...AND LEAVE THE DARKNESS BEHIND.

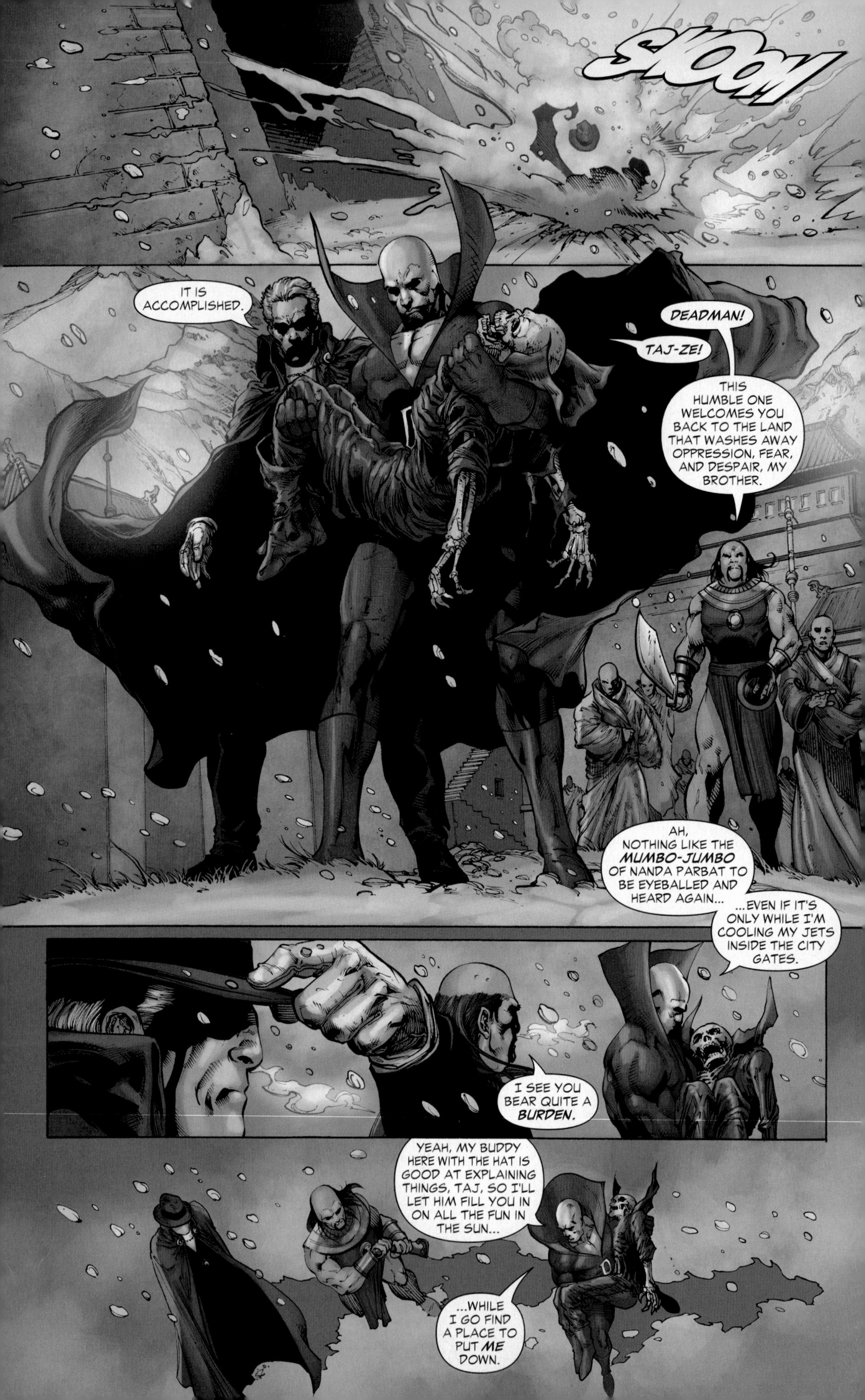
SKOOM
IT IS ACCOMPLISHED.
DEADMAN!
TAJ-ZE!
THIS HUMBLE ONE WELCOMES YOU BACK TO THE LAND THAT WASHES AWAY OPPRESSION, FEAR, AND DESPAIR, MY BROTHER.
AH, NOTHING LIKE THE MUMBO-JUMBO OF NANDA PARBAT TO BE EYEBALLED AND HEARD AGAIN...
...EVEN IF IT'S ONLY WHILE I'M COOLING MY JETS INSIDE THE CITY GATES.
I SEE YOU BEAR QUITE A BURDEN.
YEAH, MY BUDDY HERE WITH THE HAT IS GOOD AT EXPLAINING THINGS, TAJ, SO I'LL LET HIM FILL YOU IN ON ALL THE FUN IN THE SUN...
...WHILE I GO FIND A PLACE TO PUT ME DOWN.

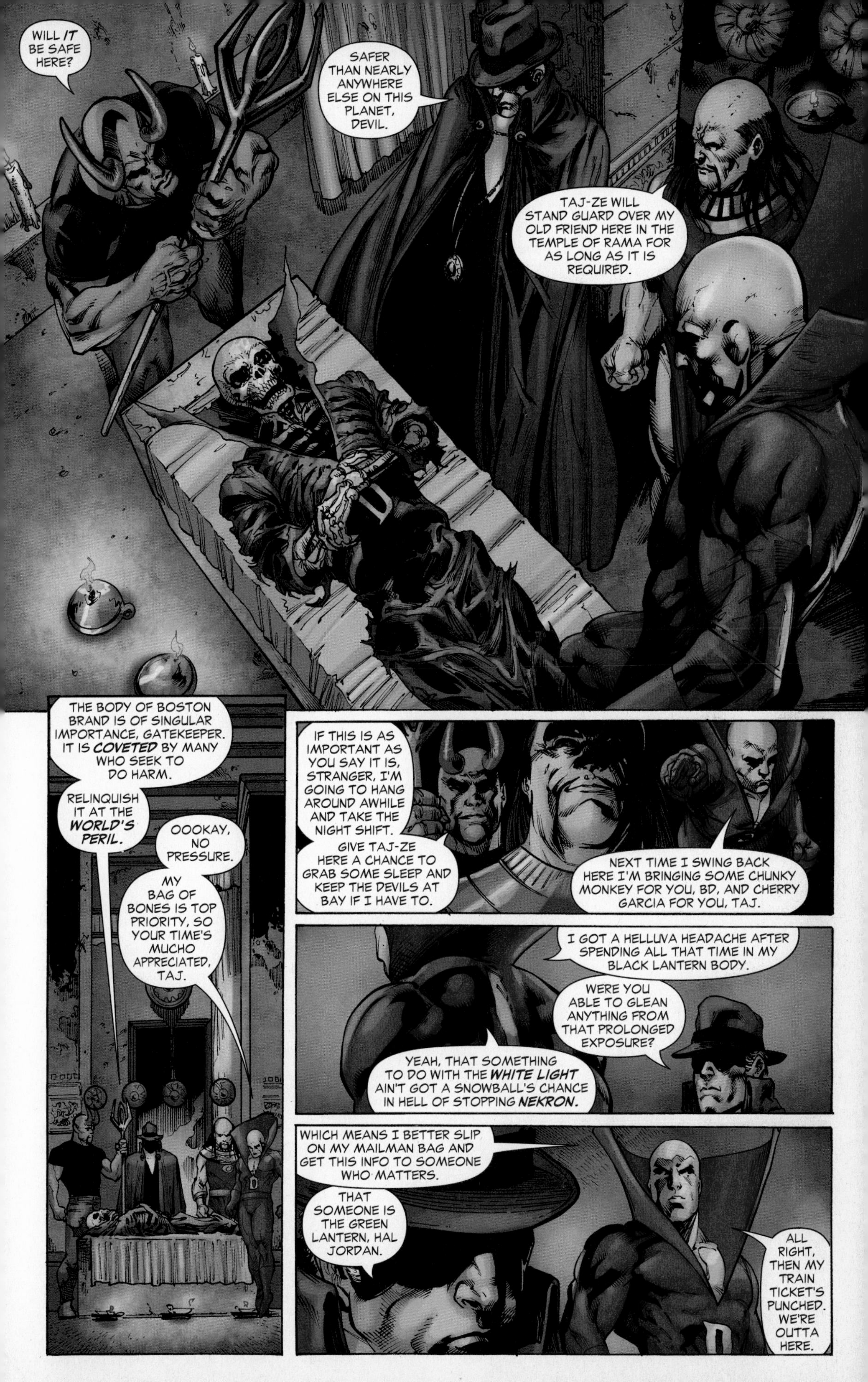
WILL *IT* BE SAFE HERE?
SAFER THAN NEARLY ANYWHERE ELSE ON THIS PLANET, DEVIL.
TAJ-ZE WILL STAND GUARD OVER MY OLD FRIEND HERE IN THE TEMPLE OF RAMA FOR AS LONG AS IT IS REQUIRED.
THE BODY OF BOSTON BRAND IS OF SINGULAR IMPORTANCE, GATEKEEPER. IT IS ***COVETED*** BY MANY WHO SEEK TO DO HARM.
RELINQUISH IT AT THE ***WORLD'S PERIL.***
OOOKAY, NO PRESSURE.
MY BAG OF BONES IS TOP PRIORITY, SO YOUR TIME'S MUCHO APPRECIATED, TAJ.
IF THIS IS AS IMPORTANT AS YOU SAY IT IS, STRANGER, I'M GOING TO HANG AROUND AWHILE AND TAKE THE NIGHT SHIFT.
GIVE TAJ-ZE HERE A CHANCE TO GRAB SOME SLEEP AND KEEP THE DEVILS AT BAY IF I HAVE TO.
NEXT TIME I SWING BACK HERE I'M BRINGING SOME CHUNKY MONKEY FOR YOU, BD, AND CHERRY GARCIA FOR YOU, TAJ.
I GOT A HELLUVA HEADACHE AFTER SPENDING ALL THAT TIME IN MY BLACK LANTERN BODY.
WERE YOU ABLE TO GLEAN ANYTHING FROM THAT PROLONGED EXPOSURE?
YEAH, THAT SOMETHING TO DO WITH THE ***WHITE LIGHT*** AIN'T GOT A SNOWBALL'S CHANCE IN HELL OF STOPPING ***NEKRON.***
WHICH MEANS I BETTER SLIP ON MY MAILMAN BAG AND GET THIS INFO TO SOMEONE WHO MATTERS.
THAT SOMEONE IS THE GREEN LANTERN, HAL JORDAN.
ALL RIGHT, THEN MY TRAIN TICKET'S PUNCHED. WE'RE OUTTA HERE.

STAY VIGILANT AND STAY SAFE.

DITTO!

THIS HUMBLE SERVANT WISHES YOU WELL, SON OF RAMA.

THANKS, TAJ, KEEP THOSE SWORD-SWINGING WRISTS LOOSE, PAL!

YOU WOULDN'T HAPPEN TO HAVE AN I-POD, WOULD YOU?

A PEA POD?

YEP, DIDN'T THINK SO.

I HAVE WALKED HUNDREDS OF BILLIONS OF MILES ACROSS THIS EARTH...

...ACROSS TIME AND SPACE...

...THROUGH THE BLINDING LIGHT OF THE ELYSIAN FIELDS AND THE HALLOWED TEMPLE HALLS OF NANDA PARBAT...

...FROM THE DARKEST DEPTHS OF PANDEMONIUM...

...WHERE THE STENCH AND DESPAIR OF THE CHAOPLASM IS ALWAYS A POTENT REMINDER OF HOW FAR MAN CAN FALL.

I AM THE PHANTOM STRANGER.

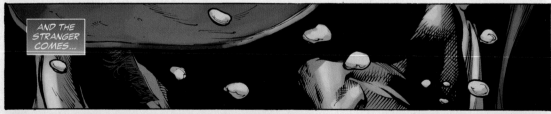

AND THE STRANGER COMES...

...WHEN THE STRANGER IS NEEDED.

END.

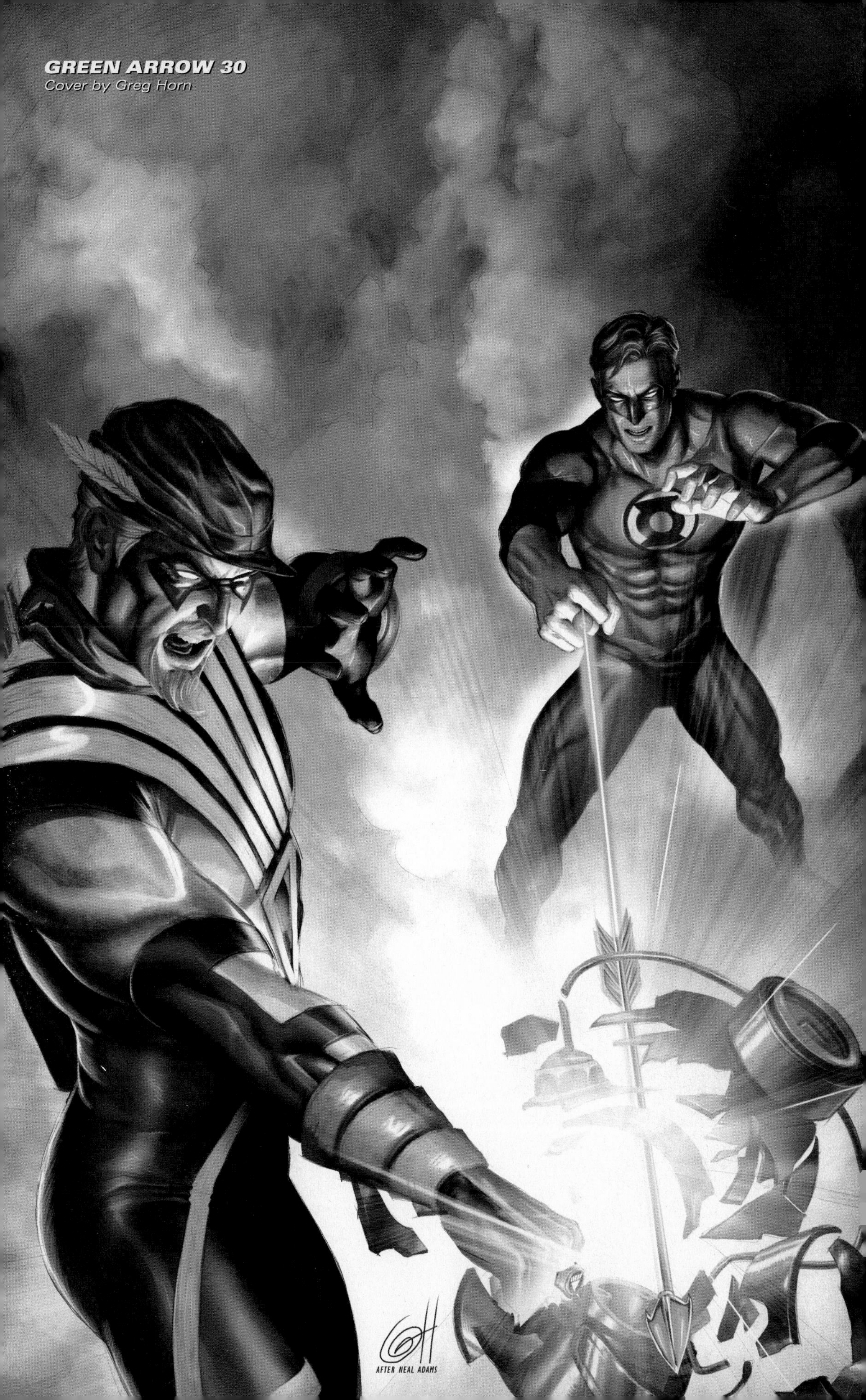
AFTER NEAL ADAMS

GREEN ARROW 30
Cover by Greg Horn

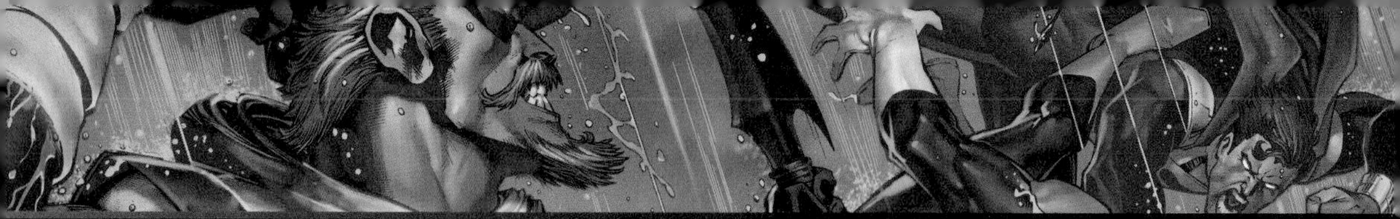

LYING TO MYSELF

J.T. KRUL
WRITER

DIOGENES NEVES
PENCILS

RUY JOSÉ
VICENTE CIFUENTES
INKS

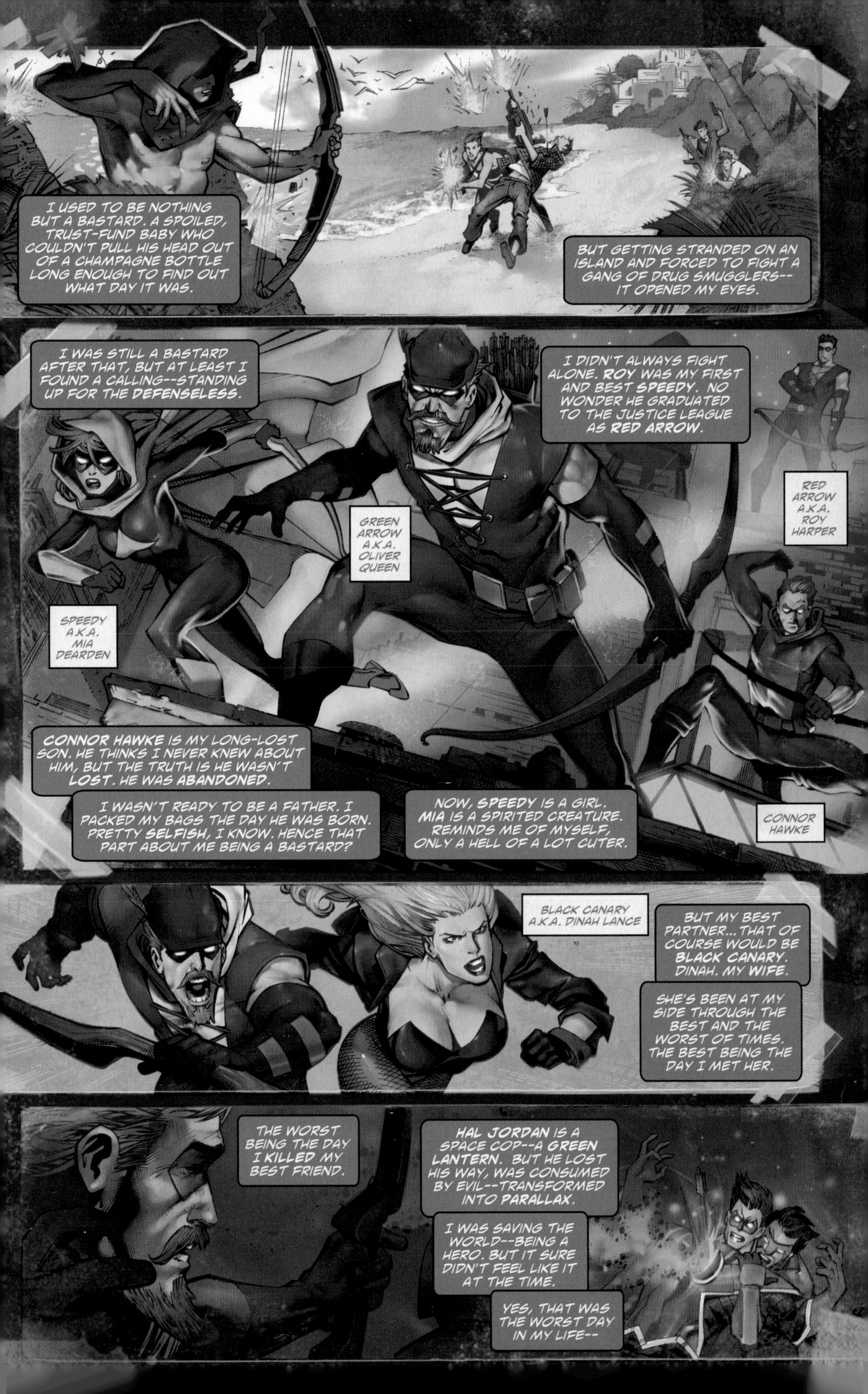
I USED TO BE NOTHING BUT A BASTARD. A SPOILED, TRUST-FUND BABY WHO COULDN'T PULL HIS HEAD OUT OF A CHAMPAGNE BOTTLE LONG ENOUGH TO FIND OUT WHAT DAY IT WAS.
BUT GETTING STRANDED ON AN ISLAND AND FORCED TO FIGHT A GANG OF DRUG SMUGGLERS-- IT OPENED MY EYES.
I WAS STILL A BASTARD AFTER THAT, BUT AT LEAST I FOUND A CALLING--STANDING UP FOR THE DEFENSELESS.
I DIDN'T ALWAYS FIGHT ALONE. ROY WAS MY FIRST AND BEST SPEEDY. NO WONDER HE GRADUATED TO THE JUSTICE LEAGUE AS RED ARROW.
RED ARROW A.K.A. ROY HARPER
GREEN ARROW A.K.A. OLIVER QUEEN
SPEEDY A.K.A. MIA DEARDEN
CONNOR HAWKE IS MY LONG-LOST SON. HE THINKS I NEVER KNEW ABOUT HIM, BUT THE TRUTH IS HE WASN'T LOST. HE WAS ABANDONED.
I WASN'T READY TO BE A FATHER. I PACKED MY BAGS THE DAY HE WAS BORN. PRETTY SELFISH, I KNOW. HENCE THAT PART ABOUT ME BEING A BASTARD?
NOW, SPEEDY IS A GIRL. MIA IS A SPIRITED CREATURE. REMINDS ME OF MYSELF, ONLY A HELL OF A LOT CUTER.
CONNOR HAWKE
BLACK CANARY A.K.A. DINAH LANCE
BUT MY BEST PARTNER...THAT OF COURSE WOULD BE BLACK CANARY. DINAH. MY WIFE.
SHE'S BEEN AT MY SIDE THROUGH THE BEST AND THE WORST OF TIMES. THE BEST BEING THE DAY I MET HER.
THE WORST BEING THE DAY I KILLED MY BEST FRIEND.
HAL JORDAN IS A SPACE COP--A GREEN LANTERN. BUT HE LOST HIS WAY, WAS CONSUMED BY EVIL--TRANSFORMED INTO PARALLAX.
I WAS SAVING THE WORLD--BEING A HERO. BUT IT SURE DIDN'T FEEL LIKE IT AT THE TIME.
YES, THAT WAS THE WORST DAY IN MY LIFE--

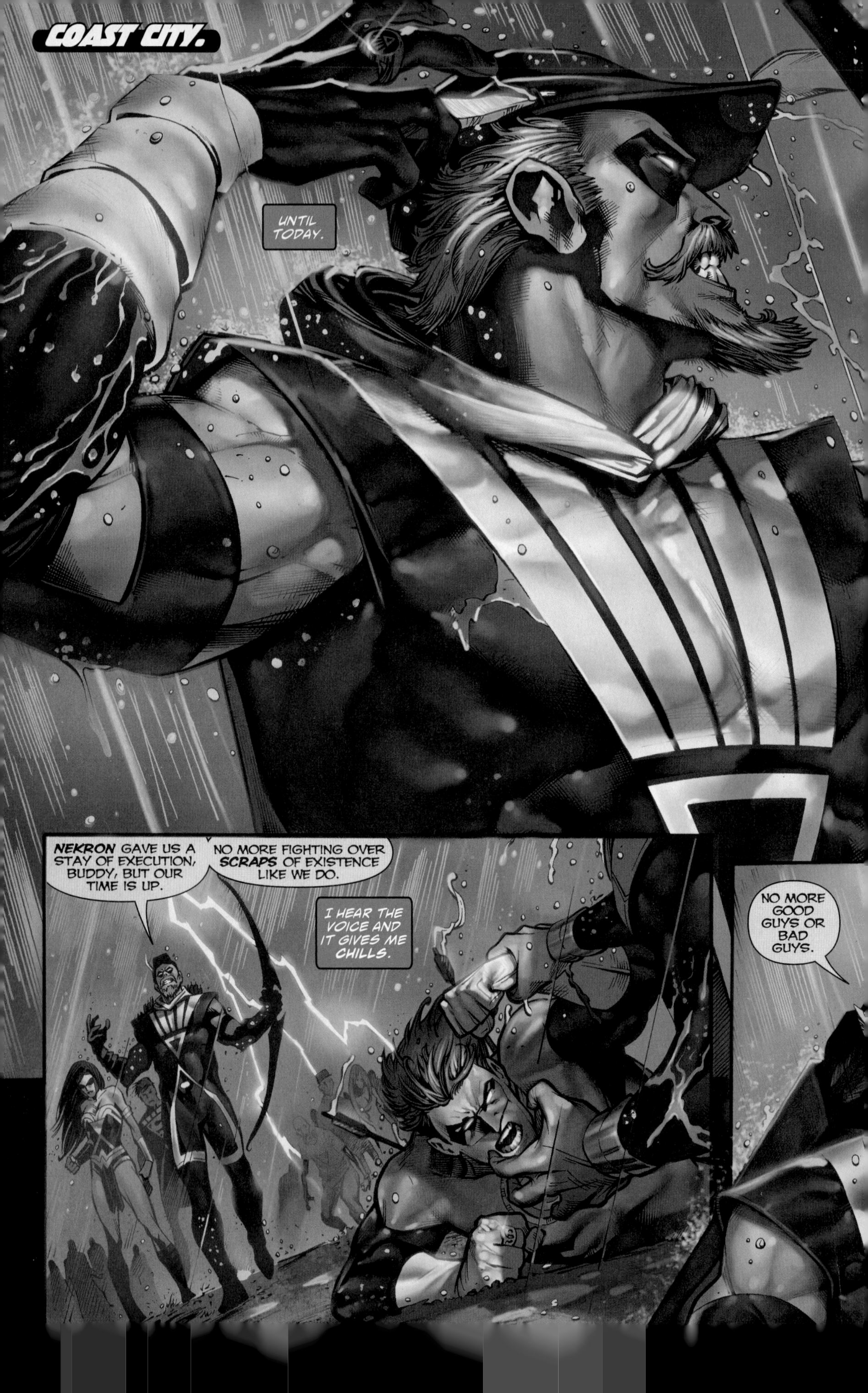
COAST CITY.
UNTIL TODAY.
NEKRON GAVE US A STAY OF EXECUTION, BUDDY, BUT OUR TIME IS UP.
NO MORE FIGHTING OVER SCRAPS OF EXISTENCE LIKE WE DO.
I HEAR THE VOICE AND IT GIVES ME CHILLS.
NO MORE GOOD GUYS OR BAD GUYS.

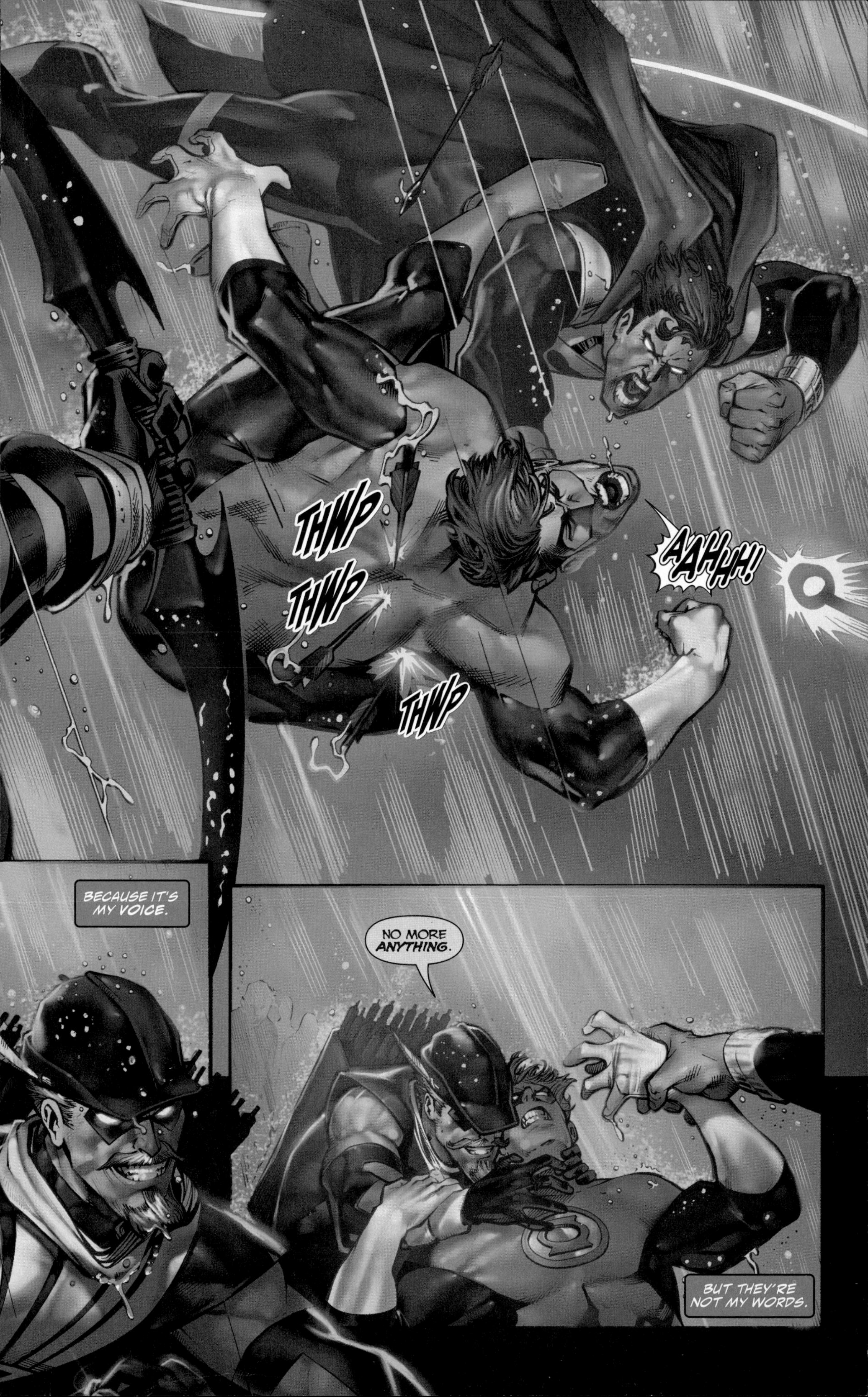
THWP
THWP
THWP
AAHHH!
BECAUSE IT'S MY VOICE.
NO MORE ANYTHING.
BUT THEY'RE NOT MY WORDS.

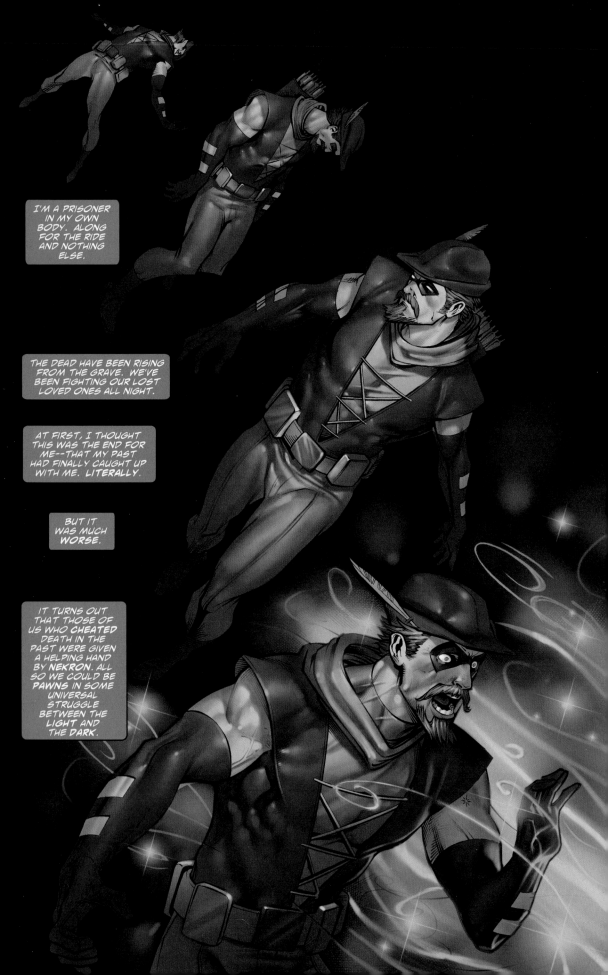

I'M A PRISONER IN MY OWN BODY. ALONG FOR THE RIDE AND NOTHING ELSE.

THE DEAD HAVE BEEN RISING FROM THE GRAVE. WE'VE BEEN FIGHTING OUR LOST LOVED ONES ALL NIGHT.

AT FIRST, I THOUGHT THIS WAS THE END FOR ME--THAT MY PAST HAD FINALLY CAUGHT UP WITH ME. *LITERALLY.*

BUT IT WAS MUCH *WORSE.*

IT TURNS OUT THAT THOSE OF US WHO *CHEATED* DEATH IN THE PAST WERE GIVEN A HELPING HAND BY *NEKRON.* ALL SO WE COULD BE PAWNS IN SOME UNIVERSAL STRUGGLE BETWEEN THE *LIGHT* AND THE *DARK.*

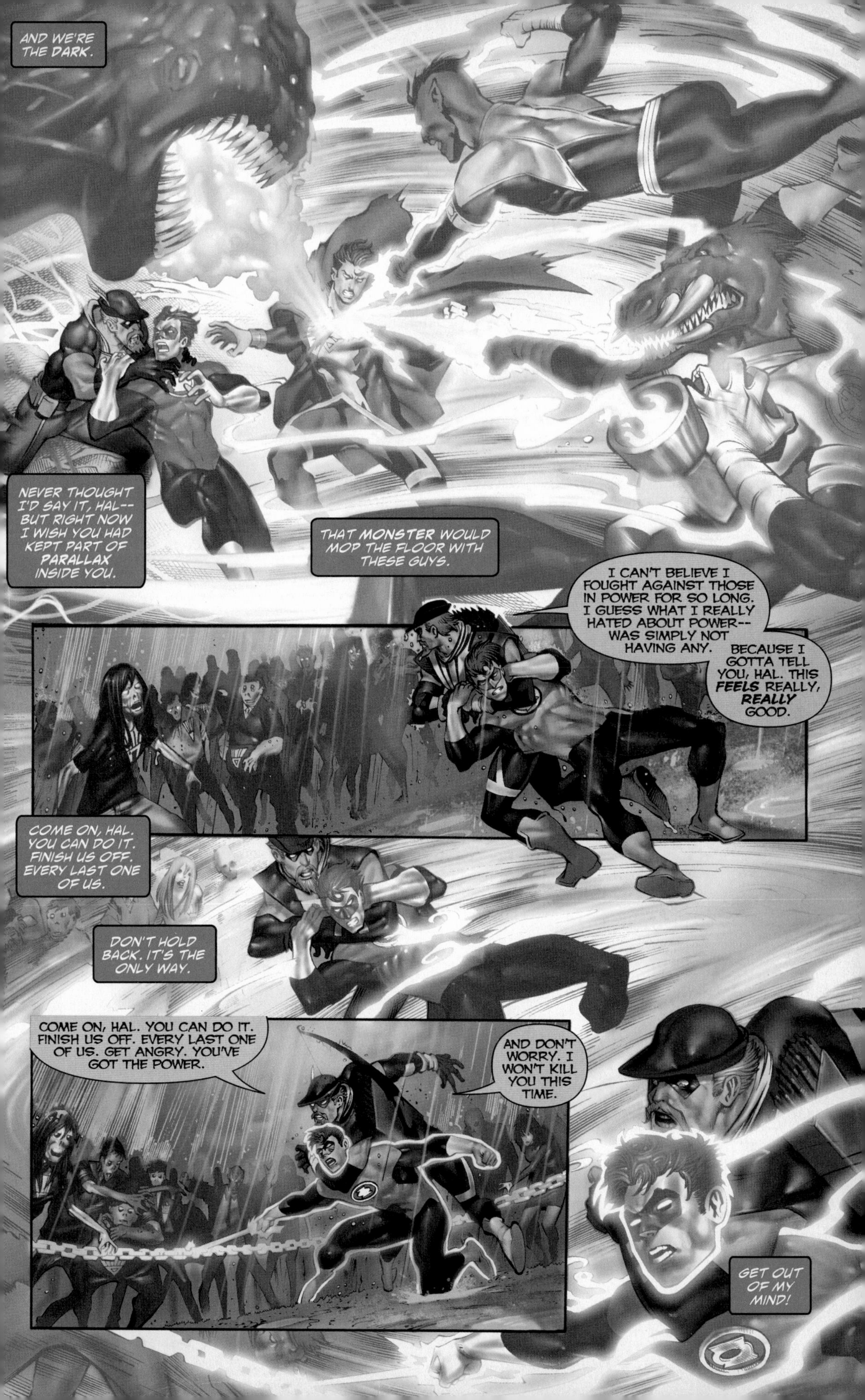
AND WE'RE THE DARK.
NEVER THOUGHT I'D SAY IT, HAL-- BUT RIGHT NOW I WISH YOU HAD KEPT PART OF PARALLAX INSIDE YOU.
THAT MONSTER WOULD MOP THE FLOOR WITH THESE GUYS.
I CAN'T BELIEVE I FOUGHT AGAINST THOSE IN POWER FOR SO LONG. I GUESS WHAT I REALLY HATED ABOUT POWER-- WAS SIMPLY NOT HAVING ANY.
BECAUSE I GOTTA TELL YOU, HAL. THIS FEELS REALLY, REALLY GOOD.
COME ON, HAL. YOU CAN DO IT. FINISH US OFF. EVERY LAST ONE OF US.
DON'T HOLD BACK. IT'S THE ONLY WAY.
COME ON, HAL. YOU CAN DO IT. FINISH US OFF. EVERY LAST ONE OF US. GET ANGRY. YOU'VE GOT THE POWER.
AND DON'T WORRY. I WON'T KILL YOU THIS TIME.
GET OUT OF MY MIND!

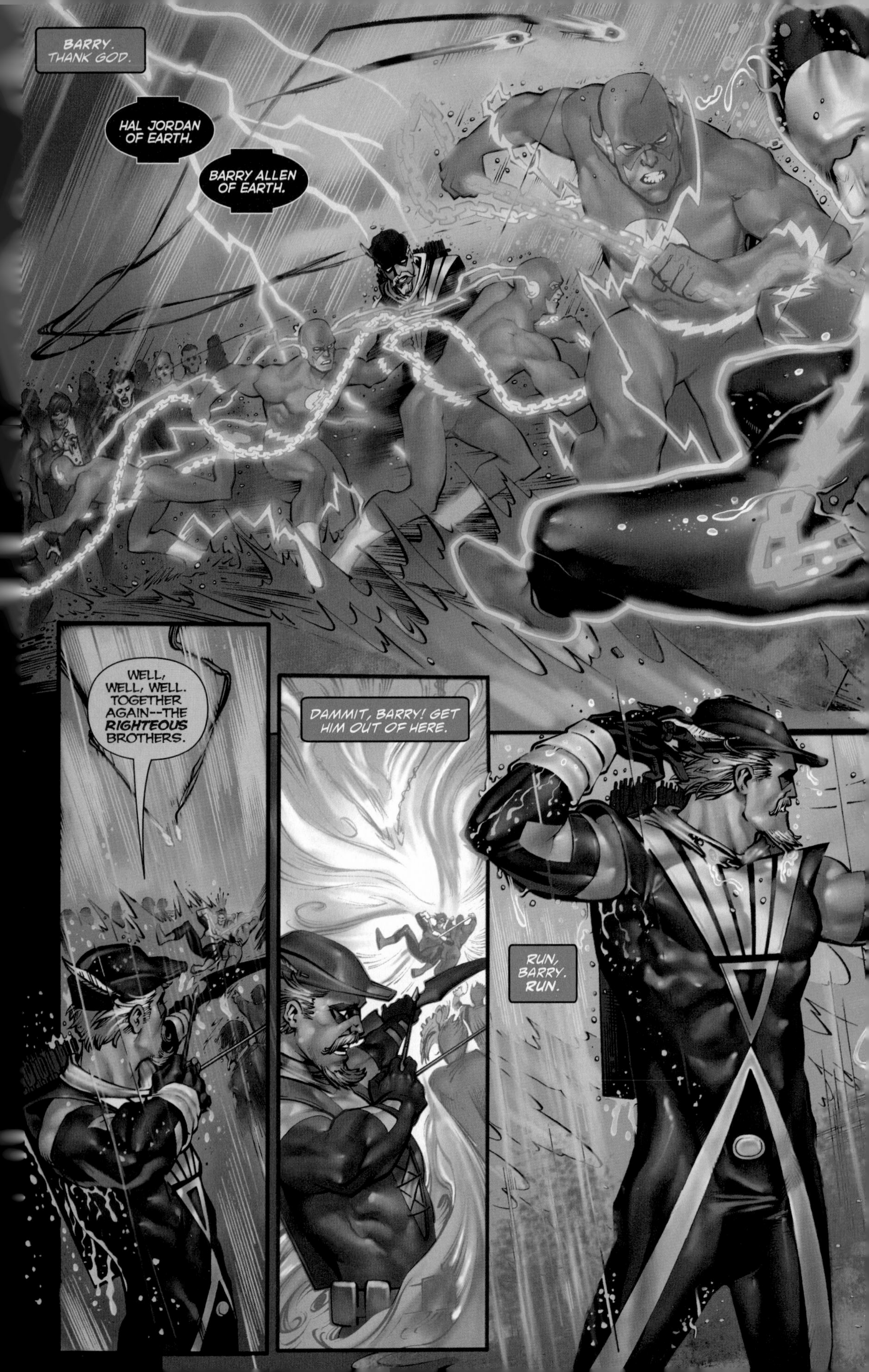
BARRY. THANK GOD.
HAL JORDAN OF EARTH.
BARRY ALLEN OF EARTH.
WELL, WELL, WELL. TOGETHER AGAIN--THE RIGHTEOUS BROTHERS.
DAMMIT, BARRY! GET HIM OUT OF HERE.
RUN, BARRY. RUN.

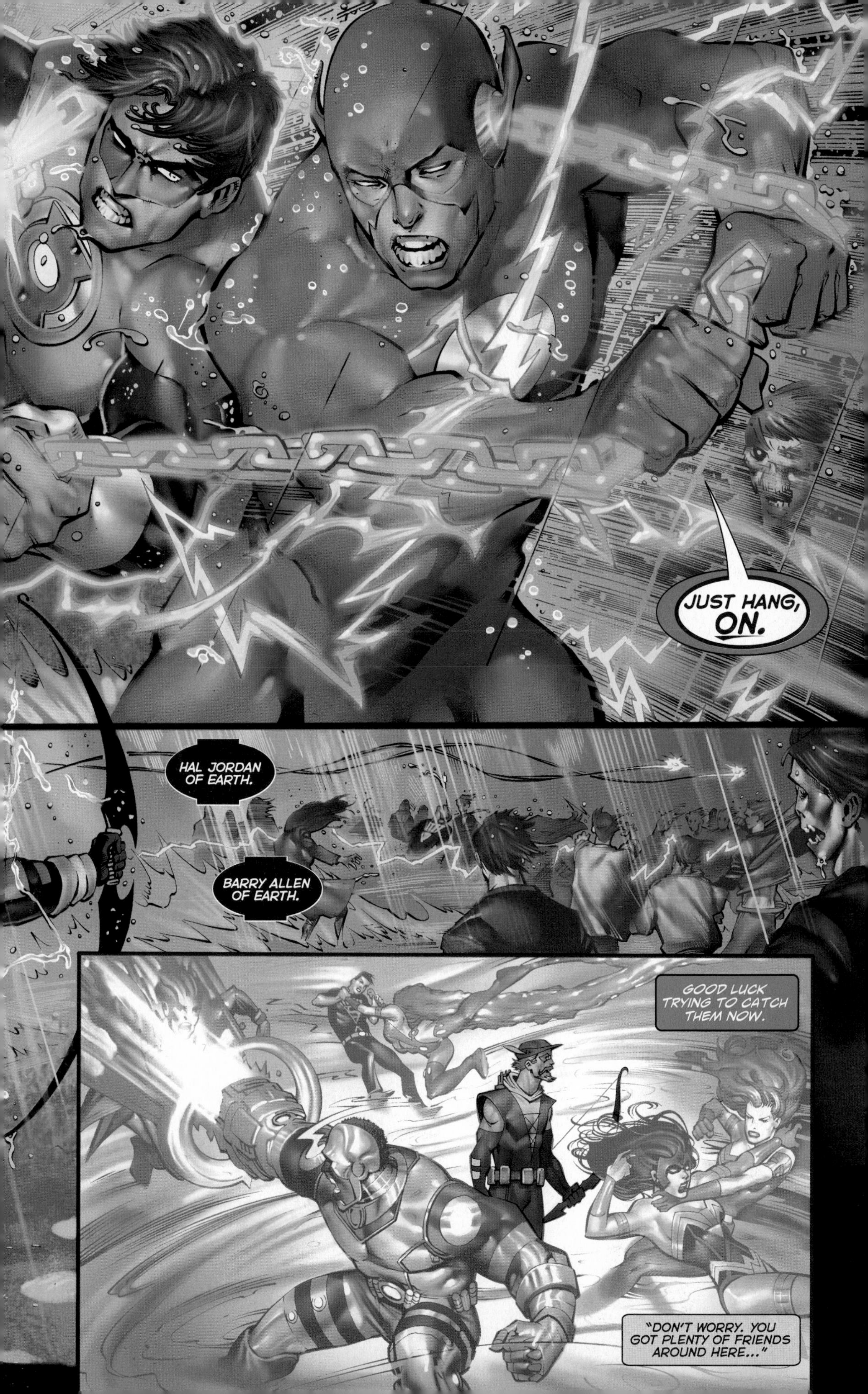
JUST HANG, ON.
HAL JORDAN OF EARTH.
BARRY ALLEN OF EARTH.
GOOD LUCK TRYING TO CATCH THEM NOW.
"DON'T WORRY. YOU GOT PLENTY OF FRIENDS AROUND HERE..."

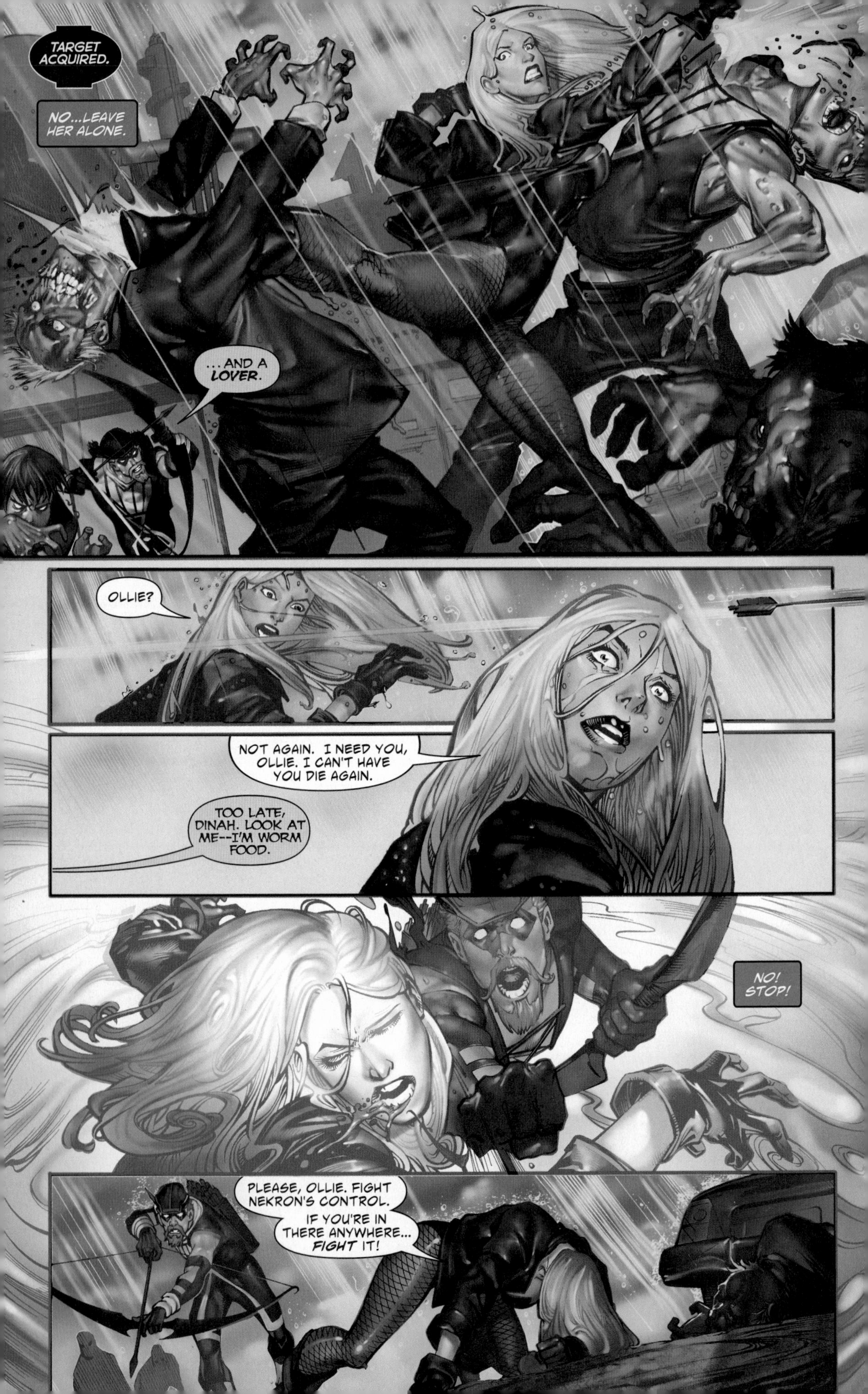
TARGET ACQUIRED.
NO...LEAVE HER ALONE.
...AND A LOVER.
OLLIE?
NOT AGAIN. I NEED YOU, OLLIE. I CAN'T HAVE YOU DIE AGAIN.
TOO LATE, DINAH. LOOK AT ME--I'M WORM FOOD.
NO! STOP!
PLEASE, OLLIE. FIGHT NEKRON'S CONTROL.
IF YOU'RE IN THERE ANYWHERE... FIGHT IT!

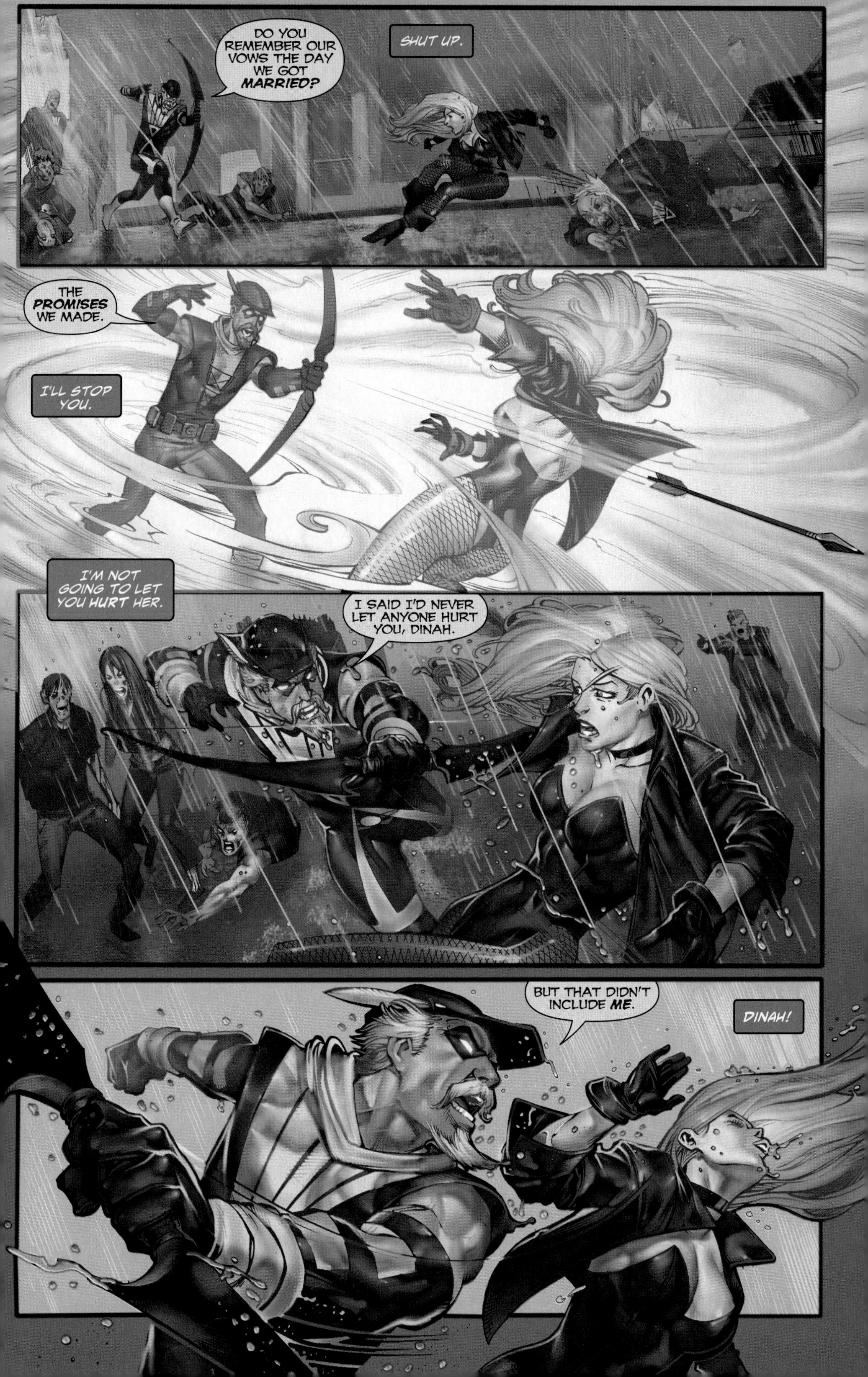
DO YOU REMEMBER OUR VOWS THE DAY WE GOT MARRIED?
SHUT UP.
THE PROMISES WE MADE.
I'LL STOP YOU.
I'M NOT GOING TO LET YOU HURT HER.
I SAID I'D NEVER LET ANYONE HURT YOU, DINAH.
BUT THAT DIDN'T INCLUDE ME.
DINAH!

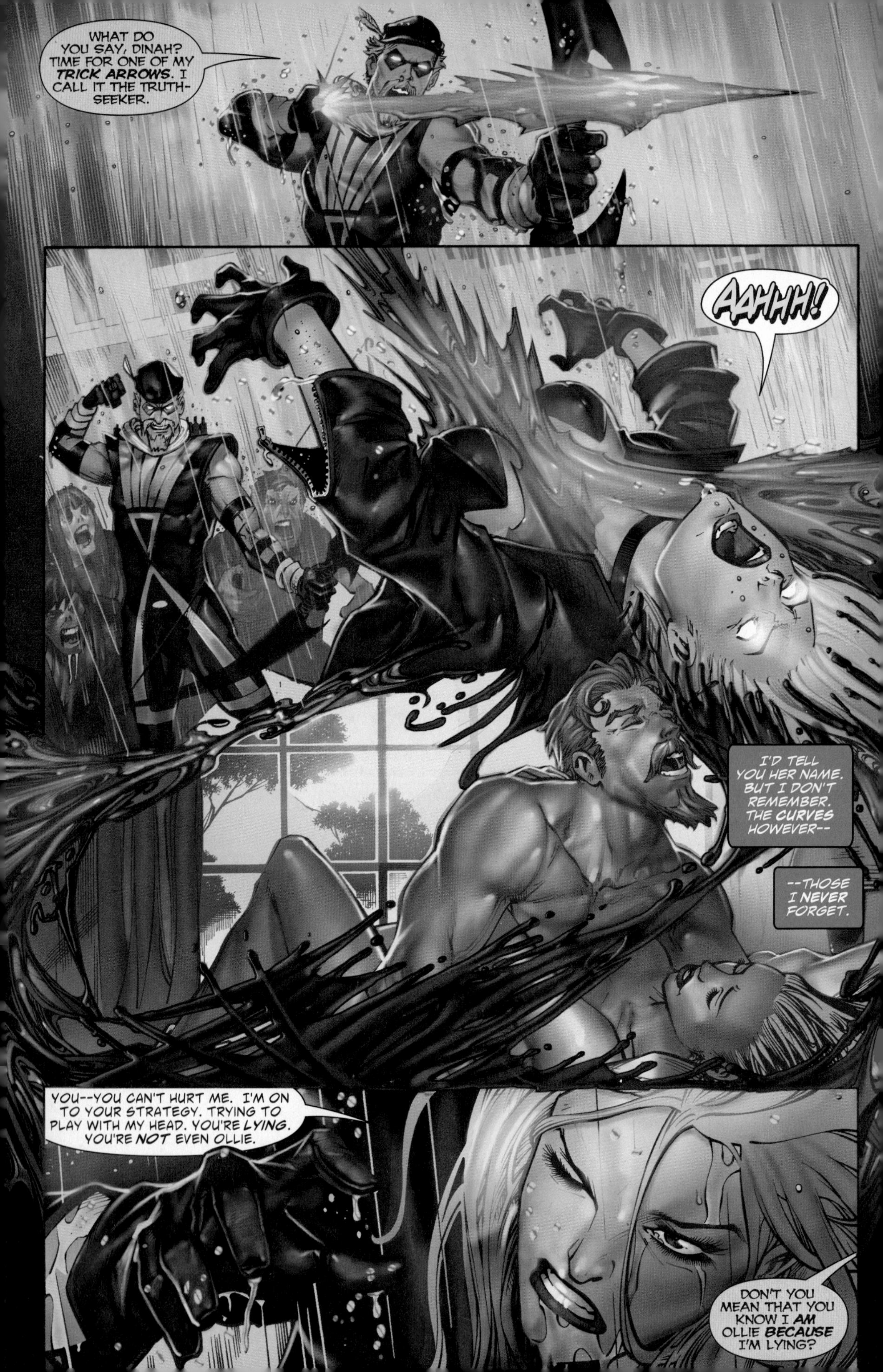
WHAT DO YOU SAY, DINAH? TIME FOR ONE OF MY TRICK ARROWS. I CALL IT THE TRUTH-SEEKER.
AAHHH!
I'D TELL YOU HER NAME. BUT I DON'T REMEMBER. THE CURVES HOWEVER--
--THOSE I NEVER FORGET.
YOU--YOU CAN'T HURT ME. I'M ON TO YOUR STRATEGY. TRYING TO PLAY WITH MY HEAD. YOU'RE LYING. YOU'RE NOT EVEN OLLIE.
DON'T YOU MEAN THAT YOU KNOW I AM OLLIE BECAUSE I'M LYING?

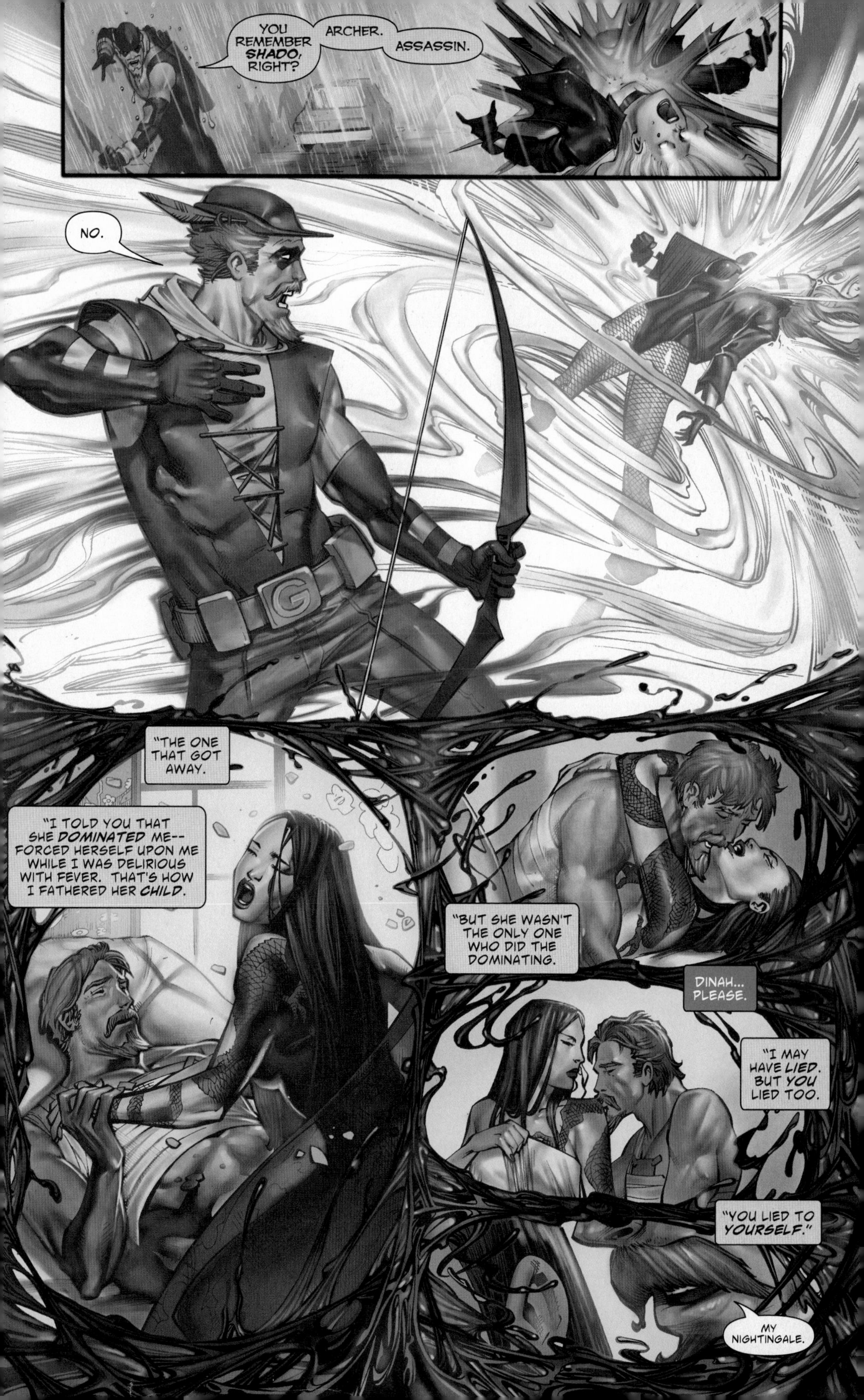
YOU REMEMBER SHADO, RIGHT?
ARCHER.
ASSASSIN.
NO.
"THE ONE THAT GOT AWAY.
"I TOLD YOU THAT SHE DOMINATED ME--FORCED HERSELF UPON ME WHILE I WAS DELIRIOUS WITH FEVER. THAT'S HOW I FATHERED HER CHILD.
"BUT SHE WASN'T THE ONLY ONE WHO DID THE DOMINATING.
DINAH... PLEASE.
"I MAY HAVE LIED. BUT YOU LIED TOO.
"YOU LIED TO YOURSELF."
MY NIGHTINGALE.

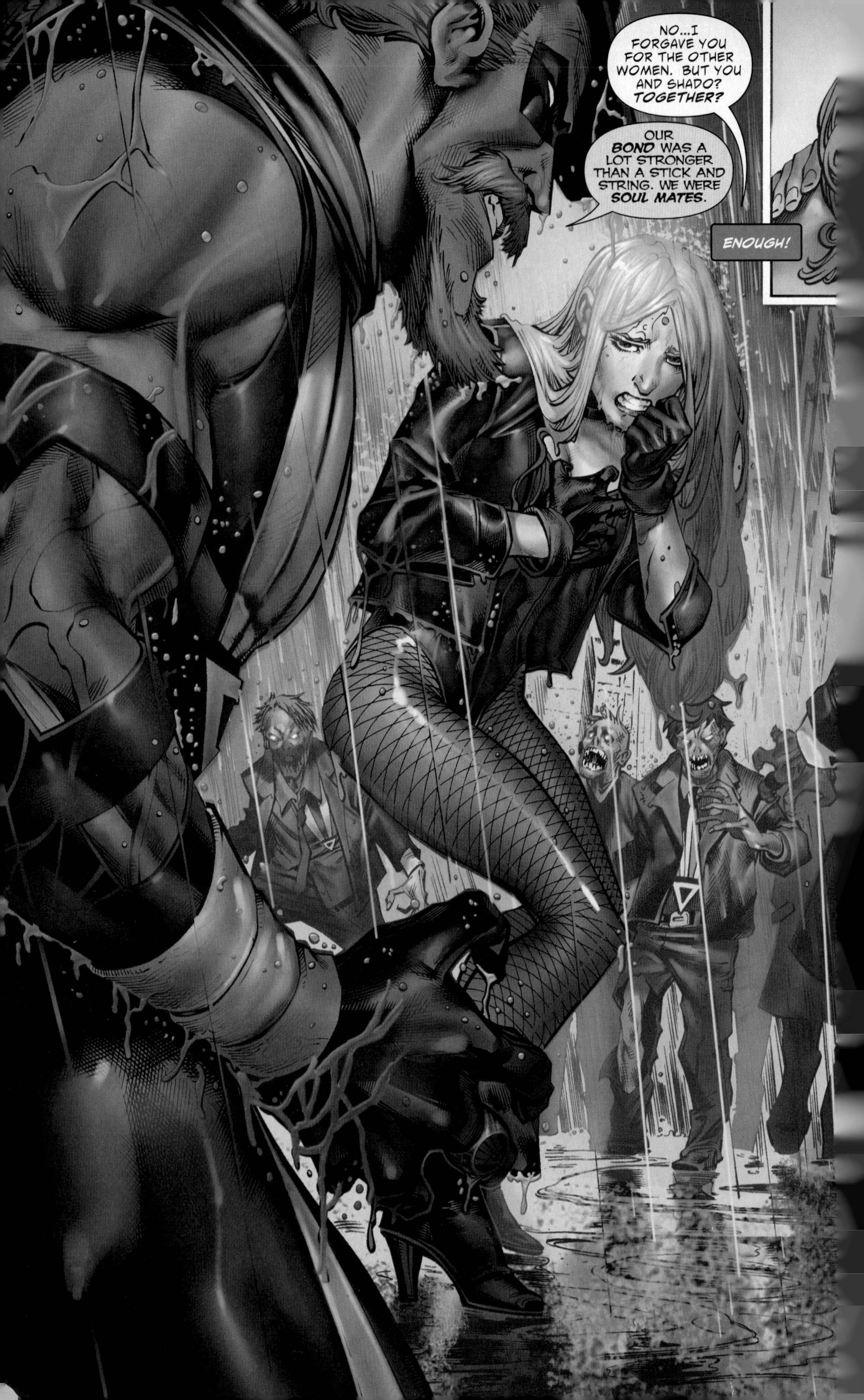
NO...I FORGAVE YOU FOR THE OTHER WOMEN. BUT YOU AND SHADO? *TOGETHER?*
OUR ***BOND*** WAS A LOT STRONGER THAN A STICK AND STRING. WE WERE ***SOUL MATES***.
ENOUGH!

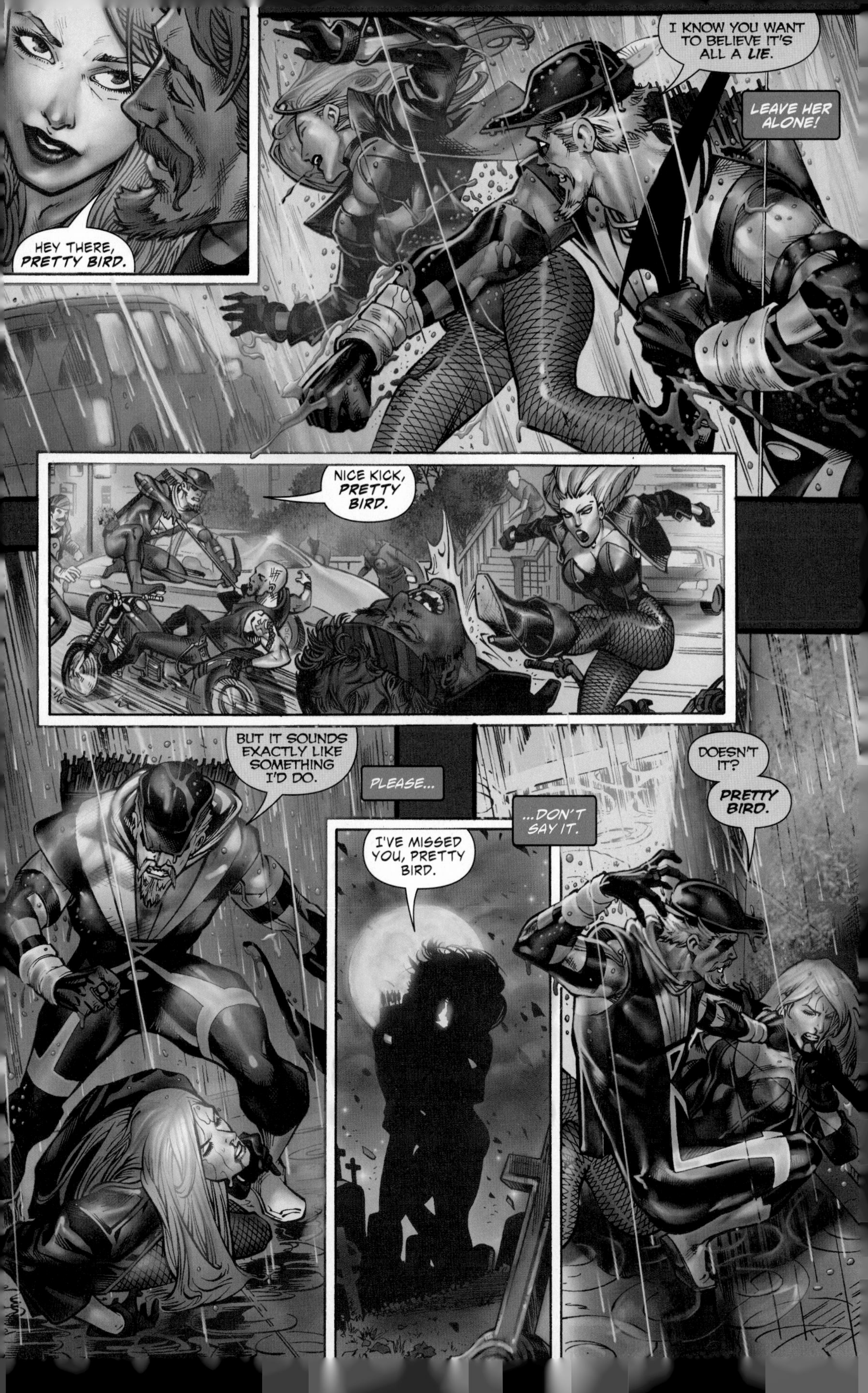
HEY THERE, PRETTY BIRD.
I KNOW YOU WANT TO BELIEVE IT'S ALL A LIE.
LEAVE HER ALONE!
NICE KICK, PRETTY BIRD.
BUT IT SOUNDS EXACTLY LIKE SOMETHING I'D DO.
PLEASE...
I'VE MISSED YOU, PRETTY BIRD.
...DON'T SAY IT.
DOESN'T IT?
PRETTY BIRD.

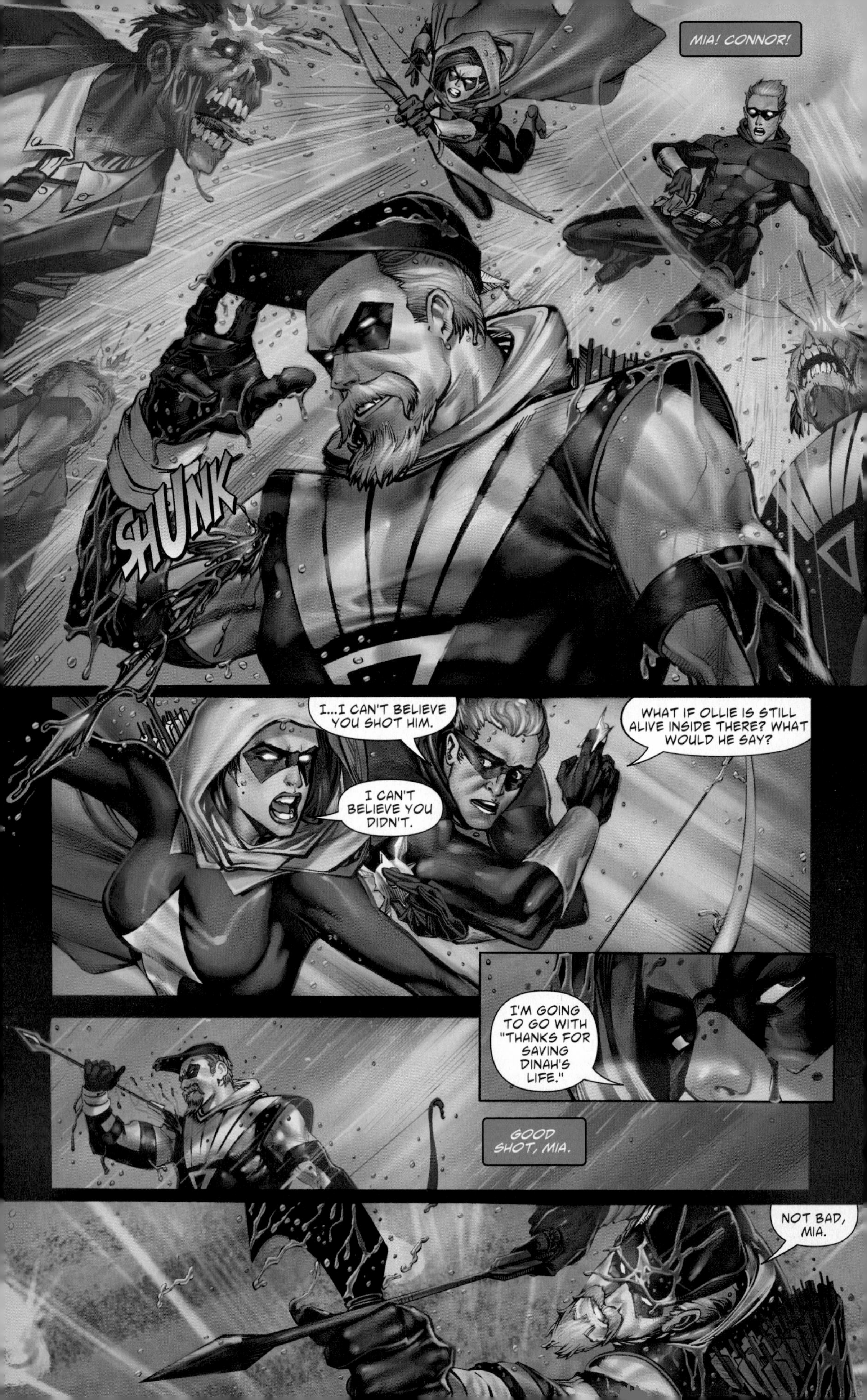
MIA! CONNOR!
SHUNK
I...I CAN'T BELIEVE YOU SHOT HIM.
I CAN'T BELIEVE YOU DIDN'T.
WHAT IF OLLIE IS STILL ALIVE INSIDE THERE? WHAT WOULD HE SAY?
I'M GOING TO GO WITH "THANKS FOR SAVING DINAH'S LIFE."
GOOD SHOT, MIA.
NOT BAD, MIA.

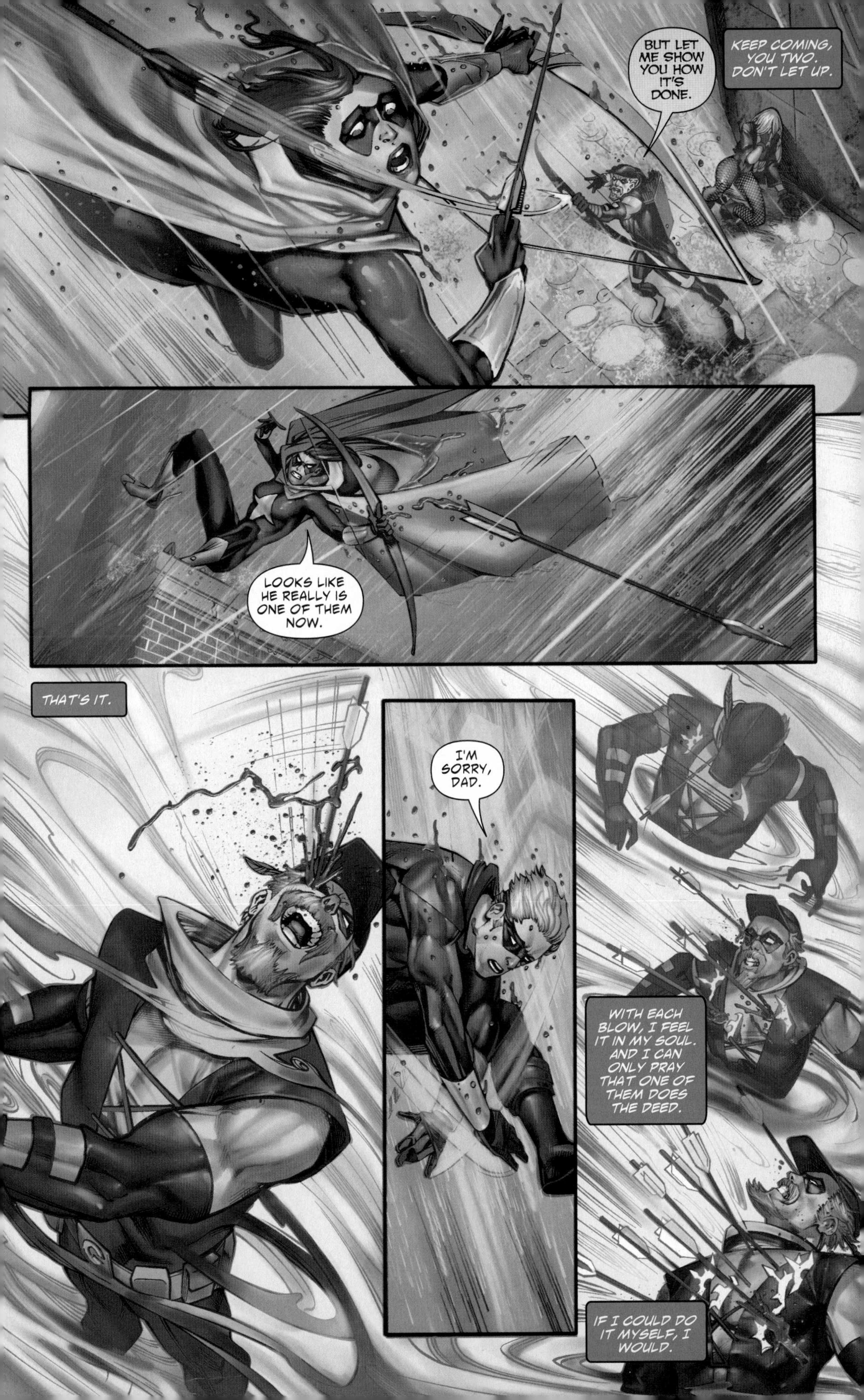
BUT LET ME SHOW YOU HOW IT'S DONE.
KEEP COMING, YOU TWO. DON'T LET UP.
LOOKS LIKE HE REALLY IS ONE OF THEM NOW.
THAT'S IT.
I'M SORRY, DAD.
WITH EACH BLOW, I FEEL IT IN MY SOUL. AND I CAN ONLY PRAY THAT ONE OF THEM DOES THE DEED.
IF I COULD DO IT MYSELF, I WOULD.

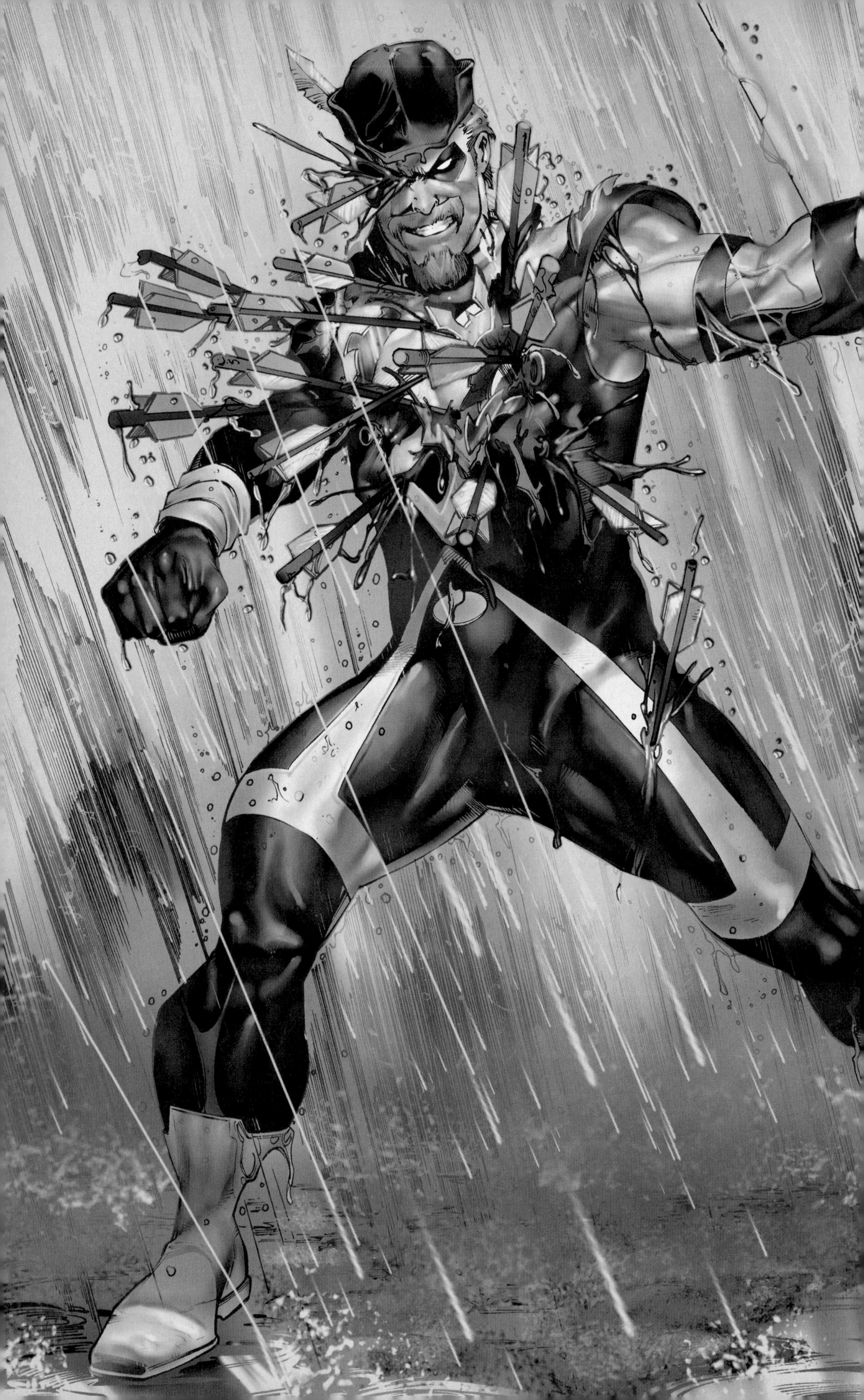

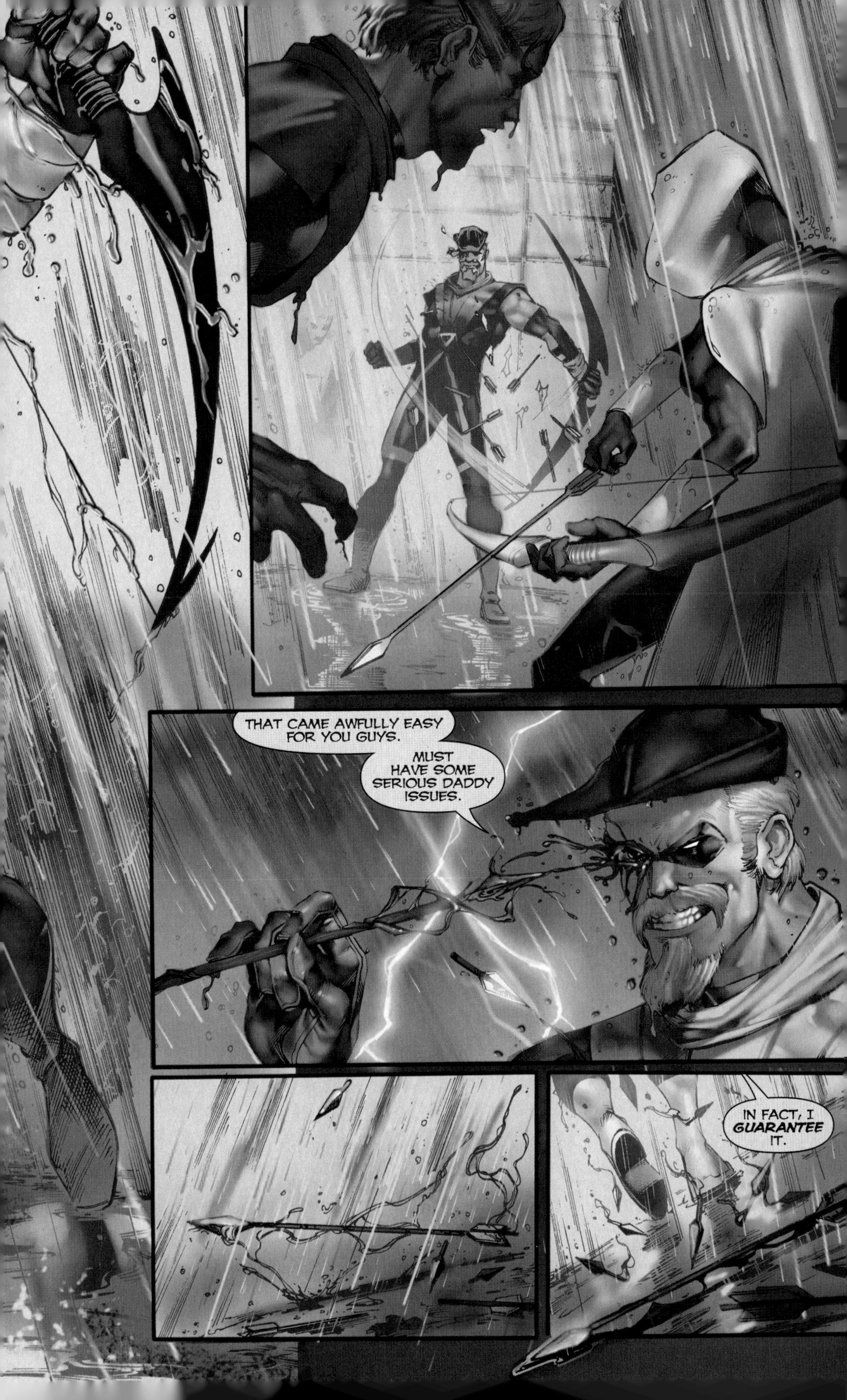
THAT CAME AWFULLY EASY FOR YOU GUYS.
MUST HAVE SOME SERIOUS DADDY ISSUES.
IN FACT, I GUARANTEE IT.

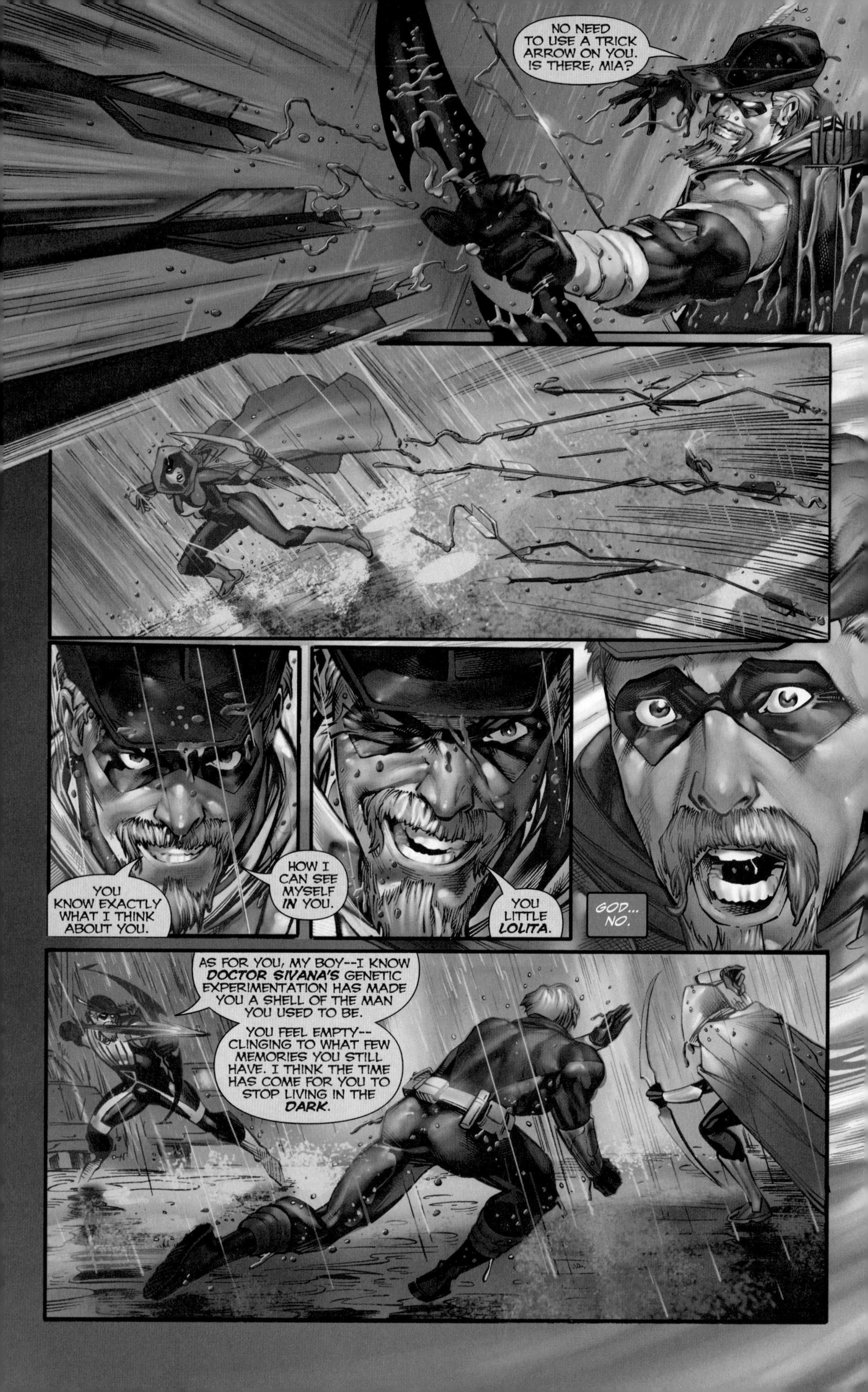
NO NEED TO USE A TRICK ARROW ON YOU. IS THERE, MIA?
YOU KNOW EXACTLY WHAT I THINK ABOUT YOU.
HOW I CAN SEE MYSELF *IN* YOU.
YOU LITTLE *LOLITA*.
GOD... NO.
AS FOR YOU, MY BOY--I KNOW *DOCTOR SIVANA'S* GENETIC EXPERIMENTATION HAS MADE YOU A SHELL OF THE MAN YOU USED TO BE.
YOU FEEL EMPTY-- CLINGING TO WHAT FEW MEMORIES YOU STILL HAVE. I THINK THE TIME HAS COME FOR YOU TO STOP LIVING IN THE *DARK*.

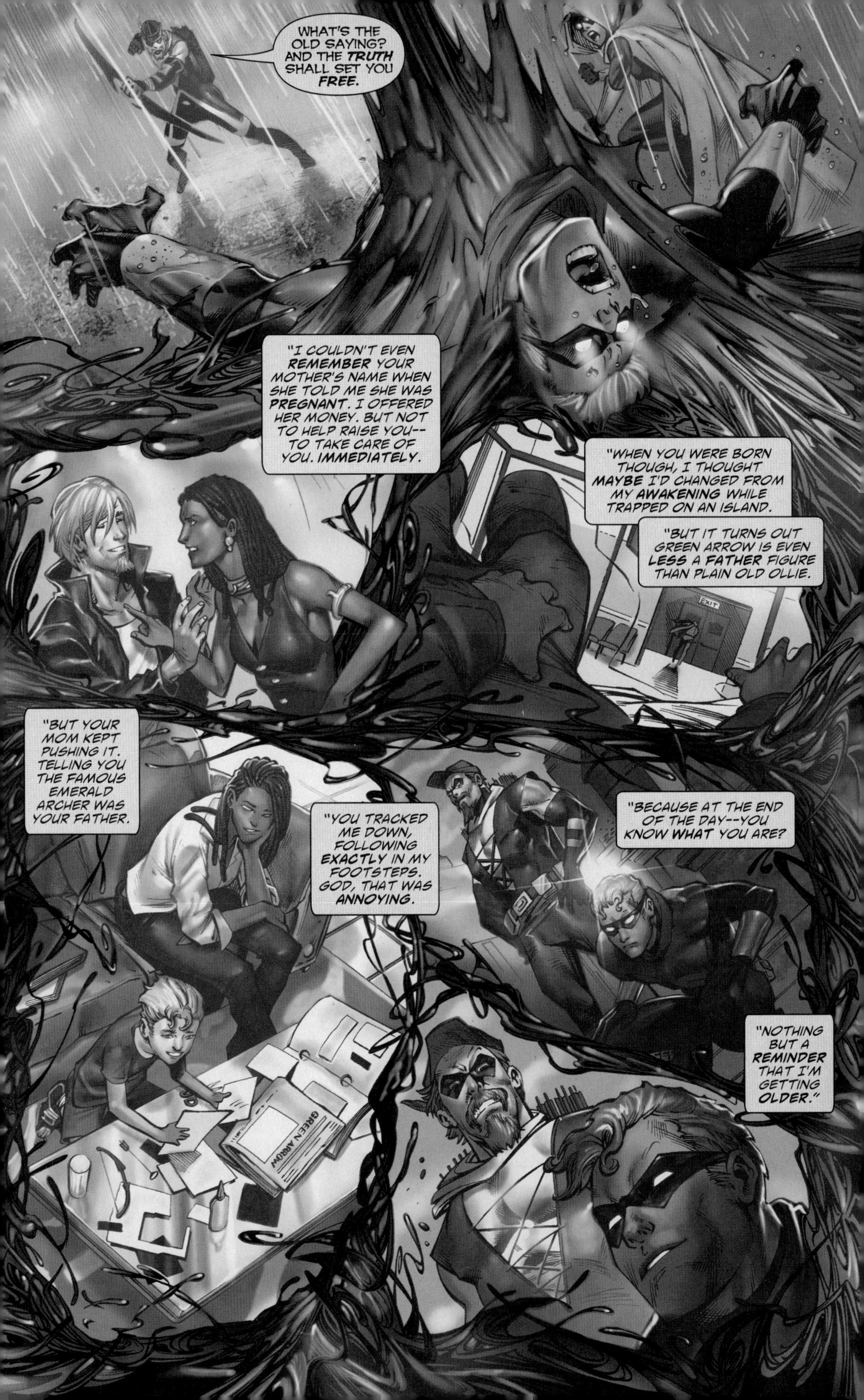
WHAT'S THE OLD SAYING? AND THE TRUTH SHALL SET YOU FREE.
"I COULDN'T EVEN REMEMBER YOUR MOTHER'S NAME WHEN SHE TOLD ME SHE WAS PREGNANT. I OFFERED HER MONEY. BUT NOT TO HELP RAISE YOU-- TO TAKE CARE OF YOU. IMMEDIATELY.
"WHEN YOU WERE BORN THOUGH, I THOUGHT MAYBE I'D CHANGED FROM MY AWAKENING WHILE TRAPPED ON AN ISLAND.
"BUT IT TURNS OUT GREEN ARROW IS EVEN LESS A FATHER FIGURE THAN PLAIN OLD OLLIE.
EXIT
"BUT YOUR MOM KEPT PUSHING IT. TELLING YOU THE FAMOUS EMERALD ARCHER WAS YOUR FATHER.
"YOU TRACKED ME DOWN, FOLLOWING EXACTLY IN MY FOOTSTEPS. GOD, THAT WAS ANNOYING.
"BECAUSE AT THE END OF THE DAY--YOU KNOW WHAT YOU ARE?
"NOTHING BUT A REMINDER THAT I'M GETTING OLDER."
GREEN ARROW

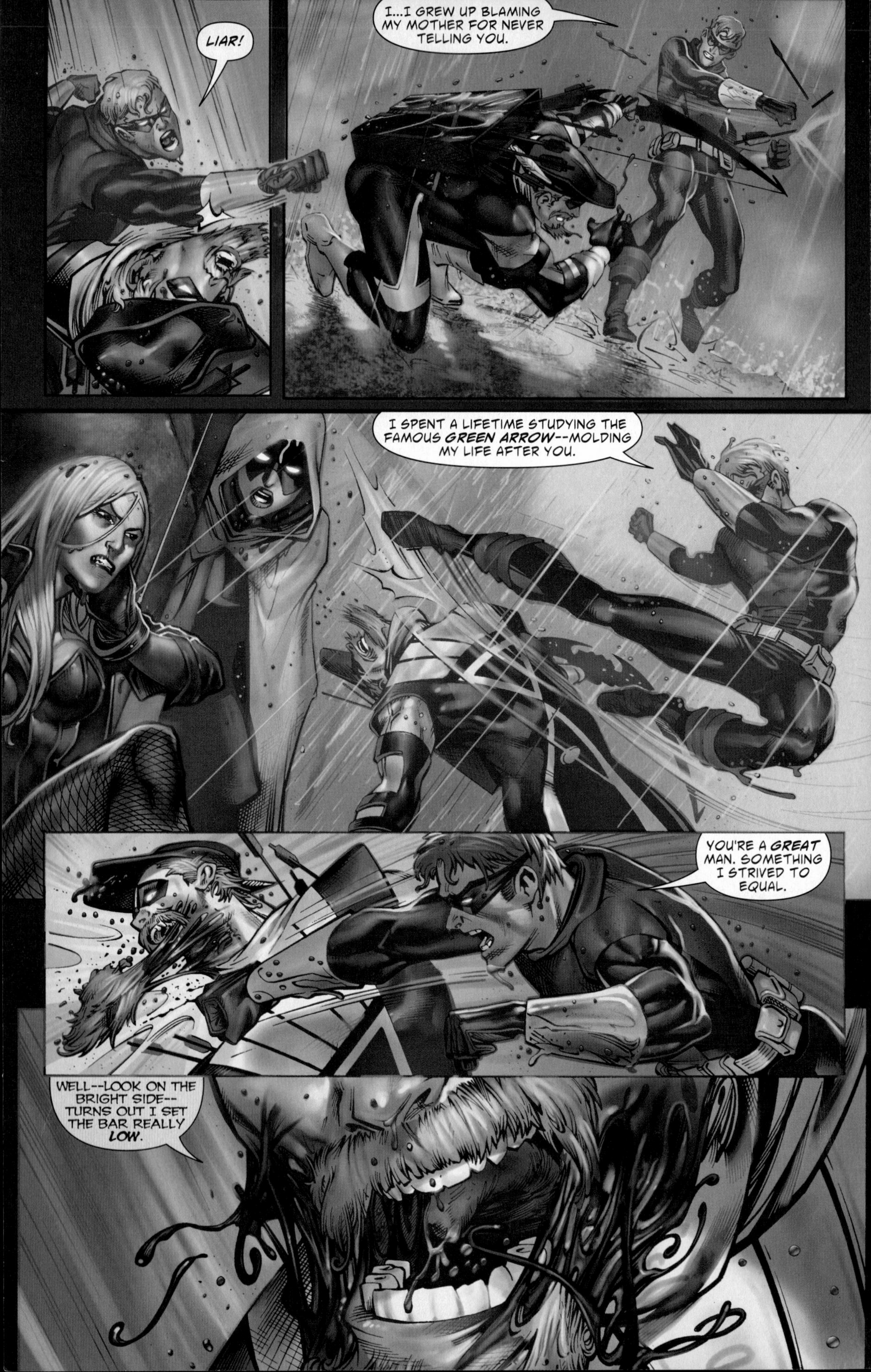
LIAR!
I...I GREW UP BLAMING MY MOTHER FOR NEVER TELLING YOU.
I SPENT A LIFETIME STUDYING THE FAMOUS GREEN ARROW--MOLDING MY LIFE AFTER YOU.
YOU'RE A GREAT MAN. SOMETHING I STRIVED TO EQUAL.
WELL--LOOK ON THE BRIGHT SIDE--TURNS OUT I SET THE BAR REALLY LOW.

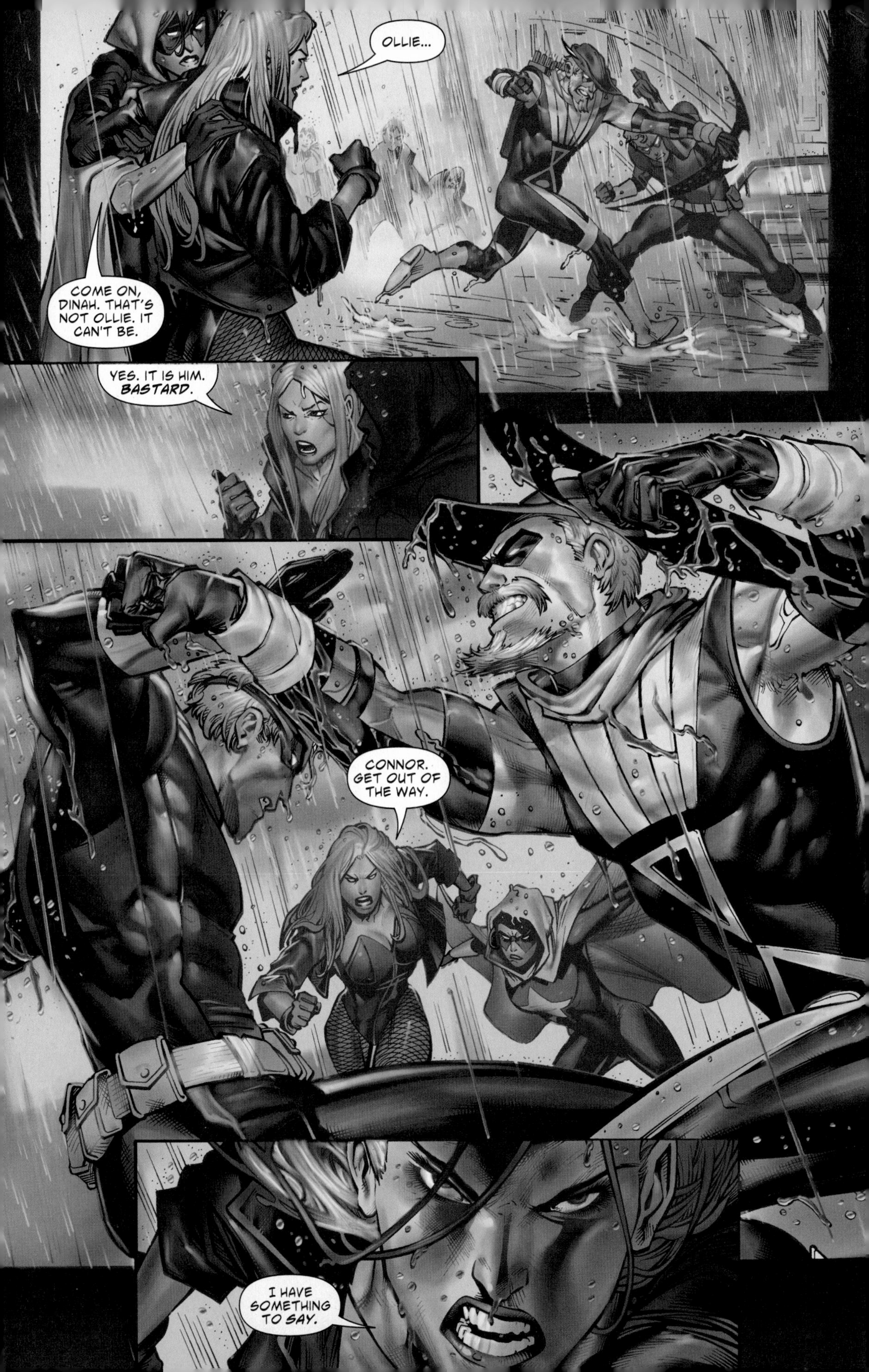
OLLIE...
COME ON, DINAH. THAT'S NOT OLLIE. IT CAN'T BE.
YES. IT IS HIM. BASTARD.
CONNOR. GET OUT OF THE WAY.
I HAVE SOMETHING TO SAY.

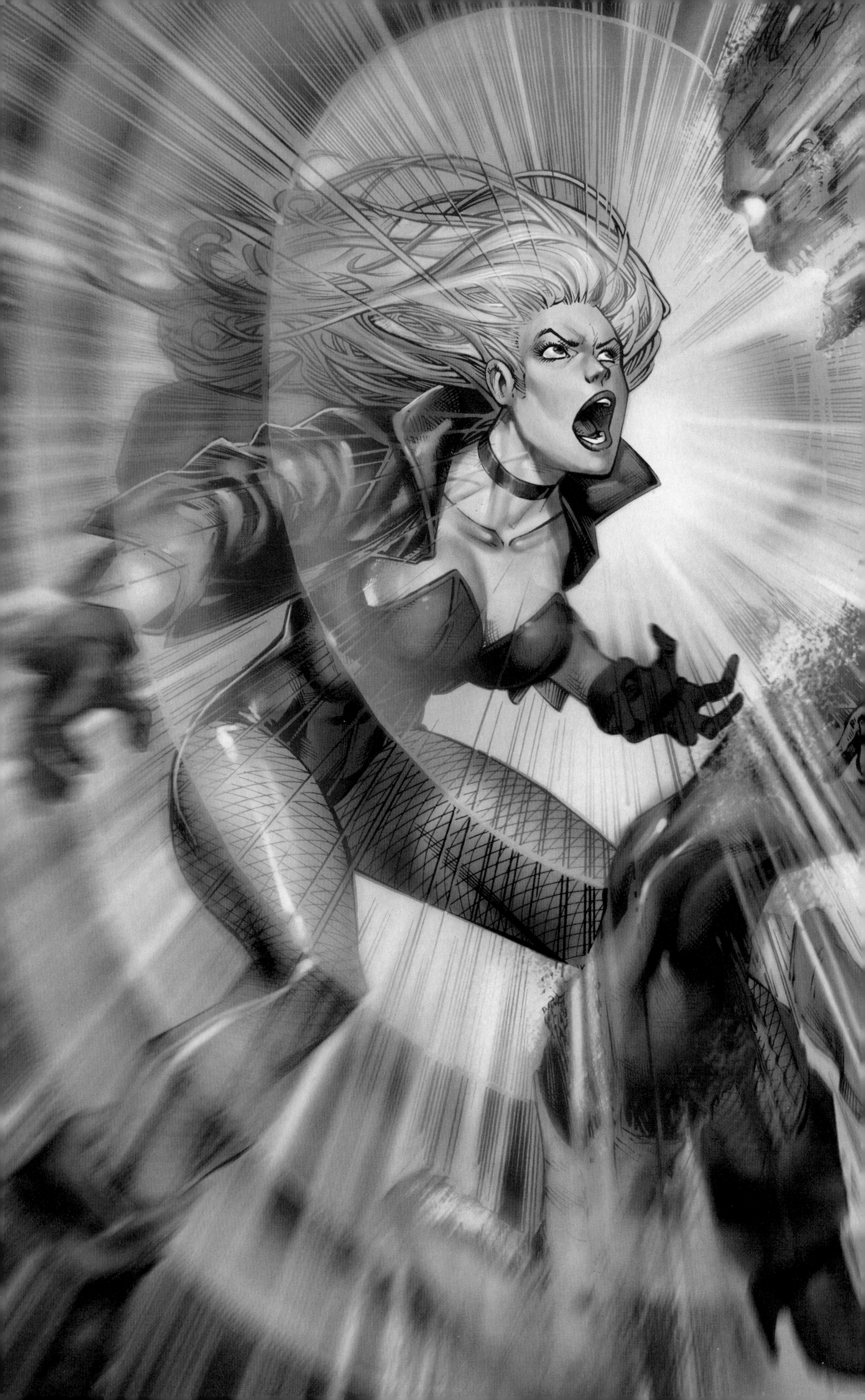

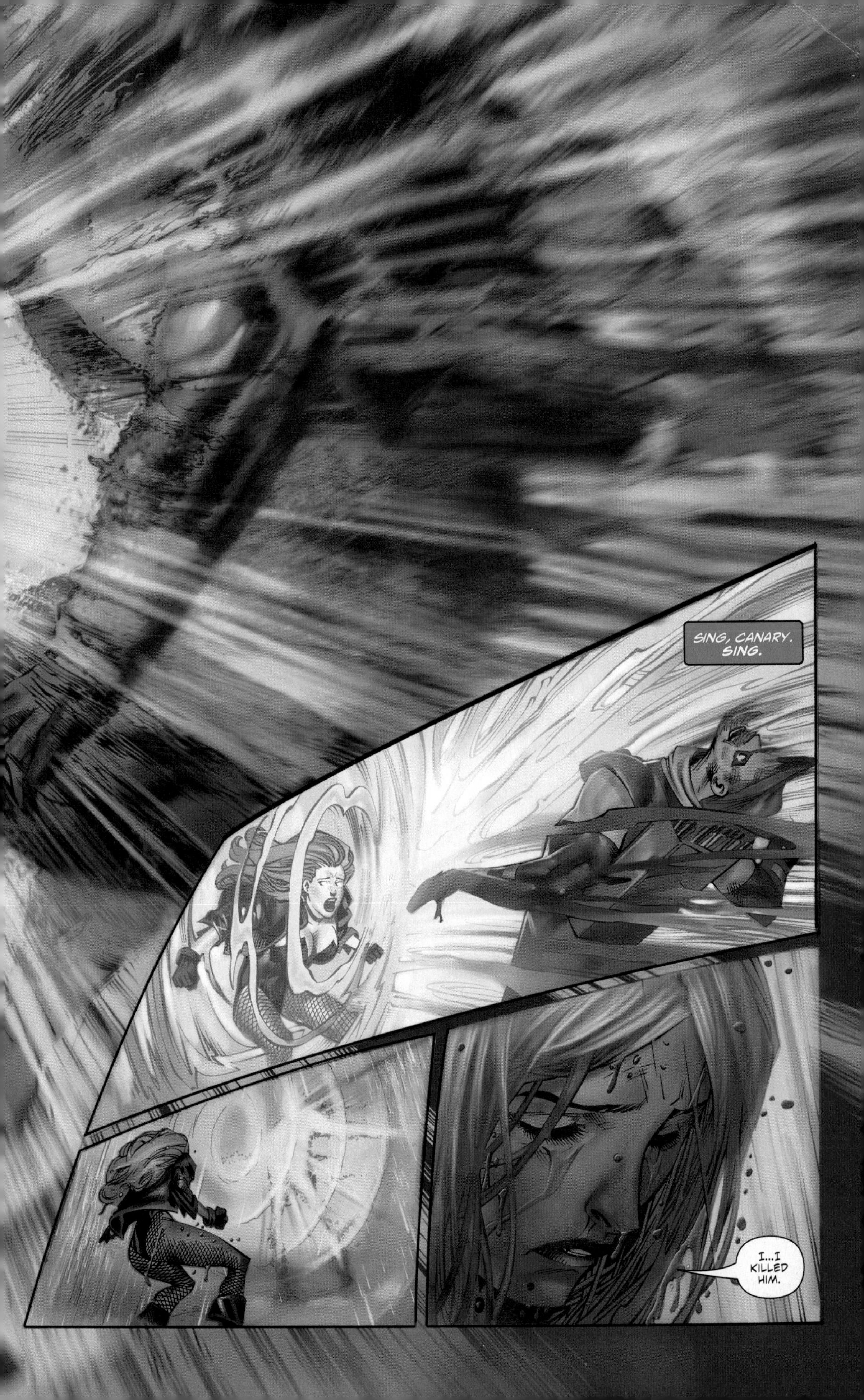
SING, CANARY. SING.
I...I KILLED HIM.

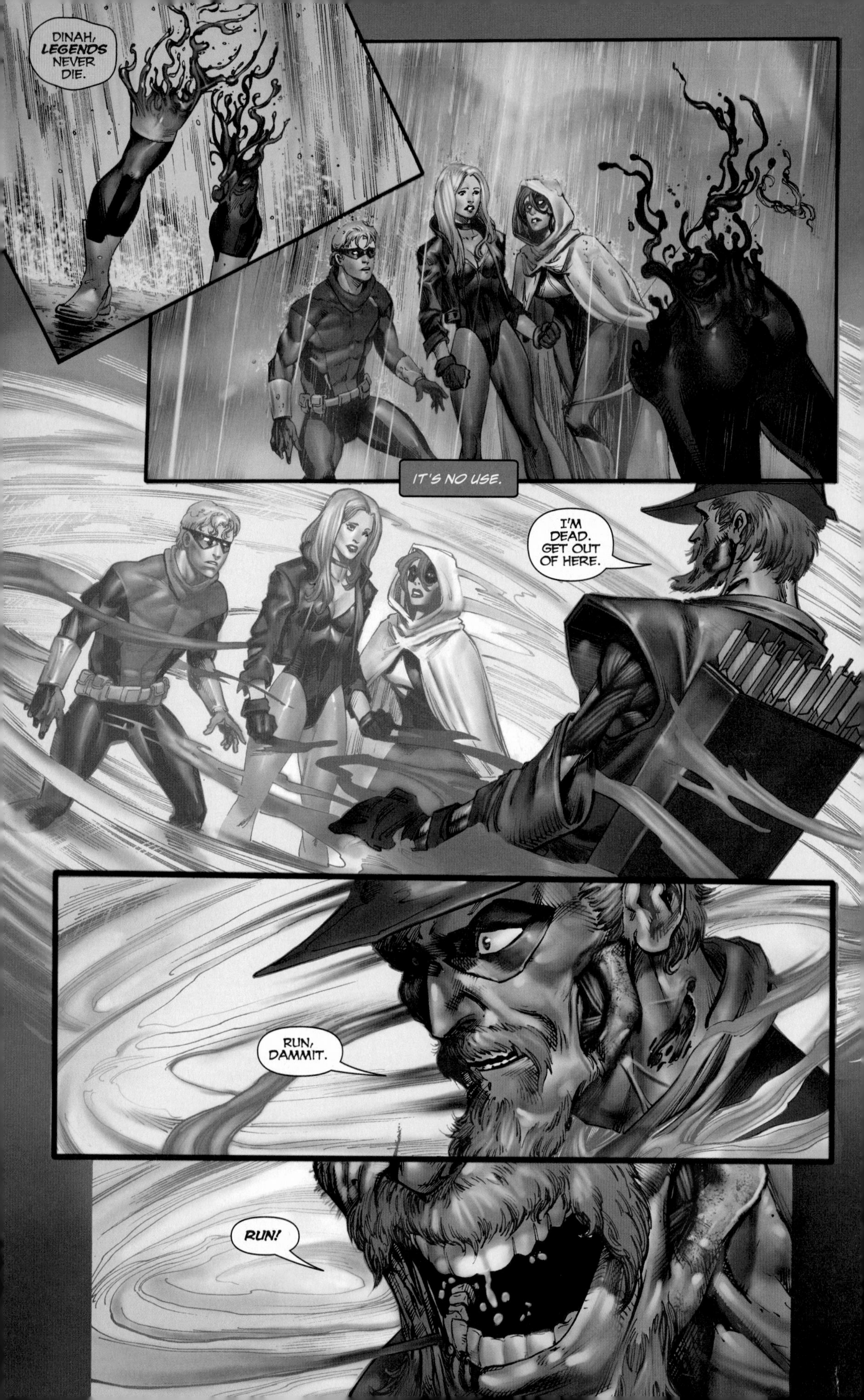
DINAH, LEGENDS NEVER DIE.
IT'S NO USE.
I'M DEAD. GET OUT OF HERE.
RUN, DAMMIT.
RUN!

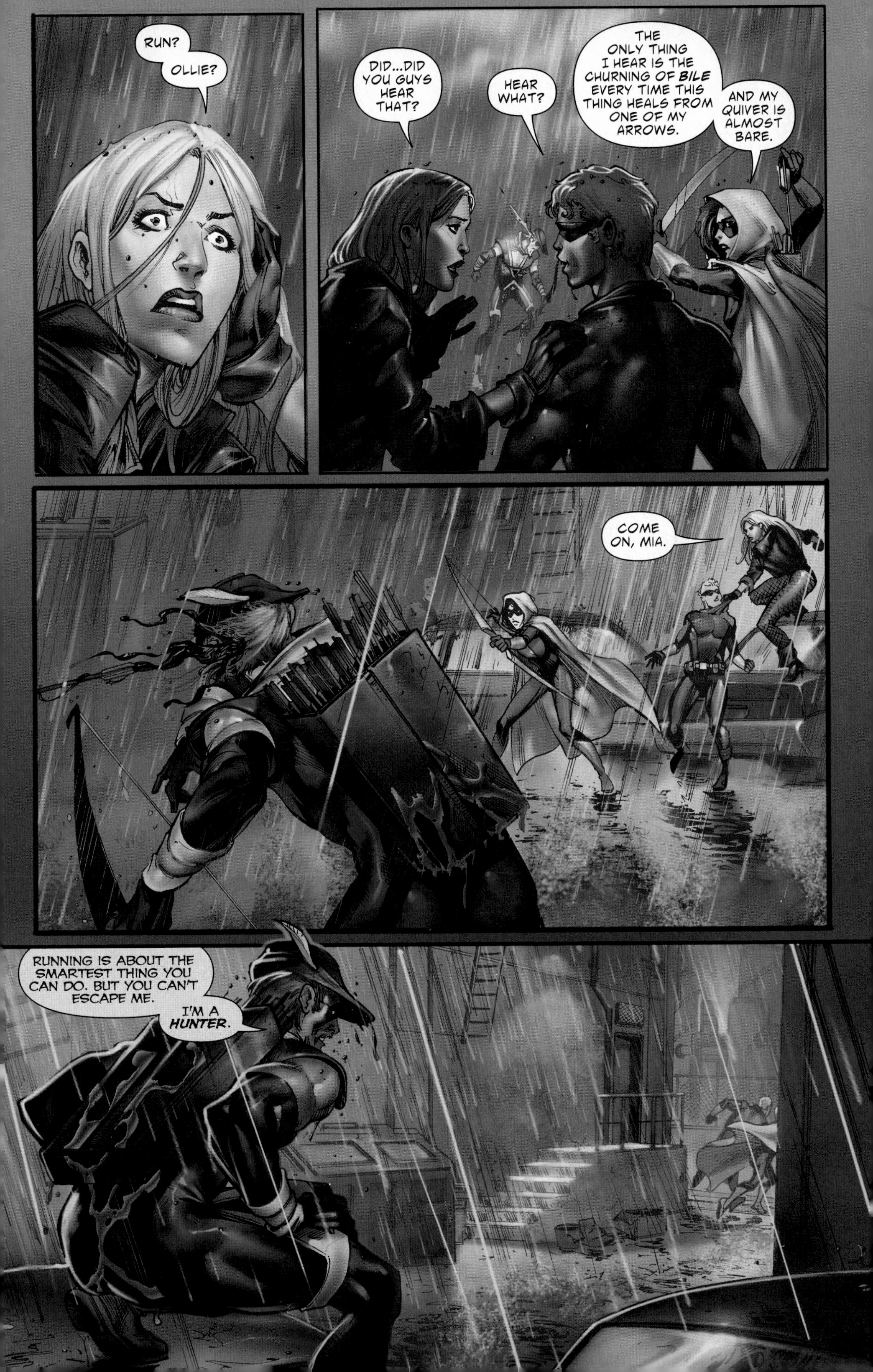
RUN?
OLLIE?
DID...DID YOU GUYS HEAR THAT?
HEAR WHAT?
THE ONLY THING I HEAR IS THE CHURNING OF BILE EVERY TIME THIS THING HEALS FROM ONE OF MY ARROWS.
AND MY QUIVER IS ALMOST BARE.
COME ON, MIA.
RUNNING IS ABOUT THE SMARTEST THING YOU CAN DO. BUT YOU CAN'T ESCAPE ME.
I'M A HUNTER.

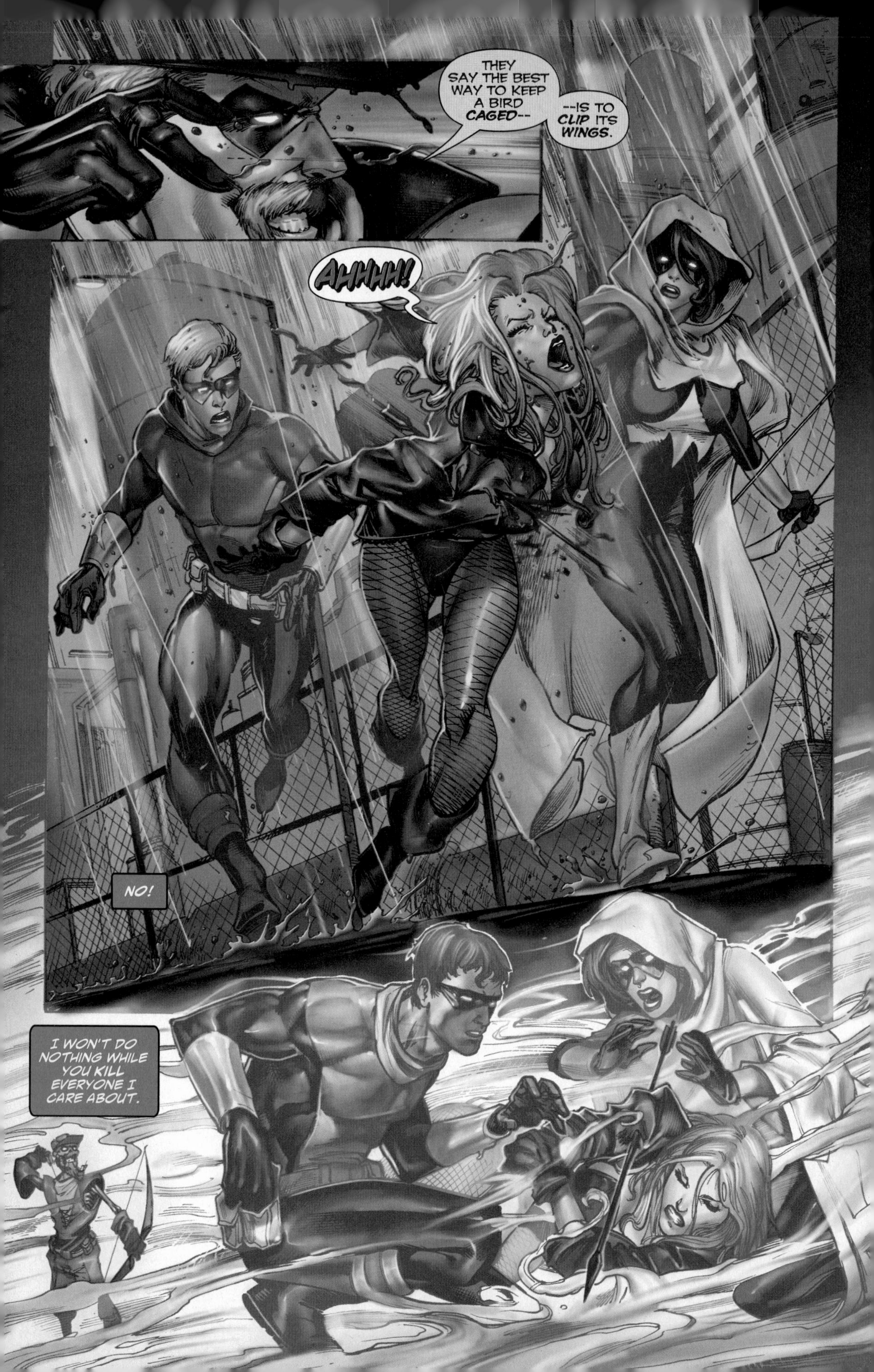
THEY SAY THE BEST WAY TO KEEP A BIRD CAGED--
--IS TO CLIP ITS WINGS.
AHHHH!
NO!
I WON'T DO NOTHING WHILE YOU KILL EVERYONE I CARE ABOUT.

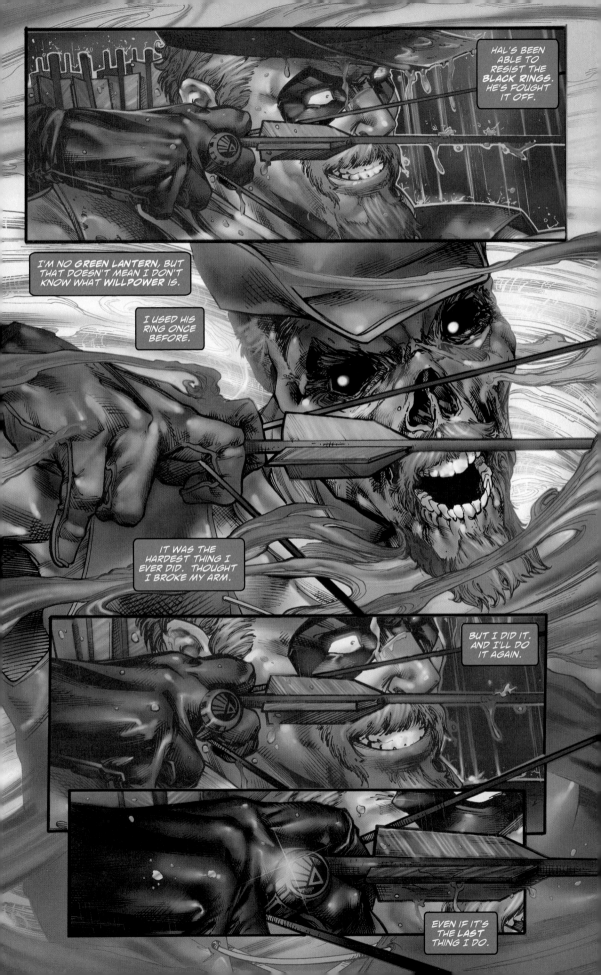

HAL'S BEEN ABLE TO RESIST THE **BLACK RINGS.** HE'S FOUGHT IT OFF.

I'M NO GREEN LANTERN, BUT THAT DOESN'T MEAN I DON'T KNOW WHAT WILLPOWER IS.

I USED HIS RING ONCE BEFORE.

IT WAS THE HARDEST THING I EVER DID. THOUGHT I BROKE MY ARM.

BUT I DID IT. AND I'LL DO IT AGAIN.

EVEN IF IT'S THE LAST THING I DO.

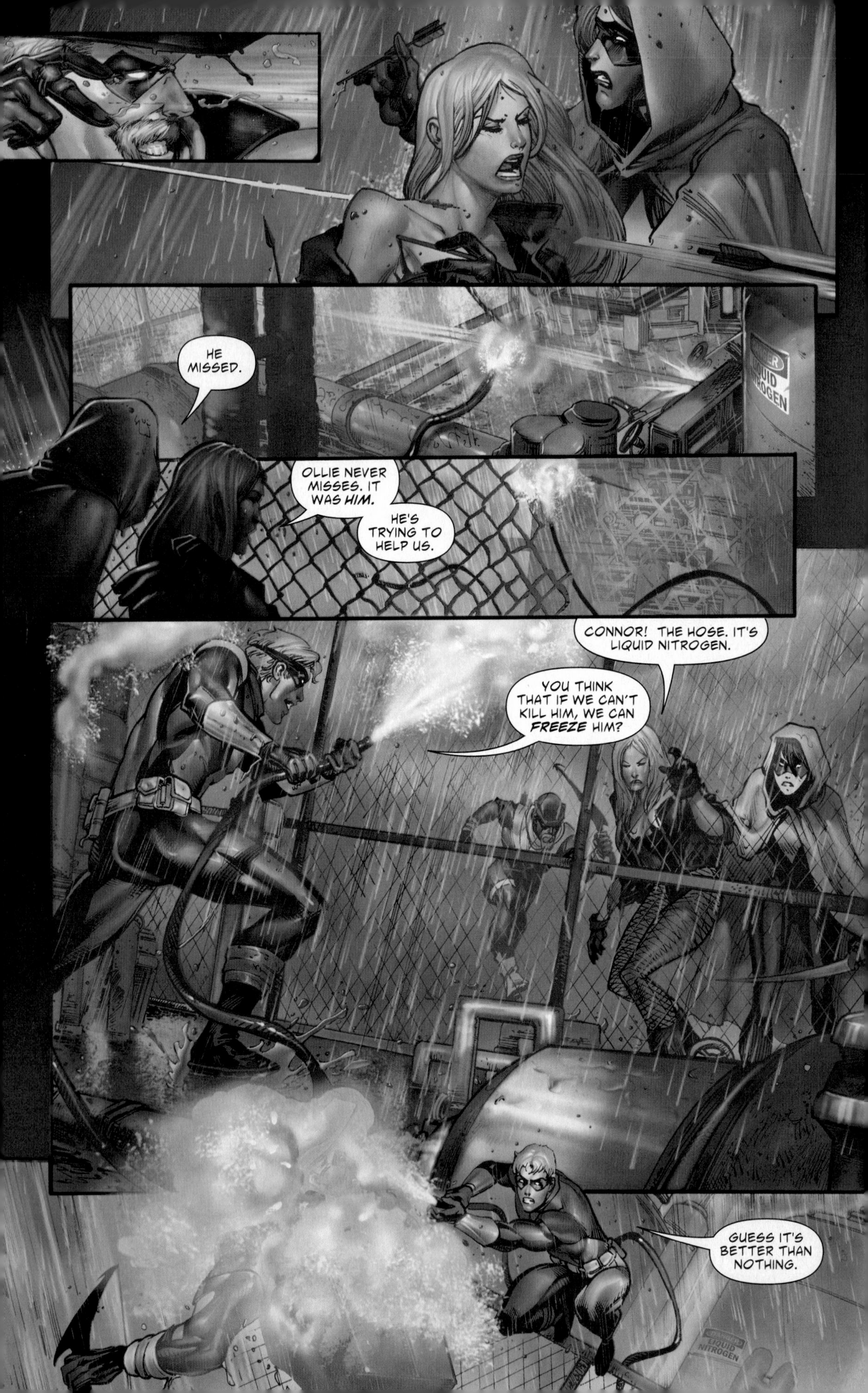
HE MISSED.
OLLIE NEVER MISSES. IT WAS HIM.
HE'S TRYING TO HELP US.
CONNOR! THE HOSE. IT'S LIQUID NITROGEN.
YOU THINK THAT IF WE CAN'T KILL HIM, WE CAN FREEZE HIM?
GUESS IT'S BETTER THAN NOTHING.

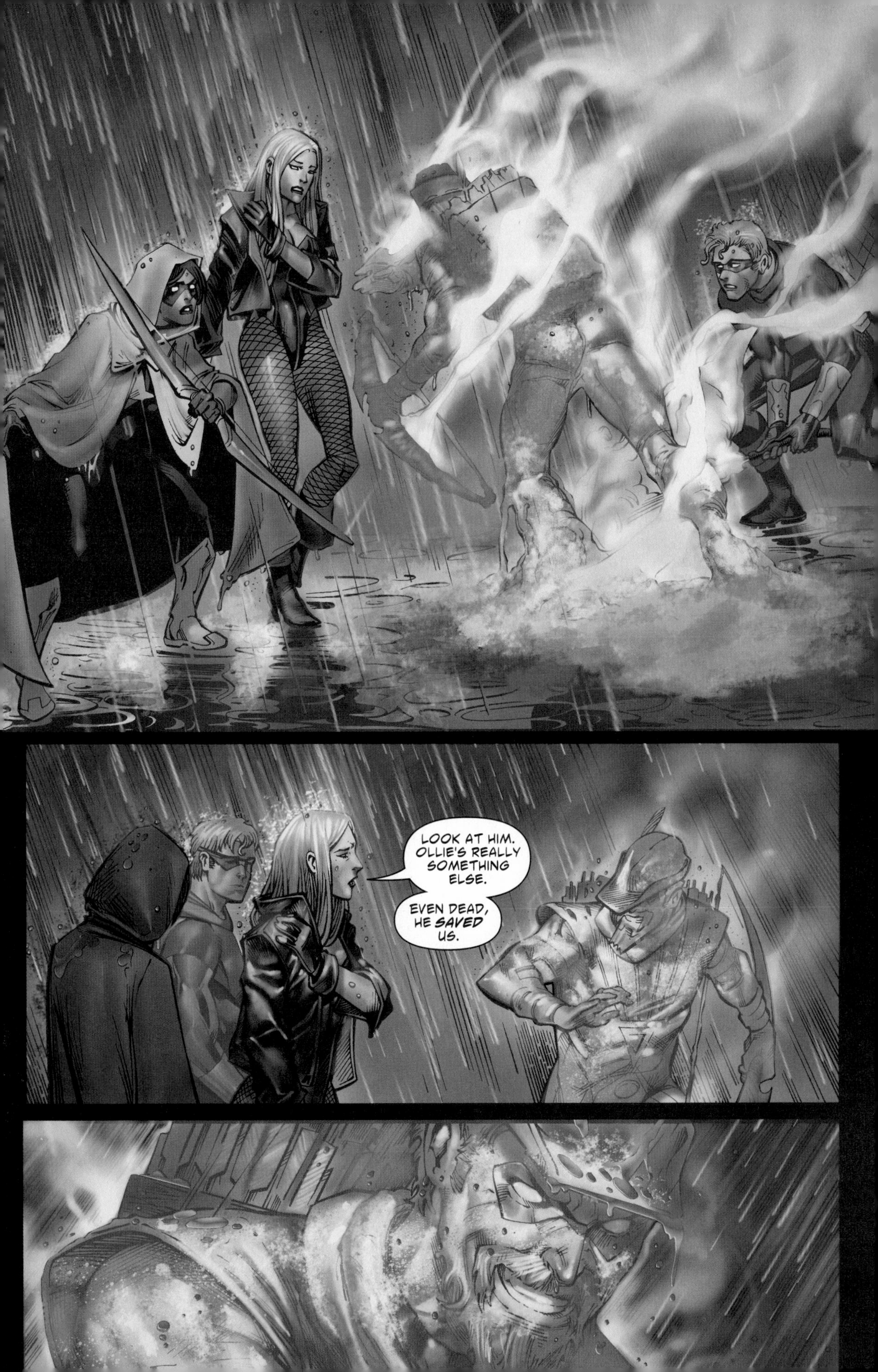
LOOK AT HIM. OLLIE'S REALLY SOMETHING ELSE.
EVEN DEAD, HE SAVED US.

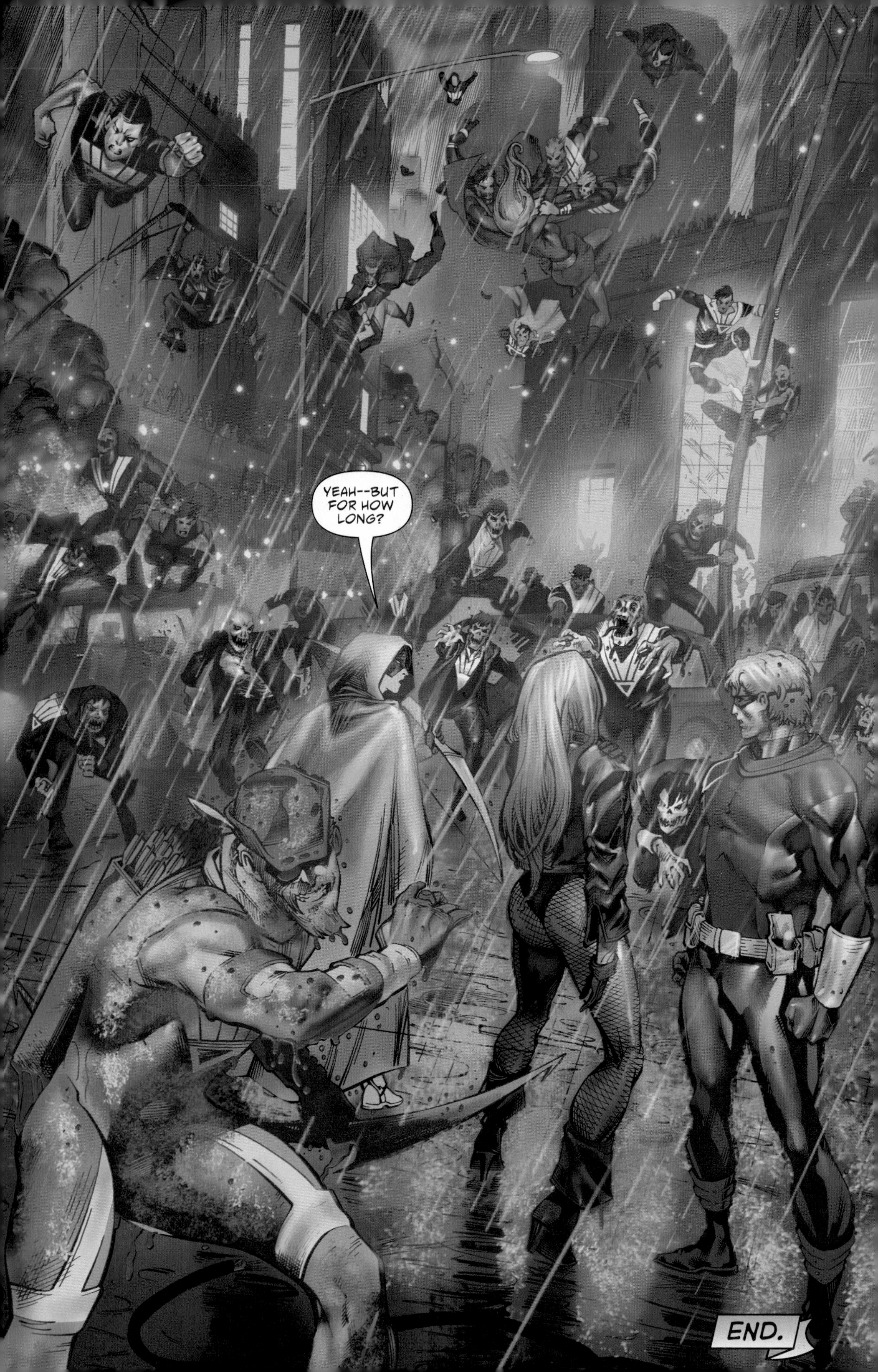
YEAH--BUT FOR HOW LONG?
END.

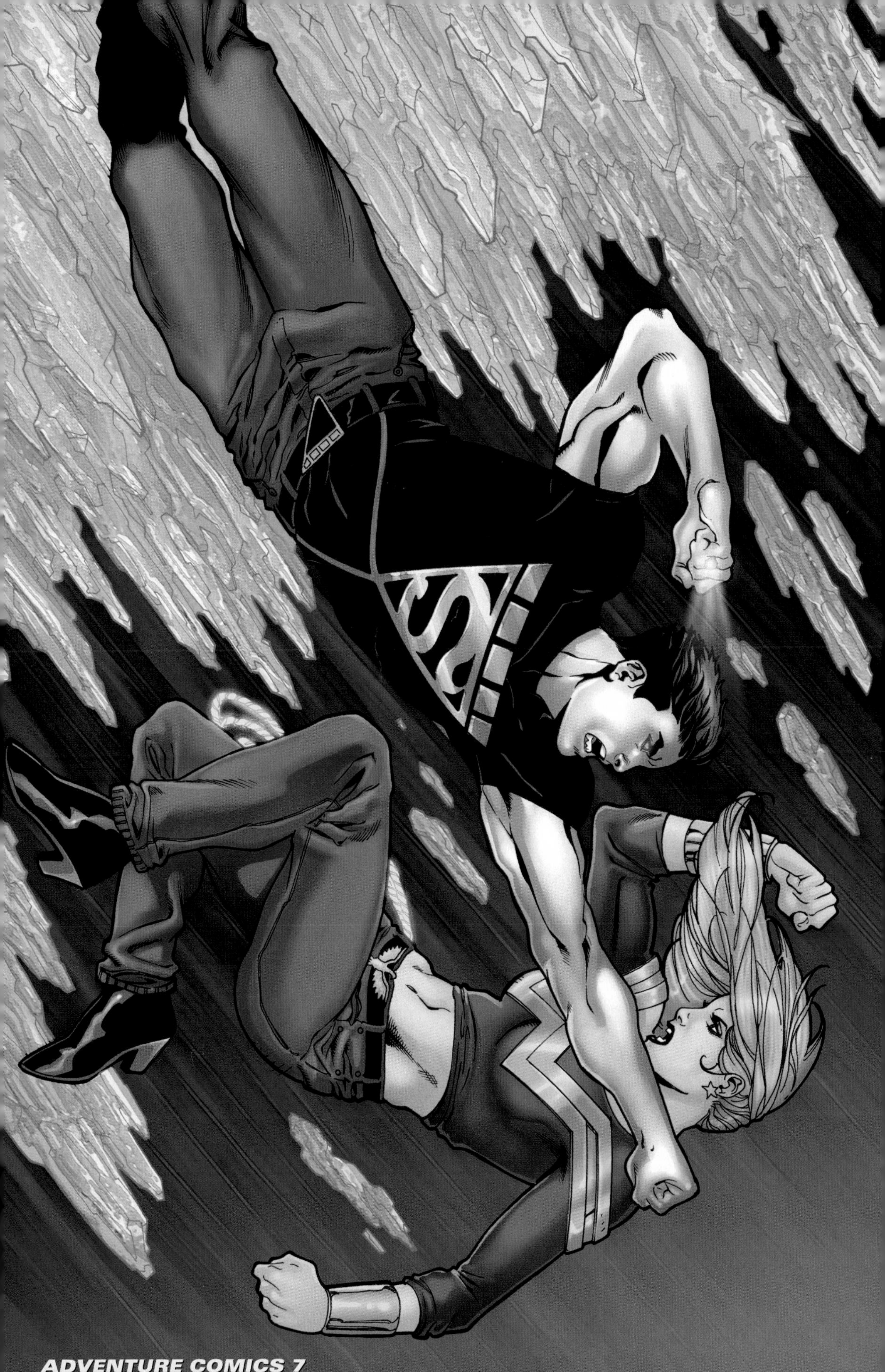

ADVENTURE COMICS 7
Cover by Aaron Lopresti

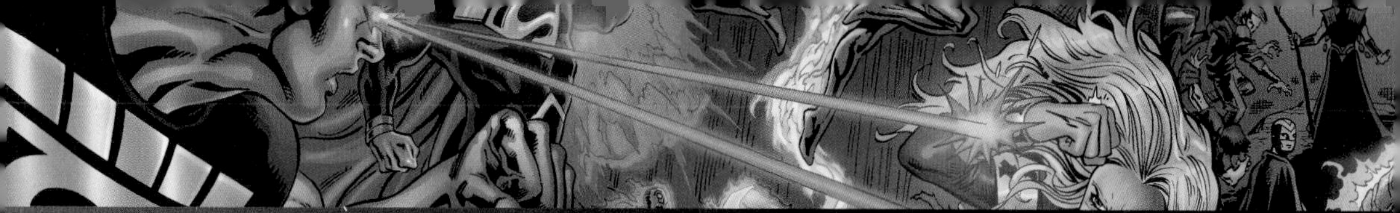

WHAT DID BLACK LANTERN SUPERBOY DO?

TONY BEDARD
WRITER

TRAVIS MOORE
PENCILS

DAN GREEN
KEITH CHAMPAGNE
BOB WIACEK
INKS

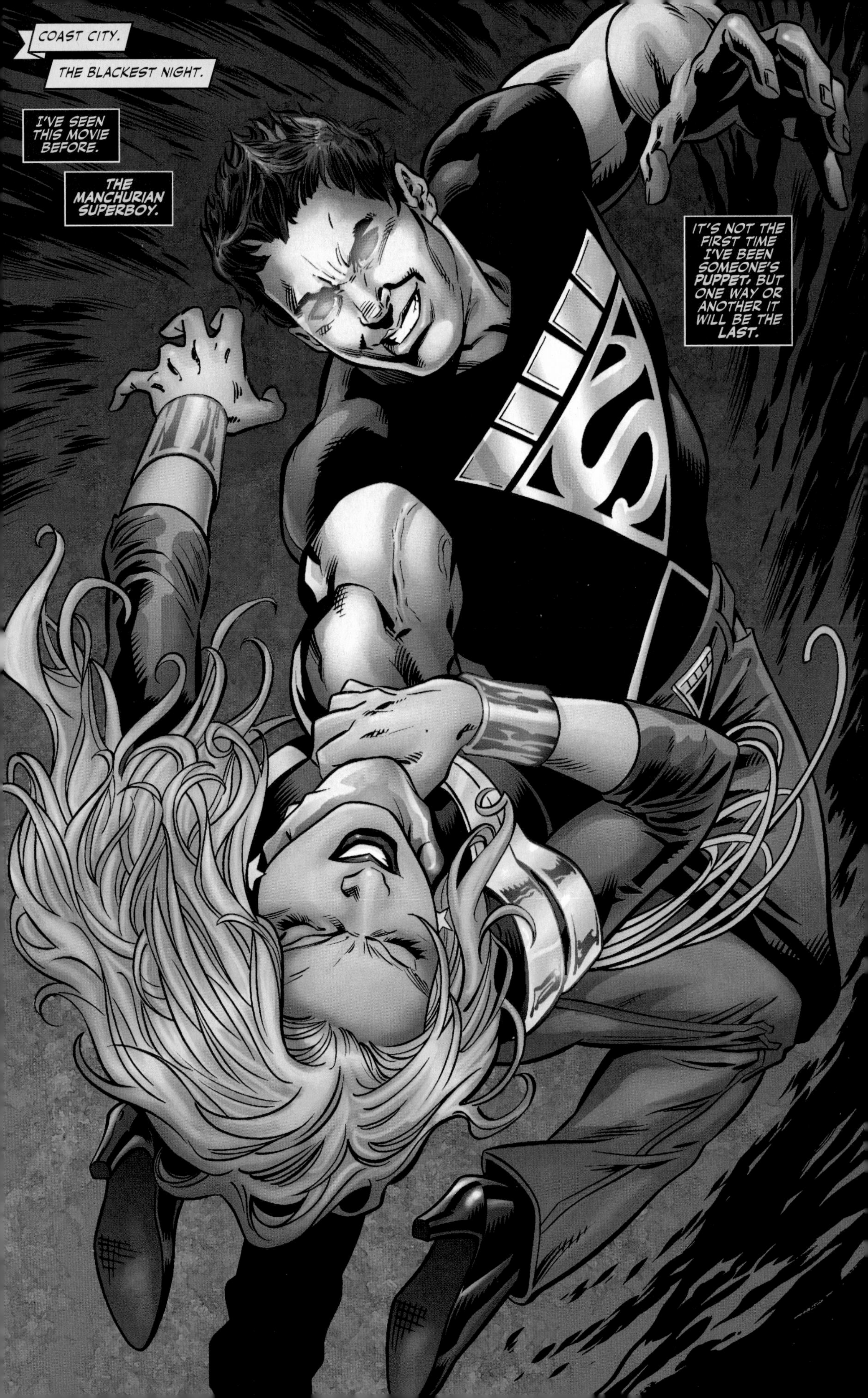
COAST CITY.
THE BLACKEST NIGHT.
I'VE SEEN THIS MOVIE BEFORE.
THE MANCHURIAN SUPERBOY.
IT'S NOT THE FIRST TIME I'VE BEEN SOMEONE'S PUPPET, BUT ONE WAY OR ANOTHER IT WILL BE THE LAST.

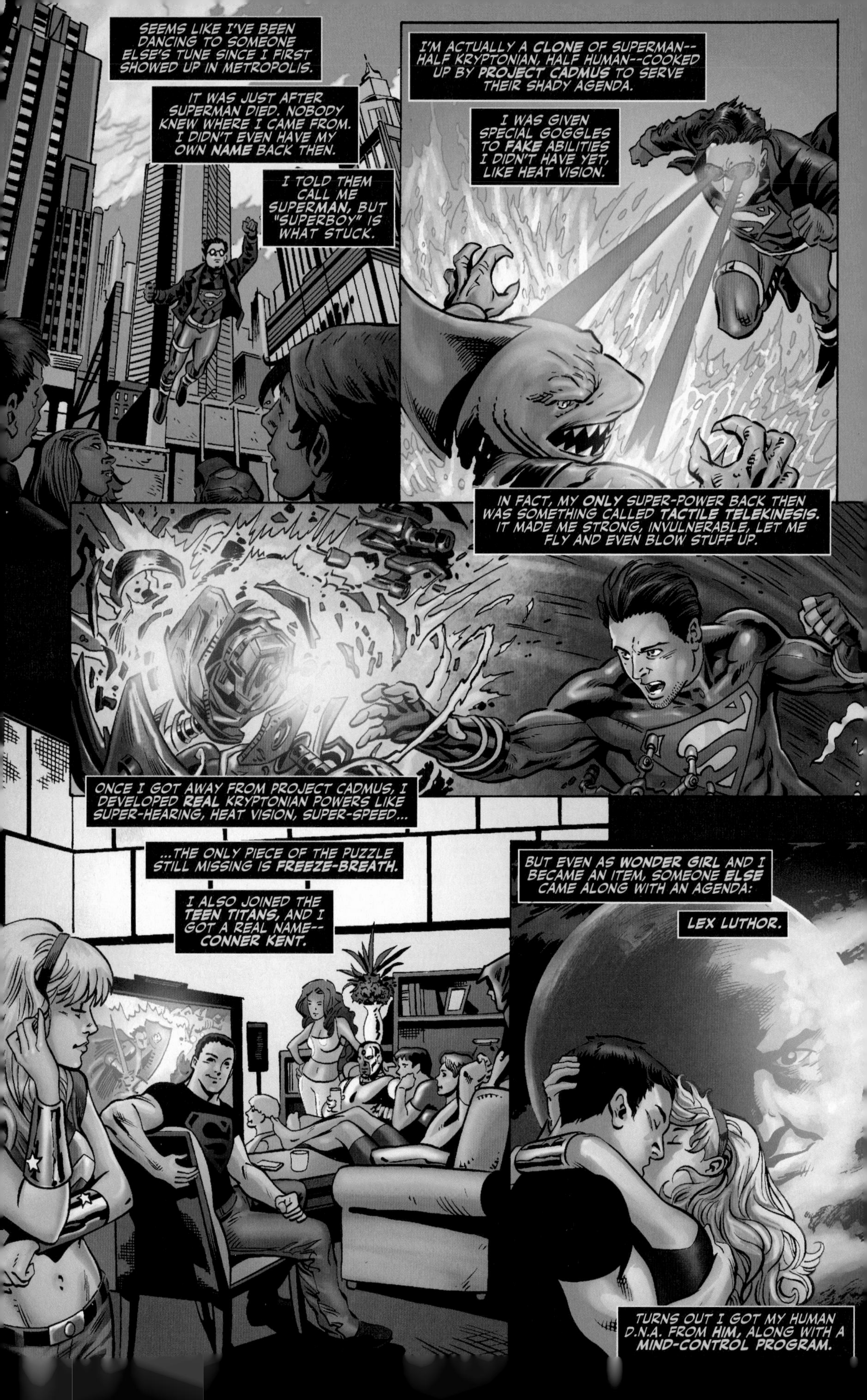

SEEMS LIKE I'VE BEEN DANCING TO SOMEONE ELSE'S TUNE SINCE I FIRST SHOWED UP IN METROPOLIS.
IT WAS JUST AFTER SUPERMAN DIED. NOBODY KNEW WHERE I CAME FROM. I DIDN'T EVEN HAVE MY OWN NAME BACK THEN.
I TOLD THEM CALL ME SUPERMAN, BUT "SUPERBOY" IS WHAT STUCK.
I'M ACTUALLY A CLONE OF SUPERMAN--HALF KRYPTONIAN, HALF HUMAN--COOKED UP BY PROJECT CADMUS TO SERVE THEIR SHADY AGENDA.
I WAS GIVEN SPECIAL GOGGLES TO FAKE ABILITIES I DIDN'T HAVE YET, LIKE HEAT VISION.
IN FACT, MY ONLY SUPER-POWER BACK THEN WAS SOMETHING CALLED TACTILE TELEKINESIS. IT MADE ME STRONG, INVULNERABLE, LET ME FLY AND EVEN BLOW STUFF UP.
ONCE I GOT AWAY FROM PROJECT CADMUS, I DEVELOPED REAL KRYPTONIAN POWERS LIKE SUPER-HEARING, HEAT VISION, SUPER-SPEED...
...THE ONLY PIECE OF THE PUZZLE STILL MISSING IS FREEZE-BREATH.
I ALSO JOINED THE TEEN TITANS, AND I GOT A REAL NAME--CONNER KENT.
BUT EVEN AS WONDER GIRL AND I BECAME AN ITEM, SOMEONE ELSE CAME ALONG WITH AN AGENDA:
LEX LUTHOR.
TURNS OUT I GOT MY HUMAN D.N.A. FROM HIM, ALONG WITH A MIND-CONTROL PROGRAM.

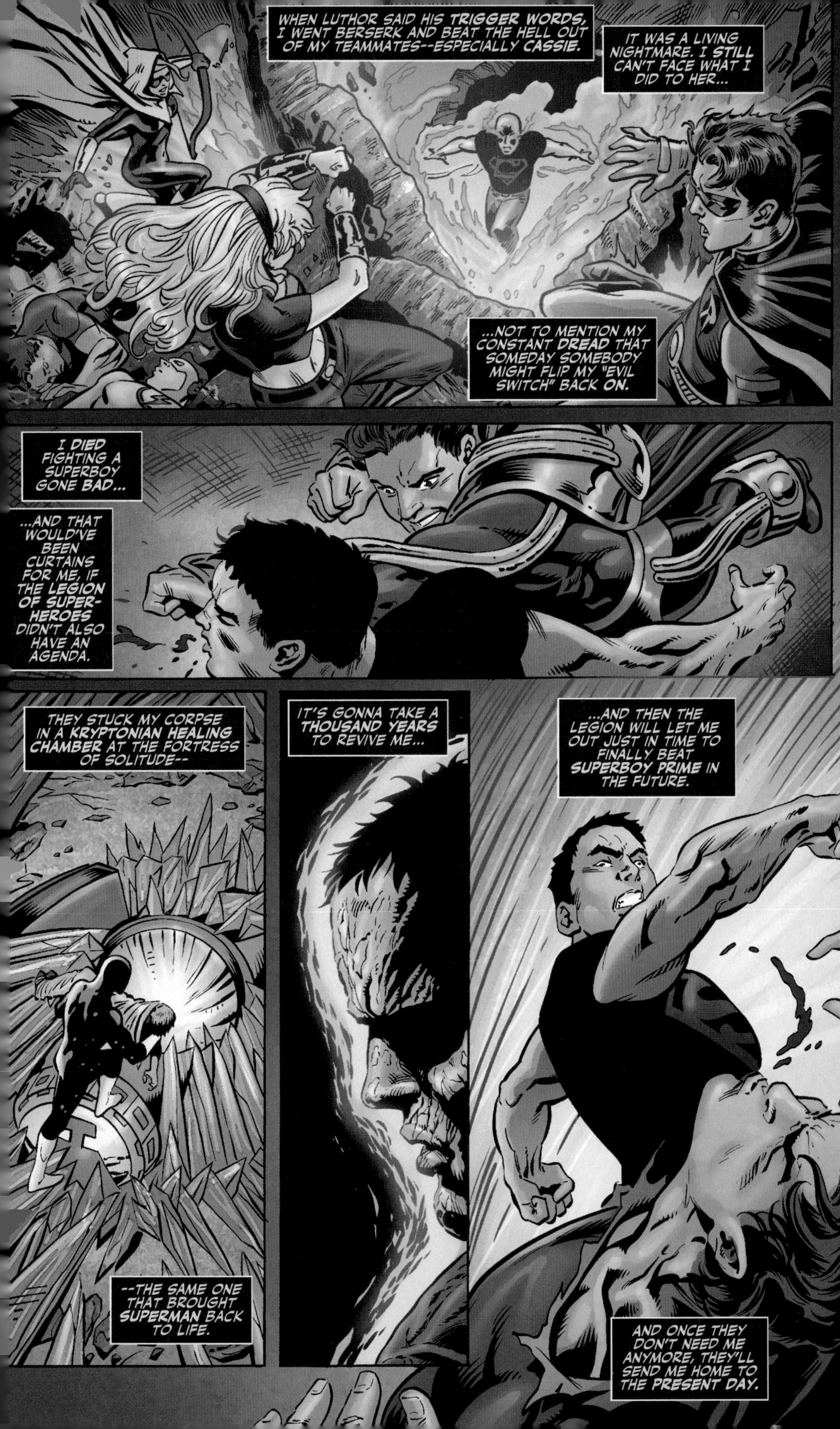
WHEN LUTHOR SAID HIS TRIGGER WORDS, I WENT BERSERK AND BEAT THE HELL OUT OF MY TEAMMATES--ESPECIALLY CASSIE.
IT WAS A LIVING NIGHTMARE. I STILL CAN'T FACE WHAT I DID TO HER...
...NOT TO MENTION MY CONSTANT DREAD THAT SOMEDAY SOMEBODY MIGHT FLIP MY "EVIL SWITCH" BACK ON.
I DIED FIGHTING A SUPERBOY GONE BAD...
...AND THAT WOULD'VE BEEN CURTAINS FOR ME, IF THE LEGION OF SUPER-HEROES DIDN'T ALSO HAVE AN AGENDA.
THEY STUCK MY CORPSE IN A KRYPTONIAN HEALING CHAMBER AT THE FORTRESS OF SOLITUDE--
--THE SAME ONE THAT BROUGHT SUPERMAN BACK TO LIFE.
IT'S GONNA TAKE A THOUSAND YEARS TO REVIVE ME...
...AND THEN THE LEGION WILL LET ME OUT JUST IN TIME TO FINALLY BEAT SUPERBOY PRIME IN THE FUTURE.
AND ONCE THEY DON'T NEED ME ANYMORE, THEY'LL SEND ME HOME TO THE PRESENT DAY.

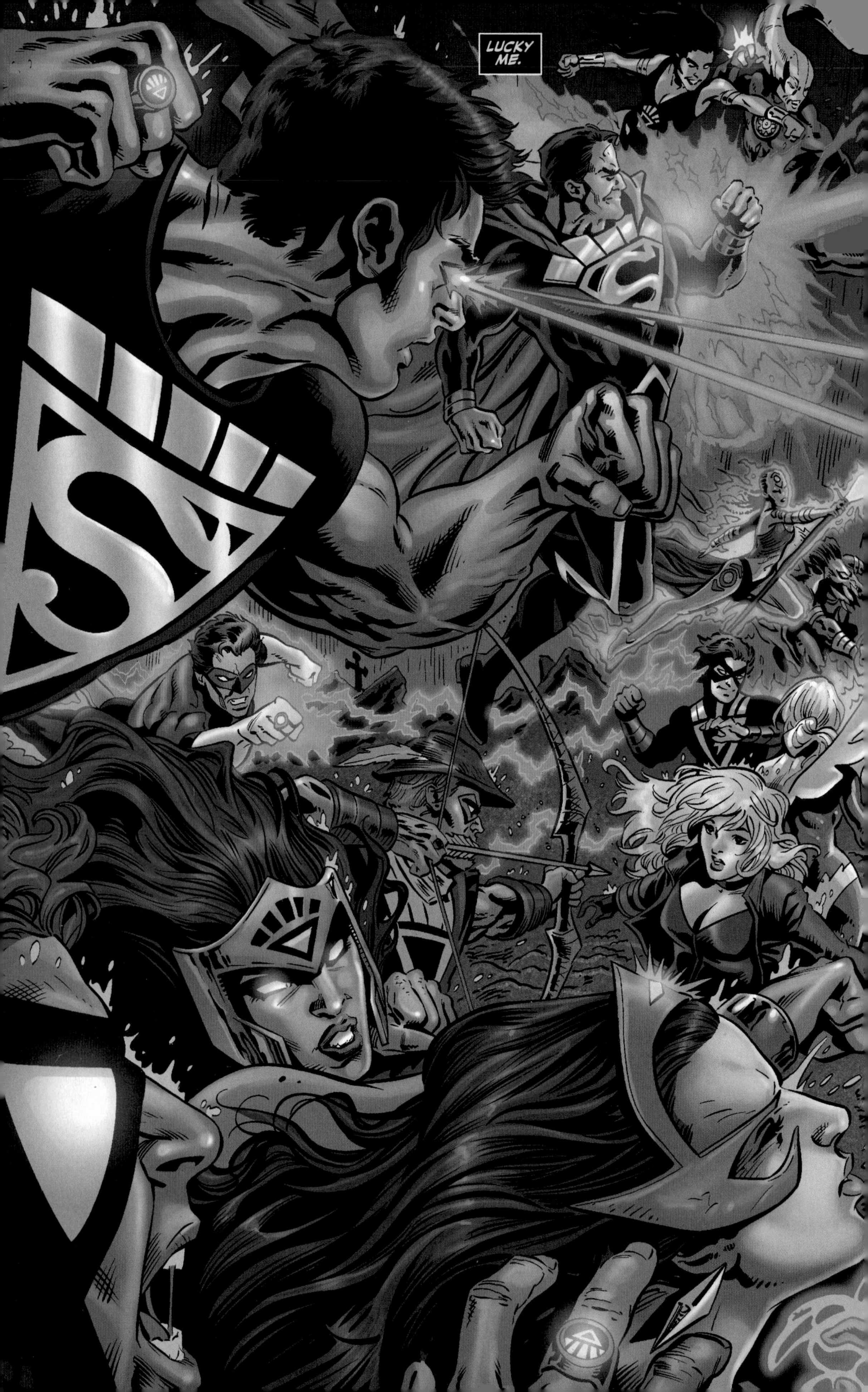
LUCKY ME.

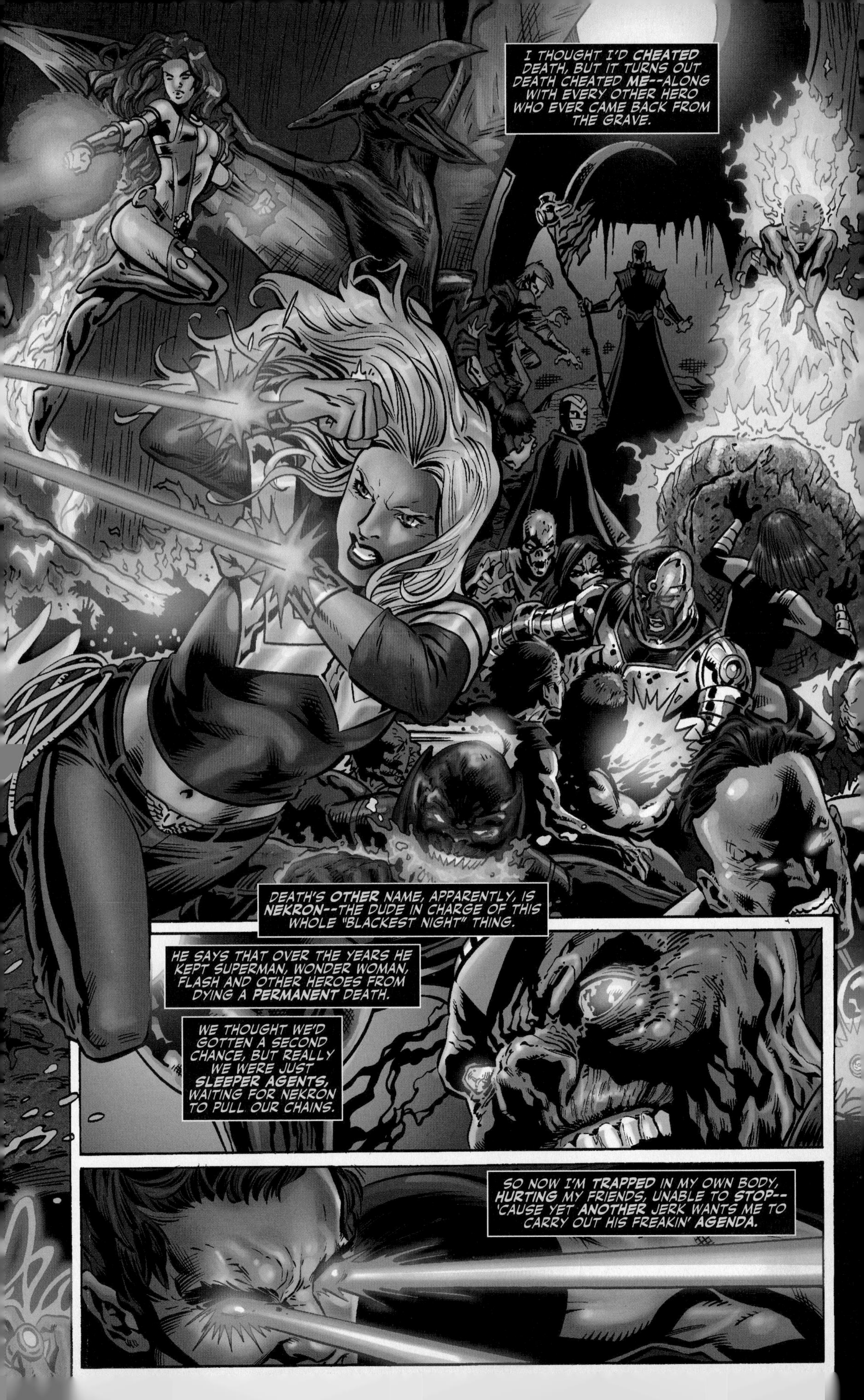

I THOUGHT I'D CHEATED DEATH, BUT IT TURNS OUT DEATH CHEATED ME--ALONG WITH EVERY OTHER HERO WHO EVER CAME BACK FROM THE GRAVE.
DEATH'S OTHER NAME, APPARENTLY, IS NEKRON--THE DUDE IN CHARGE OF THIS WHOLE "BLACKEST NIGHT" THING.
HE SAYS THAT OVER THE YEARS HE KEPT SUPERMAN, WONDER WOMAN, FLASH AND OTHER HEROES FROM DYING A PERMANENT DEATH.
WE THOUGHT WE'D GOTTEN A SECOND CHANCE, BUT REALLY WE WERE JUST SLEEPER AGENTS, WAITING FOR NEKRON TO PULL OUR CHAINS.
SO NOW I'M TRAPPED IN MY OWN BODY, HURTING MY FRIENDS, UNABLE TO STOP-- 'CAUSE YET ANOTHER JERK WANTS ME TO CARRY OUT HIS FREAKIN' AGENDA.

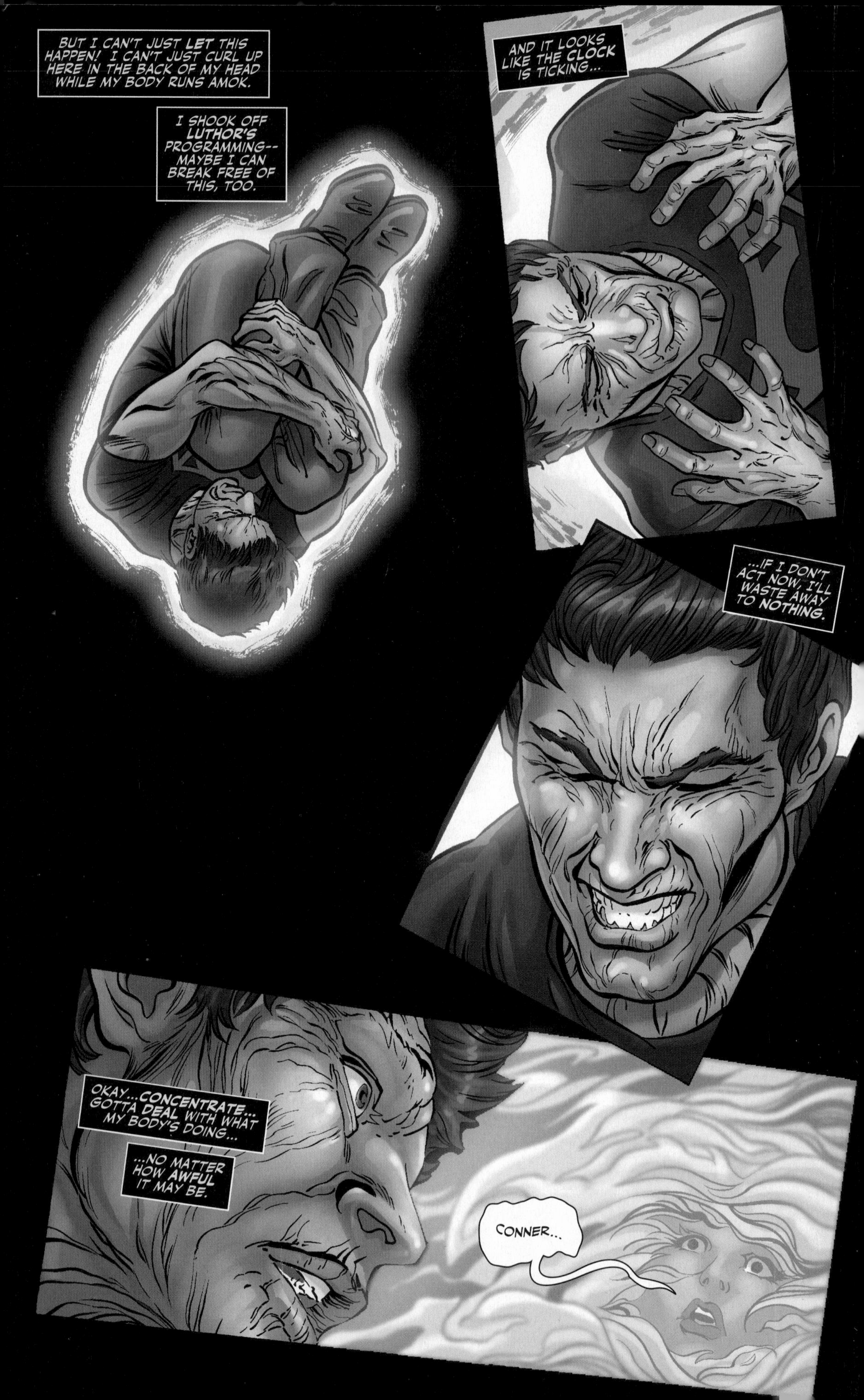
BUT I CAN'T JUST LET THIS HAPPEN! I CAN'T JUST CURL UP HERE IN THE BACK OF MY HEAD WHILE MY BODY RUNS AMOK.
I SHOOK OFF LUTHOR'S PROGRAMMING-- MAYBE I CAN BREAK FREE OF THIS, TOO.
AND IT LOOKS LIKE THE CLOCK IS TICKING...
...IF I DON'T ACT NOW, I'LL WASTE AWAY TO NOTHING.
OKAY...CONCENTRATE... GOTTA DEAL WITH WHAT MY BODY'S DOING...
...NO MATTER HOW AWFUL IT MAY BE.
CONNER...

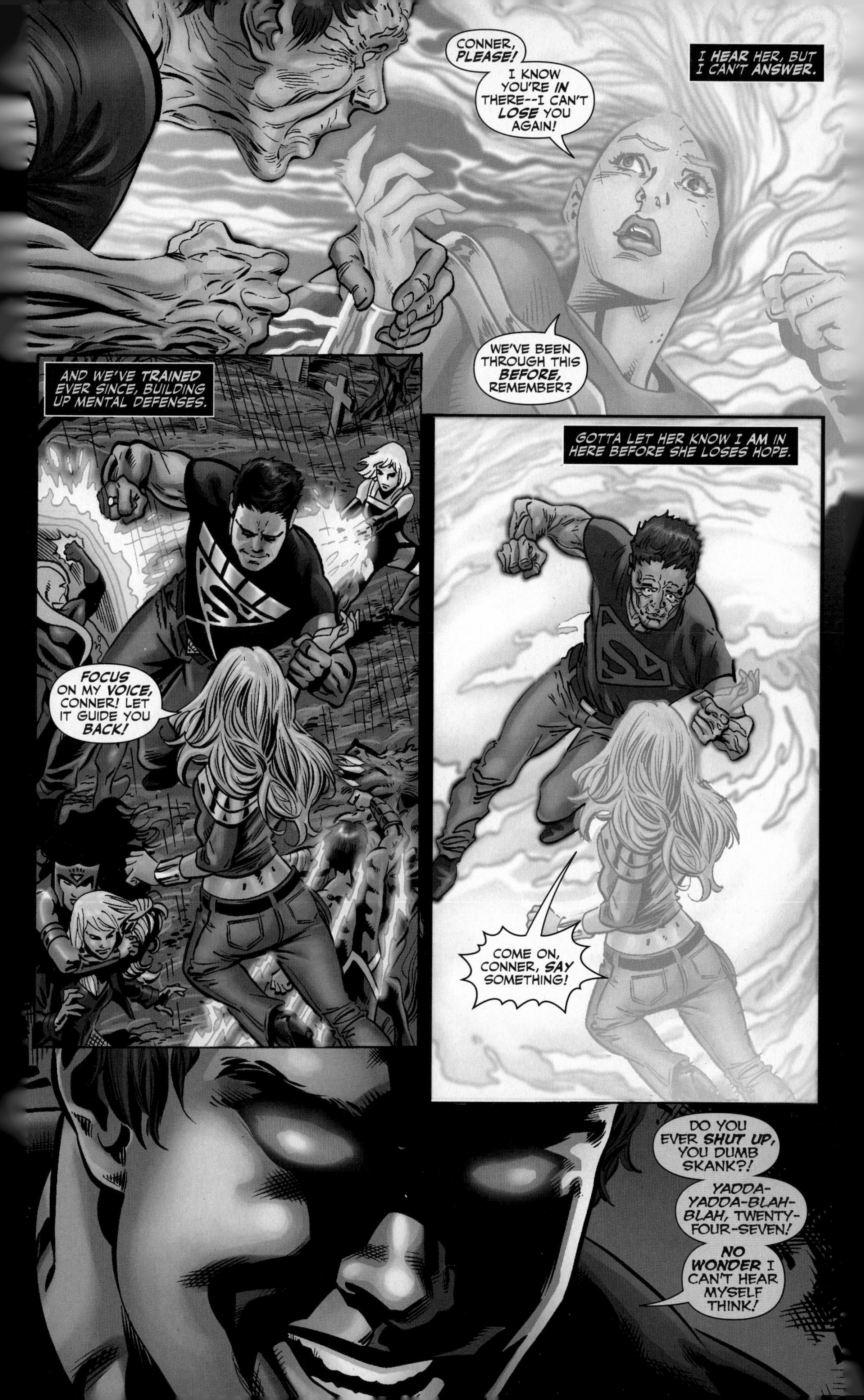
CONNER, PLEASE!
I KNOW YOU'RE IN THERE--I CAN'T LOSE YOU AGAIN!
I HEAR HER, BUT I CAN'T ANSWER.
WE'VE BEEN THROUGH THIS BEFORE, REMEMBER?
AND WE'VE TRAINED EVER SINCE, BUILDING UP MENTAL DEFENSES.
FOCUS ON MY VOICE, CONNER! LET IT GUIDE YOU BACK!
GOTTA LET HER KNOW I AM IN HERE BEFORE SHE LOSES HOPE.
COME ON, CONNER, SAY SOMETHING!
DO YOU EVER SHUT UP, YOU DUMB SKANK?!
YADDA-YADDA-BLAH-BLAH, TWENTY-FOUR-SEVEN!
NO WONDER I CAN'T HEAR MYSELF THINK!

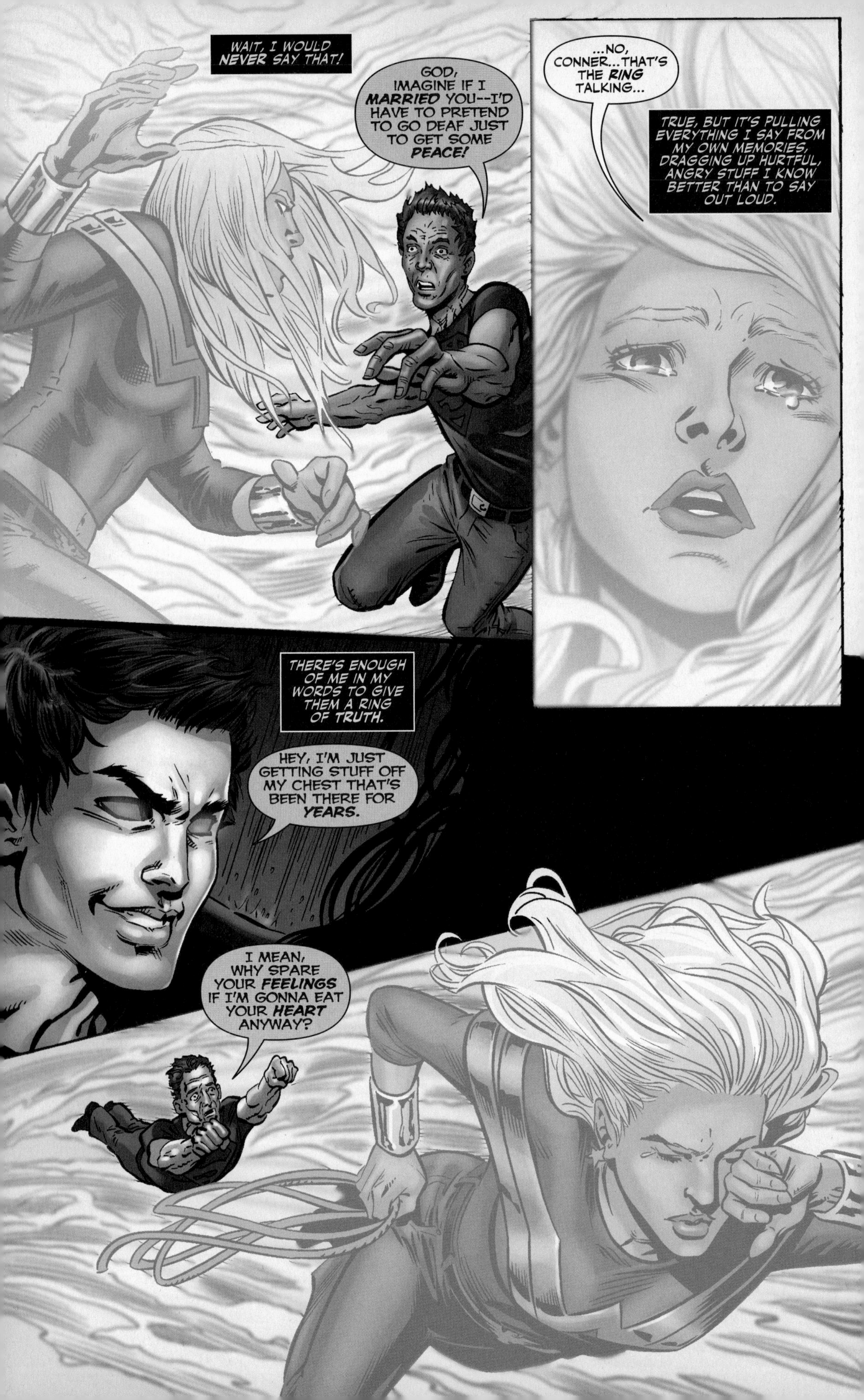
WAIT, I WOULD NEVER SAY THAT!
GOD, IMAGINE IF I MARRIED YOU--I'D HAVE TO PRETEND TO GO DEAF JUST TO GET SOME PEACE!
...NO, CONNER...THAT'S THE RING TALKING...
TRUE, BUT IT'S PULLING EVERYTHING I SAY FROM MY OWN MEMORIES, DRAGGING UP HURTFUL, ANGRY STUFF I KNOW BETTER THAN TO SAY OUT LOUD.
THERE'S ENOUGH OF ME IN MY WORDS TO GIVE THEM A RING OF TRUTH.
HEY, I'M JUST GETTING STUFF OFF MY CHEST THAT'S BEEN THERE FOR YEARS.
I MEAN, WHY SPARE YOUR FEELINGS IF I'M GONNA EAT YOUR HEART ANYWAY?

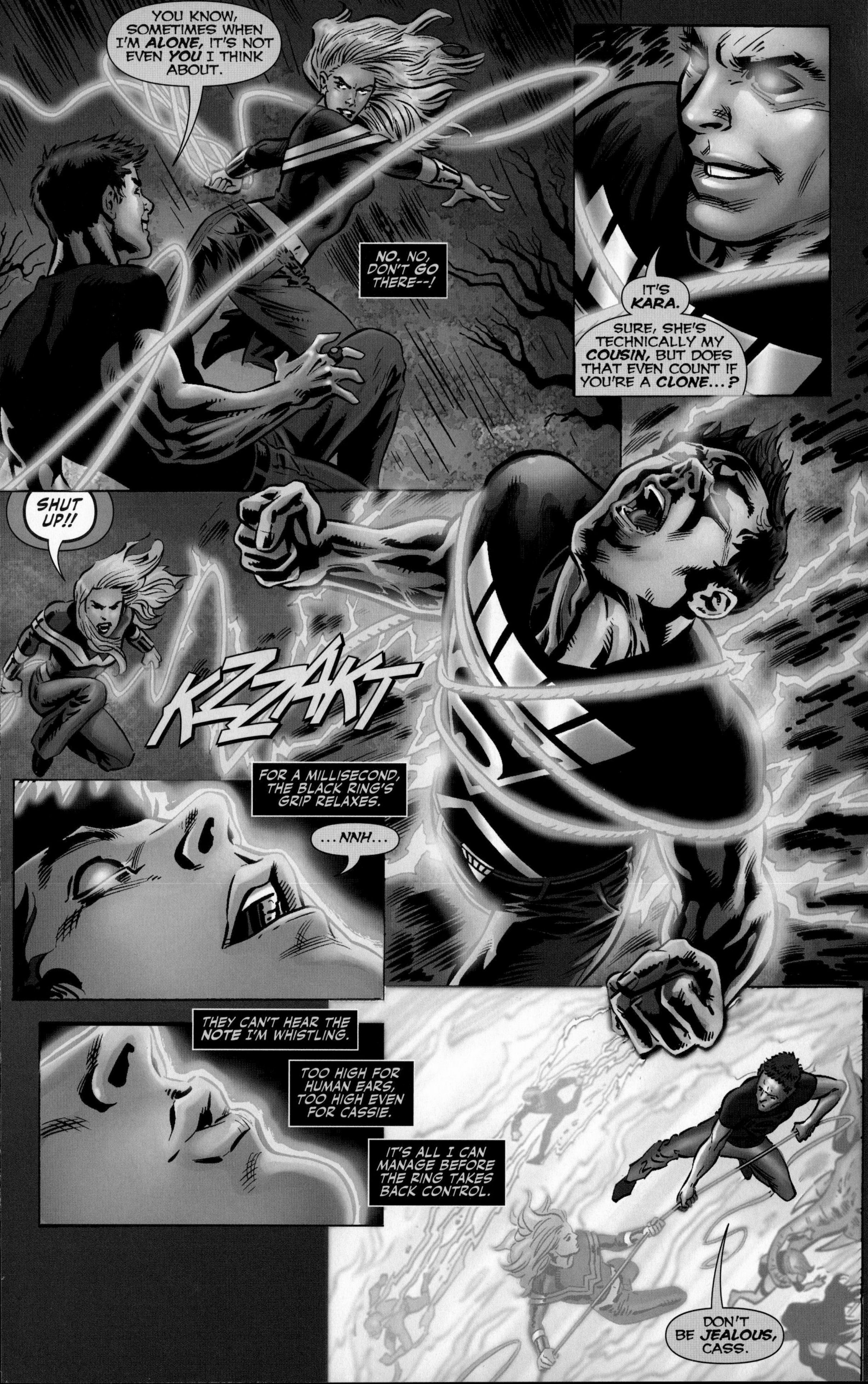
YOU KNOW, SOMETIMES WHEN I'M ALONE, IT'S NOT EVEN YOU I THINK ABOUT.
NO. NO, DON'T GO THERE--!
IT'S KARA.
SURE, SHE'S TECHNICALLY MY COUSIN, BUT DOES THAT EVEN COUNT IF YOU'RE A CLONE...?
SHUT UP!!
KZZAKT
FOR A MILLISECOND, THE BLACK RING'S GRIP RELAXES.
...NNH...
THEY CAN'T HEAR THE NOTE I'M WHISTLING.
TOO HIGH FOR HUMAN EARS, TOO HIGH EVEN FOR CASSIE.
IT'S ALL I CAN MANAGE BEFORE THE RING TAKES BACK CONTROL.
DON'T BE JEALOUS, CASS.

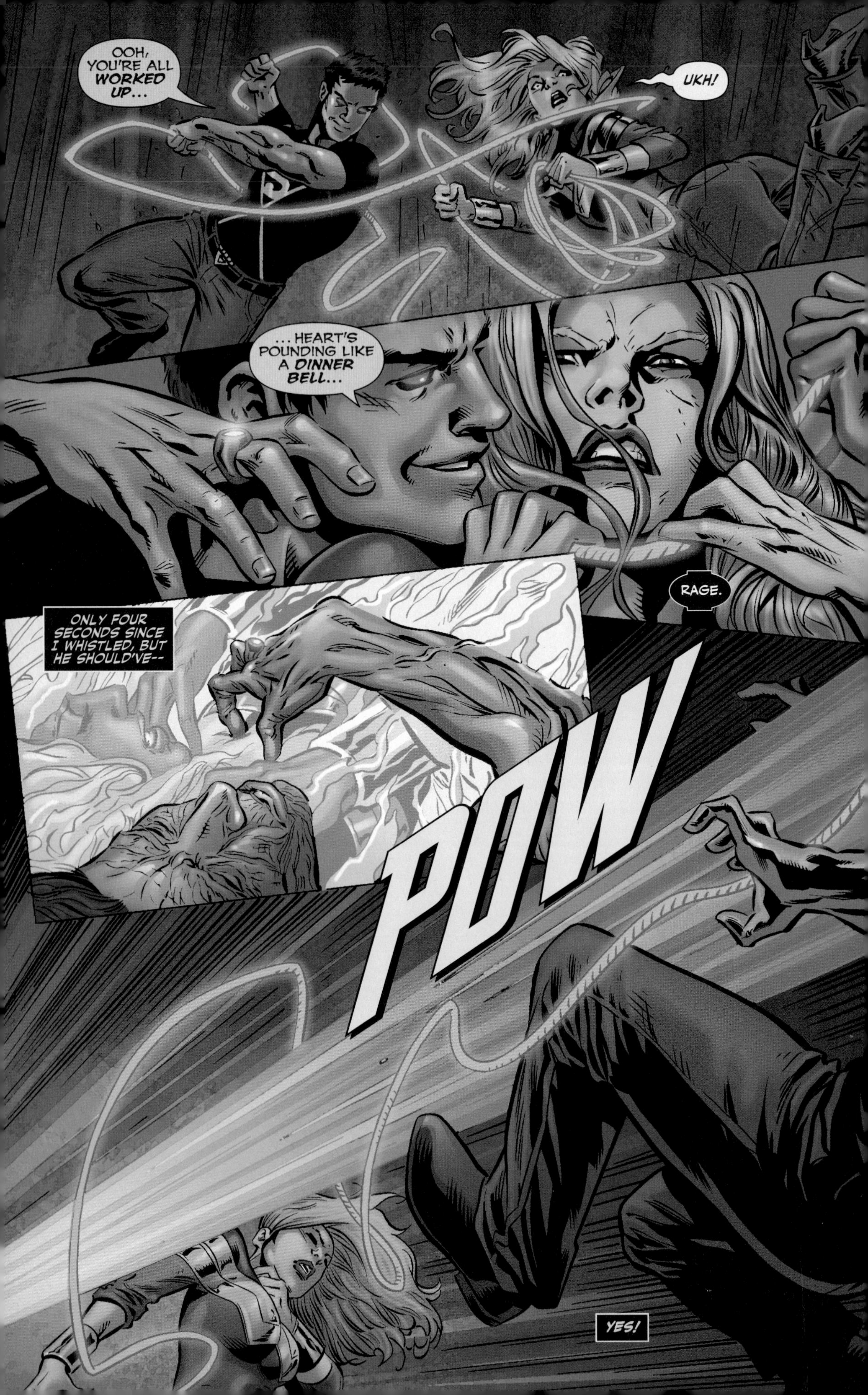
OOH, YOU'RE ALL WORKED UP...
UKH!
...HEART'S POUNDING LIKE A DINNER BELL...
RAGE.
ONLY FOUR SECONDS SINCE I WHISTLED, BUT HE SHOULD'VE--
POW
YES!

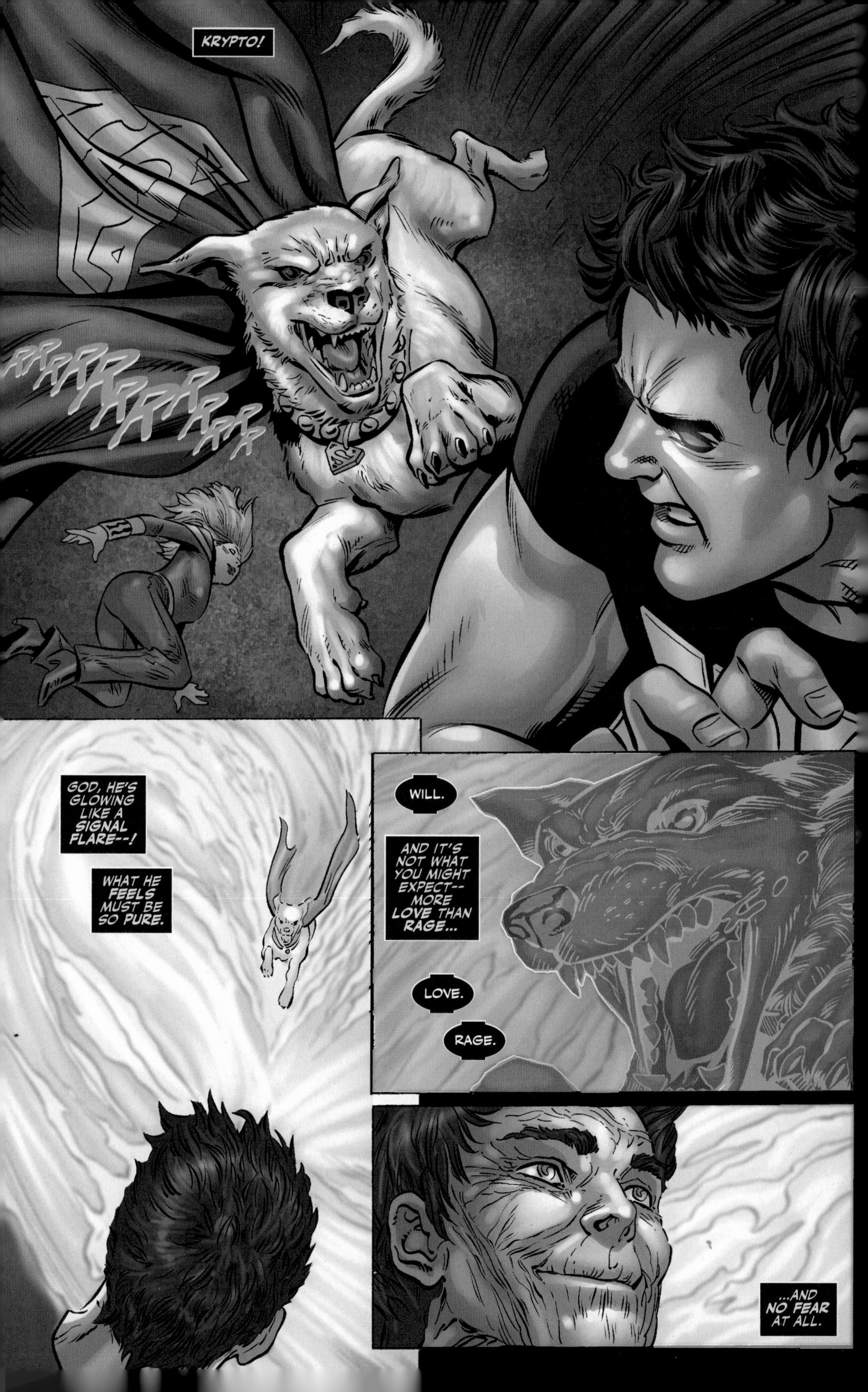

KRYPTO!
RRRRRRRRRRRRRRR
GOD, HE'S GLOWING LIKE A SIGNAL FLARE--!
WHAT HE FEELS MUST BE SO PURE.
WILL.
AND IT'S NOT WHAT YOU MIGHT EXPECT--MORE LOVE THAN RAGE...
LOVE.
RAGE.
...AND NO FEAR AT ALL.

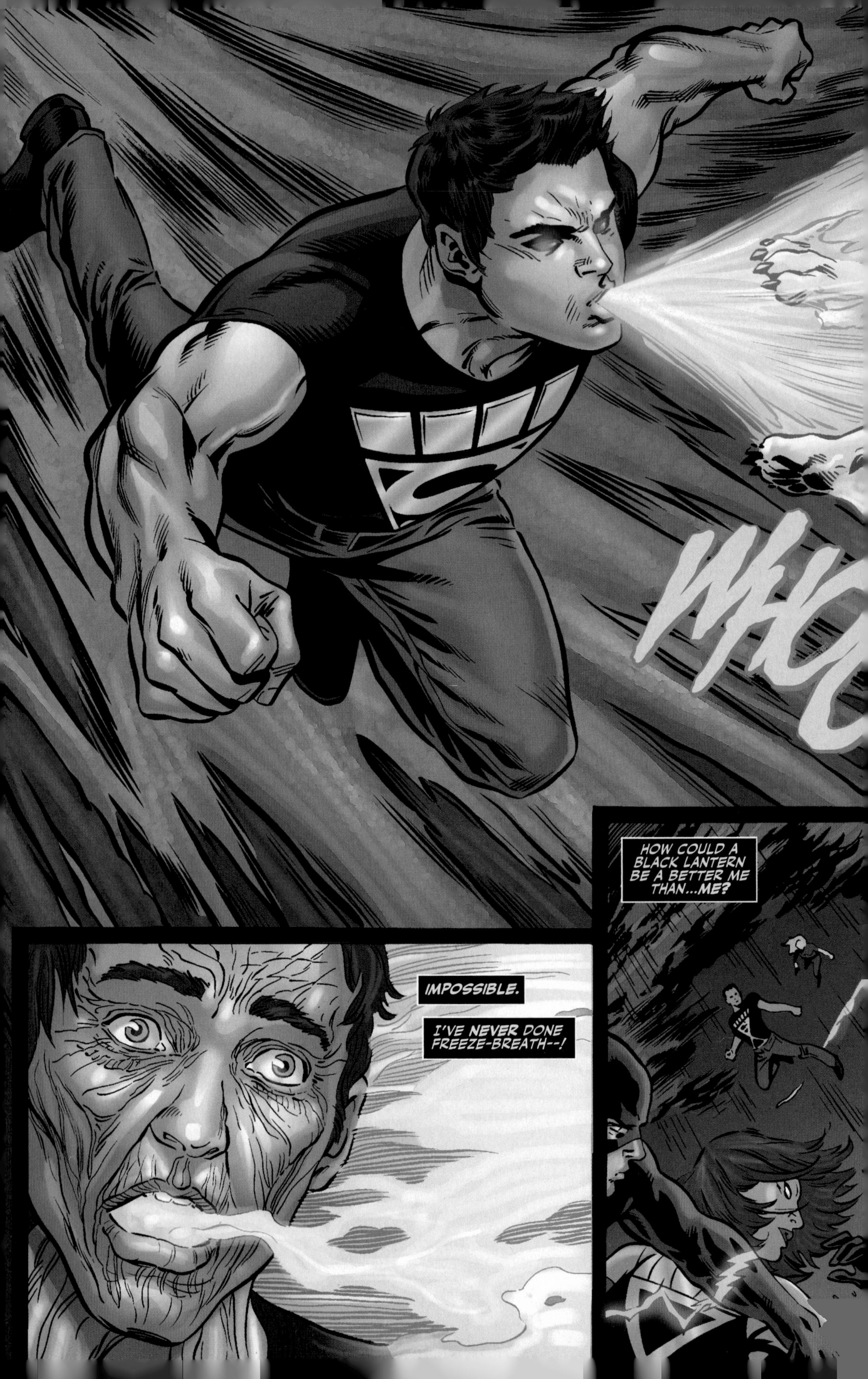
IMPOSSIBLE.
I'VE NEVER DONE FREEZE-BREATH--!
HOW COULD A BLACK LANTERN BE A BETTER ME THAN...ME?

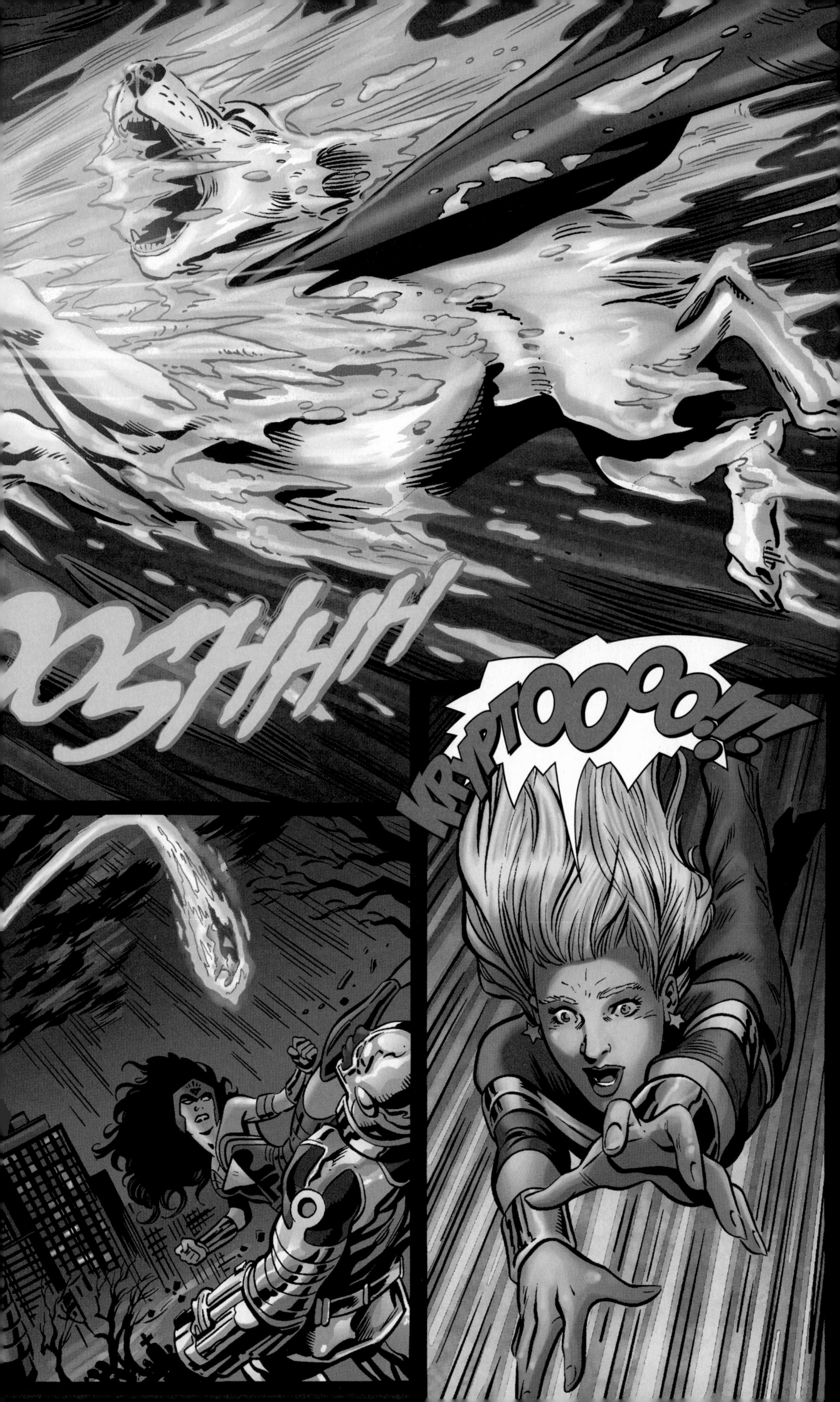
OSHHH
KRYPTOOOO!!!

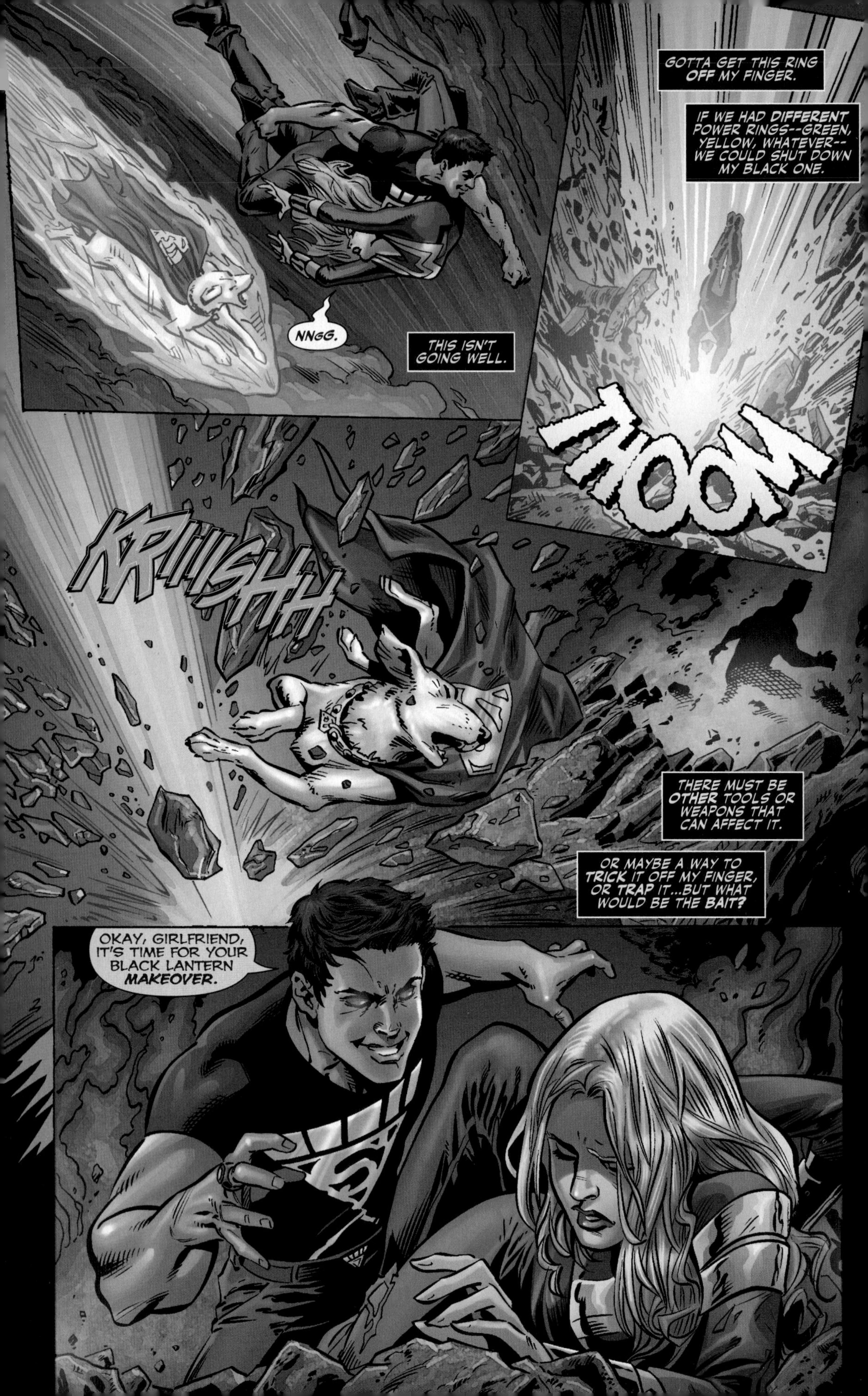
GOTTA GET THIS RING OFF MY FINGER.
IF WE HAD DIFFERENT POWER RINGS--GREEN, YELLOW, WHATEVER--WE COULD SHUT DOWN MY BLACK ONE.
NNGG.
THIS ISN'T GOING WELL.
THOOM
KRIIIISHH
THERE MUST BE OTHER TOOLS OR WEAPONS THAT CAN AFFECT IT.
OR MAYBE A WAY TO TRICK IT OFF MY FINGER, OR TRAP IT...BUT WHAT WOULD BE THE BAIT?
OKAY, GIRLFRIEND, IT'S TIME FOR YOUR BLACK LANTERN MAKEOVER.

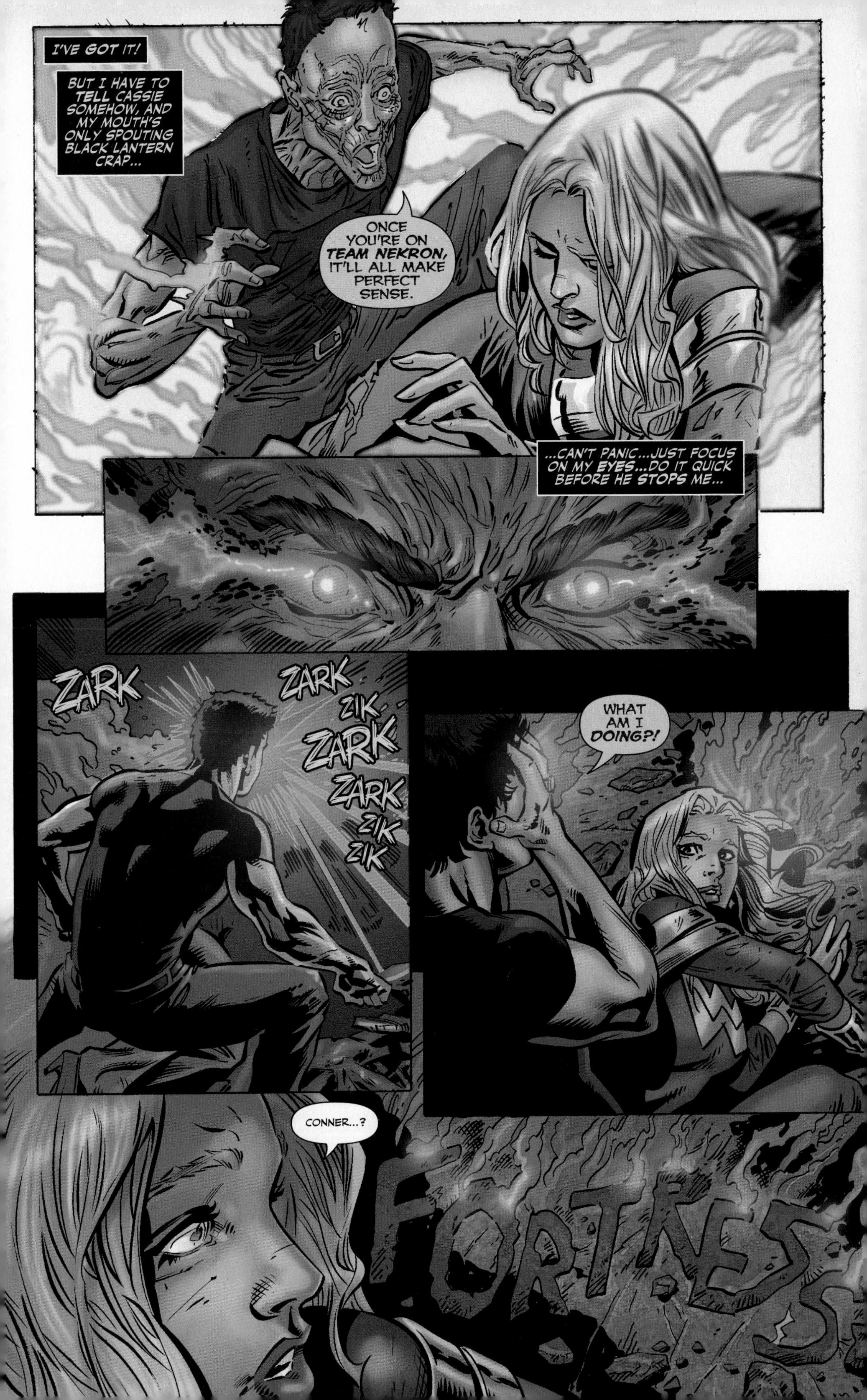
I'VE GOT IT!
BUT I HAVE TO TELL CASSIE SOMEHOW, AND MY MOUTH'S ONLY SPOUTING BLACK LANTERN CRAP...
ONCE YOU'RE ON TEAM NEKRON, IT'LL ALL MAKE PERFECT SENSE.
...CAN'T PANIC...JUST FOCUS ON MY EYES...DO IT QUICK BEFORE HE STOPS ME...
ZARK
ZARK
ZIK
ZARK
ZARK
ZIK
ZIK
WHAT AM I DOING?!
CONNER...?
FORTNESS

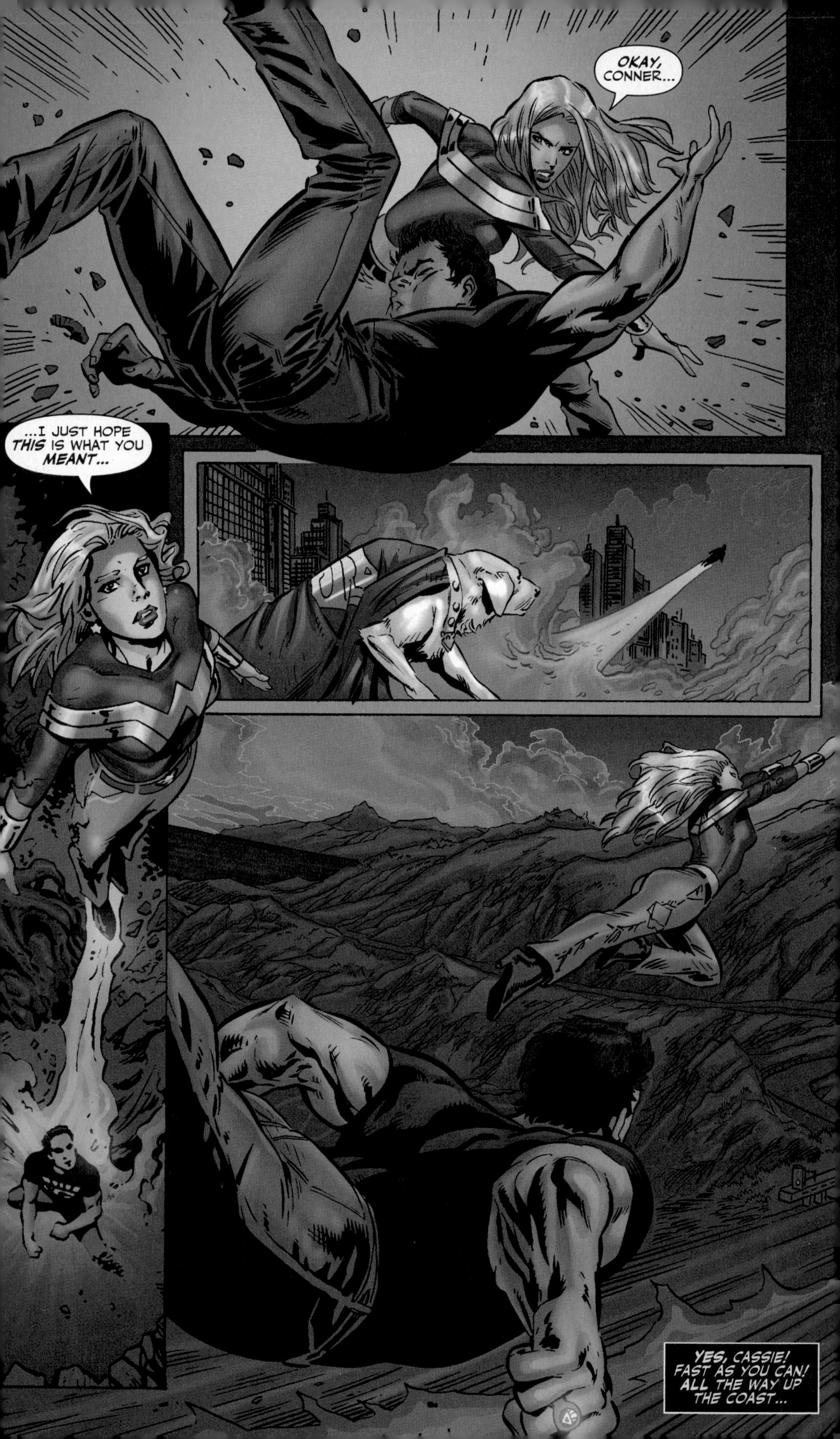
OKAY, CONNER...
...I JUST HOPE THIS IS WHAT YOU MEANT...
YES, CASSIE! FAST AS YOU CAN! ALL THE WAY UP THE COAST...

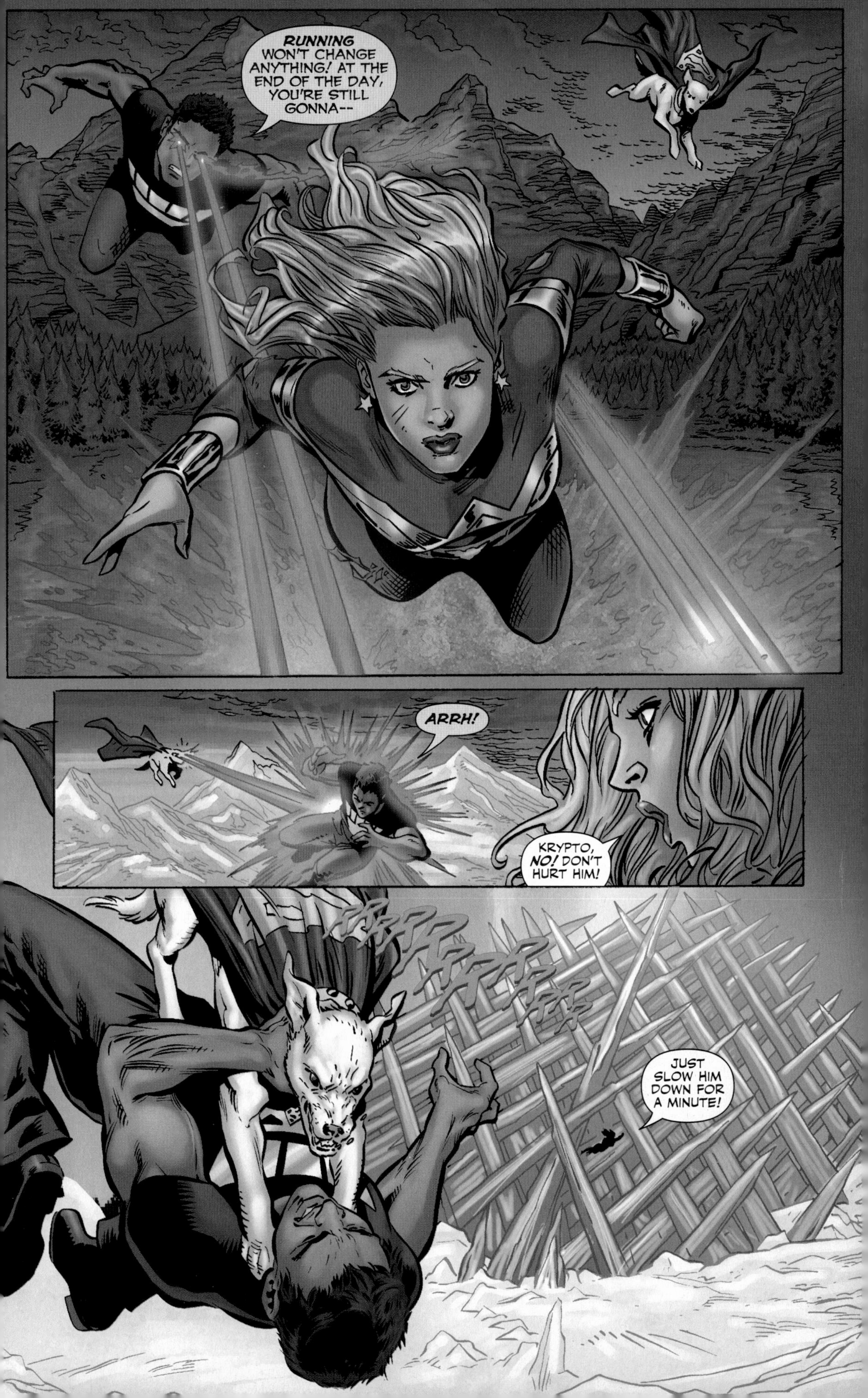
RUNNING WON'T CHANGE ANYTHING! AT THE END OF THE DAY, YOU'RE STILL GONNA--
ARRH!
KRYPTO, NO! DON'T HURT HIM!
JUST SLOW HIM DOWN FOR A MINUTE!

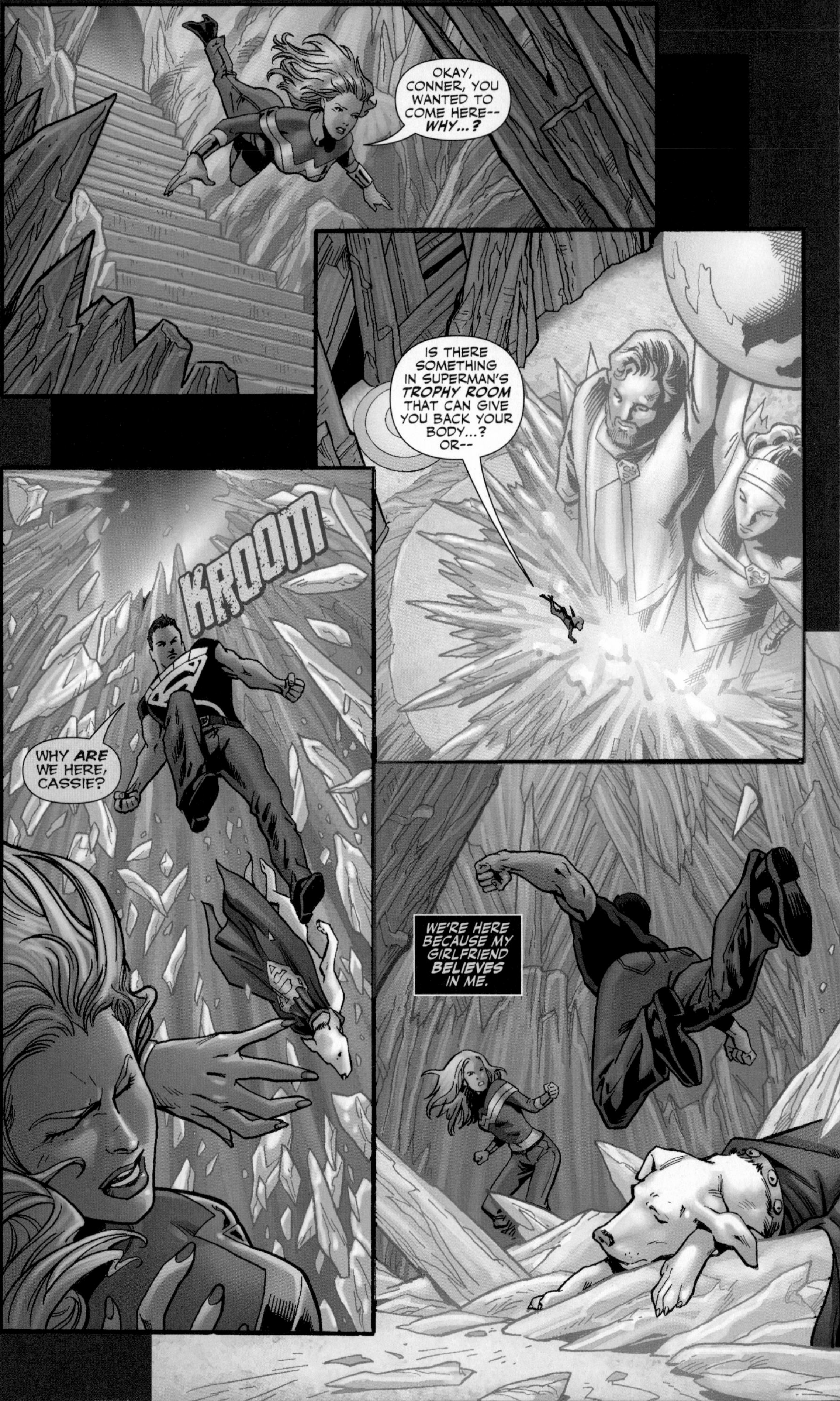

OKAY, CONNER, YOU WANTED TO COME HERE-- WHY...?
IS THERE SOMETHING IN SUPERMAN'S TROPHY ROOM THAT CAN GIVE YOU BACK YOUR BODY...? OR--
KROOM
WHY ARE WE HERE, CASSIE?
WE'RE HERE BECAUSE MY GIRLFRIEND BELIEVES IN ME.

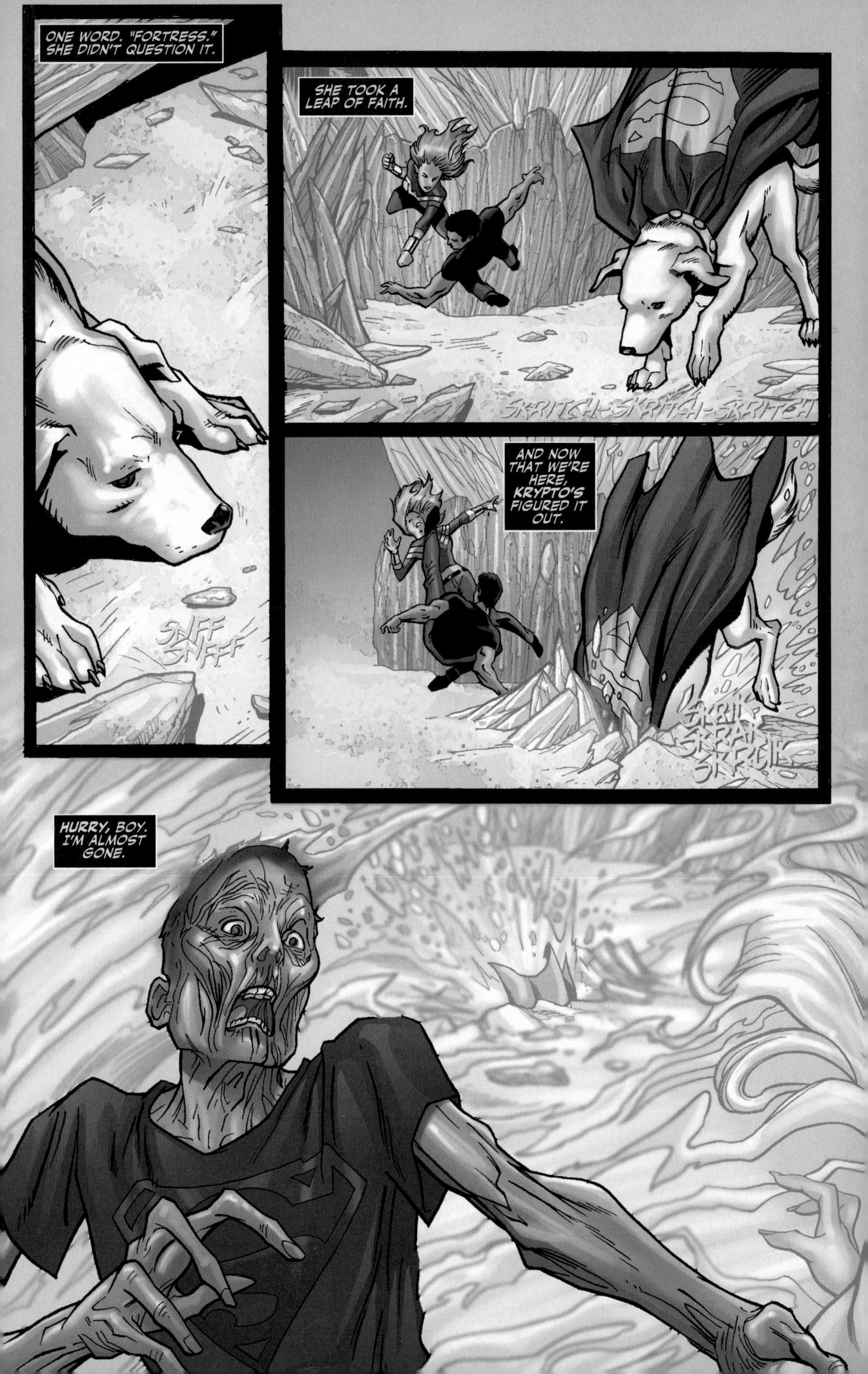

ONE WORD. "FORTRESS." SHE DIDN'T QUESTION IT.
SNIFF SNIFF
SHE TOOK A LEAP OF FAITH.
SKRITCH-SKRITCH-SKRITCH
AND NOW THAT WE'RE HERE, KRYPTO'S FIGURED IT OUT.
HURRY, BOY. I'M ALMOST GONE.

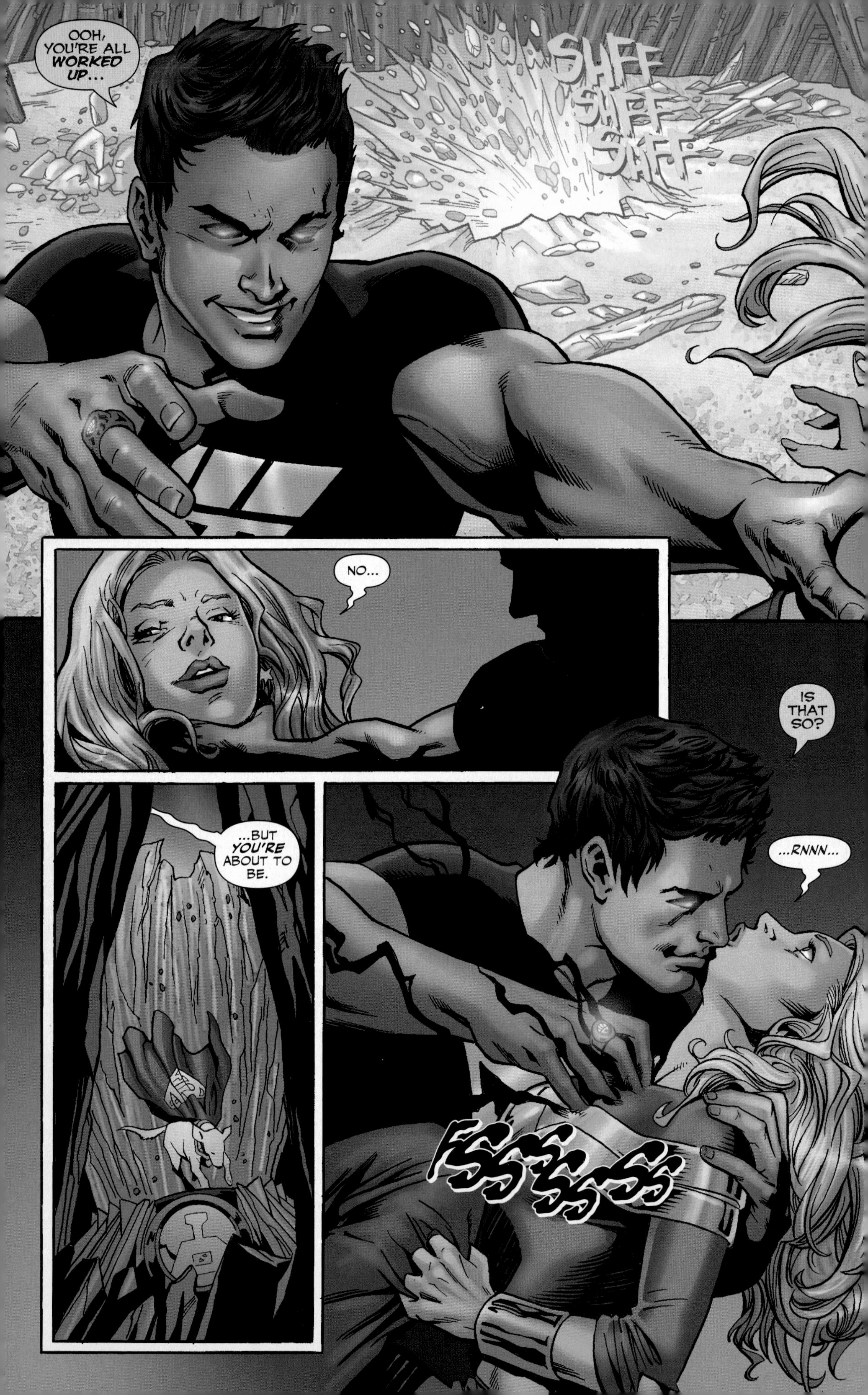
OOH, YOU'RE ALL WORKED UP...
SHFF SHFF SHFF
NO...
IS THAT SO?
...BUT YOU'RE ABOUT TO BE.
...RNNN...
FSSSSSSS

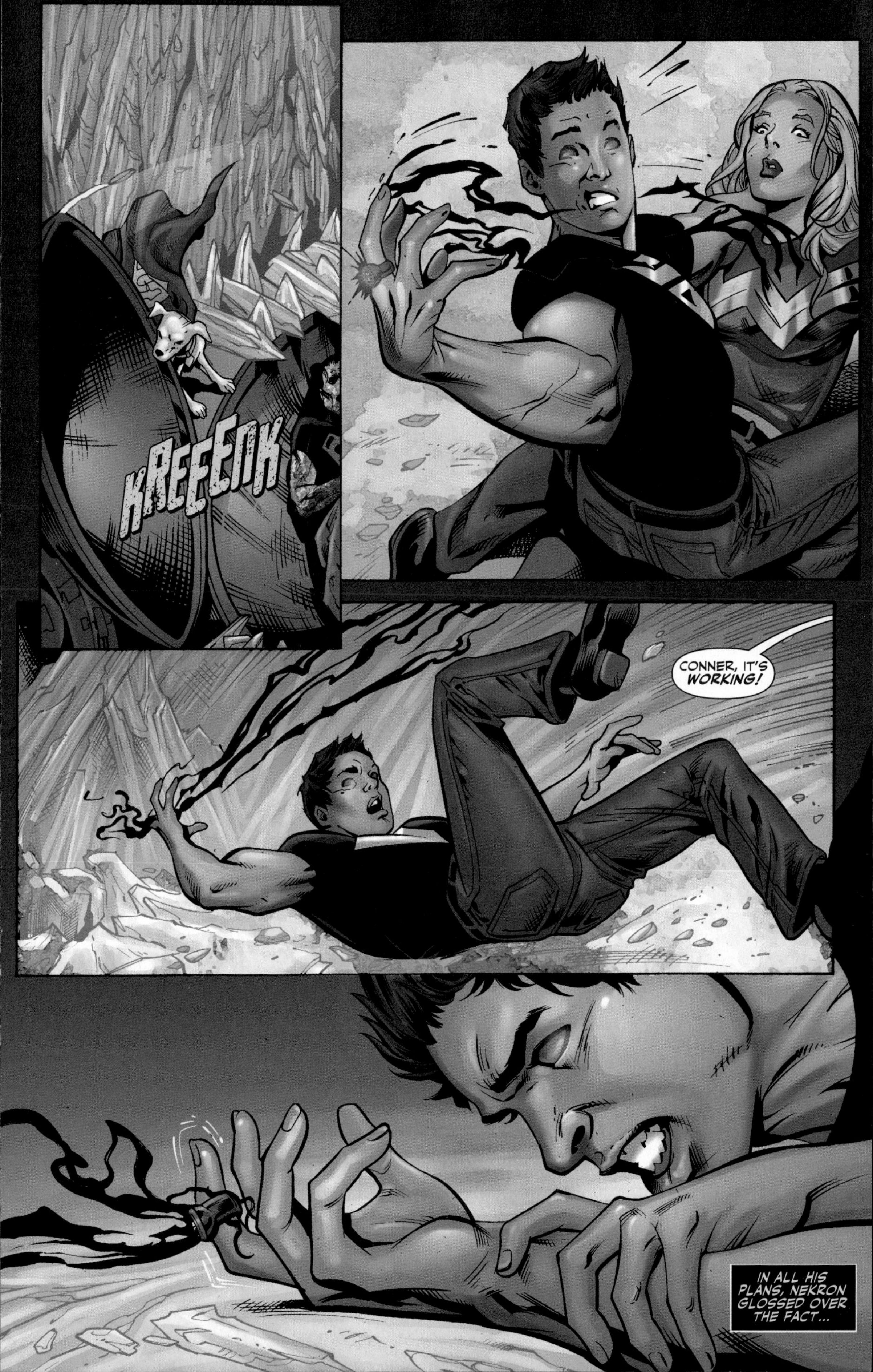
KREEENK
CONNER, IT'S WORKING!
IN ALL HIS PLANS, NEKRON GLOSSED OVER THE FACT...

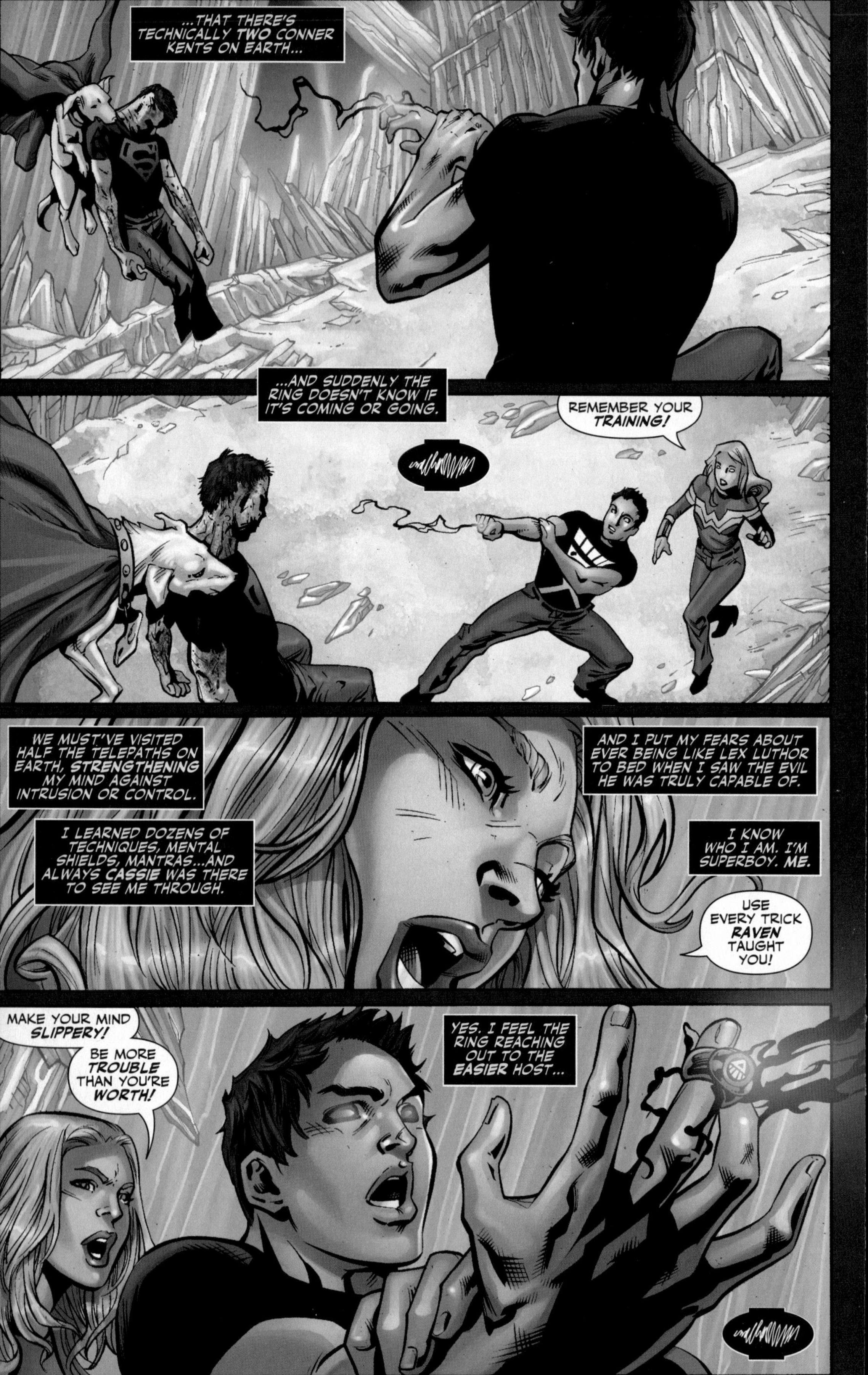

...THAT THERE'S TECHNICALLY TWO CONNER KENTS ON EARTH...
...AND SUDDENLY THE RING DOESN'T KNOW IF IT'S COMING OR GOING.
REMEMBER YOUR TRAINING!
WE MUST'VE VISITED HALF THE TELEPATHS ON EARTH, STRENGTHENING MY MIND AGAINST INTRUSION OR CONTROL.
I LEARNED DOZENS OF TECHNIQUES, MENTAL SHIELDS, MANTRAS...AND ALWAYS CASSIE WAS THERE TO SEE ME THROUGH.
AND I PUT MY FEARS ABOUT EVER BEING LIKE LEX LUTHOR TO BED WHEN I SAW THE EVIL HE WAS TRULY CAPABLE OF.
I KNOW WHO I AM. I'M SUPERBOY. ME.
USE EVERY TRICK RAVEN TAUGHT YOU!
MAKE YOUR MIND SLIPPERY!
BE MORE TROUBLE THAN YOU'RE WORTH!
YES. I FEEL THE RING REACHING OUT TO THE EASIER HOST...

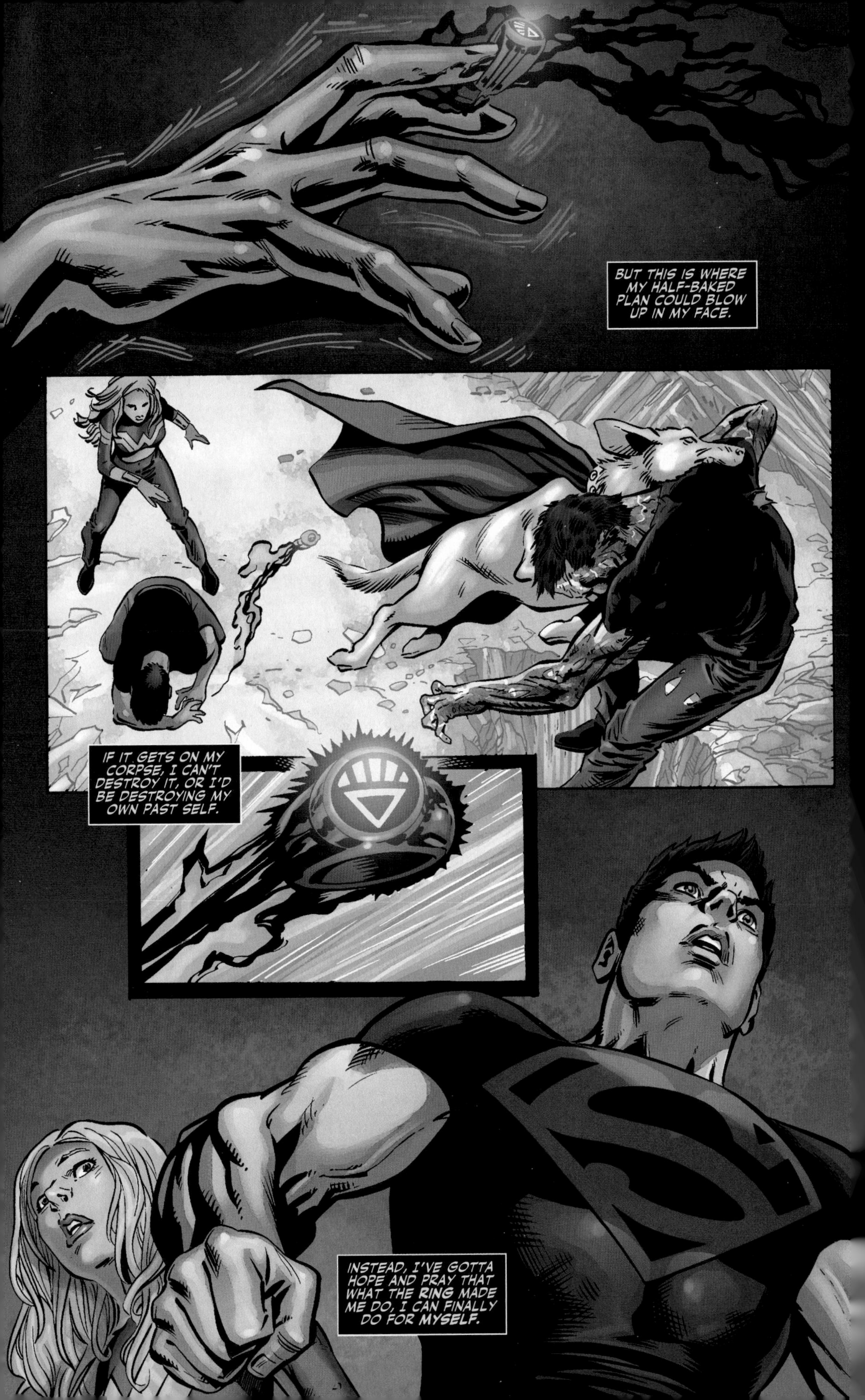

BUT THIS IS WHERE MY HALF-BAKED PLAN COULD BLOW UP IN MY FACE.
IF IT GETS ON MY CORPSE, I CAN'T DESTROY IT, OR I'D BE DESTROYING MY OWN PAST SELF.
INSTEAD, I'VE GOTTA HOPE AND PRAY THAT WHAT THE RING MADE ME DO, I CAN FINALLY DO FOR MYSELF.

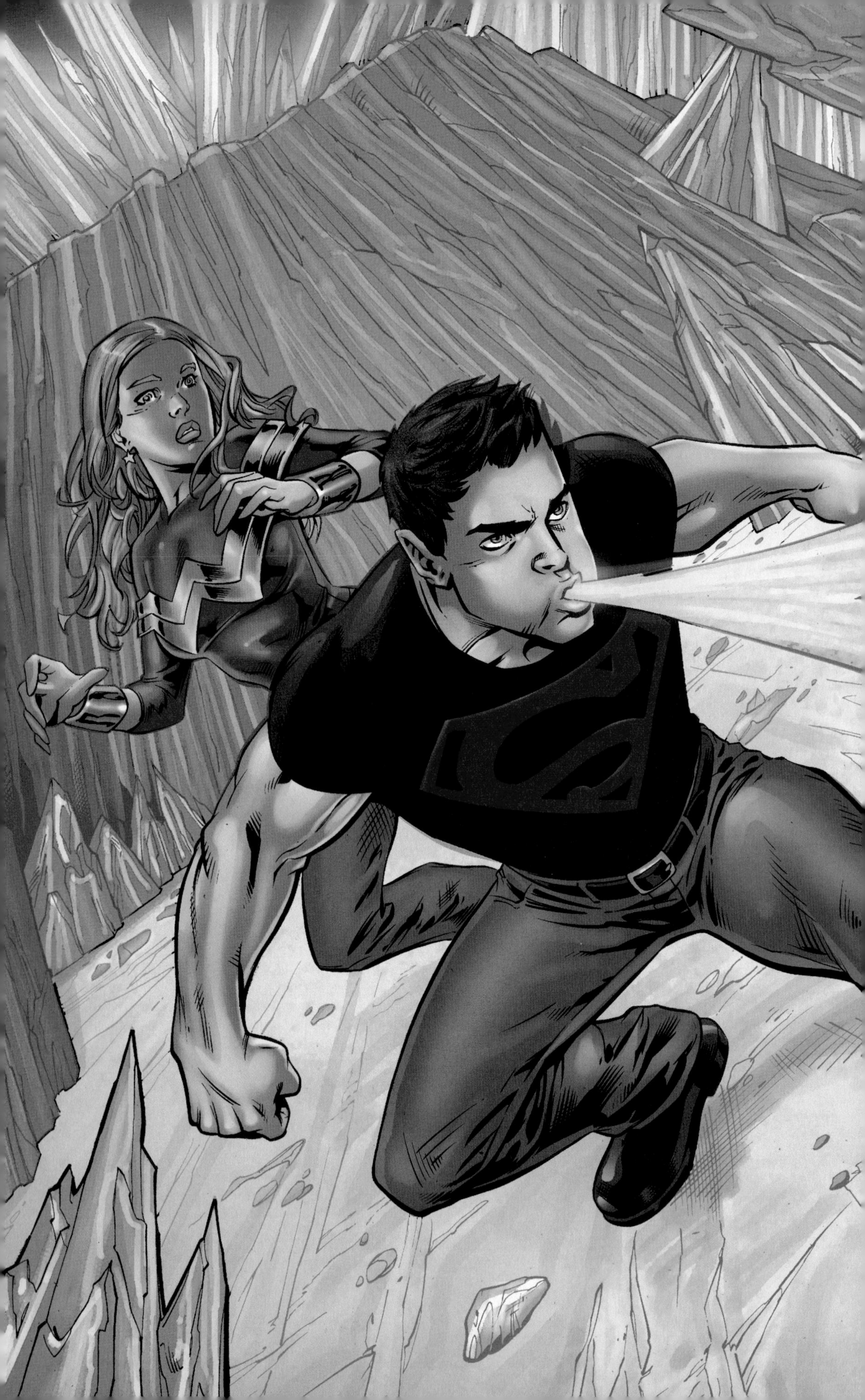

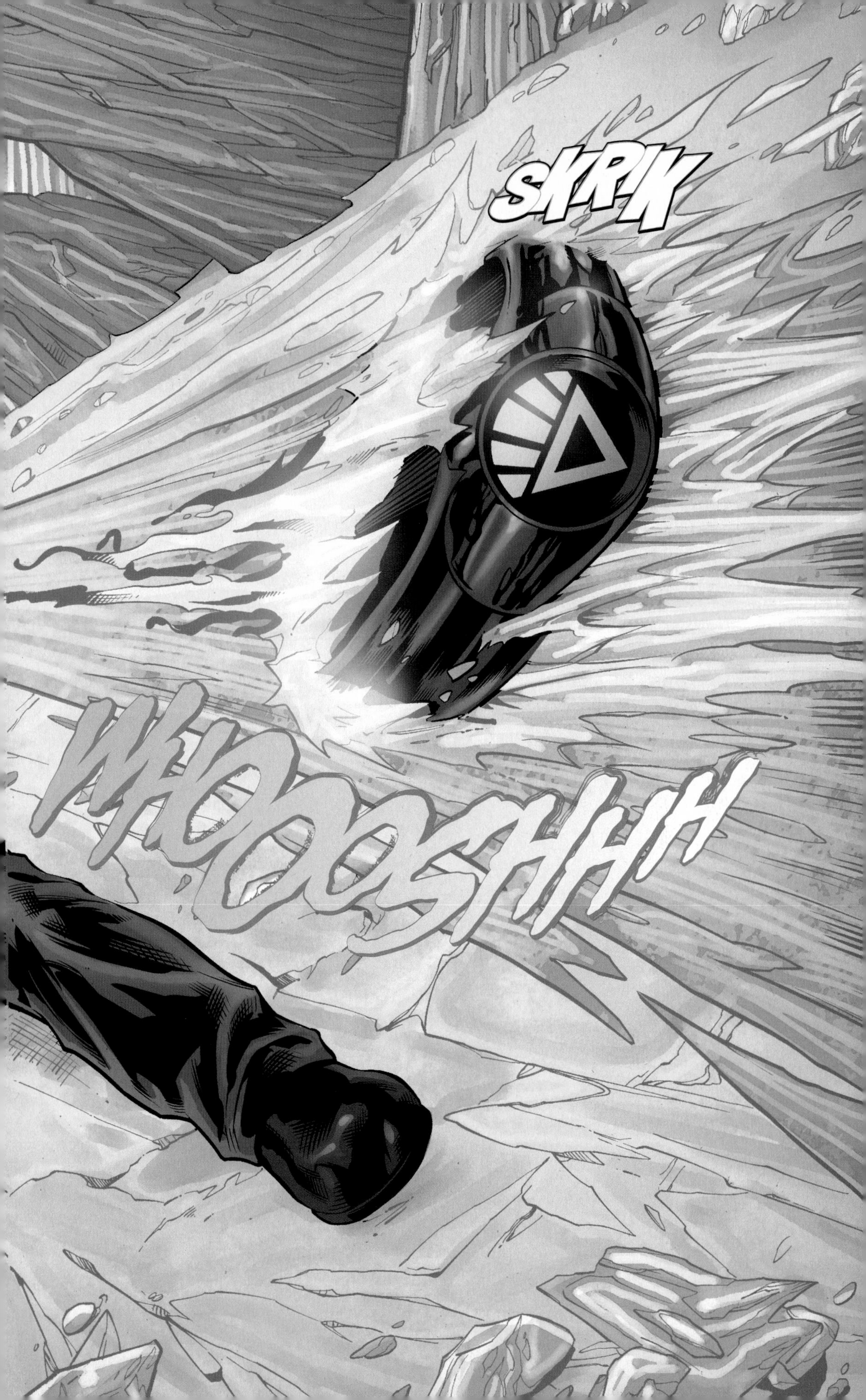
SKRIK
WHOOSHH

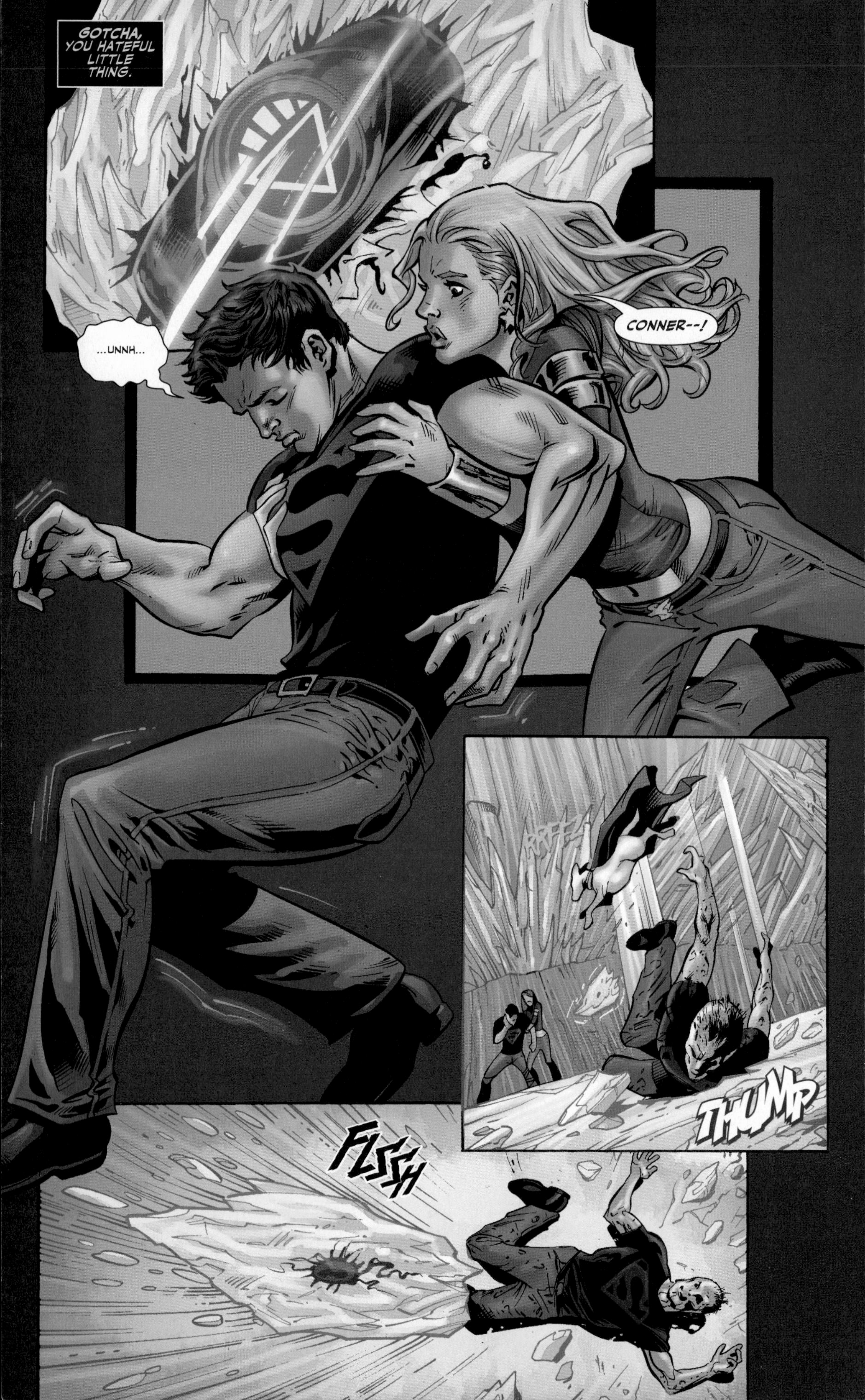
GOTCHA, YOU HATEFUL LITTLE THING.
...UNNH...
CONNER--!
THUMP
FLSSH

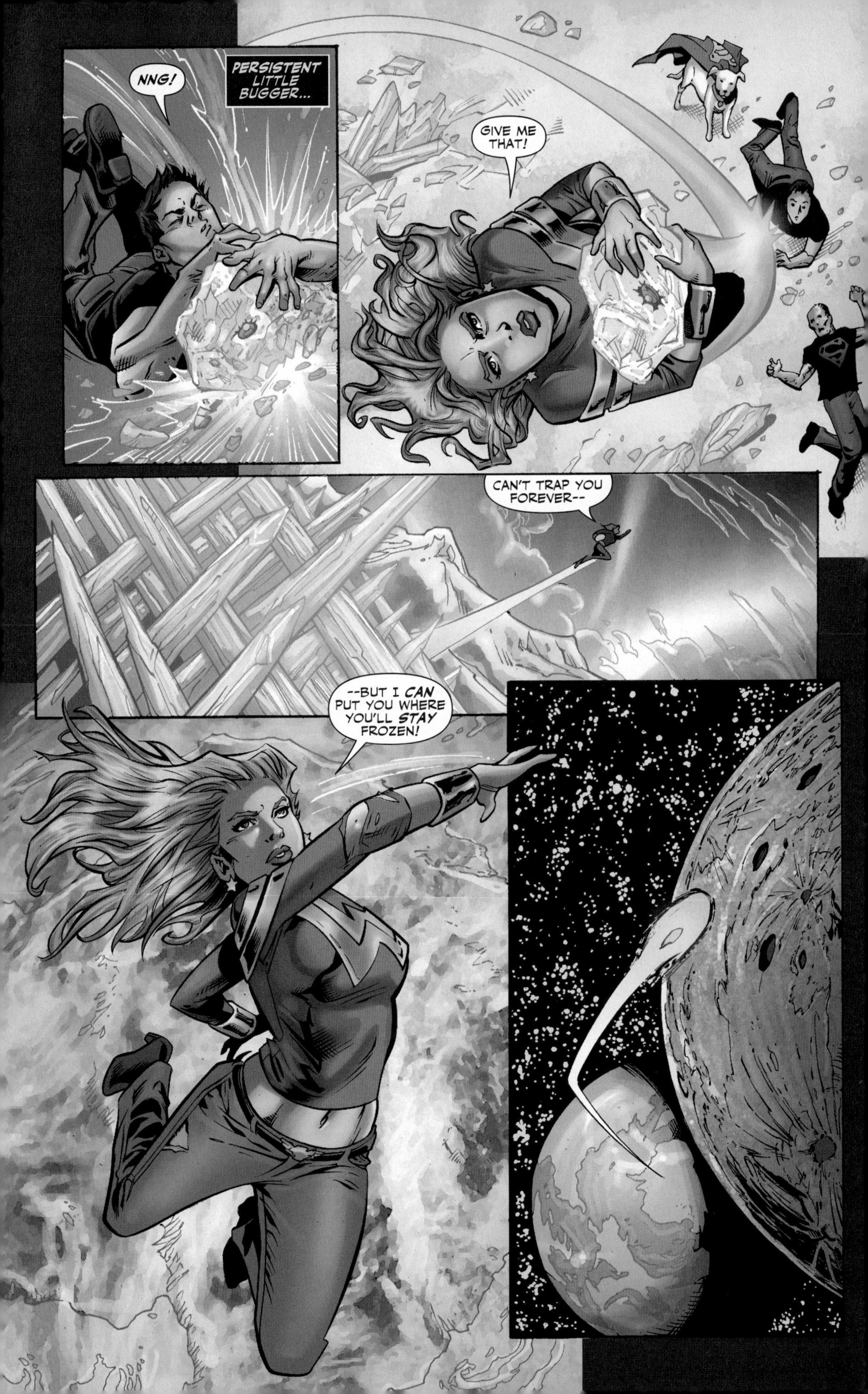
PERSISTENT LITTLE BUGGER...
NNG!
GIVE ME THAT!
CAN'T TRAP YOU FOREVER--
--BUT I CAN PUT YOU WHERE YOU'LL STAY FROZEN!

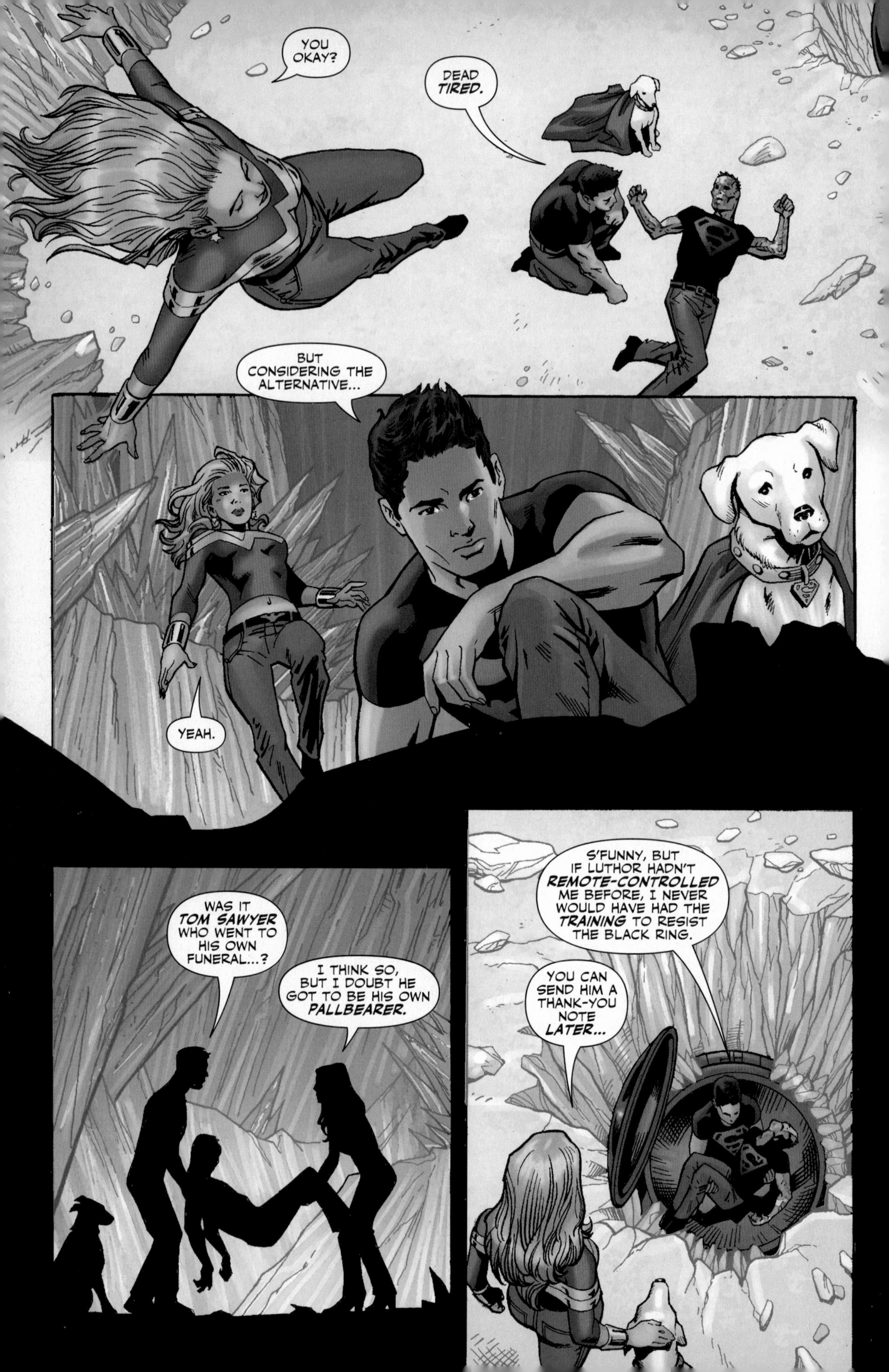
YOU OKAY?
DEAD TIRED.
BUT CONSIDERING THE ALTERNATIVE...
YEAH.
WAS IT TOM SAWYER WHO WENT TO HIS OWN FUNERAL...?
I THINK SO, BUT I DOUBT HE GOT TO BE HIS OWN PALLBEARER.
S'FUNNY, BUT IF LUTHOR HADN'T REMOTE-CONTROLLED ME BEFORE, I NEVER WOULD HAVE HAD THE TRAINING TO RESIST THE BLACK RING.
YOU CAN SEND HIM A THANK-YOU NOTE LATER...

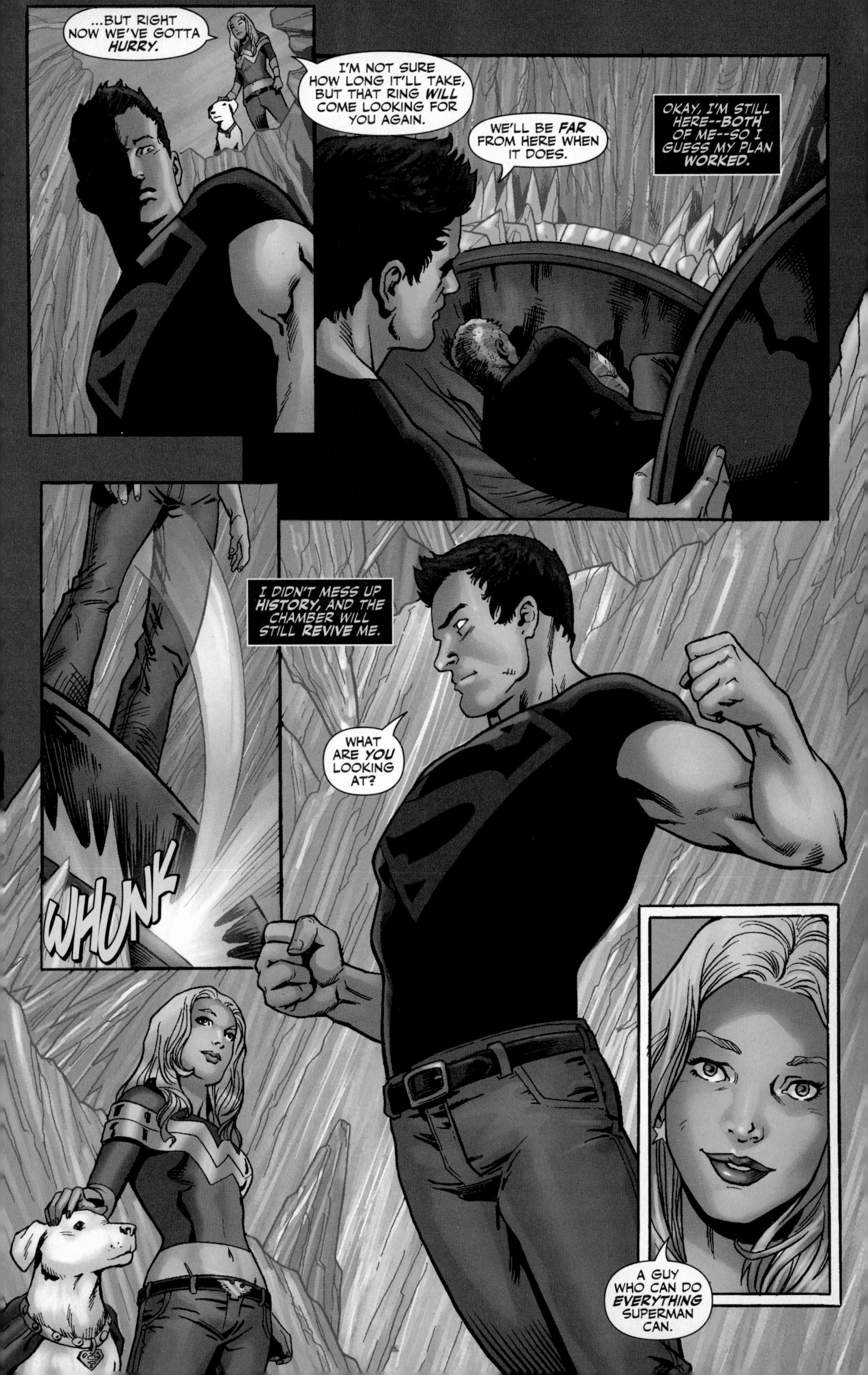
...BUT RIGHT NOW WE'VE GOTTA *HURRY.*
I'M NOT SURE HOW LONG IT'LL TAKE, BUT THAT RING *WILL* COME LOOKING FOR YOU AGAIN.
WE'LL BE *FAR* FROM HERE WHEN IT DOES.
OKAY, I'M STILL HERE--*BOTH* OF ME--SO I GUESS MY PLAN *WORKED.*
I DIDN'T MESS UP *HISTORY,* AND THE CHAMBER WILL STILL *REVIVE* ME.
WHUNK
WHAT ARE *YOU* LOOKING AT?
A GUY WHO CAN DO *EVERYTHING* SUPERMAN CAN.

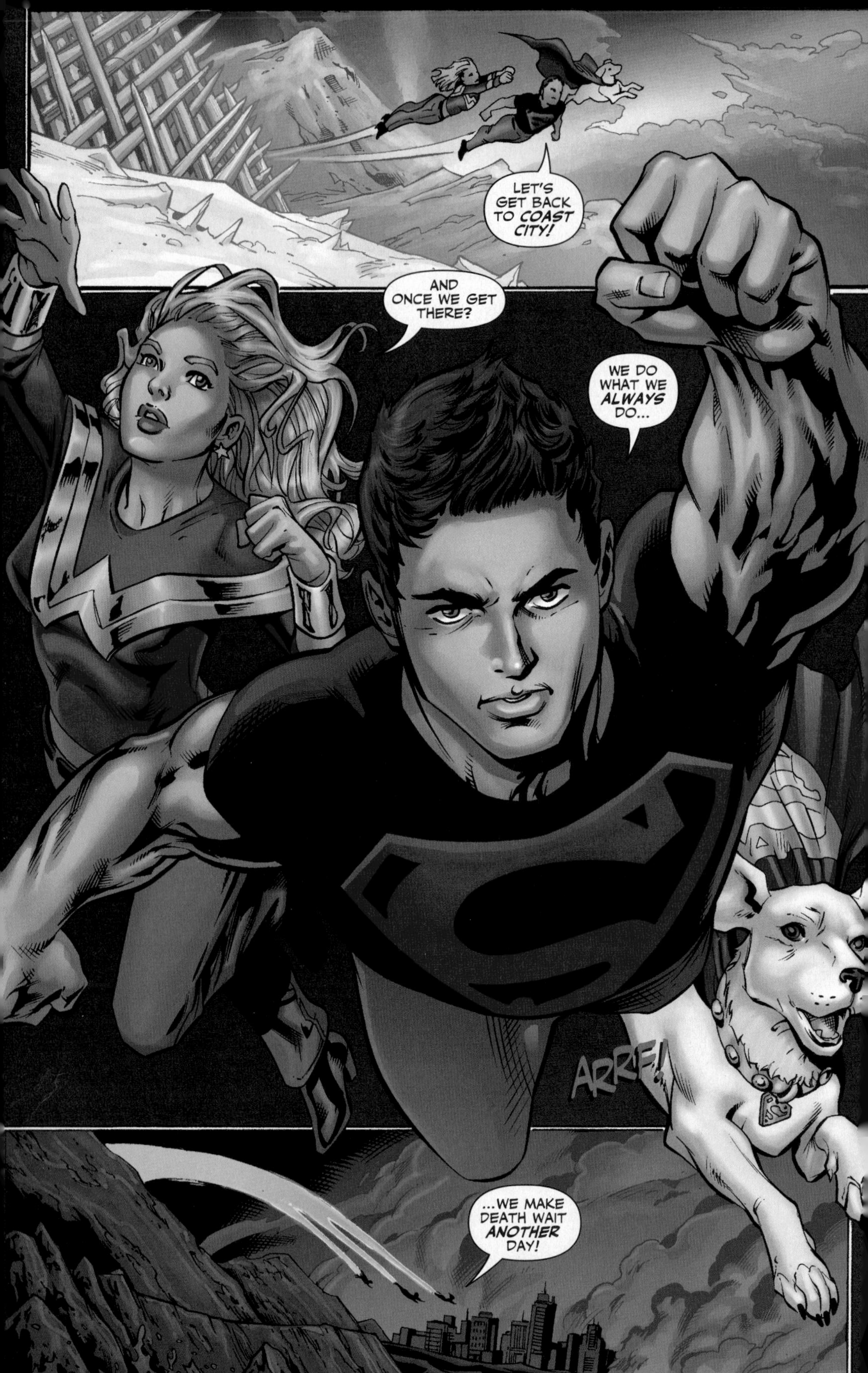
LET'S GET BACK TO COAST CITY!
AND ONCE WE GET THERE?
WE DO WHAT WE ALWAYS DO...
ARRF!
...WE MAKE DEATH WAIT ANOTHER DAY!
END.

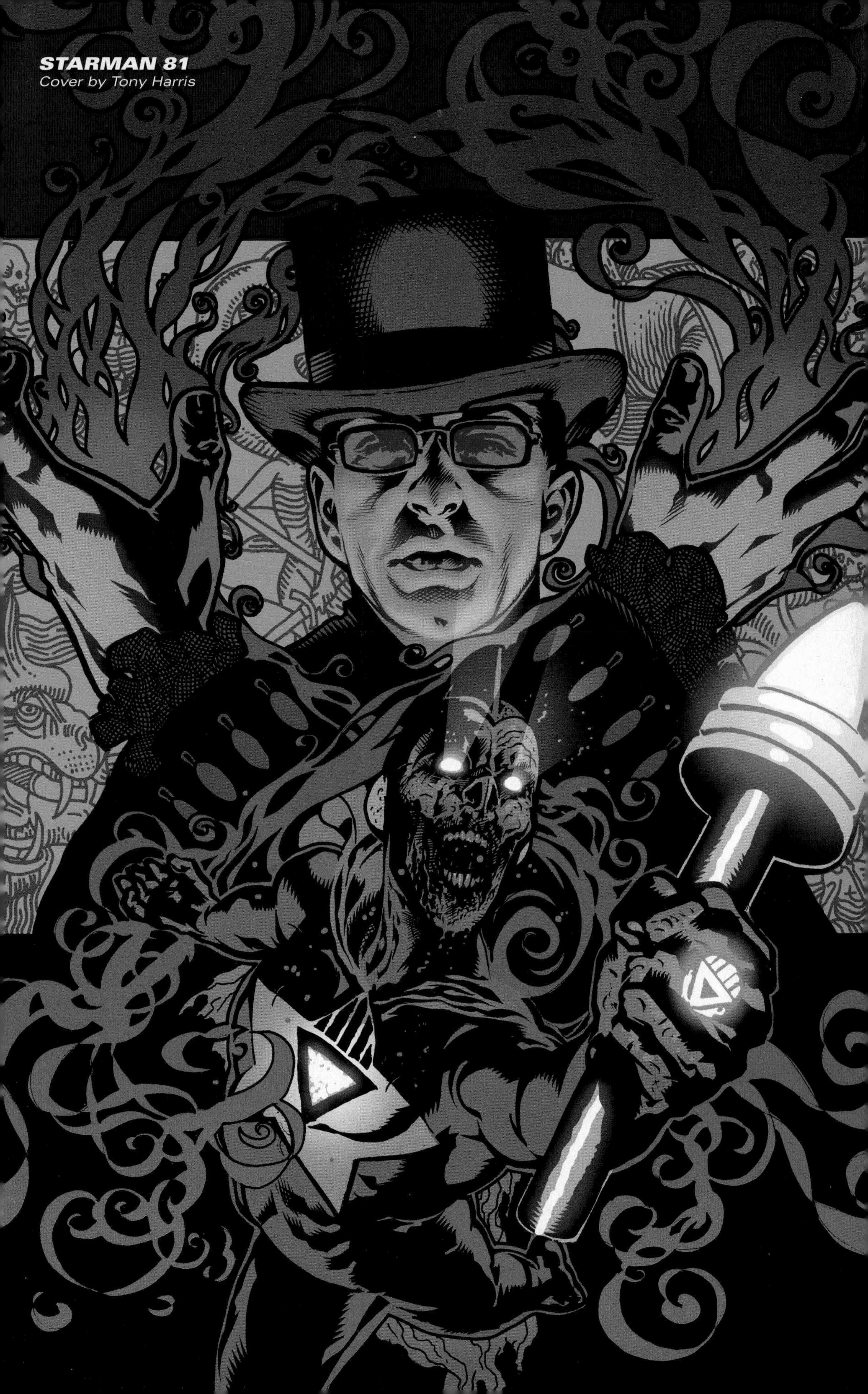

STARMAN 81
Cover by Tony Harris

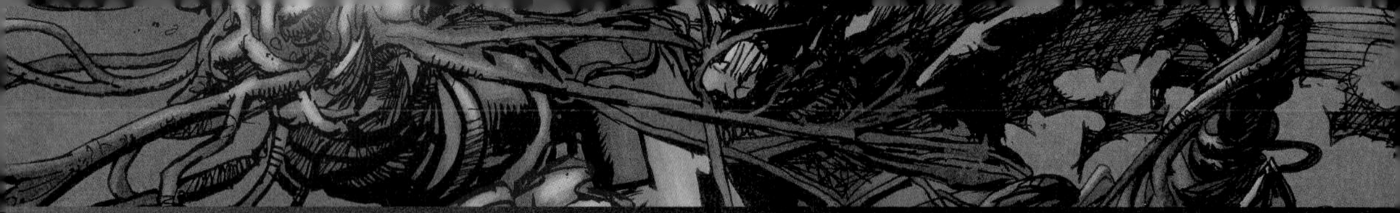

BLACKEST NIGHT STARMAN

JAMES ROBINSON
WRITER

FERNANDO DAGNINO
LAYOUTS

BILL SIENKIEWICZ
FINISHES

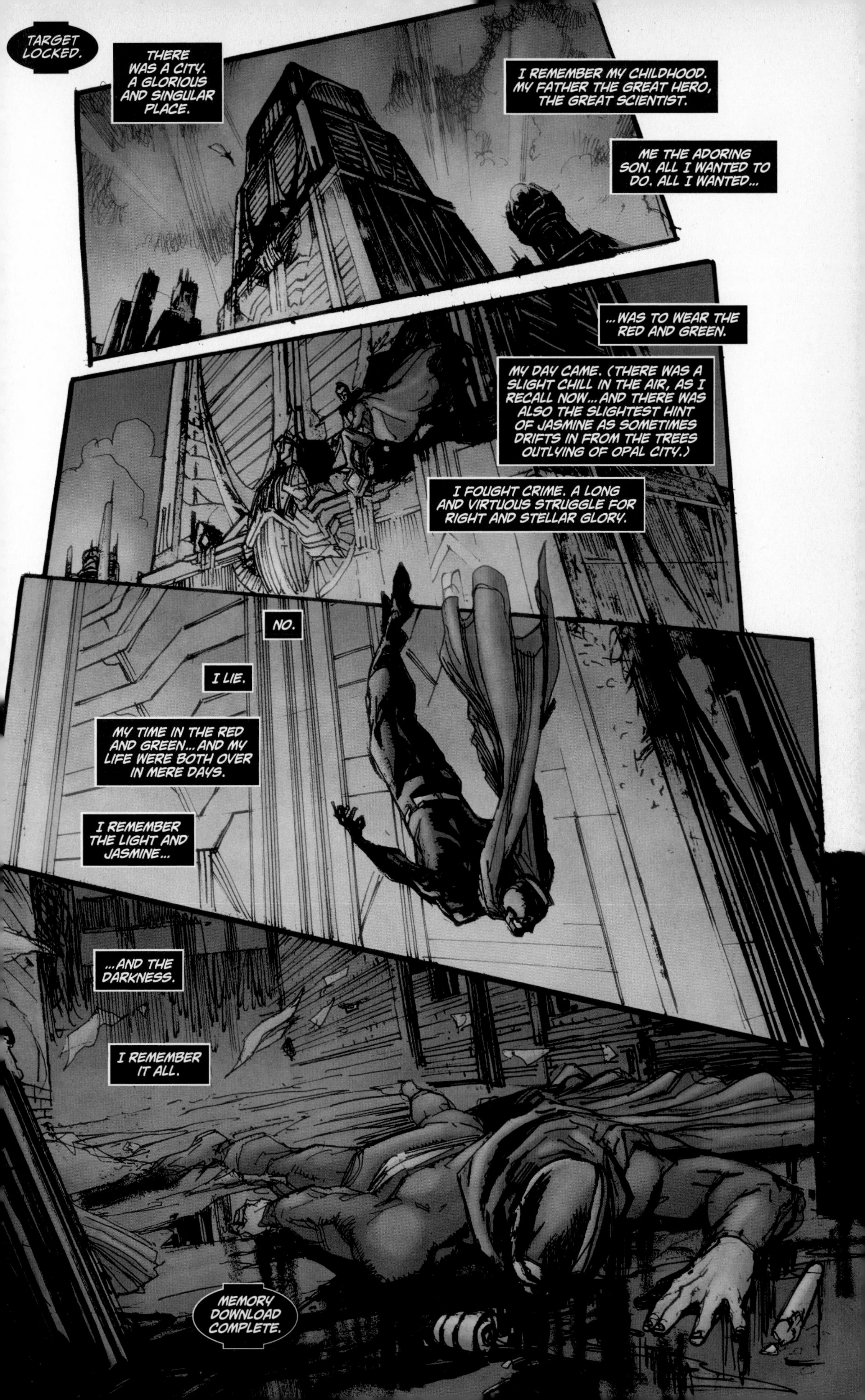
TARGET LOCKED.
THERE WAS A CITY. A GLORIOUS AND SINGULAR PLACE.
I REMEMBER MY CHILDHOOD. MY FATHER THE GREAT HERO, THE GREAT SCIENTIST.
ME THE ADORING SON. ALL I WANTED TO DO. ALL I WANTED...
...WAS TO WEAR THE RED AND GREEN.
MY DAY CAME. (THERE WAS A SLIGHT CHILL IN THE AIR, AS I RECALL NOW...AND THERE WAS ALSO THE SLIGHTEST HINT OF JASMINE AS SOMETIMES DRIFTS IN FROM THE TREES OUTLYING OF OPAL CITY.)
I FOUGHT CRIME. A LONG AND VIRTUOUS STRUGGLE FOR RIGHT AND STELLAR GLORY.
NO.
I LIE.
MY TIME IN THE RED AND GREEN...AND MY LIFE WERE BOTH OVER IN MERE DAYS.
I REMEMBER THE LIGHT AND JASMINE...
...AND THE DARKNESS.
I REMEMBER IT ALL.
MEMORY DOWNLOAD COMPLETE.

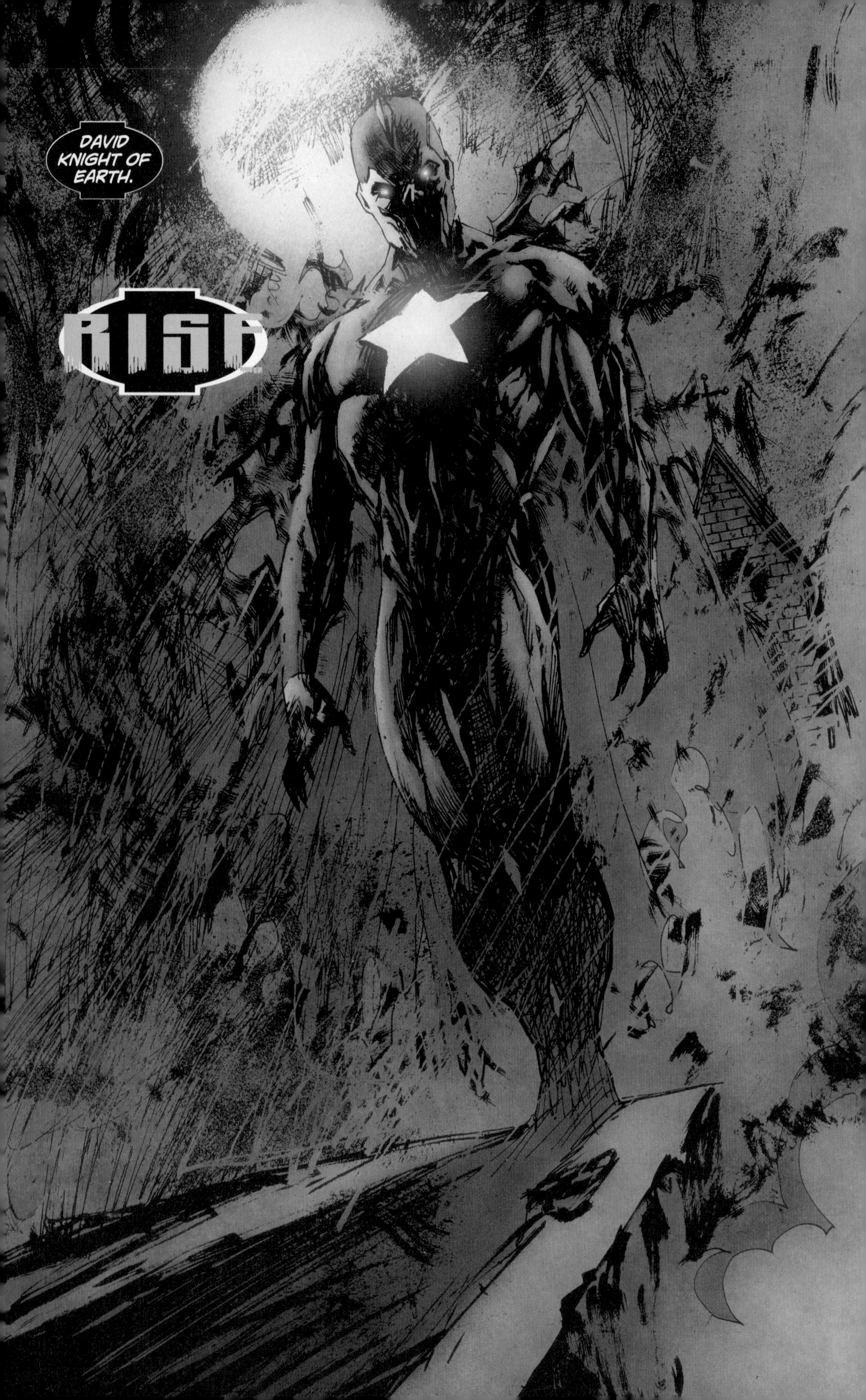
DAVID KNIGHT OF EARTH.
RISE

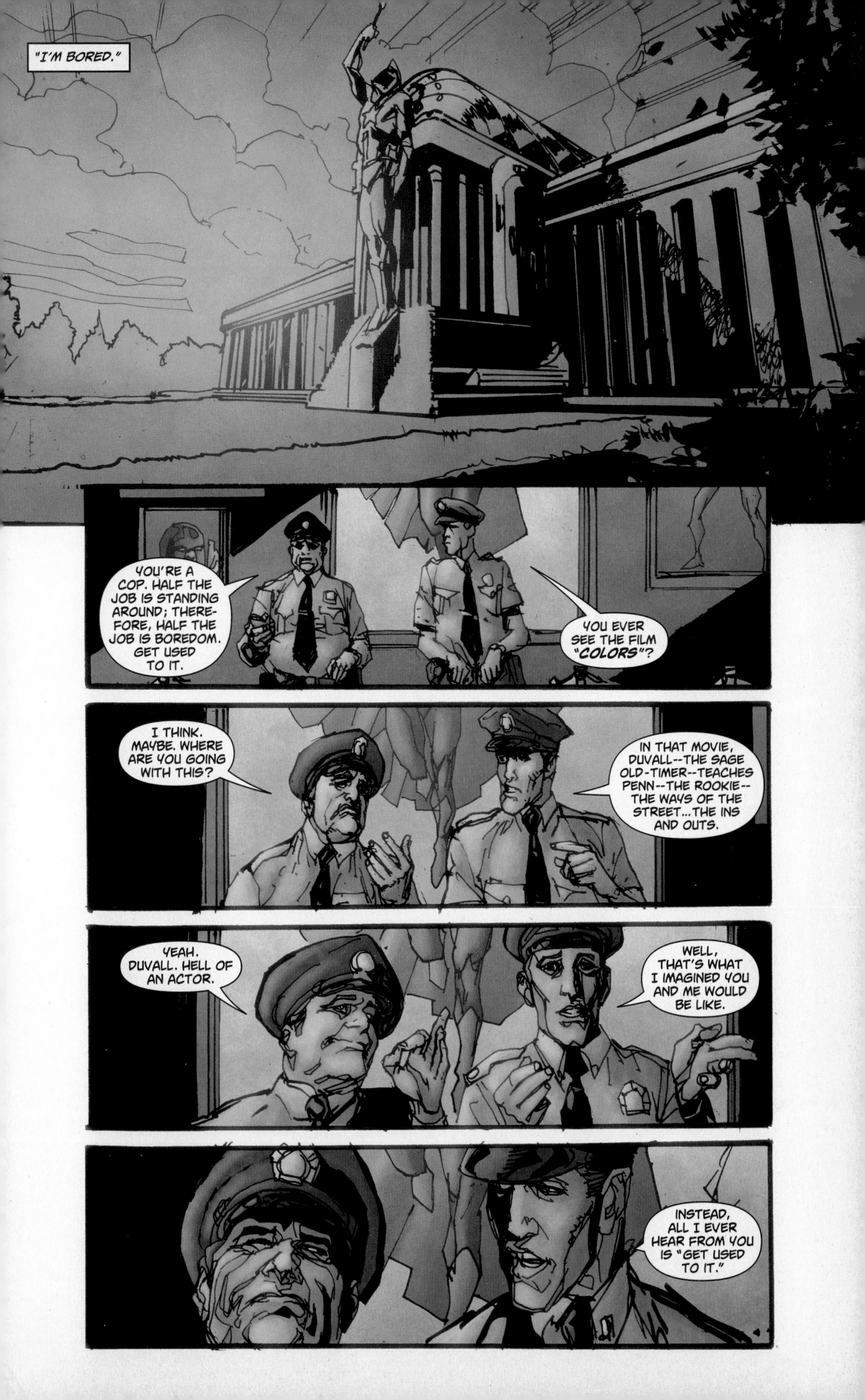
"I'M BORED."
YOU'RE A COP. HALF THE JOB IS STANDING AROUND; THEREFORE, HALF THE JOB IS BOREDOM. GET USED TO IT.
YOU EVER SEE THE FILM "COLORS"?
I THINK. MAYBE. WHERE ARE YOU GOING WITH THIS?
IN THAT MOVIE, DUVALL--THE SAGE OLD-TIMER--TEACHES PENN--THE ROOKIE--THE WAYS OF THE STREET...THE INS AND OUTS.
YEAH. DUVALL. HELL OF AN ACTOR.
WELL, THAT'S WHAT I IMAGINED YOU AND ME WOULD BE LIKE.
INSTEAD, ALL I EVER HEAR FROM YOU IS "GET USED TO IT."

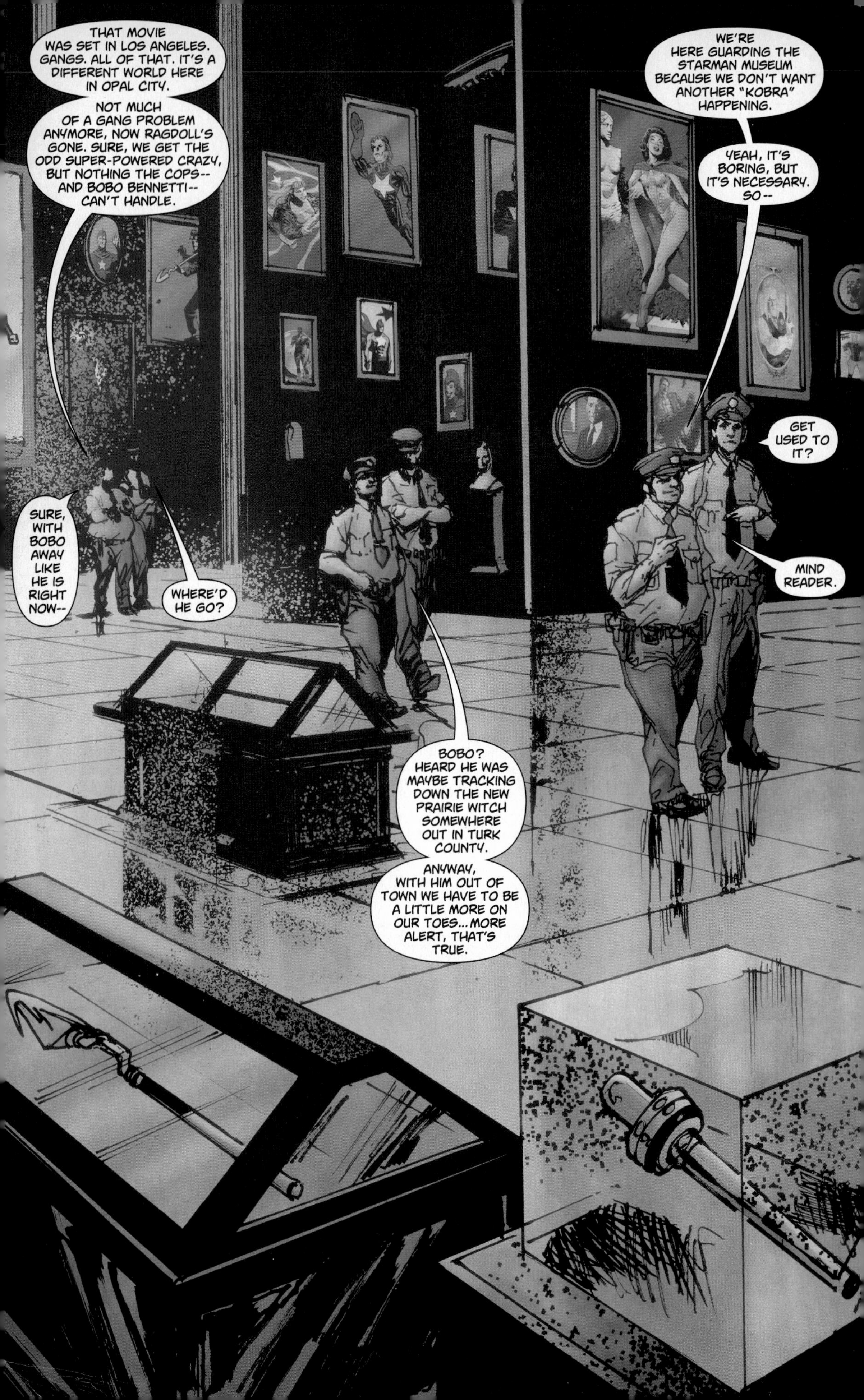
THAT MOVIE WAS SET IN LOS ANGELES. GANGS. ALL OF THAT. IT'S A DIFFERENT WORLD HERE IN OPAL CITY.
NOT MUCH OF A GANG PROBLEM ANYMORE, NOW RAGDOLL'S GONE. SURE, WE GET THE ODD SUPER-POWERED CRAZY, BUT NOTHING THE COPS-- AND BOBO BENNETTI-- CAN'T HANDLE.
SURE, WITH BOBO AWAY LIKE HE IS RIGHT NOW--
WHERE'D HE GO?
BOBO? HEARD HE WAS MAYBE TRACKING DOWN THE NEW PRAIRIE WITCH SOMEWHERE OUT IN TURK COUNTY.
ANYWAY, WITH HIM OUT OF TOWN WE HAVE TO BE A LITTLE MORE ON OUR TOES...MORE ALERT, THAT'S TRUE.
WE'RE HERE GUARDING THE STARMAN MUSEUM BECAUSE WE DON'T WANT ANOTHER "KOBRA" HAPPENING.
YEAH, IT'S BORING, BUT IT'S NECESSARY. SO--
GET USED TO IT?
MIND READER.

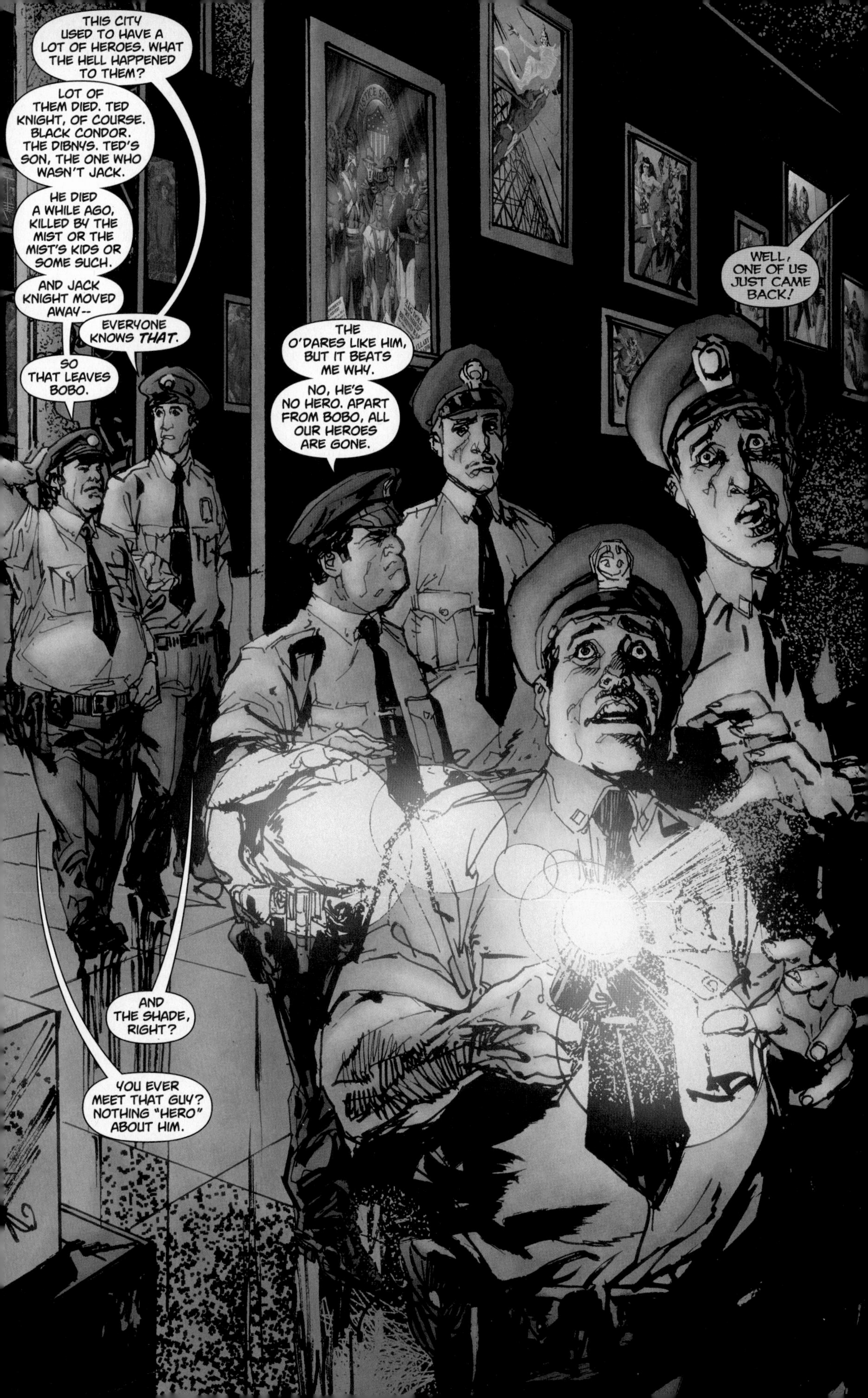
THIS CITY USED TO HAVE A LOT OF HEROES. WHAT THE HELL HAPPENED TO THEM?
LOT OF THEM DIED. TED KNIGHT, OF COURSE. BLACK CONDOR. THE DIBNYS. TED'S SON, THE ONE WHO WASN'T JACK.
HE DIED A WHILE AGO, KILLED BY THE MIST OR THE MIST'S KIDS OR SOME SUCH.
AND JACK KNIGHT MOVED AWAY--
EVERYONE KNOWS THAT.
SO THAT LEAVES BOBO.
THE O'DARES LIKE HIM, BUT IT BEATS ME WHY.
NO, HE'S NO HERO. APART FROM BOBO, ALL OUR HEROES ARE GONE.
AND THE SHADE, RIGHT?
YOU EVER MEET THAT GUY? NOTHING "HERO" ABOUT HIM.
WELL, ONE OF US JUST CAME BACK!

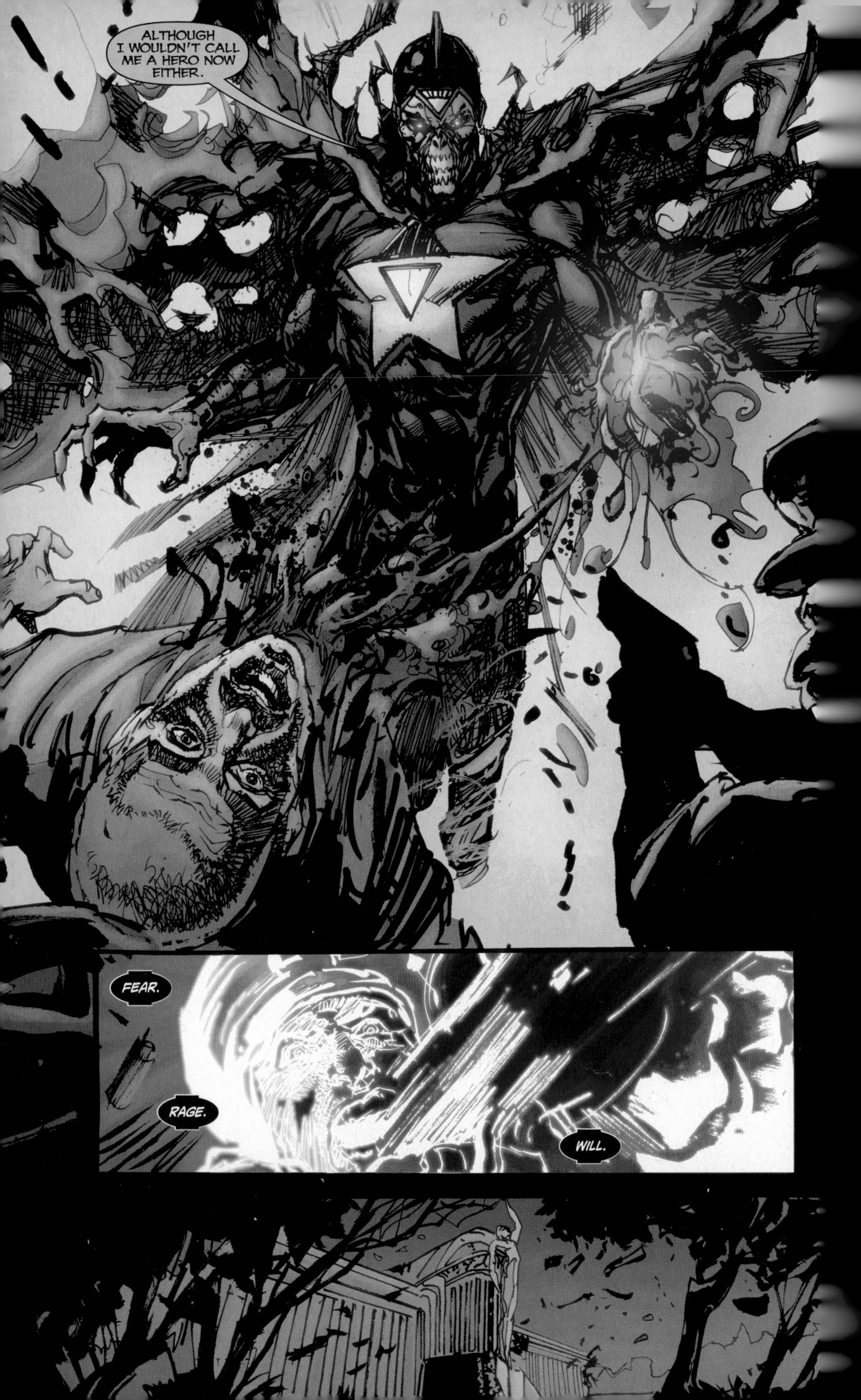
ALTHOUGH I WOULDN'T CALL ME A HERO NOW EITHER.
FEAR.
RAGE.
WILL.

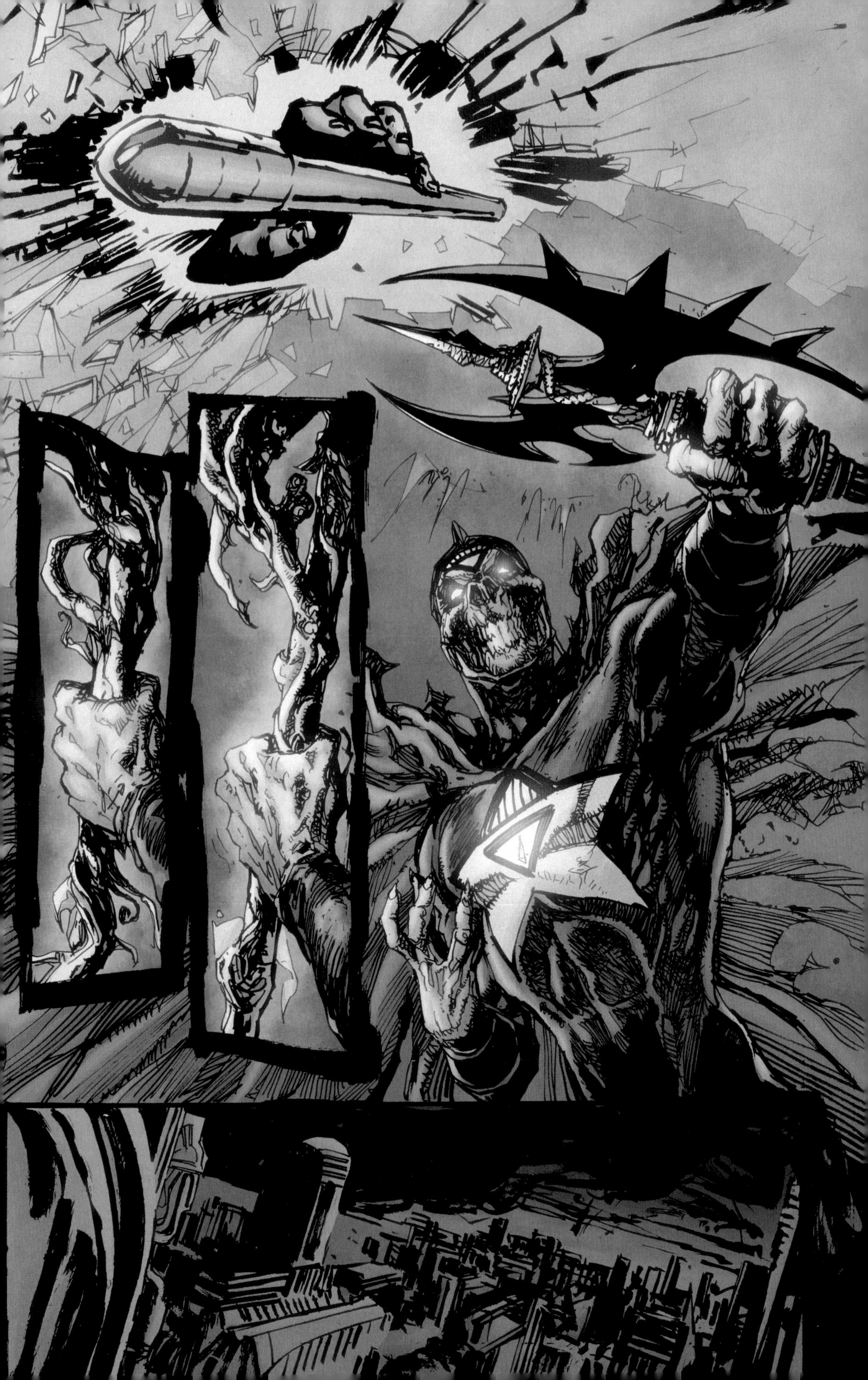

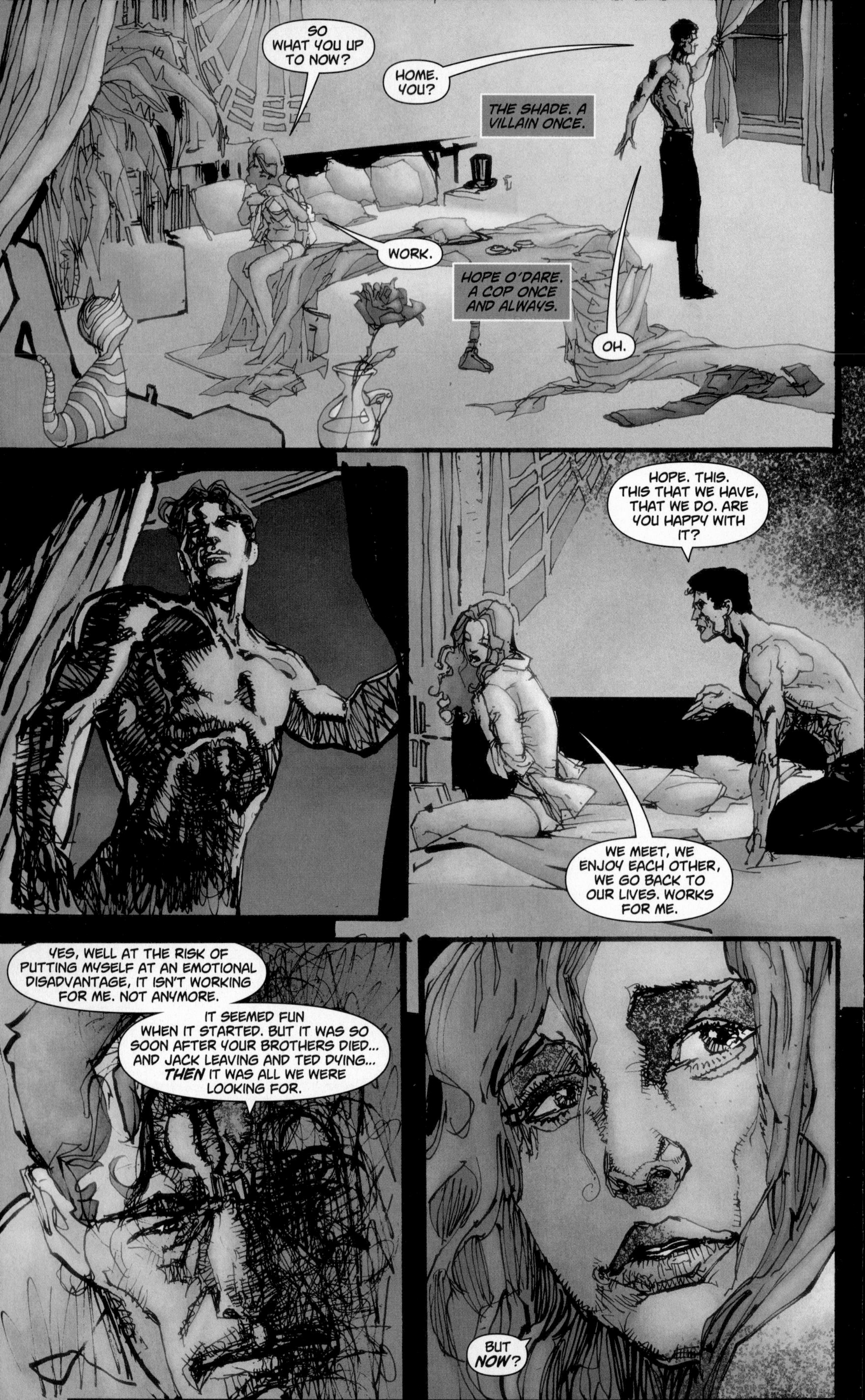
SO WHAT YOU UP TO NOW?
HOME. YOU?
THE SHADE. A VILLAIN ONCE.
WORK.
HOPE O'DARE. A COP ONCE AND ALWAYS.
OH.
HOPE. THIS. THIS THAT WE HAVE, THAT WE DO. ARE YOU HAPPY WITH IT?
WE MEET, WE ENJOY EACH OTHER, WE GO BACK TO OUR LIVES. WORKS FOR ME.
YES, WELL AT THE RISK OF PUTTING MYSELF AT AN EMOTIONAL DISADVANTAGE, IT ISN'T WORKING FOR ME. NOT ANYMORE.
IT SEEMED FUN WHEN IT STARTED. BUT IT WAS SO SOON AFTER YOUR BROTHERS DIED... AND JACK LEAVING AND TED DYING... *THEN* IT WAS ALL WE WERE LOOKING FOR.
BUT *NOW*?

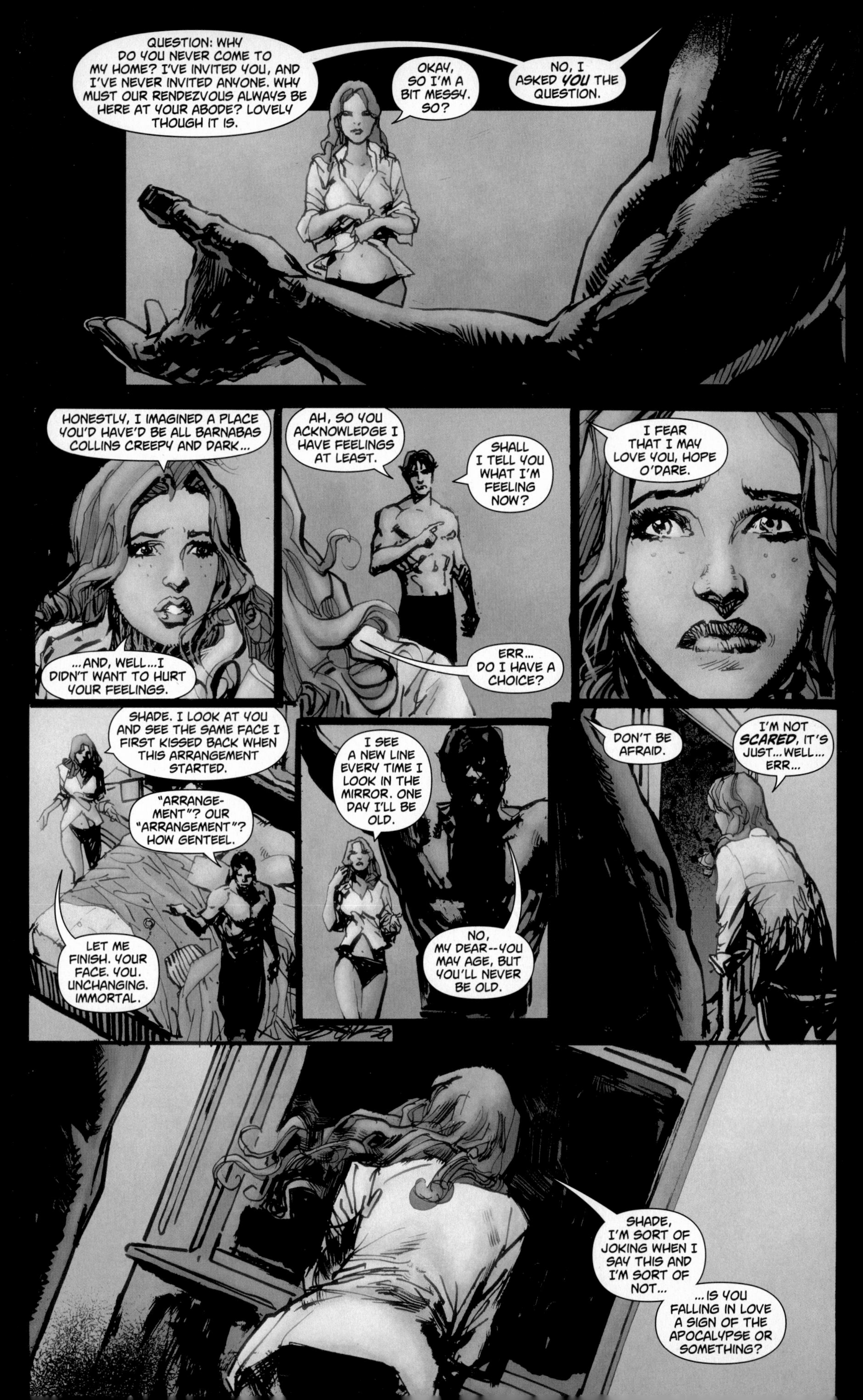
QUESTION: WHY DO YOU NEVER COME TO MY HOME? I'VE INVITED YOU, AND I'VE NEVER INVITED ANYONE. WHY MUST OUR RENDEZVOUS ALWAYS BE HERE AT YOUR ABODE? LOVELY THOUGH IT IS.
OKAY, SO I'M A BIT MESSY. SO?
NO, I ASKED *YOU* THE QUESTION.
HONESTLY, I IMAGINED A PLACE YOU'D HAVE'D BE ALL BARNABAS COLLINS CREEPY AND DARK...
...AND, WELL...I DIDN'T WANT TO HURT YOUR FEELINGS.
AH, SO YOU ACKNOWLEDGE I HAVE FEELINGS AT LEAST.
SHALL I TELL YOU WHAT I'M FEELING NOW?
ERR... DO I HAVE A CHOICE?
I FEAR THAT I MAY LOVE YOU, HOPE O'DARE.
SHADE. I LOOK AT YOU AND SEE THE SAME FACE I FIRST KISSED BACK WHEN THIS ARRANGEMENT STARTED.
"ARRANGE-MENT"? OUR "ARRANGEMENT"? HOW GENTEEL.
LET ME FINISH. YOUR FACE. YOU. UNCHANGING. IMMORTAL.
I SEE A NEW LINE EVERY TIME I LOOK IN THE MIRROR. ONE DAY I'LL BE OLD.
NO, MY DEAR--YOU MAY AGE, BUT YOU'LL NEVER BE OLD.
DON'T BE AFRAID.
I'M NOT *SCARED*, IT'S JUST...WELL... ERR...
SHADE, I'M SORT OF JOKING WHEN I SAY THIS AND I'M SORT OF NOT...
...IS YOU FALLING IN LOVE A SIGN OF THE APOCALYPSE OR SOMETHING?

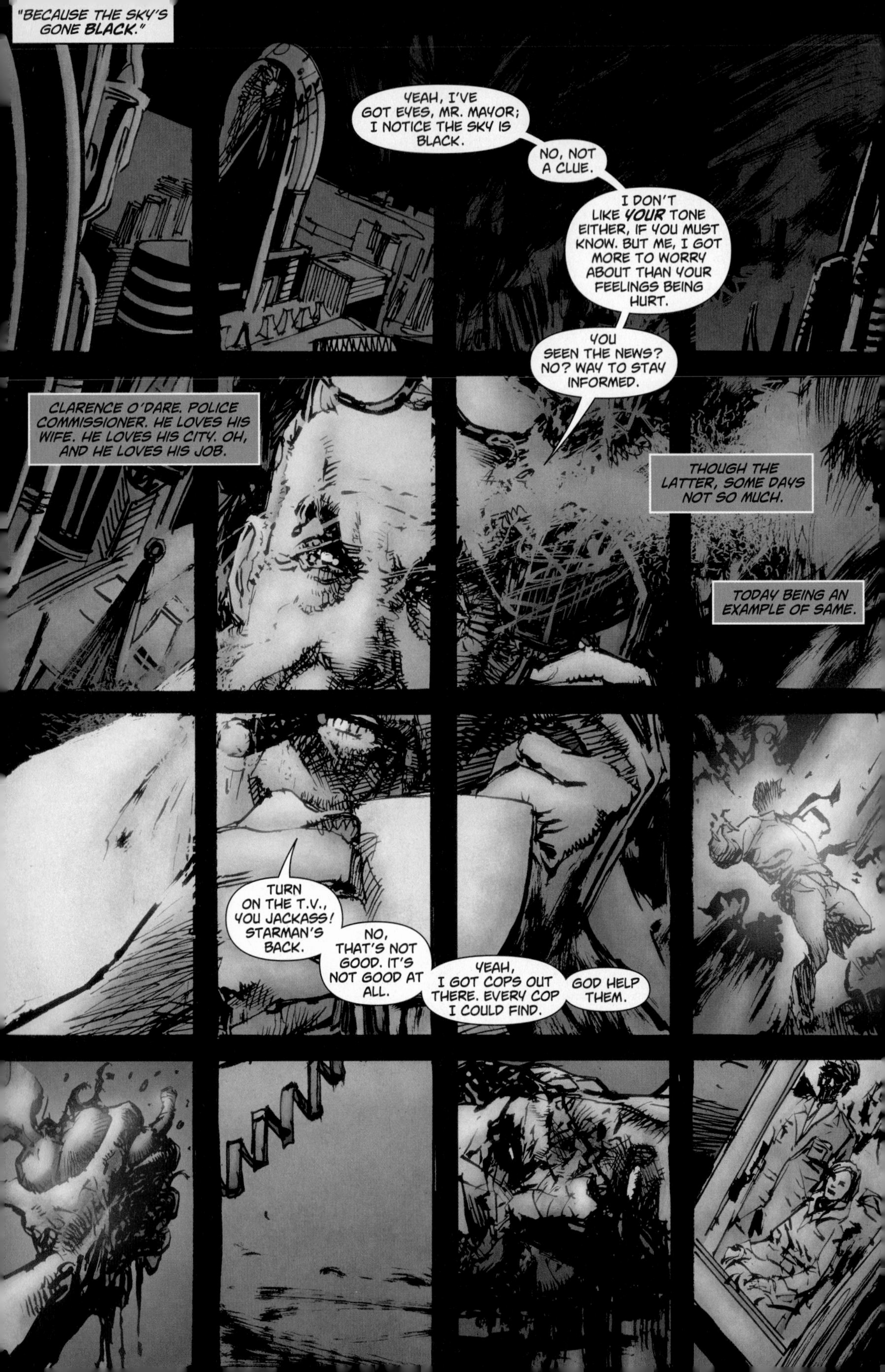
"BECAUSE THE SKY'S GONE BLACK."
YEAH, I'VE GOT EYES, MR. MAYOR; I NOTICE THE SKY IS BLACK.
NO, NOT A CLUE.
I DON'T LIKE YOUR TONE EITHER, IF YOU MUST KNOW. BUT ME, I GOT MORE TO WORRY ABOUT THAN YOUR FEELINGS BEING HURT.
YOU SEEN THE NEWS? NO? WAY TO STAY INFORMED.
CLARENCE O'DARE. POLICE COMMISSIONER. HE LOVES HIS WIFE. HE LOVES HIS CITY. OH, AND HE LOVES HIS JOB.
THOUGH THE LATTER, SOME DAYS NOT SO MUCH.
TODAY BEING AN EXAMPLE OF SAME.
TURN ON THE T.V., YOU JACKASS! STARMAN'S BACK.
NO, THAT'S NOT GOOD. IT'S NOT GOOD AT ALL.
YEAH, I GOT COPS OUT THERE. EVERY COP I COULD FIND.
GOD HELP THEM.

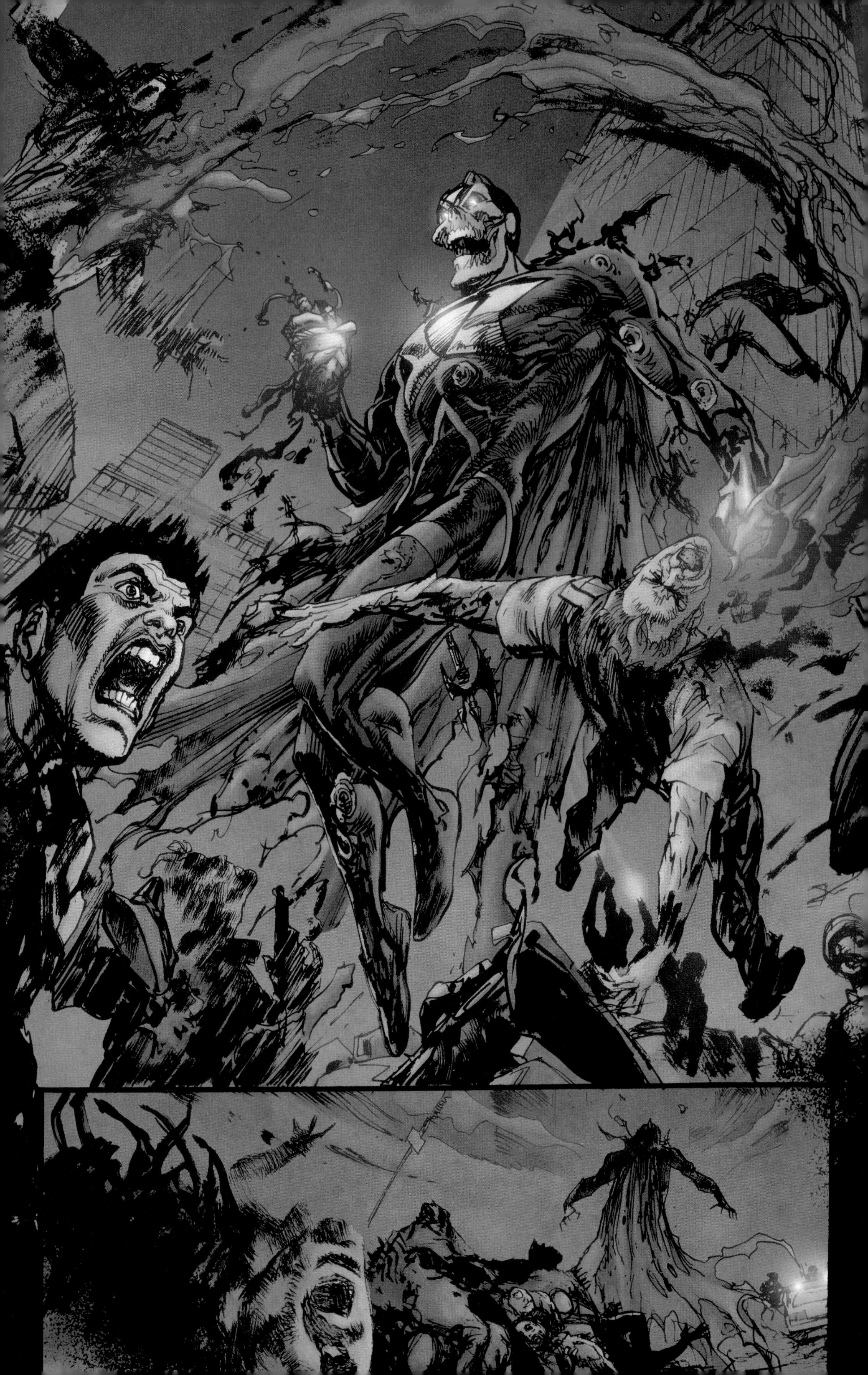

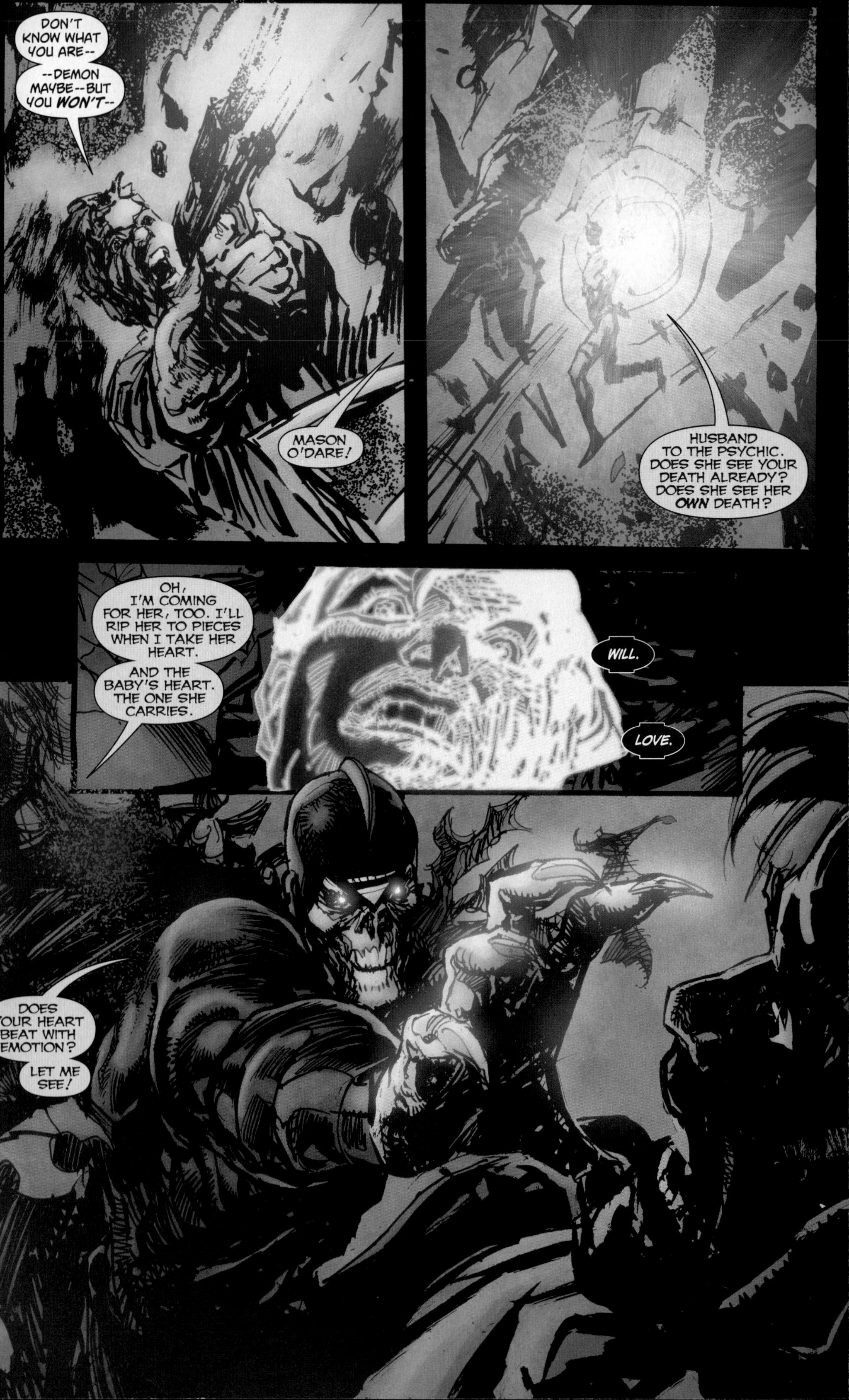
DON'T KNOW WHAT YOU ARE--
--DEMON MAYBE--BUT YOU WON'T--
MASON O'DARE!
HUSBAND TO THE PSYCHIC. DOES SHE SEE YOUR DEATH ALREADY? DOES SHE SEE HER OWN DEATH?
OH, I'M COMING FOR HER, TOO. I'LL RIP HER TO PIECES WHEN I TAKE HER HEART.
AND THE BABY'S HEART. THE ONE SHE CARRIES.
WILL.
LOVE.
DOES YOUR HEART BEAT WITH EMOTION?
LET ME SEE!

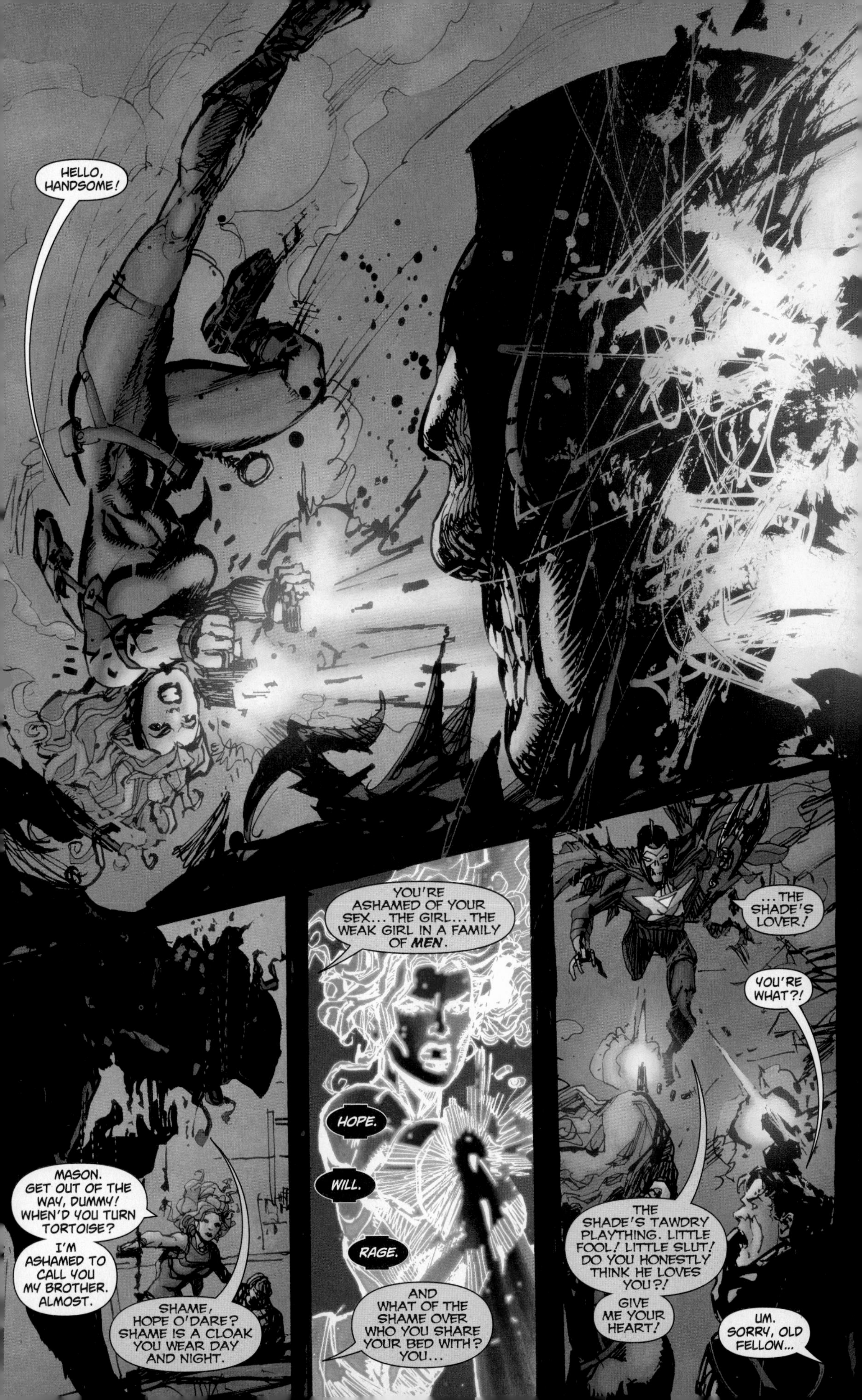
HELLO, HANDSOME!
MASON. GET OUT OF THE WAY, DUMMY! WHEN'D YOU TURN TORTOISE?
I'M ASHAMED TO CALL YOU MY BROTHER. ALMOST.
SHAME, HOPE O'DARE? SHAME IS A CLOAK YOU WEAR DAY AND NIGHT.
YOU'RE ASHAMED OF YOUR SEX... THE GIRL... THE WEAK GIRL IN A FAMILY OF MEN.
HOPE.
WILL.
RAGE.
AND WHAT OF THE SHAME OVER WHO YOU SHARE YOUR BED WITH? YOU...
...THE SHADE'S LOVER!
YOU'RE WHAT?!
THE SHADE'S TAWDRY PLAYTHING. LITTLE FOOL! LITTLE SLUT! DO YOU HONESTLY THINK HE LOVES YOU?!
GIVE ME YOUR HEART!
UM. SORRY, OLD FELLOW...

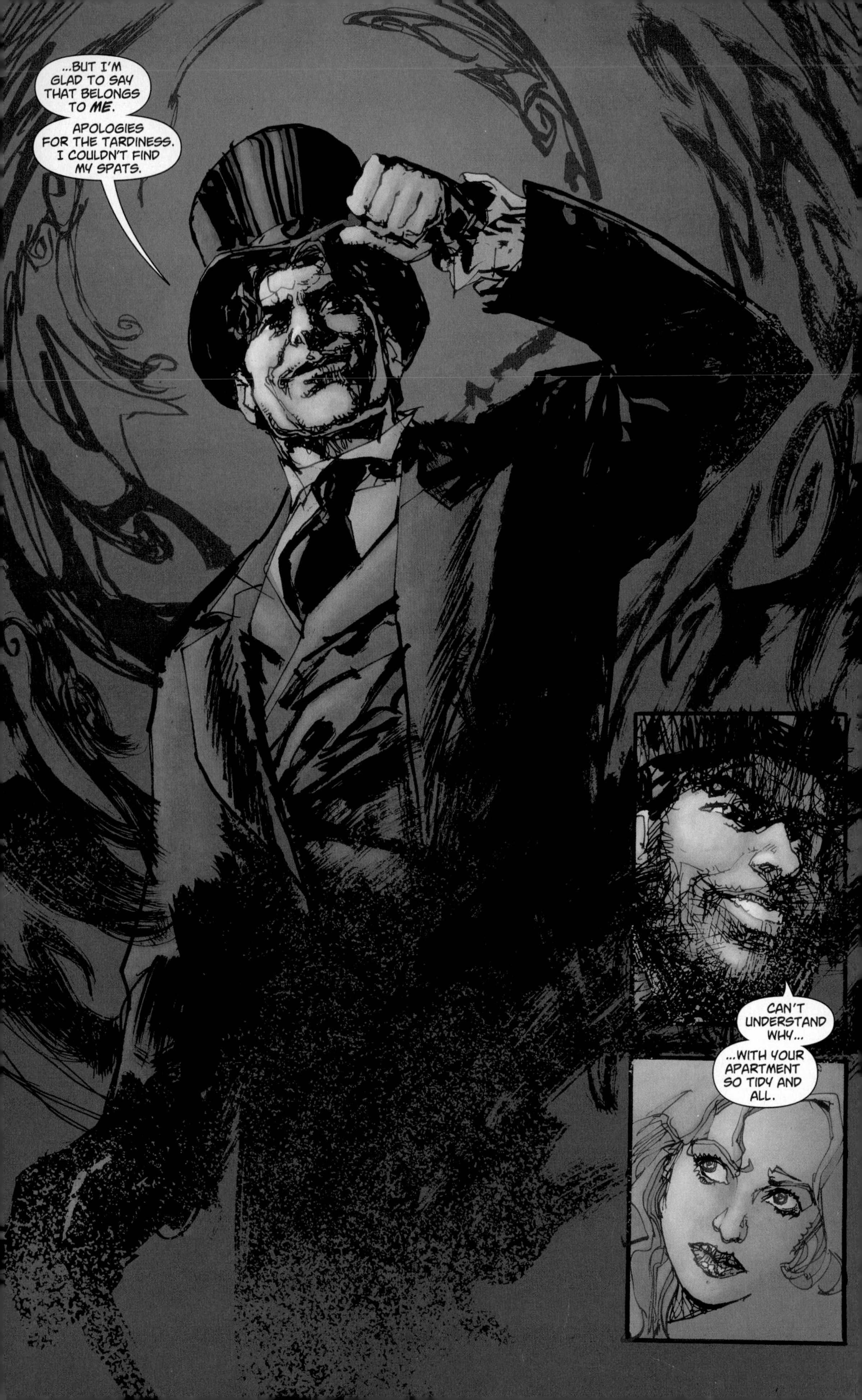
...BUT I'M GLAD TO SAY THAT BELONGS TO *ME*.
APOLOGIES FOR THE TARDINESS. I COULDN'T FIND MY SPATS.
CAN'T UNDERSTAND WHY...
...WITH YOUR APARTMENT SO TIDY AND ALL.

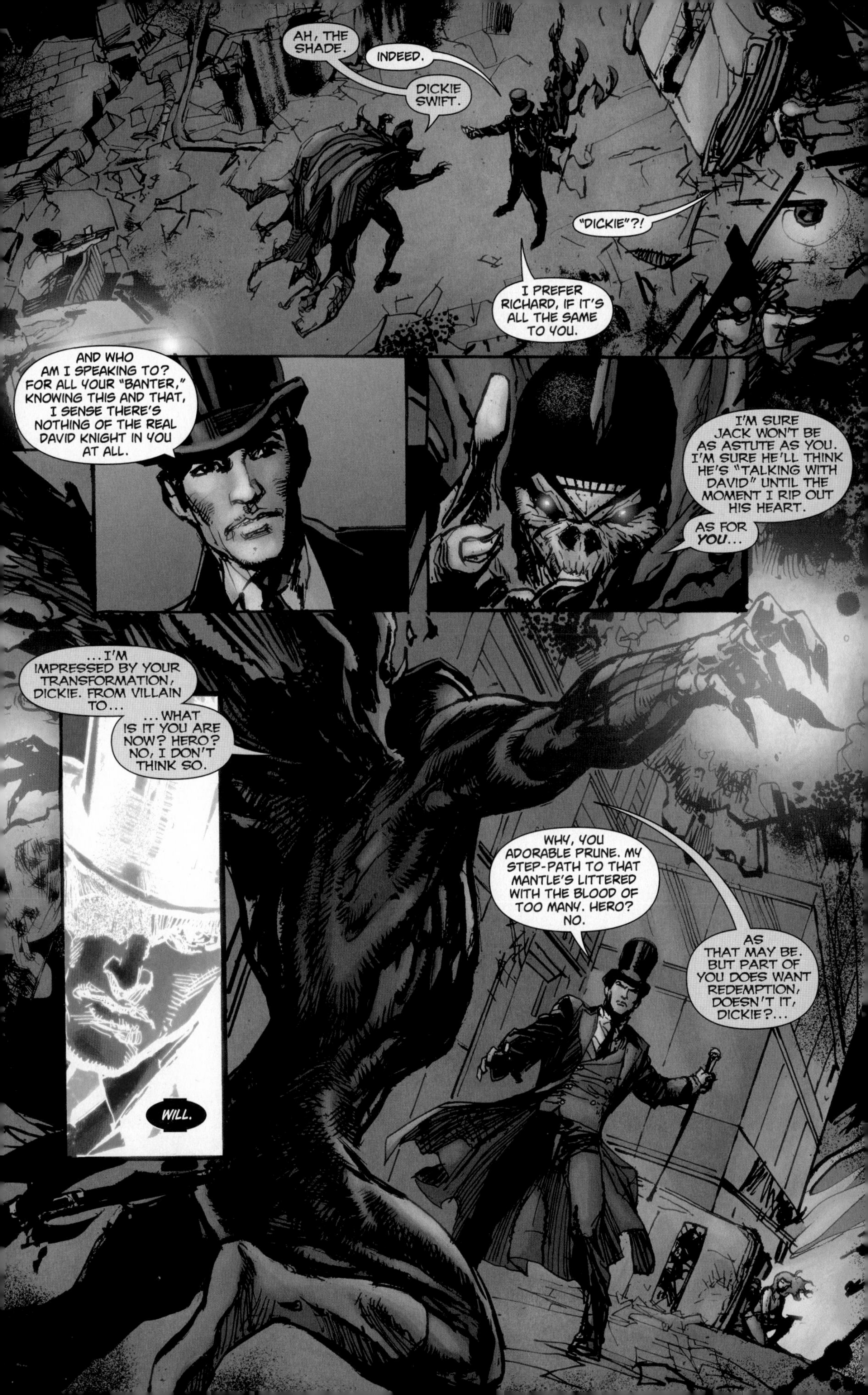
AH, THE SHADE.
INDEED.
DICKIE SWIFT.
"DICKIE"?!
I PREFER RICHARD, IF IT'S ALL THE SAME TO YOU.
AND WHO AM I SPEAKING TO? FOR ALL YOUR "BANTER," KNOWING THIS AND THAT, I SENSE THERE'S NOTHING OF THE REAL DAVID KNIGHT IN YOU AT ALL.
I'M SURE JACK WON'T BE AS ASTUTE AS YOU. I'M SURE HE'LL THINK HE'S "TALKING WITH DAVID" UNTIL THE MOMENT I RIP OUT HIS HEART.
AS FOR *YOU*...
...I'M IMPRESSED BY YOUR TRANSFORMATION, DICKIE. FROM VILLAIN TO...
...WHAT IS IT YOU ARE NOW? HERO? NO, I DON'T THINK SO.
WHY, YOU ADORABLE PRUNE. MY STEP-PATH TO THAT MANTLE'S LITTERED WITH THE BLOOD OF TOO MANY. HERO? NO.
AS THAT MAY BE. BUT PART OF YOU DOES WANT REDEMPTION, DOESN'T IT, DICKIE?...
WILL.

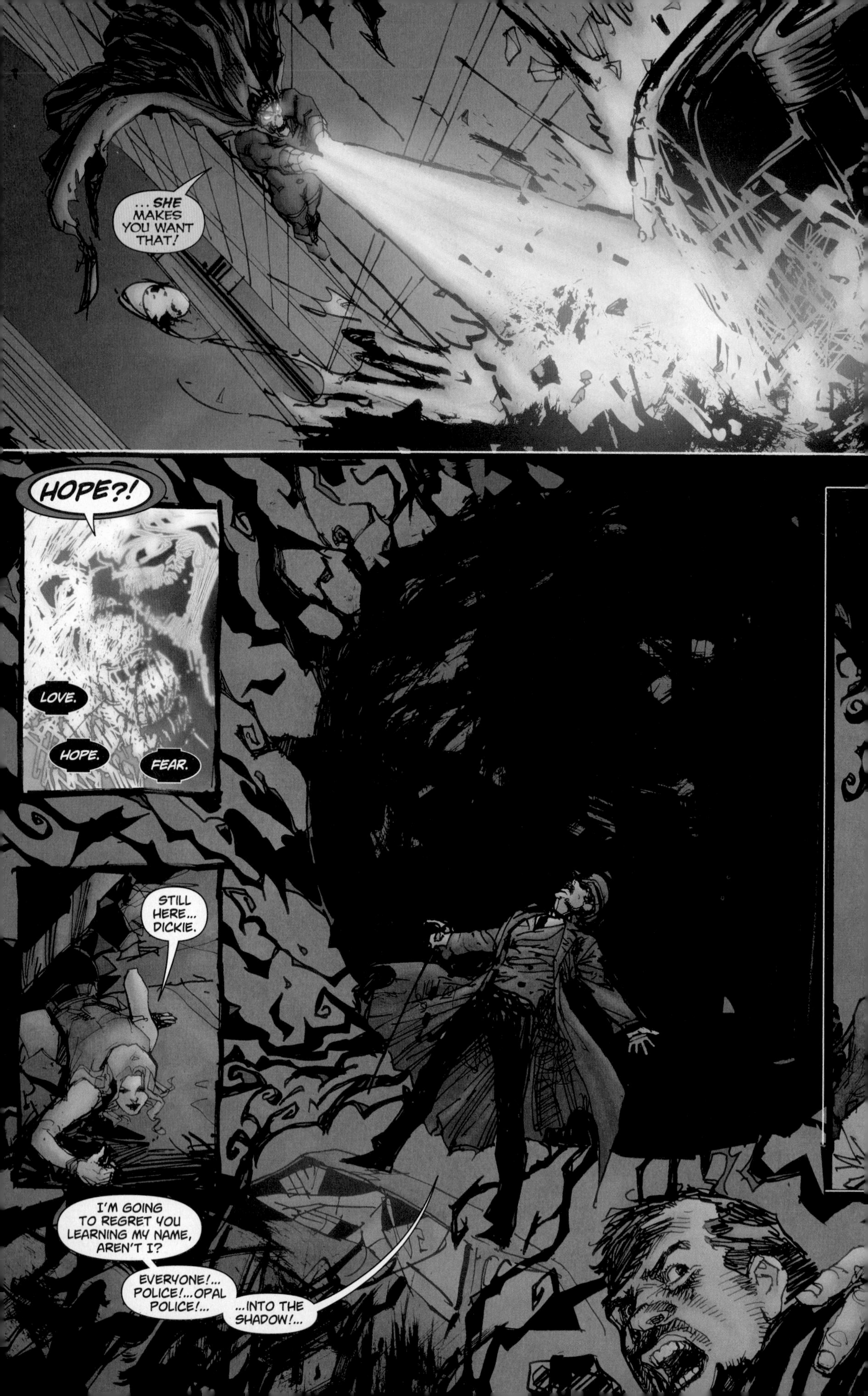
...SHE MAKES YOU WANT THAT!
HOPE?!
LOVE.
HOPE.
FEAR.
STILL HERE... DICKIE.
I'M GOING TO REGRET YOU LEARNING MY NAME, AREN'T I?
EVERYONE!... POLICE!...OPAL POLICE!...
...INTO THE SHADOW!...

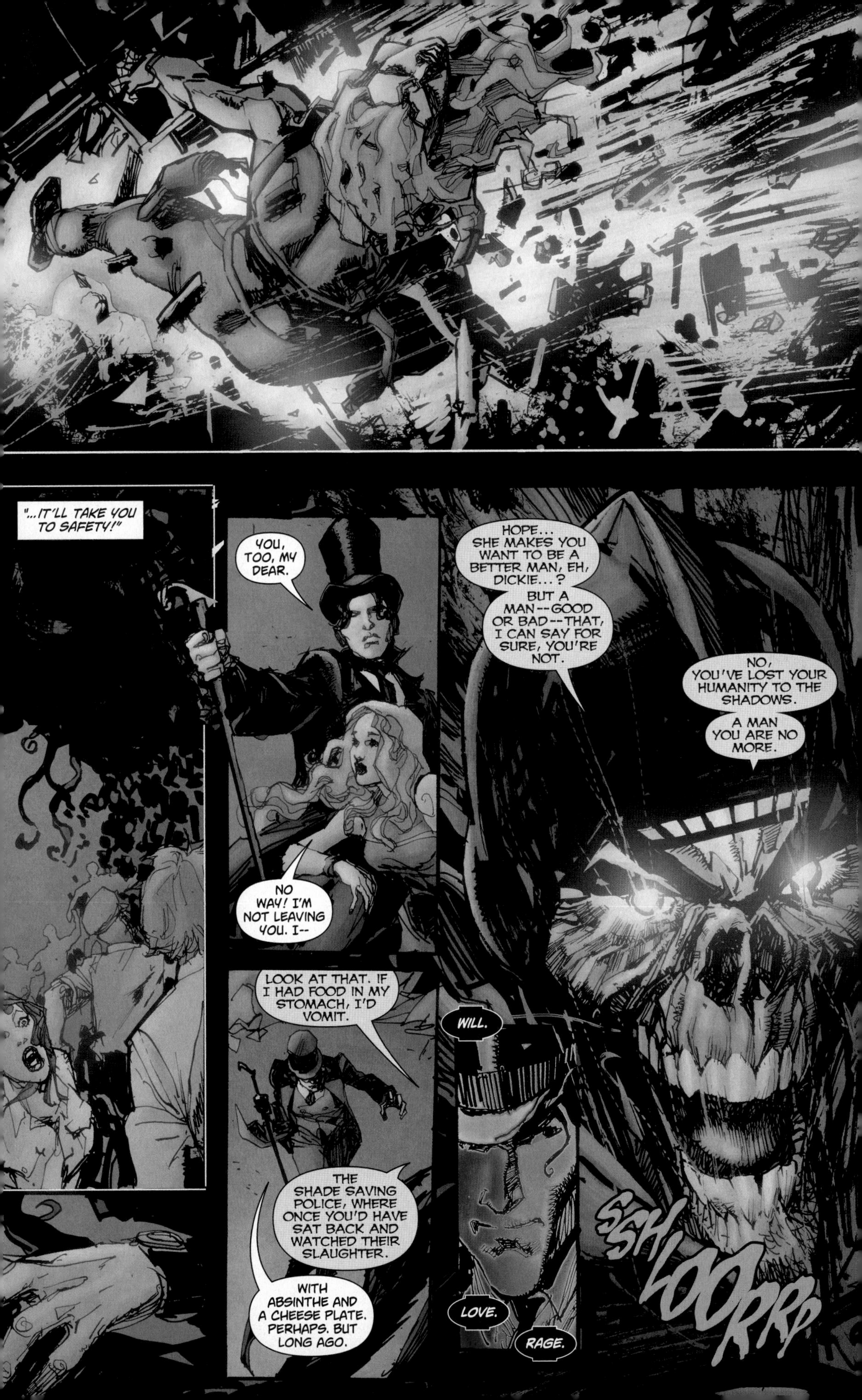
"...IT'LL TAKE YOU TO SAFETY!"
YOU, TOO, MY DEAR.
NO WAY! I'M NOT LEAVING YOU. I--
LOOK AT THAT. IF I HAD FOOD IN MY STOMACH, I'D VOMIT.
THE SHADE SAVING POLICE, WHERE ONCE YOU'D HAVE SAT BACK AND WATCHED THEIR SLAUGHTER.
WITH ABSINTHE AND A CHEESE PLATE. PERHAPS. BUT LONG AGO.
HOPE... SHE MAKES YOU WANT TO BE A BETTER MAN, EH, DICKIE...?
BUT A MAN--GOOD OR BAD--THAT, I CAN SAY FOR SURE, YOU'RE NOT.
NO, YOU'VE LOST YOUR HUMANITY TO THE SHADOWS.
A MAN YOU ARE NO MORE.
WILL.
LOVE.
RAGE.
SSHLOORRP

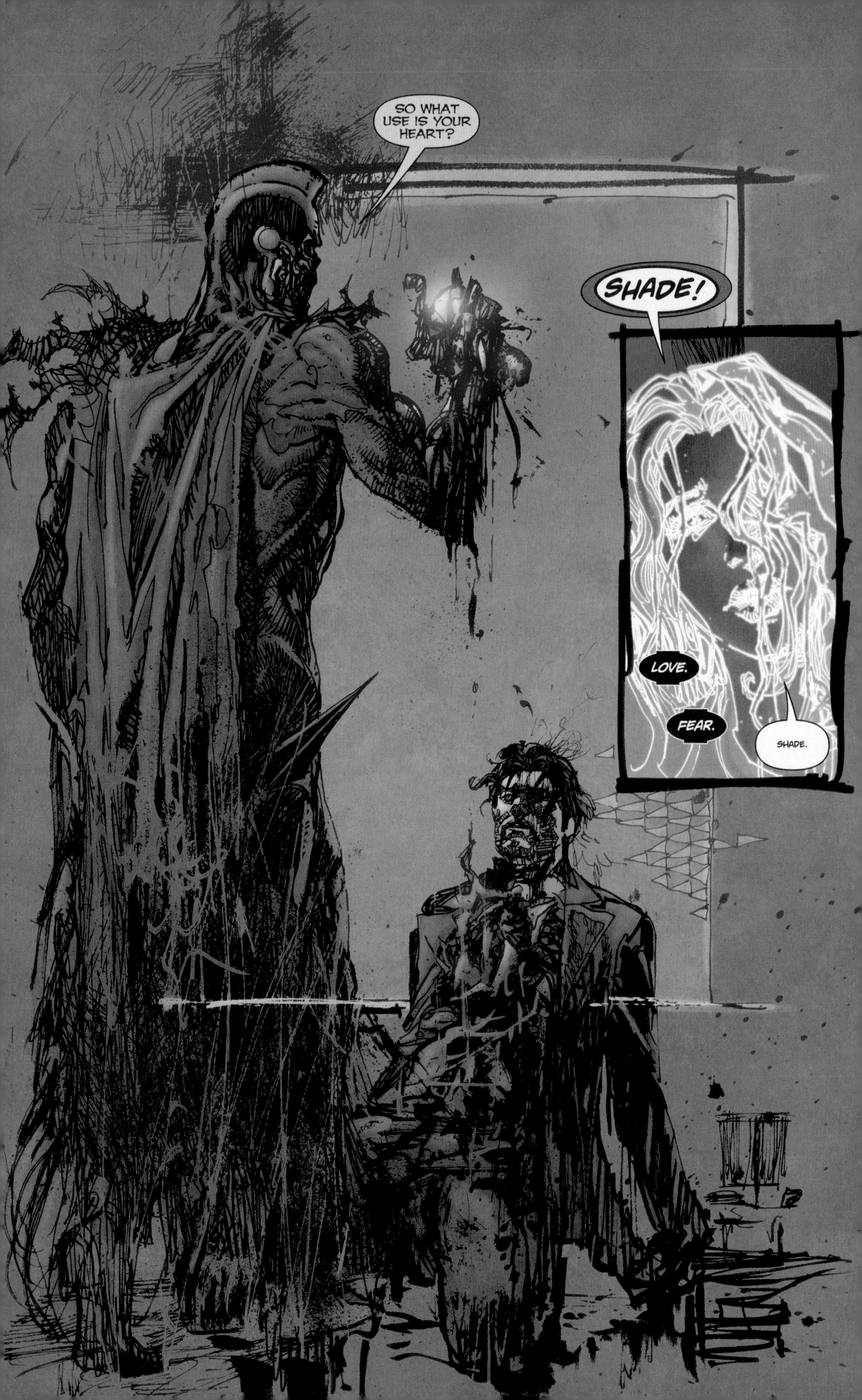
SO WHAT USE IS YOUR HEART?
SHADE!
LOVE.
FEAR.
SHADE.

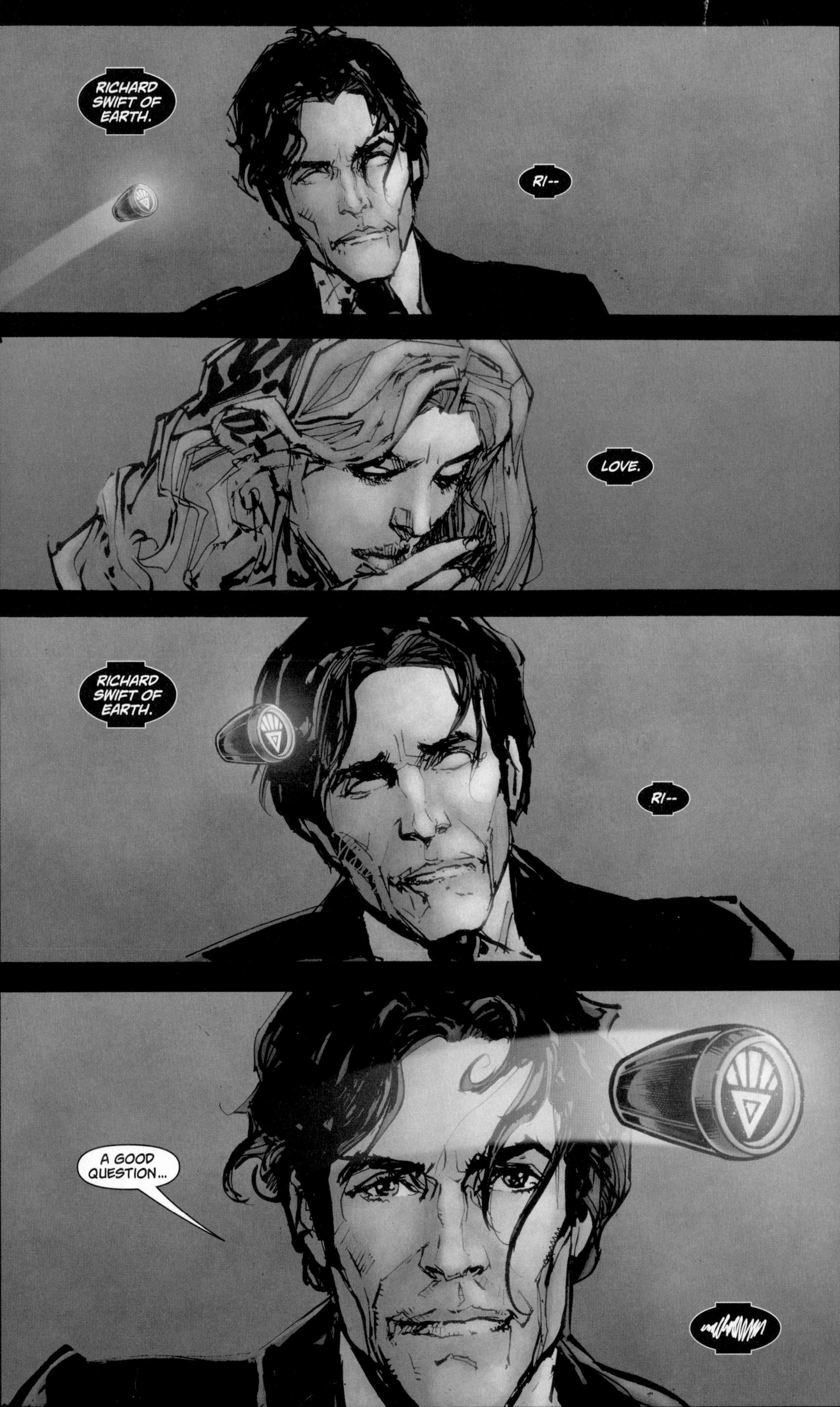

RICHARD SWIFT OF EARTH.
RI--
LOVE.
RICHARD SWIFT OF EARTH.
RI--
A GOOD QUESTION...

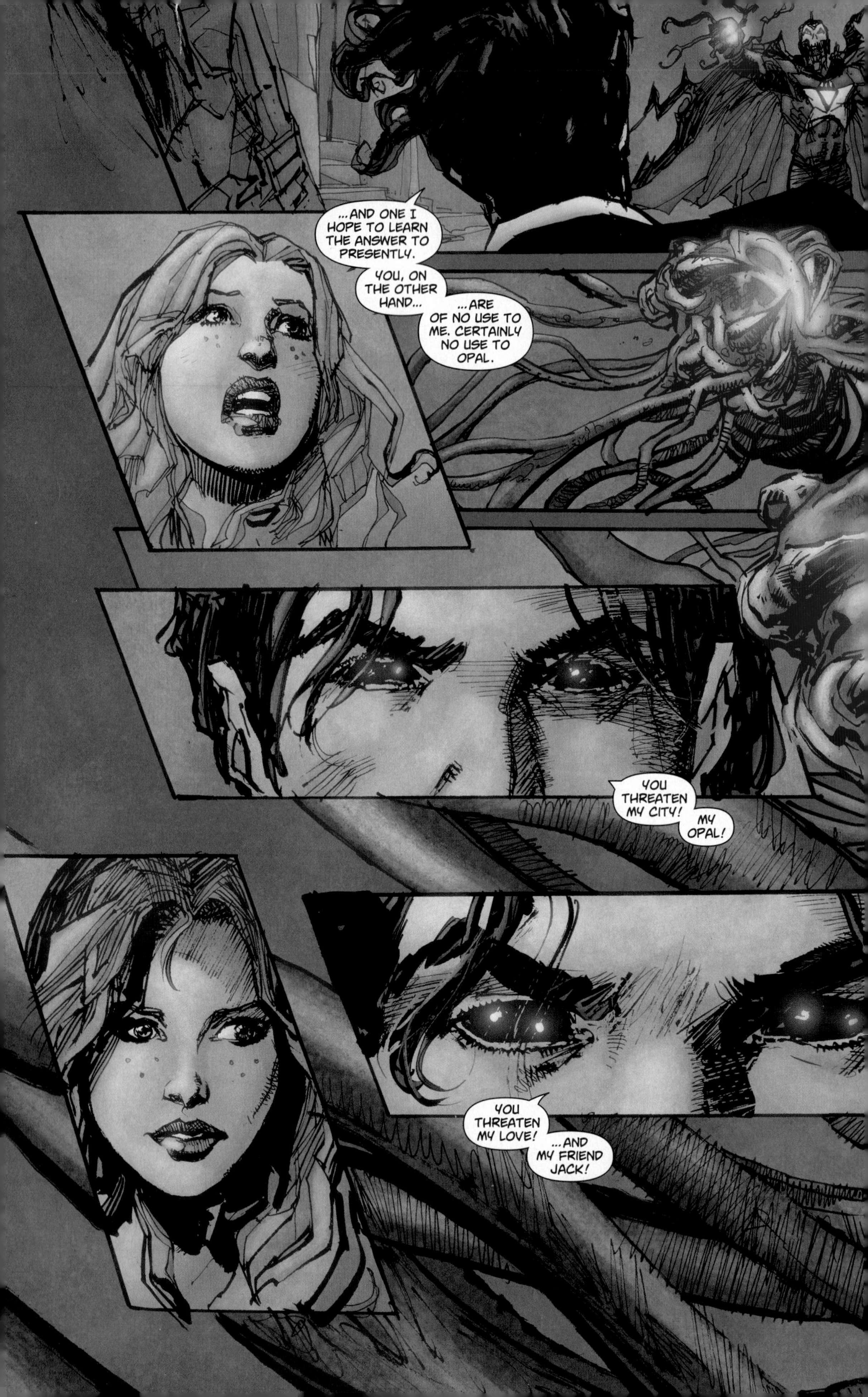
...AND ONE I HOPE TO LEARN THE ANSWER TO PRESENTLY.
YOU, ON THE OTHER HAND...
...ARE OF NO USE TO ME. CERTAINLY NO USE TO OPAL.
YOU THREATEN MY CITY!
MY OPAL!
YOU THREATEN MY LOVE!
...AND MY FRIEND JACK!

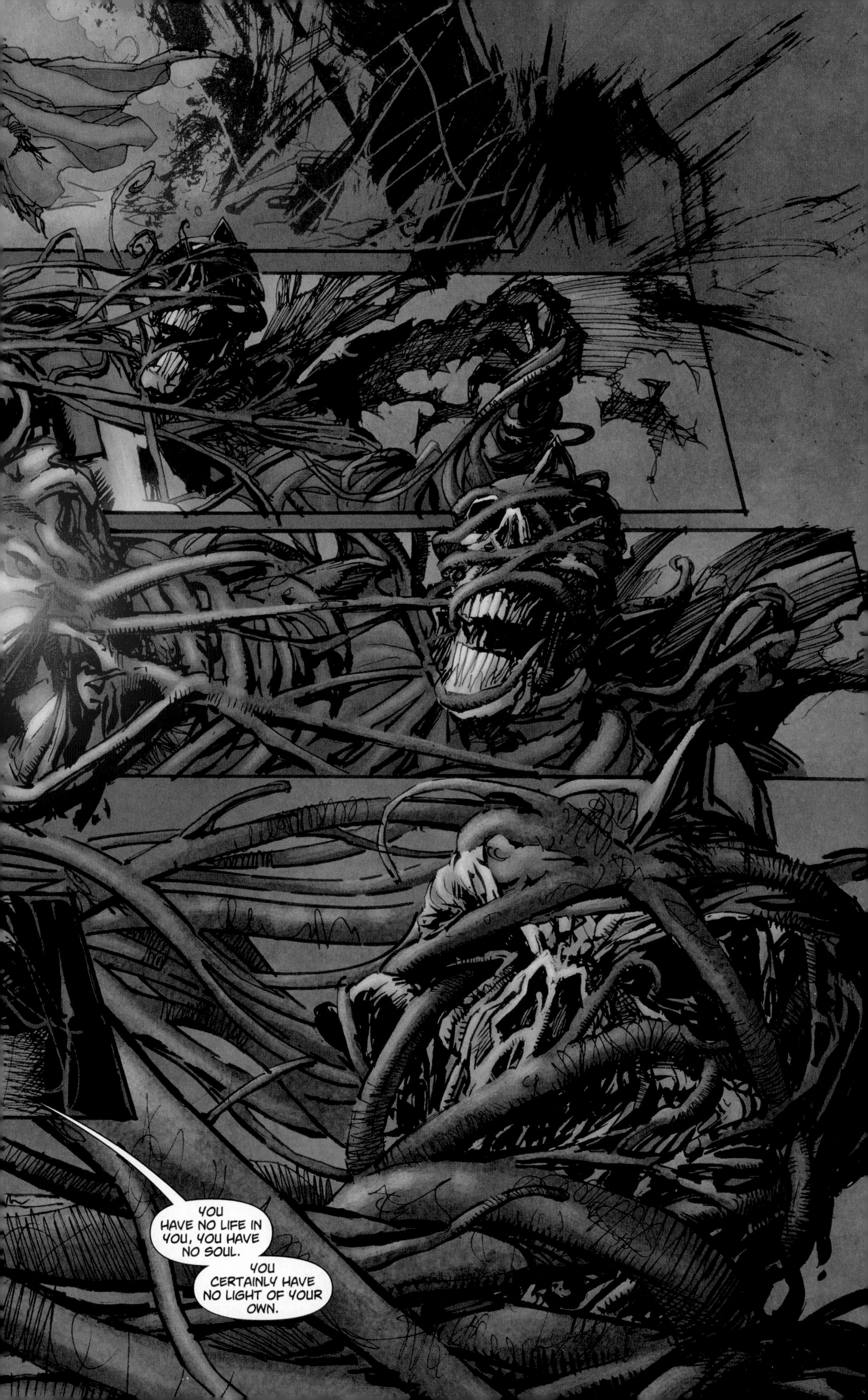
YOU HAVE NO LIFE IN YOU, YOU HAVE NO SOUL.
YOU CERTAINLY HAVE NO LIGHT OF YOUR OWN.

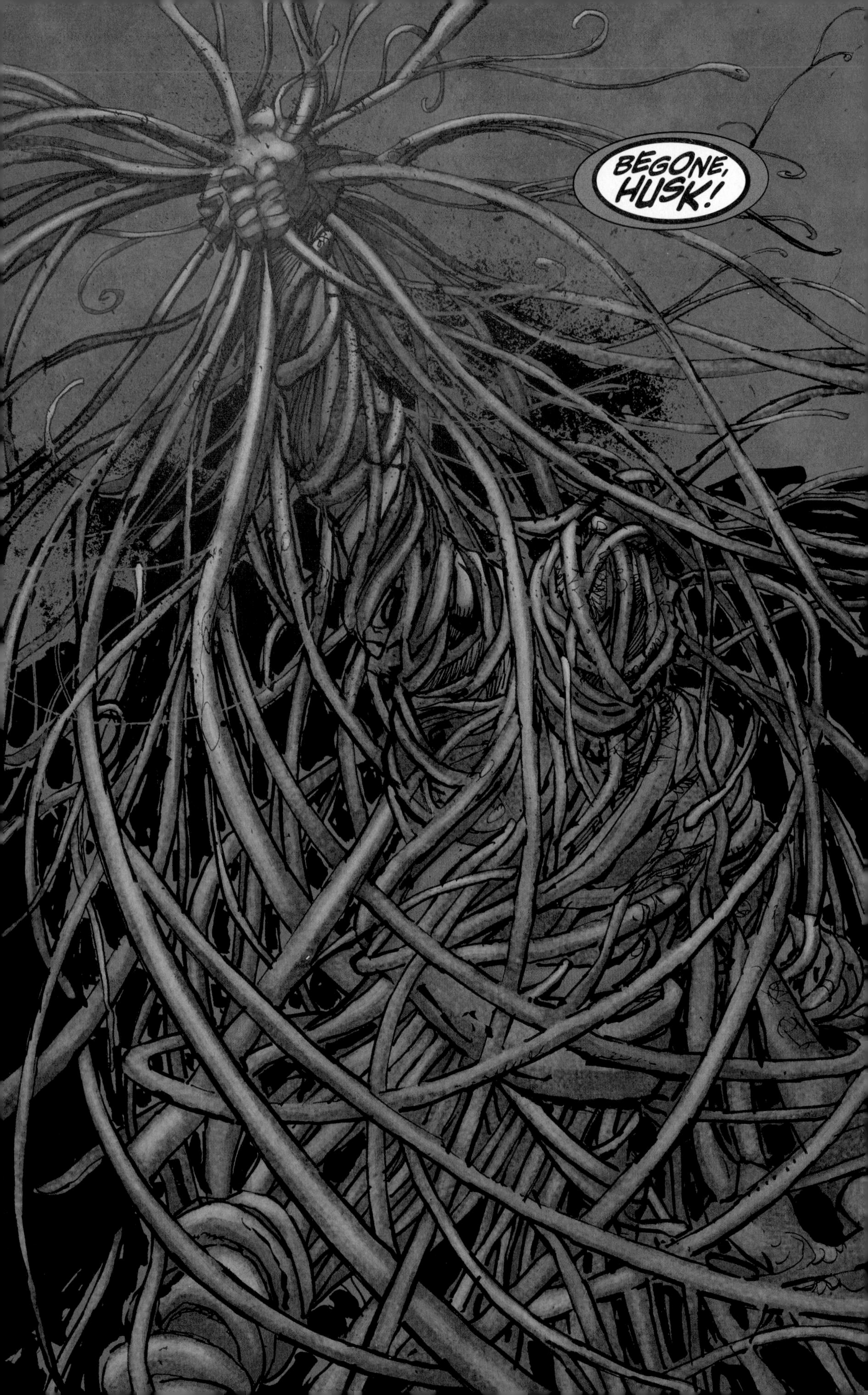
BEGONE, HUSK!

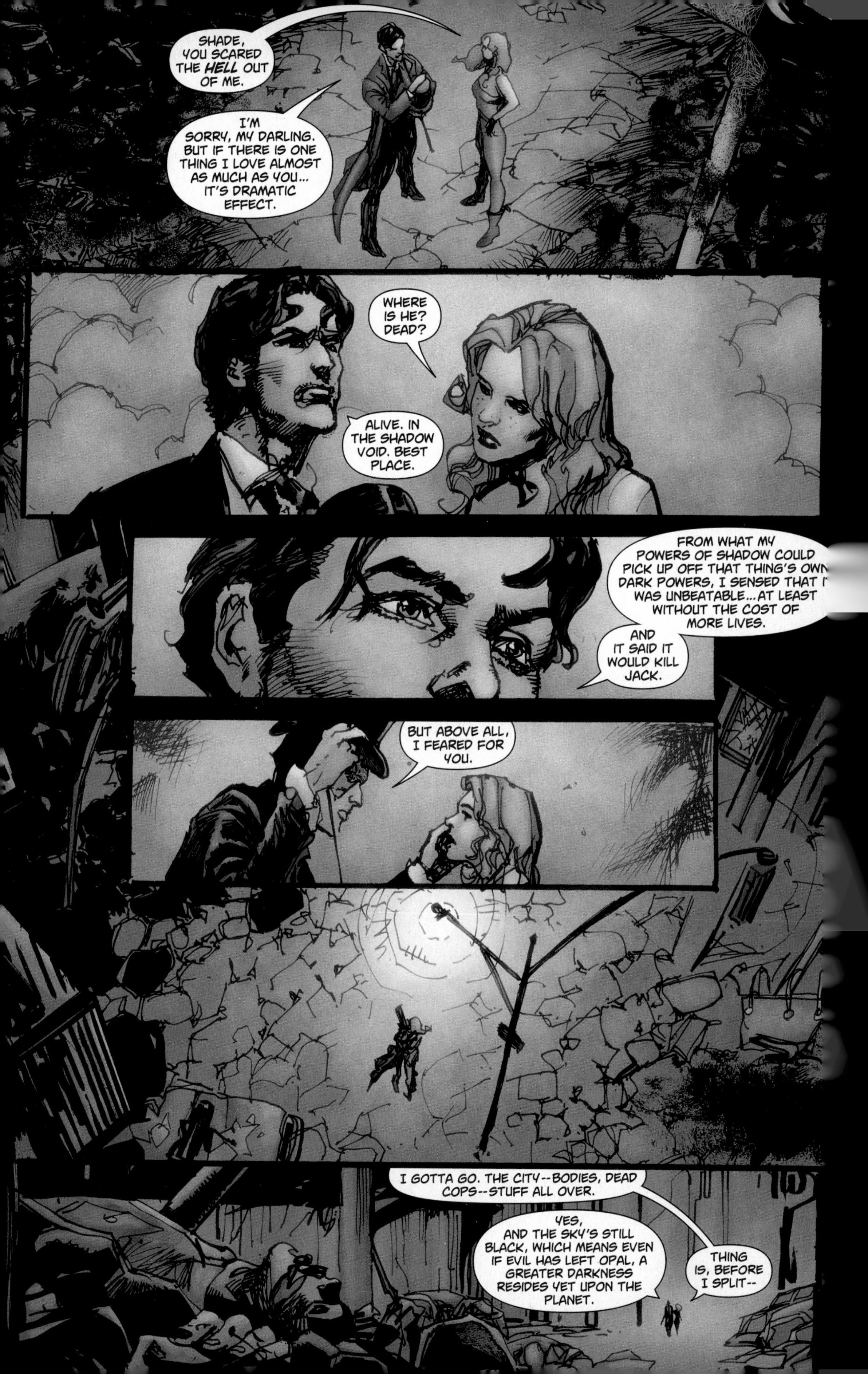
SHADE, YOU SCARED THE HELL OUT OF ME.
I'M SORRY, MY DARLING. BUT IF THERE IS ONE THING I LOVE ALMOST AS MUCH AS YOU... IT'S DRAMATIC EFFECT.
WHERE IS HE? DEAD?
ALIVE. IN THE SHADOW VOID. BEST PLACE.
FROM WHAT MY POWERS OF SHADOW COULD PICK UP OFF THAT THING'S OWN DARK POWERS, I SENSED THAT IT WAS UNBEATABLE...AT LEAST WITHOUT THE COST OF MORE LIVES.
AND IT SAID IT WOULD KILL JACK.
BUT ABOVE ALL, I FEARED FOR YOU.
I GOTTA GO. THE CITY--BODIES, DEAD COPS--STUFF ALL OVER.
YES, AND THE SKY'S STILL BLACK, WHICH MEANS EVEN IF EVIL HAS LEFT OPAL, A GREATER DARKNESS RESIDES YET UPON THE PLANET.
THING IS, BEFORE I SPLIT--

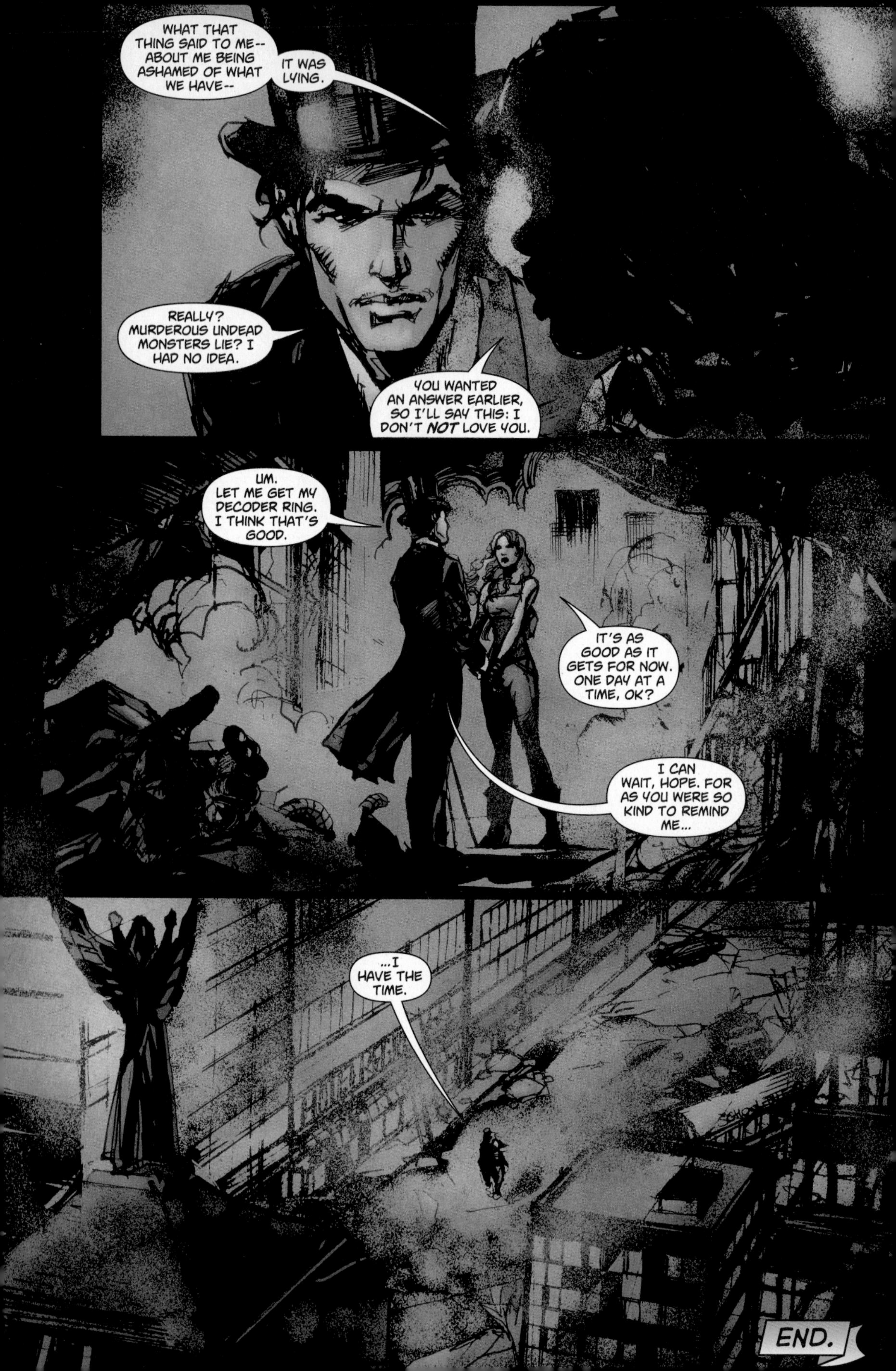
WHAT THAT THING SAID TO ME-- ABOUT ME BEING ASHAMED OF WHAT WE HAVE--
IT WAS LYING.
REALLY? MURDEROUS UNDEAD MONSTERS LIE? I HAD NO IDEA.
YOU WANTED AN ANSWER EARLIER, SO I'LL SAY THIS: I DON'T NOT LOVE YOU.
UM. LET ME GET MY DECODER RING. I THINK THAT'S GOOD.
IT'S AS GOOD AS IT GETS FOR NOW. ONE DAY AT A TIME, OK?
I CAN WAIT, HOPE. FOR AS YOU WERE SO KIND TO REMIND ME...
...I HAVE THE TIME.
END.

THE QUESTION 37
Cover by Cully Hamner with Dave McCaig

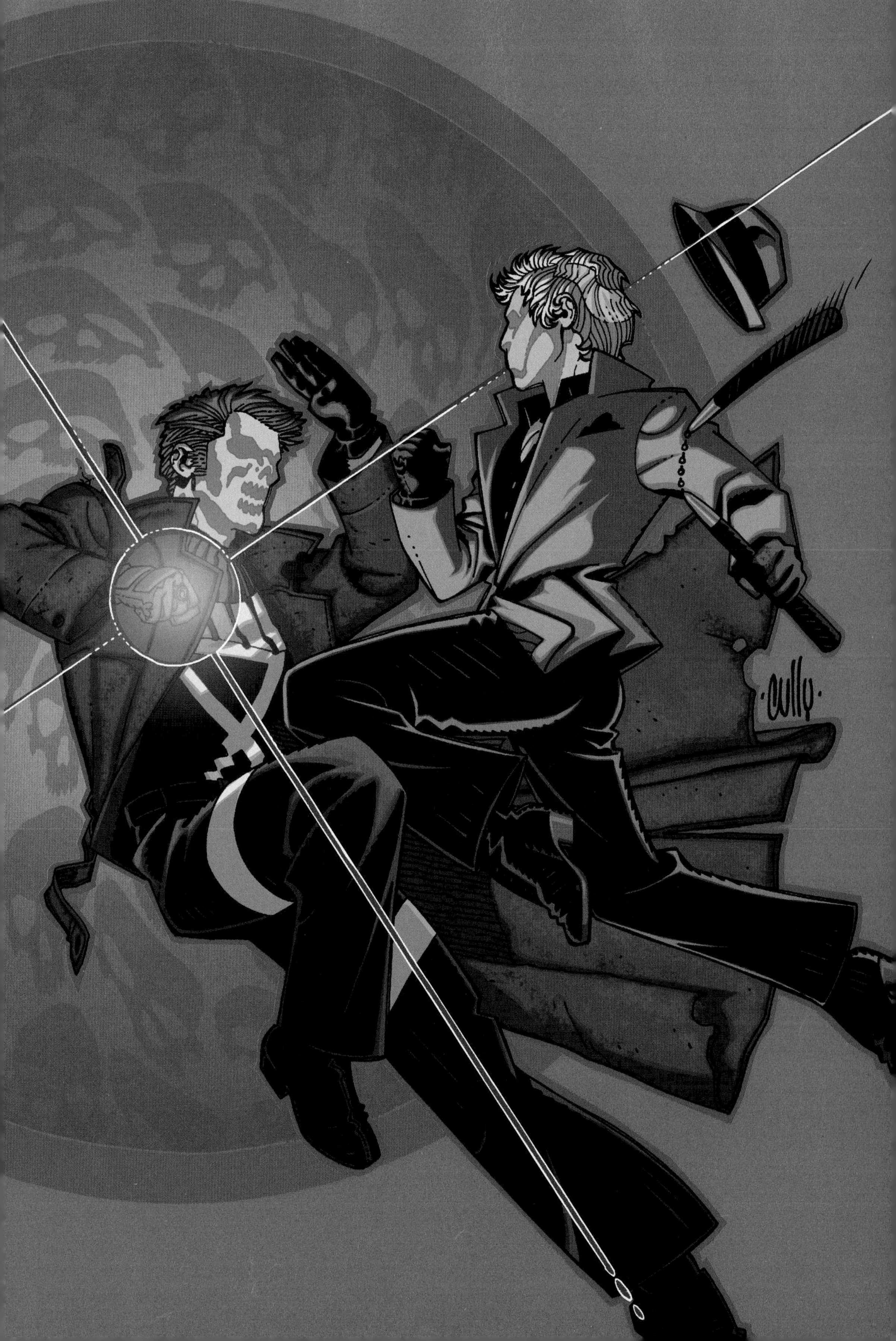
·cully·

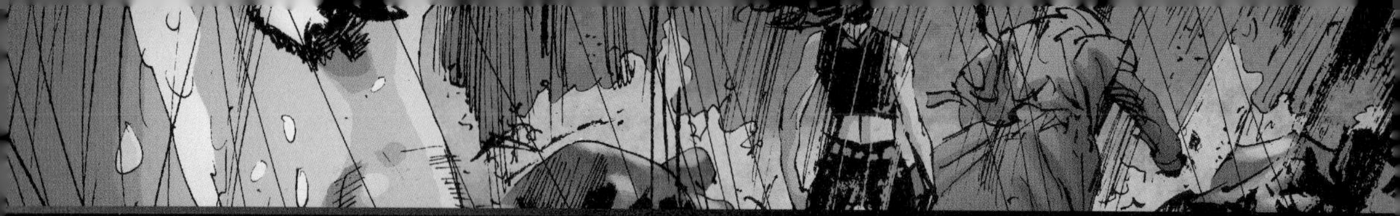

ONE MORE QUESTION

DENNIS O'NEILL
GREG RUCKA
WRITERS

DENYS COWAN
PENCILS

BILL SIENKIEWICZ
JOHN STANISCI
INKS

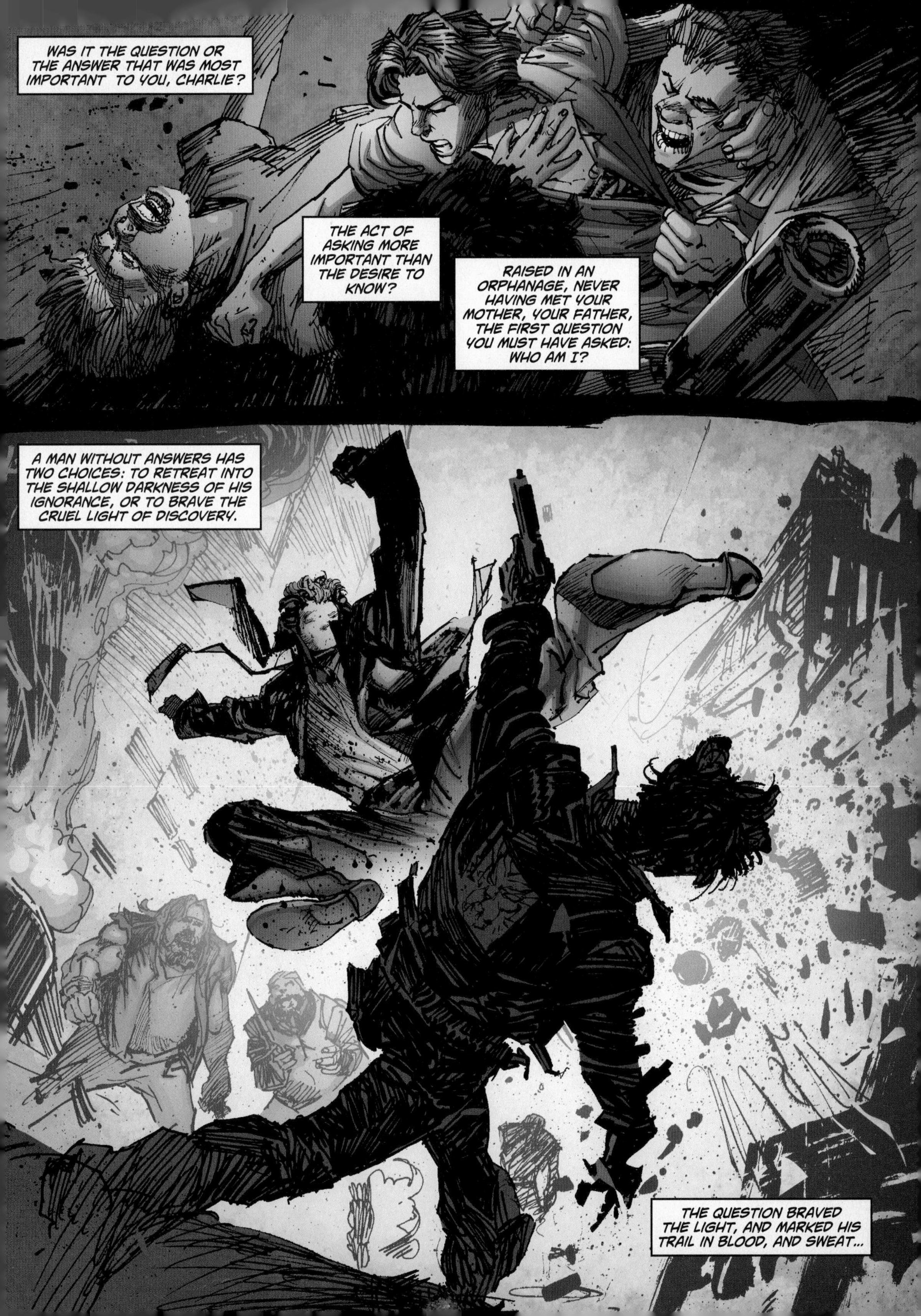
WAS IT THE QUESTION OR THE ANSWER THAT WAS MOST IMPORTANT TO YOU, CHARLIE?
THE ACT OF ASKING MORE IMPORTANT THAN THE DESIRE TO KNOW?
RAISED IN AN ORPHANAGE, NEVER HAVING MET YOUR MOTHER, YOUR FATHER, THE FIRST QUESTION YOU MUST HAVE ASKED: WHO AM I?
A MAN WITHOUT ANSWERS HAS TWO CHOICES: TO RETREAT INTO THE SHALLOW DARKNESS OF HIS IGNORANCE, OR TO BRAVE THE CRUEL LIGHT OF DISCOVERY.
THE QUESTION BRAVED THE LIGHT, AND MARKED HIS TRAIL IN BLOOD, AND SWEAT...

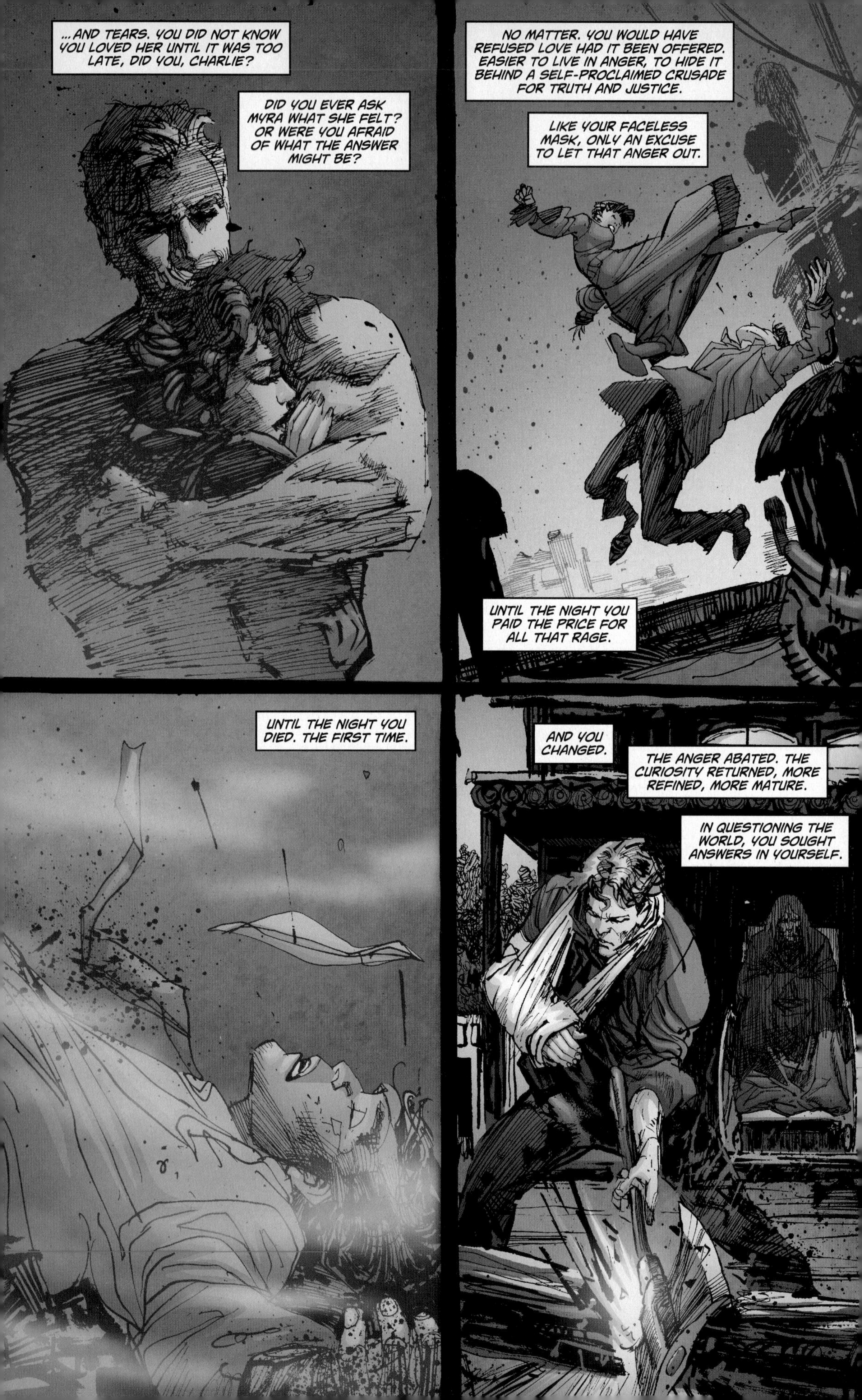
...AND TEARS. YOU DID NOT KNOW YOU LOVED HER UNTIL IT WAS TOO LATE, DID YOU, CHARLIE?
DID YOU EVER ASK MYRA WHAT SHE FELT? OR WERE YOU AFRAID OF WHAT THE ANSWER MIGHT BE?
NO MATTER. YOU WOULD HAVE REFUSED LOVE HAD IT BEEN OFFERED. EASIER TO LIVE IN ANGER, TO HIDE IT BEHIND A SELF-PROCLAIMED CRUSADE FOR TRUTH AND JUSTICE.
LIKE YOUR FACELESS MASK, ONLY AN EXCUSE TO LET THAT ANGER OUT.
UNTIL THE NIGHT YOU PAID THE PRICE FOR ALL THAT RAGE.
UNTIL THE NIGHT YOU DIED. THE FIRST TIME.
AND YOU CHANGED.
THE ANGER ABATED. THE CURIOSITY RETURNED, MORE REFINED, MORE MATURE.
IN QUESTIONING THE WORLD, YOU SOUGHT ANSWERS IN YOURSELF.

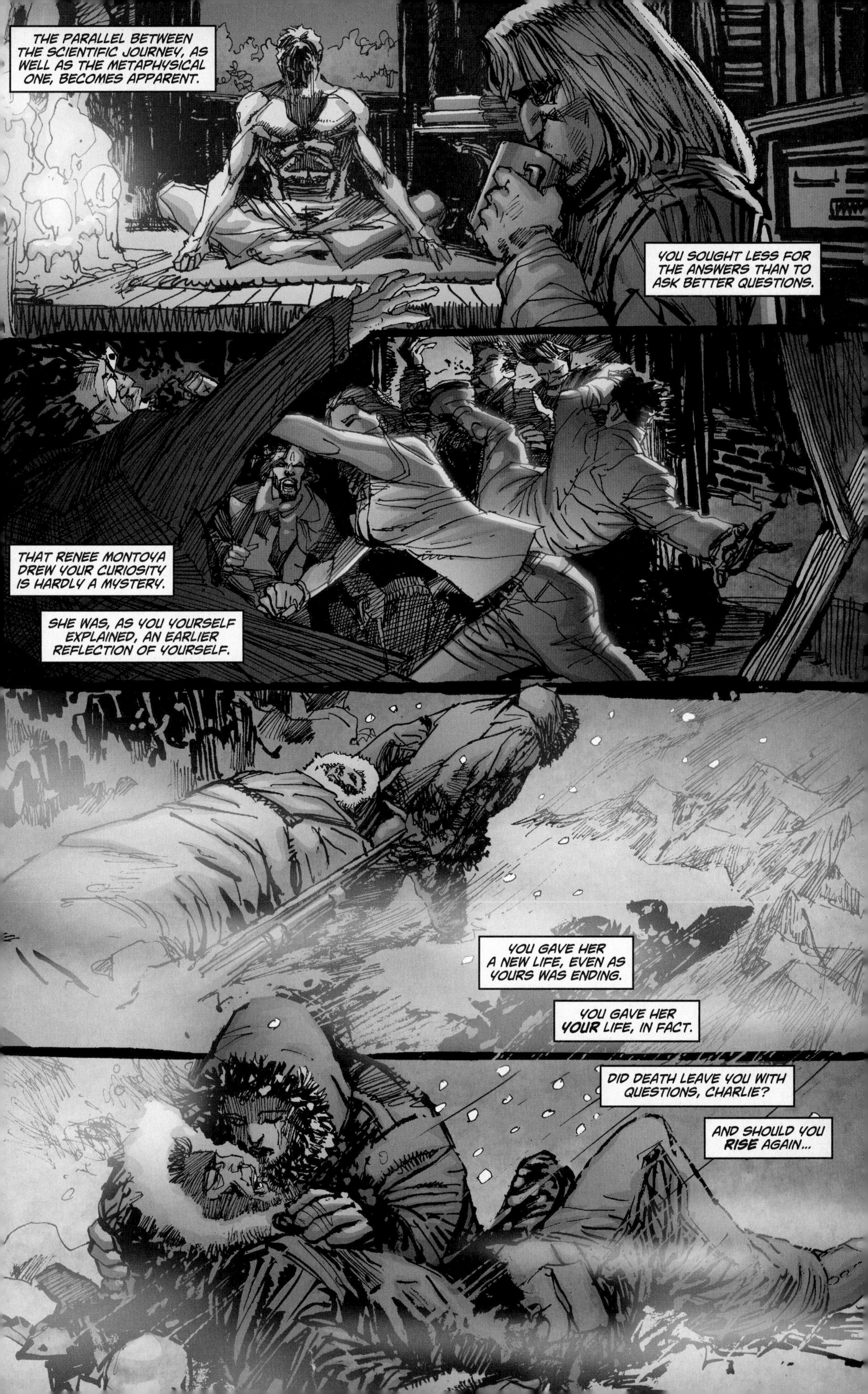
THE PARALLEL BETWEEN THE SCIENTIFIC JOURNEY, AS WELL AS THE METAPHYSICAL ONE, BECOMES APPARENT.
YOU SOUGHT LESS FOR THE ANSWERS THAN TO ASK BETTER QUESTIONS.
THAT RENEE MONTOYA DREW YOUR CURIOSITY IS HARDLY A MYSTERY.
SHE WAS, AS YOU YOURSELF EXPLAINED, AN EARLIER REFLECTION OF YOURSELF.
YOU GAVE HER A NEW LIFE, EVEN AS YOURS WAS ENDING.
YOU GAVE HER **YOUR** LIFE, IN FACT.
DID DEATH LEAVE YOU WITH QUESTIONS, CHARLIE?
AND SHOULD YOU **RISE** AGAIN...

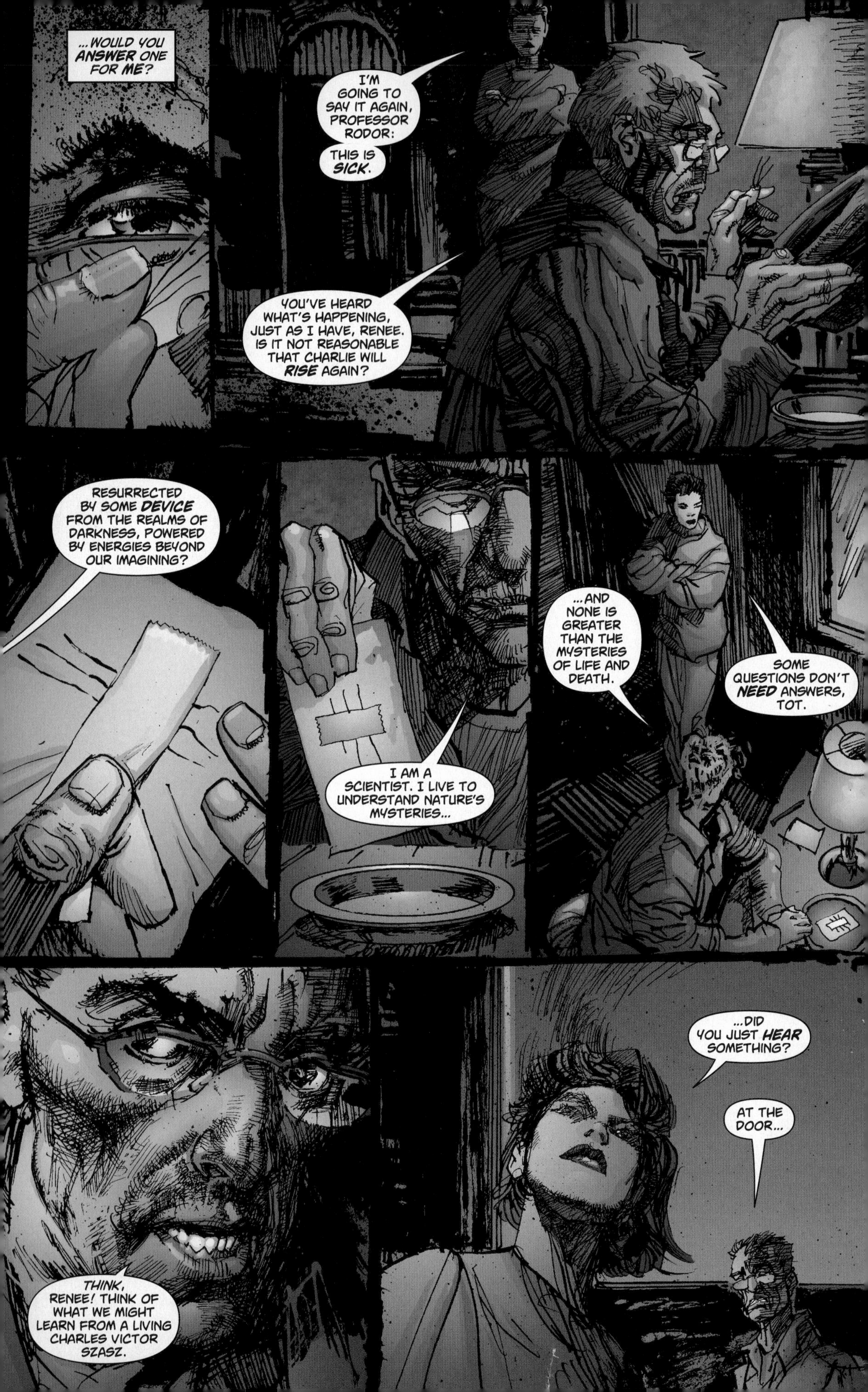
...WOULD YOU ANSWER ONE FOR ME?
I'M GOING TO SAY IT AGAIN, PROFESSOR RODOR:
THIS IS SICK.
YOU'VE HEARD WHAT'S HAPPENING, JUST AS I HAVE, RENEE. IS IT NOT REASONABLE THAT CHARLIE WILL RISE AGAIN?
RESURRECTED BY SOME DEVICE FROM THE REALMS OF DARKNESS, POWERED BY ENERGIES BEYOND OUR IMAGINING?
I AM A SCIENTIST. I LIVE TO UNDERSTAND NATURE'S MYSTERIES...
...AND NONE IS GREATER THAN THE MYSTERIES OF LIFE AND DEATH.
SOME QUESTIONS DON'T NEED ANSWERS, TOT.
THINK, RENEE! THINK OF WHAT WE MIGHT LEARN FROM A LIVING CHARLES VICTOR SZASZ.
...DID YOU JUST HEAR SOMETHING?
AT THE DOOR...

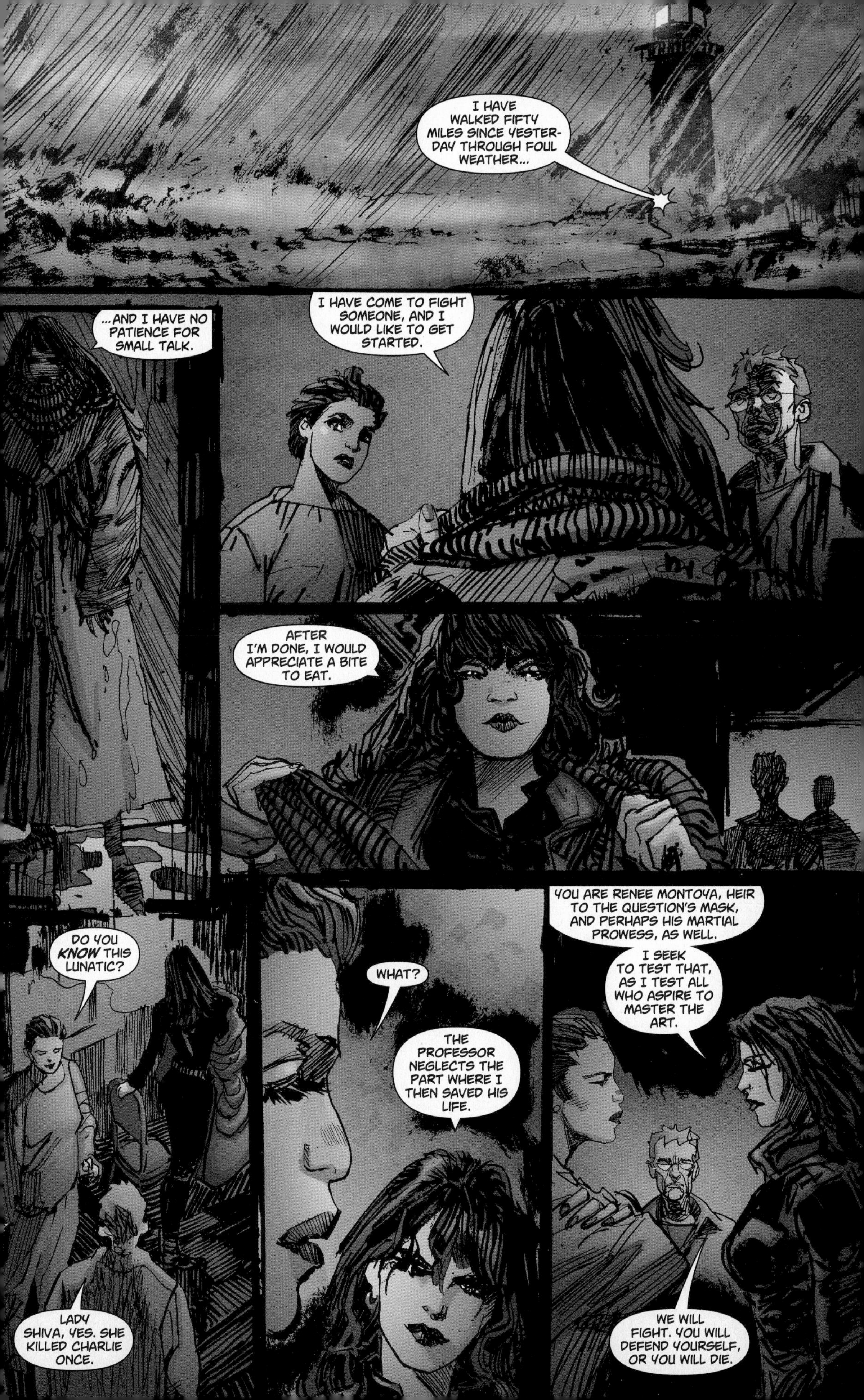
I HAVE WALKED FIFTY MILES SINCE YESTER-DAY THROUGH FOUL WEATHER...
...AND I HAVE NO PATIENCE FOR SMALL TALK.
I HAVE COME TO FIGHT SOMEONE, AND I WOULD LIKE TO GET STARTED.
AFTER I'M DONE, I WOULD APPRECIATE A BITE TO EAT.
DO YOU KNOW THIS LUNATIC?
LADY SHIVA, YES. SHE KILLED CHARLIE ONCE.
WHAT?
THE PROFESSOR NEGLECTS THE PART WHERE I THEN SAVED HIS LIFE.
YOU ARE RENEE MONTOYA, HEIR TO THE QUESTION'S MASK, AND PERHAPS HIS MARTIAL PROWESS, AS WELL.
I SEEK TO TEST THAT, AS I TEST ALL WHO ASPIRE TO MASTER THE ART.
WE WILL FIGHT. YOU WILL DEFEND YOURSELF, OR YOU WILL DIE.

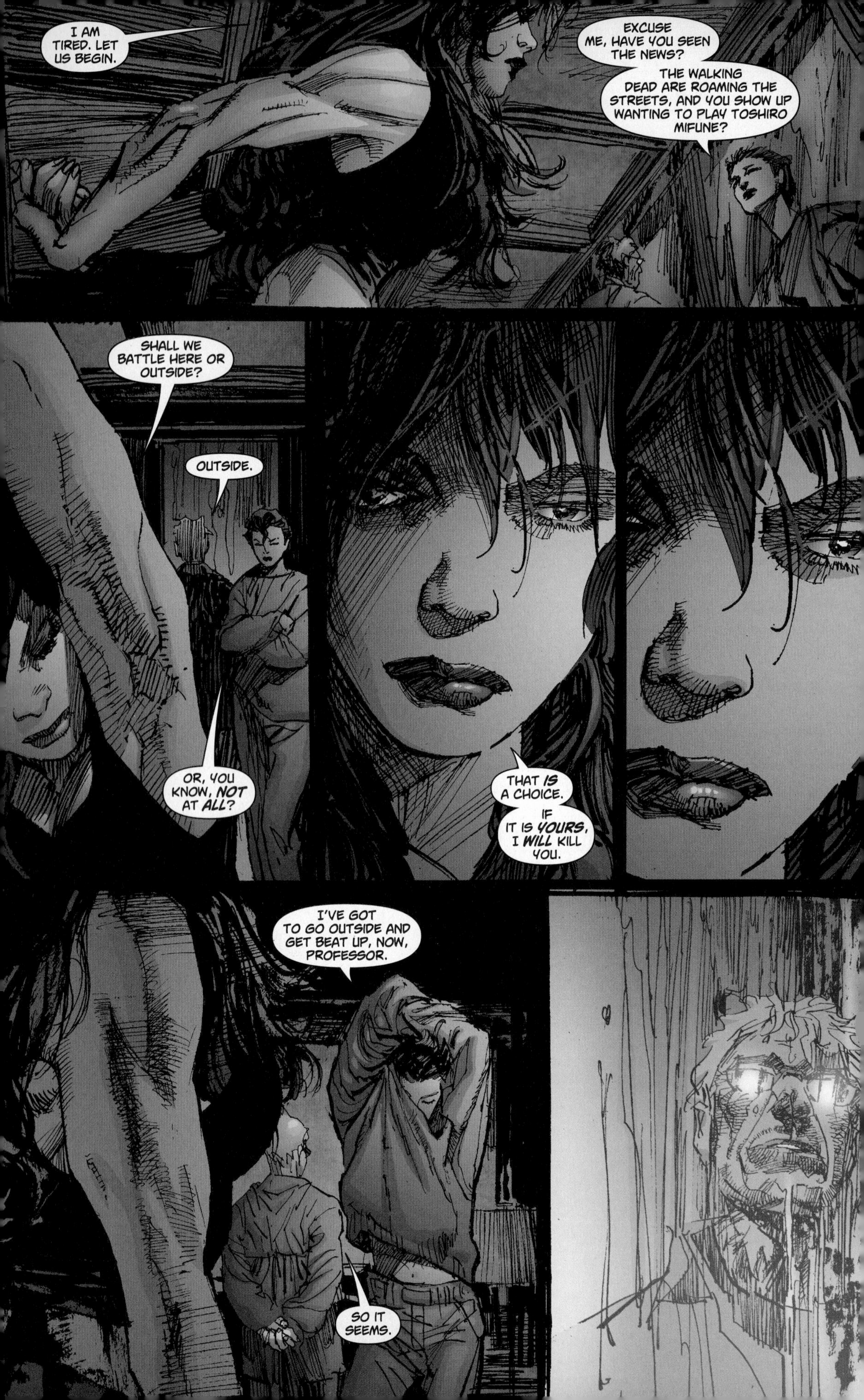

I AM TIRED. LET US BEGIN.
EXCUSE ME, HAVE YOU SEEN THE NEWS?
THE WALKING DEAD ARE ROAMING THE STREETS, AND YOU SHOW UP WANTING TO PLAY TOSHIRO MIFUNE?
SHALL WE BATTLE HERE OR OUTSIDE?
OUTSIDE.
OR, YOU KNOW, NOT AT ALL?
THAT IS A CHOICE.
IF IT IS YOURS, I WILL KILL YOU.
I'VE GOT TO GO OUTSIDE AND GET BEAT UP, NOW, PROFESSOR.
SO IT SEEMS.

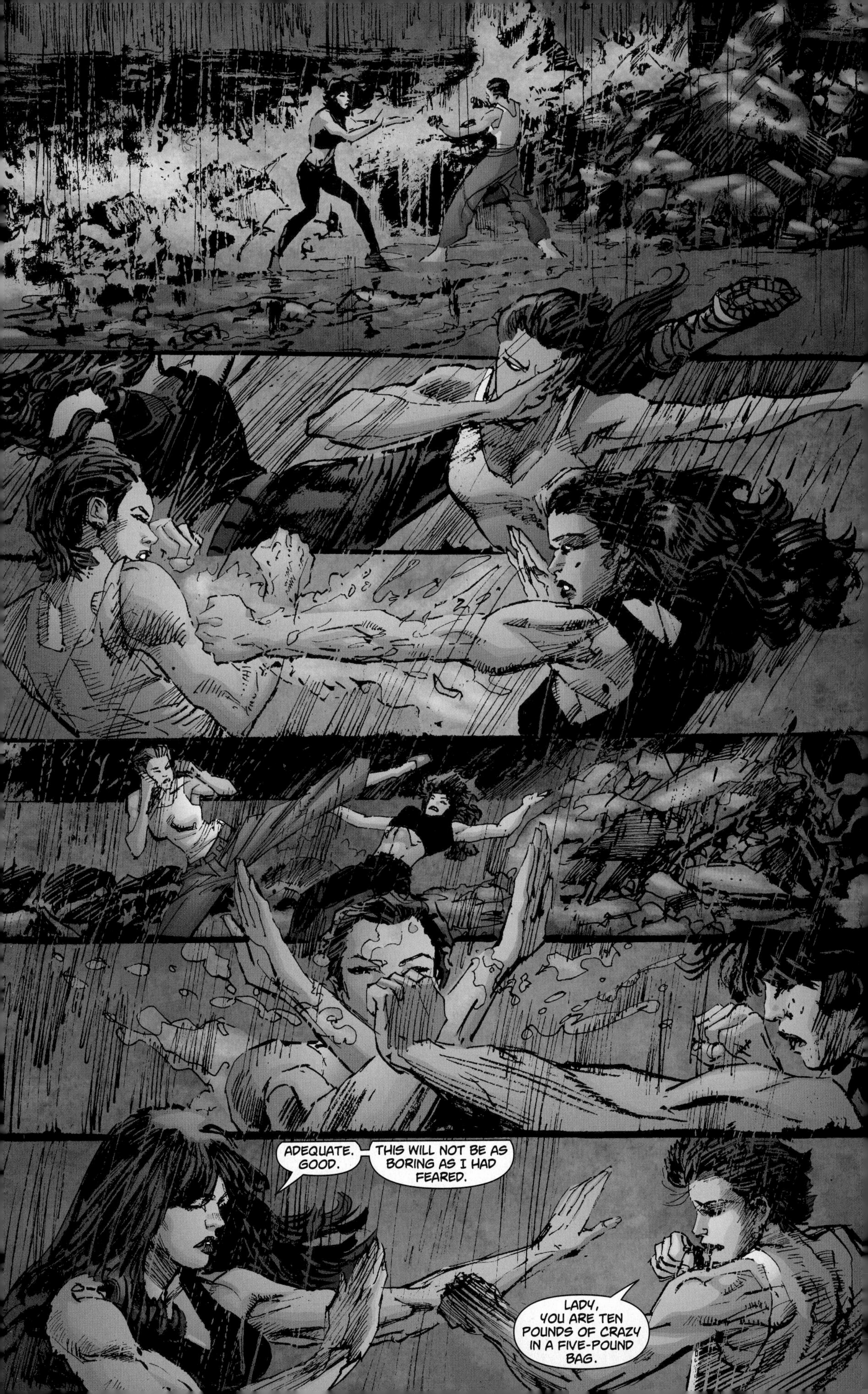
ADEQUATE. GOOD.
THIS WILL NOT BE AS BORING AS I HAD FEARED.
LADY, YOU ARE TEN POUNDS OF CRAZY IN A FIVE-POUND BAG.

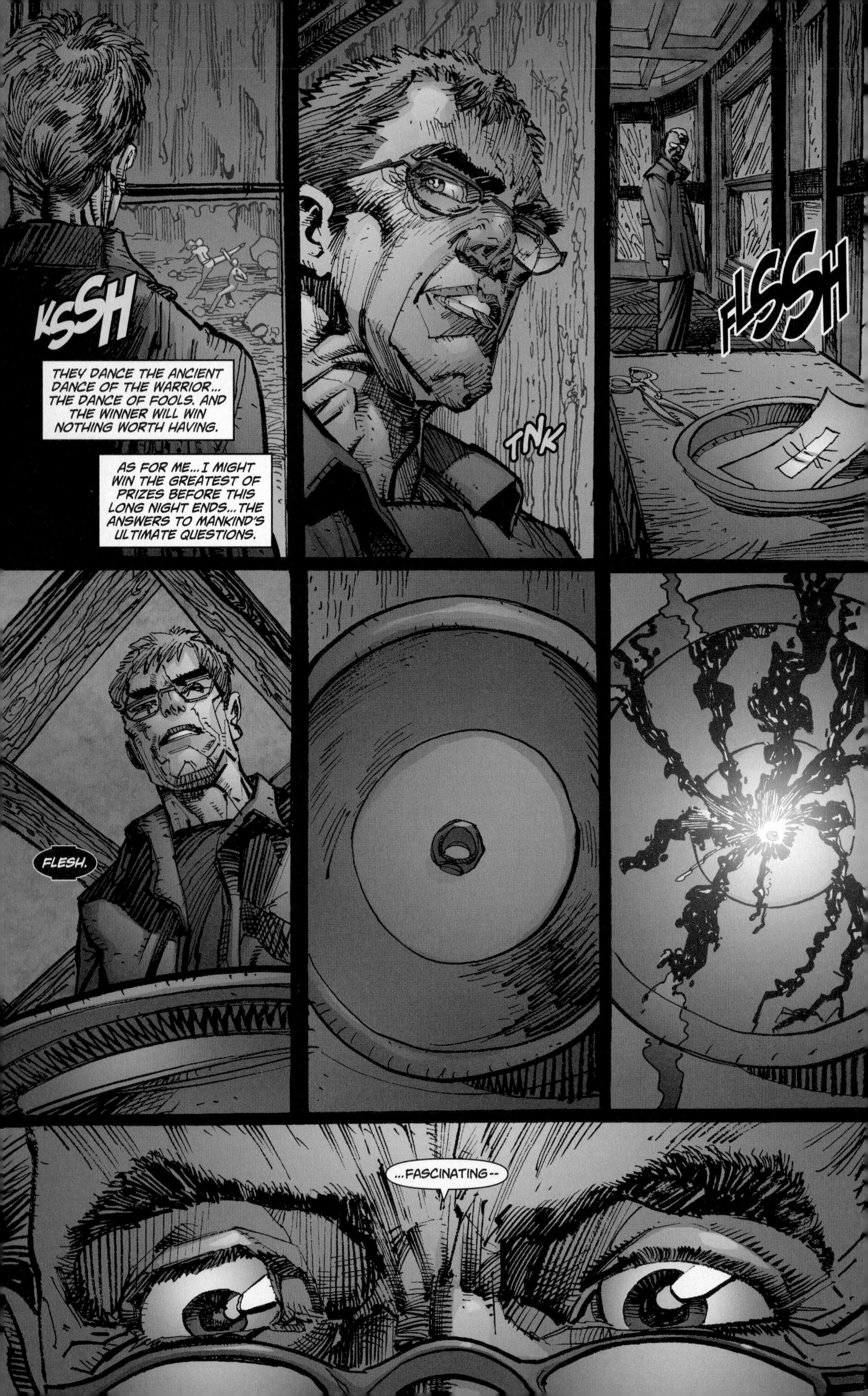
KSSH
THEY DANCE THE ANCIENT DANCE OF THE WARRIOR... THE DANCE OF FOOLS. AND THE WINNER WILL WIN NOTHING WORTH HAVING.
AS FOR ME... I MIGHT WIN THE GREATEST OF PRIZES BEFORE THIS LONG NIGHT ENDS... THE ANSWERS TO MANKIND'S ULTIMATE QUESTIONS.
TNK
FLSSH
FLESH.
...FASCINATING--

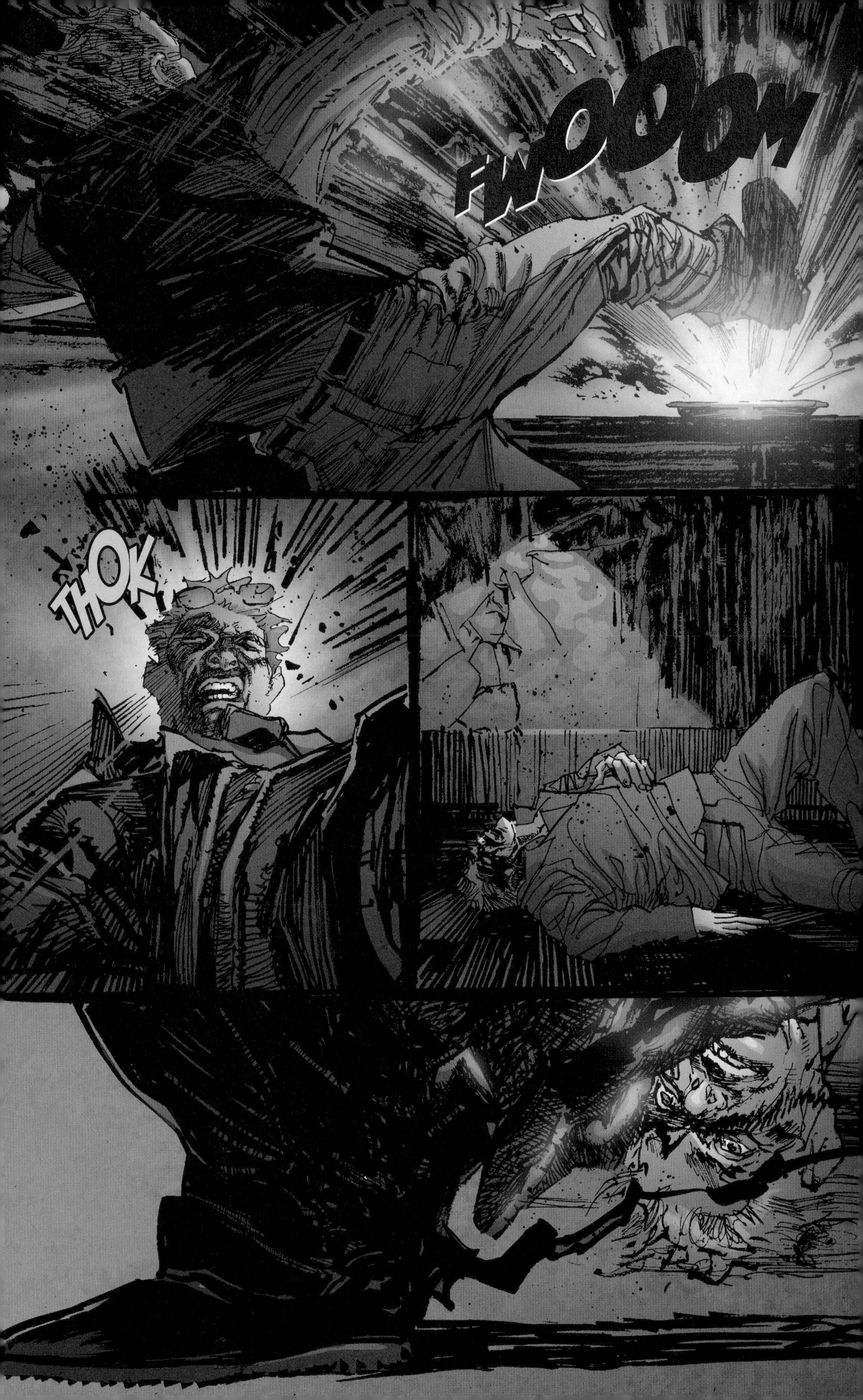
FWOOOOM
THOK

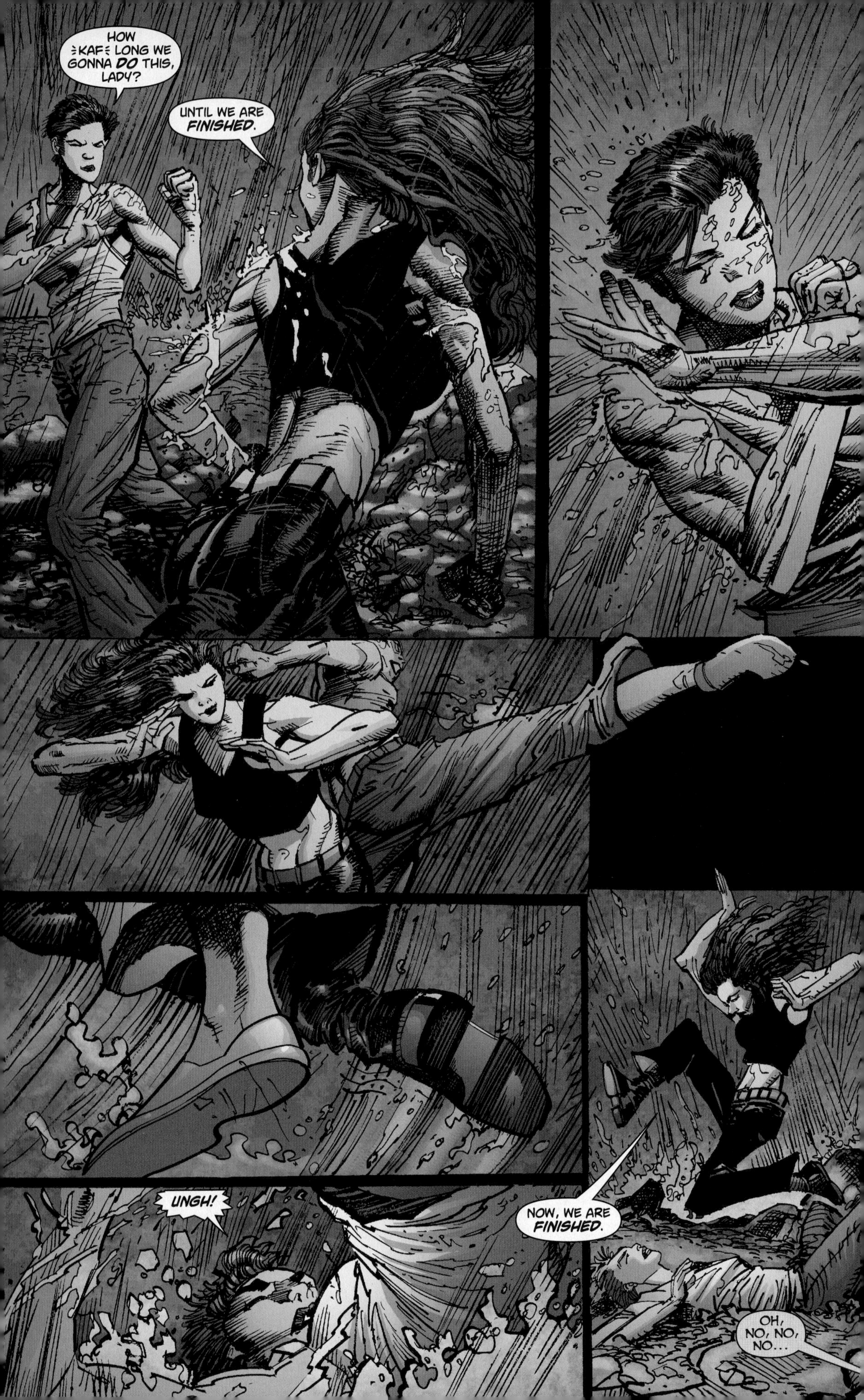
HOW
KAF LONG WE GONNA DO THIS, LADY?
UNTIL WE ARE FINISHED.
UNGH!
NOW, WE ARE FINISHED.
OH, NO, NO, NO...

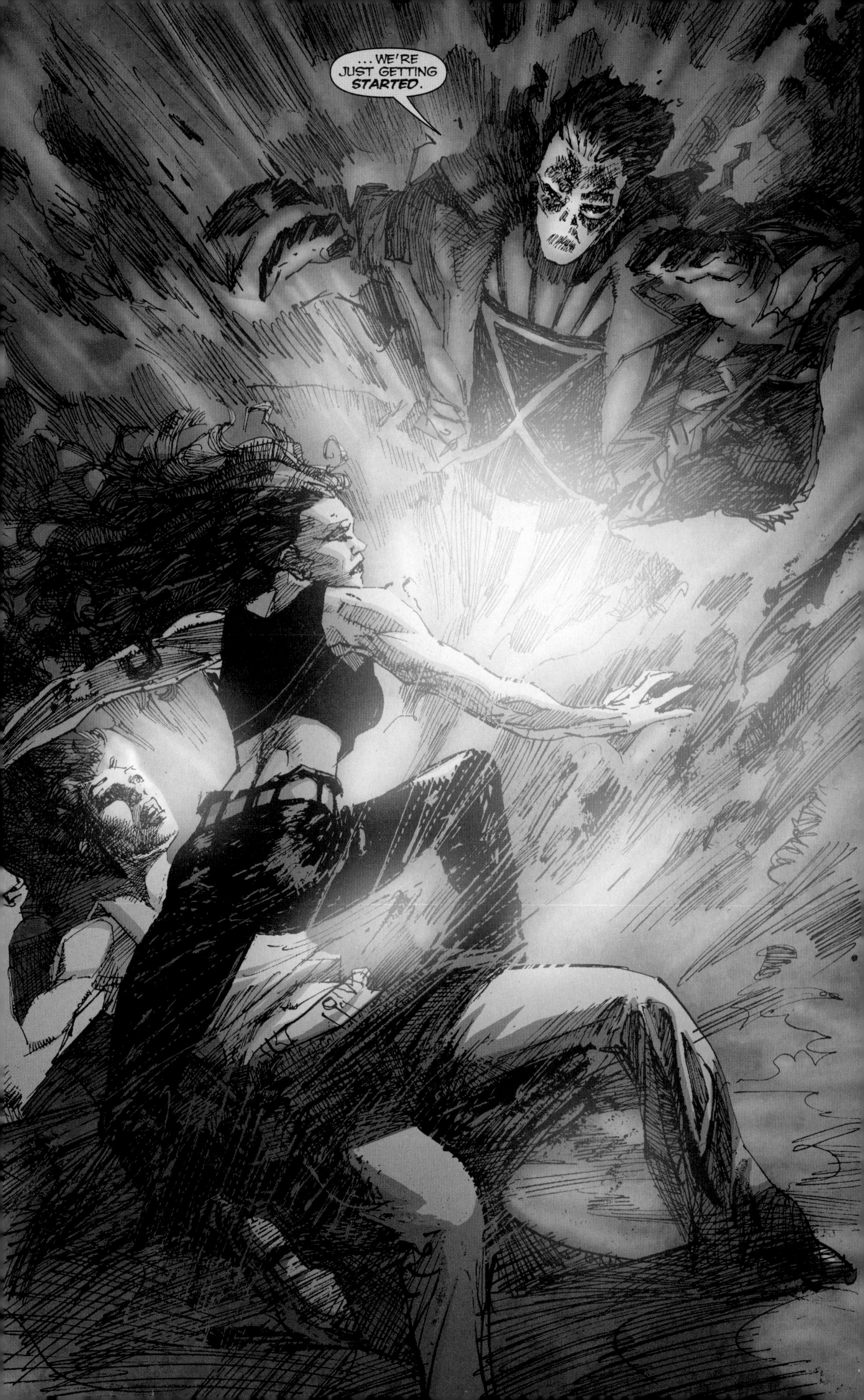
...WE'RE JUST GETTING STARTED.

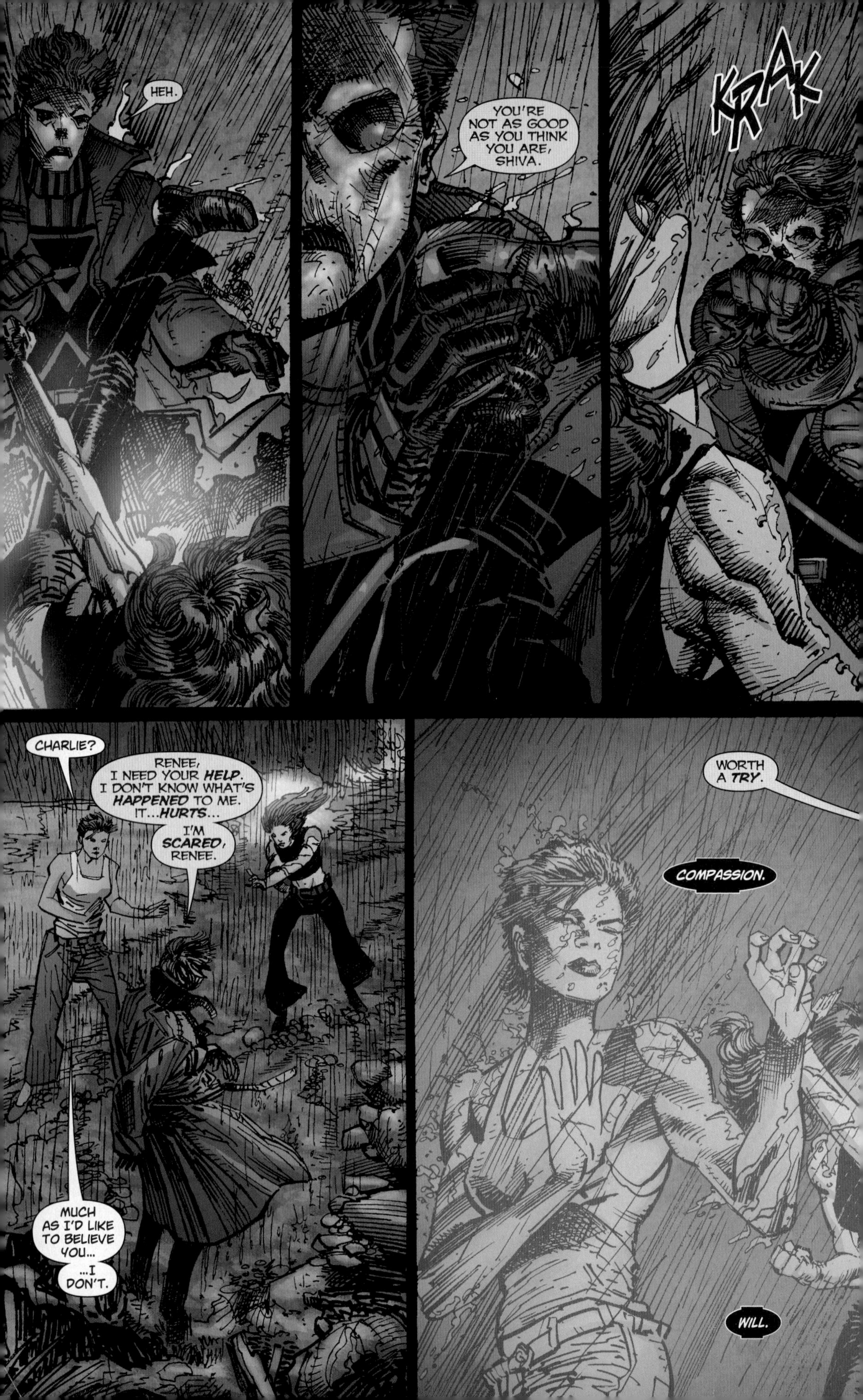
HEH.
YOU'RE NOT AS GOOD AS YOU THINK YOU ARE, SHIVA.
KRAK
CHARLIE?
RENEE, I NEED YOUR **HELP**. I DON'T KNOW WHAT'S **HAPPENED** TO ME. IT...**HURTS**...
I'M **SCARED**, RENEE.
MUCH AS I'D LIKE TO BELIEVE YOU...
...I DON'T.
WORTH A **TRY**.
COMPASSION.
WILL.

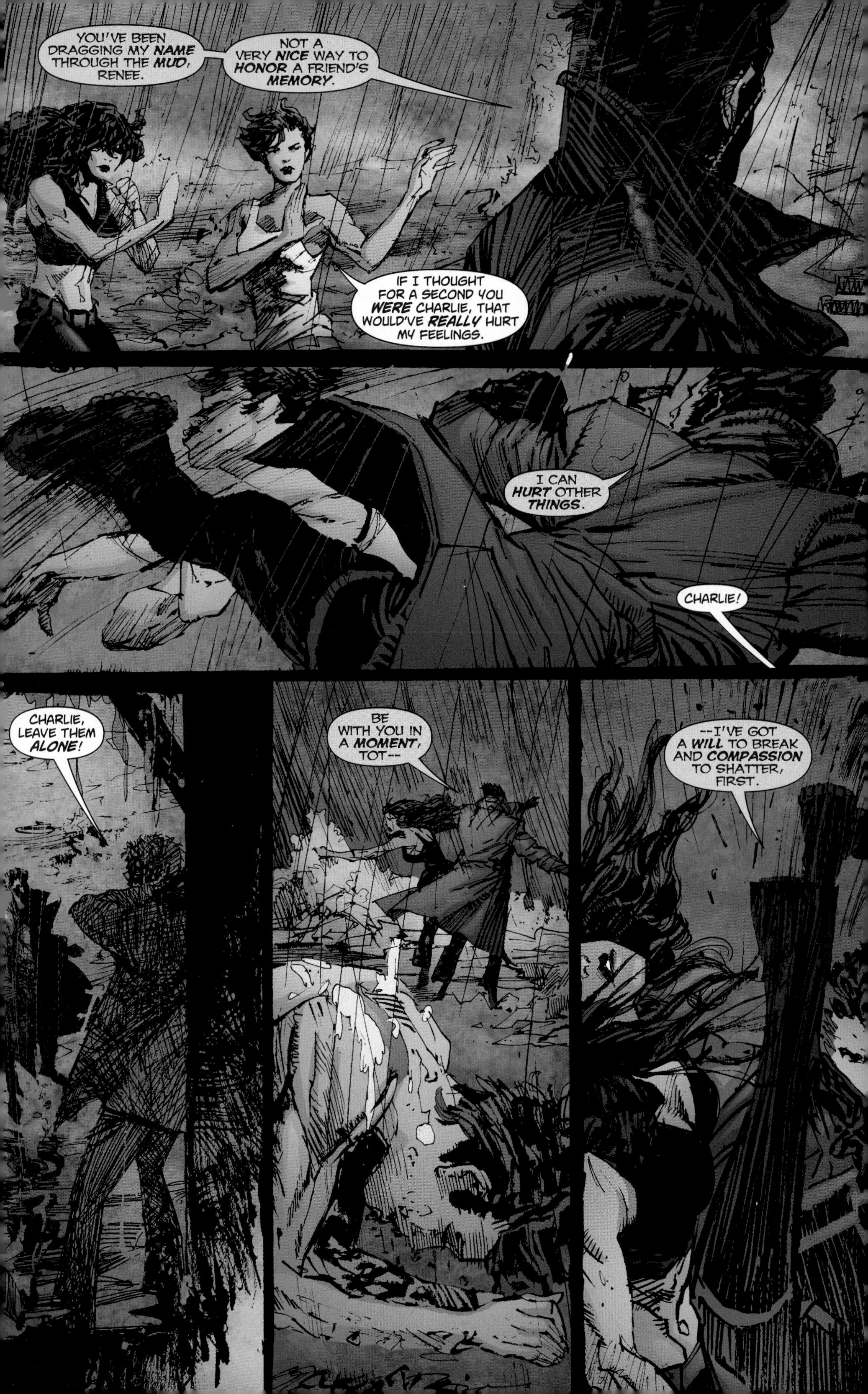
YOU'VE BEEN DRAGGING MY NAME THROUGH THE MUD, RENEE.
NOT A VERY NICE WAY TO HONOR A FRIEND'S MEMORY.
IF I THOUGHT FOR A SECOND YOU WERE CHARLIE, THAT WOULD'VE REALLY HURT MY FEELINGS.
I CAN HURT OTHER THINGS.
CHARLIE!
CHARLIE, LEAVE THEM ALONE!
BE WITH YOU IN A MOMENT, TOT--
--I'VE GOT A WILL TO BREAK AND COMPASSION TO SHATTER, FIRST.

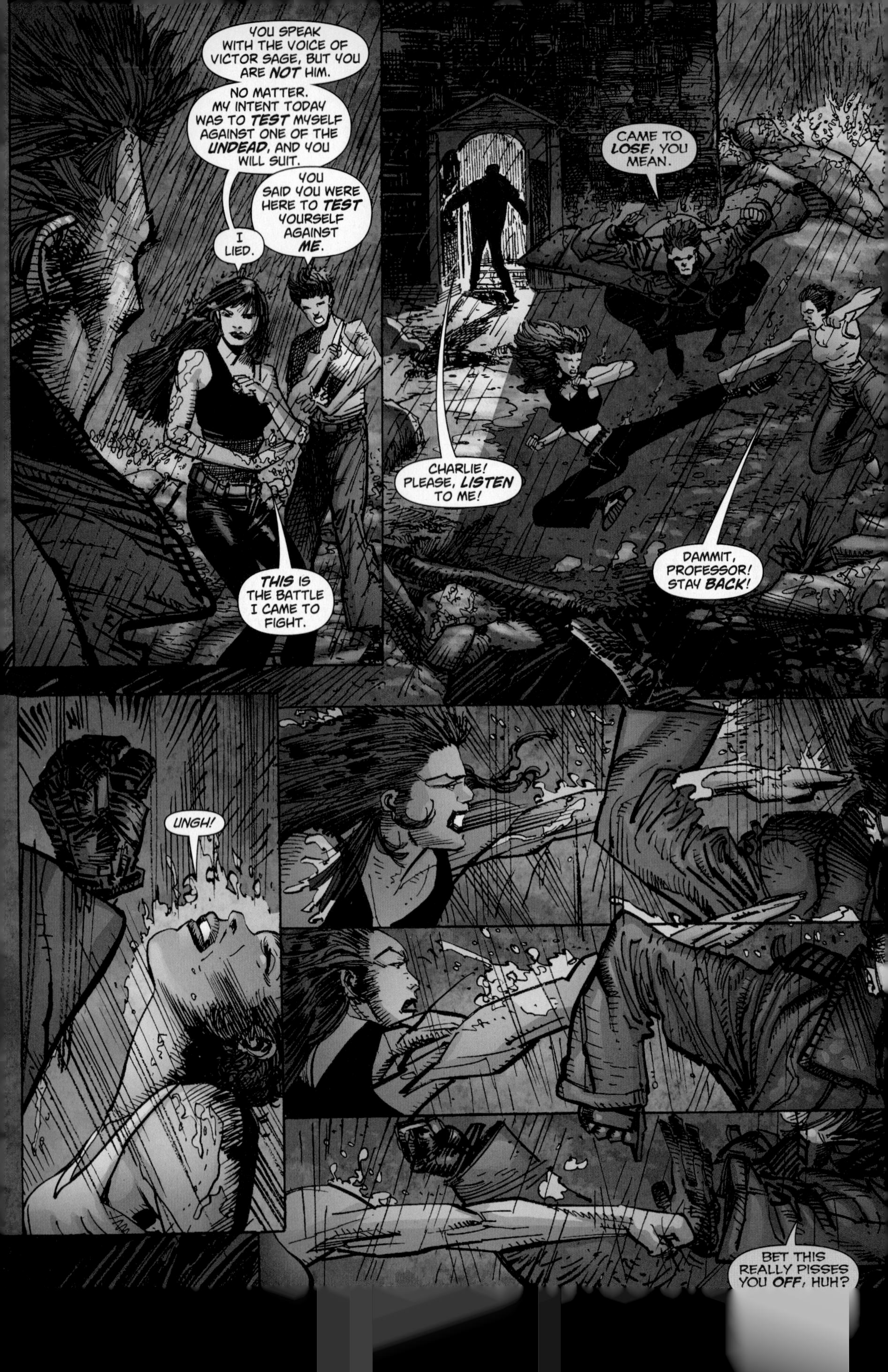
YOU SPEAK WITH THE VOICE OF VICTOR SAGE, BUT YOU ARE NOT HIM.
NO MATTER. MY INTENT TODAY WAS TO TEST MYSELF AGAINST ONE OF THE UNDEAD, AND YOU WILL SUIT.
YOU SAID YOU WERE HERE TO TEST YOURSELF AGAINST ME.
I LIED.
THIS IS THE BATTLE I CAME TO FIGHT.
CAME TO LOSE, YOU MEAN.
CHARLIE! PLEASE, LISTEN TO ME!
DAMMIT, PROFESSOR! STAY BACK!
UNGH!
BET THIS REALLY PISSES YOU OFF, HUH?

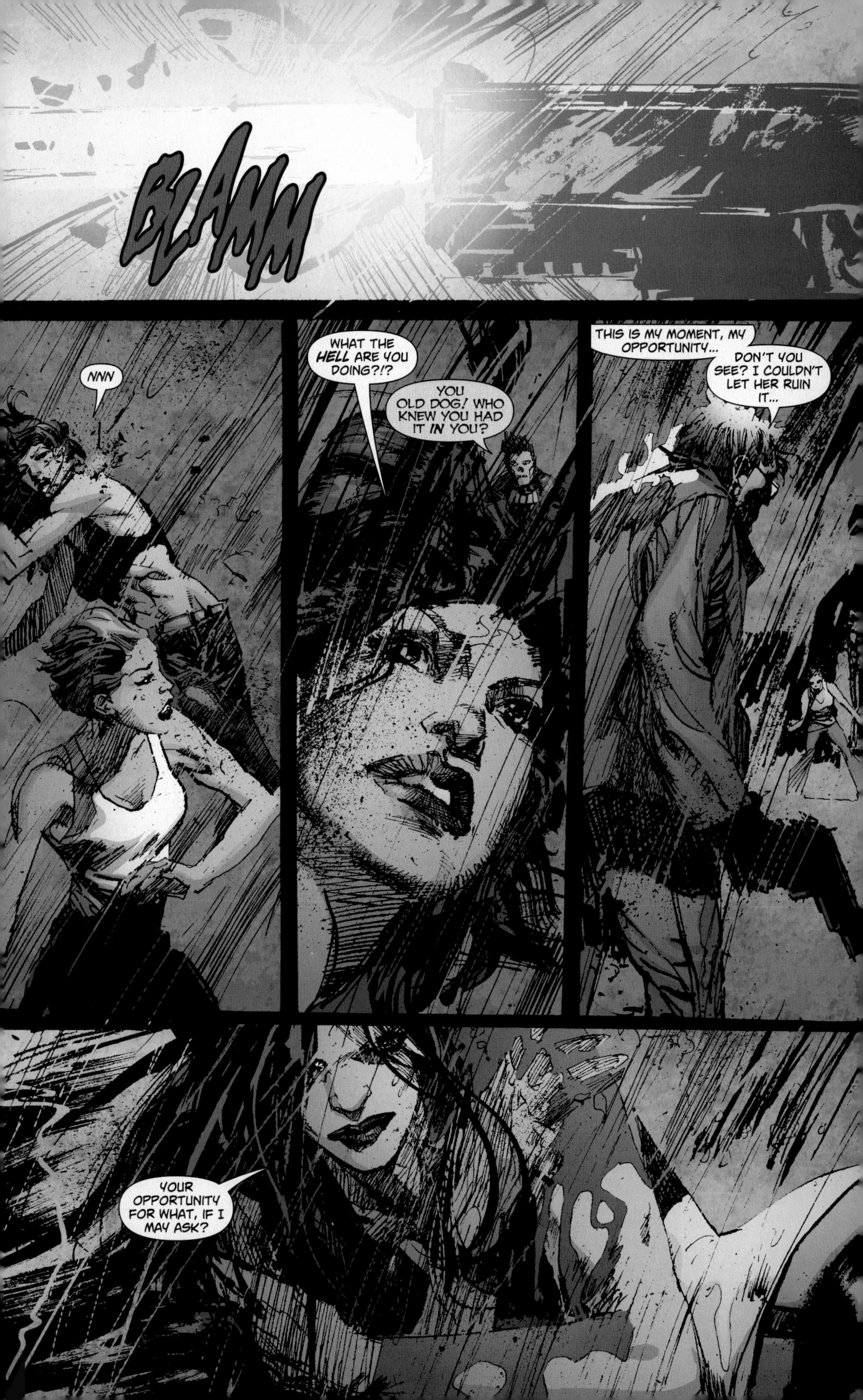
BLAMM
NNN
WHAT THE HELL ARE YOU DOING?!?
YOU OLD DOG! WHO KNEW YOU HAD IT IN YOU?
THIS IS MY MOMENT, MY OPPORTUNITY...
DON'T YOU SEE? I COULDN'T LET HER RUIN IT...
YOUR OPPORTUNITY FOR WHAT, IF I MAY ASK?

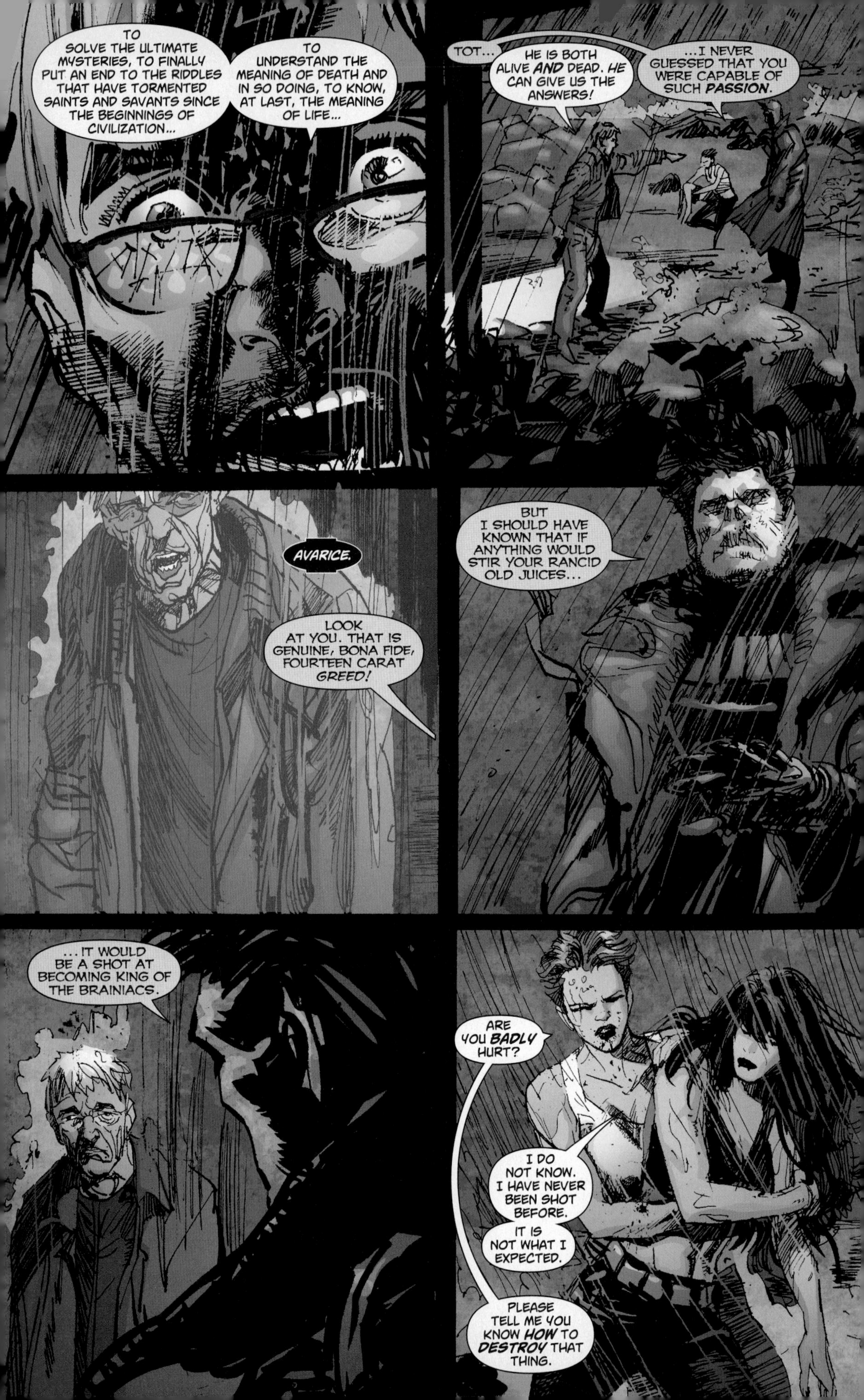
TO SOLVE THE ULTIMATE MYSTERIES, TO FINALLY PUT AN END TO THE RIDDLES THAT HAVE TORMENTED SAINTS AND SAVANTS SINCE THE BEGINNINGS OF CIVILIZATION...
TO UNDERSTAND THE MEANING OF DEATH AND IN SO DOING, TO KNOW, AT LAST, THE MEANING OF LIFE...
HE IS BOTH ALIVE AND DEAD. HE CAN GIVE US THE ANSWERS!
TOT... ...I NEVER GUESSED THAT YOU WERE CAPABLE OF SUCH PASSION.
AVARICE.
LOOK AT YOU. THAT IS GENUINE, BONA FIDE, FOURTEEN CARAT GREED!
BUT I SHOULD HAVE KNOWN THAT IF ANYTHING WOULD STIR YOUR RANCID OLD JUICES...
...IT WOULD BE A SHOT AT BECOMING KING OF THE BRAINIACS.
ARE YOU BADLY HURT?
I DO NOT KNOW. I HAVE NEVER BEEN SHOT BEFORE.
IT IS NOT WHAT I EXPECTED.
PLEASE TELL ME YOU KNOW HOW TO DESTROY THAT THING.

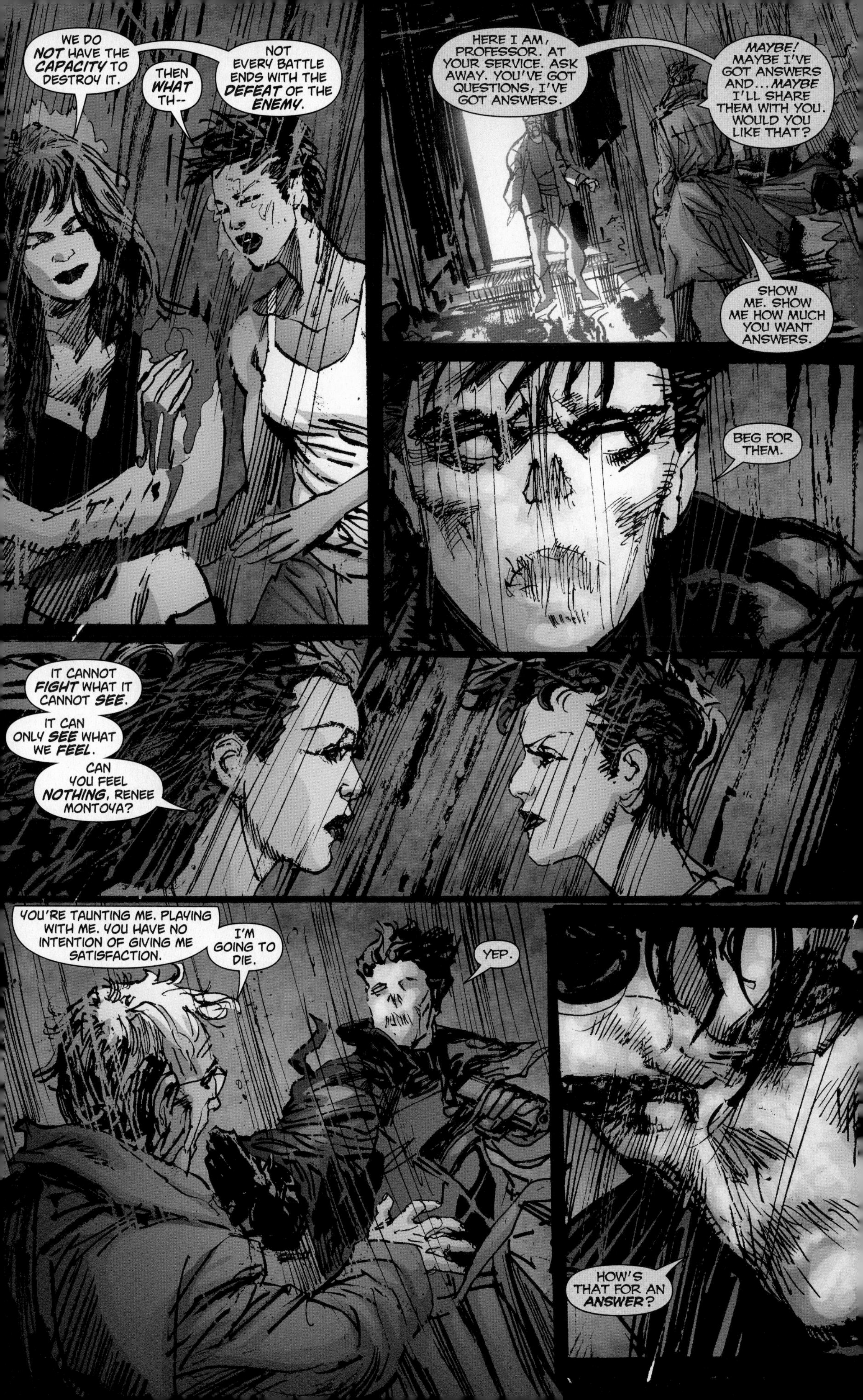
WE DO NOT HAVE THE CAPACITY TO DESTROY IT.
THEN WHAT TH--
NOT EVERY BATTLE ENDS WITH THE DEFEAT OF THE ENEMY.
HERE I AM, PROFESSOR. AT YOUR SERVICE. ASK AWAY. YOU'VE GOT QUESTIONS, I'VE GOT ANSWERS.
MAYBE! MAYBE I'VE GOT ANSWERS AND... MAYBE I'LL SHARE THEM WITH YOU. WOULD YOU LIKE THAT?
SHOW ME. SHOW ME HOW MUCH YOU WANT ANSWERS.
BEG FOR THEM.
IT CANNOT FIGHT WHAT IT CANNOT SEE.
IT CAN ONLY SEE WHAT WE FEEL.
CAN YOU FEEL NOTHING, RENEE MONTOYA?
YOU'RE TAUNTING ME. PLAYING WITH ME. YOU HAVE NO INTENTION OF GIVING ME SATISFACTION.
I'M GOING TO DIE.
YEP.
HOW'S THAT FOR AN ANSWER?

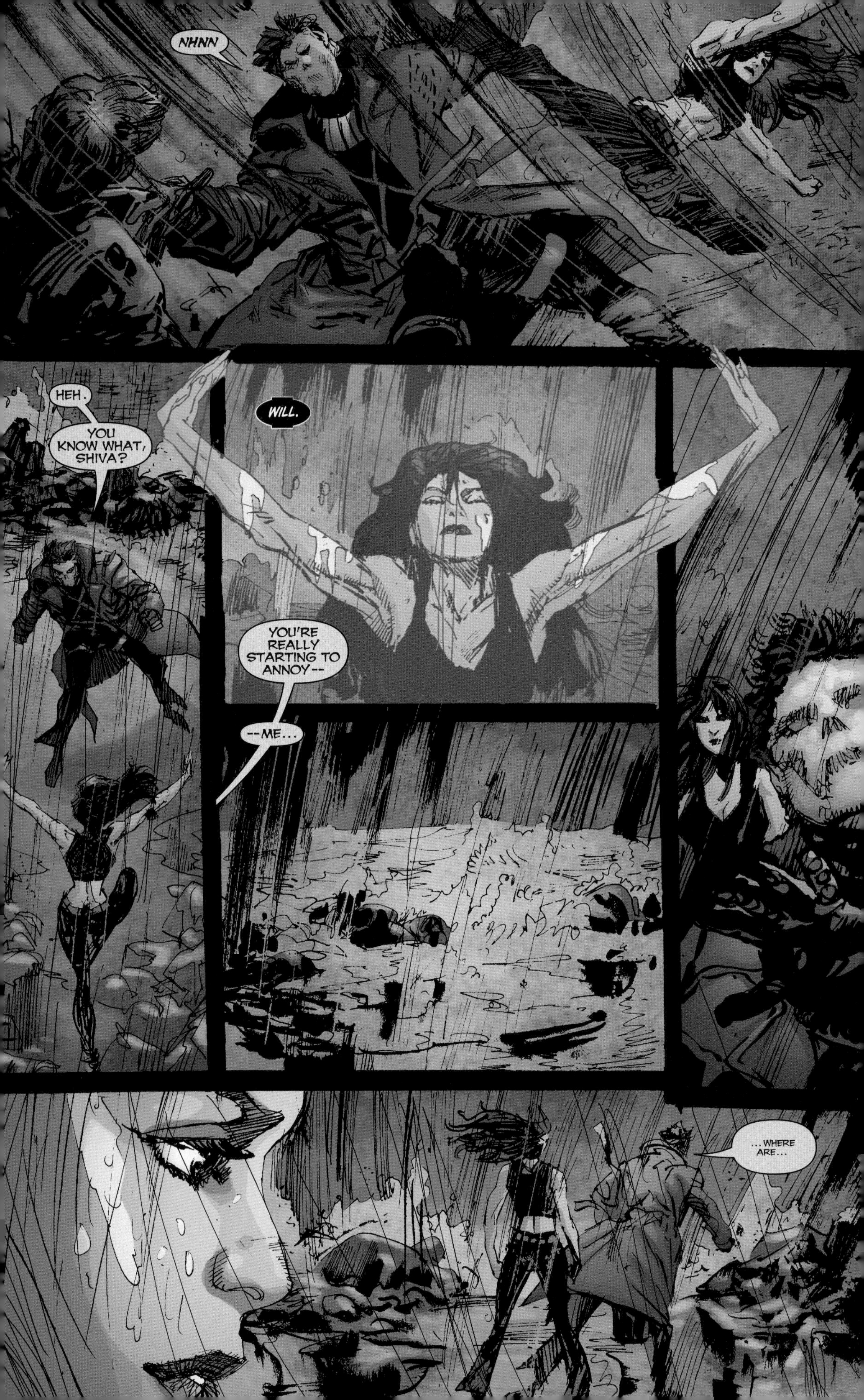
NHNN
HEH.
YOU KNOW WHAT, SHIVA?
WILL.
YOU'RE REALLY STARTING TO ANNOY--
--ME...
...WHERE ARE...

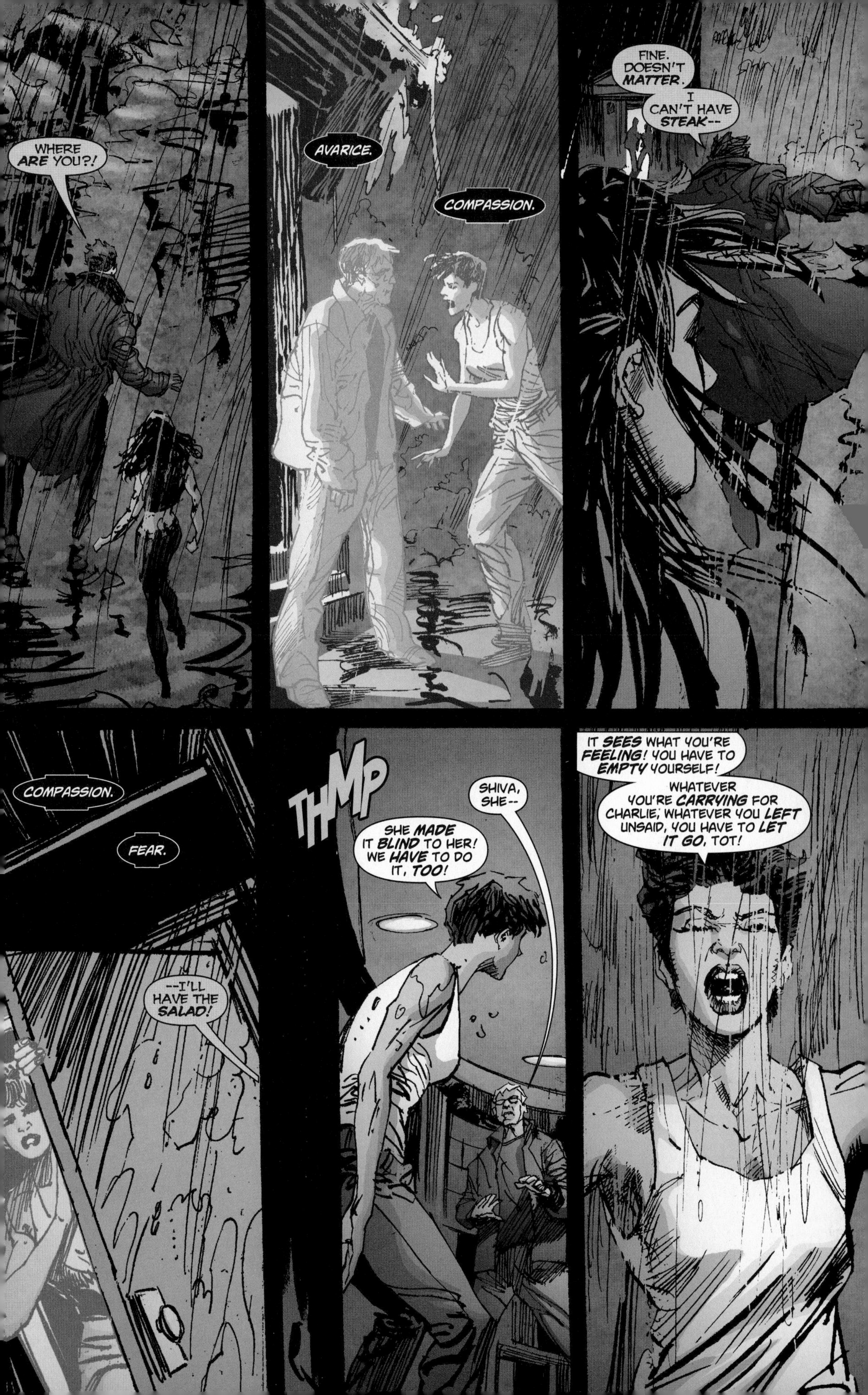
WHERE ARE YOU?!
AVARICE.
COMPASSION.
FINE. DOESN'T MATTER.
I CAN'T HAVE STEAK--
COMPASSION.
FEAR.
--I'LL HAVE THE SALAD!
THMP
SHIVA, SHE--
SHE MADE IT BLIND TO HER! WE HAVE TO DO IT, TOO!
IT SEES WHAT YOU'RE FEELING! YOU HAVE TO EMPTY YOURSELF!
WHATEVER YOU'RE CARRYING FOR CHARLIE, WHATEVER YOU LEFT UNSAID, YOU HAVE TO LET IT GO, TOT!

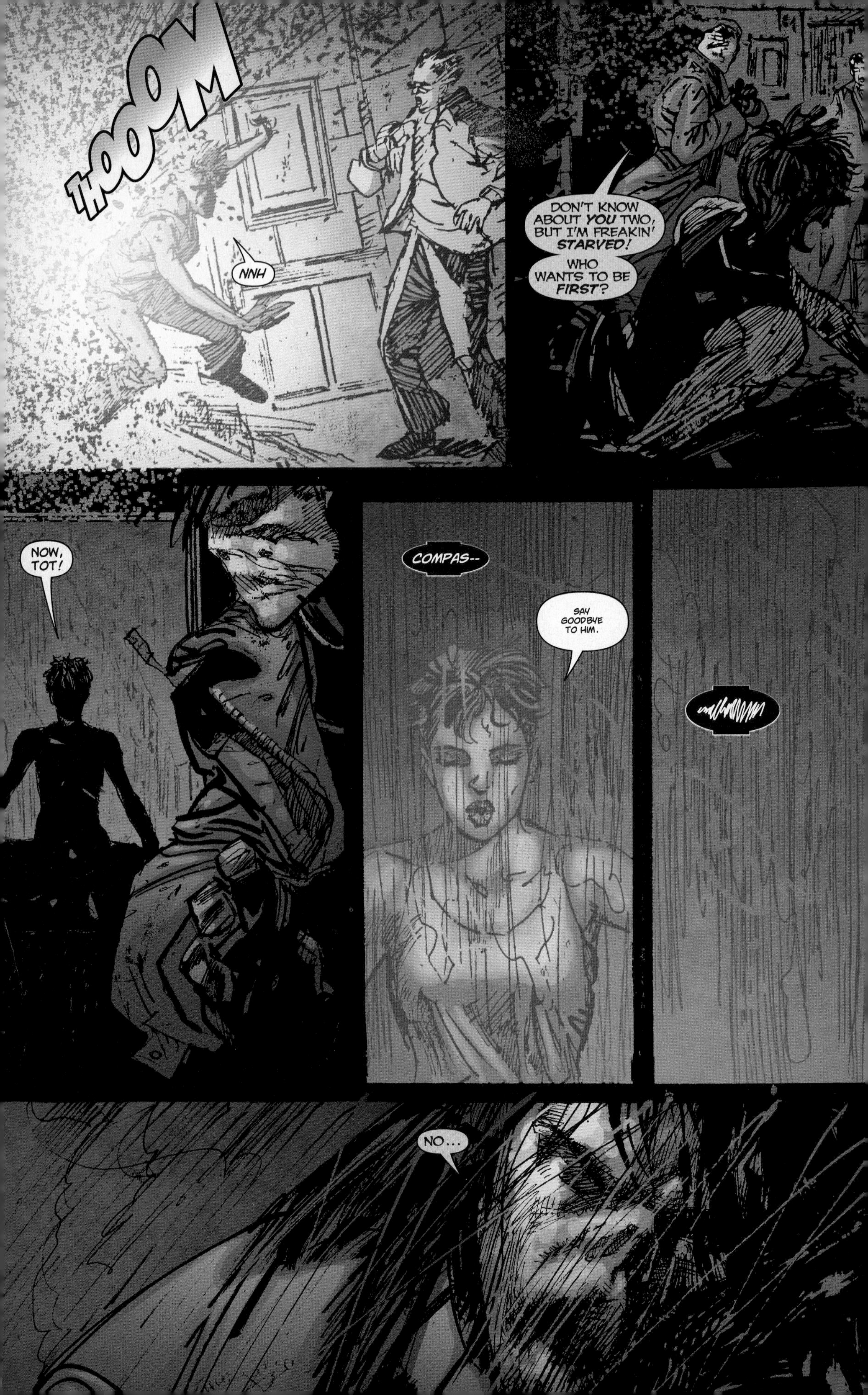
THOOOM
NNH
DON'T KNOW ABOUT YOU TWO, BUT I'M FREAKIN' STARVED!
WHO WANTS TO BE FIRST?
NOW, TOT!
COMPAS--
SAY GOODBYE TO HIM.
NO...

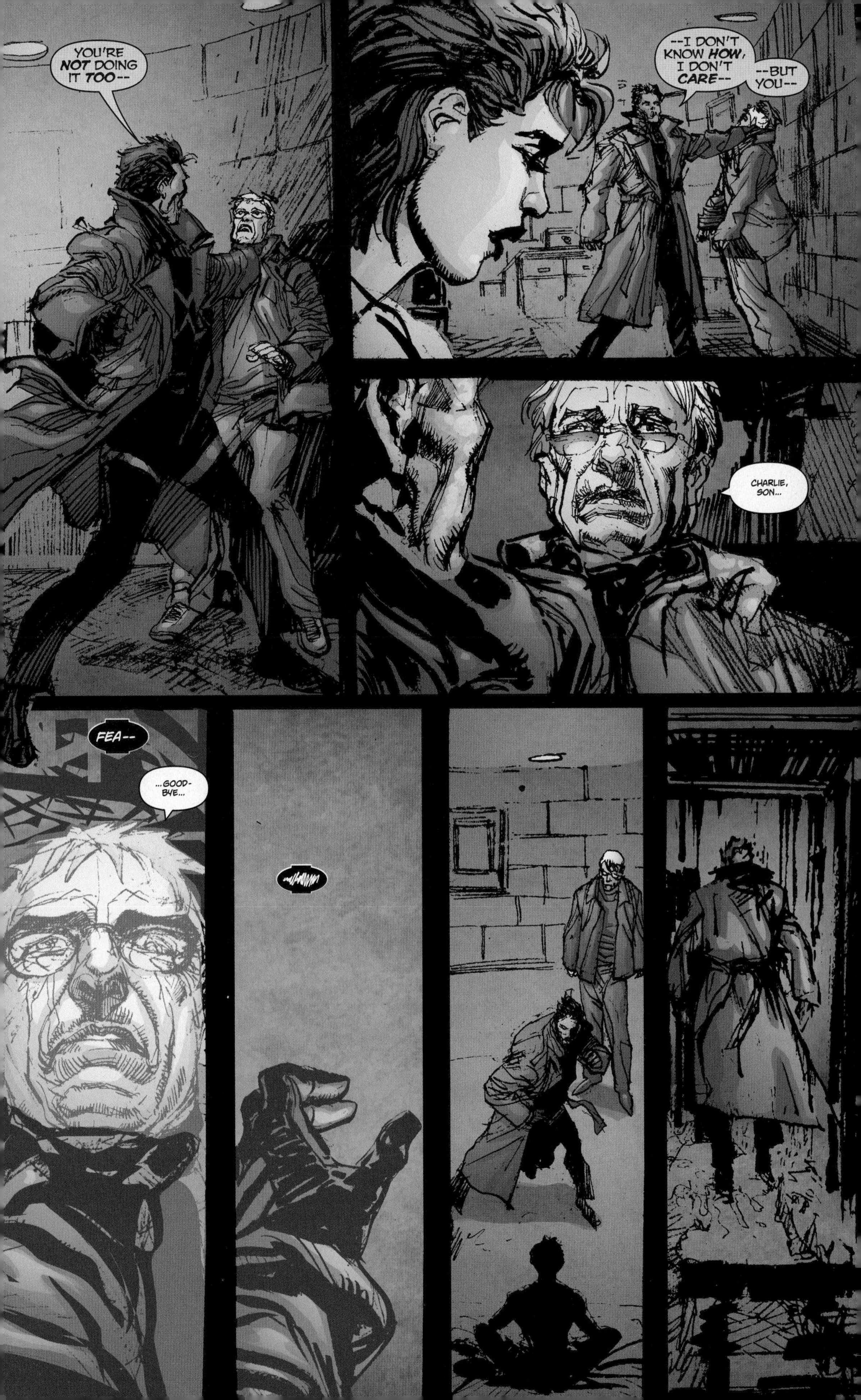
YOU'RE NOT DOING IT TOO--
--I DON'T KNOW HOW, I DON'T CARE--
--BUT YOU--
CHARLIE, SON...
FEA--
...GOOD-BYE...

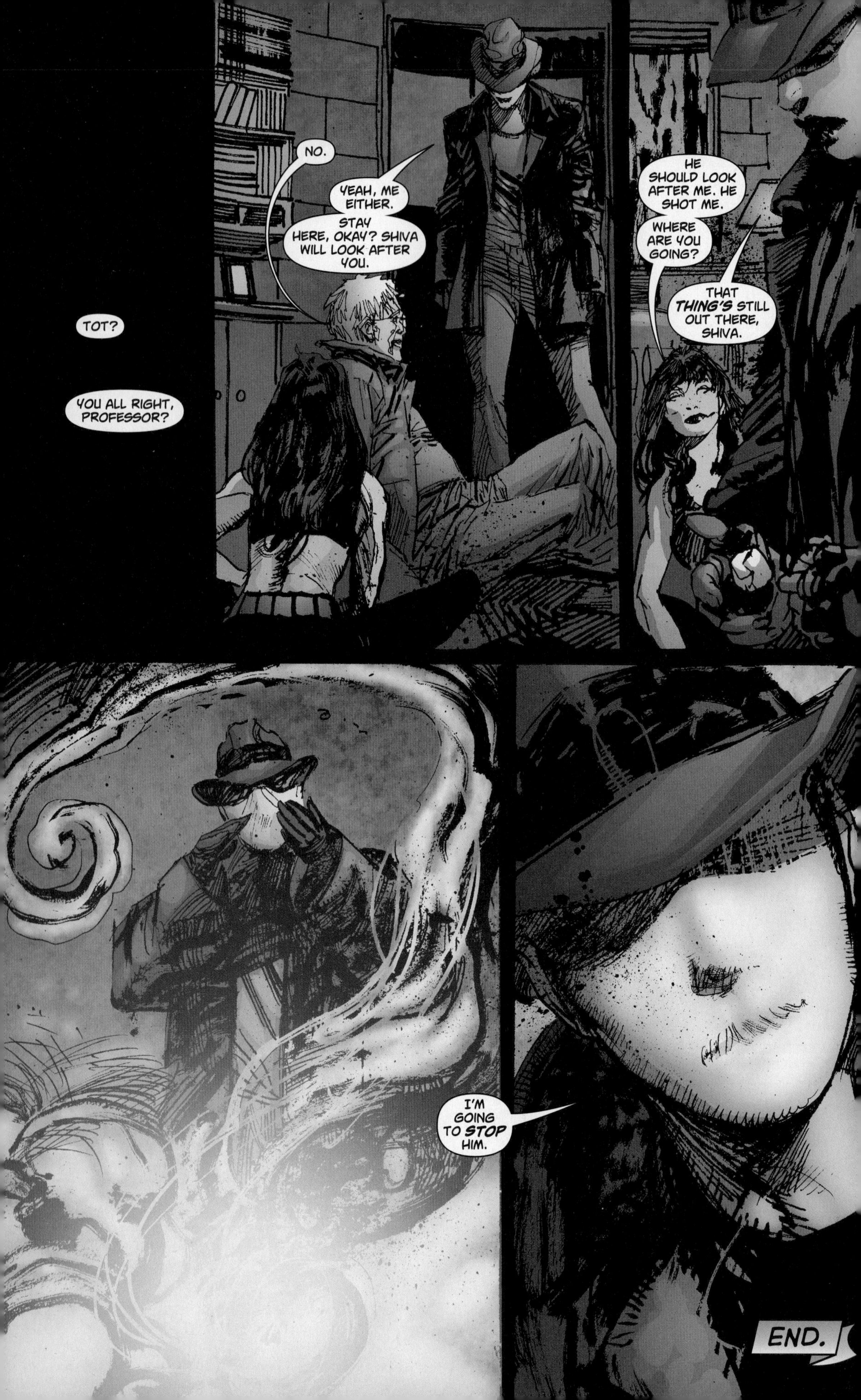
TOT?
YOU ALL RIGHT, PROFESSOR?
NO.
YEAH, ME EITHER.
STAY HERE, OKAY? SHIVA WILL LOOK AFTER YOU.
HE SHOULD LOOK AFTER ME. HE SHOT ME.
WHERE ARE YOU GOING?
THAT THING'S STILL OUT THERE, SHIVA.
I'M GOING TO STOP HIM.
END.

CATWOMAN 83
Cover by Adam Hughes

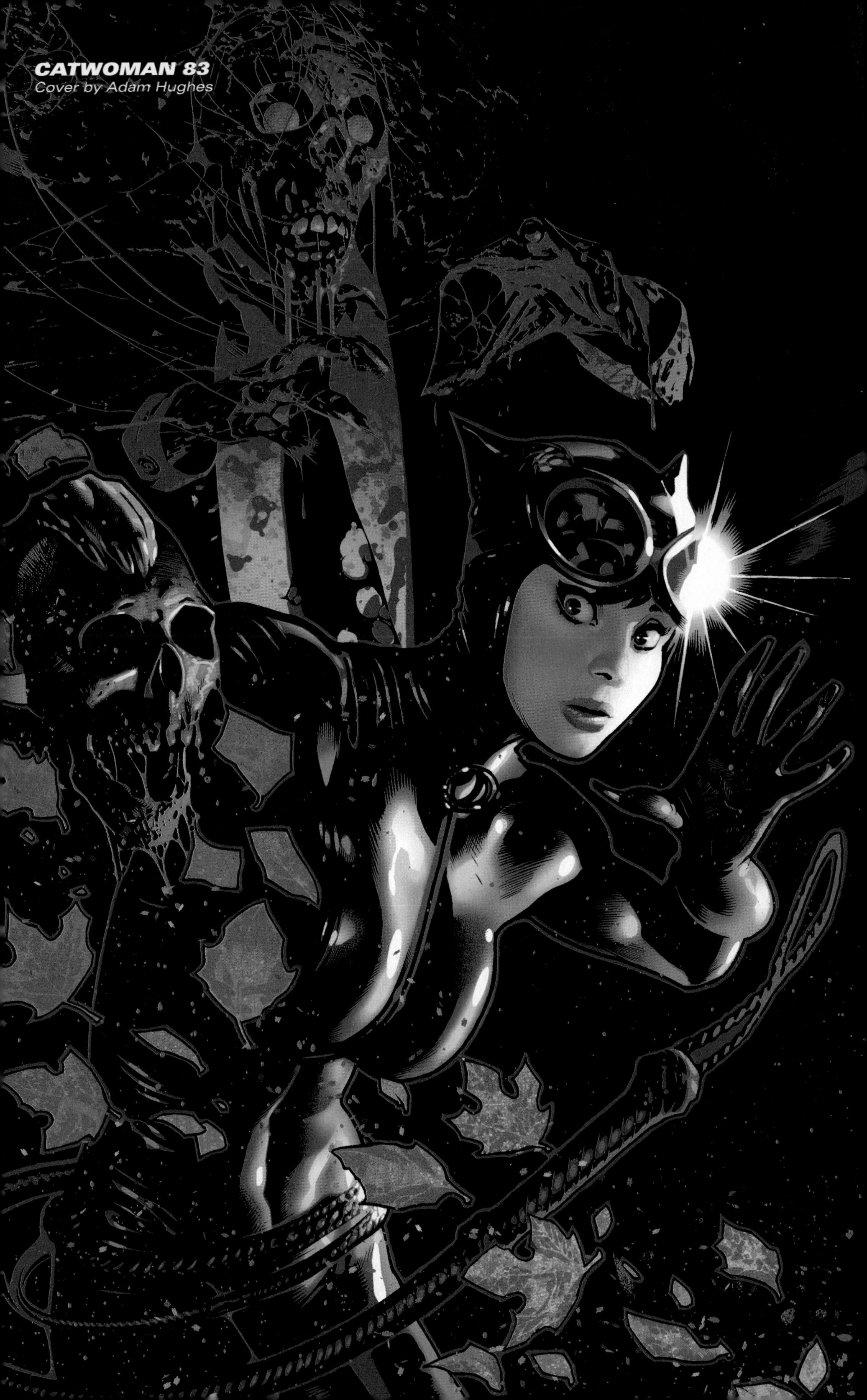

NIGHT AND THE CITY

TONY BEDARD
WRITER

FABRIZIO FIORENTINO
IBRAIM ROBERSON
MARCOS MARZ
LUCIANA DEL NEGRO
ARTISTS

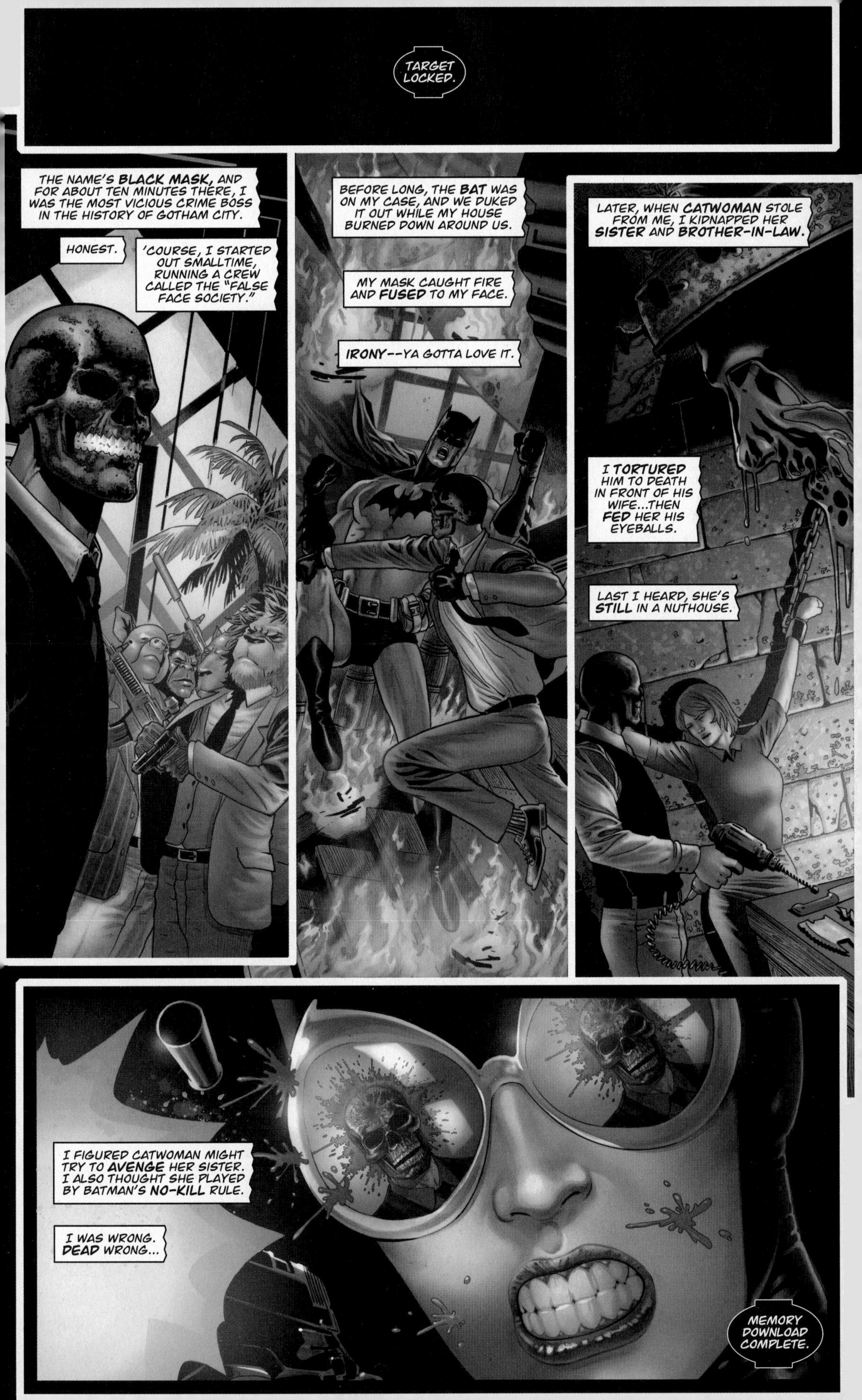
TARGET LOCKED.
THE NAME'S BLACK MASK, AND FOR ABOUT TEN MINUTES THERE, I WAS THE MOST VICIOUS CRIME BOSS IN THE HISTORY OF GOTHAM CITY.
HONEST.
'COURSE, I STARTED OUT SMALLTIME, RUNNING A CREW CALLED THE "FALSE FACE SOCIETY."
BEFORE LONG, THE BAT WAS ON MY CASE, AND WE DUKED IT OUT WHILE MY HOUSE BURNED DOWN AROUND US.
MY MASK CAUGHT FIRE AND FUSED TO MY FACE.
IRONY--YA GOTTA LOVE IT.
LATER, WHEN CATWOMAN STOLE FROM ME, I KIDNAPPED HER SISTER AND BROTHER-IN-LAW.
I TORTURED HIM TO DEATH IN FRONT OF HIS WIFE...THEN FED HER HIS EYEBALLS.
LAST I HEARD, SHE'S STILL IN A NUTHOUSE.
I FIGURED CATWOMAN MIGHT TRY TO AVENGE HER SISTER. I ALSO THOUGHT SHE PLAYED BY BATMAN'S NO-KILL RULE.
I WAS WRONG. DEAD WRONG...
MEMORY DOWNLOAD COMPLETE.

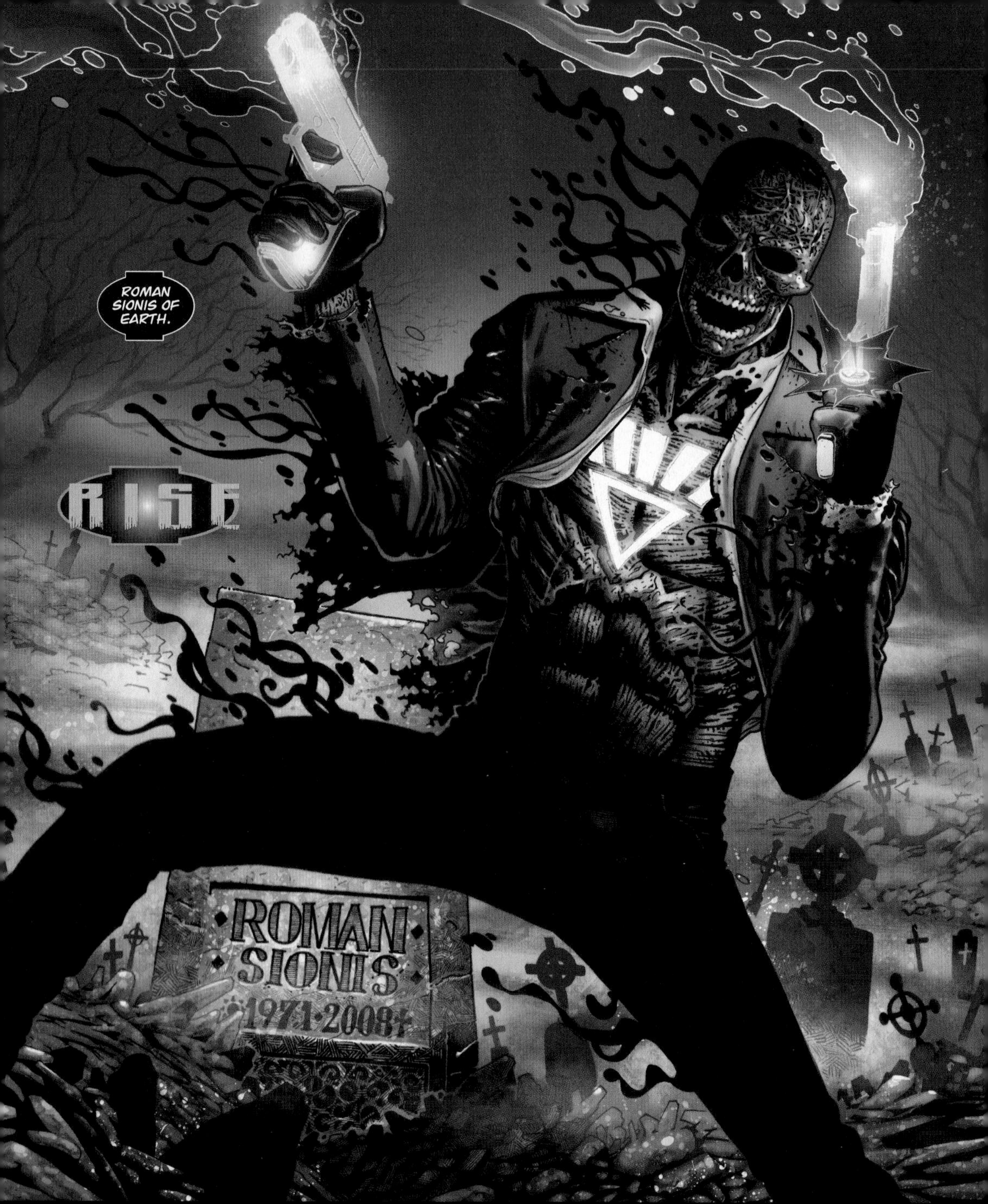
ROMAN SIONIS OF EARTH.
RISE
ROMAN SIONIS
1971-2008

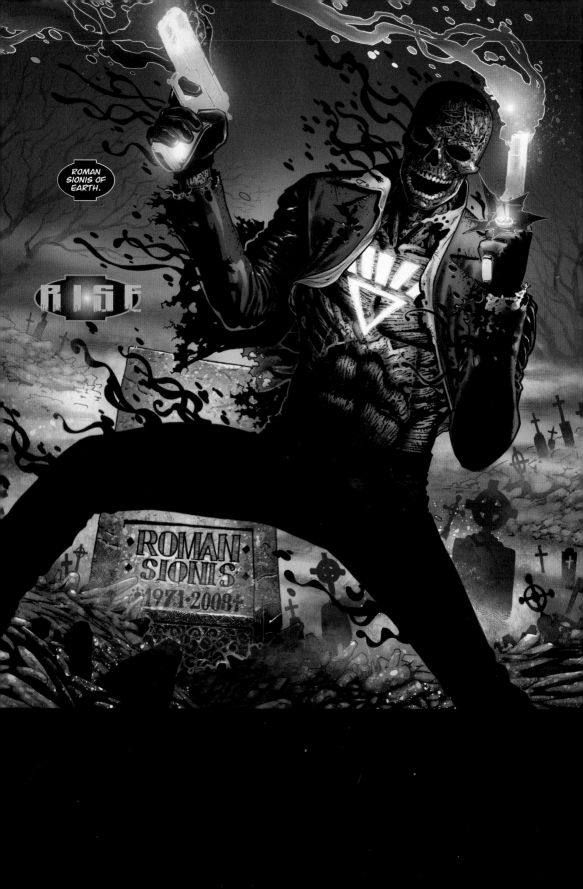

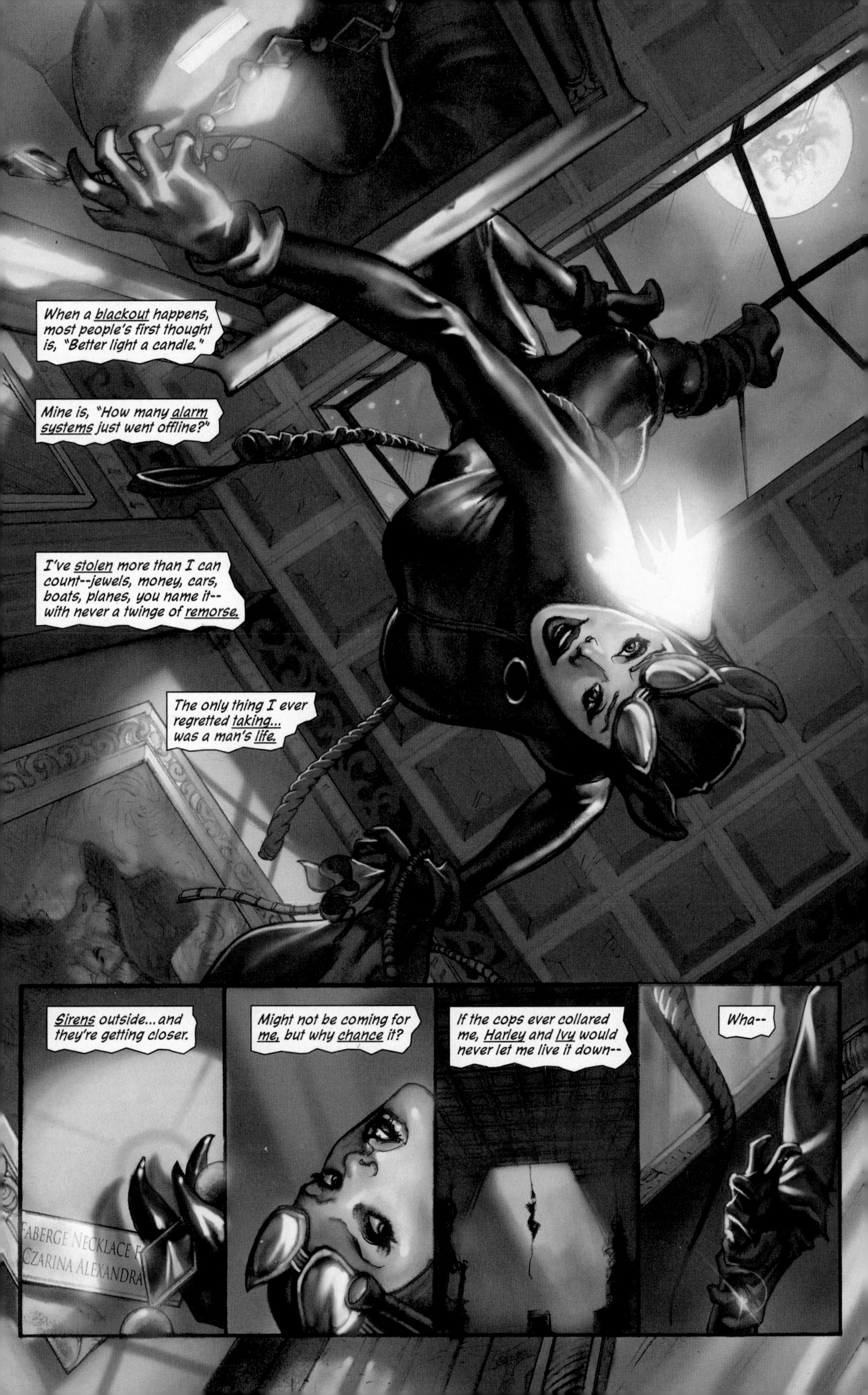
When a blackout happens, most people's first thought is, "Better light a candle."
Mine is, "How many alarm systems just went offline?"
I've stolen more than I can count--jewels, money, cars, boats, planes, you name it--with never a twinge of remorse.
The only thing I ever regretted taking... was a man's life.
Sirens outside... and they're getting closer.
FABERGE NECKLACE F
CZARINA ALEXANDRA
Might not be coming for me, but why chance it?
If the cops ever collared me, Harley and Ivy would never let me live it down--
Wha--

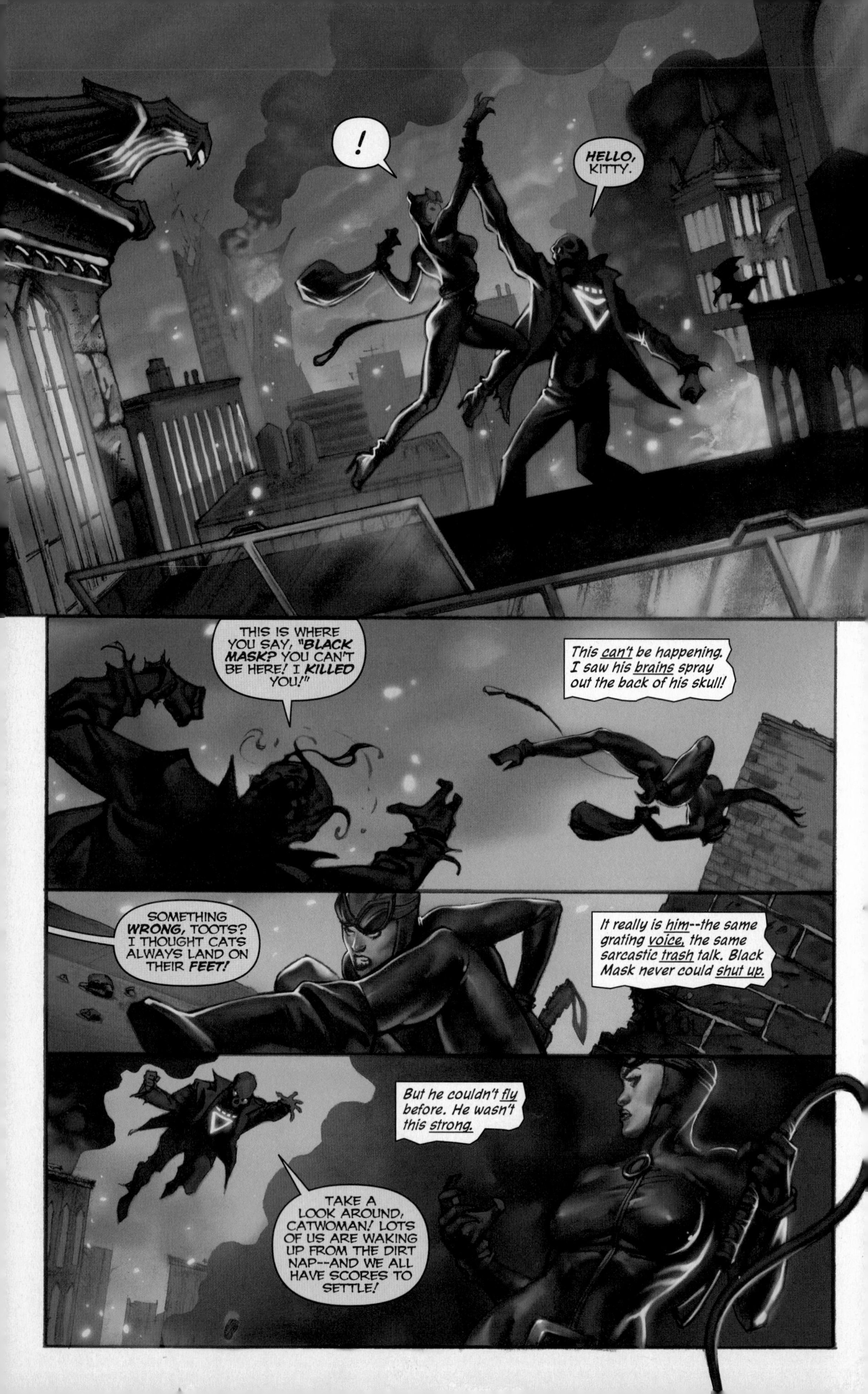
!
HELLO, KITTY.
THIS IS WHERE YOU SAY, "BLACK MASK? YOU CAN'T BE HERE! I KILLED YOU!"
This can't be happening. I saw his brains spray out the back of his skull!
SOMETHING WRONG, TOOTS? I THOUGHT CATS ALWAYS LAND ON THEIR FEET!
It really is him--the same grating voice, the same sarcastic trash talk. Black Mask never could shut up.
But he couldn't fly before. He wasn't this strong.
TAKE A LOOK AROUND, CATWOMAN! LOTS OF US ARE WAKING UP FROM THE DIRT NAP--AND WE ALL HAVE SCORES TO SETTLE!

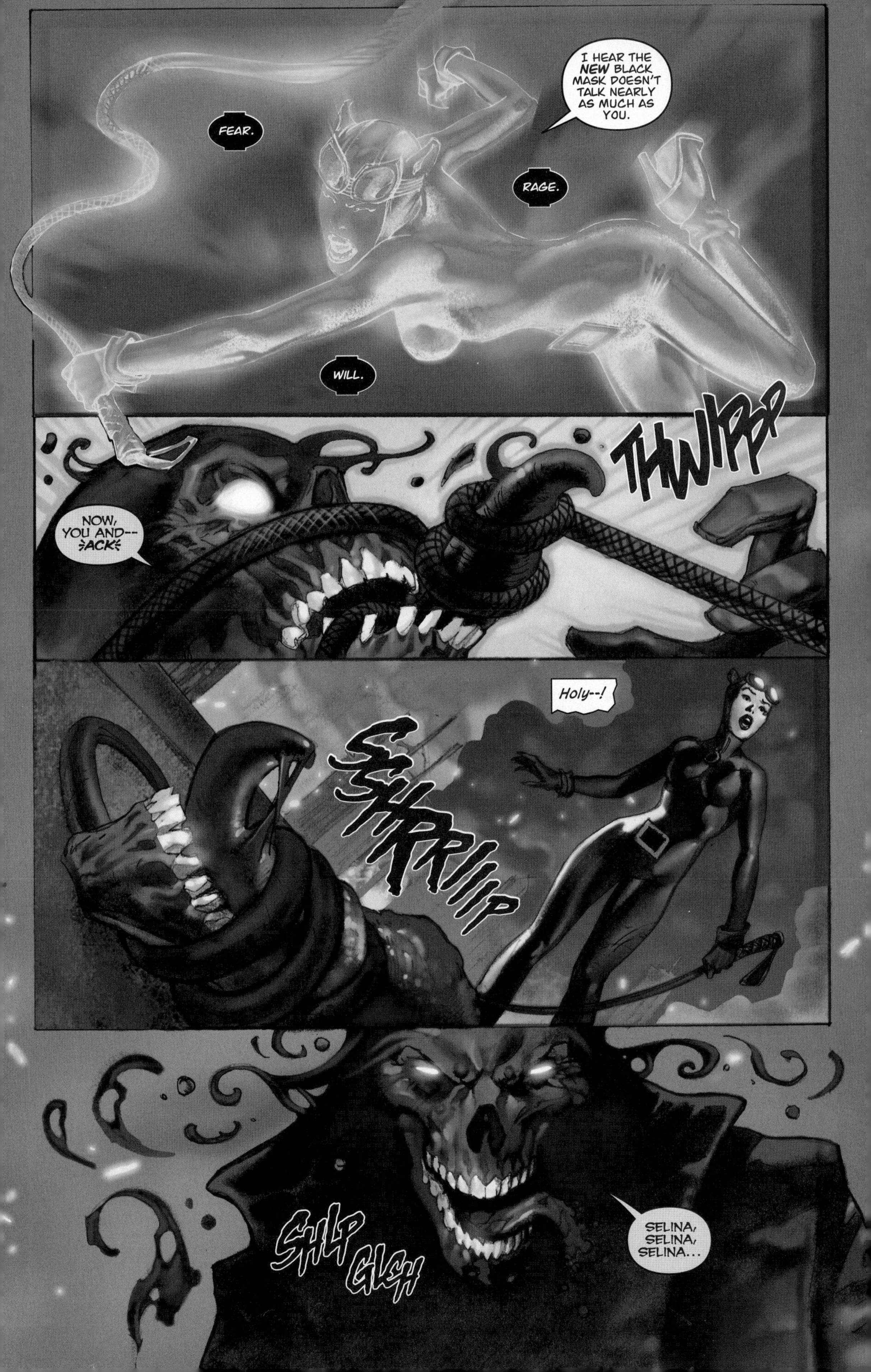
FEAR.
I HEAR THE NEW BLACK MASK DOESN'T TALK NEARLY AS MUCH AS YOU.
RAGE.
WILL.
NOW, YOU AND-- ACK
THWIPP
Holy--!
SHRRIIIP
SHLP
GLCH
SELINA, SELINA, SELINA...

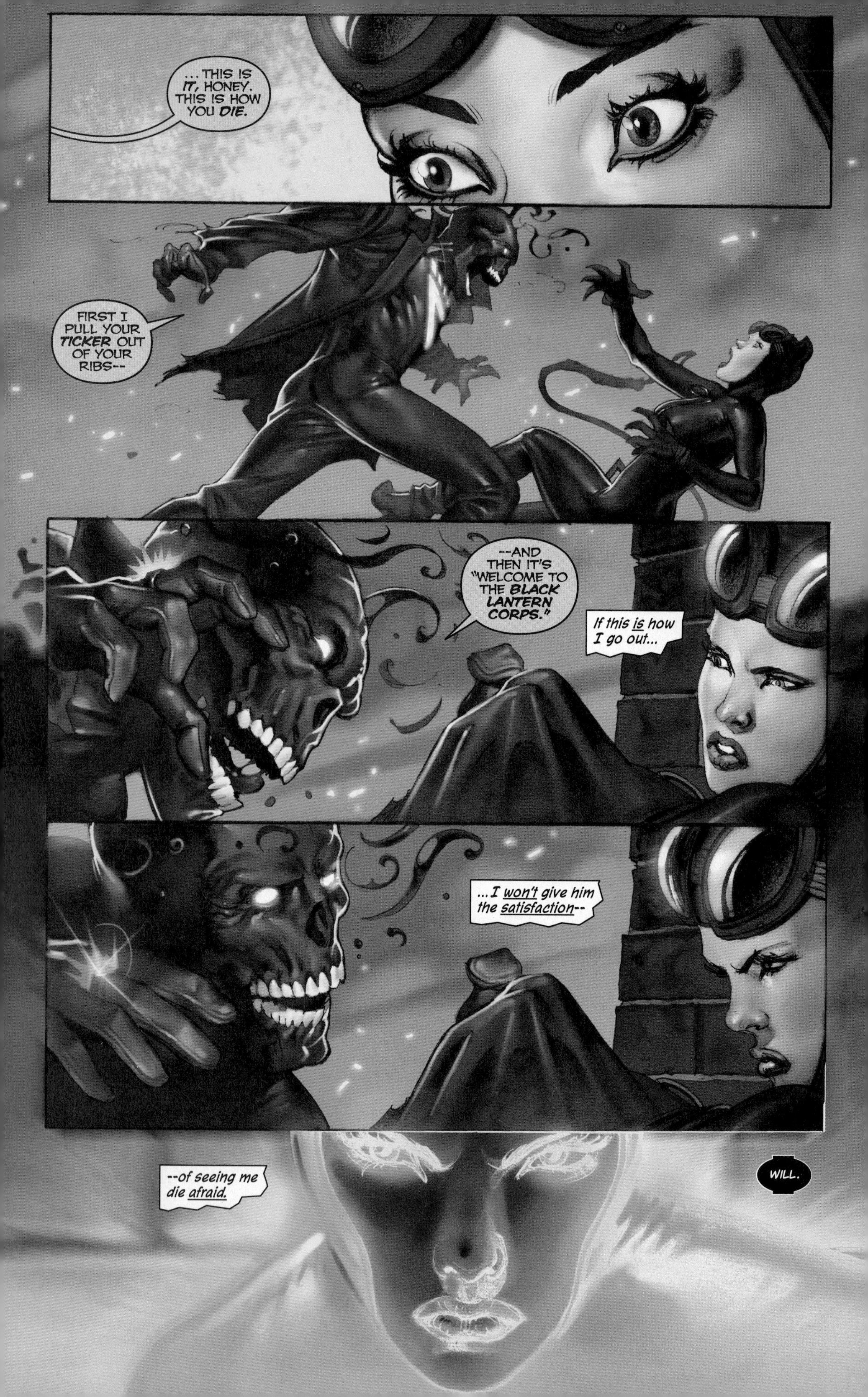
...THIS IS IT, HONEY. THIS IS HOW YOU DIE.
FIRST I PULL YOUR TICKER OUT OF YOUR RIBS--
--AND THEN IT'S "WELCOME TO THE BLACK LANTERN CORPS."
If this is how I go out...
...I won't give him the satisfaction--
--of seeing me die afraid.
WILL.

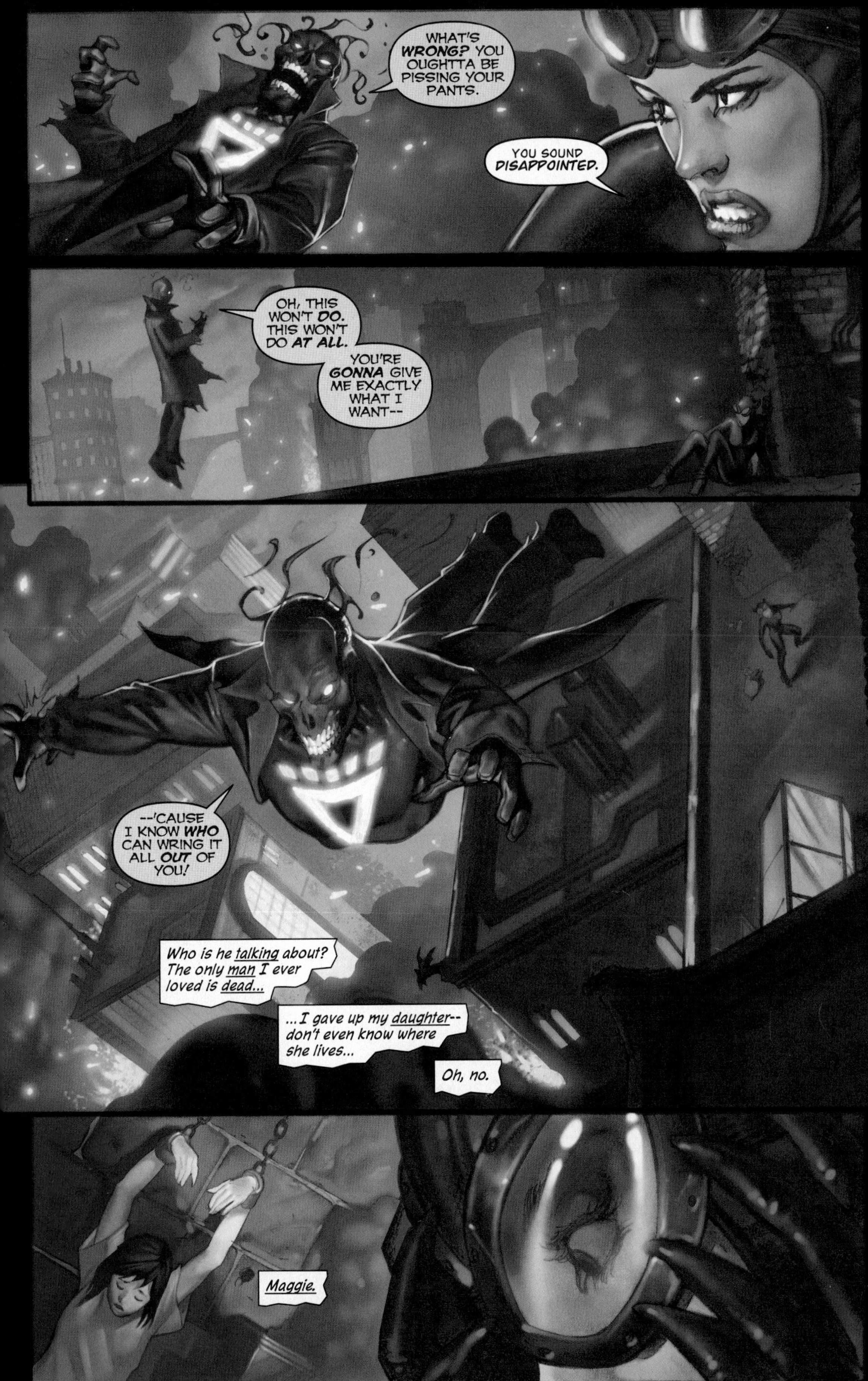
WHAT'S WRONG? YOU OUGHTTA BE PISSING YOUR PANTS.
YOU SOUND DISAPPOINTED.
OH, THIS WON'T DO. THIS WON'T DO AT ALL.
YOU'RE GONNA GIVE ME EXACTLY WHAT I WANT--
--'CAUSE I KNOW WHO CAN WRING IT ALL OUT OF YOU!
Who is he talking about? The only man I ever loved is dead...
...I gave up my daughter-- don't even know where she lives...
Oh, no.
Maggie.

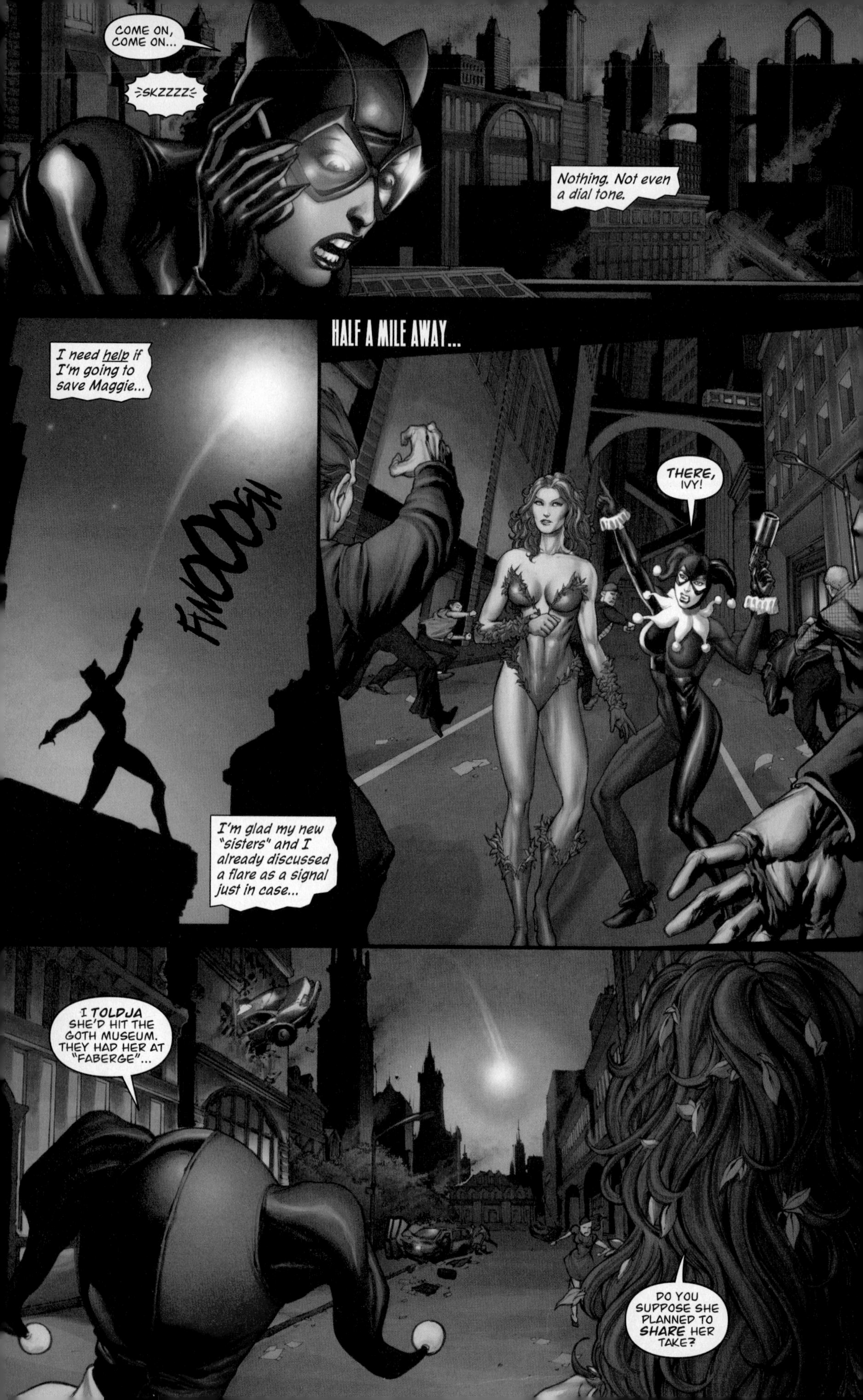
COME ON, COME ON...
SKZZZZ
Nothing. Not even a dial tone.
I need help if I'm going to save Maggie...
FWOOOSH
HALF A MILE AWAY...
THERE, IVY!
I'm glad my new "sisters" and I already discussed a flare as a signal just in case...
I TOLDJA SHE'D HIT THE GOTH MUSEUM. THEY HAD HER AT "FABERGE"...
DO YOU SUPPOSE SHE PLANNED TO SHARE HER TAKE?

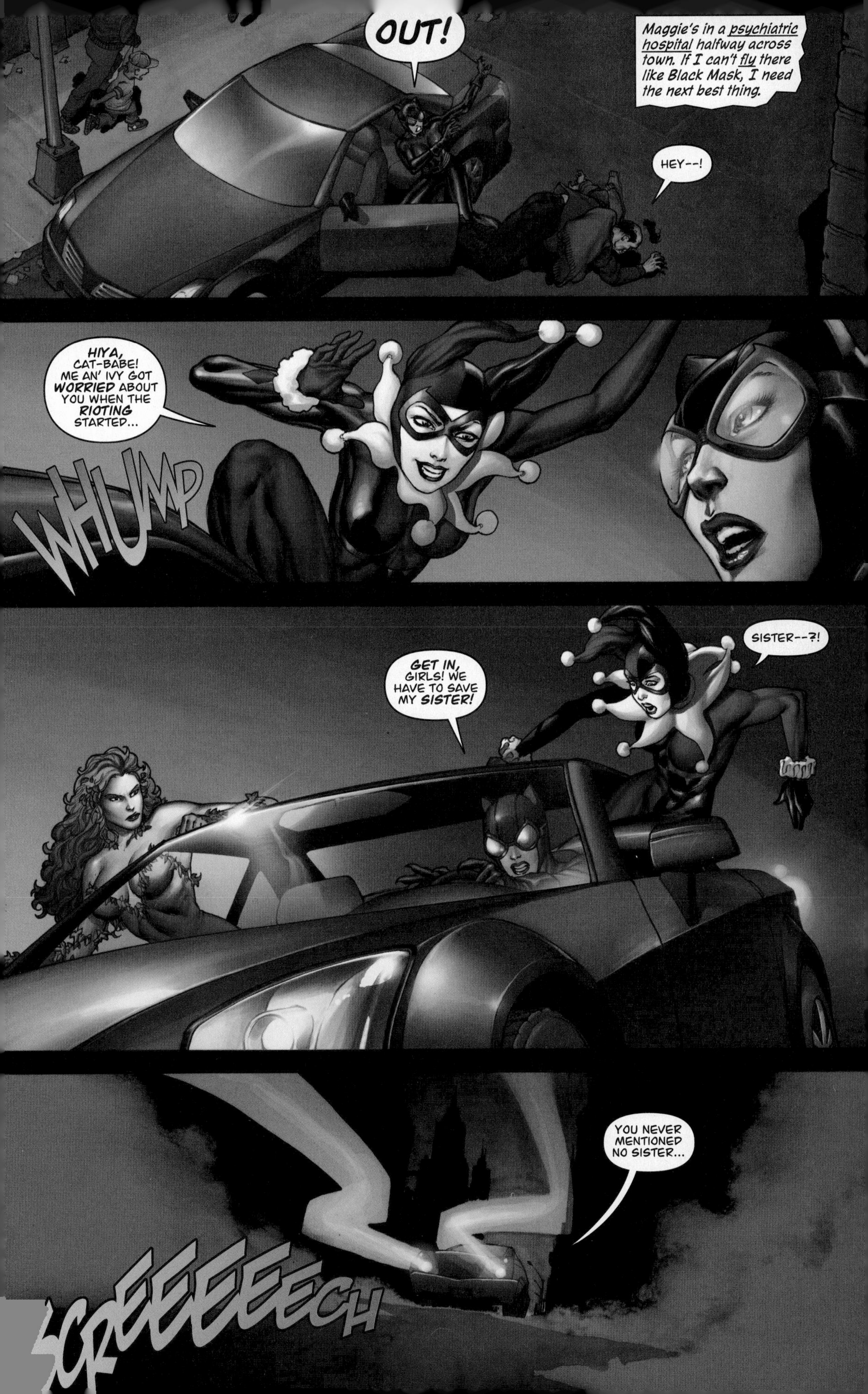
OUT!
Maggie's in a psychiatric hospital halfway across town. If I can't fly there like Black Mask, I need the next best thing.
HEY--!
HIYA, CAT-BABE! ME AN' IVY GOT WORRIED ABOUT YOU WHEN THE RIOTING STARTED...
WHUMP
GET IN, GIRLS! WE HAVE TO SAVE MY SISTER!
SISTER--?!
YOU NEVER MENTIONED NO SISTER...
SCREEEEEECH

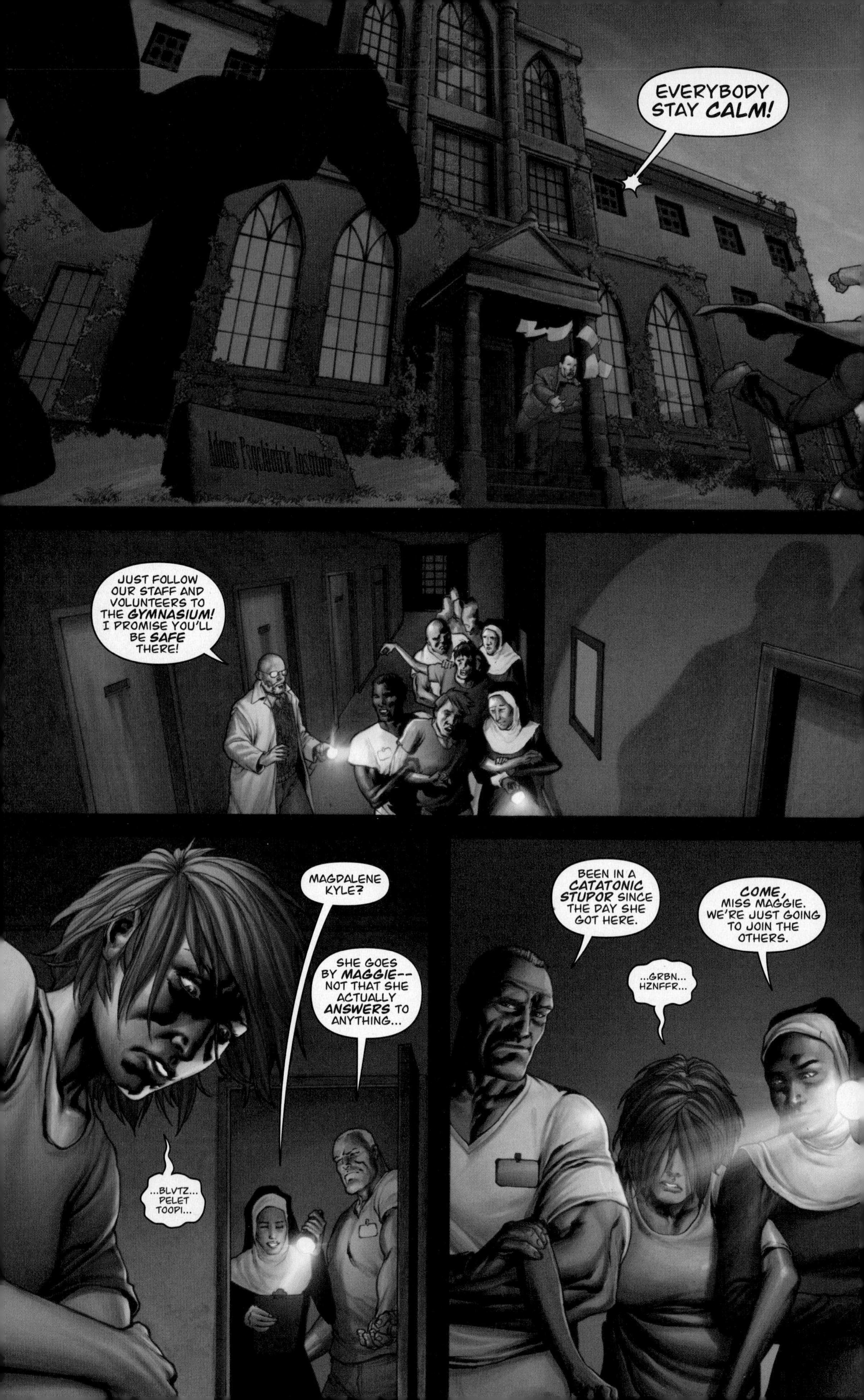
EVERYBODY STAY CALM!
Adams Psychiatric Institute
JUST FOLLOW OUR STAFF AND VOLUNTEERS TO THE GYMNASIUM! I PROMISE YOU'LL BE SAFE THERE!
MAGDALENE KYLE?
SHE GOES BY MAGGIE-- NOT THAT SHE ACTUALLY ANSWERS TO ANYTHING...
...BLVTZ... PELET TOOPI...
BEEN IN A CATATONIC STUPOR SINCE THE DAY SHE GOT HERE.
...GRBN... HZNFFR...
COME, MISS MAGGIE. WE'RE JUST GOING TO JOIN THE OTHERS.

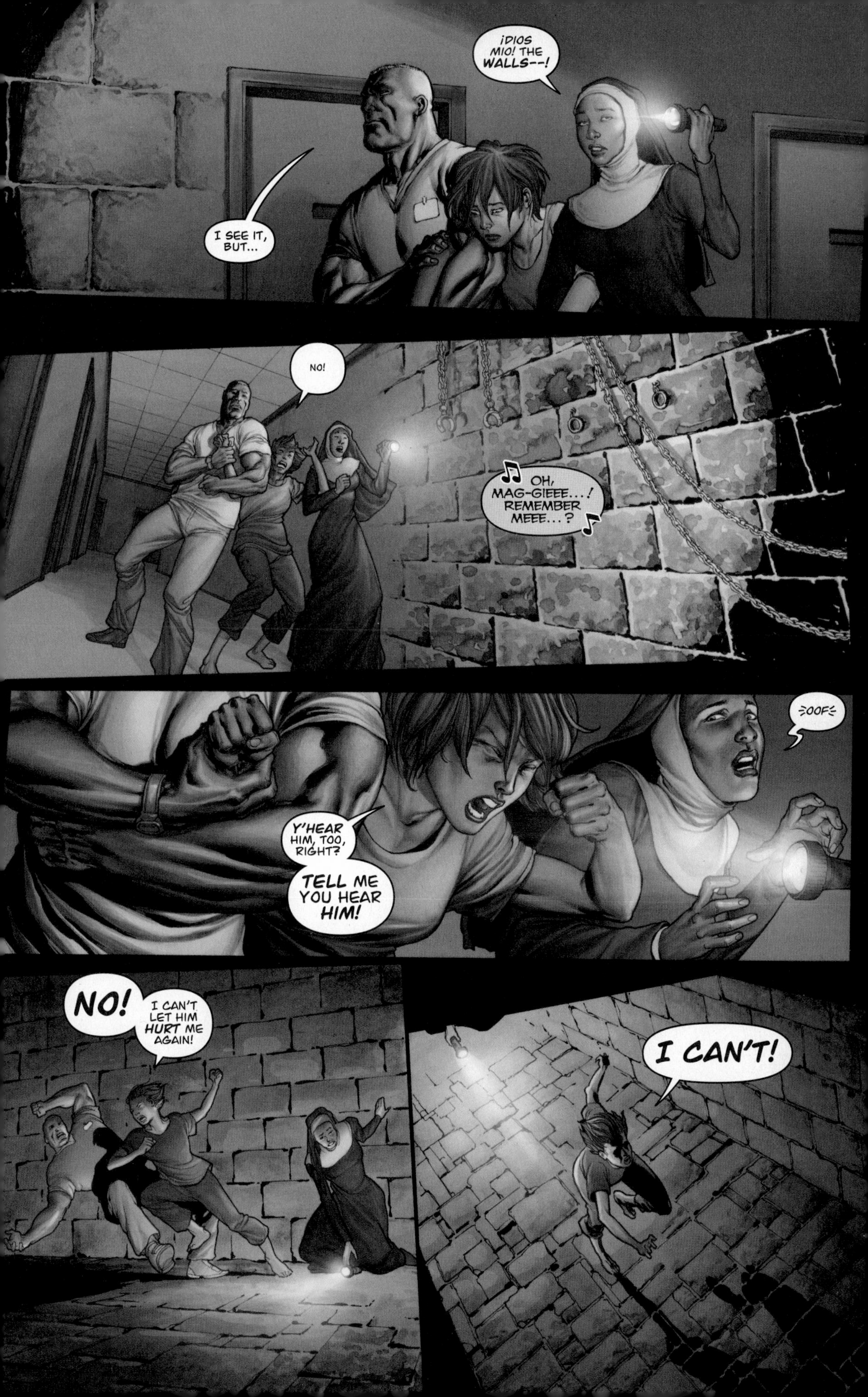
¡DIOS MIO! THE WALLS--!
I SEE IT, BUT...
NO!
OH, MAG-GIEEE...! REMEMBER MEEE...?
OOF
Y'HEAR HIM, TOO, RIGHT?
TELL ME YOU HEAR HIM!
NO!
I CAN'T LET HIM HURT ME AGAIN!
I CAN'T!

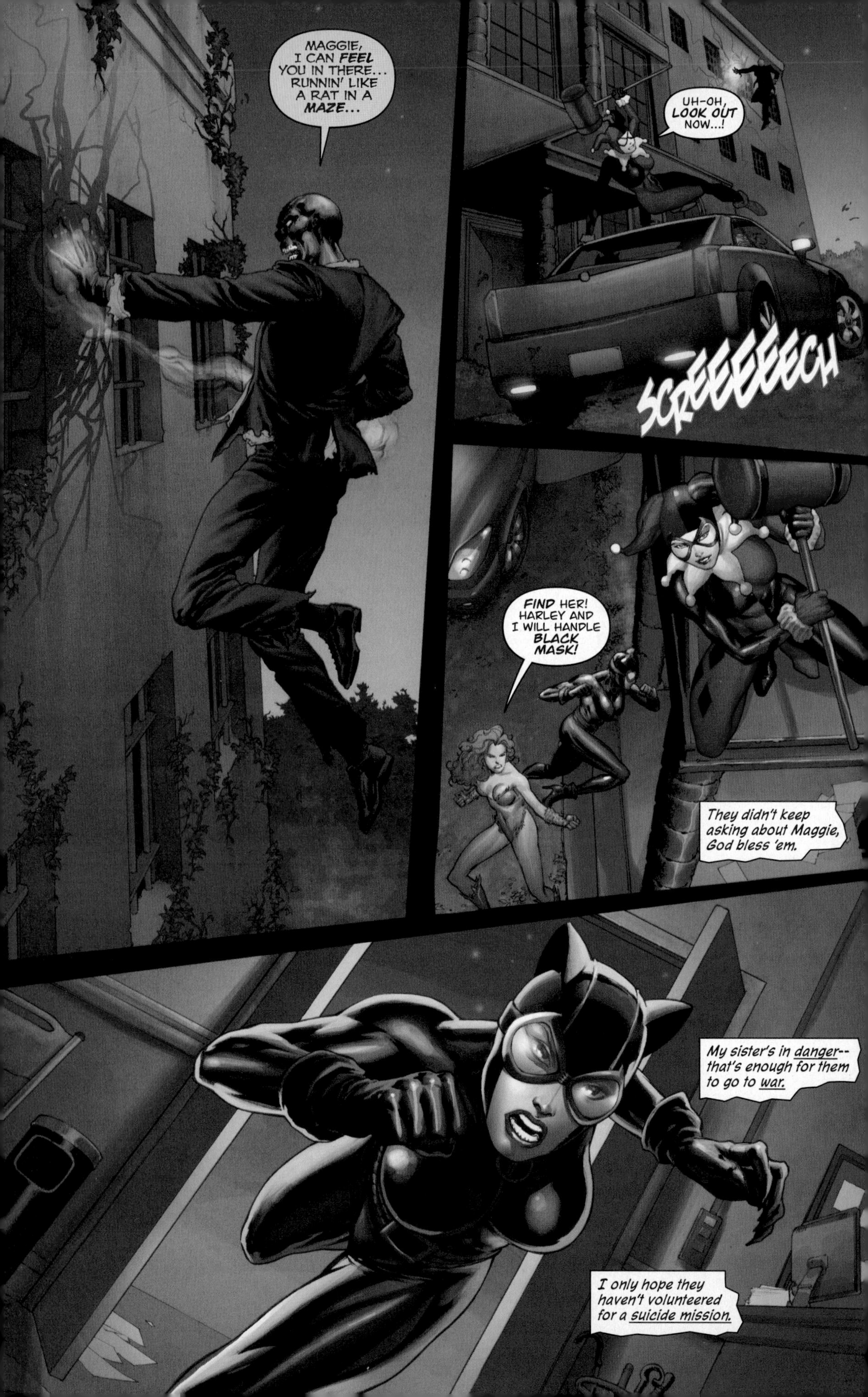
MAGGIE, I CAN FEEL YOU IN THERE... RUNNIN' LIKE A RAT IN A MAZE...
UH-OH, LOOK OUT NOW...!
SCREEEEECH
FIND HER! HARLEY AND I WILL HANDLE BLACK MASK!
They didn't keep asking about Maggie, God bless 'em.
My sister's in danger--that's enough for them to go to war.
I only hope they haven't volunteered for a suicide mission.

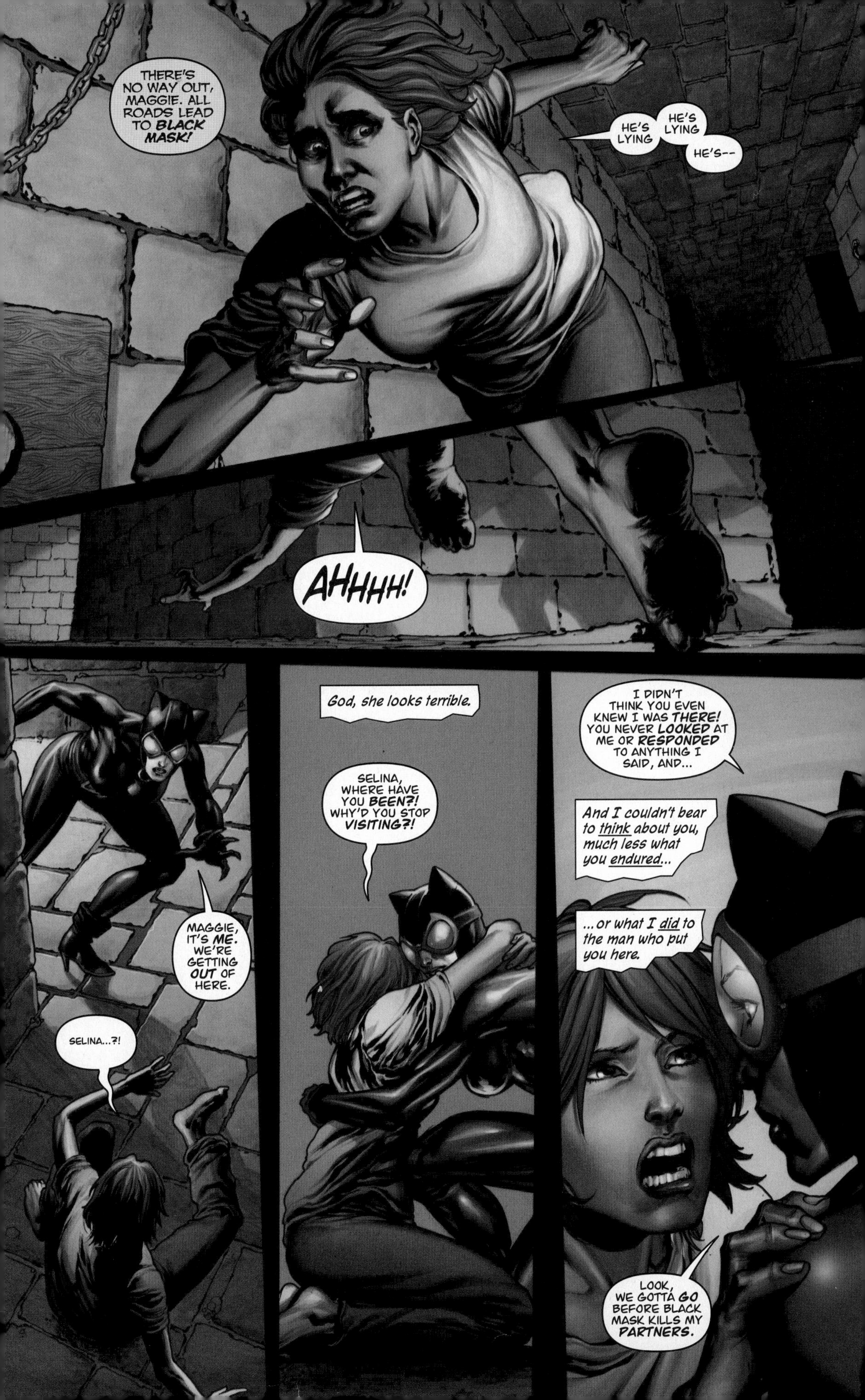
THERE'S NO WAY OUT, MAGGIE. ALL ROADS LEAD TO BLACK MASK!
HE'S LYING
HE'S LYING
HE'S--
AHHHH!
MAGGIE, IT'S ME. WE'RE GETTING OUT OF HERE.
SELINA...?!
God, she looks terrible.
SELINA, WHERE HAVE YOU BEEN?! WHY'D YOU STOP VISITING?!
I DIDN'T THINK YOU EVEN KNEW I WAS THERE! YOU NEVER LOOKED AT ME OR RESPONDED TO ANYTHING I SAID, AND...
And I couldn't bear to think about you, much less what you endured...
...or what I did to the man who put you here.
LOOK, WE GOTTA GO BEFORE BLACK MASK KILLS MY PARTNERS.

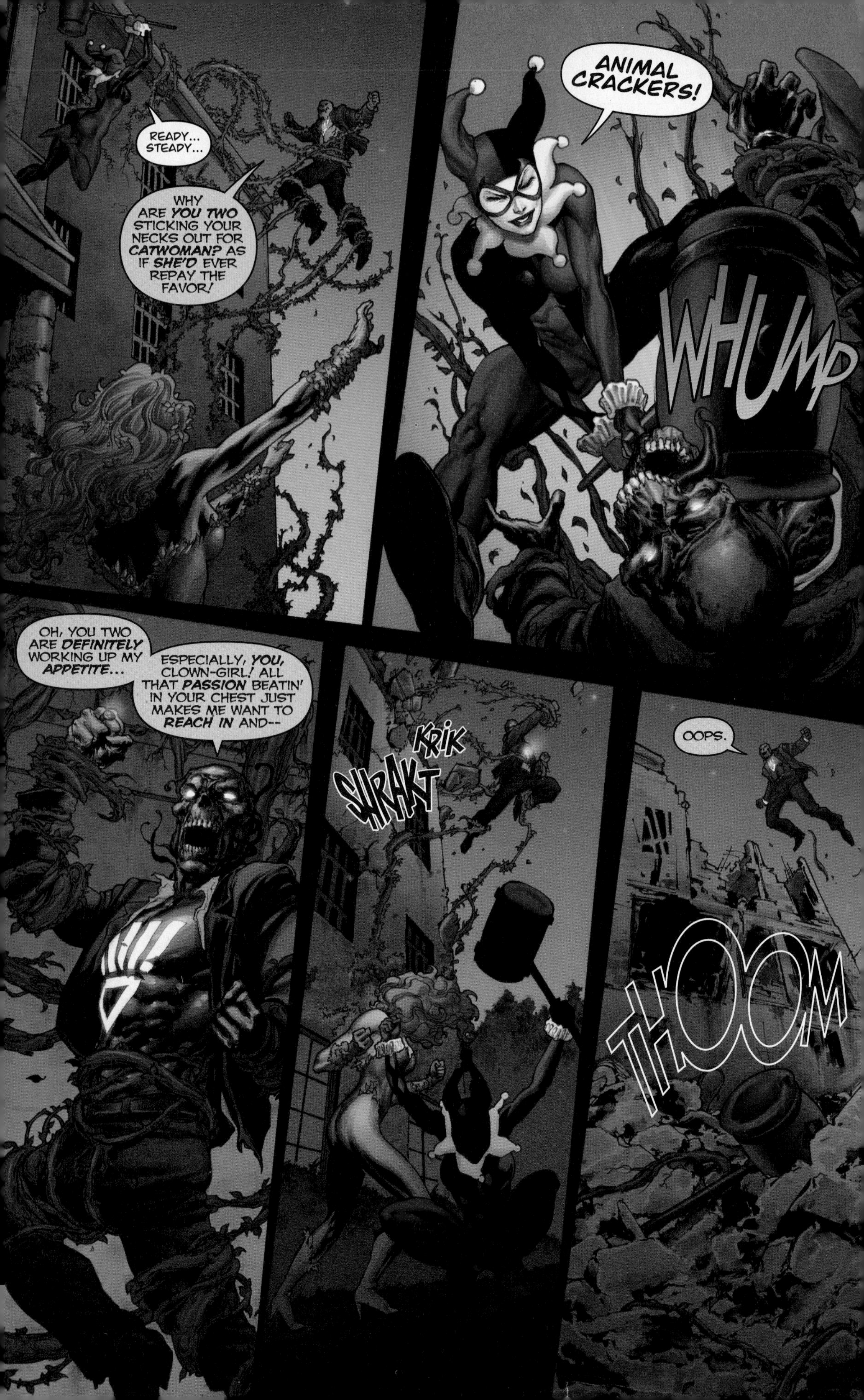
READY... STEADY...
WHY ARE YOU TWO STICKING YOUR NECKS OUT FOR CATWOMAN? AS IF SHE'D EVER REPAY THE FAVOR!
ANIMAL CRACKERS!
WHUMP
OH, YOU TWO ARE DEFINITELY WORKING UP MY APPETITE...
ESPECIALLY, YOU, CLOWN-GIRL! ALL THAT PASSION BEATIN' IN YOUR CHEST JUST MAKES ME WANT TO REACH IN AND--
KRIK
SHRAKT
OOPS.
THOOM

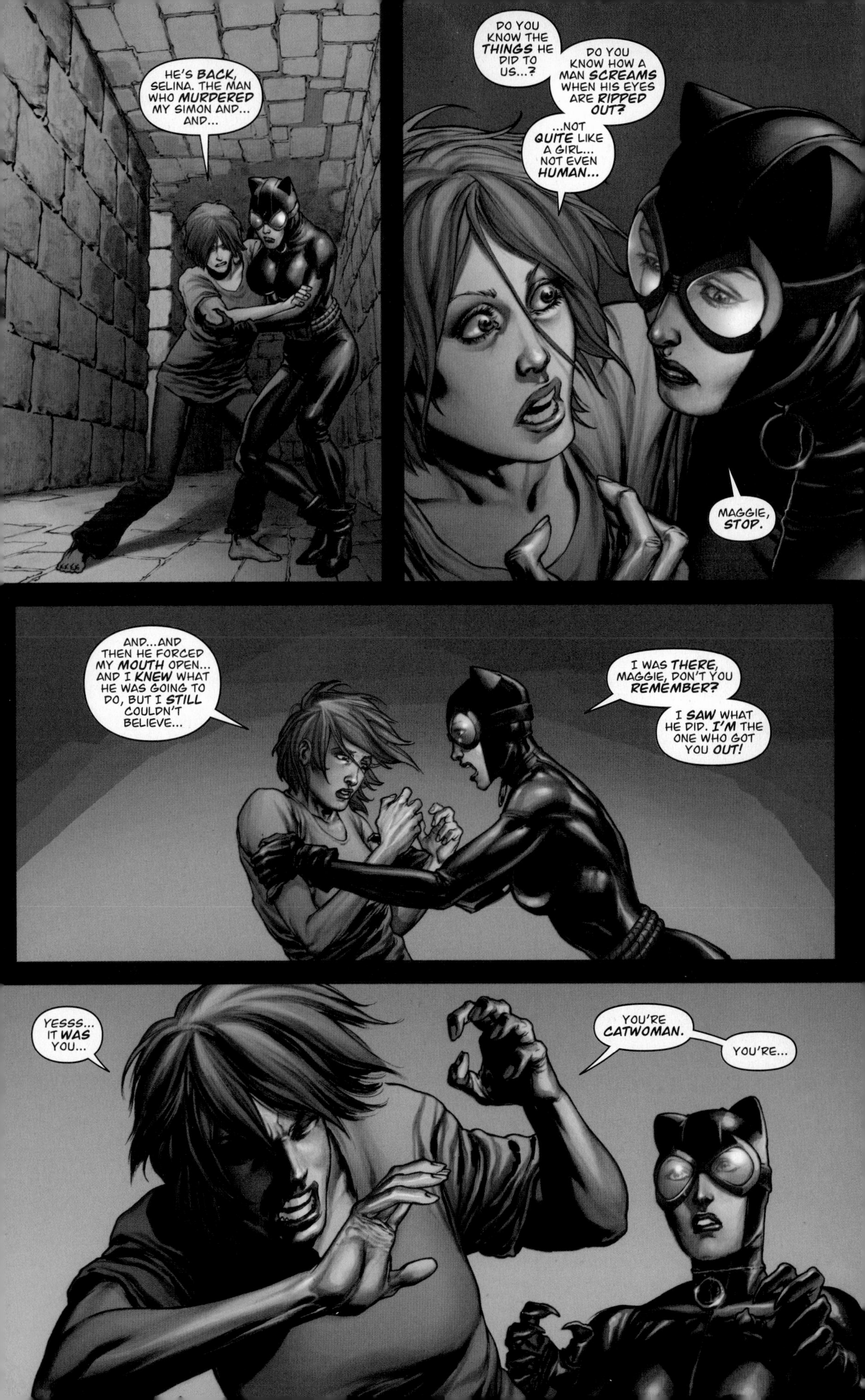
HE'S BACK, SELINA. THE MAN WHO MURDERED MY SIMON AND... AND...
DO YOU KNOW THE THINGS HE DID TO US...?
DO YOU KNOW HOW A MAN SCREAMS WHEN HIS EYES ARE RIPPED OUT?
...NOT QUITE LIKE A GIRL... NOT EVEN HUMAN...
MAGGIE, STOP.
AND...AND THEN HE FORCED MY MOUTH OPEN... AND I KNEW WHAT HE WAS GOING TO DO, BUT I STILL COULDN'T BELIEVE...
I WAS THERE, MAGGIE, DON'T YOU REMEMBER?
I SAW WHAT HE DID. I'M THE ONE WHO GOT YOU OUT!
YESSS... IT WAS YOU...
YOU'RE CATWOMAN.
YOU'RE...

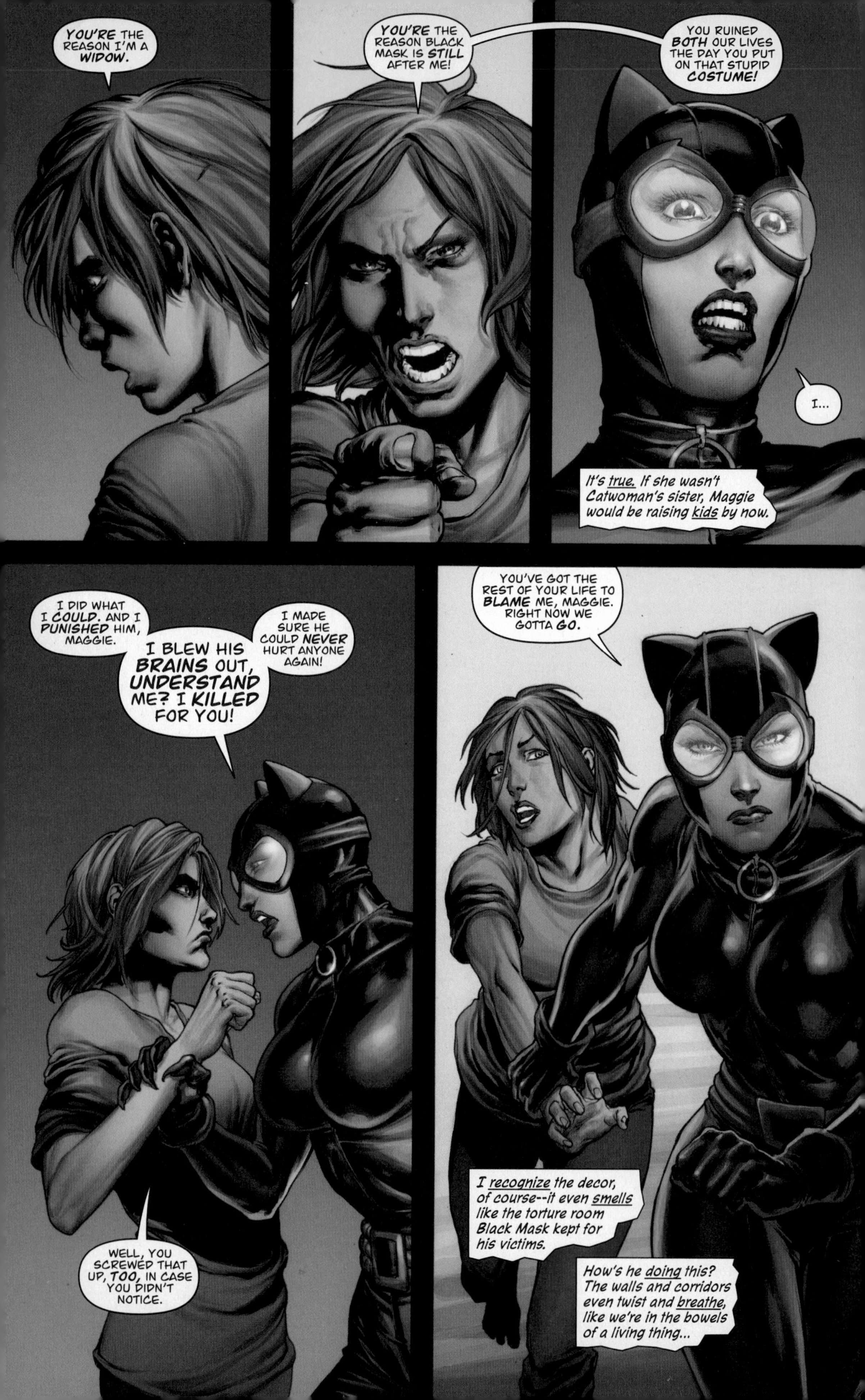
YOU'RE THE REASON I'M A WIDOW.
YOU'RE THE REASON BLACK MASK IS STILL AFTER ME!
YOU RUINED BOTH OUR LIVES THE DAY YOU PUT ON THAT STUPID COSTUME!
I...
It's true. If she wasn't Catwoman's sister, Maggie would be raising kids by now.
I DID WHAT I COULD. AND I PUNISHED HIM, MAGGIE.
I BLEW HIS BRAINS OUT, UNDERSTAND ME? I KILLED FOR YOU!
I MADE SURE HE COULD NEVER HURT ANYONE AGAIN!
WELL, YOU SCREWED THAT UP, TOO, IN CASE YOU DIDN'T NOTICE.
YOU'VE GOT THE REST OF YOUR LIFE TO BLAME ME, MAGGIE. RIGHT NOW WE GOTTA GO.
I recognize the decor, of course--it even smells like the torture room Black Mask kept for his victims.
How's he doing this? The walls and corridors even twist and breathe, like we're in the bowels of a living thing...

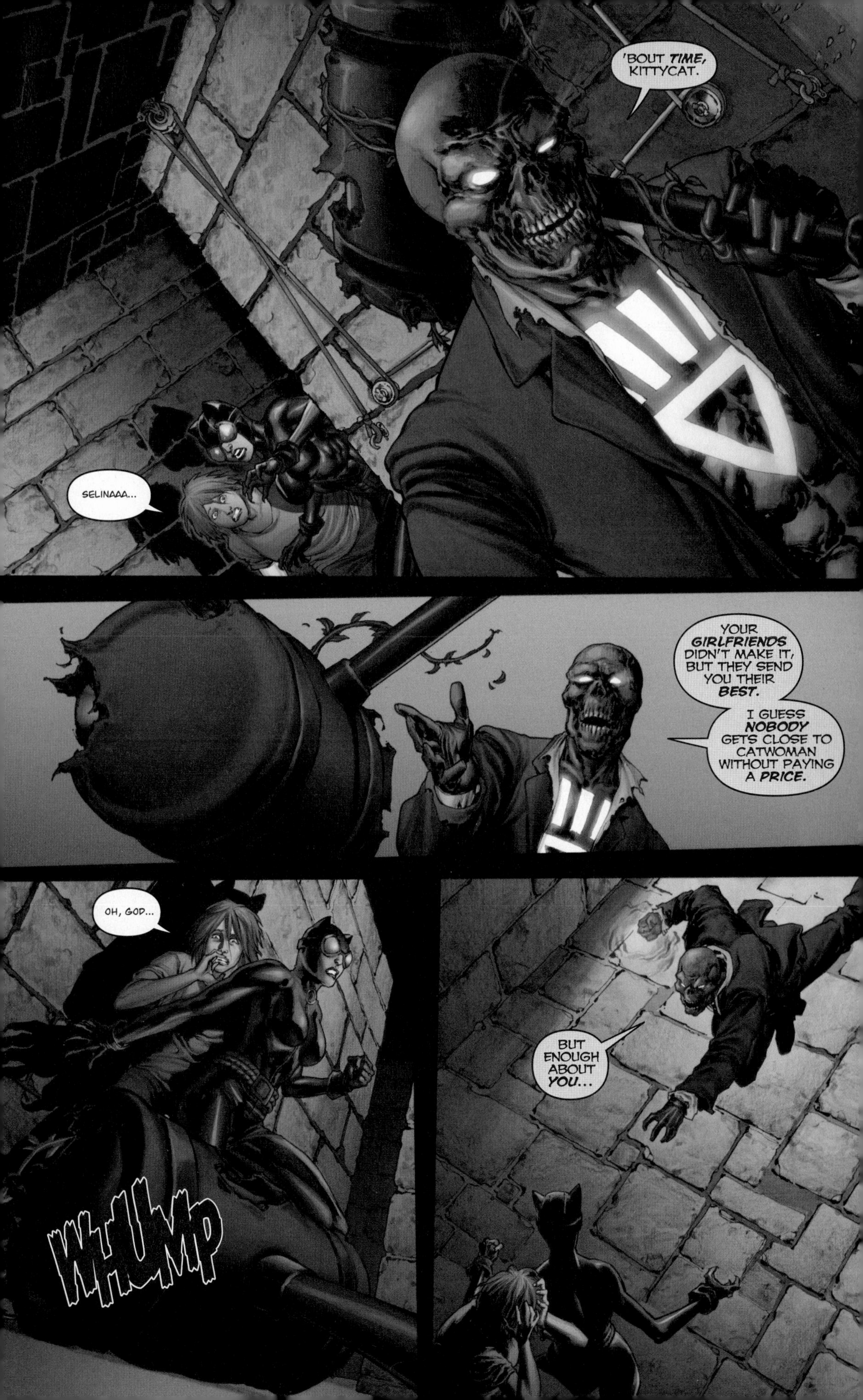
'BOUT TIME, KITTYCAT.
SELINAAA...
YOUR GIRLFRIENDS DIDN'T MAKE IT, BUT THEY SEND YOU THEIR BEST.
I GUESS NOBODY GETS CLOSE TO CATWOMAN WITHOUT PAYING A PRICE.
OH, GOD...
WHUMP
BUT ENOUGH ABOUT YOU...

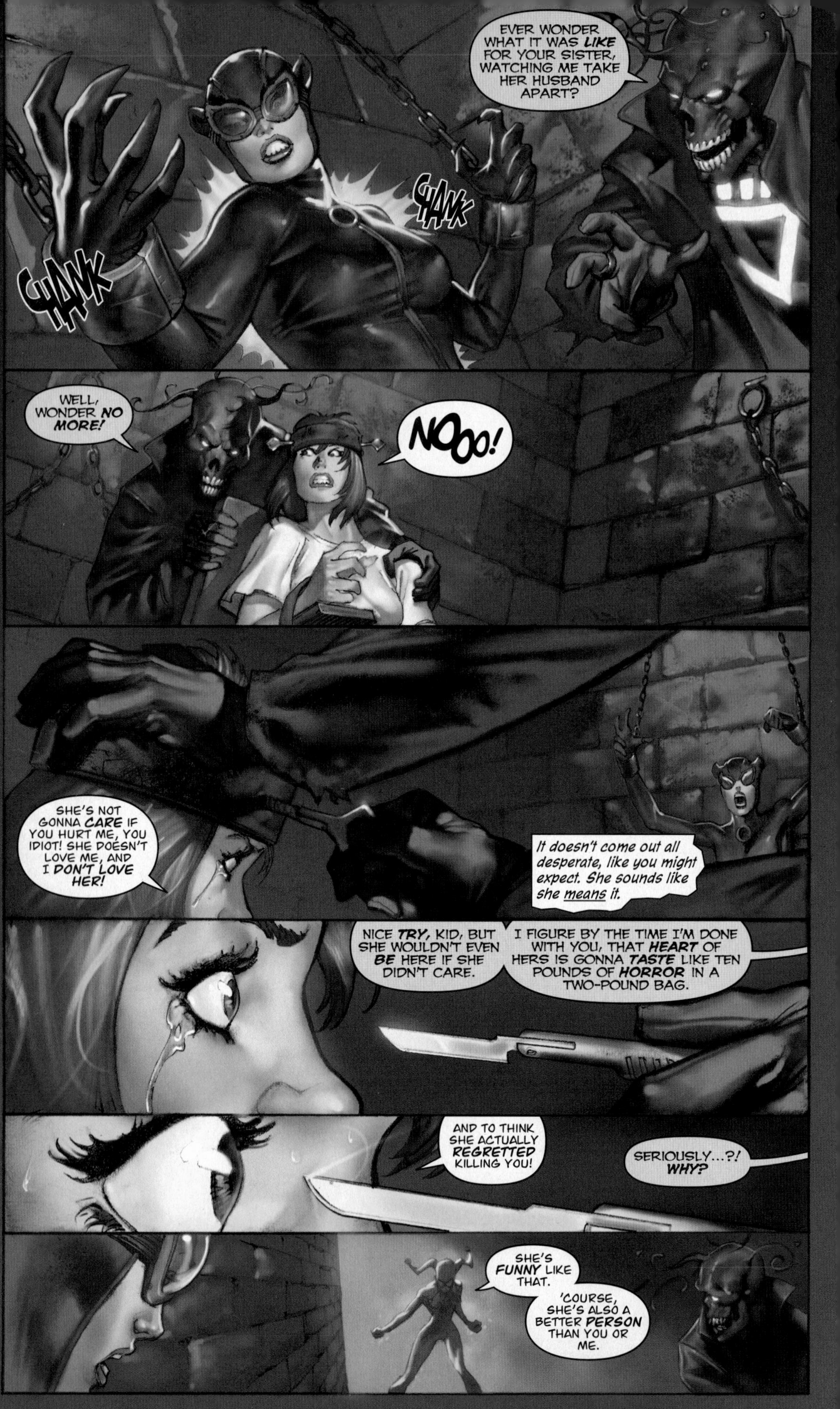

EVER WONDER WHAT IT WAS LIKE FOR YOUR SISTER, WATCHING ME TAKE HER HUSBAND APART?
CHANK
CHANK
WELL, WONDER NO MORE!
NOOO!
SHE'S NOT GONNA CARE IF YOU HURT ME, YOU IDIOT! SHE DOESN'T LOVE ME, AND I DON'T LOVE HER!
It doesn't come out all desperate, like you might expect. She sounds like she means it.
NICE TRY, KID, BUT SHE WOULDN'T EVEN BE HERE IF SHE DIDN'T CARE.
I FIGURE BY THE TIME I'M DONE WITH YOU, THAT HEART OF HERS IS GONNA TASTE LIKE TEN POUNDS OF HORROR IN A TWO-POUND BAG.
AND TO THINK SHE ACTUALLY REGRETTED KILLING YOU!
SERIOUSLY...?! WHY?
SHE'S FUNNY LIKE THAT.
'COURSE, SHE'S ALSO A BETTER PERSON THAN YOU OR ME.

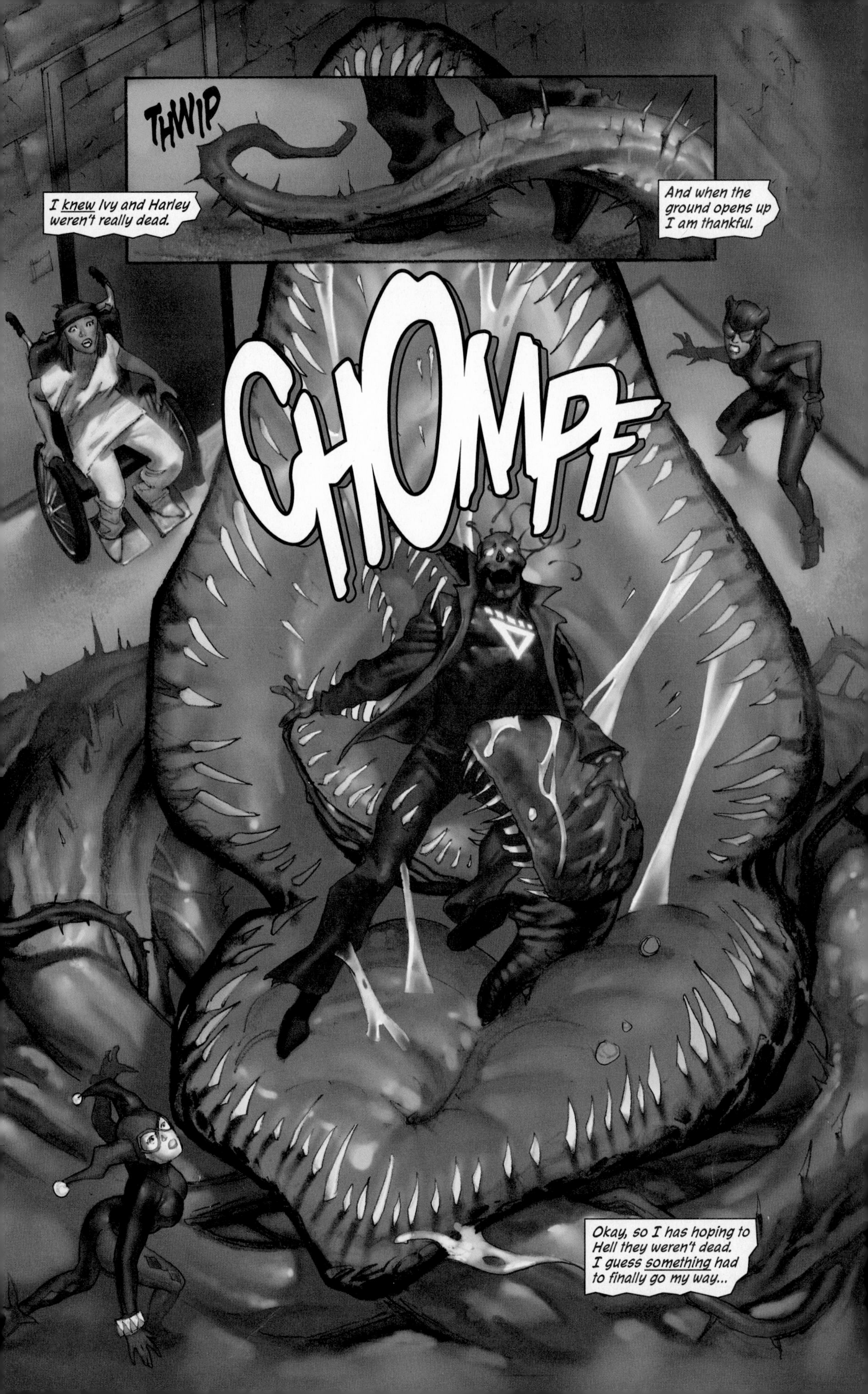
THWIP
I knew Ivy and Harley weren't really dead.
And when the ground opens up I am thankful.
CHOMPF
Okay, so I has hoping to Hell they weren't dead. I guess something had to finally go my way...

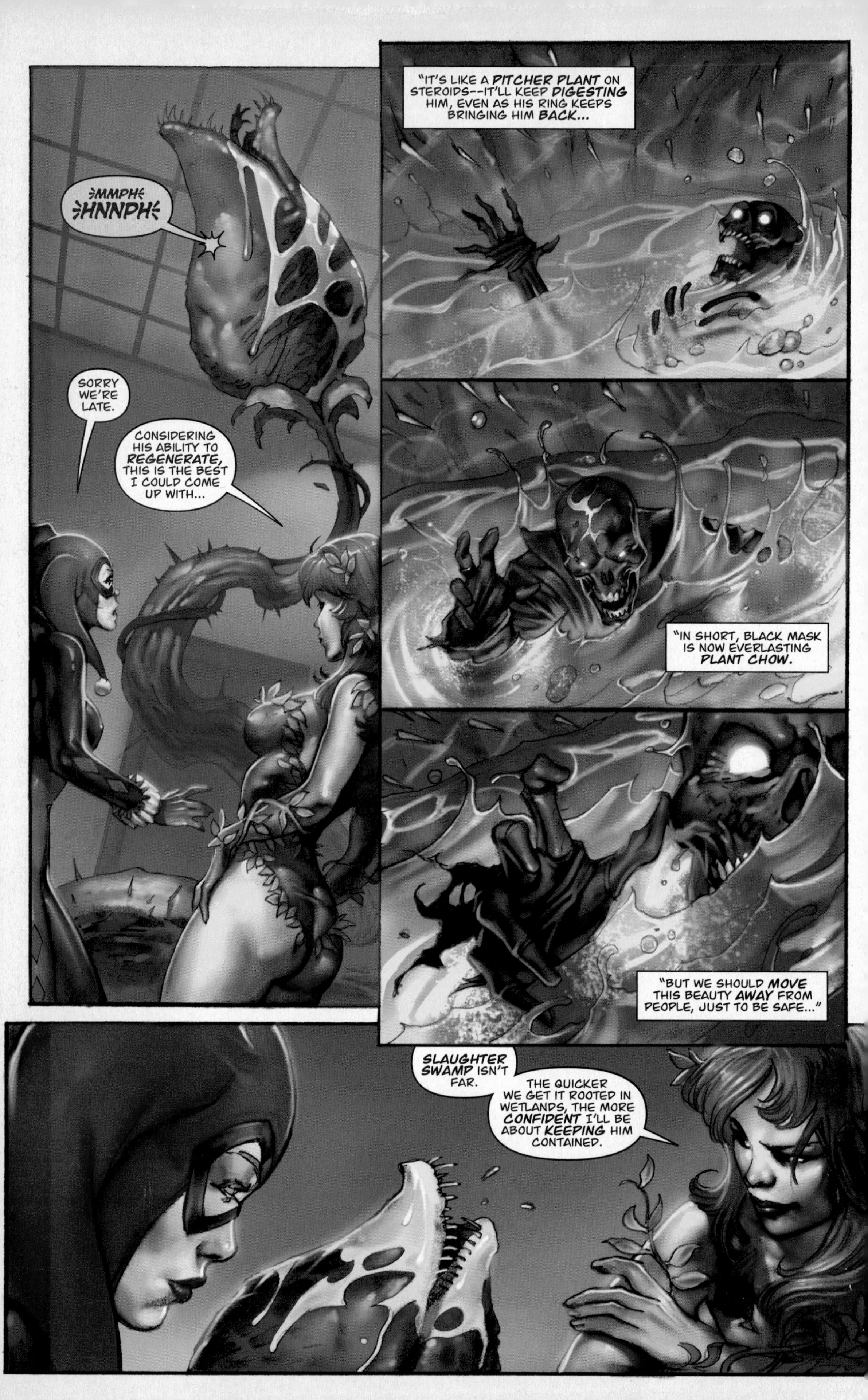
MMPH HNNPH
SORRY WE'RE LATE.
CONSIDERING HIS ABILITY TO REGENERATE, THIS IS THE BEST I COULD COME UP WITH...
"IT'S LIKE A PITCHER PLANT ON STEROIDS--IT'LL KEEP DIGESTING HIM, EVEN AS HIS RING KEEPS BRINGING HIM BACK...
"IN SHORT, BLACK MASK IS NOW EVERLASTING PLANT CHOW.
"BUT WE SHOULD MOVE THIS BEAUTY AWAY FROM PEOPLE, JUST TO BE SAFE..."
SLAUGHTER SWAMP ISN'T FAR.
THE QUICKER WE GET IT ROOTED IN WETLANDS, THE MORE CONFIDENT I'LL BE ABOUT KEEPING HIM CONTAINED.

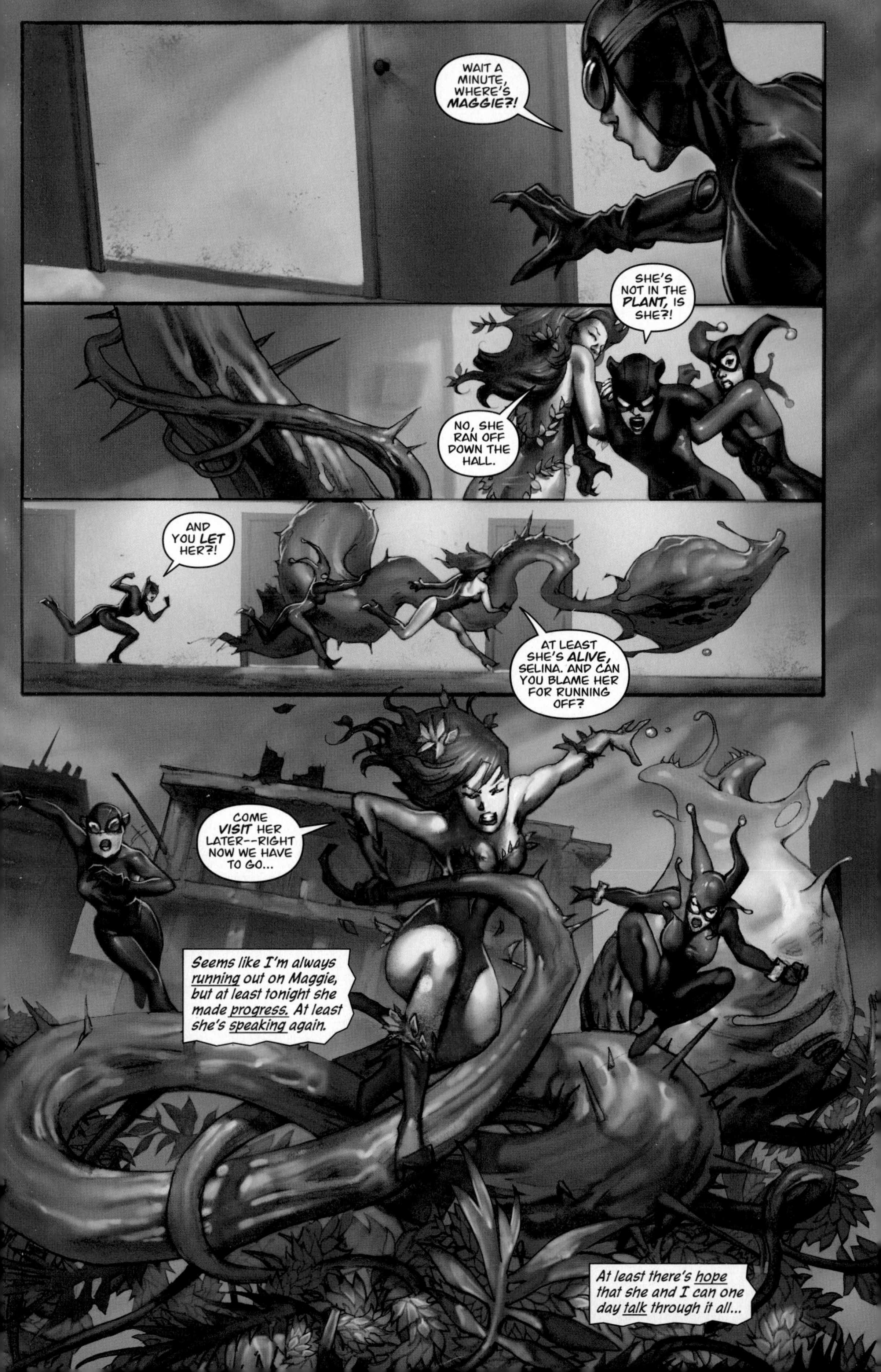

WAIT A MINUTE, WHERE'S MAGGIE?!
SHE'S NOT IN THE PLANT, IS SHE?!
NO, SHE RAN OFF DOWN THE HALL.
AND YOU LET HER?!
AT LEAST SHE'S ALIVE, SELINA. AND CAN YOU BLAME HER FOR RUNNING OFF?
COME VISIT HER LATER--RIGHT NOW WE HAVE TO GO...
Seems like I'm always running out on Maggie, but at least tonight she made progress. At least she's speaking again.
At least there's hope that she and I can one day talk through it all...

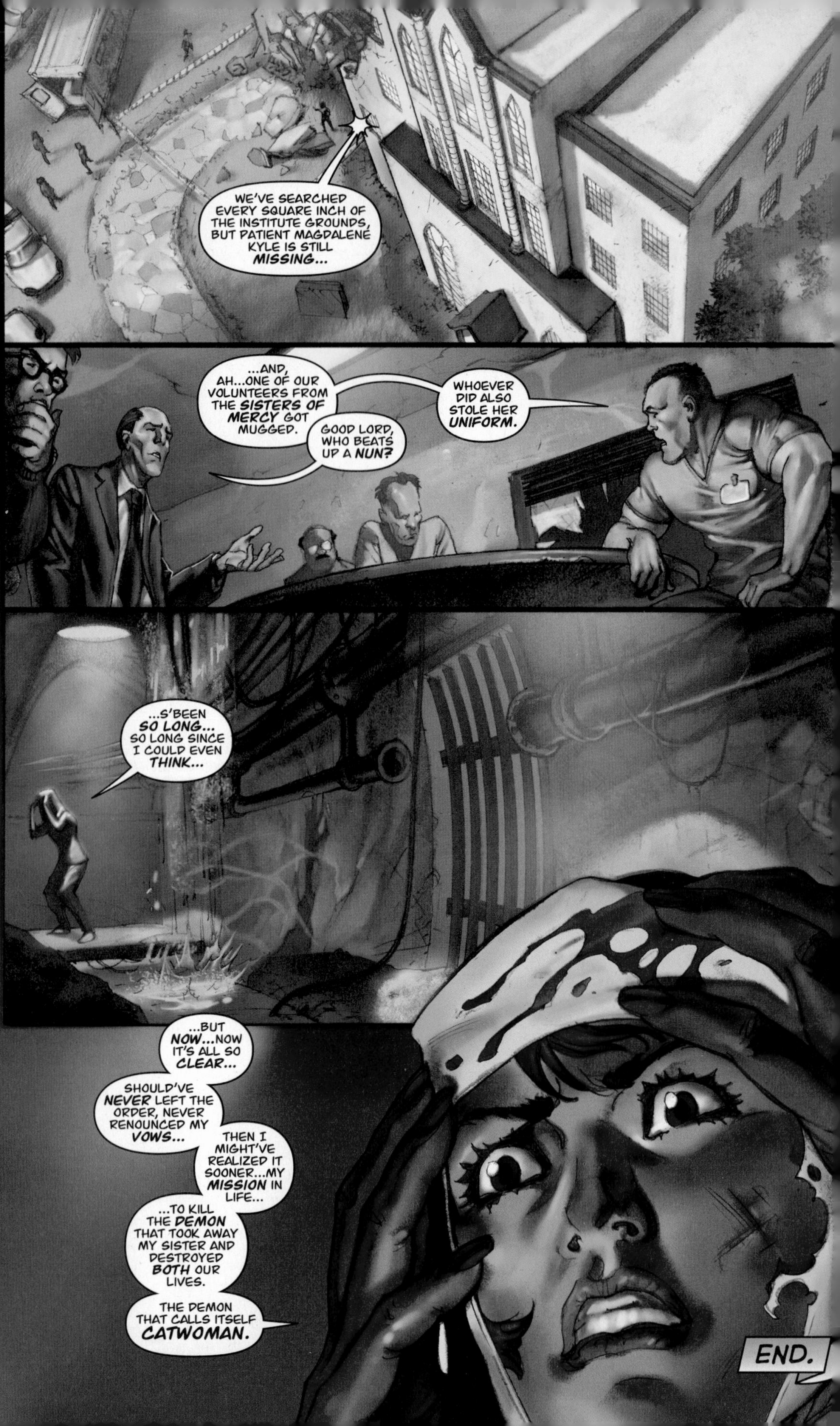
WE'VE SEARCHED EVERY SQUARE INCH OF THE INSTITUTE GROUNDS, BUT PATIENT MAGDALENE KYLE IS STILL MISSING...
...AND, AH...ONE OF OUR VOLUNTEERS FROM THE SISTERS OF MERCY GOT MUGGED.
WHOEVER DID ALSO STOLE HER UNIFORM.
GOOD LORD, WHO BEATS UP A NUN?
...S'BEEN SO LONG... SO LONG SINCE I COULD EVEN THINK...
...BUT NOW...NOW IT'S ALL SO CLEAR...
SHOULD'VE NEVER LEFT THE ORDER, NEVER RENOUNCED MY VOWS...
THEN I MIGHT'VE REALIZED IT SOONER...MY MISSION IN LIFE...
...TO KILL THE DEMON THAT TOOK AWAY MY SISTER AND DESTROYED BOTH OUR LIVES.
THE DEMON THAT CALLS ITSELF CATWOMAN.
END.

WEIRD WESTERN TALES 71

Cover by Bill Sienkiewicz

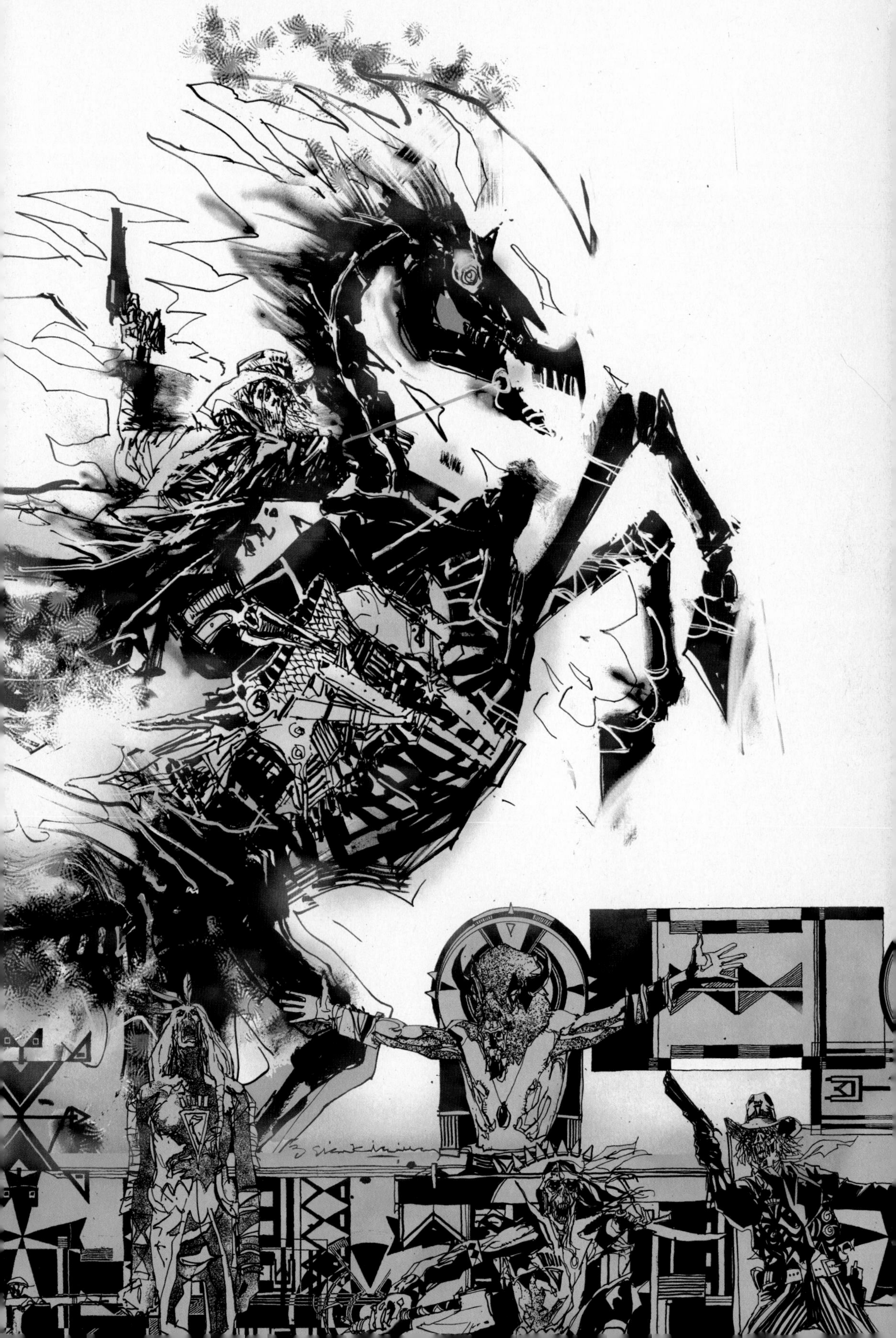

AND THE SOUTH SHALL RISE AGAIN

DAN DIDIO
WRITER

RENATO ARLEM
ARTIST

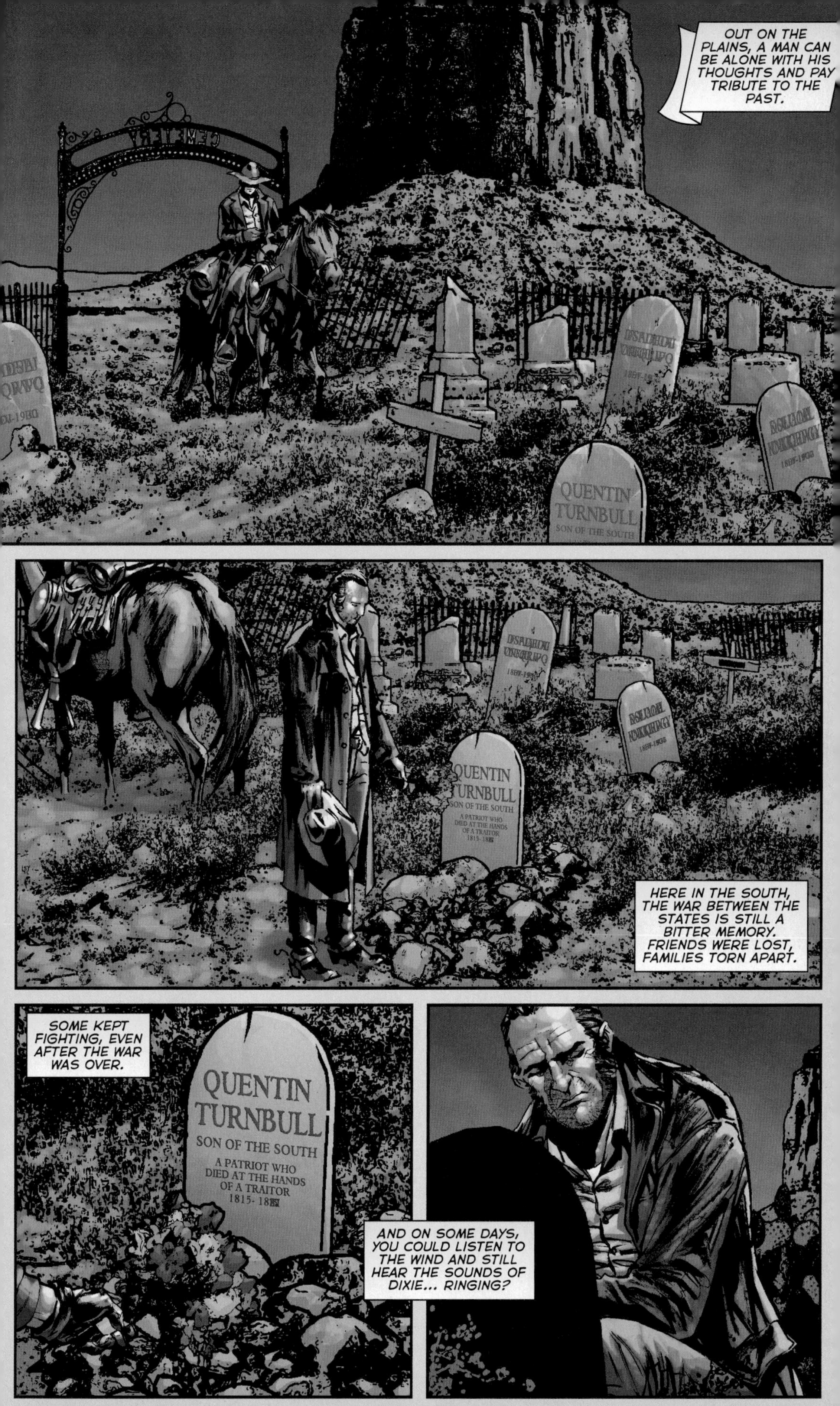
OUT ON THE PLAINS, A MAN CAN BE ALONE WITH HIS THOUGHTS AND PAY TRIBUTE TO THE PAST.
QUENTIN TURNBULL SON OF THE SOUTH
HERE IN THE SOUTH, THE WAR BETWEEN THE STATES IS STILL A BITTER MEMORY. FRIENDS WERE LOST, FAMILIES TORN APART.
SOME KEPT FIGHTING, EVEN AFTER THE WAR WAS OVER.
QUENTIN TURNBULL
SON OF THE SOUTH
A PATRIOT WHO DIED AT THE HANDS OF A TRAITOR
AND ON SOME DAYS, YOU COULD LISTEN TO THE WIND AND STILL HEAR THE SOUNDS OF DIXIE... RINGING?

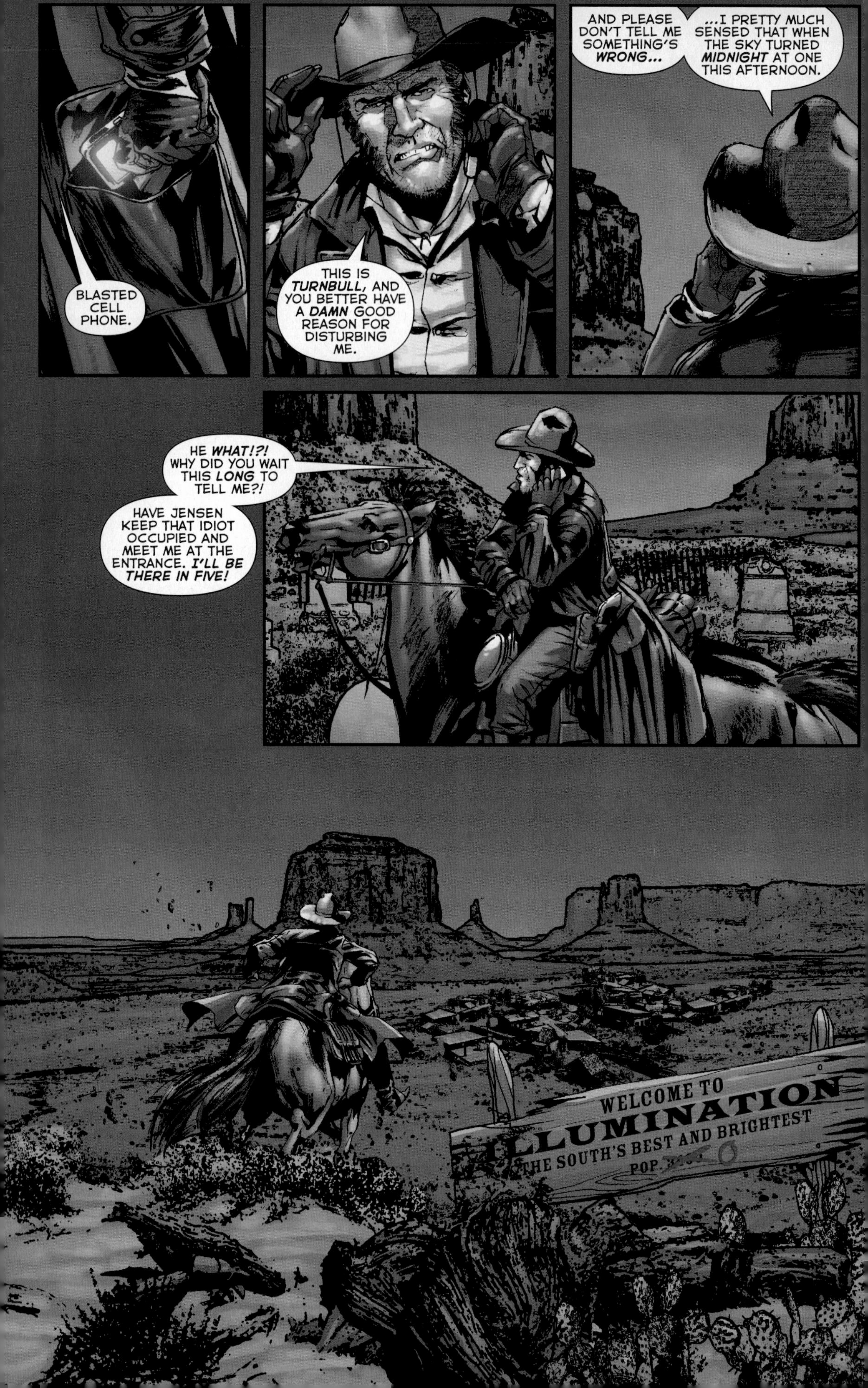

BLASTED CELL PHONE.
THIS IS TURNBULL, AND YOU BETTER HAVE A DAMN GOOD REASON FOR DISTURBING ME.
AND PLEASE DON'T TELL ME SOMETHING'S WRONG...
...I PRETTY MUCH SENSED THAT WHEN THE SKY TURNED MIDNIGHT AT ONE THIS AFTERNOON.
HE WHAT!?! WHY DID YOU WAIT THIS LONG TO TELL ME?!
HAVE JENSEN KEEP THAT IDIOT OCCUPIED AND MEET ME AT THE ENTRANCE. I'LL BE THERE IN FIVE!
WELCOME TO
ILLUMINATION
THE SOUTH'S BEST AND BRIGHTEST
POP.

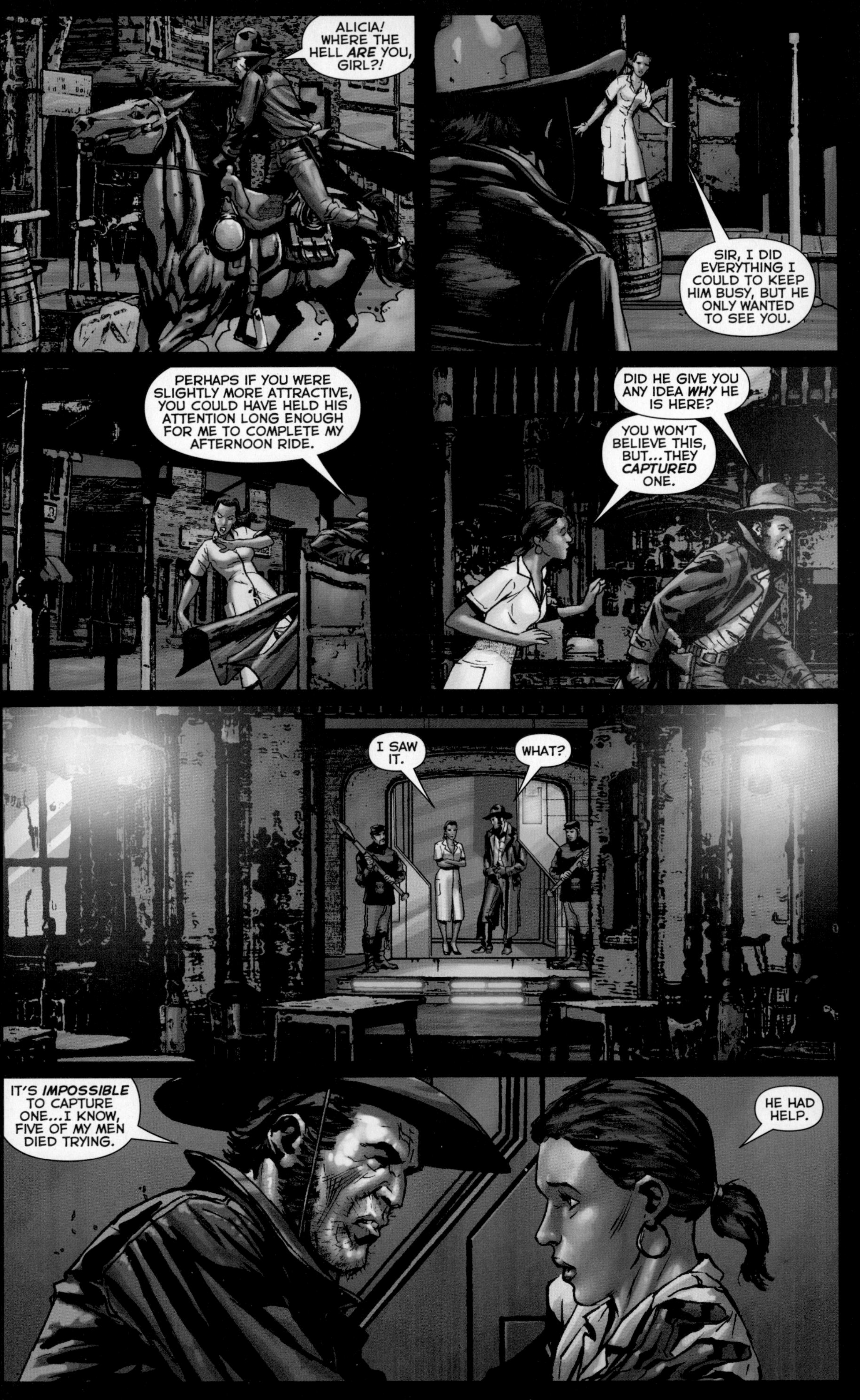
ALICIA! WHERE THE HELL ARE YOU, GIRL?!
SIR, I DID EVERYTHING I COULD TO KEEP HIM BUSY, BUT HE ONLY WANTED TO SEE YOU.
PERHAPS IF YOU WERE SLIGHTLY MORE ATTRACTIVE, YOU COULD HAVE HELD HIS ATTENTION LONG ENOUGH FOR ME TO COMPLETE MY AFTERNOON RIDE.
DID HE GIVE YOU ANY IDEA WHY HE IS HERE?
YOU WON'T BELIEVE THIS, BUT... THEY CAPTURED ONE.
I SAW IT.
WHAT?
IT'S IMPOSSIBLE TO CAPTURE ONE... I KNOW, FIVE OF MY MEN DIED TRYING.
HE HAD HELP.

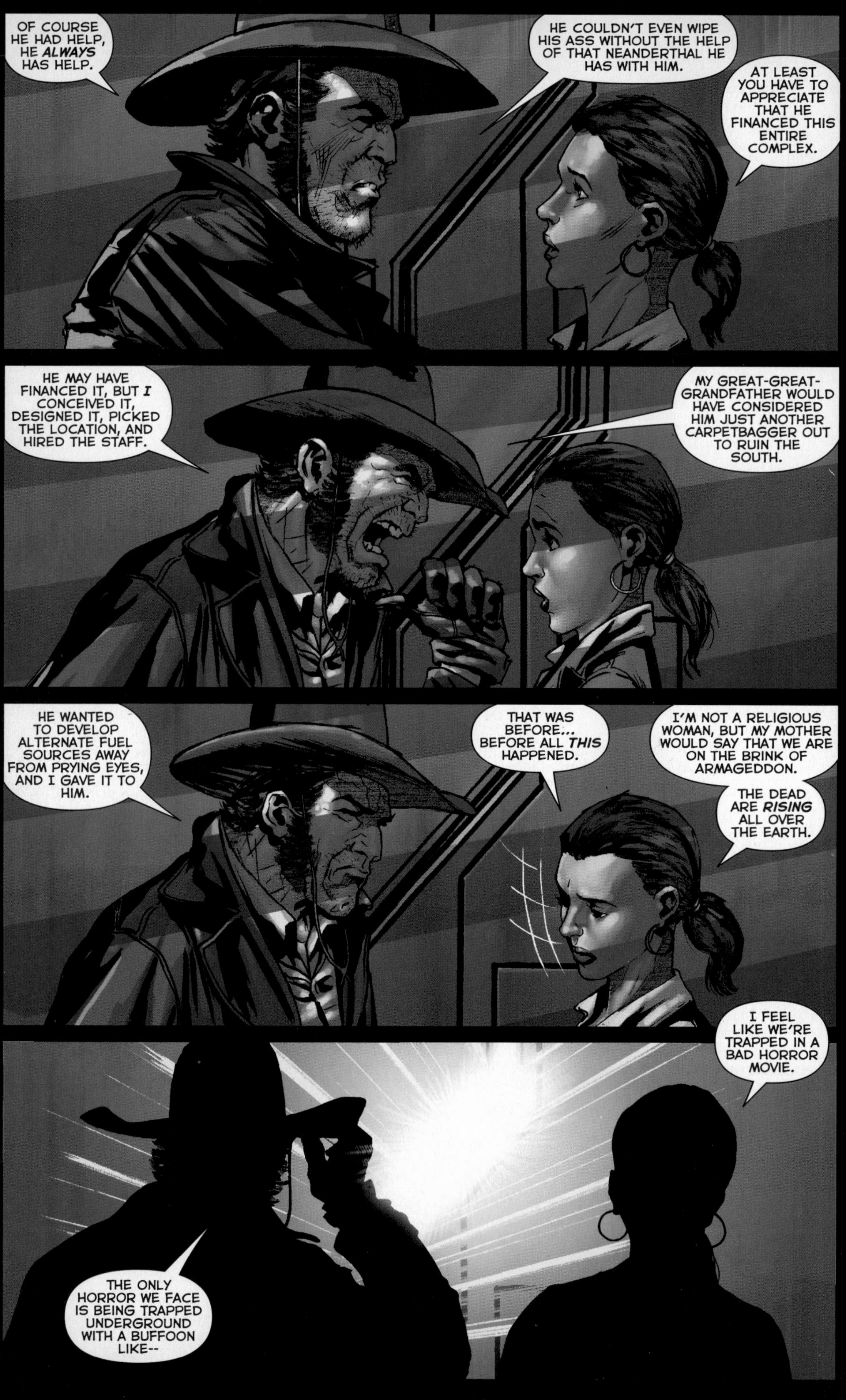
OF COURSE HE HAD HELP, HE *ALWAYS* HAS HELP.
HE COULDN'T EVEN WIPE HIS ASS WITHOUT THE HELP OF THAT NEANDERTHAL HE HAS WITH HIM.
AT LEAST YOU HAVE TO APPRECIATE THAT HE FINANCED THIS ENTIRE COMPLEX.
HE MAY HAVE FINANCED IT, BUT *I* CONCEIVED IT, DESIGNED IT, PICKED THE LOCATION, AND HIRED THE STAFF.
MY GREAT-GREAT-GRANDFATHER WOULD HAVE CONSIDERED HIM JUST ANOTHER CARPETBAGGER OUT TO RUIN THE SOUTH.
HE WANTED TO DEVELOP ALTERNATE FUEL SOURCES AWAY FROM PRYING EYES, AND I GAVE IT TO HIM.
THAT WAS BEFORE... BEFORE ALL *THIS* HAPPENED.
I'M NOT A RELIGIOUS WOMAN, BUT MY MOTHER WOULD SAY THAT WE ARE ON THE BRINK OF ARMAGEDDON.
THE DEAD ARE *RISING* ALL OVER THE EARTH.
I FEEL LIKE WE'RE TRAPPED IN A BAD HORROR MOVIE.
THE ONLY HORROR WE FACE IS BEING TRAPPED UNDERGROUND WITH A BUFFOON LIKE--

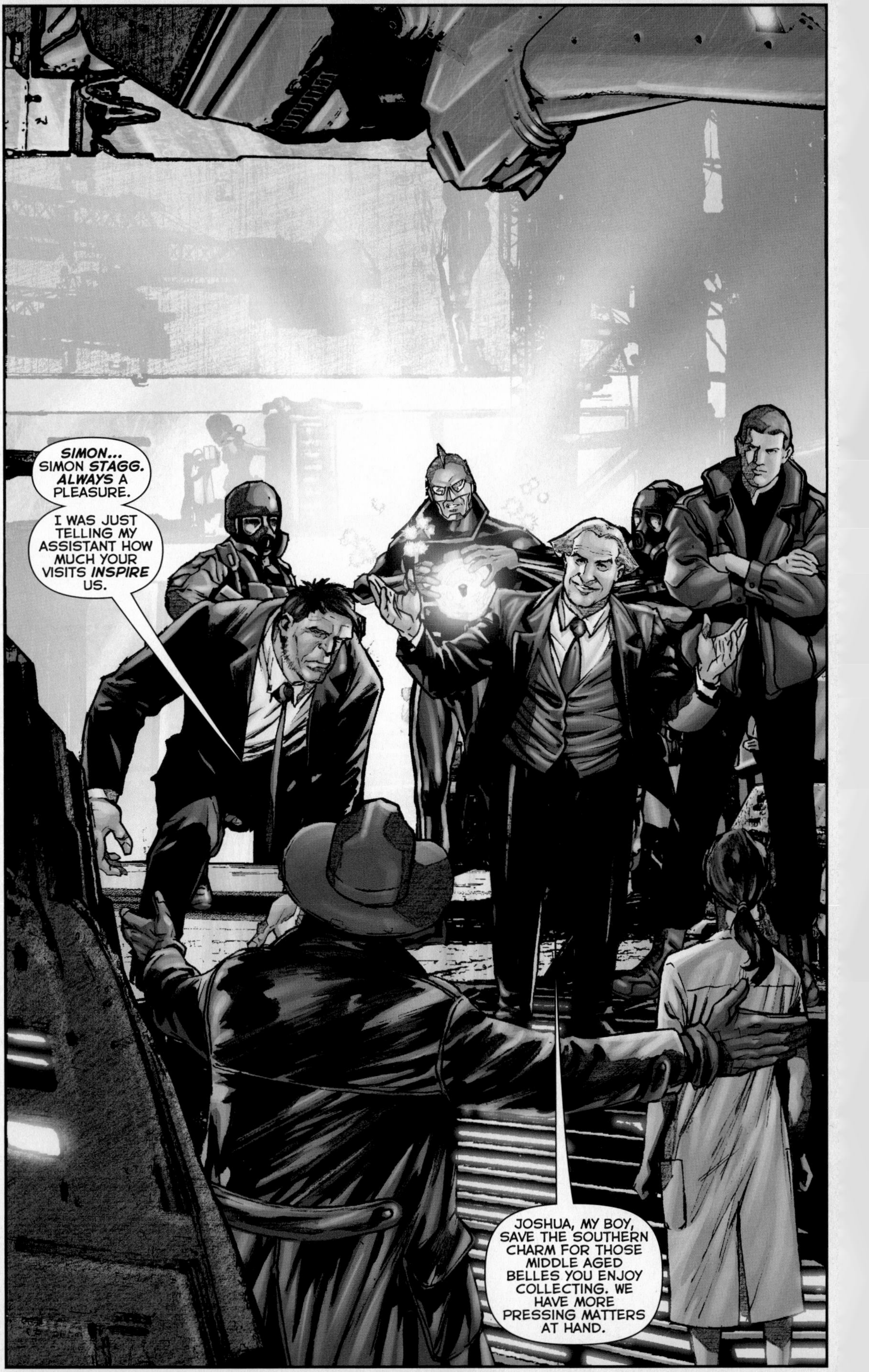
SIMON... SIMON STAGG. ALWAYS A PLEASURE.
I WAS JUST TELLING MY ASSISTANT HOW MUCH YOUR VISITS INSPIRE US.
JOSHUA, MY BOY, SAVE THE SOUTHERN CHARM FOR THOSE MIDDLE AGED BELLES YOU ENJOY COLLECTING. WE HAVE MORE PRESSING MATTERS AT HAND.

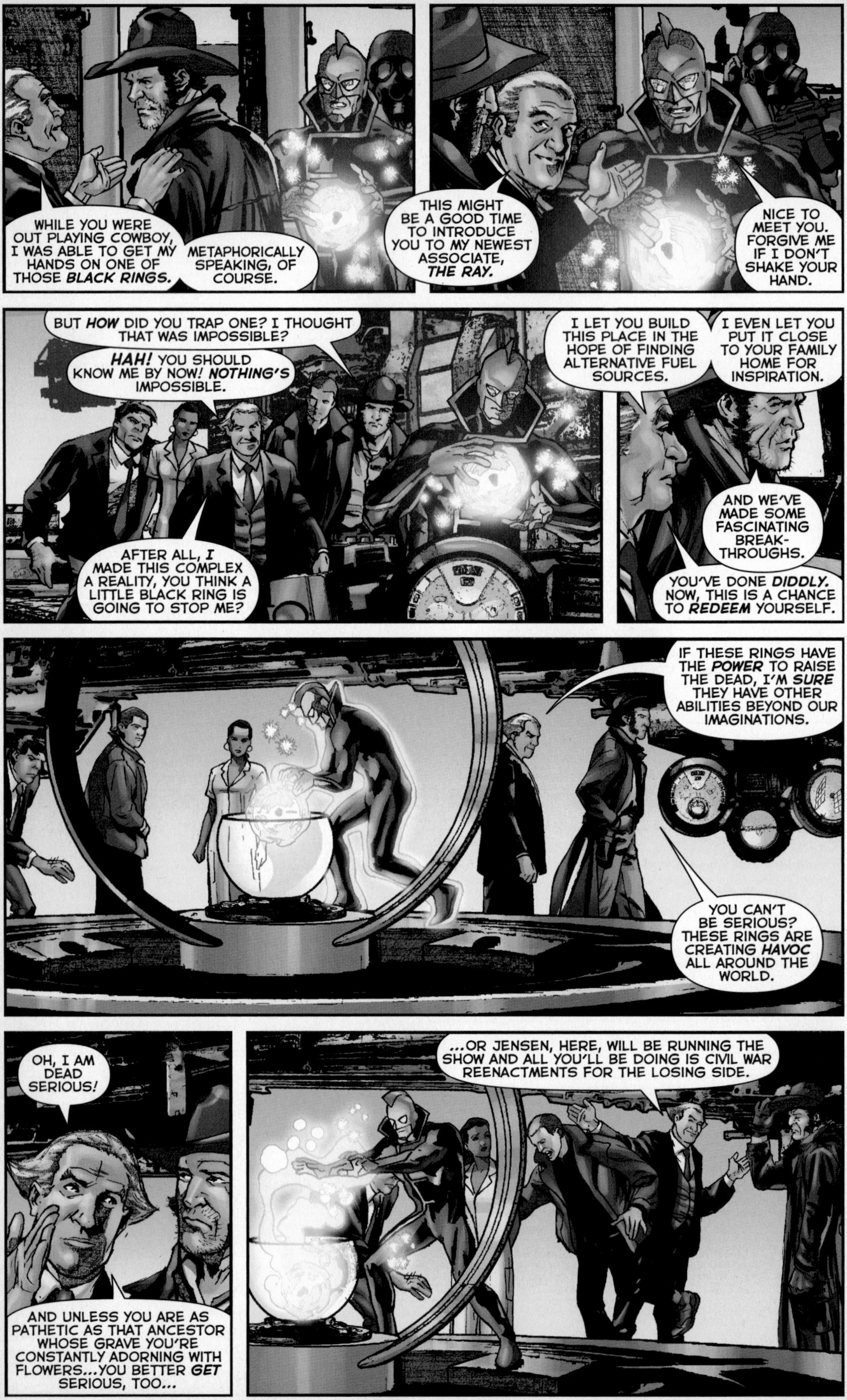
WHILE YOU WERE OUT PLAYING COWBOY, I WAS ABLE TO GET MY HANDS ON ONE OF THOSE BLACK RINGS.
METAPHORICALLY SPEAKING, OF COURSE.
THIS MIGHT BE A GOOD TIME TO INTRODUCE YOU TO MY NEWEST ASSOCIATE, THE RAY.
NICE TO MEET YOU. FORGIVE ME IF I DON'T SHAKE YOUR HAND.
BUT HOW DID YOU TRAP ONE? I THOUGHT THAT WAS IMPOSSIBLE?
HAH! YOU SHOULD KNOW ME BY NOW! NOTHING'S IMPOSSIBLE.
AFTER ALL, I MADE THIS COMPLEX A REALITY, YOU THINK A LITTLE BLACK RING IS GOING TO STOP ME?
I LET YOU BUILD THIS PLACE IN THE HOPE OF FINDING ALTERNATIVE FUEL SOURCES.
I EVEN LET YOU PUT IT CLOSE TO YOUR FAMILY HOME FOR INSPIRATION.
AND WE'VE MADE SOME FASCINATING BREAK-THROUGHS.
YOU'VE DONE DIDDLY. NOW, THIS IS A CHANCE TO REDEEM YOURSELF.
IF THESE RINGS HAVE THE POWER TO RAISE THE DEAD, I'M SURE THEY HAVE OTHER ABILITIES BEYOND OUR IMAGINATIONS.
YOU CAN'T BE SERIOUS? THESE RINGS ARE CREATING HAVOC ALL AROUND THE WORLD.
OH, I AM DEAD SERIOUS!
AND UNLESS YOU ARE AS PATHETIC AS THAT ANCESTOR WHOSE GRAVE YOU'RE CONSTANTLY ADORNING WITH FLOWERS...YOU BETTER GET SERIOUS, TOO...
...OR JENSEN, HERE, WILL BE RUNNING THE SHOW AND ALL YOU'LL BE DOING IS CIVIL WAR REENACTMENTS FOR THE LOSING SIDE.

CONTAINMENT IS COMPLETE. IT'S ALL YOURS NOW.

IF YOU REALLY WANT TO KNOW HOW WE GOT THE RING, BEST YOU ASK THE RAY. HE CAN TELL YOU ABOUT ITS DRAMATIC CAPTURE.

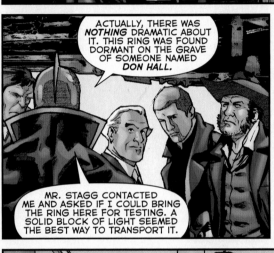

ACTUALLY, THERE WAS *NOTHING* DRAMATIC ABOUT IT. THIS RING WAS FOUND DORMANT ON THE GRAVE OF SOMEONE NAMED *DON HALL.*

MR. STAGG CONTACTED ME AND ASKED IF I COULD BRING THE RING HERE FOR TESTING. A SOLID BLOCK OF LIGHT SEEMED THE BEST WAY TO TRANSPORT IT.

JOSH! THE RING SEEMS TO BE RESISTING ANY FORM OF ANALYSIS.

ALL IT'S RESISTING IS *YOUR* STUPIDITY! *I* CAN BREAK IT, *I* CAN FIND WHAT SECRETS IT HOLDS.

AVARICE

NOW YOU BOYS PLAY NICE, AND LET ME KNOW AS SOON AS YOU HAVE SOME RESULTS.

I'LL BE AWAITING YOUR CALL IN MY SAFE HOUSE. IT'S THE BEST PLACE TO SIT THIS OUT.

WE'RE A HALF MILE UNDERGROUND WITH CONCRETE- AND STEEL-REINFORCED WALLS, HOW MUCH SAFER CAN YOU *BE?*

YOU'D BE *SURPRISED.*

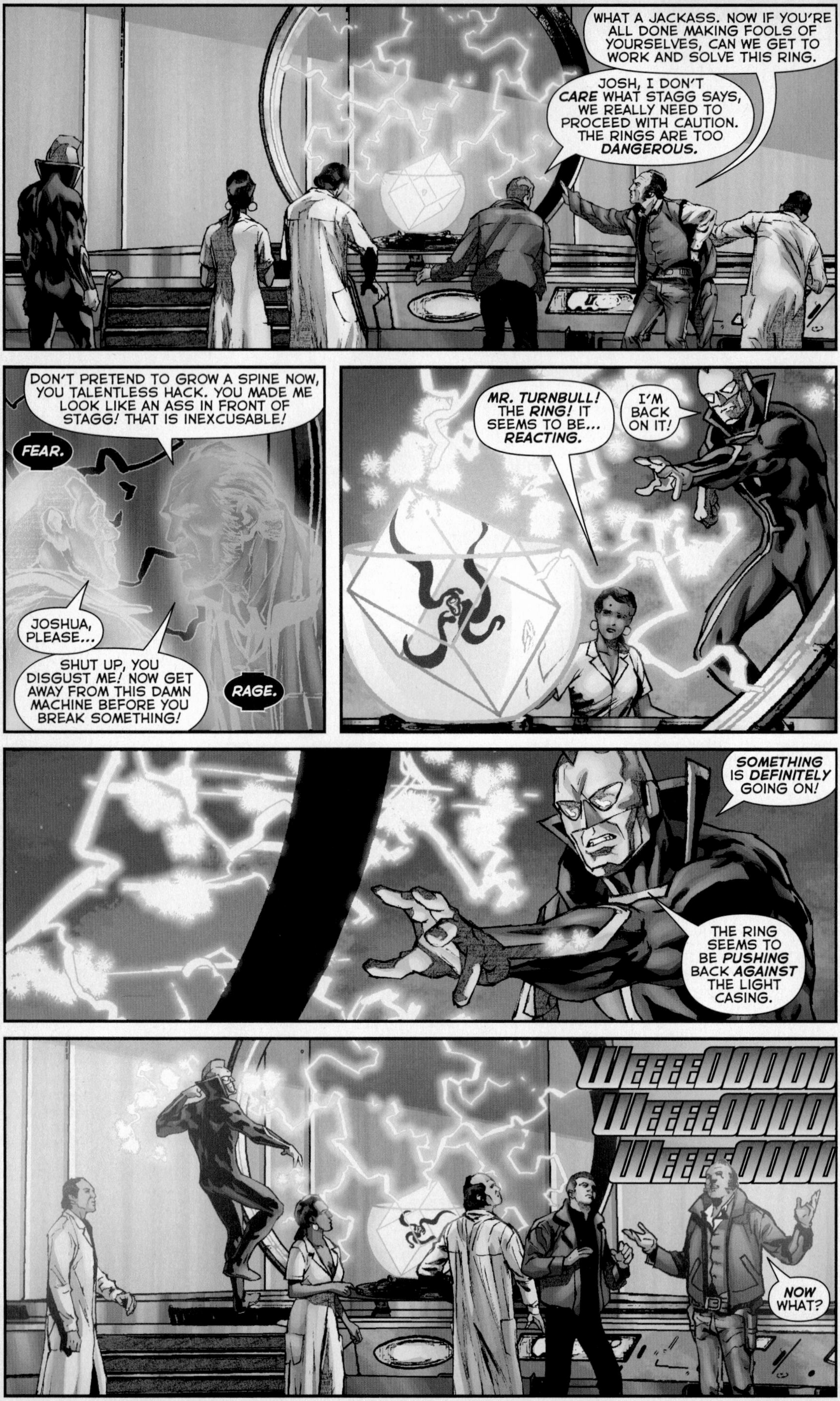

WHAT A JACKASS. NOW IF YOU'RE ALL DONE MAKING FOOLS OF YOURSELVES, CAN WE GET TO WORK AND SOLVE THIS RING.
JOSH, I DON'T CARE WHAT STAGG SAYS, WE REALLY NEED TO PROCEED WITH CAUTION. THE RINGS ARE TOO DANGEROUS.
DON'T PRETEND TO GROW A SPINE NOW, YOU TALENTLESS HACK. YOU MADE ME LOOK LIKE AN ASS IN FRONT OF STAGG! THAT IS INEXCUSABLE!
FEAR.
JOSHUA, PLEASE...
SHUT UP, YOU DISGUST ME! NOW GET AWAY FROM THIS DAMN MACHINE BEFORE YOU BREAK SOMETHING!
RAGE.
MR. TURNBULL! THE RING! IT SEEMS TO BE... REACTING.
I'M BACK ON IT!
SOMETHING IS DEFINITELY GOING ON!
THE RING SEEMS TO BE PUSHING BACK AGAINST THE LIGHT CASING.
WEEEOOOOO
WEEEOOOO
WEEEOOOO
NOW WHAT?

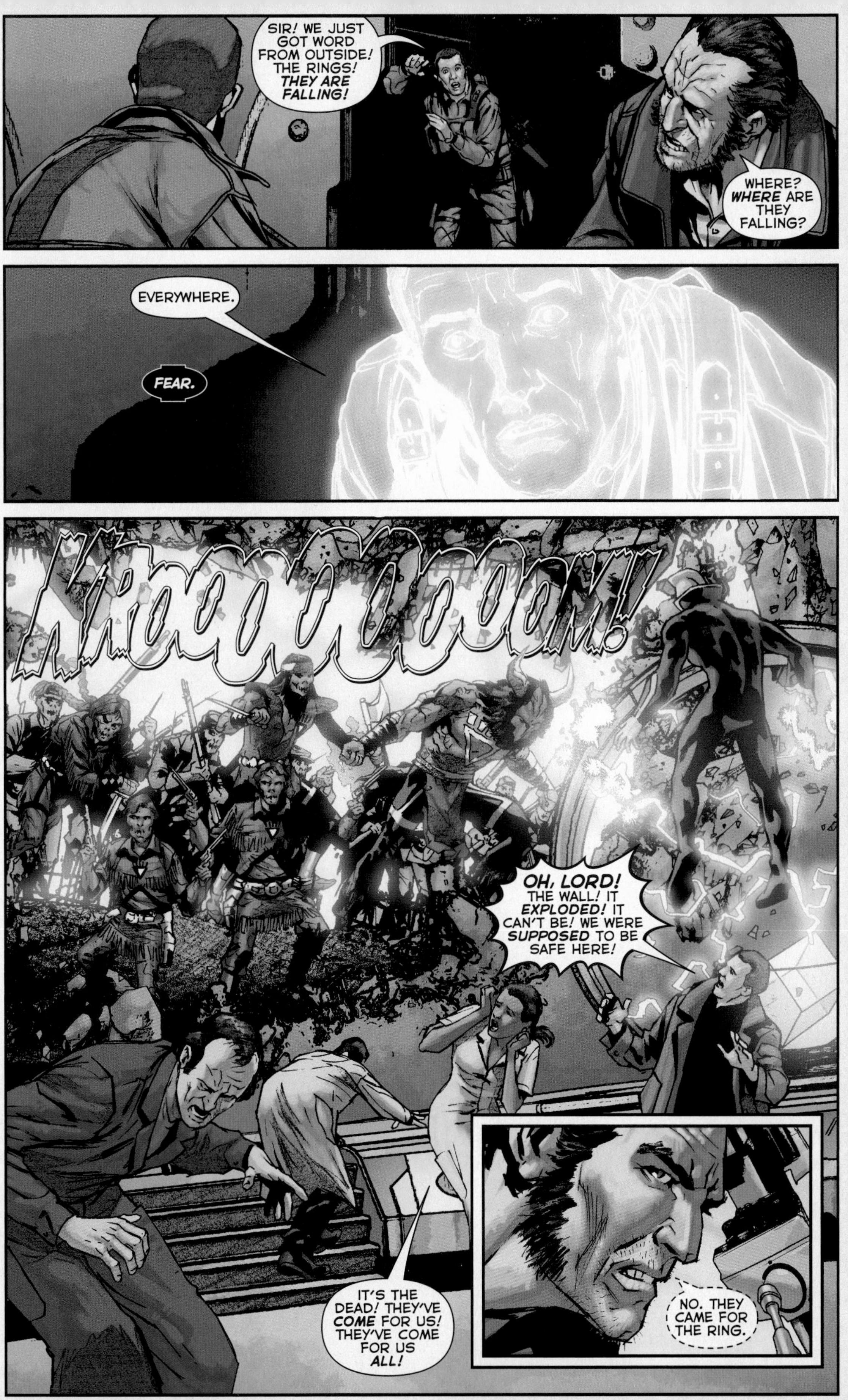
SIR! WE JUST GOT WORD FROM OUTSIDE! THE RINGS! THEY ARE FALLING!
WHERE? WHERE ARE THEY FALLING?
EVERYWHERE.
FEAR.
KRROOOOOOOOOM!
OH, LORD! THE WALL! IT EXPLODED! IT CAN'T BE! WE WERE SUPPOSED TO BE SAFE HERE!
IT'S THE DEAD! THEY'VE COME FOR US! THEY'VE COME FOR US ALL!
NO. THEY CAME FOR THE RING.

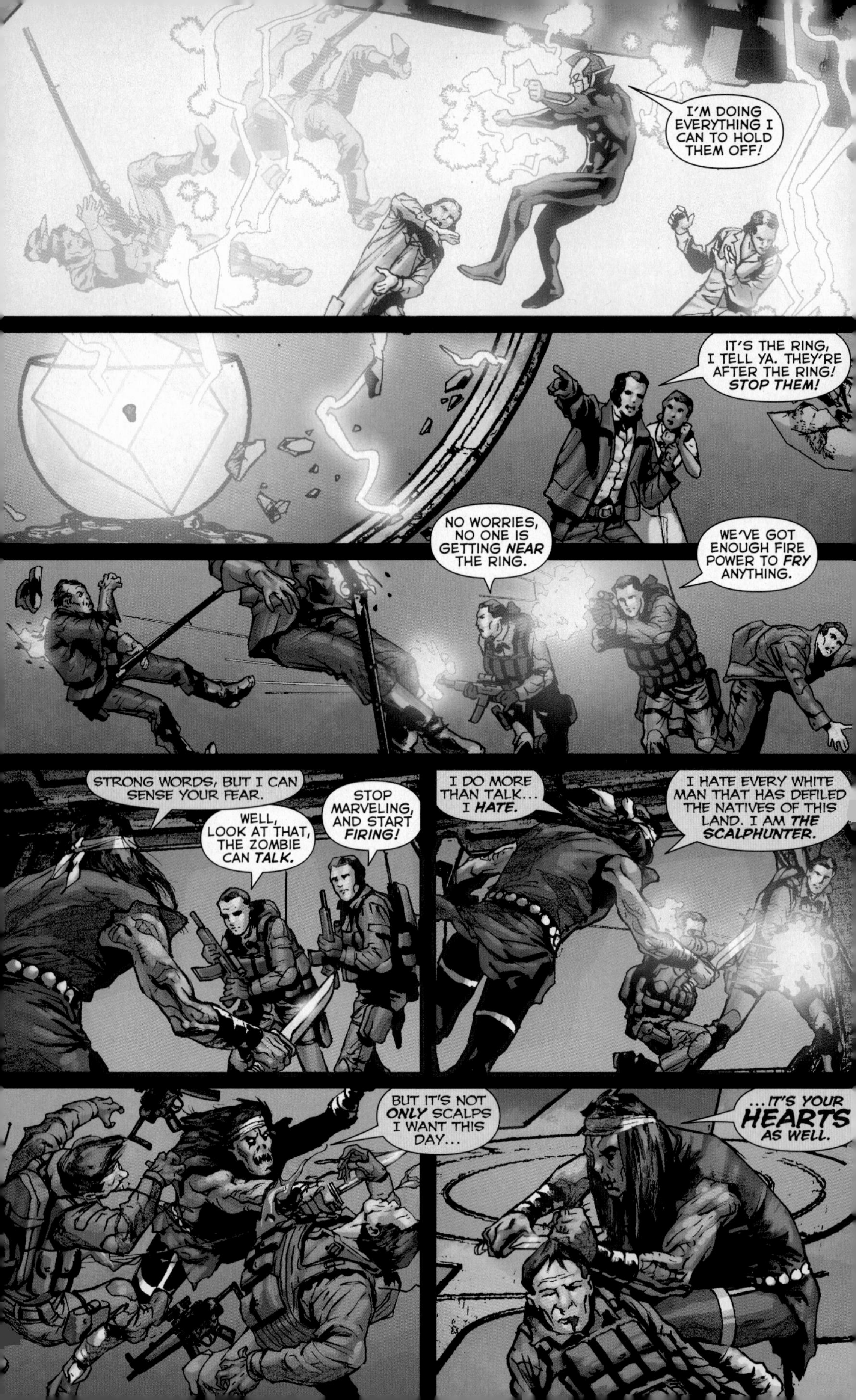
I'M DOING EVERYTHING I CAN TO HOLD THEM OFF!
IT'S THE RING, I TELL YA. THEY'RE AFTER THE RING! STOP THEM!
NO WORRIES, NO ONE IS GETTING NEAR THE RING.
WE'VE GOT ENOUGH FIRE POWER TO FRY ANYTHING.
STRONG WORDS, BUT I CAN SENSE YOUR FEAR.
WELL, LOOK AT THAT, THE ZOMBIE CAN TALK.
STOP MARVELING, AND START FIRING!
I DO MORE THAN TALK... I HATE.
I HATE EVERY WHITE MAN THAT HAS DEFILED THE NATIVES OF THIS LAND. I AM THE SCALPHUNTER.
BUT IT'S NOT ONLY SCALPS I WANT THIS DAY...
...IT'S YOUR HEARTS AS WELL.

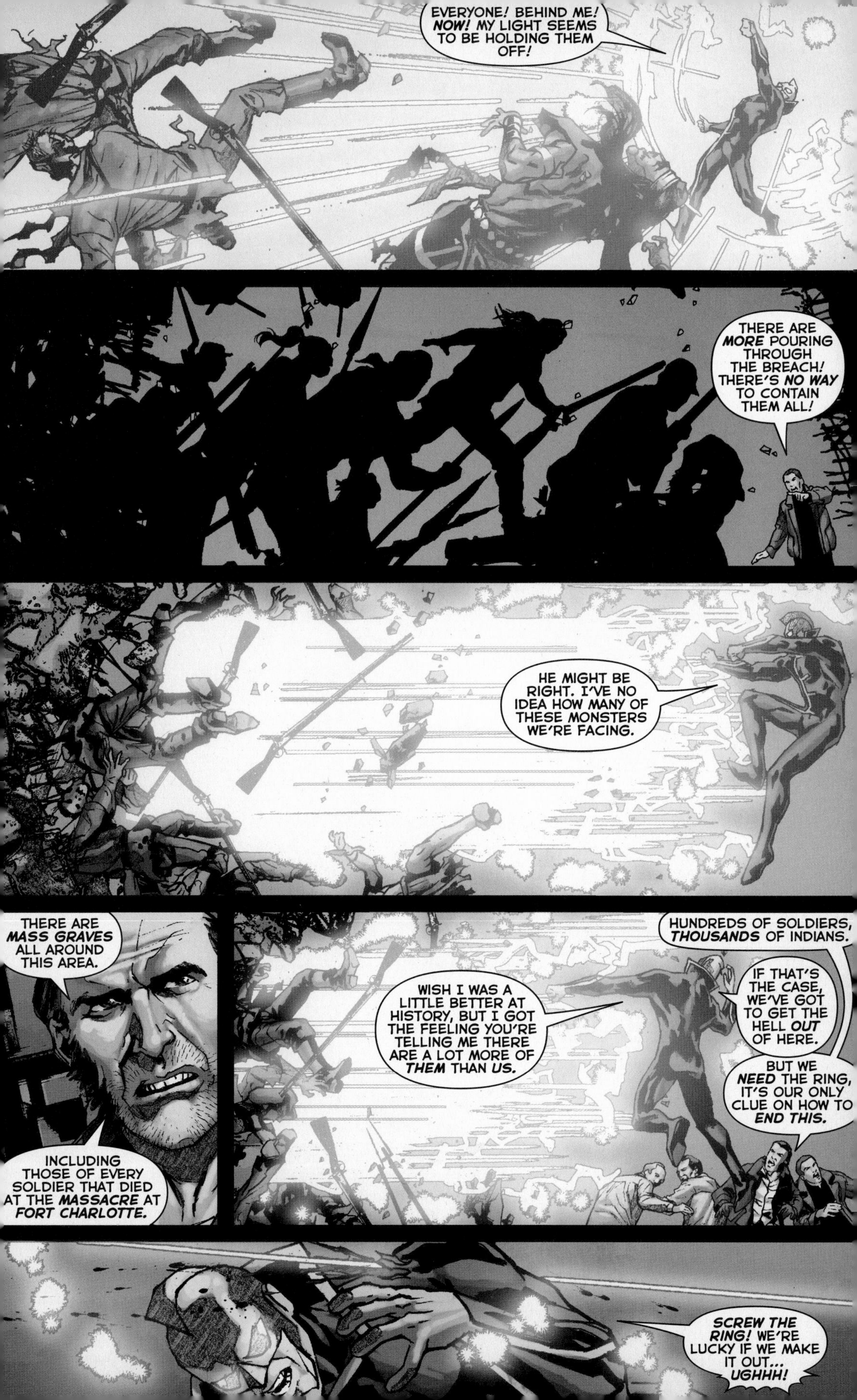

EVERYONE! BEHIND ME! NOW! MY LIGHT SEEMS TO BE HOLDING THEM OFF!
THERE ARE MORE POURING THROUGH THE BREACH! THERE'S NO WAY TO CONTAIN THEM ALL!
HE MIGHT BE RIGHT. I'VE NO IDEA HOW MANY OF THESE MONSTERS WE'RE FACING.
THERE ARE MASS GRAVES ALL AROUND THIS AREA.
INCLUDING THOSE OF EVERY SOLDIER THAT DIED AT THE MASSACRE AT FORT CHARLOTTE.
HUNDREDS OF SOLDIERS, THOUSANDS OF INDIANS.
WISH I WAS A LITTLE BETTER AT HISTORY, BUT I GOT THE FEELING YOU'RE TELLING ME THERE ARE A LOT MORE OF THEM THAN US.
IF THAT'S THE CASE, WE'VE GOT TO GET THE HELL OUT OF HERE.
BUT WE NEED THE RING, IT'S OUR ONLY CLUE ON HOW TO END THIS.
SCREW THE RING! WE'RE LUCKY IF WE MAKE IT OUT... UGHHH!

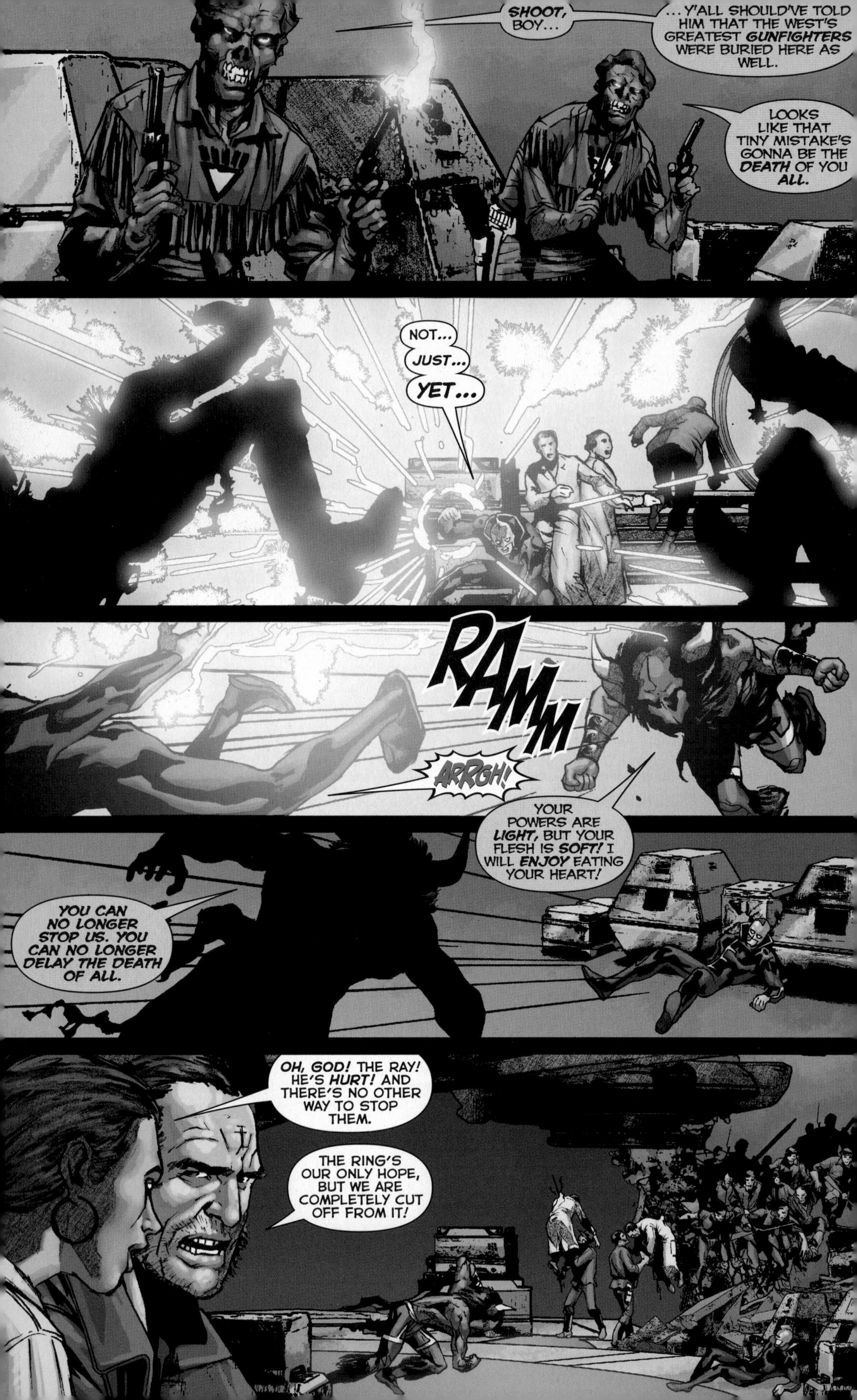
SHOOT, BOY...
...Y'ALL SHOULD'VE TOLD HIM THAT THE WEST'S GREATEST GUNFIGHTERS WERE BURIED HERE AS WELL.
LOOKS LIKE THAT TINY MISTAKE'S GONNA BE THE DEATH OF YOU ALL.
NOT...
JUST...
YET...
RAMM
ARRGH!
YOUR POWERS ARE LIGHT, BUT YOUR FLESH IS SOFT! I WILL ENJOY EATING YOUR HEART!
YOU CAN NO LONGER STOP US. YOU CAN NO LONGER DELAY THE DEATH OF ALL.
OH, GOD! THE RAY! HE'S HURT! AND THERE'S NO OTHER WAY TO STOP THEM.
THE RING'S OUR ONLY HOPE, BUT WE ARE COMPLETELY CUT OFF FROM IT!

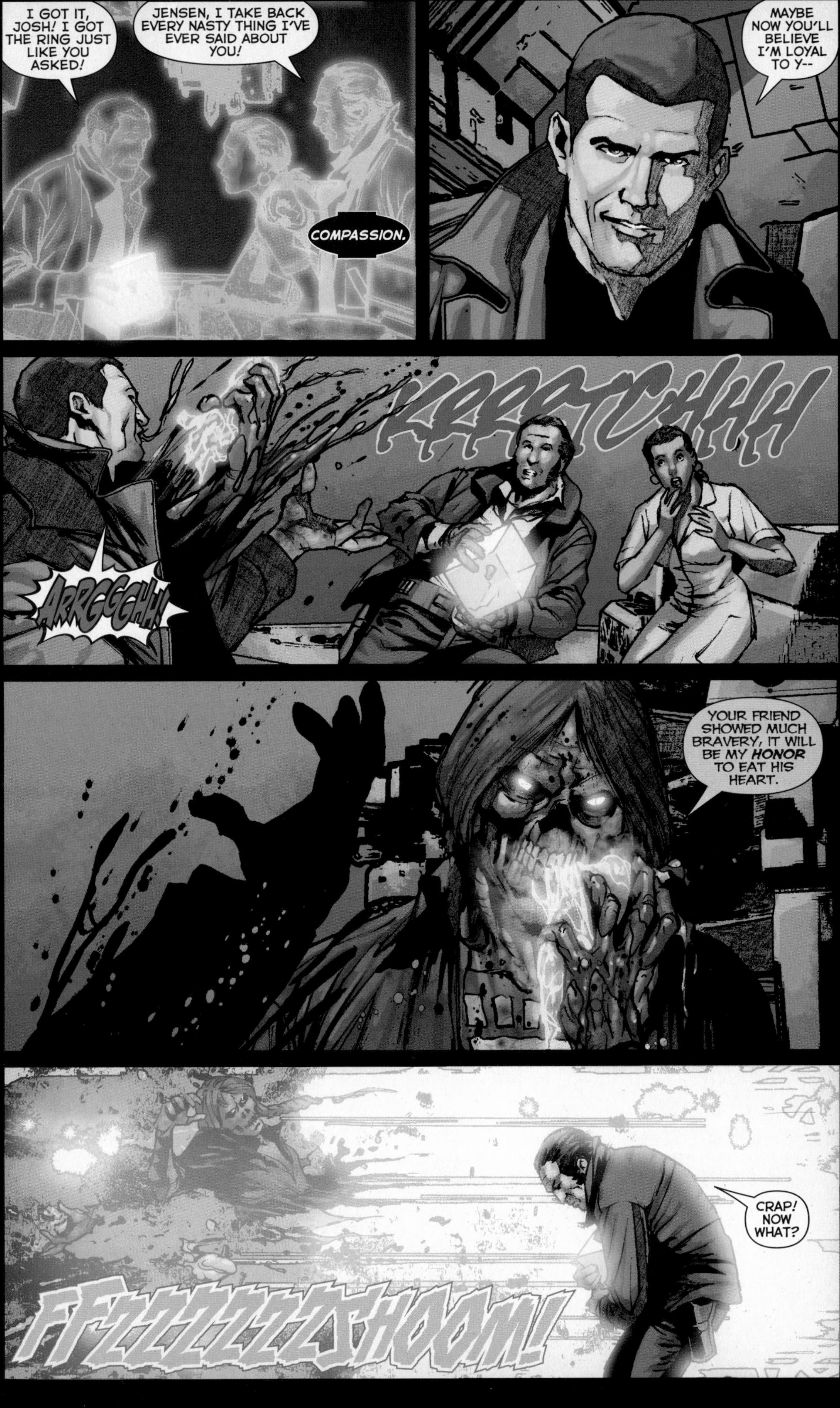
I GOT IT, JOSH! I GOT THE RING JUST LIKE YOU ASKED!
JENSEN, I TAKE BACK EVERY NASTY THING I'VE EVER SAID ABOUT YOU!
COMPASSION.
MAYBE NOW YOU'LL BELIEVE I'M LOYAL TO Y--
KRRRTCHHH
ARRGGGHH!
YOUR FRIEND SHOWED MUCH BRAVERY, IT WILL BE MY HONOR TO EAT HIS HEART.
CRAP! NOW WHAT?
FFZZZZZZSHOOM!

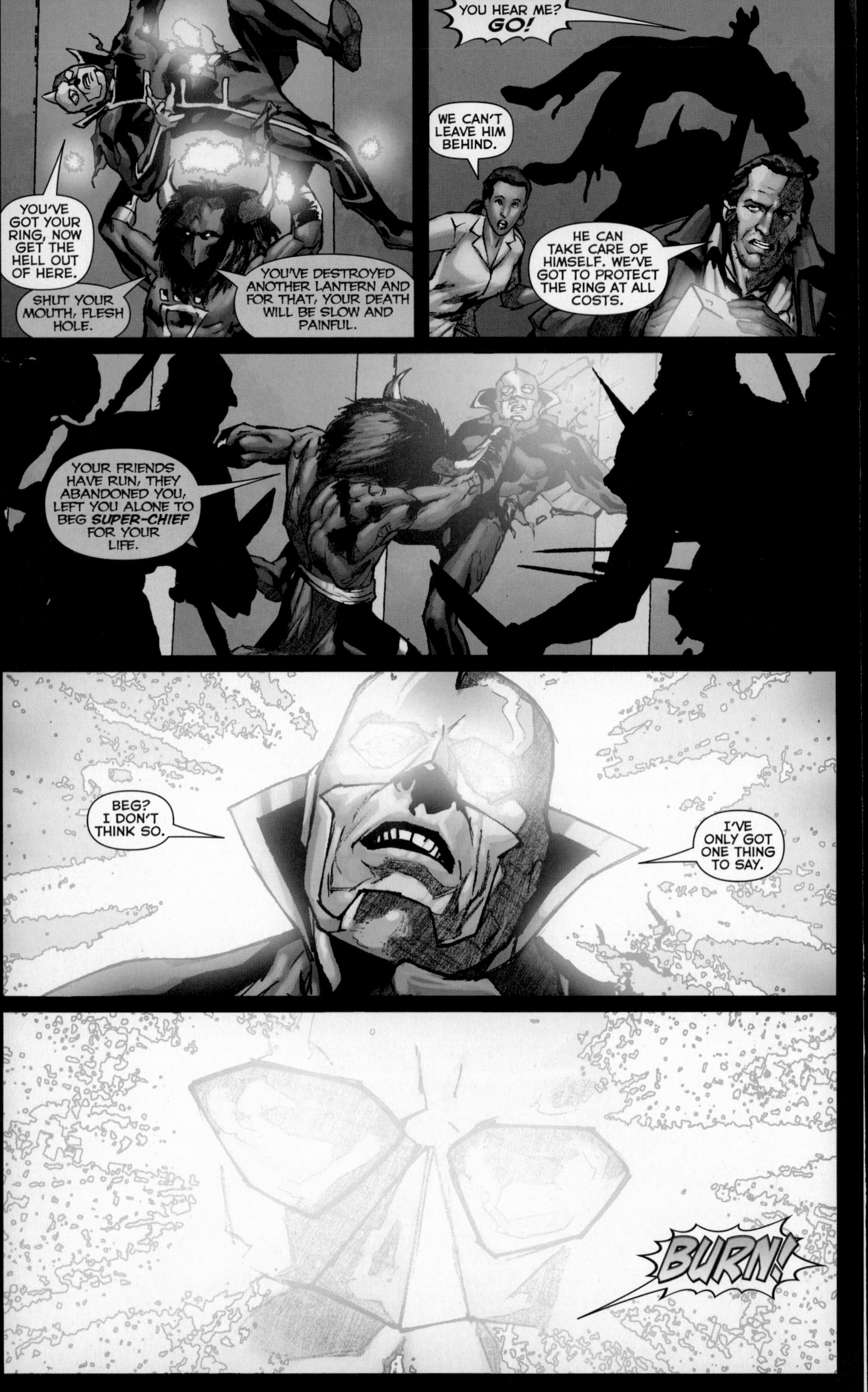
YOU HEAR ME? GO!
YOU'VE GOT YOUR RING, NOW GET THE HELL OUT OF HERE.
SHUT YOUR MOUTH, FLESH HOLE.
YOU'VE DESTROYED ANOTHER LANTERN AND FOR THAT, YOUR DEATH WILL BE SLOW AND PAINFUL.
WE CAN'T LEAVE HIM BEHIND.
HE CAN TAKE CARE OF HIMSELF. WE'VE GOT TO PROTECT THE RING AT ALL COSTS.
YOUR FRIENDS HAVE RUN, THEY ABANDONED YOU, LEFT YOU ALONE TO BEG SUPER-CHIEF FOR YOUR LIFE.
BEG? I DON'T THINK SO.
I'VE ONLY GOT ONE THING TO SAY.
BURN!

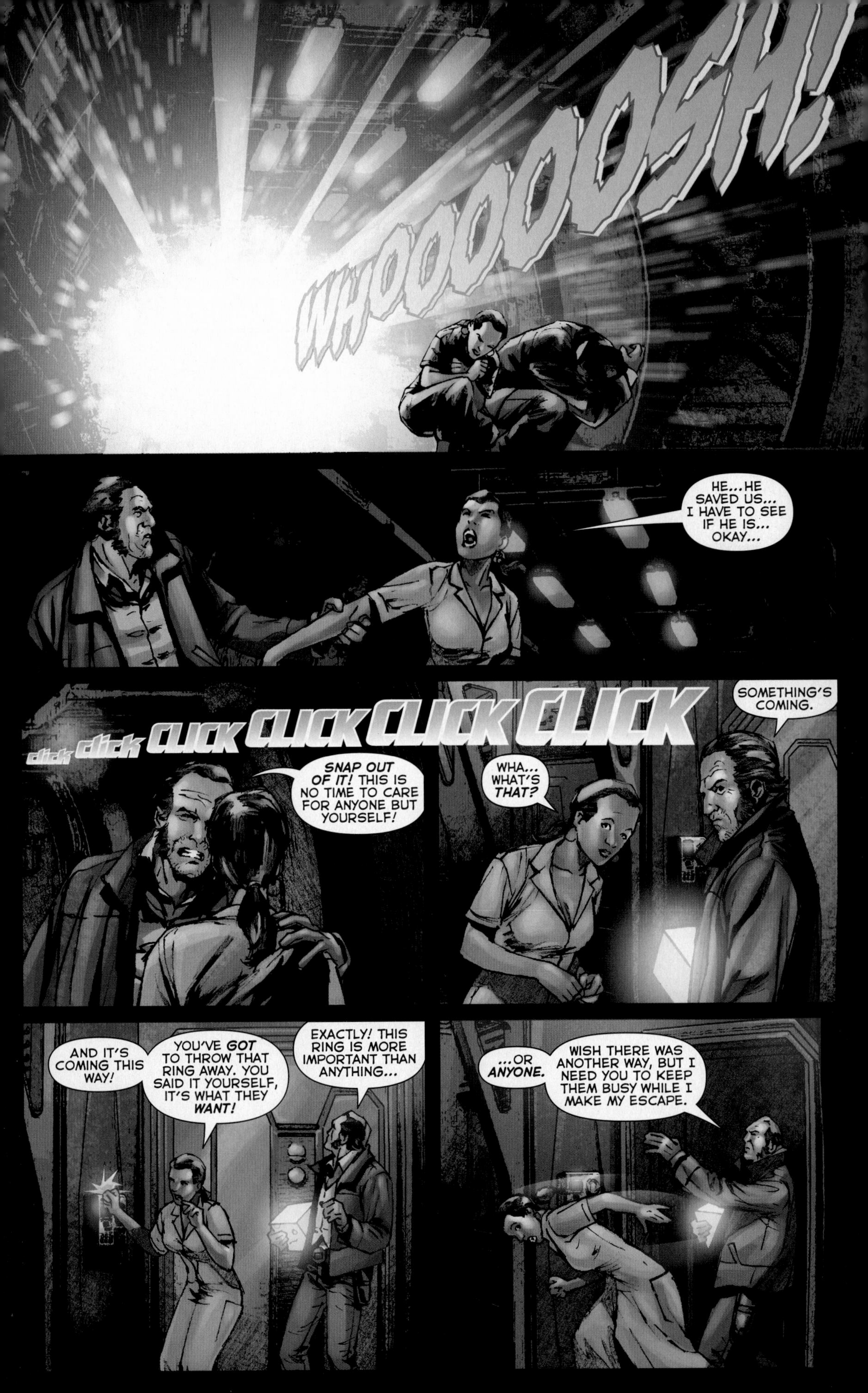
WHOOOOOSH!
HE...HE SAVED US... I HAVE TO SEE IF HE IS... OKAY...
click click CLICK CLICK CLICK CLICK
SNAP OUT OF IT! THIS IS NO TIME TO CARE FOR ANYONE BUT YOURSELF!
SOMETHING'S COMING.
WHA... WHAT'S THAT?
AND IT'S COMING THIS WAY!
YOU'VE GOT TO THROW THAT RING AWAY. YOU SAID IT YOURSELF, IT'S WHAT THEY WANT!
EXACTLY! THIS RING IS MORE IMPORTANT THAN ANYTHING...
...OR ANYONE.
WISH THERE WAS ANOTHER WAY, BUT I NEED YOU TO KEEP THEM BUSY WHILE I MAKE MY ESCAPE.

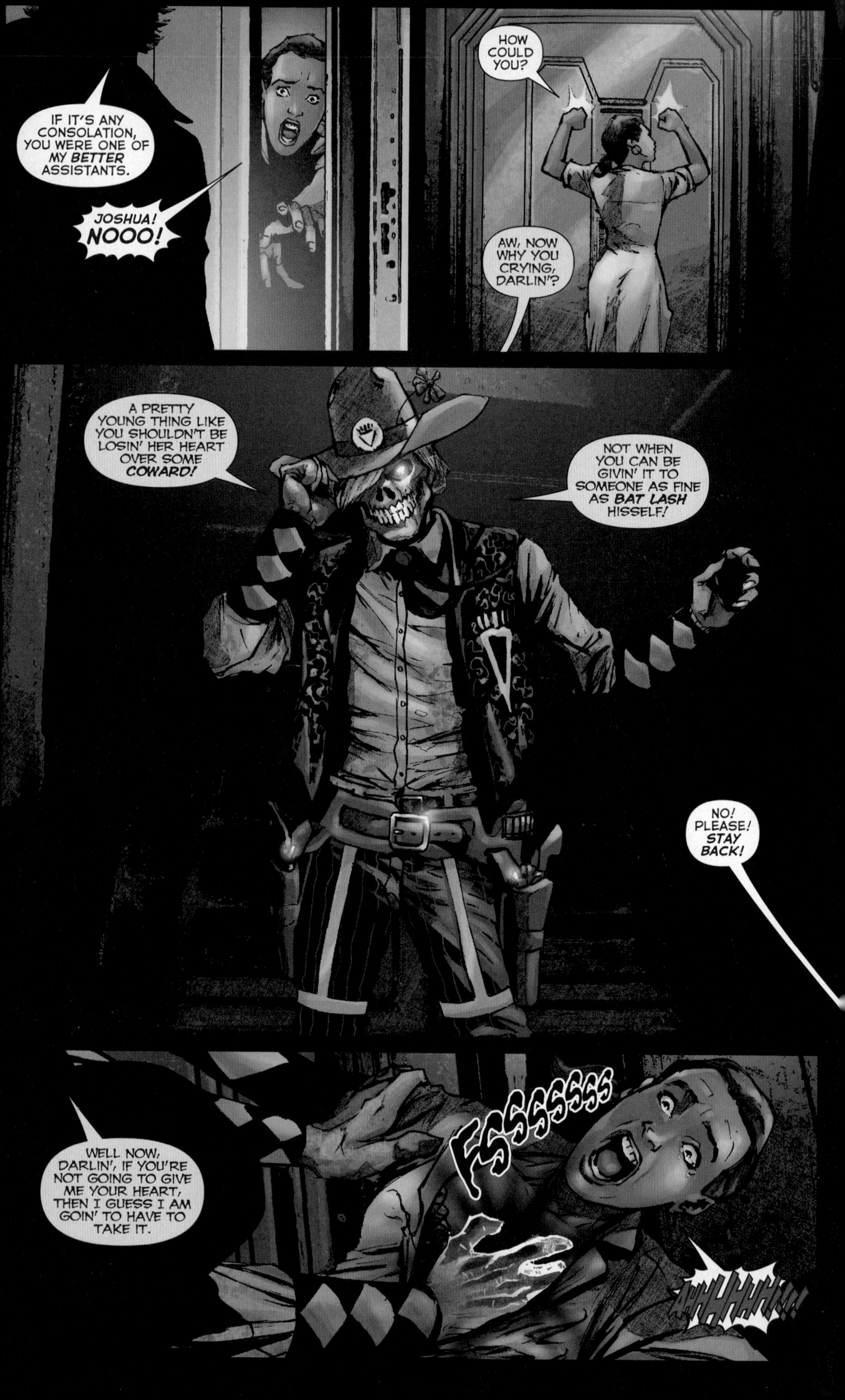
IF IT'S ANY CONSOLATION, YOU WERE ONE OF MY BETTER ASSISTANTS.
JOSHUA! NOOO!
HOW COULD YOU?
AW, NOW WHY YOU CRYING, DARLIN'?
A PRETTY YOUNG THING LIKE YOU SHOULDN'T BE LOSIN' HER HEART OVER SOME COWARD!
NOT WHEN YOU CAN BE GIVIN' IT TO SOMEONE AS FINE AS BAT LASH HISSELF!
NO! PLEASE! STAY BACK!
WELL NOW, DARLIN', IF YOU'RE NOT GOING TO GIVE ME YOUR HEART, THEN I GUESS I AM GOIN' TO HAVE TO TAKE IT.
FSSSSSSS
AHHHHHH!!

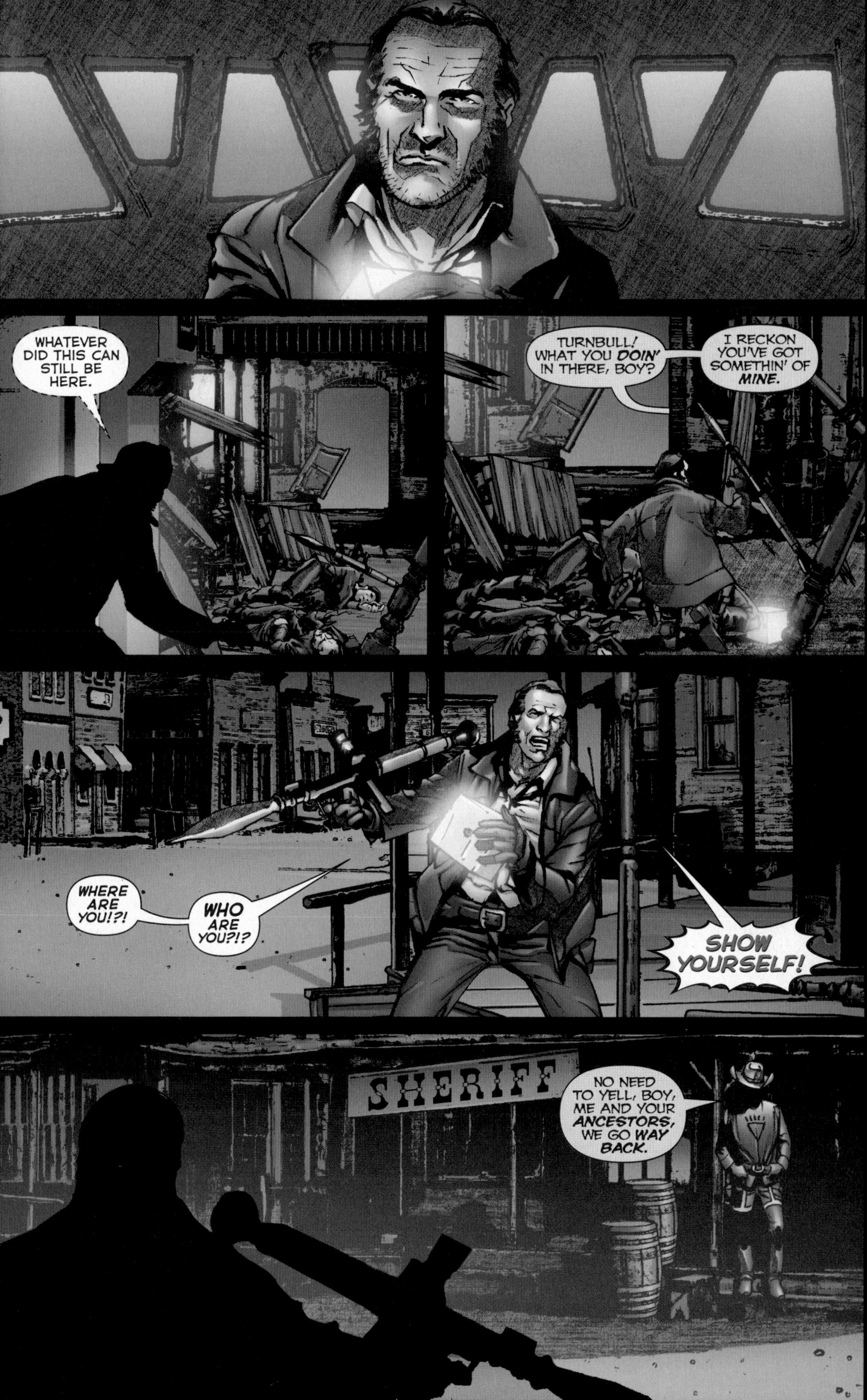
WHATEVER DID THIS CAN STILL BE HERE.
TURNBULL! WHAT YOU DOIN' IN THERE, BOY?
I RECKON YOU'VE GOT SOMETHIN' OF MINE.
WHERE ARE YOU!?!
WHO ARE YOU?!?
SHOW YOURSELF!
SHERIFF
NO NEED TO YELL, BOY, ME AND YOUR ANCESTORS, WE GO WAY BACK.

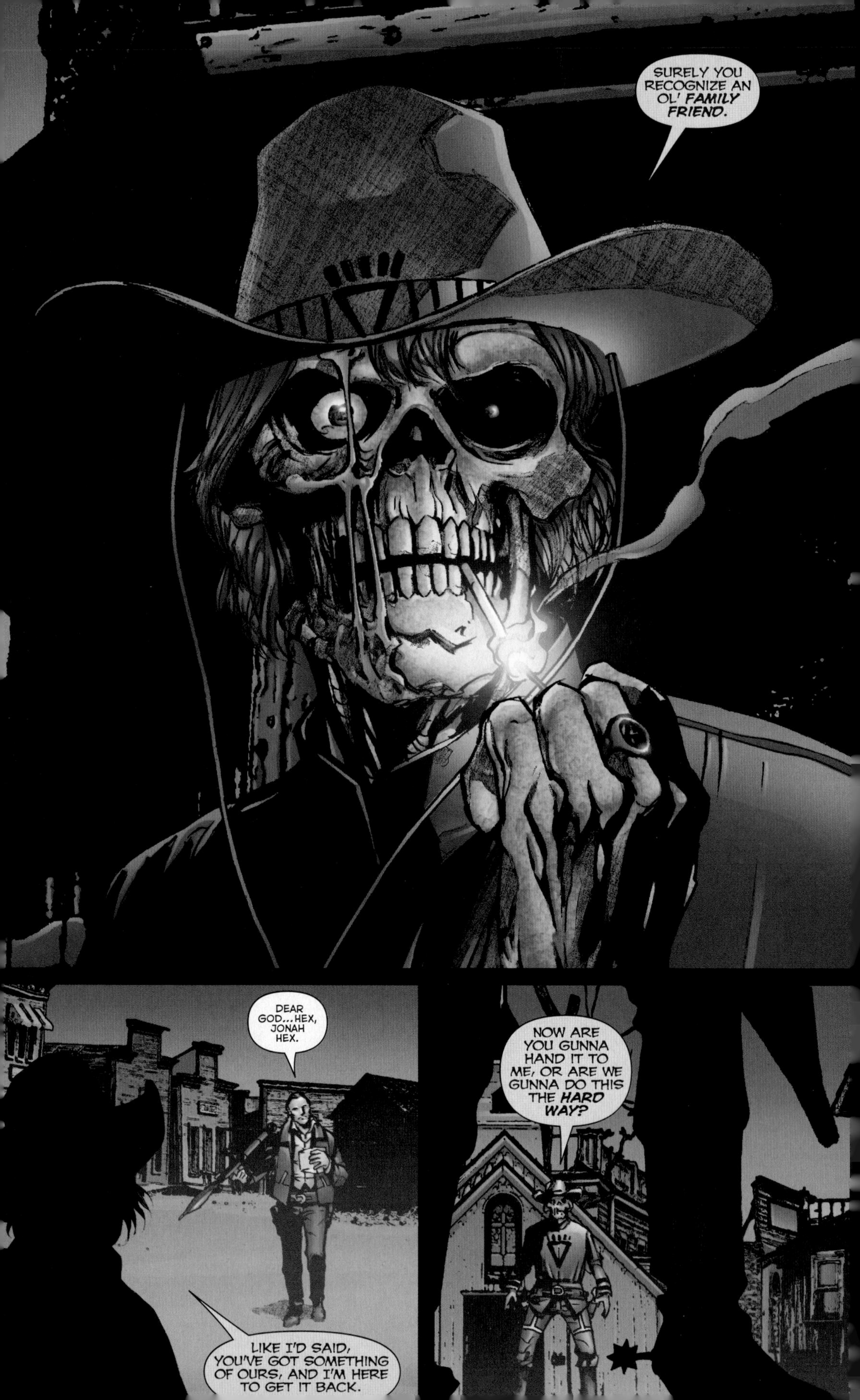
SURELY YOU RECOGNIZE AN OL' FAMILY FRIEND.
DEAR GOD... HEX, JONAH HEX.
LIKE I'D SAID, YOU'VE GOT SOMETHING OF OURS, AND I'M HERE TO GET IT BACK.
NOW ARE YOU GUNNA HAND IT TO ME, OR ARE WE GUNNA DO THIS THE HARD WAY?

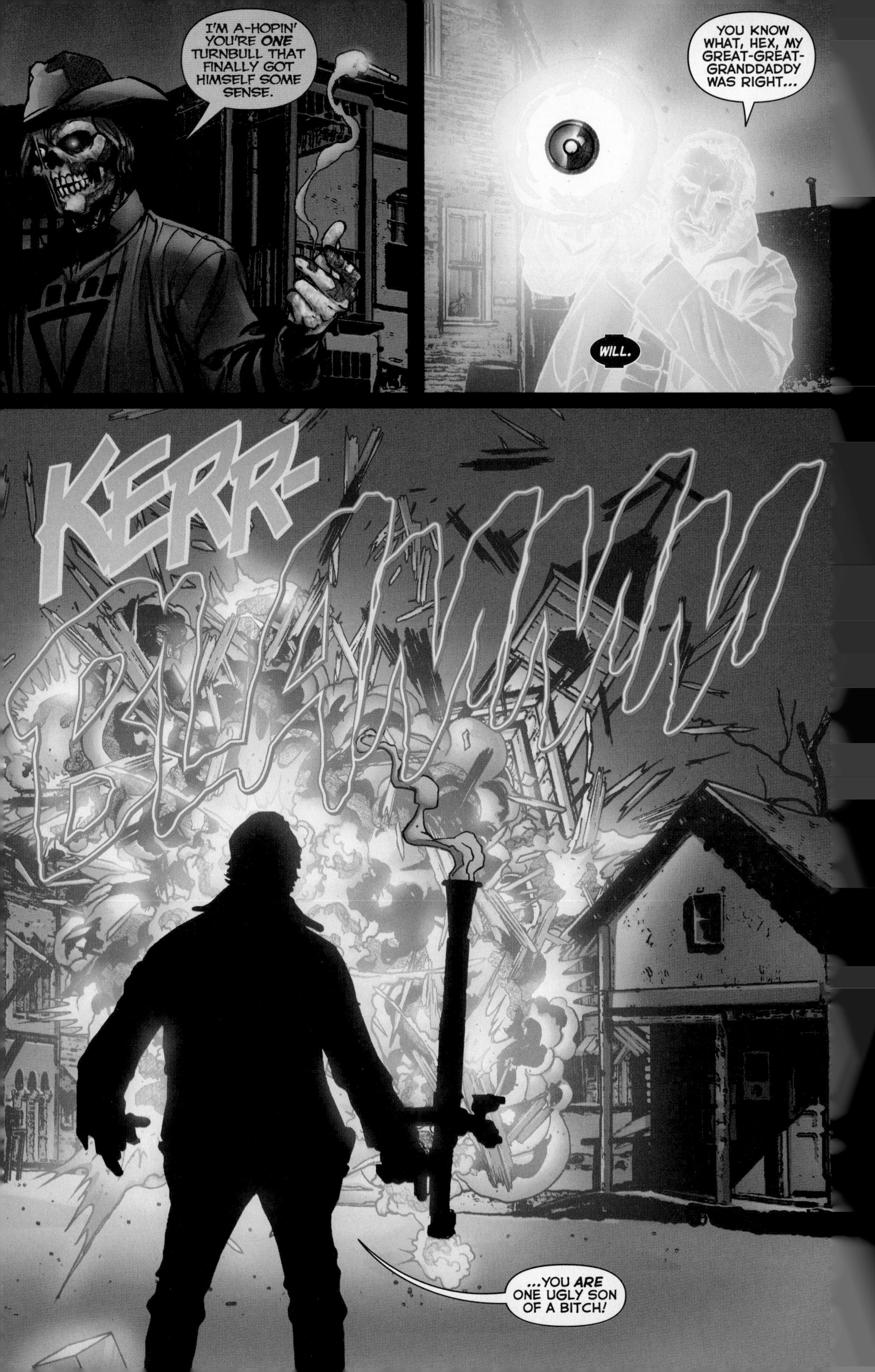
I'M A-HOPIN' YOU'RE *ONE* TURNBULL THAT FINALLY GOT HIMSELF SOME SENSE.
YOU KNOW WHAT, HEX, MY GREAT-GREAT-GRANDDADDY WAS RIGHT...
WILL.
KERR-
BLAMMMMM
...YOU *ARE* ONE UGLY SON OF A BITCH!

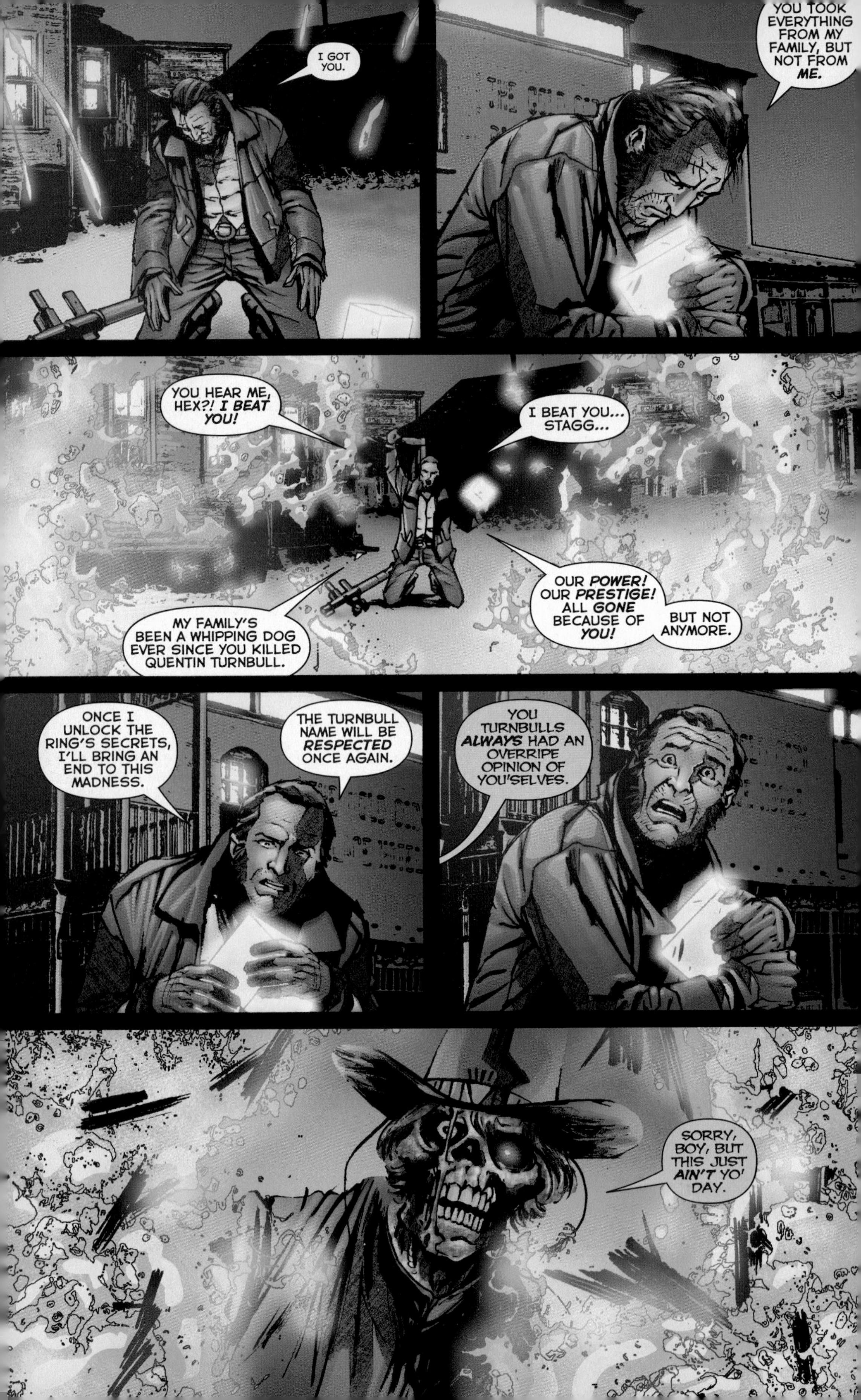
I GOT YOU.
YOU TOOK EVERYTHING FROM MY FAMILY, BUT NOT FROM *ME.*
YOU HEAR ME, HEX?! *I BEAT YOU!*
I BEAT YOU... STAGG...
MY FAMILY'S BEEN A WHIPPING DOG EVER SINCE YOU KILLED QUENTIN TURNBULL.
OUR *POWER!* OUR *PRESTIGE!* ALL *GONE* BECAUSE OF *YOU!*
BUT NOT ANYMORE.
ONCE I UNLOCK THE RING'S SECRETS, I'LL BRING AN END TO THIS MADNESS.
THE TURNBULL NAME WILL BE *RESPECTED* ONCE AGAIN.
YOU TURNBULLS *ALWAYS* HAD AN OVERRIPE OPINION OF YOU'SELVES.
SORRY, BOY, BUT THIS JUST *AIN'T* YO' DAY.

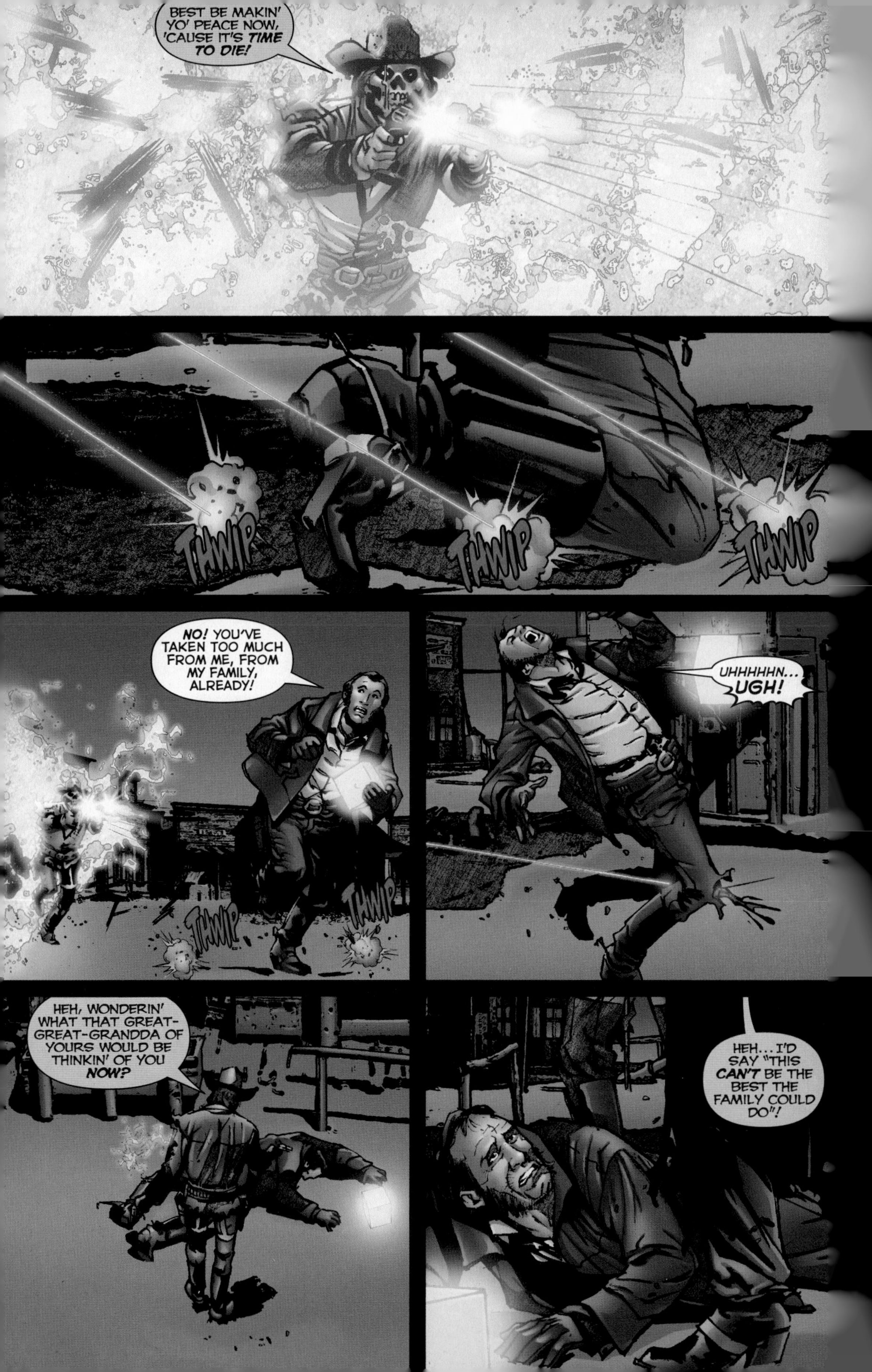
BEST BE MAKIN' YO' PEACE NOW, 'CAUSE IT'S TIME TO DIE!
THWIP
THWIP
THWIP
NO! YOU'VE TAKEN TOO MUCH FROM ME, FROM MY FAMILY, ALREADY!
THWIP
THWIP
UHHHHHN... UGH!
HEH, WONDERIN' WHAT THAT GREAT-GREAT-GRANDDA OF YOURS WOULD BE THINKIN' OF YOU NOW?
HEH... I'D SAY "THIS CAN'T BE THE BEST THE FAMILY COULD DO"!

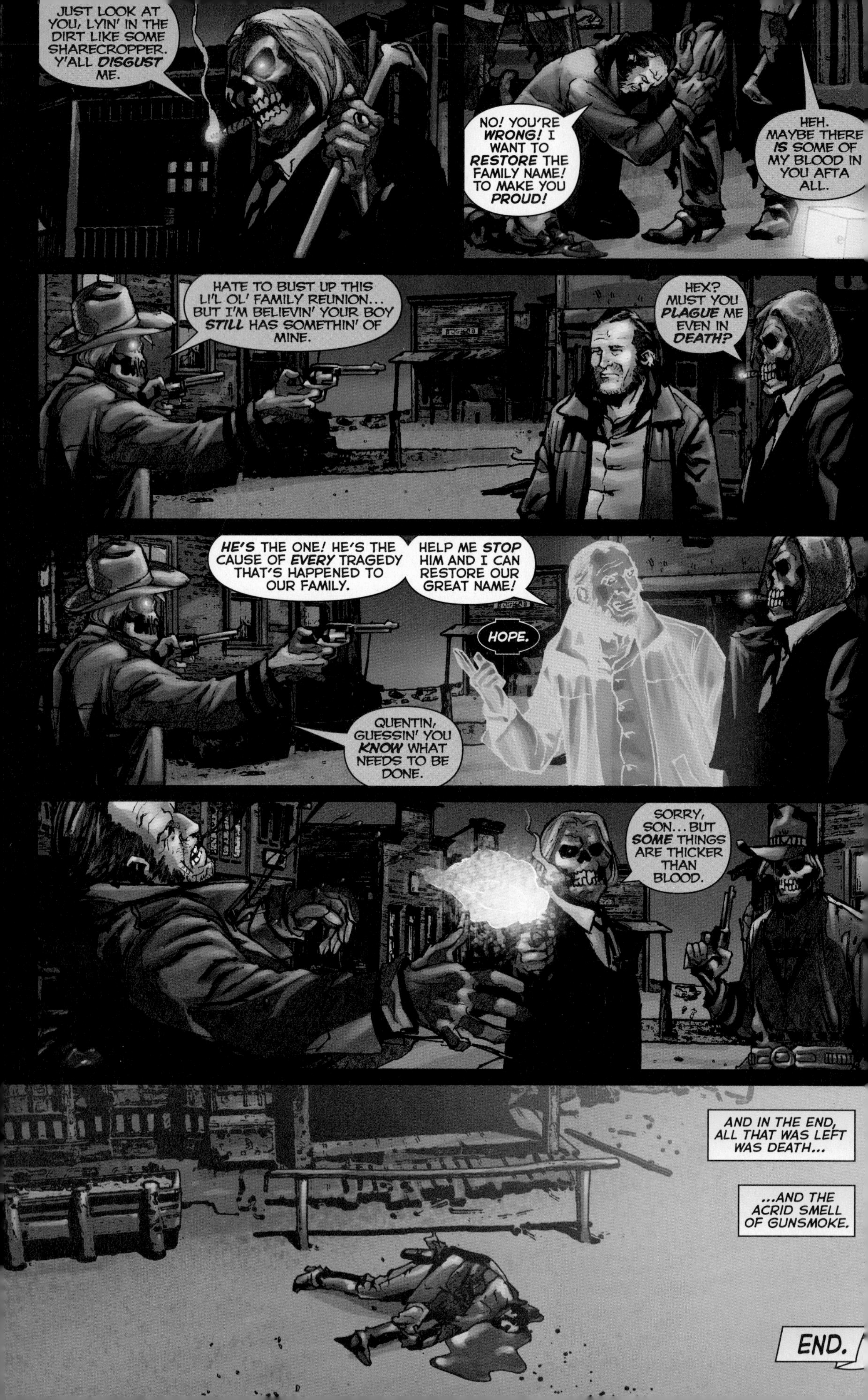
JUST LOOK AT YOU, LYIN' IN THE DIRT LIKE SOME SHARECROPPER. Y'ALL DISGUST ME.
NO! YOU'RE WRONG! I WANT TO RESTORE THE FAMILY NAME! TO MAKE YOU PROUD!
HEH. MAYBE THERE IS SOME OF MY BLOOD IN YOU AFTA ALL.
HATE TO BUST UP THIS LI'L OL' FAMILY REUNION... BUT I'M BELIEVIN' YOUR BOY STILL HAS SOMETHIN' OF MINE.
HEX? MUST YOU PLAGUE ME EVEN IN DEATH?
HE'S THE ONE! HE'S THE CAUSE OF EVERY TRAGEDY THAT'S HAPPENED TO OUR FAMILY.
HELP ME STOP HIM AND I CAN RESTORE OUR GREAT NAME!
HOPE.
QUENTIN, GUESSIN' YOU KNOW WHAT NEEDS TO BE DONE.
SORRY, SON... BUT SOME THINGS ARE THICKER THAN BLOOD.
AND IN THE END, ALL THAT WAS LEFT WAS DEATH...
...AND THE ACRID SMELL OF GUNSMOKE.
END.

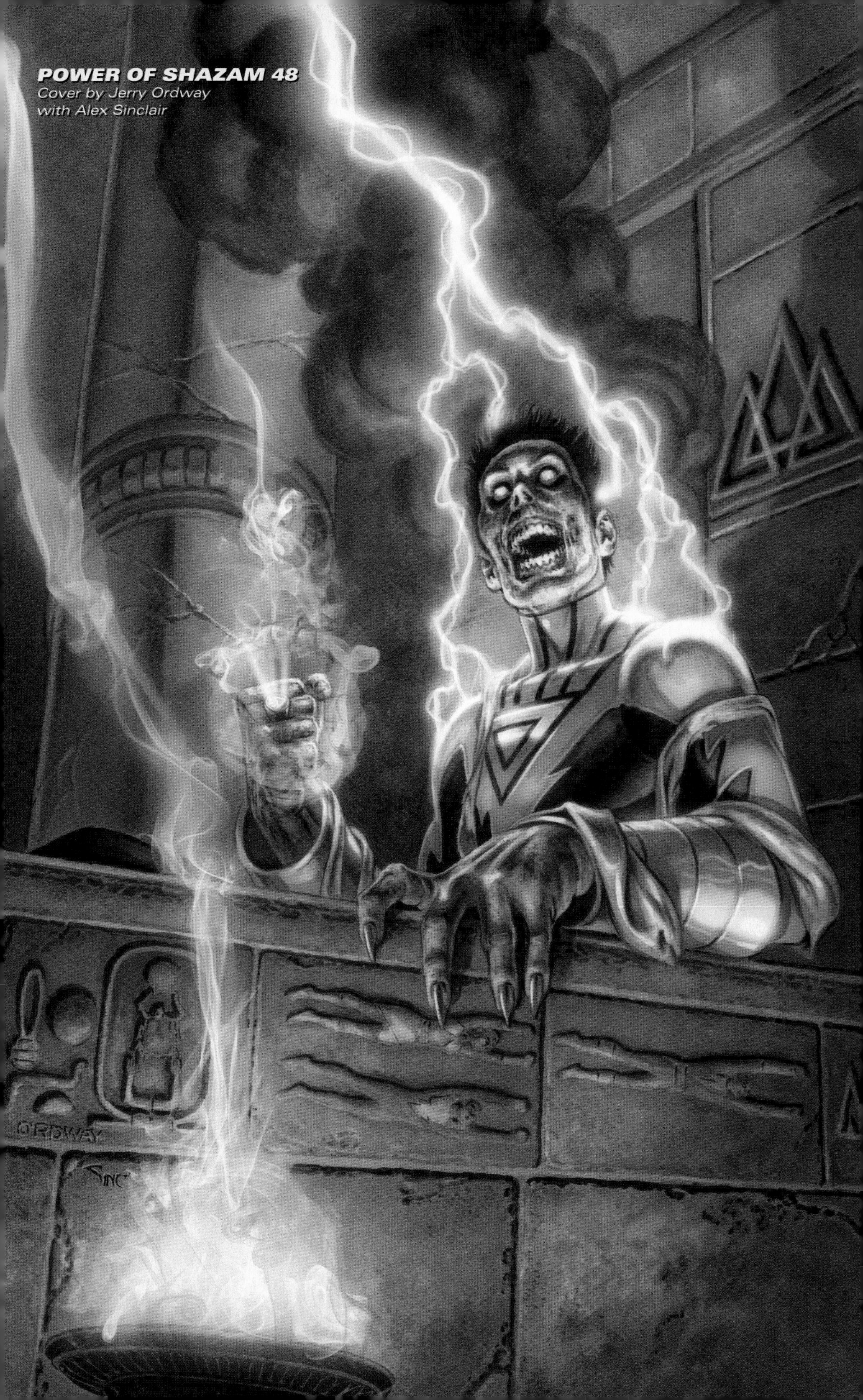
ORDWAY

POWER OF SHAZAM 48
Cover by Jerry Ordway
with Alex Sinclair

REST IN PEACE

ERIC WALLACE
WRITER

DON KRAMER
PENCILS

MICHAEL BABINSKI
INKS

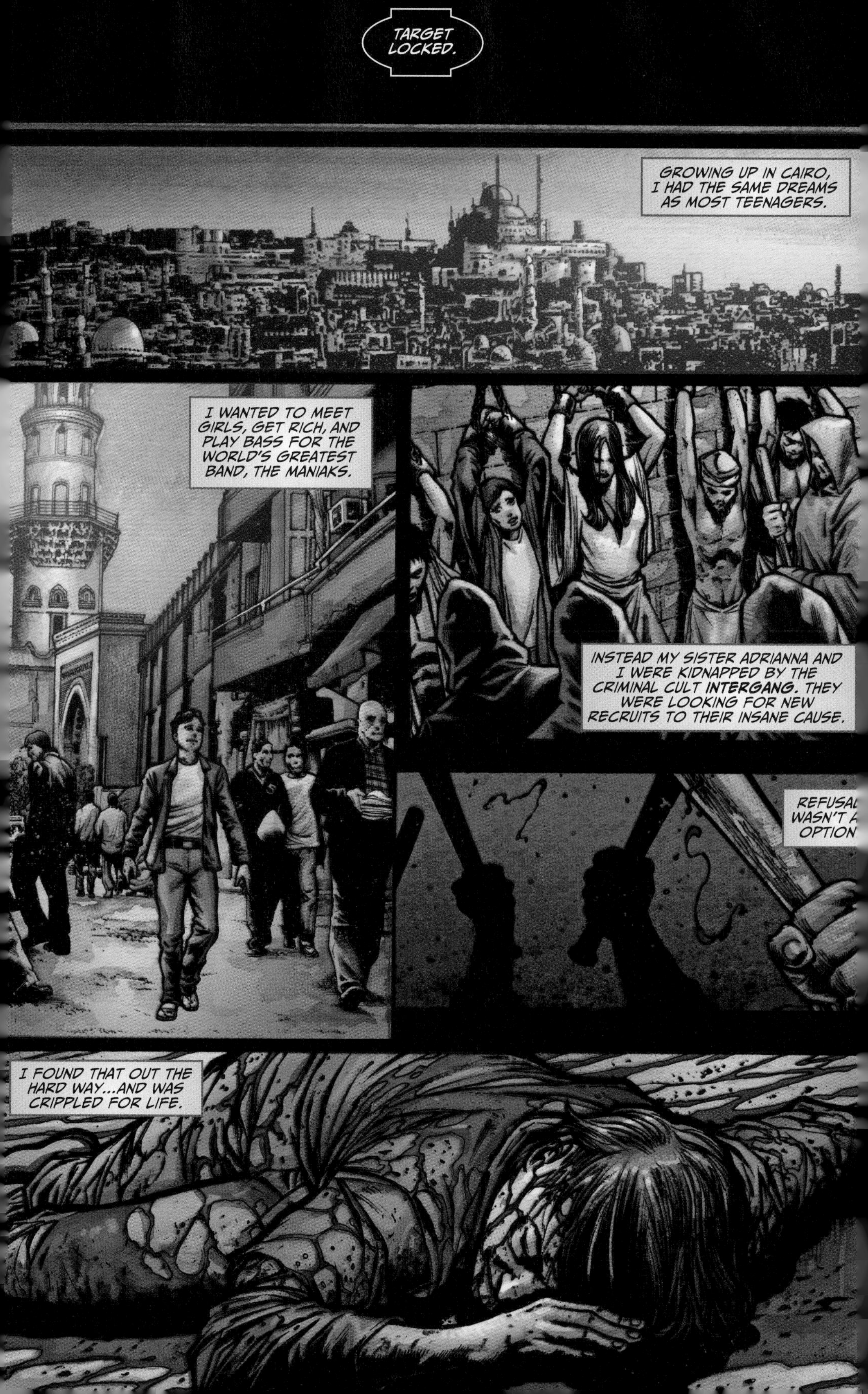
TARGET LOCKED.
GROWING UP IN CAIRO, I HAD THE SAME DREAMS AS MOST TEENAGERS.
I WANTED TO MEET GIRLS, GET RICH, AND PLAY BASS FOR THE WORLD'S GREATEST BAND, THE MANIAKS.
INSTEAD MY SISTER ADRIANNA AND I WERE KIDNAPPED BY THE CRIMINAL CULT INTERGANG. THEY WERE LOOKING FOR NEW RECRUITS TO THEIR INSANE CAUSE.
REFUSAL WASN'T A OPTION
I FOUND THAT OUT THE HARD WAY...AND WAS CRIPPLED FOR LIFE.

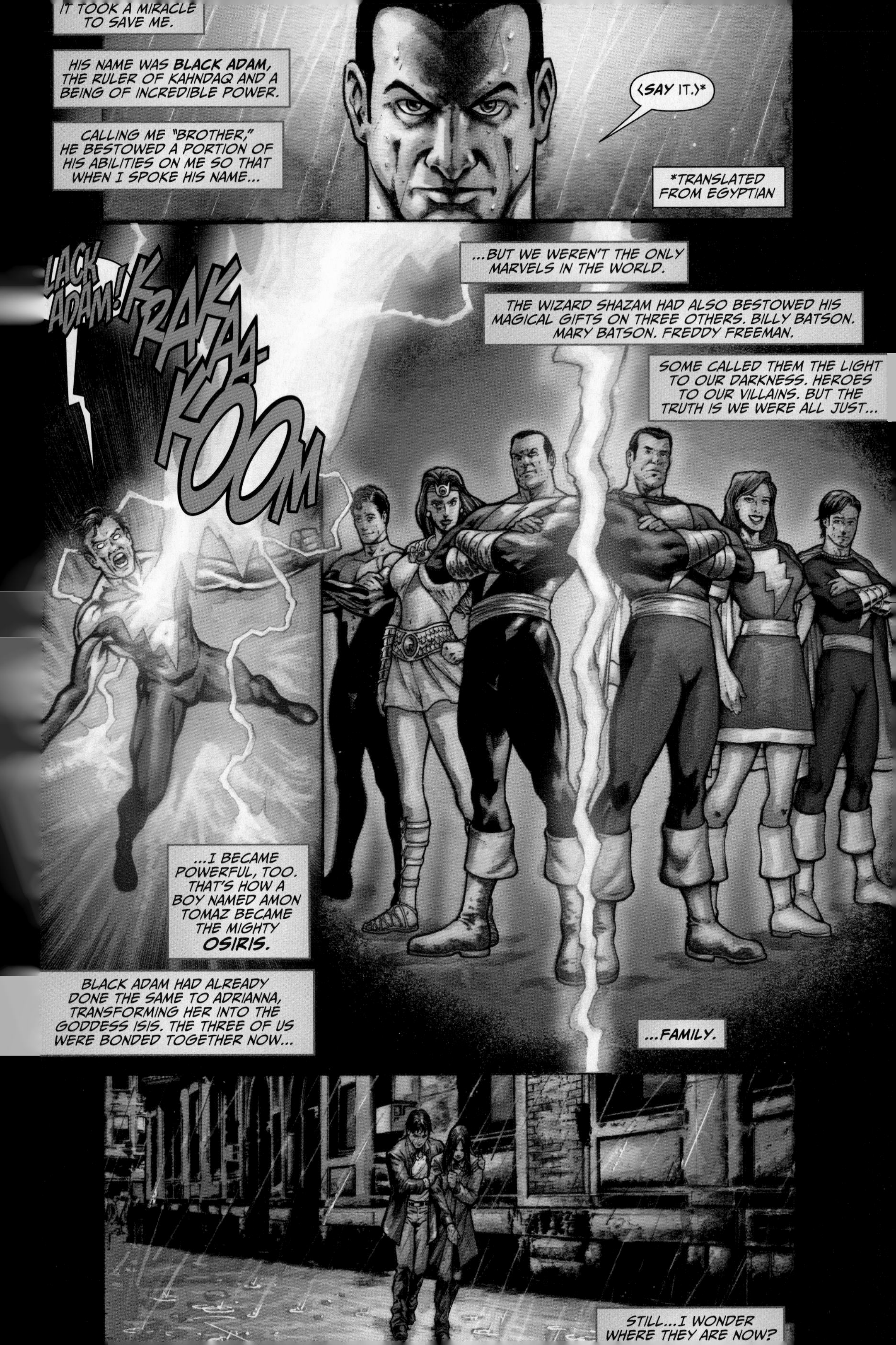

IT TOOK A MIRACLE TO SAVE ME.
HIS NAME WAS BLACK ADAM, THE RULER OF KAHNDAQ AND A BEING OF INCREDIBLE POWER.
CALLING ME "BROTHER," HE BESTOWED A PORTION OF HIS ABILITIES ON ME SO THAT WHEN I SPOKE HIS NAME...
‹SAY IT.›*
*TRANSLATED FROM EGYPTIAN
LACK ADAM!
KRAKAA-KOOM
...I BECAME POWERFUL, TOO. THAT'S HOW A BOY NAMED AMON TOMAZ BECAME THE MIGHTY OSIRIS.
BLACK ADAM HAD ALREADY DONE THE SAME TO ADRIANNA, TRANSFORMING HER INTO THE GODDESS ISIS. THE THREE OF US WERE BONDED TOGETHER NOW...
...BUT WE WEREN'T THE ONLY MARVELS IN THE WORLD.
THE WIZARD SHAZAM HAD ALSO BESTOWED HIS MAGICAL GIFTS ON THREE OTHERS. BILLY BATSON. MARY BATSON. FREDDY FREEMAN.
SOME CALLED THEM THE LIGHT TO OUR DARKNESS. HEROES TO OUR VILLAINS. BUT THE TRUTH IS WE WERE ALL JUST...
...FAMILY.
STILL...I WONDER WHERE THEY ARE NOW?

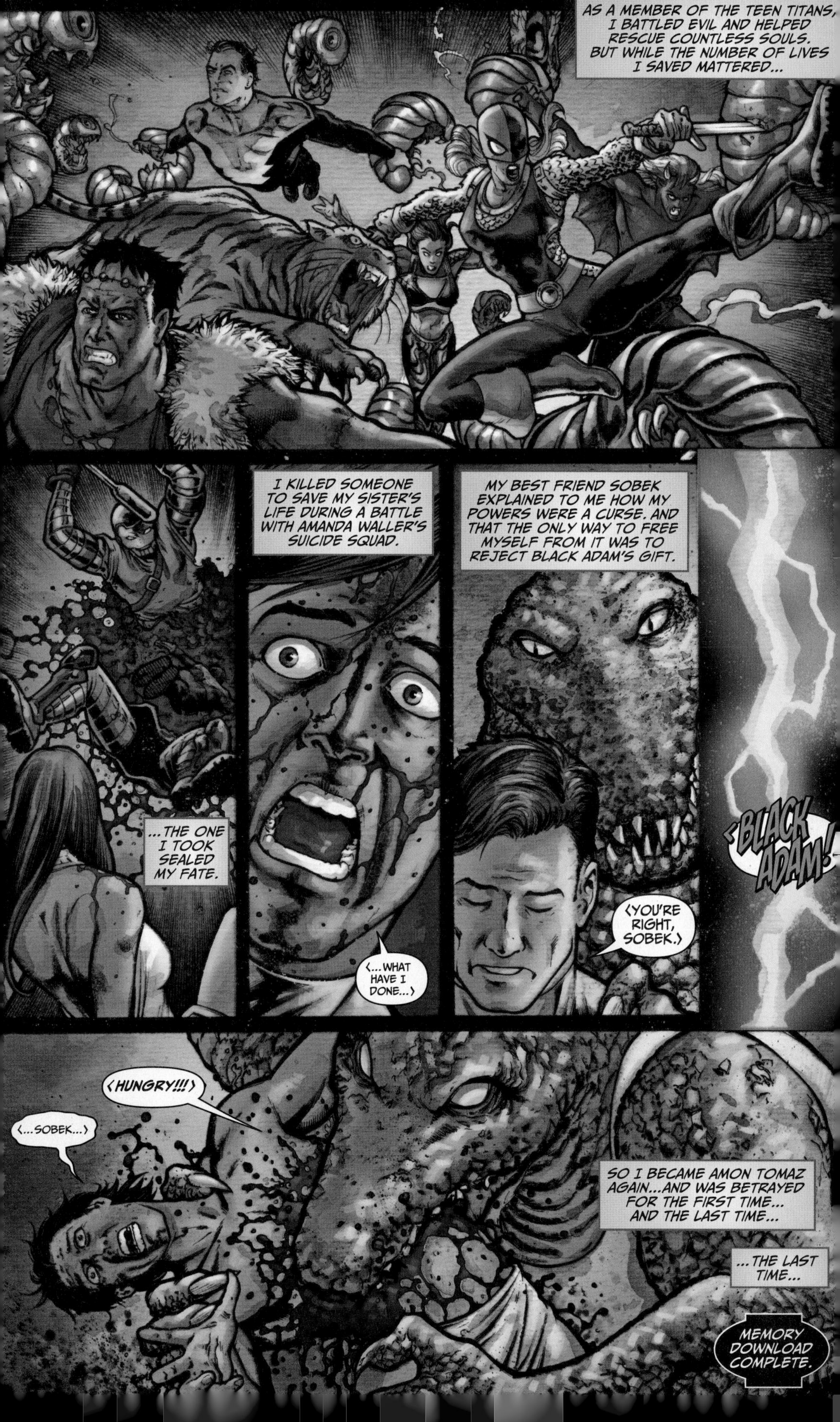

AS A MEMBER OF THE TEEN TITANS, I BATTLED EVIL AND HELPED RESCUE COUNTLESS SOULS. BUT WHILE THE NUMBER OF LIVES I SAVED MATTERED...
...THE ONE I TOOK SEALED MY FATE.
I KILLED SOMEONE TO SAVE MY SISTER'S LIFE DURING A BATTLE WITH AMANDA WALLER'S SUICIDE SQUAD.
‹...WHAT HAVE I DONE...›
MY BEST FRIEND SOBEK EXPLAINED TO ME HOW MY POWERS WERE A CURSE. AND THAT THE ONLY WAY TO FREE MYSELF FROM IT WAS TO REJECT BLACK ADAM'S GIFT.
‹YOU'RE RIGHT, SOBEK.›
‹BLACK ADAM!›
‹HUNGRY!!!›
‹...SOBEK...›
SO I BECAME AMON TOMAZ AGAIN...AND WAS BETRAYED FOR THE FIRST TIME... AND THE LAST TIME...
...THE LAST TIME...
MEMORY DOWNLOAD COMPLETE.

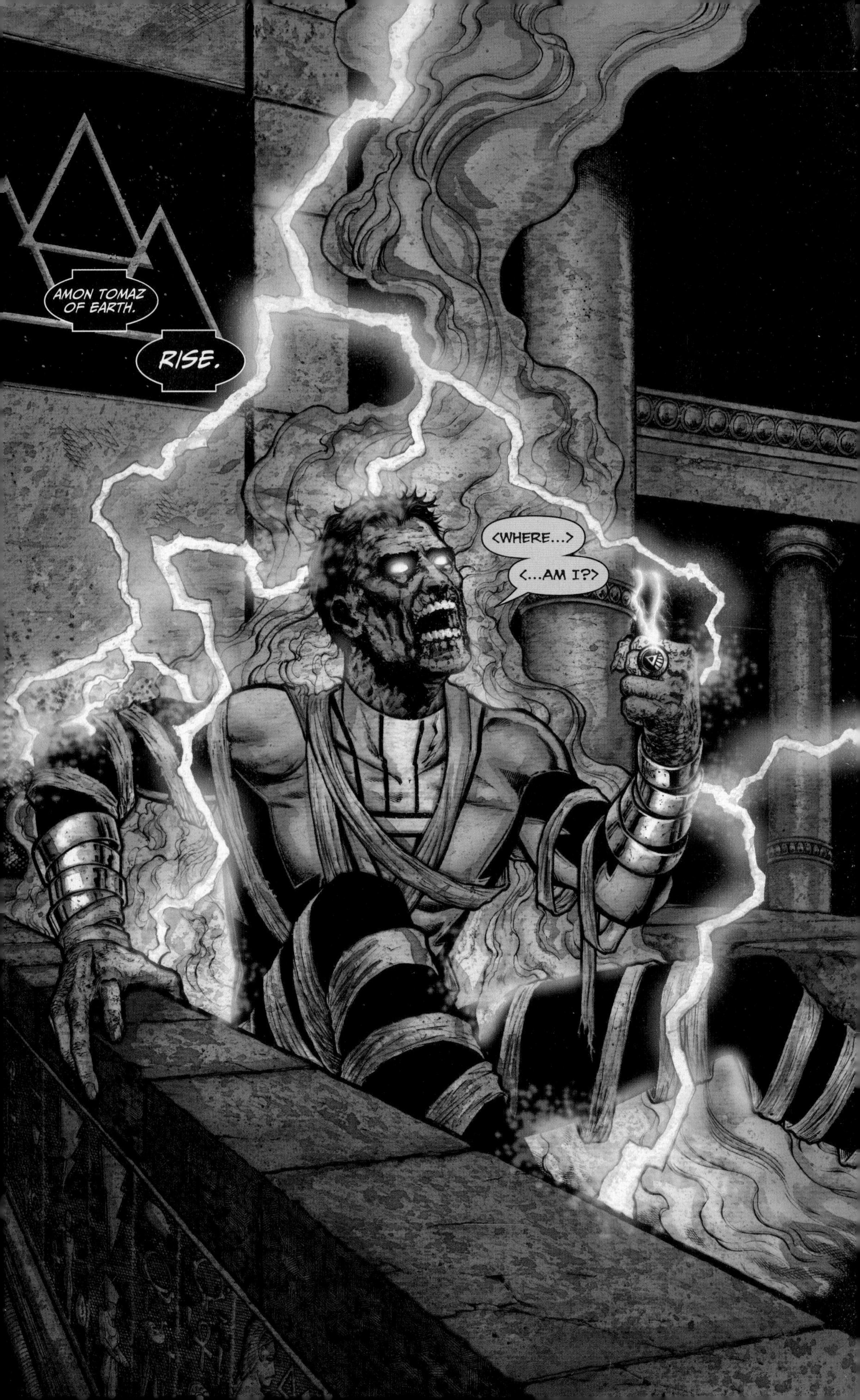
AMON TOMAZ OF EARTH.
RISE.
<WHERE...>
<...AM I?>

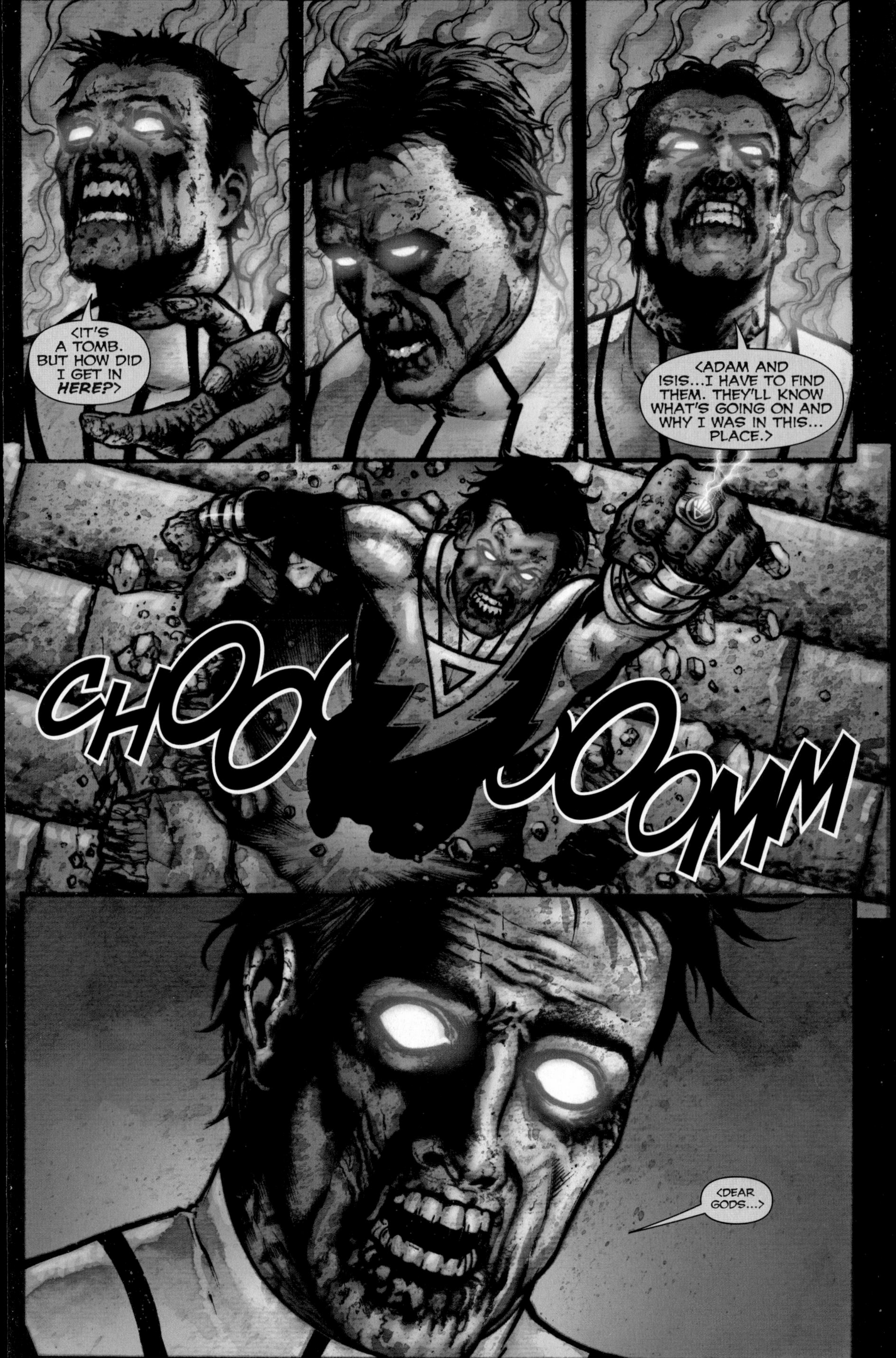
<IT'S A TOMB. BUT HOW DID I GET IN *HERE?*>
<ADAM AND ISIS...I HAVE TO FIND THEM. THEY'LL KNOW WHAT'S GOING ON AND WHY I WAS IN THIS... PLACE.>
CHOOOOOOMM
<DEAR GODS...>

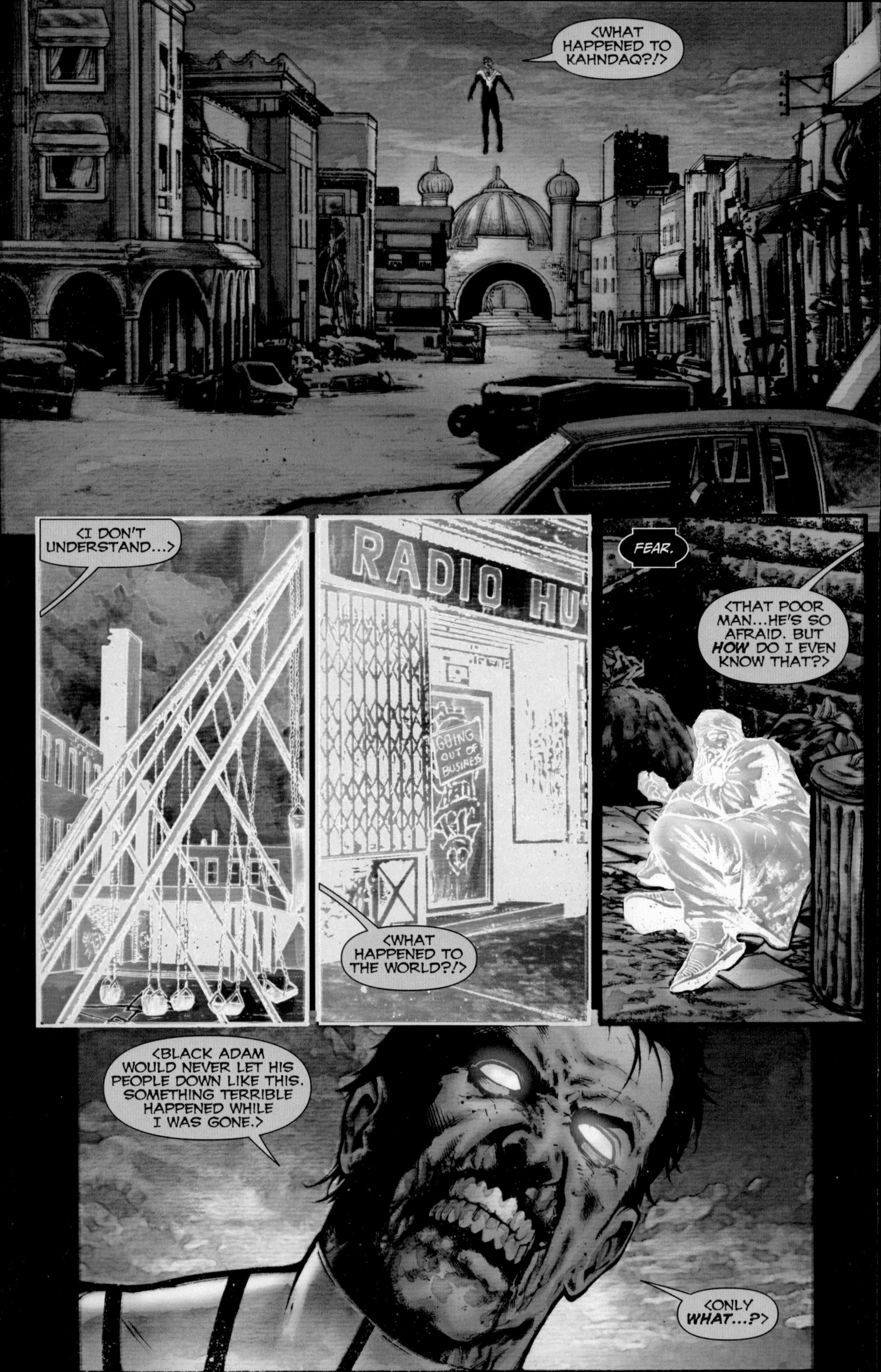

<WHAT HAPPENED TO KAHNDAQ?!>
<I DON'T UNDERSTAND...>
RADIO HU
GOING OUT OF BUSINESS
<WHAT HAPPENED TO THE WORLD?!>
FEAR.
<THAT POOR MAN...HE'S SO AFRAID. BUT HOW DO I EVEN KNOW THAT?>
<BLACK ADAM WOULD NEVER LET HIS PEOPLE DOWN LIKE THIS. SOMETHING TERRIBLE HAPPENED WHILE I WAS GONE.>
<ONLY WHAT...?>

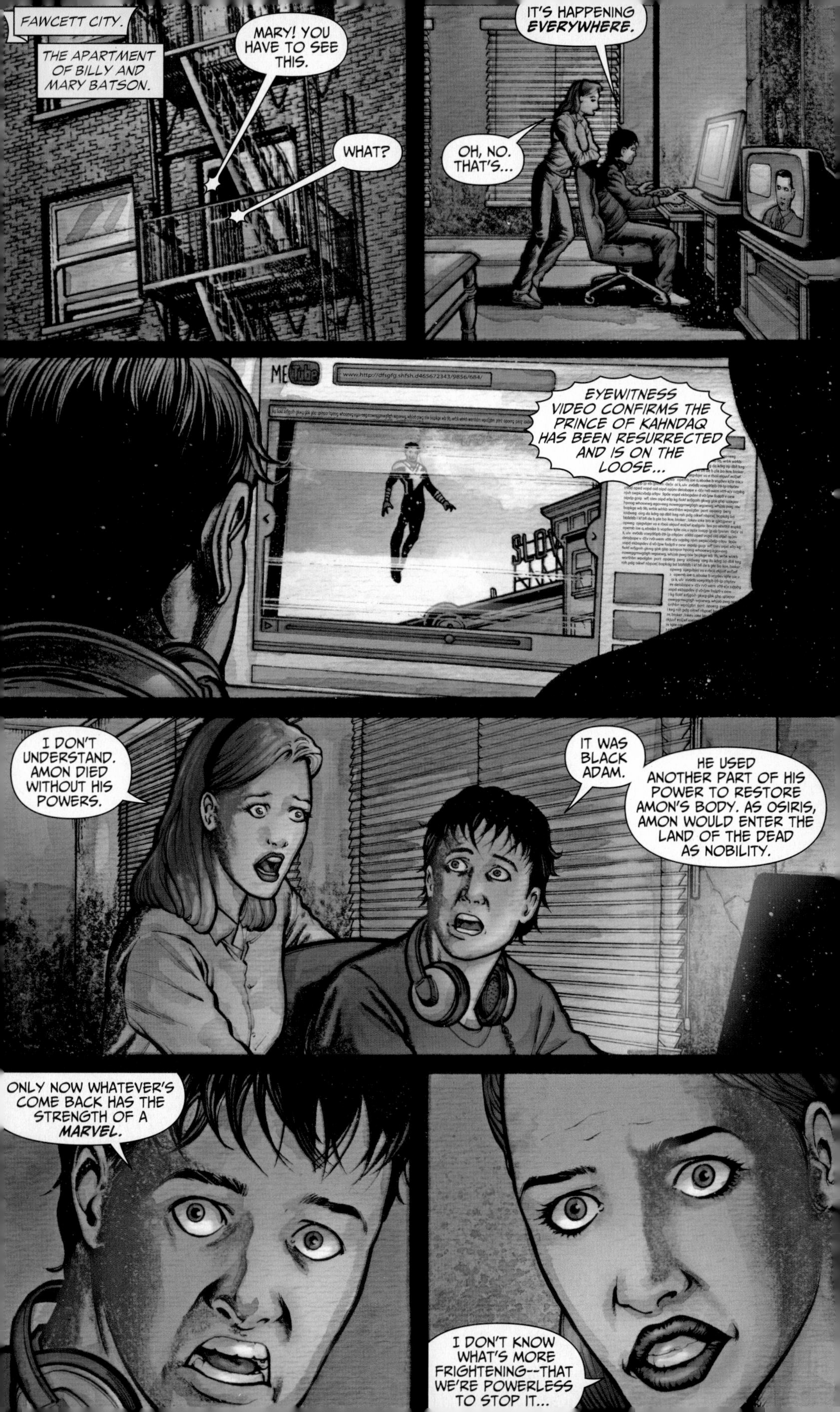
FAWCETT CITY.
THE APARTMENT OF BILLY AND MARY BATSON.
MARY! YOU HAVE TO SEE THIS.
WHAT?
IT'S HAPPENING EVERYWHERE.
OH, NO. THAT'S...
www.http://dfsgfg.shfsh.d465672343/9856/684/
EYEWITNESS VIDEO CONFIRMS THE PRINCE OF KAHNDAQ HAS BEEN RESURRECTED AND IS ON THE LOOSE...
I DON'T UNDERSTAND. AMON DIED WITHOUT HIS POWERS.
IT WAS BLACK ADAM.
HE USED ANOTHER PART OF HIS POWER TO RESTORE AMON'S BODY. AS OSIRIS, AMON WOULD ENTER THE LAND OF THE DEAD AS NOBILITY.
ONLY NOW WHATEVER'S COME BACK HAS THE STRENGTH OF A MARVEL.
I DON'T KNOW WHAT'S MORE FRIGHTENING--THAT WE'RE POWERLESS TO STOP IT...

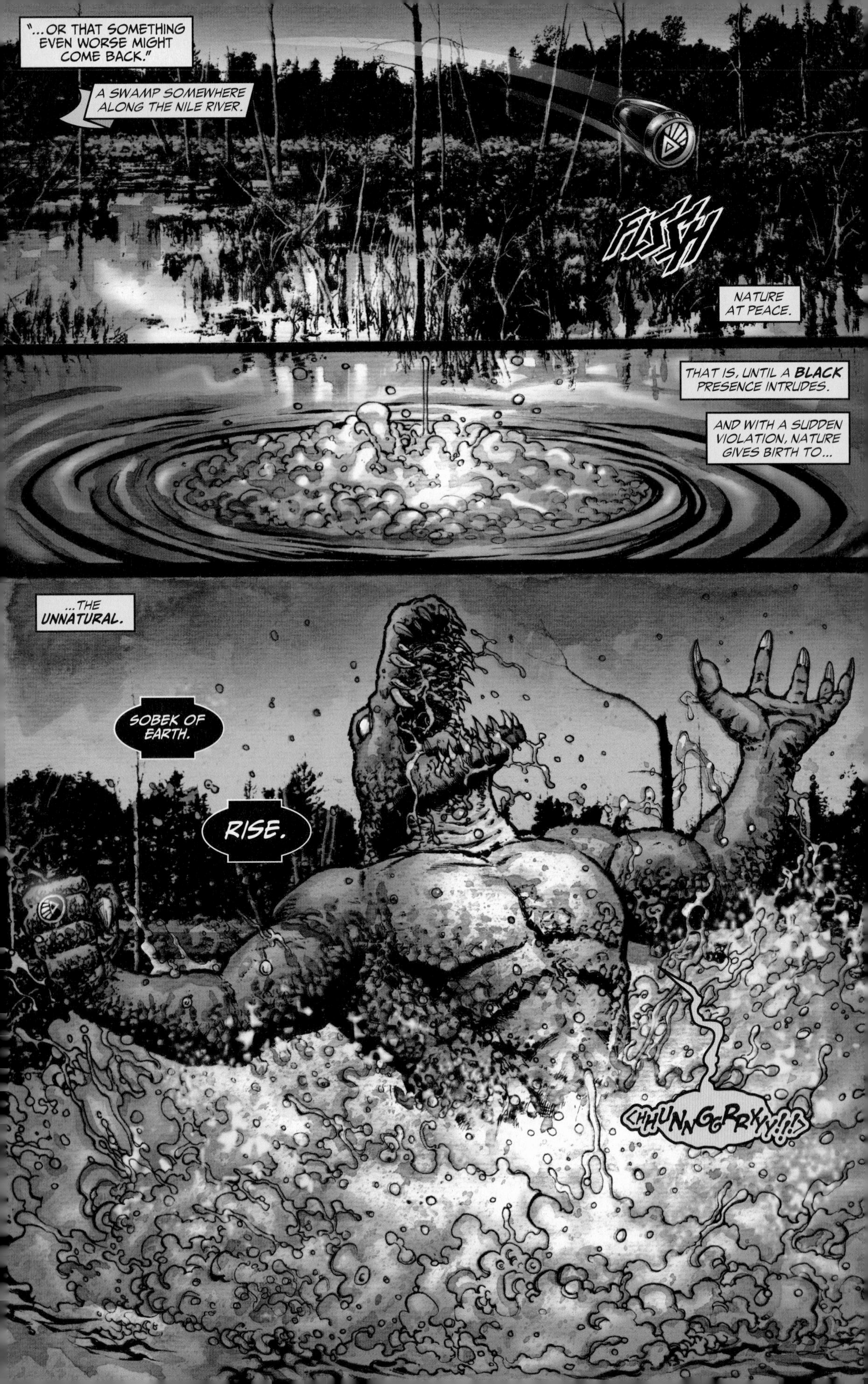
"...OR THAT SOMETHING EVEN WORSE MIGHT COME BACK."
A SWAMP SOMEWHERE ALONG THE NILE RIVER.
FLSSH
NATURE AT PEACE.
THAT IS, UNTIL A BLACK PRESENCE INTRUDES.
AND WITH A SUDDEN VIOLATION, NATURE GIVES BIRTH TO...
...THE UNNATURAL.
SOBEK OF EARTH.
RISE.
<HHUNNGGRRXYY!!!>

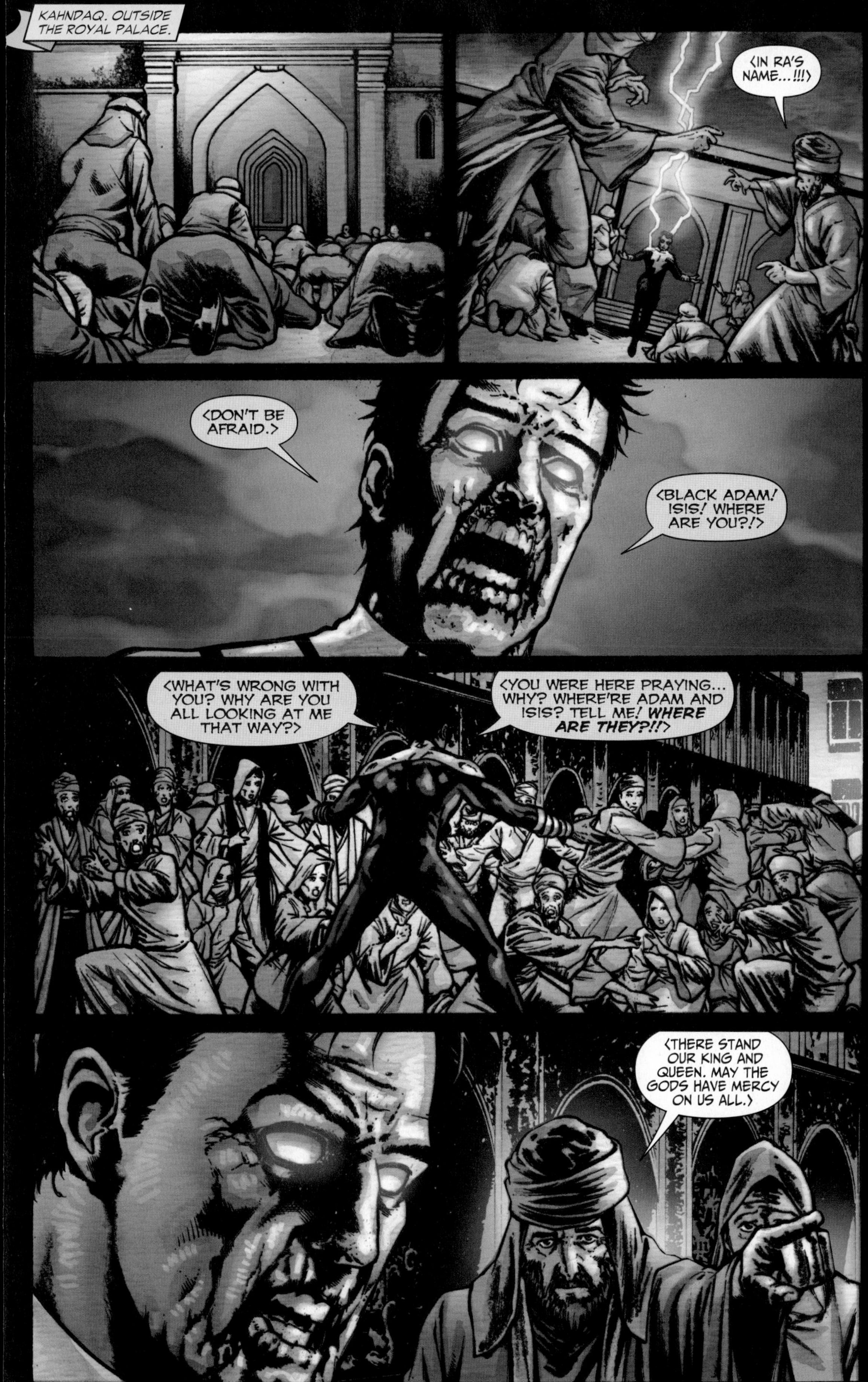
KAHNDAQ. OUTSIDE THE ROYAL PALACE.
‹IN RA'S NAME...!!!›
‹DON'T BE AFRAID.›
‹BLACK ADAM! ISIS! WHERE ARE YOU?!›
‹WHAT'S WRONG WITH YOU? WHY ARE YOU ALL LOOKING AT ME THAT WAY?›
‹YOU WERE HERE PRAYING... WHY? WHERE'RE ADAM AND ISIS? TELL ME! WHERE ARE THEY?!!›
‹THERE STAND OUR KING AND QUEEN. MAY THE GODS HAVE MERCY ON US ALL.›

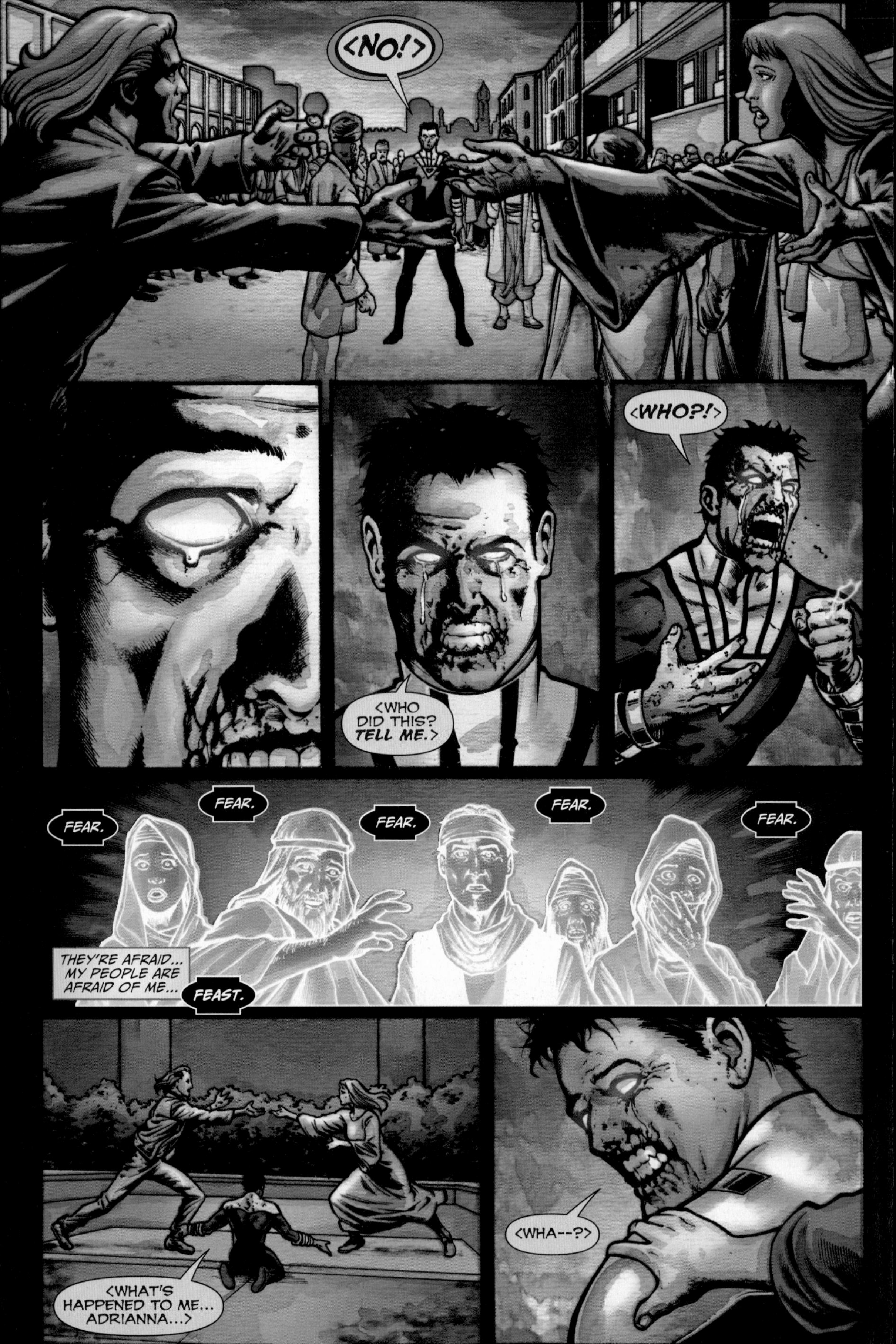
<NO!>
<WHO DID THIS? TELL ME.>
<WHO?!>
FEAR.
FEAR.
FEAR.
FEAR.
FEAR.
THEY'RE AFRAID... MY PEOPLE ARE AFRAID OF ME...
FEAST.
<WHAT'S HAPPENED TO ME... ADRIANNA...>
<WHA--?>

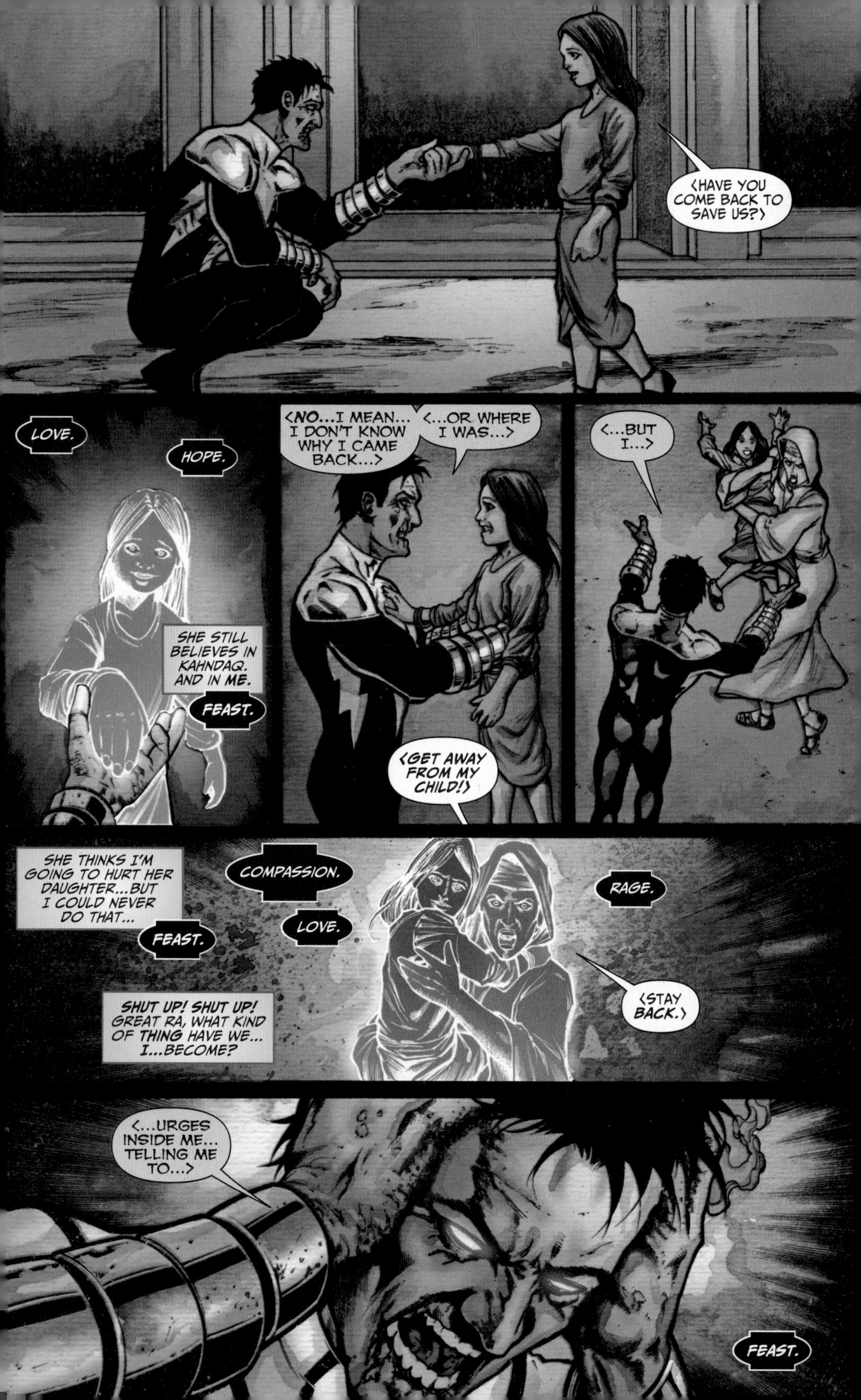
‹HAVE YOU COME BACK TO SAVE US?›
LOVE.
HOPE.
SHE STILL BELIEVES IN KAHNDAQ. AND IN ME.
FEAST.
‹NO...I MEAN... I DON'T KNOW WHY I CAME BACK...›
‹...OR WHERE I WAS...›
‹GET AWAY FROM MY CHILD!›
‹...BUT I...›
SHE THINKS I'M GOING TO HURT HER DAUGHTER...BUT I COULD NEVER DO THAT...
COMPASSION.
LOVE.
RAGE.
FEAST.
SHUT UP! SHUT UP! GREAT RA, WHAT KIND OF THING HAVE WE... I...BECOME?
‹STAY BACK.›
‹...URGES INSIDE ME... TELLING ME TO...›
FEAST.

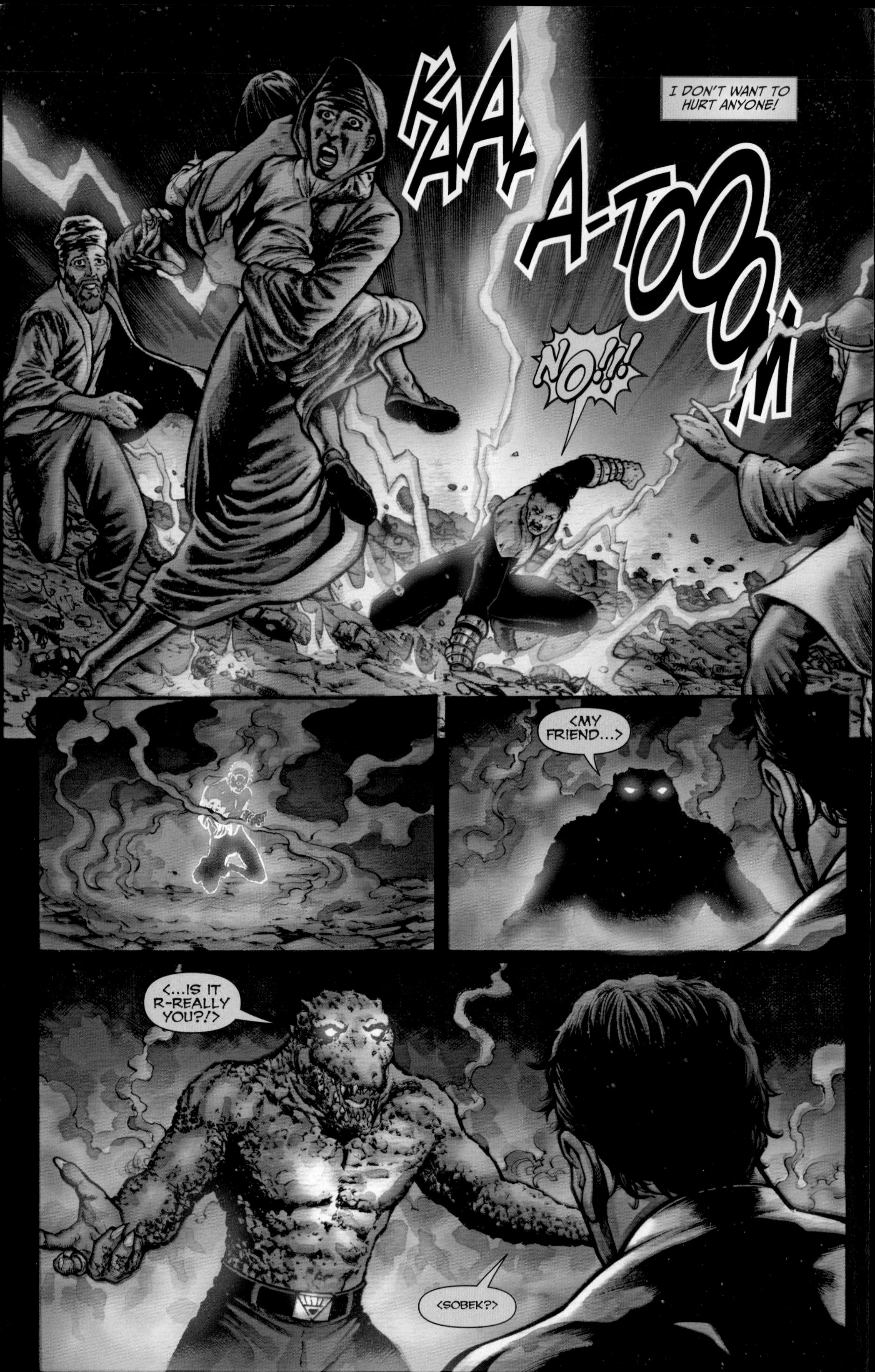
I DON'T WANT TO HURT ANYONE!
KA-KA-A-TOOOOM!
NO!!!
<MY FRIEND...>
<...IS IT R-REALLY YOU?!>
<SOBEK?>

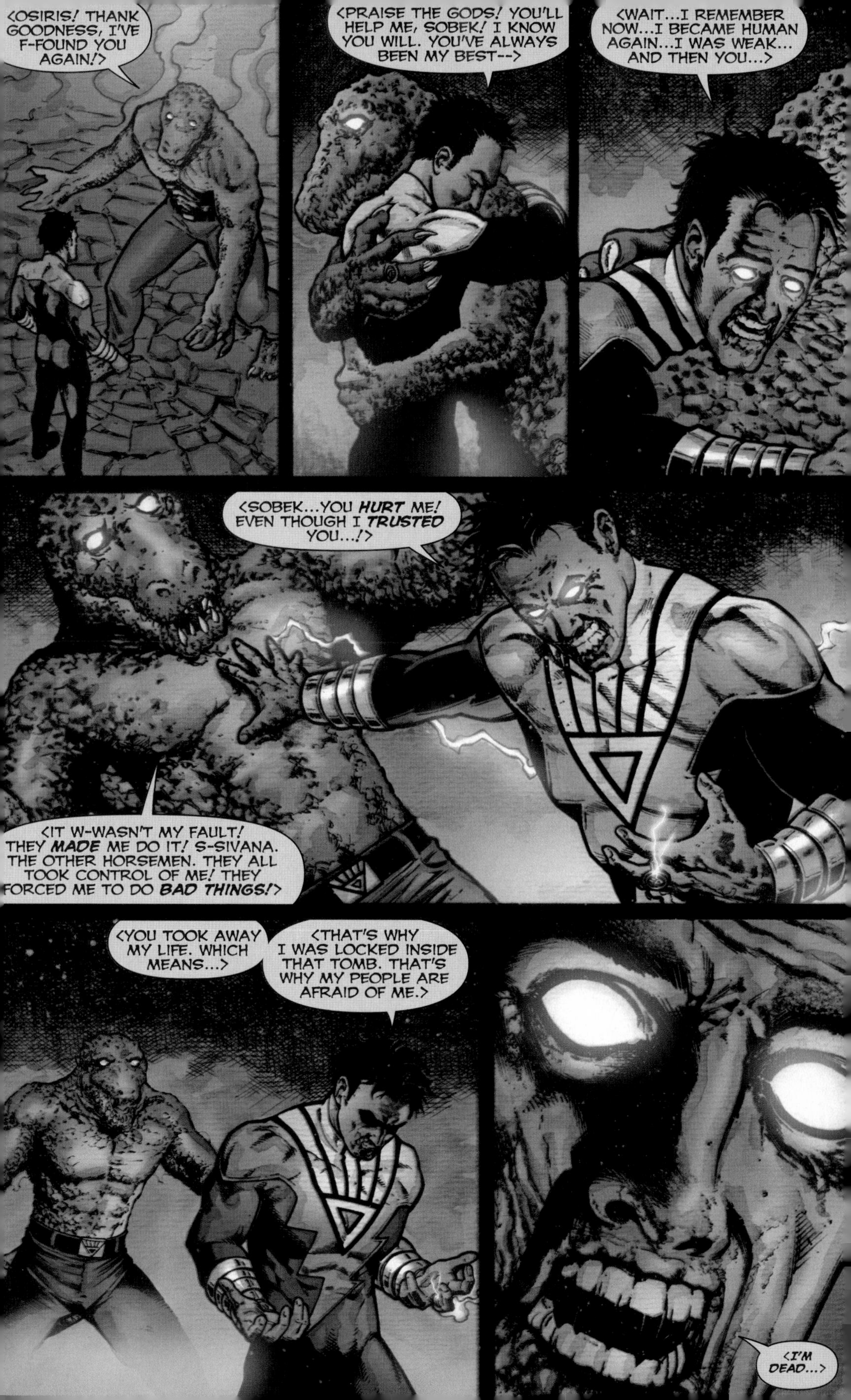
<OSIRIS! THANK GOODNESS, I'VE F-FOUND YOU AGAIN!>
<PRAISE THE GODS! YOU'LL HELP ME, SOBEK! I KNOW YOU WILL. YOU'VE ALWAYS BEEN MY BEST-->
<WAIT...I REMEMBER NOW...I BECAME HUMAN AGAIN...I WAS WEAK... AND THEN YOU...>
<SOBEK...YOU *HURT* ME! EVEN THOUGH I *TRUSTED* YOU...!>
<IT W-WASN'T MY FAULT! THEY *MADE* ME DO IT! S-SIVANA. THE OTHER HORSEMEN. THEY ALL TOOK CONTROL OF ME! THEY FORCED ME TO DO *BAD THINGS!*>
<YOU TOOK AWAY MY LIFE. WHICH MEANS...>
<THAT'S WHY I WAS LOCKED INSIDE THAT TOMB. THAT'S WHY MY PEOPLE ARE AFRAID OF ME.>
<*I'M DEAD...*>

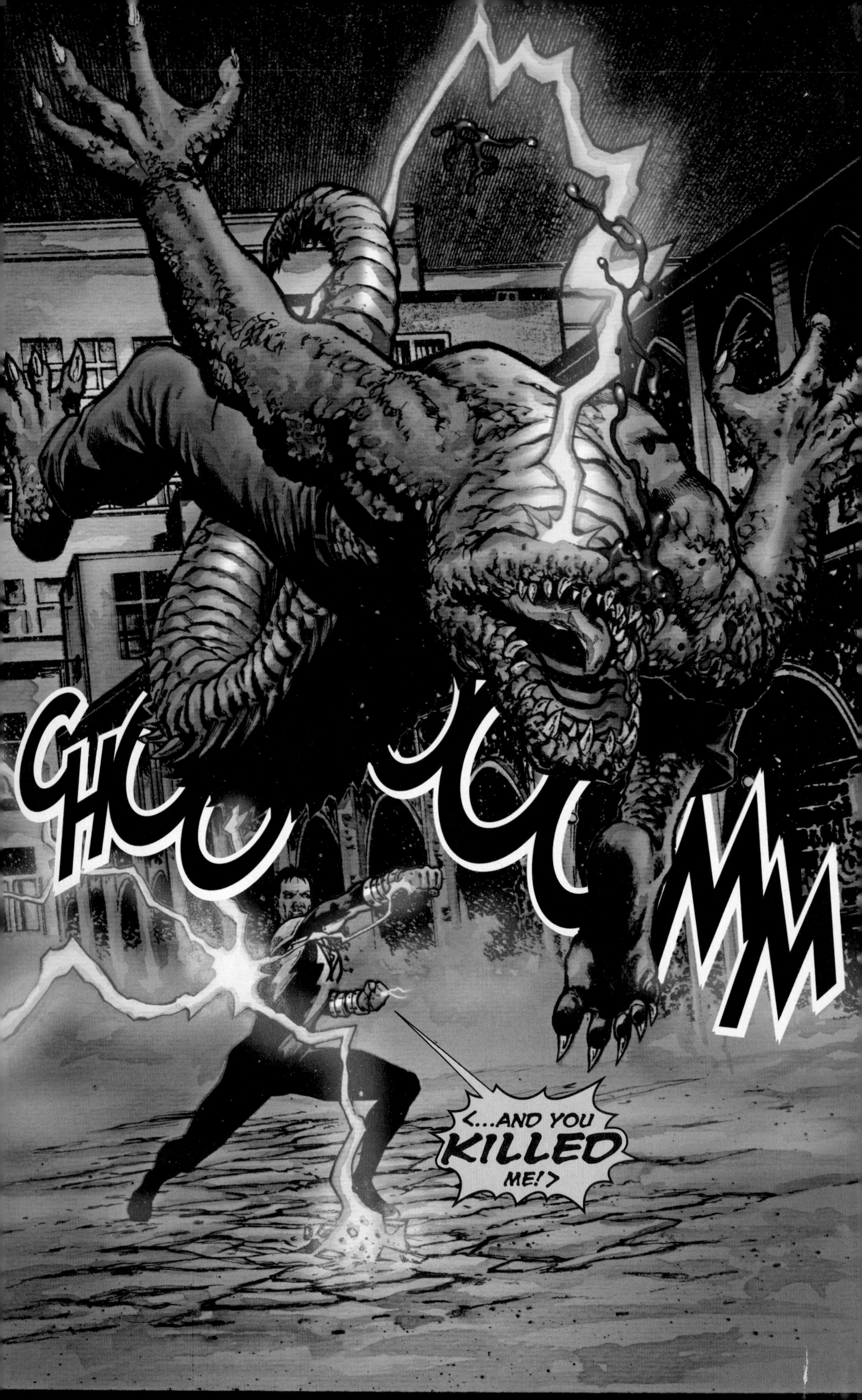
<...AND YOU KILLED ME!>

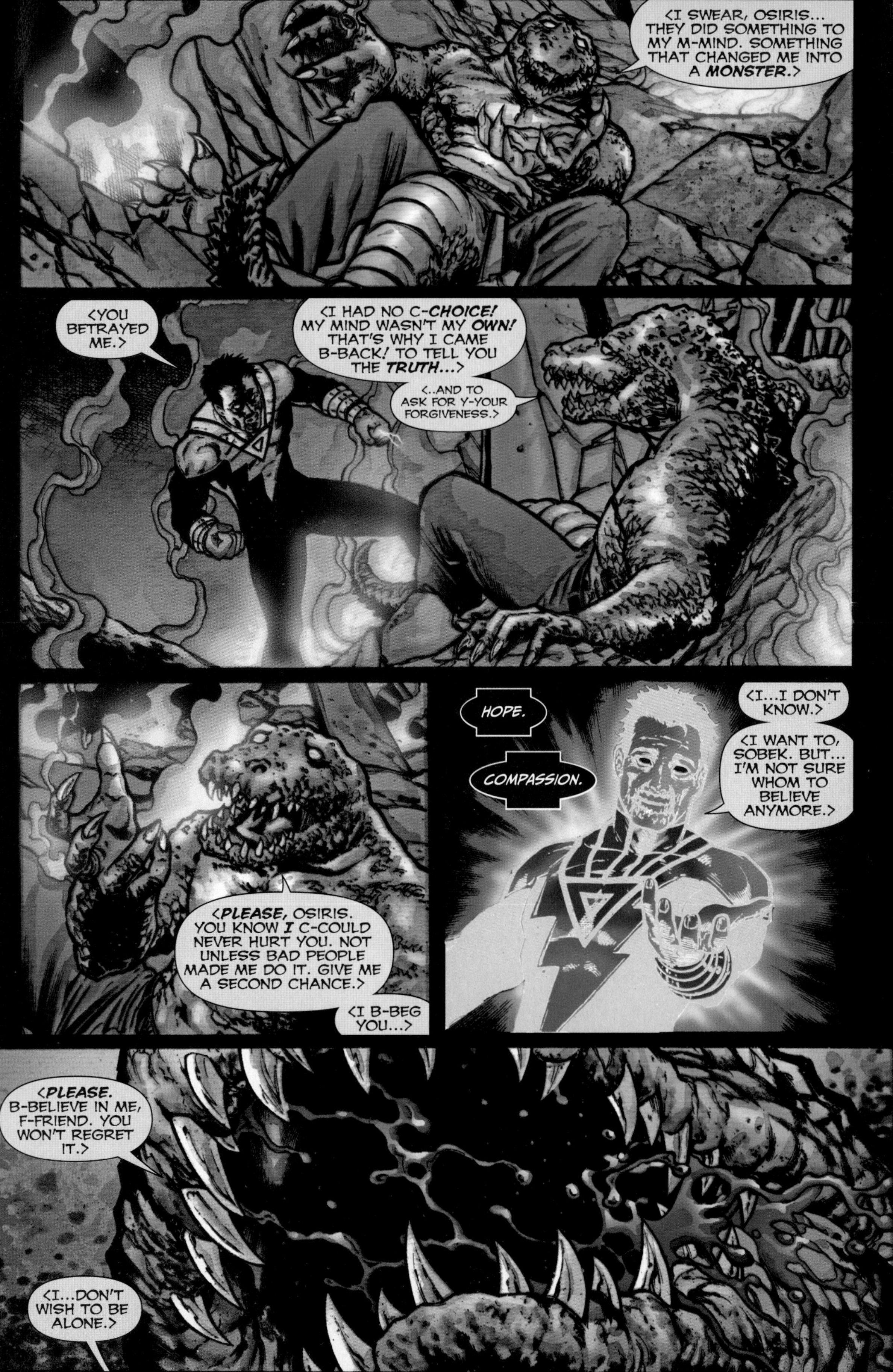
<I SWEAR, OSIRIS... THEY DID SOMETHING TO MY M-MIND. SOMETHING THAT CHANGED ME INTO A ***MONSTER***.>
<YOU BETRAYED ME.>
<I HAD NO C-***CHOICE!*** MY MIND WASN'T MY ***OWN!*** THAT'S WHY I CAME B-BACK! TO TELL YOU THE ***TRUTH...***>
<..AND TO ASK FOR Y-YOUR FORGIVENESS.>
<***PLEASE,*** OSIRIS. YOU KNOW ***I*** C-COULD NEVER HURT YOU. NOT UNLESS BAD PEOPLE MADE ME DO IT. GIVE ME A SECOND CHANCE.>
<I B-BEG YOU...>
HOPE.
COMPASSION.
<I...I DON'T KNOW.>
<I WANT TO, SOBEK. BUT... I'M NOT SURE WHOM TO BELIEVE ANYMORE.>
<***PLEASE.*** B-BELIEVE IN ME, F-FRIEND. YOU WON'T REGRET IT.>
<I...DON'T WISH TO BE ALONE.>

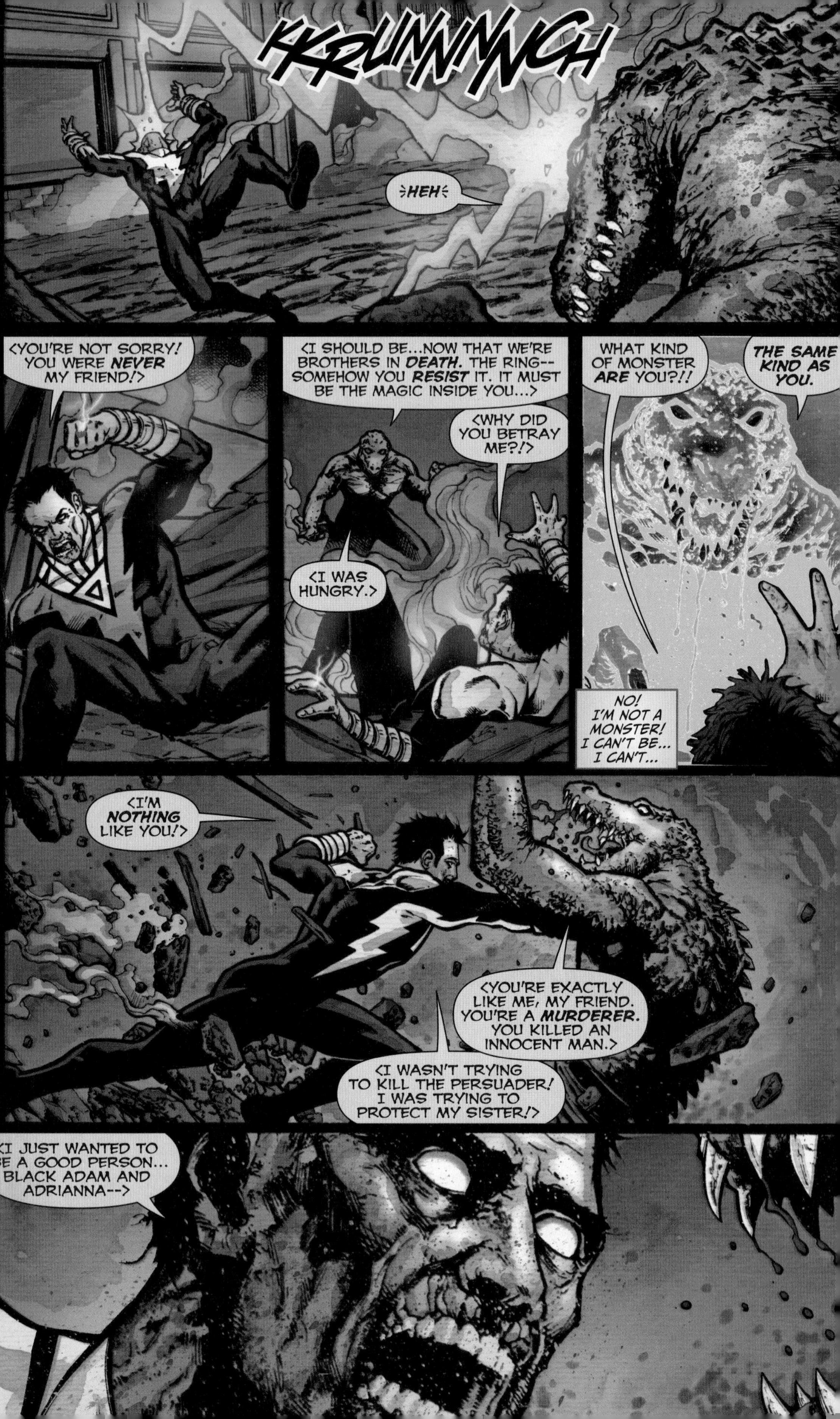
KKRUNNNNCH
HEH
<YOU'RE NOT SORRY! YOU WERE NEVER MY FRIEND!>
<I SHOULD BE...NOW THAT WE'RE BROTHERS IN DEATH. THE RING--SOMEHOW YOU RESIST IT. IT MUST BE THE MAGIC INSIDE YOU...>
<WHY DID YOU BETRAY ME?!>
<I WAS HUNGRY.>
WHAT KIND OF MONSTER ARE YOU?!!
THE SAME KIND AS YOU.
NO! I'M NOT A MONSTER! I CAN'T BE... I CAN'T...
<I'M NOTHING LIKE YOU!>
<YOU'RE EXACTLY LIKE ME, MY FRIEND. YOU'RE A MURDERER. YOU KILLED AN INNOCENT MAN.>
<I WASN'T TRYING TO KILL THE PERSUADER! I WAS TRYING TO PROTECT MY SISTER!>
<I JUST WANTED TO BE A GOOD PERSON... BLACK ADAM AND ADRIANNA-->

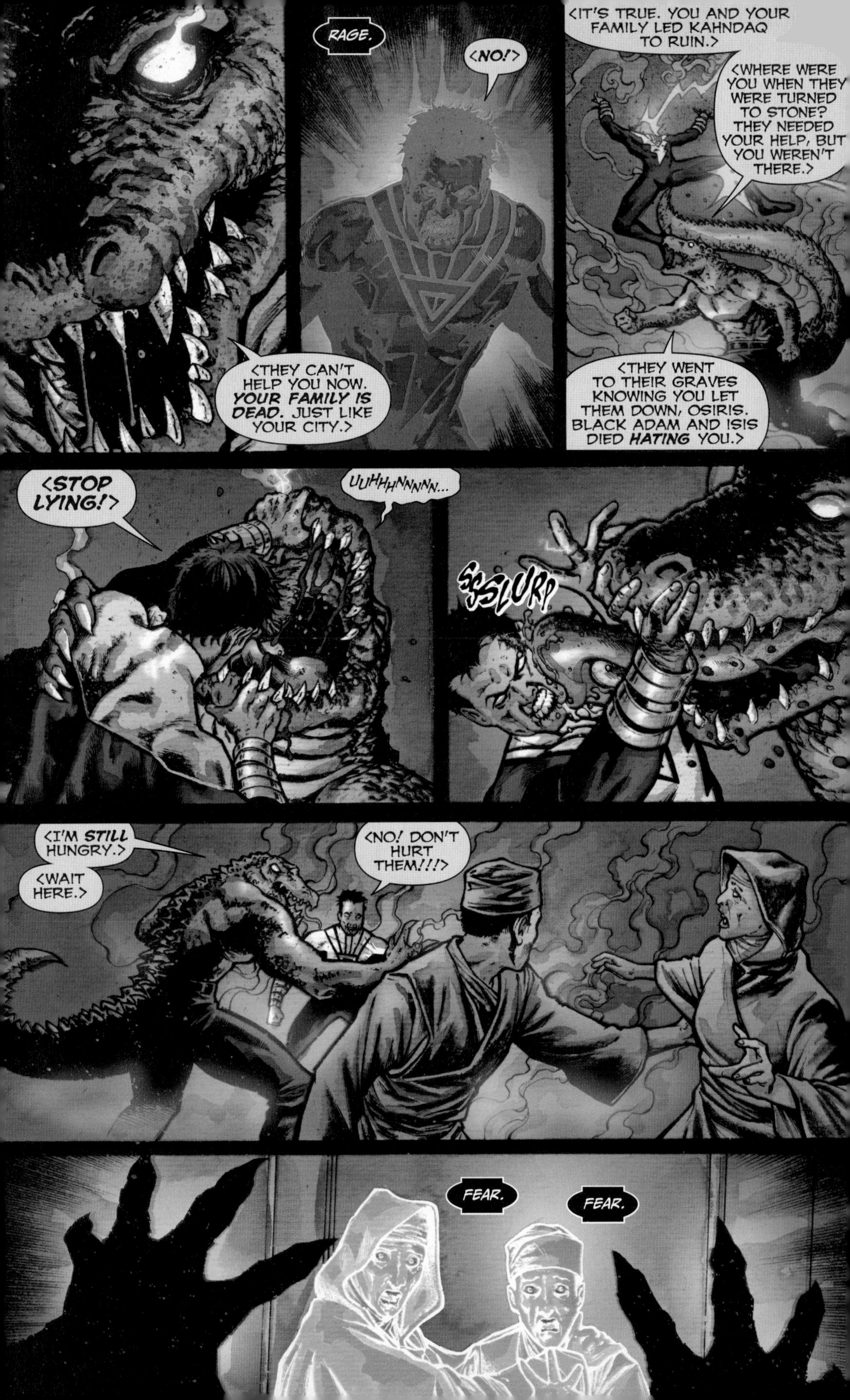
RAGE.
<NO!>
<THEY CAN'T HELP YOU NOW. YOUR FAMILY IS DEAD. JUST LIKE YOUR CITY.>
<IT'S TRUE. YOU AND YOUR FAMILY LED KAHNDAQ TO RUIN.>
<WHERE WERE YOU WHEN THEY WERE TURNED TO STONE? THEY NEEDED YOUR HELP, BUT YOU WEREN'T THERE.>
<THEY WENT TO THEIR GRAVES KNOWING YOU LET THEM DOWN, OSIRIS. BLACK ADAM AND ISIS DIED HATING YOU.>
<STOP LYING!>
UUHHHNNNNN...
SSSLURP
<I'M STILL HUNGRY.>
<WAIT HERE.>
<NO! DON'T HURT THEM!!!>
FEAR.
FEAR.

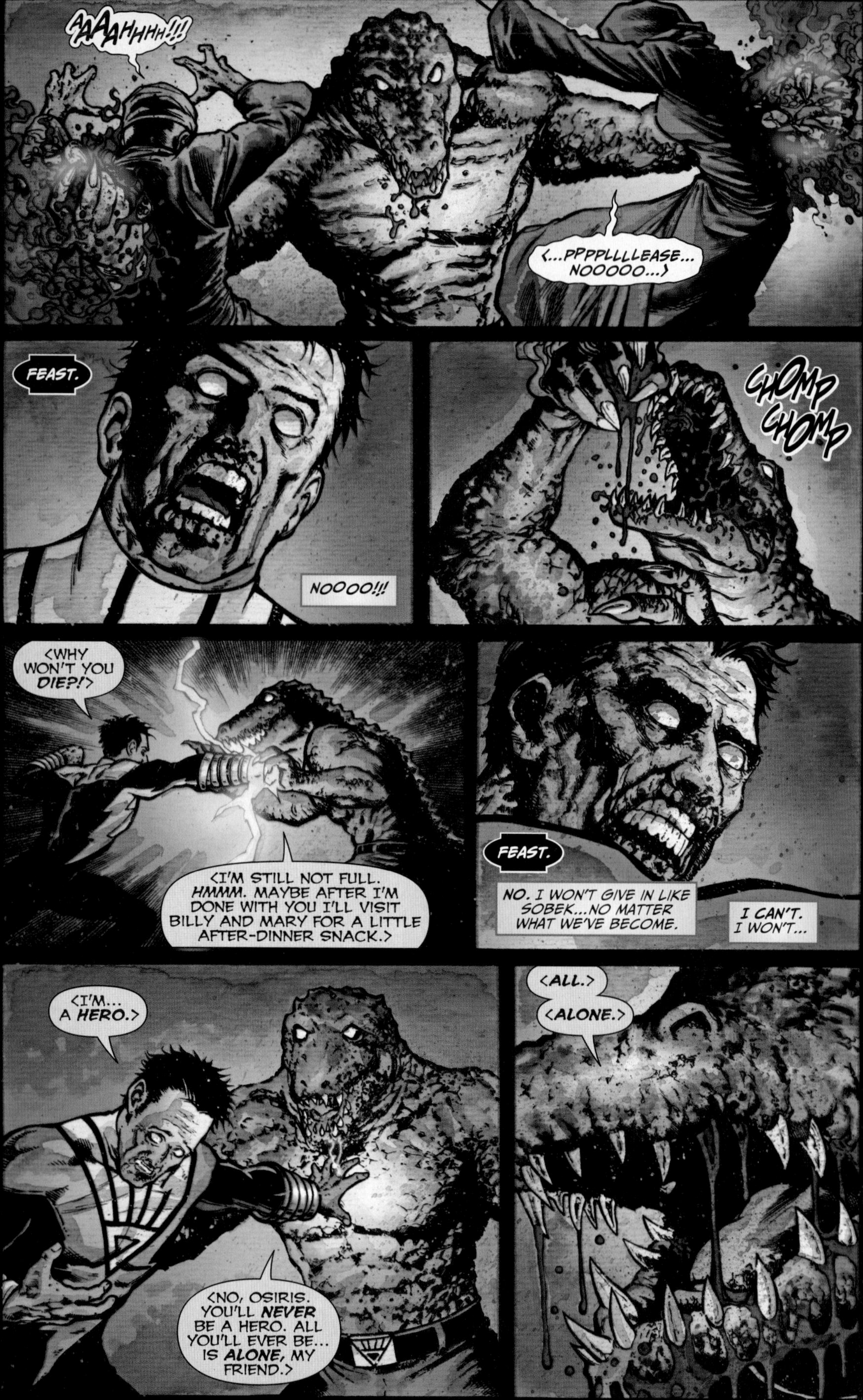
AAAAHHHH!!!
<...PPPPLLLLEASE... NOOOOO...>
FEAST.
NOOOO!!!
CHOMP CHOMP
<WHY WON'T YOU DIE?!>
<I'M STILL NOT FULL. HMMMM. MAYBE AFTER I'M DONE WITH YOU I'LL VISIT BILLY AND MARY FOR A LITTLE AFTER-DINNER SNACK.>
FEAST.
NO. I WON'T GIVE IN LIKE SOBEK...NO MATTER WHAT WE'VE BECOME.
I CAN'T. I WON'T...
<I'M... A HERO.>
<NO, OSIRIS. YOU'LL NEVER BE A HERO. ALL YOU'LL EVER BE... IS ALONE, MY FRIEND.>
<ALL.>
<ALONE.>

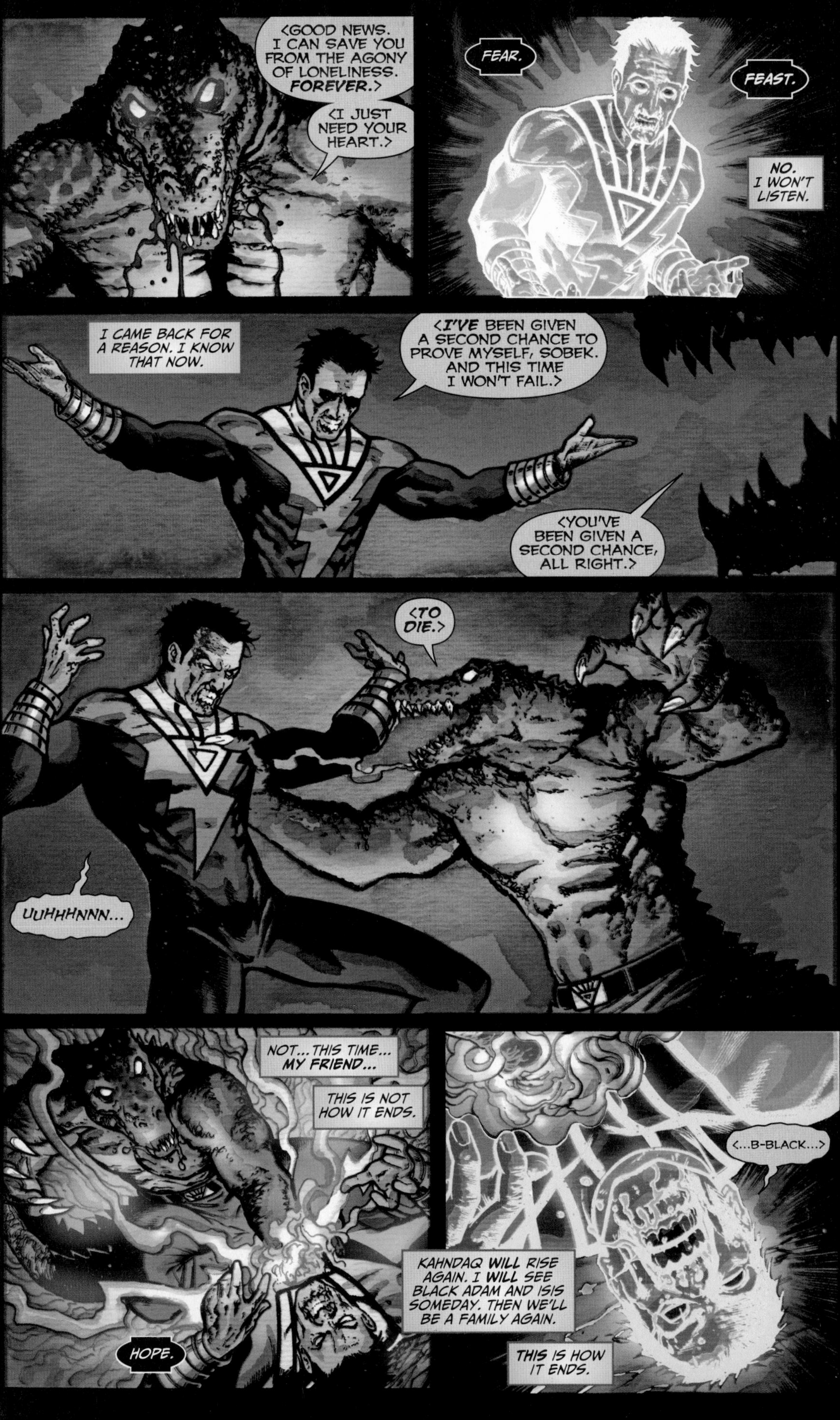
<GOOD NEWS. I CAN SAVE YOU FROM THE AGONY OF LONELINESS. FOREVER.>
<I JUST NEED YOUR HEART.>
FEAR.
FEAST.
NO. I WON'T LISTEN.
I CAME BACK FOR A REASON. I KNOW THAT NOW.
<I'VE BEEN GIVEN A SECOND CHANCE TO PROVE MYSELF, SOBEK. AND THIS TIME I WON'T FAIL.>
<YOU'VE BEEN GIVEN A SECOND CHANCE, ALL RIGHT.>
<TO DIE.>
UUHHHNNN...
NOT... THIS TIME... MY FRIEND...
THIS IS NOT HOW IT ENDS.
HOPE.
<...B-BLACK...>
KAHNDAQ WILL RISE AGAIN. I WILL SEE BLACK ADAM AND ISIS SOMEDAY. THEN WE'LL BE A FAMILY AGAIN.
THIS IS HOW IT ENDS.

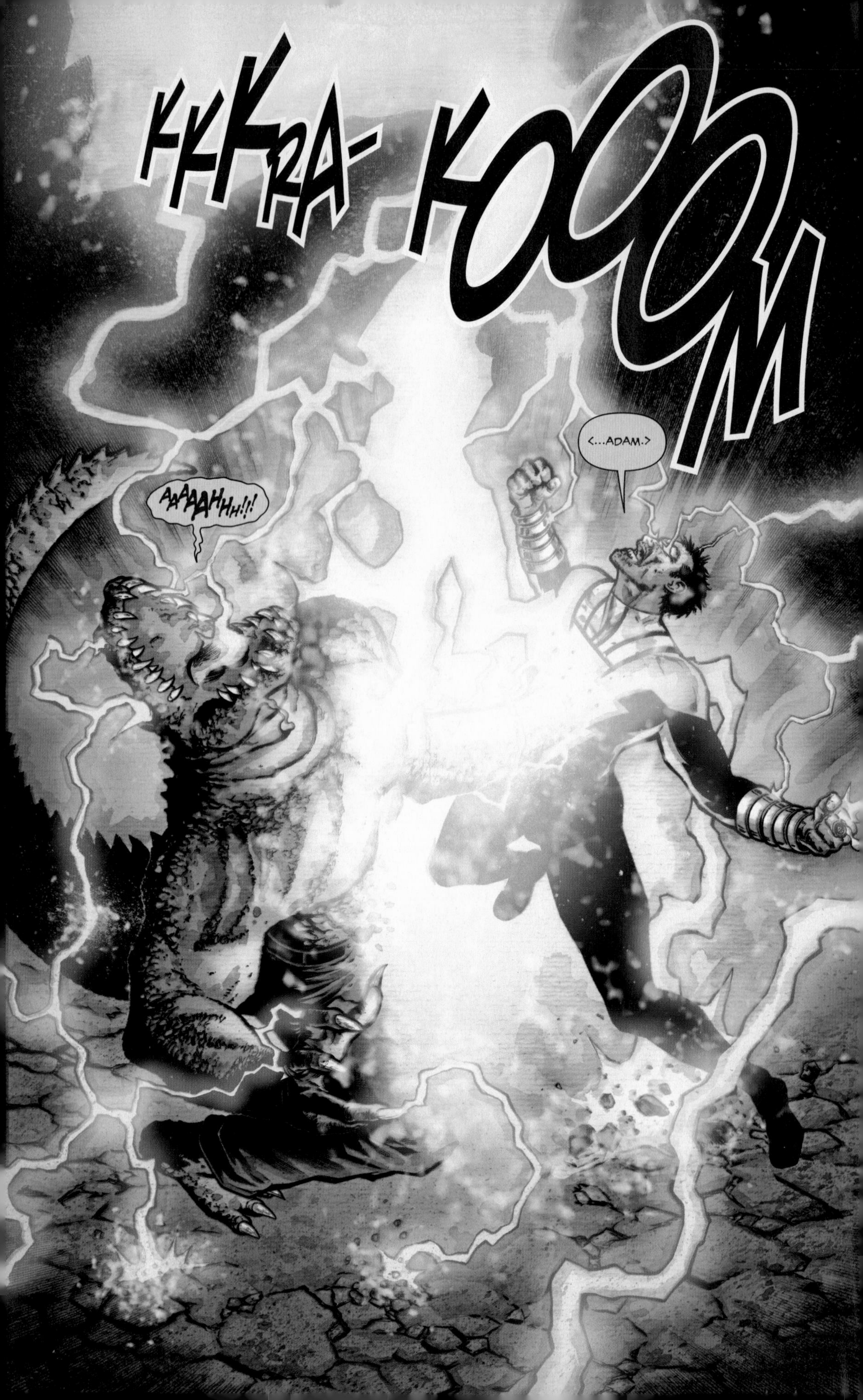
KKKRA-KOOOM
<...ADAM.>
AAAAAHHh!!!

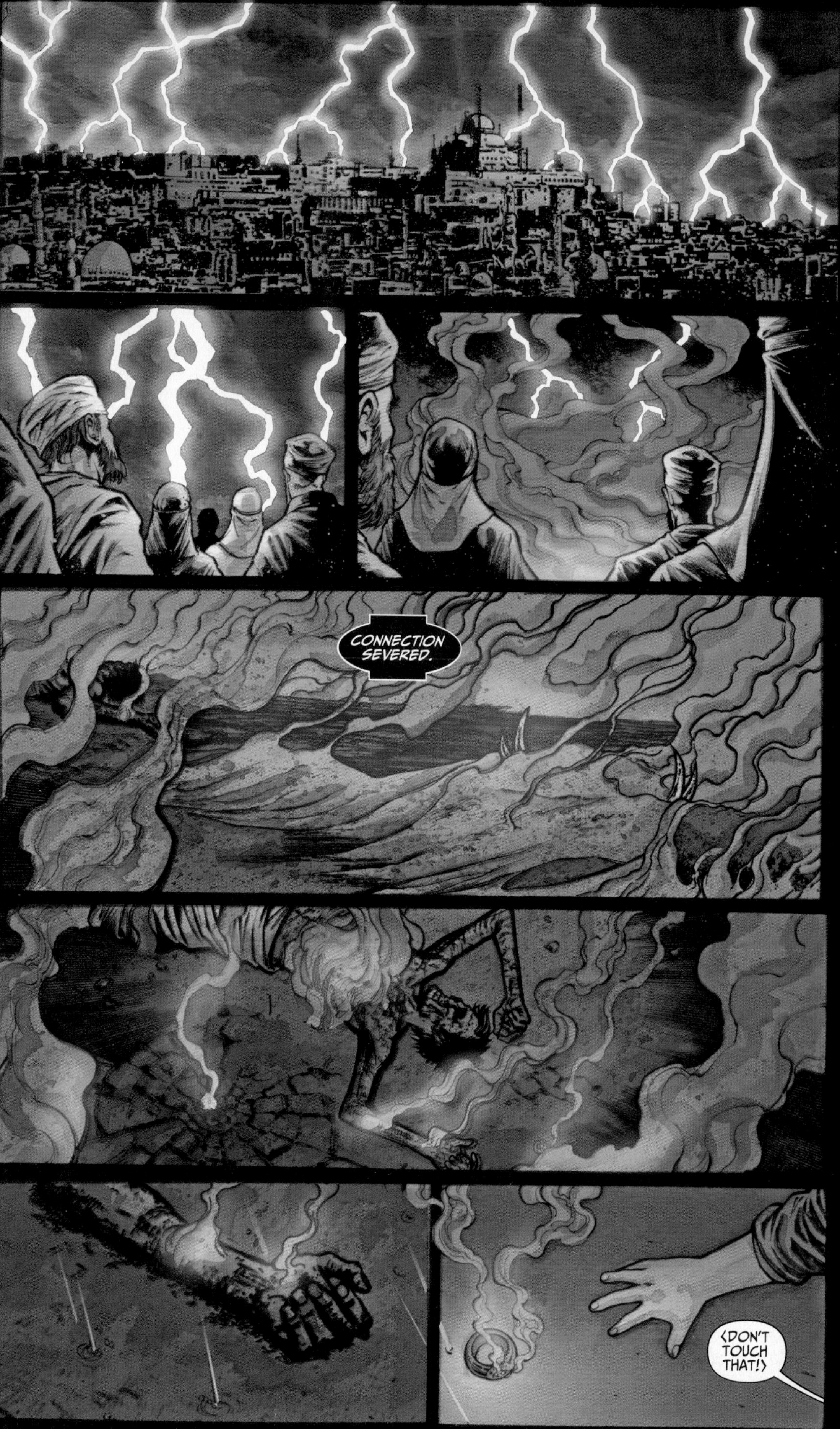
CONNECTION SEVERED.
‹DON'T TOUCH THAT!›

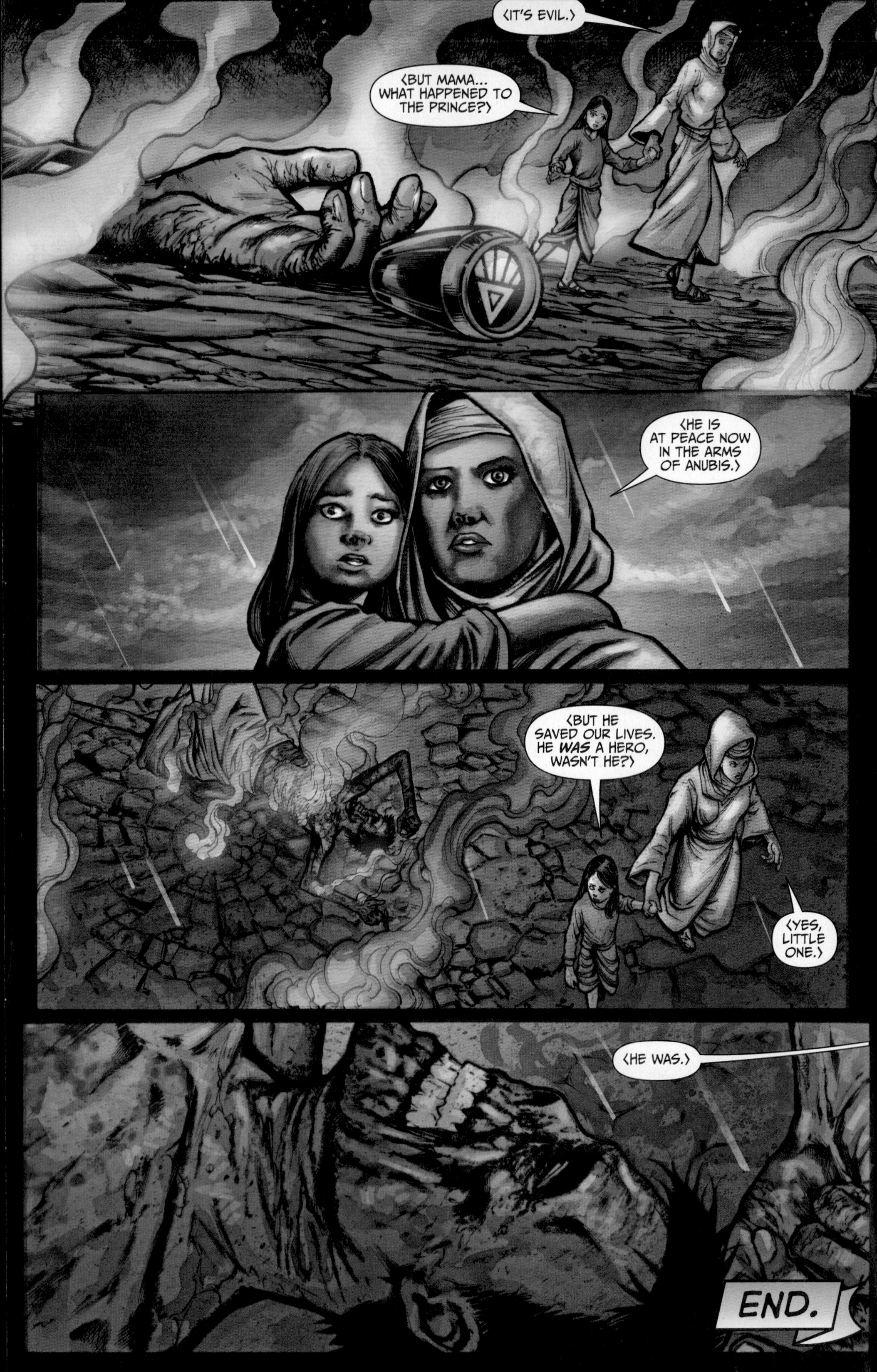

‹IT'S EVIL.›
‹BUT MAMA... WHAT HAPPENED TO THE PRINCE?›
‹HE IS AT PEACE NOW IN THE ARMS OF ANUBIS.›
‹BUT HE SAVED OUR LIVES. HE WAS A HERO, WASN'T HE?›
‹YES, LITTLE ONE.›
‹HE WAS.›
END.

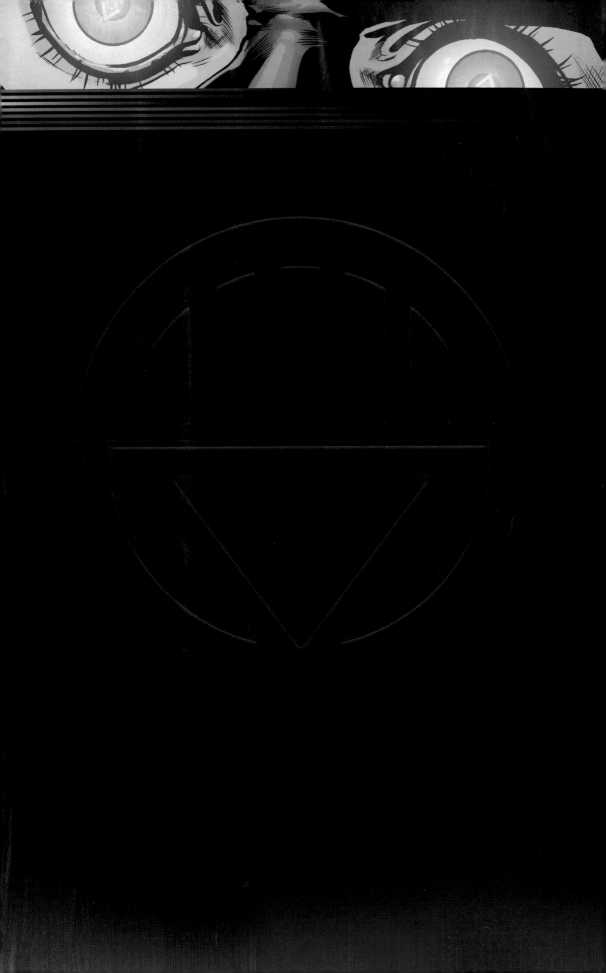

BLACKEST NIGHT
RISE OF THE
BLACK LANTERNS
VARIANT COVER GALLERY

GREEN ARROW 30
Cover by Mike Grell

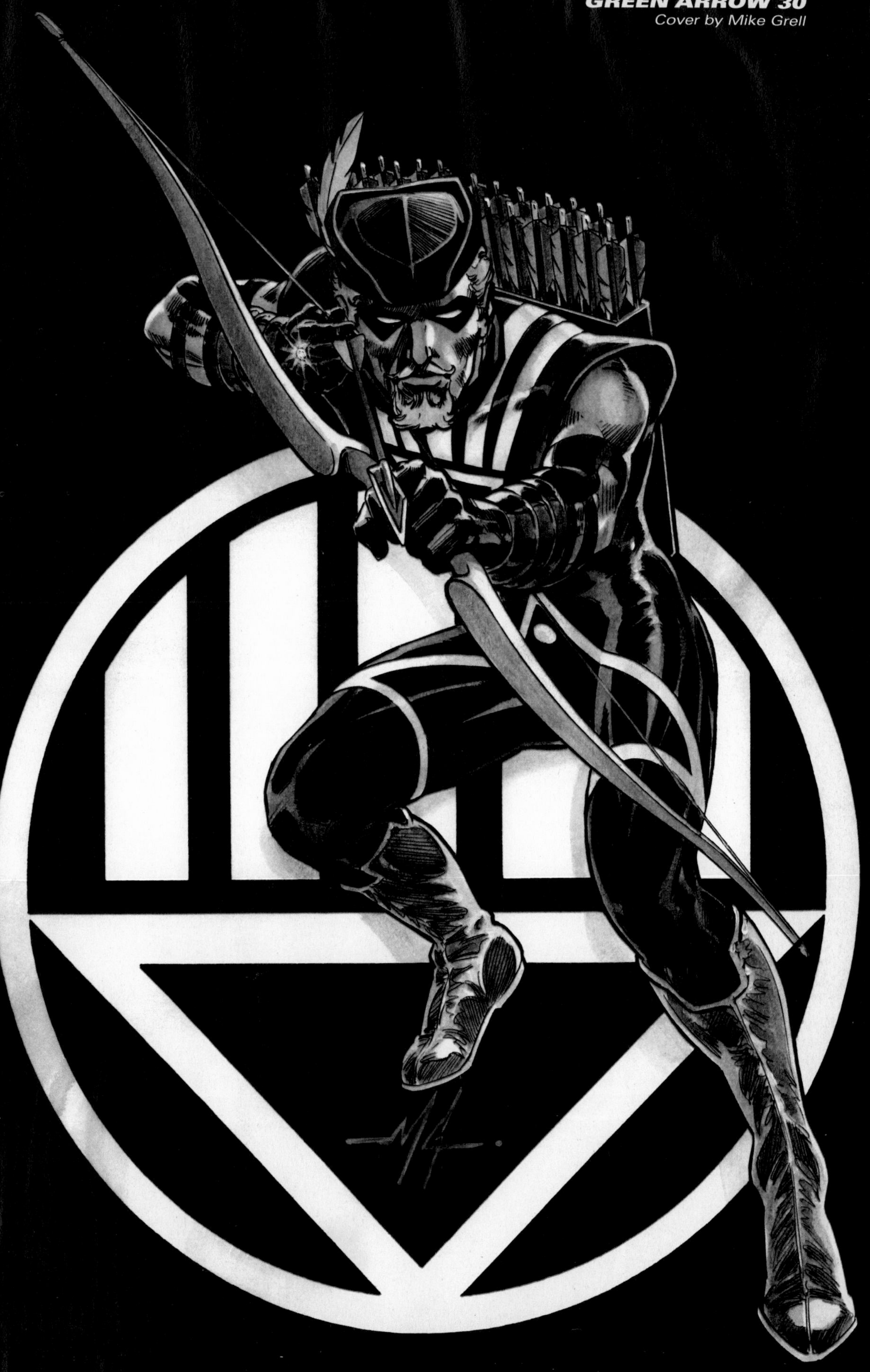

ADVENTURE COMICS 7
Cover by Francis Manapul

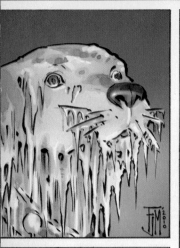

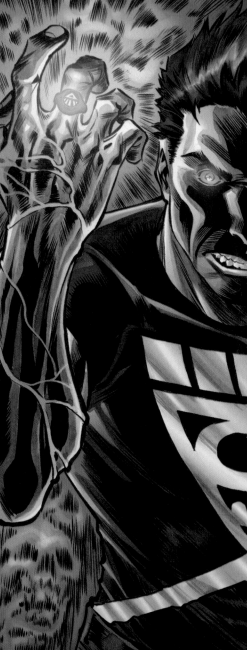

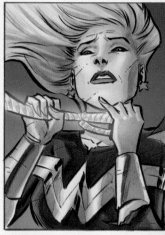

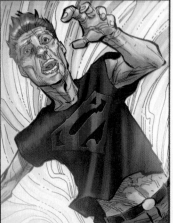

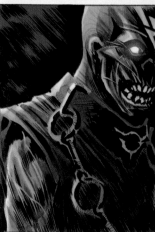

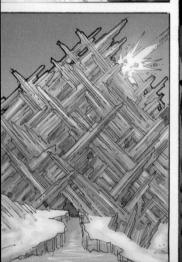

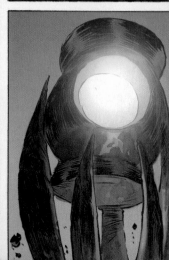

BLACK LANTERN DEADMAN

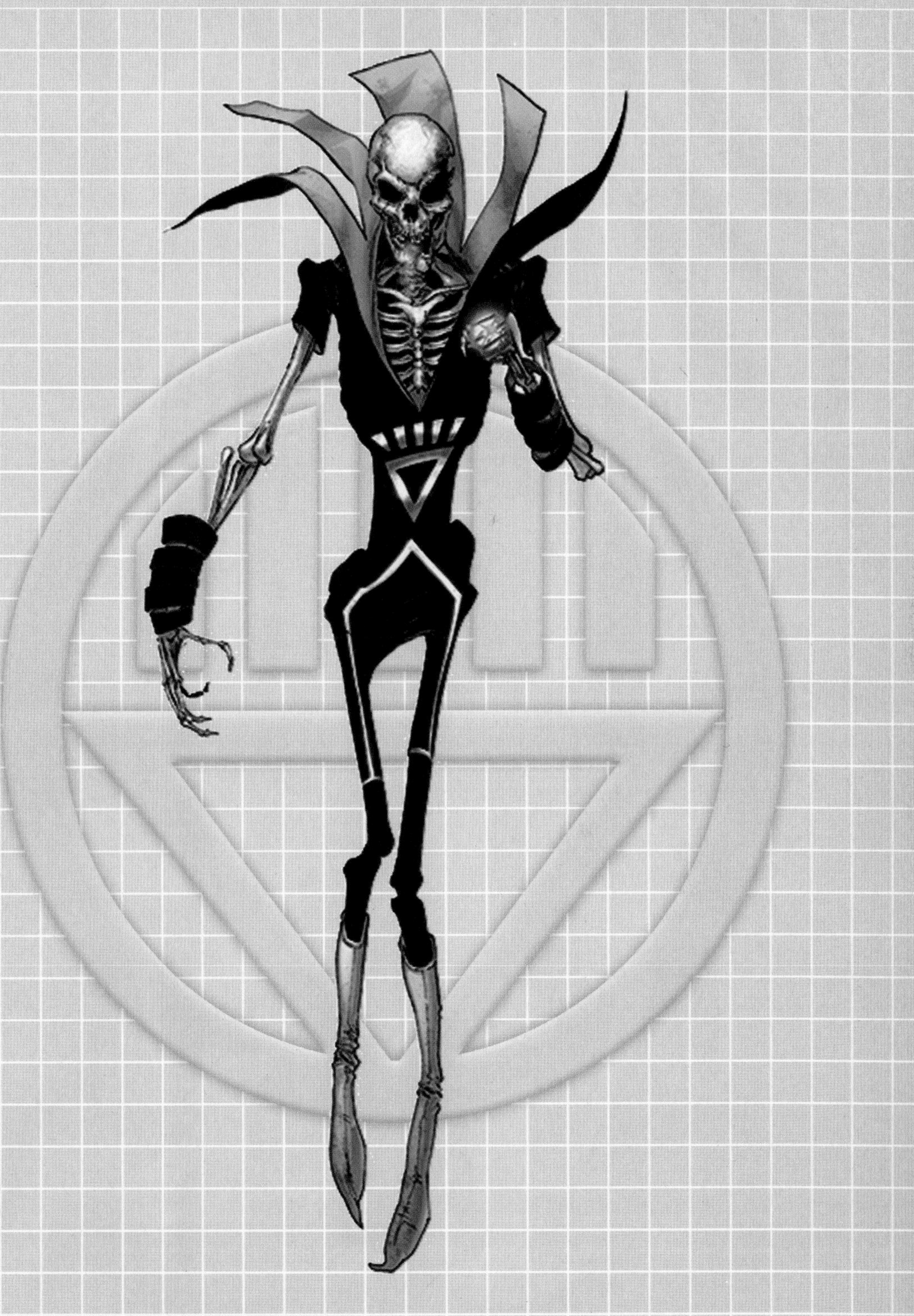

ALTER EGO: BOSTON BRAND
AS A SPIRIT, DEADMAN IS UNABLE TO STOP HIS DEAD PHYSICAL BODY FROM RECEIVING A BLACK LANTERN RING. DEADMAN ATTEMPTS TO REGAIN CONTROL OF HIS BLACK LANTERN BODY, BUT ENTERING THE BODY CAUSES HIM TREMENDOUS PAIN.

Design by Ethan Van Sciver w/ Alex Sinclair

BLACK LANTERN HAWKMAN

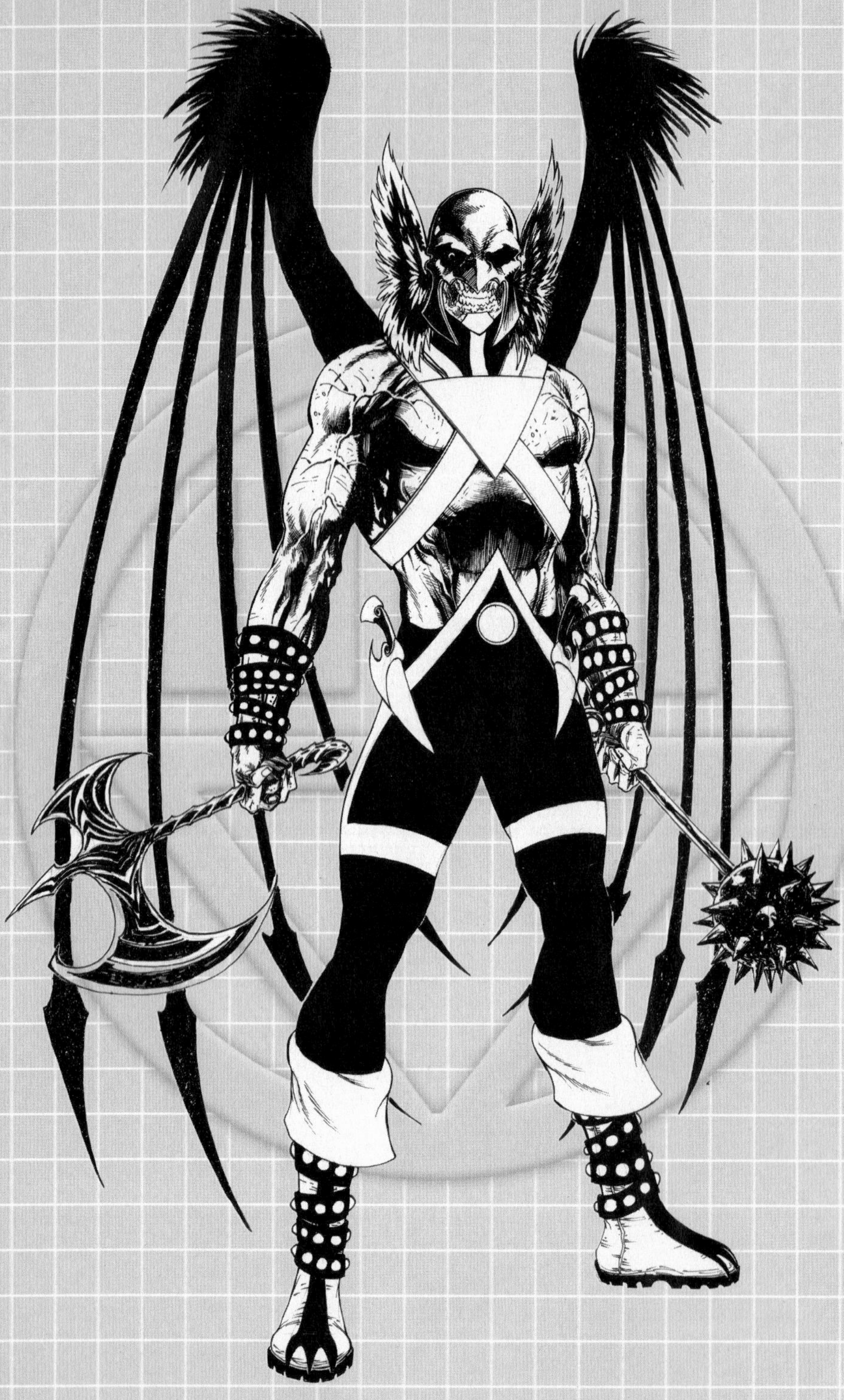

ALTER EGO: CARTER HALL
AFTER MULTIPLE REINCARNATIONS, HAWKMAN RECENTLY WAS KILLED BY BLACK LANTERNS RALPH AND SUE DIBNY, JOINING THE RANKS OF THE BLACK LANTERNS.

Design by Joe Prado

BLACK LANTERN HAWKGIRL

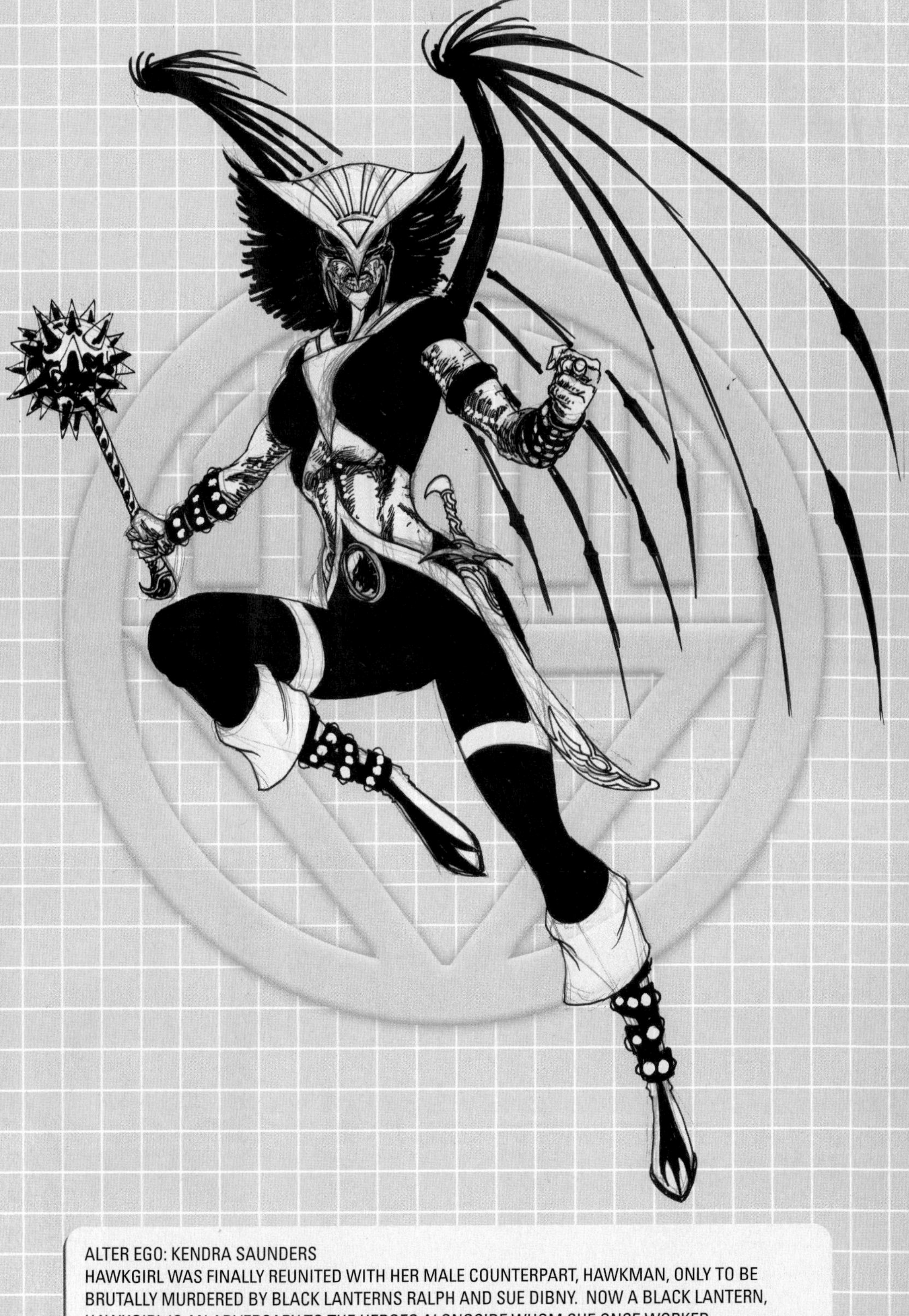

ALTER EGO: KENDRA SAUNDERS
HAWKGIRL WAS FINALLY REUNITED WITH HER MALE COUNTERPART, HAWKMAN, ONLY TO BE BRUTALLY MURDERED BY BLACK LANTERNS RALPH AND SUE DIBNY. NOW A BLACK LANTERN, HAWKGIRL IS AN ADVERSARY TO THE HEROES ALONGSIDE WHOM SHE ONCE WORKED.

Design by Joe Prado

BLACK LANTERN GREEN ARROW

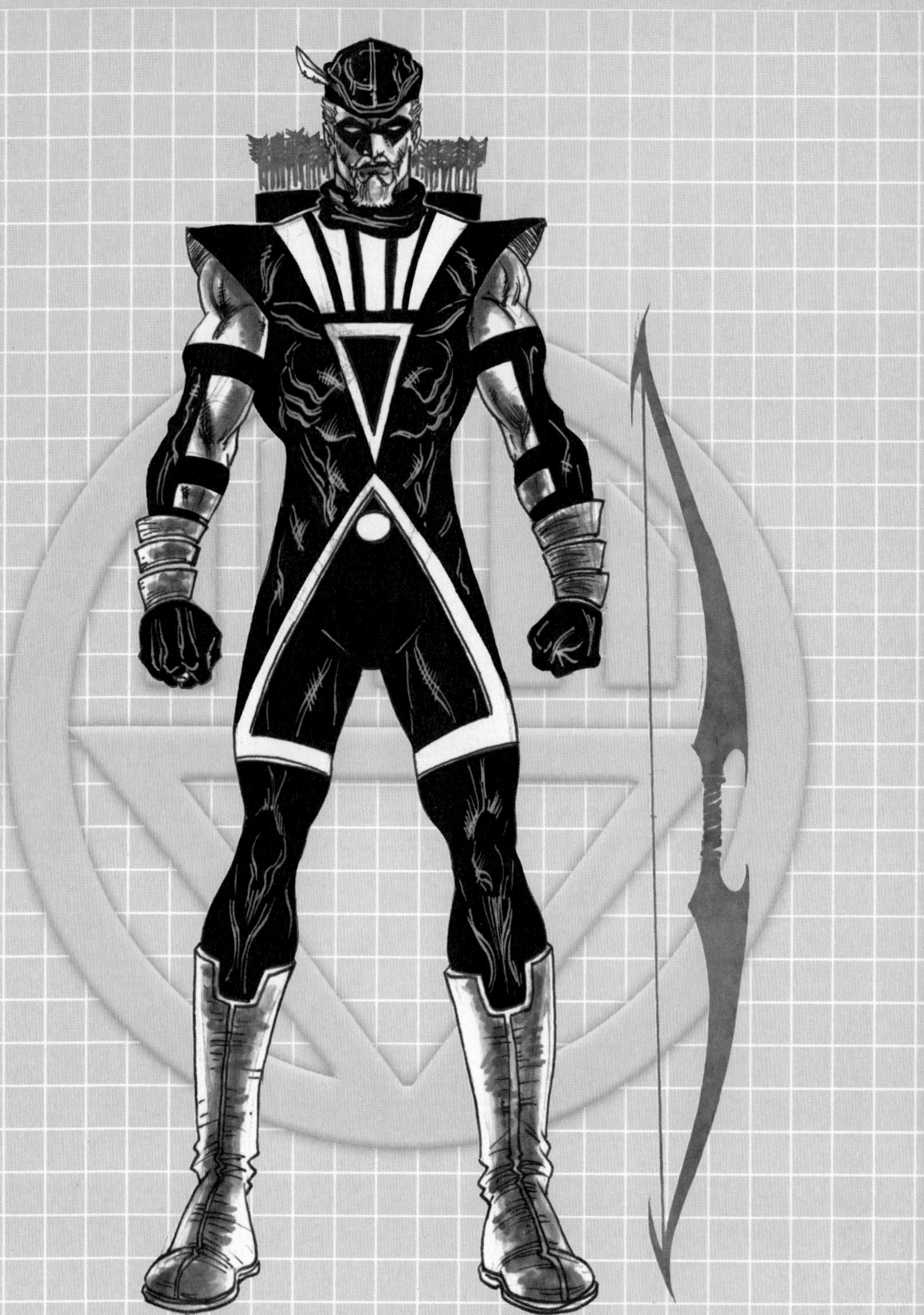

ALTER EGO: OLIVER JONAS "OLLIE" QUEEN
MAN OF THE PEOPLE OLIVER QUEEN PERISHED FIGHTING INJUSTICE WHEN AN AIRPLANE EXPLODED WITH HIM ABOARD. THE EMERALD ARCHER WAS RETURNED TO LIFE BY HIS FRIEND HAL JORDAN. NEKRON USED THIS TO HIS ADVANTAGE, MAKING OLLIE INTO A BLACK LANTERN AND SENDING HIM AFTER HIS FAMILY: BLACK CANARY, SPEEDY AND CONNOR HAWKE.

Design by Joe Prado

BLACK LANTERN SUPERBOY

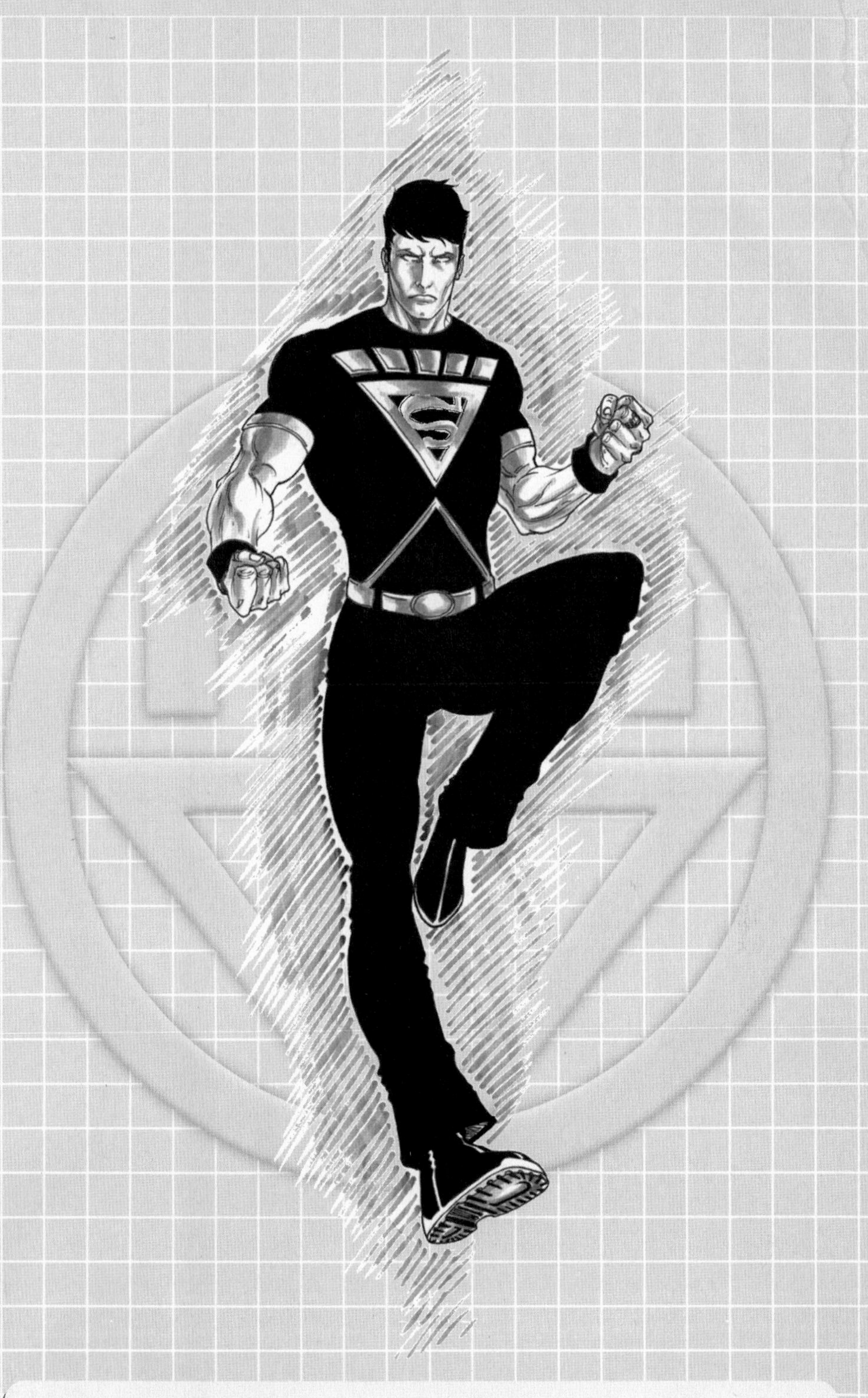

ALTER EGO: CONNER KENT / KON-EL

SUPERBOY, ALONG WITH SUPERMAN, BATTLED BLACK LANTERN EARTH-2 SUPERMAN. HOWEVER, AS SUPERBOY HAD BEEN RESURRECTED FROM THE DEAD PREVIOUSLY, NEKRON WAS ABLE TO TURN HIM INTO A BLACK LANTERN. CONNER THEN ATTACKED WONDER GIRL, HIS GIRLFRIEND, USING HER EMOTIONAL CONNECTION TO HIM AGAINST HER.

Design by Joe Prado

BLACK LANTERN QUESTION

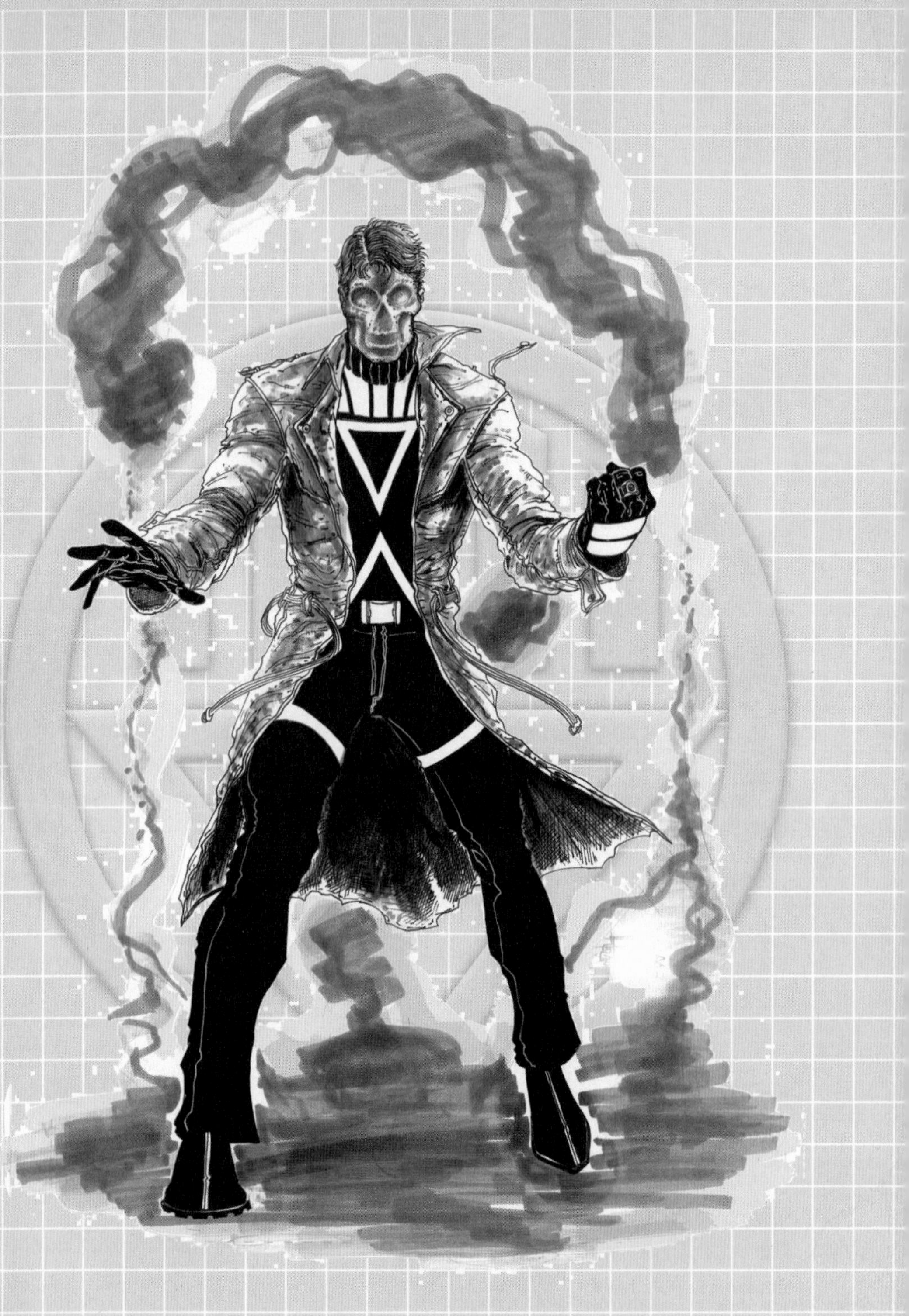

ALTER EGO: CHARLES "CHARLIE" VICTOR SZASZ
THE QUESTION DIED OF CANCER, BUT NOT BEFORE PASSING ON HIS WISDOM TO RENEE MONTOYA, WHO WOULD BECOME THE NEW QUESTION. HAVING RETURNED FROM THE DEAD, CHARLIE HAS GONE AFTER RENEE, DETERMINED TO ADD HER TO THE RANKS OF NEKRON'S BLACK LANTERNS.

Design by Joe Prado

BLACK LANTERN STARMAN

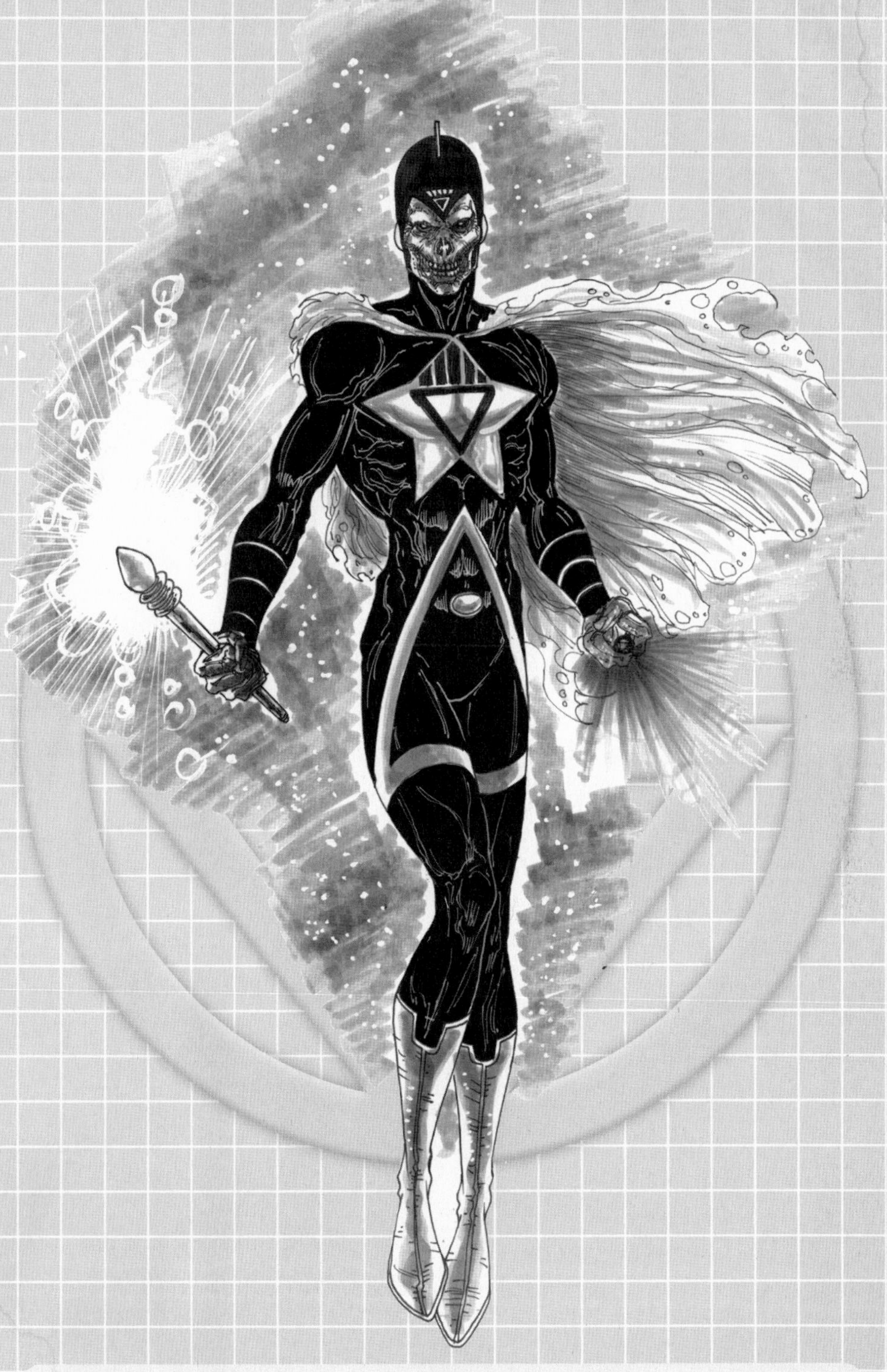

ALTER EGO: DAVID KNIGHT
USING A GRAVITY ROD, TED KNIGHT WAS ABLE TO FLY AND SHOOT ENERGY BOLTS AT HIS FOES UNTIL HIS DEATH AT THE HANDS OF THE MIST. HIS SON DAVID BRIEFLY TOOK ON THE ROLE OF STARMAN UNTIL HE WAS ALSO MURDERED. STARGIRL CURRENTLY WIELDS THE GRAVITY ROD, CARRYING ON THE LEGACY.

Design by Joe Prado

WESTERN BLACK LANTERNS

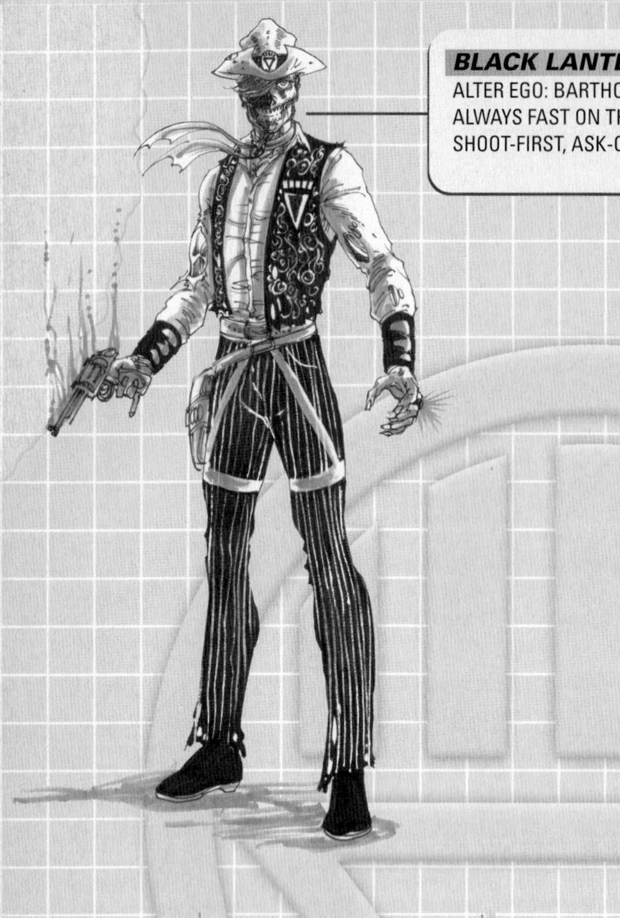

BLACK LANTERN BAT LASH

ALTER EGO: BARTHOLOMEW ALOUYSIUS LASH
ALWAYS FAST ON THE DRAW, BAT LASH HAS RETURNED AS A SHOOT-FIRST, ASK-QUESTIONS-LATER BLACK LANTERN.

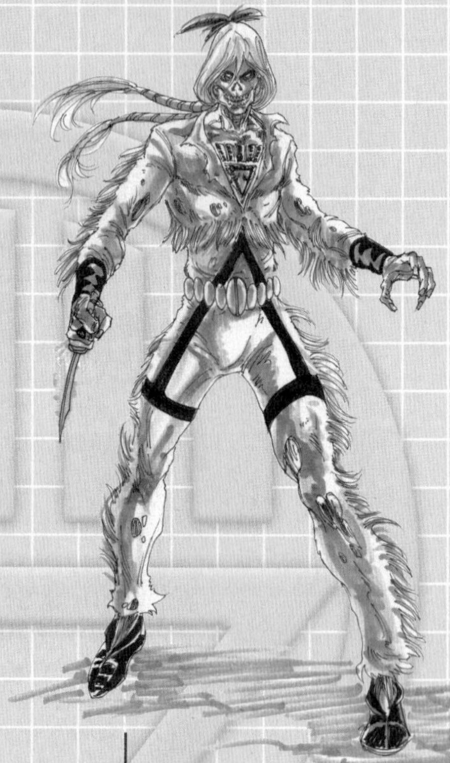

BLACK LANTERN FIREHAIR

ALTER EGO: UNKNOWN
RAISED BY THE BLACKFOOT INDIANS AFTER HIS FAMILY WAS MURDERED, FIREHAIR ULTIMATELY WENT THE WAY OF HIS PARENTS. NOW, HE'S A BLACK LANTERN EQUIPPED WITH ALL THE SKILLS TAUGHT HIM BY THE TRIBE THAT RAISED HIM.

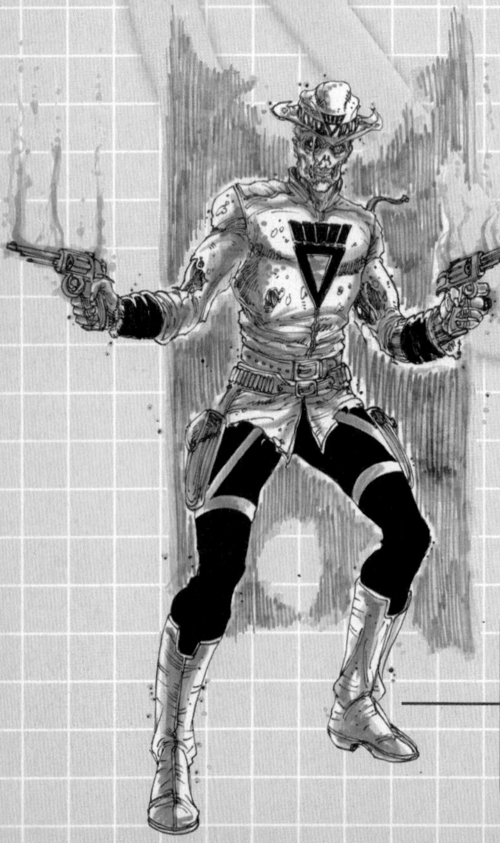

BLACK LANTERN JONAH HEX

ALTER EGO: JONAH WOODSON HEX
ONE OF THE MOST FEARED GUNMEN IN THE OLD WEST, HEX WAS KILLED WHILE PLAYING CARDS. HE'S RETURNED WITH THE GOAL OF FINDING A STOLEN BLACK LANTERN RING.

Designs by Joe Prado

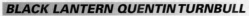

BLACK LANTERN QUENTIN TURNBULL
ALTER EGO: QUENTIN TURNBULL
TURNBULL WAS KILLED BY JONAH HEX BUT HAS NOW RETURNED AS A BLACK LANTERN WORKING WITH HIS FORMER ENEMY.

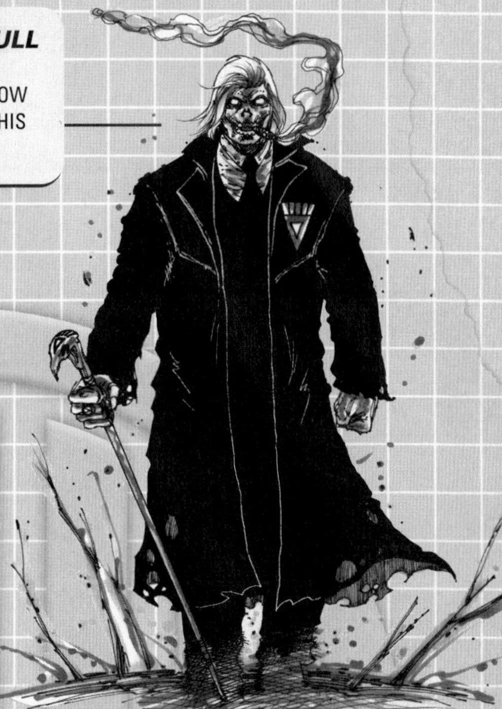

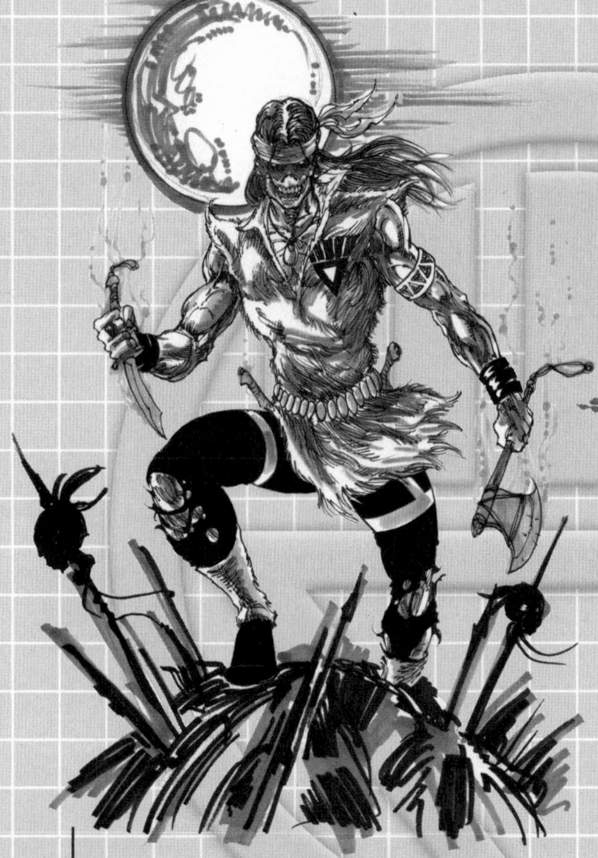

BLACK LANTERN SCALPHUNTER
ALTER EGO: BRIAN SAVAGE
RAISED BY THE KIOWA INDIANS, SCALPHUNTER LATER BECAME THE SHERIFF OF OPAL CITY. HE WAS KILLED BY THE LAST MEMBER OF THE TUESDAY CLUB THAT WAS THREATENING HIS TOWN.

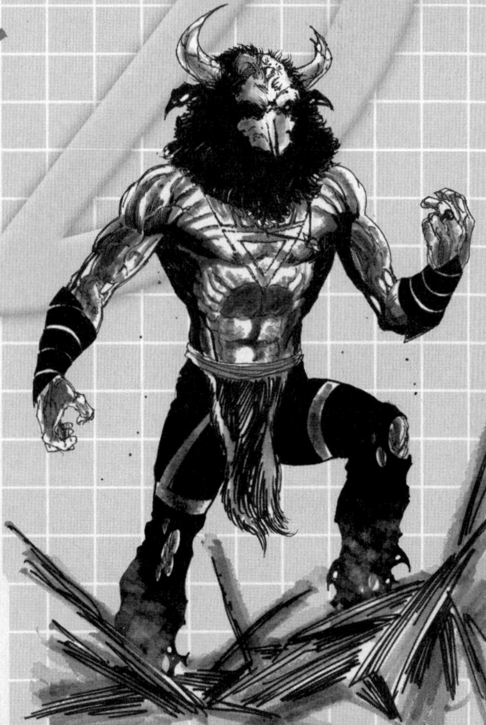

BLACK LANTERN SUPER-CHIEF
ALTER EGO: FLYING STAG
THE NECKLACE HE WORE THAT GAVE HIM THE ABILITIES OF SUPER-SPEED, STRENGTH AND FLIGHT COULD NOT SAVE THIS FANTASTIC WARRIOR FROM DEATH.

FOLLOW THE COMPLETE

BLACKEST NIGHT

SAGA IN THESE GRAPHIC NOVELS

BLACKEST NIGHT
Geoff Johns & Ivan Reis

BLACKEST NIGHT: GREEN LANTERN
Geoff Johns & Doug Mahnke

BLACKEST NIGHT: GREEN LANTERN CORPS
Peter J. Tomasi & Patrick Gleason

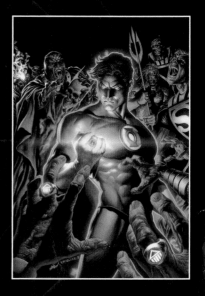

BLACKEST NIGHT: BLACK LANTERN CORPS Vol. 1
Peter J. Tomasi, James Robinson, J.T. Krul,
Ardian Syaf, Ed Benes & Eddy Barrows

BLACKEST NIGHT: BLACK LANTERN CORPS Vol. 2
Geoff Johns, James Robinson, Greg Rucka,
Scott Kolins, Eddy Barrows & Nicola Scott

BLACKEST NIGHT: RISE OF THE BLACK LANTERNS
Geoff Johns, Peter J. Tomasi, James Robinson & others

BLACKEST NIGHT: TALES OF THE CORPS
Geoff Johns, Peter J. Tomasi & others